Mr. Justice White during his first full term. Photographed by Fabian Bachrach, 1963
(Courtesy of NFL Properties)

THE MAN WHO ONCE WAS WHIZZER WHITE

A Portrait of Justice Byron R. White

DENNIS J. HUTCHINSON

THE FREE PRESS

New York   London   Toronto   Singapore   Sydney

A Division of Simon & Schuster Inc.
1230 Avenue of the Americas
New York, NY 10020

Designed by Carla Bolte

Manufactured in the United States of America

10 9 8 7 6 5 4 3 2 1

Library of Congress Cataloging-in-Publication Data

Hutchinson, Dennis J.
  The man who once was Whizzer White : a portrait of Justice Byron
R. White / Dennis J. Hutchinson.
    p.   cm.
  Includes bibliographical references and index.
  1. White, Byron R., 1917–   . 2. Judges—United States—
Biography. [1. United States. Supreme Court—Biography.]
I. Title.
KF8745.W48H88   1998
347.73'2634—dc21
  [B]   97–47302
                                                          CIP

ISBN 0–684–82794–8

Permission to quote from copyrighted material: Calvin Trillin, to reprint "Adieu, Whizzer," by Calvin Trillin, © 1993 by Calvin Trillin, reprinted with permission; *Rocky Mountain News*, to reprint "On judges and justice: Byron White reflects on court and critics," by Clifford May, © 1996 by the *Rocky Mountain News*, reprinted with permission; Time, Inc., to reprint excerpts from "A Modest All-American Who Sits on the Highest Bench," by Alfred Wright, reprinted courtesy of *Sports Illustrated*, December 10, 1962, © 1962 by Time, Inc.; The University of Chicago Press, for excerpts from *A River Runs Through It and Other Stories*, by Norman Maclean, © 1976 by The University of Chicago, all rights reserved, reprinted with permission; The University of Chicago Press, for an adaptation of "The Ideal New Frontier Justice," by Dennis J. Hutchinson, published in *The Supreme Court Review*, 1997, © 1998 by The University of Chicago, all rights reserved, reprinted with permission; *The Green Bag*, for an adaptation of "Whizzer White at Yale," by Dennis J. Hutchinson, published in vol. 1 (n.s.), no. 2, © 1998, reprinted with permission.

To

Katy, David, and Jane

Love will abide.

PART III. LAW AND POLITICS

10. Denver: Law and Local Politics 223

11. The Kennedy Campaign 241

12. Kennedy Justice 260

13. Kennedy Judges 287

14. "The Ideal New Frontier Judge" 310

PART IV. THE SUPREME COURT

15. The Warren Court: White, J., Dissenting . . . 335

16. October Term 1971 355

17. October Term 1981 382

18. October Term 1991 407

19. "The End of the Ride" 432

20. Service As Legacy 444

Appendixes

A. White-Patterson Meeting 459
B. Letter of October 20, 1975 463
C. June 1996 Interview 466
D. Law Clerks 471

Notes   477
Sources   517
Acknowledgments   539
Case Index   541
General Index   547

CONTENTS

Author's Note   ix

Prologue 1

PART I. COLORADO

1. Wellington 11

2. "No Clippings" 25

3. Whizzermania 43

4. The Decision 71

PART II. GRADUATE WORK

5. Pittsburgh: "Golden Boy" 97

6. "A Yank at Oxford" 123

7. Yale and Detroit 145

8. The Navy 172

9. Supreme Court: October Term 1946 194

AUTHOR'S NOTE

Statements set off by quotation marks, aside from reprinted material and oral histories, are statements made to me, or supported by contemporaneous notes, or verified by me; quotations in italics are generally paraphrases or renditions of statements made long enough ago that I deem exact quotation unreliable.

PROLOGUE

A FEW DAYS after John F. Kennedy was inaugurated as president of the United States, in January 1961, Byron R. White, the deputy attorney general, and one of his assistants slipped out of the Department of Justice building for a quick lunch at Hammel's, a nearby restaurant. After the sandwiches, while the coffee was being poured, their waitress looked carefully at White and asked, "Say, aren't you Whizzer White?" White took a sip of coffee, measured her slowly, and replied in a soft voice, "I was."

The incident was quickly told and retold throughout the department and soon became an early piece of folklore about the new administration. The symbolism was irresistible. White embodied the new administration—he was an intellectually distinguished, physically vigorous volunteer modestly serving the public. In a government that soon included more than a dozen former Rhodes scholars, White's résumé was unmatched. A junior Phi Beta Kappa, he had been a consensus all-American football player, a Rhodes scholar, the highest-paid player in the history of the National Football League (and rushing leader for two years), a decorated navy veteran, number one man academically in his Yale Law School class, law clerk to the chief justice of the United States, and a quiet community leader in Denver, Colorado. To top it off, he not only wore his past lightly but seemed to dismiss it, or at least its recollection.

The irony is that White's modesty served to fuse his past to his present. By denying the significance of his achievements as a young man, he unintentionally enhanced his stature in the administration and in the eyes of those whom it enthralled. It is not too much to say that White's image propelled him to the top of the short list for the first vacancy on the Supreme Court of the United

1

States when it arose, fourteen months after the inauguration. In fact, President Kennedy hardly considered anyone else for the position. When White announced his retirement thirty-one years later, after serving longer than all but nine of the one-hundred-plus justices in the Court's history, President Bill Clinton stated that "he has had a truly remarkable life"—an allusion to his pre-Court biography as much as to three decades of public service. But if White was asked whether he would write his memoirs, his standard reply was a cryptic "I have."

Although he had given a singularly candid interview to *Sports Illustrated* a few months after joining the Court, the statement more likely recalls Justice Louis D. Brandeis, who gave the same response to the same question—implying that the text was to be found in the *United States Reports,* the official publication of the Court's opinions. Brandeis's point, and perhaps White's, was that the Court, and thus its members, speak only through their opinions, and that elaborations of the record are inappropriate, if not unethical. White was infuriated by *The Brethren,* published in 1979 by Bob Woodward and Scott Armstrong, which provided backstage accounts of the Court's decision-making process plus offstage gossip. When journalists asked White for interviews, his standard reply was, "What could we talk about?"

More is at issue than discretion. Neither temperament nor conviction suit him to public introspection. In the words of his closest friend, Ira C. Rothgerber Jr., "He is a shy man with an aggressive, and encompassing, view of his own privacy." Never at ease as a public speaker and not given to easy reminiscence, he is not inclined to public self-assessment. Following White's retirement, in 1993, Judge Louis Oberdorfer, a colleague from law school and the Kennedy administration, hosted a small dinner party for the justice and his wife, Marion. When the time came for the guest of honor to speak, his self-effacing remarks recalled memorable and telling incidents about everyone in the room except himself.

At a deeper level, White has a reflexive suspicion of intellectuals, especially philosophers and historians. He is notorious among curators and archivists for refusing to be interviewed for oral history collections. The list of refusals includes the Fred M. Vinson Oral History Project of the University of Kentucky Library, the Oral History Program of the John F. Kennedy Library in Boston, the Local History Department of the Fort Collins, Colorado, Public Library, and even the Oral History Collection of his hometown public library, in Wellington, Colorado. Although he donated his judicial papers to the Manuscript Division of the Library of Congress several years ago, his gift may turn out to be more symbolic than substantial. According to former staff members, White destroyed the bulk of his papers prior to the beginning of October Term 1986. With twenty-five terms of accumulated cases files in a storage area of the Court, the justice and three of his law clerks spent successive weekends running files through a paper shredder obtained specifically for the occasion. (One of the clerks, who had academic ambitions, recalls vividly putting one file after another marked *Miranda v. Arizona* through the shredder: "I thought, Well, here's an article; here's an entire book. I couldn't believe how much history was going down the chute.") White gave no explanation for the project, other than that "it was time to clean up the place."

The timing of the project is significant. October term 1986 marked Justice White's twenty-fifth full term on the Supreme Court. Journalists and academics predictably used the occasion for retrospectives on his career, which he did not welcome. The *University of Colorado Law Review* planned an entire issue devoted to his career. With advice from Denver lawyers who knew him well, the student editors mapped out almost a dozen articles covering each phase of White's life and work on the Court. To flesh out the biographical details available from the old *Sports Illustrated* interview, the editor in chief of the law review telephoned White's older brother, Dr. Clayton S. (Sam) White, president emeritus of the Lovelace Medical Foundation in Albuquerque, New Mexico. Twenty minutes later, the editor received a chilling one-sentence telephone call from Justice White: "Don't ever call any member of my family again." The editor was shaken, because he had initiated the contact at the suggestion of Ira Rothgerber, a Denver lawyer widely thought to know the justice better and longer than anyone else in the state. "Well," Rothgerber later recalled, "I blew that one. Byron was getting very publicity shy then." The published issue of the law review skated over White's early life and began the biographical coverage with a nostalgic essay by a former law partner in Denver.

As the '86 term wore on, demands to honor White grew. Near the end of the term, two dinners were held at the Supreme Court in Justice White's honor, the first a reunion of his former law clerks, the second a seventieth-birthday dinner hosted by the family. On both occasions, history was an unwelcome guest. At the reunion, Judge Oberdorfer gave a brief talk summarizing White's career and attempting to analyze the principal influences on his thinking. Later, selections from football-game films featuring White were run in one of the conference rooms. As *Newsweek* later reported, White "walked out of his own party when law clerks began screening old newsreels of his gridiron heroics." At the second party, the justice announced to his hundred-plus guests, who included friends from Colorado and the Kennedy administration, that the purpose of the occasion was to have a good time and that there would be no speeches. With that, he turned off the microphone and directed a member of the Supreme Court police force to unplug and remove the device. Only by invoking personal privilege was White's son, Charles Byron (Barney) White, a Denver lawyer, able to recover the mike in order to make brief remarks in honor of his father. Other anniversary celebrations followed when the Whites returned to Colorado for the summer—a seventieth-birthday party in Denver and a gala sponsored by the Wellington High School Alumni Association honoring his twenty-five years on the Court, attended by three hundred people. In the fall, the University of Colorado held a fiftieth-anniversary reunion in Boulder for the surviving members of the Cotton Bowl team.

The next time that the claims of history asserted themselves was in 1993, when White retired from the Court after thirty-one years and two months— the fourth-longest tenure of any justice this century. Print and broadcast journalists requested a formal news conference along the lines of the retirement conferences held by Lewis F. Powell in 1987 and Thurgood Marshall in 1991. White declined. Unbeknownst to the media at the time, he had also completely moved his offices from the Supreme Court building to the Federal Judicial Center by the day of his formal retirement, the first member of the Court not to retain chambers in the building as a retired justice since it was first occupied, in 1935. After the move, subsequent requests for individual interviews from journalists were met with the response that no interviews would be granted for one year. The strategy was designed to punish the forgetful and to defeat the newsworthiness of any product obtained by those who remembered. White's first interview was with a sports reporter for the *Denver Post,* published January 30, 1994—less than seven months after retirement. The next, and the first touching on issues involving the Supreme Court, was published June 30, 1996, again in a Denver newspaper, the *Rocky Mountain News.*

Byron White's relations with the press have been troubled since he was in college. It is hard to imagine, and few can now remember, that the terse, publicity-shy member of the Supreme Court of the United States was the most publicized football player in the country for more than one year—during his senior season, in the fall of 1937, which culminated in the second Cotton Bowl, on January 1, 1938, and throughout the spring and summer of 1938, when he weighed the choice of accepting a Rhodes Scholarship or a $15,800 offer to play football for the Pittsburgh franchise in the National Football League. He eventually was able to do both. He postponed the scholarship by one term in order to play for Pittsburgh, where he was shamelessly marketed by his undercapitalized owner and where the value of his play was the subject of constant, sometimes daily, attention. Oxford University provided no respite. He was dogged constantly by tabloid reporters from Fleet Street, including some who camped outside his rooms in violation of college regulations. It is no surprise that when he returned to Denver in 1947, after completing Yale Law School and clerking for Chief Justice Vinson, he told Ira Rothgerber he had only three goals: "to practice law, raise a family, and keep my name out of the goddamn newspapers."

His experience in Washington drove his animosities deeper. Although he treated journalists who covered the Department of Justice and the Court with courtesy—no one in the media with whom I have talked will speak ill of him on that score—he privately viewed most of the press corps with scorn. When he decided to retire, he telephoned Rothgerber and predicated his revelation with ironic rue: "Ira, I hate to confirm anything, *anything*, published in the *Washington Post*, but I have in fact decided to retire."

What unites Byron White's disdain for both journalists and historians is the obvious common thread of the professions—the presumption that someone who has not experienced an event can accurately rehearse it and, worse, pass judgment on its participants. From the time he was in college he has criticized, often in blunt terms, secondhand accounts of people or events by those "who don't know what they're talking about," usually because they lacked direct personal exposure to necessary evidence. Why, then, would he strip his files before donating them to a public archive? The answer is that a higher value prevails: materials generated in confidence must not be compromised—at least by him. The governing regime is as simple as the children's game of "scissors cut paper, paper covers stone." In Byron White's world, simple rules are rigidly observed. What makes his behavior sometimes seem unpredictable is that he makes little effort to explain the hierarchy of the controlling principles.

I was one of Justice White's three law clerks during October term 1975. Our relationship over time consisted of annually exchanging Christmas cards and visiting briefly at the occasional reunion of former clerks. When I met with him on March 9, 1993, and told him that I had agreed to undertake his biography, he responded that the work would be "unauthorized"—that I would be "on my own." Because life studies sometimes are cooperative without being wholly authorized, I wrote seeking his permission to obtain photocopies of his academic record at Yale Law School, in order to resolve the question, on which there were contradictory reports, of his enrollment in the fall term of 1941. He wrote in reply: "You are on your own, as I indicated before. I would not like to do anything to suggest that what you are doing is an authorized biography." At the same time, he took no steps to inhibit friends or former colleagues and staff members from agreeing to be interviewed for the project. The man who viewed *The Brethren* with unrelieved contempt, largely because he assumed former law clerks compromised the confidentiality of the institution they served, replied to one of his former clerks who asked his view of cooperation with my work: "He is on his own as far as I am concerned, and I would not think of trying to muzzle any ex-clerk." Justice White's concept of authorization cut both ways. He would neither cooperate nor attempt to exert any control.

The result is the most complete portrait, under the circumstances, that I can provide at this time. It should go without saying that neither Justice White nor his immediate family has provided information in connection with the work. That is not to say that they could not have helped, even archivally. The Whites retain scrapbooks, begun by the justice's mother, apparently covering his entire public career. The Office of the Curator at the Supreme Court manages an archive of seventy-three photographs of White at various stages of his life. After examining that archive with the curator's permission, I requested that several of the photos be made available for this volume; I was told by staff to expect a response within one week, but I never heard from the curator's office, which releases photos or even their facsimiles only with the justices' approval.

The behavior, especially in Washington, D.C., bespeaks someone with something to hide, but even the most skeptical investigative reporter states that "Byron White is the straightest straight arrow I have covered in twenty-five years. His personal integrity is impeccable, in the extreme." One of his lifelong fishing companions says with mixed admiration and bemusement: "He won't even let me pick him up at the airport and give him a ride to the lodge. He wants his independence. But mainly I know he doesn't want anybody to be able to say that he accepted favors from some businessman whose industry might appear before him someday."

The fame that was thrust upon him before he reached the age of twenty-one was not accompanied by glamour, comfort, or their expectation. Athletes of the 1930s and 1940s, both collegiate and professional, lived sparely and played games marked by routine physical brutality. Inconspicuous physical courage was just as necessary as speed or strength. White seldom drew explicit lessons from his preprofessional career, but those who worked closely with him felt that his own playing fields (not unlike the Duke of Wellington's) tempered his character. At various points in his career—advising Robert Kennedy on his brother's presidential campaign, facing down a belligerent governor during the Freedom Rides in 1961, bucking fashionable opinion both on substance and on internal institutional procedures as a member of the Supreme Court—White was willing to face tough choices squarely and was not to be swayed by conventional wisdom. "He was a man who knew himself and knew his convictions and didn't care too much what others thought," in Rothgerber's view. Yet White's inherent modesty and distaste for the limelight made invisible or obscure the evidence that would make him less enigmatic. "He is a very private man," observes a federal judge who has known him and several other members of the Supreme Court for decades. "And it has cost him."

Byron White is a complex figure who does little to clarify himself. His discomfort with journalists and historians made him an unappealing subject. His Supreme Court jurisprudence had a problematic side—it resided, as Judge Oberdorfer has said, "mainly in between the lines." Supreme Court justices are effective beyond the result in an individual case, however, only when they explain and justify their decisions. White's writing has often been elliptical, even opaque, earning the just complaint of colleague, journalist, and scholar alike. Judge Oberdorfer, who knows the man well, is nonetheless correct. White's personality and character fit inexactly into handy categories—unreconstructed New Dealer, legal realist, anti-intellectual former athlete. His brother, who knows him better than anyone else, underscores the point (pulling his eyes into a hard squint for emphasis): "You have to get one thing straight: my brother is unique. No one else has ever had a career like his. If you don't get that, you can't understand him."

Justice Holmes remarked that "judges do and must legislate, but they do so only interstitially; they are confined from the molar to molecular motions." Critics—both friendly and hostile—admired Byron White for his attention to the particulars of each case and his insistence, echoing Holmes, that law was created case by case and not theory by theory. "No one better manifested the saying that law is made retail and not wholesale," according to White's long-time friend Erwin N. Griswold. And so a term-by-term perspective allows White's work on the Court to be set in the context of other events in his public life, including, but not limited to, his never-forgotten athletic past. Byron White believed more than most justices during his tenure that the proper focus of adjudication was on the individual case as much as on its location in larger doctrine: the lower-court record always came first, the issue second. He was an incrementalist first and foremost, perhaps to a fault. Indeed, one of his law clerks from the early 1970s—loyal but not uncritical—insists that White is best found in "the elusive originality embedded in the particular, the judicial achievement that is most like that of the practicing lawyer." His energies term by term were often deployed on the case that drew only routine interest in others, or that he saw as fundamentally miscast due to the nature of the factual record or prudential constraints.

White's judicial career is distinguished more by application of well-developed convictions and talents than by evolution or dramatic discovery. The pattern that emerges from the welter of particulars is of a judge who holds no romantic illusions about his role or his capacity as a social engineer. In an era that lionized the judicial reformer, from Chief Justice Earl Warren to Justice William J. Brennan, Byron White was a nonconformist. He dissented in two of the most famous decisions of his tenure—*Miranda v. Arizona* in 1966, which provided police officers with a litany to recite to everyone they arrested, and *Roe v. Wade* in 1973, which established a constitutional right for women in early pregnancy to choose between abortion and giving birth. White also resisted judicial invalidation of congressional responses to campaign-financing abuses (in *Buckley v. Valeo*) and, later, to the unchecked discretion of the administrative state. As he told an old friend halfway through his career, "Judges have an exaggerated view of their role in our polity."

Dennis J. Hutchinson
Chicago
Labor Day 1997

Part I

COLORADO

1

WELLINGTON

THE TRAJECTORY of immigration for Byron White's ancestors resembled that of many during the mid-nineteenth century—a straight line west through Pennsylvania along the National Road, with progress punctuated by military service and economic dislocation. The earliest recorded ancestor is Ephraim Godfrey White, who was born in 1823 of German immigrant stock, "in poverty and amid the rugged hills of Somerset County, Pennsylvania," according to a privately published family history. He apprenticed as a harness maker but enlisted illegally at age sixteen to fight in the Second Seminole War. When he finished serving under Gen. Zachary Taylor in Florida, he returned to Pennsylvania, but quickly enlisted to fight in the Mexican War, where he fought under Taylor and Gen. Winfield Scott and was wounded in action. Again he returned to Petersburg, Pennsylvania, where he married Naomi Kemp, a native of Ireland, in 1848. Economic opportunities for a saddler and harness maker were beginning to decline along the western gateways of the National Road, which Petersburg straddled, as railroads supplanted the stagecoach trade. Ephraim White's tax assessments in the early 1850s were among the lowest in his township, and he owned no land and only one head of livestock before 1855. At the same time, the Iowa Territory was undergoing rapid development, and advertisements for cheap land there circulated widely along the National Road. The development went hand in hand with the expansion of railroads, three of which traversed

11

Iowa, from the Mississippi River to the Missouri River, by 1857. Sometime in 1855 or 1856, Ephraim White migrated to Agency, Wapello County, Iowa, in the southeastern corner of the territory, with his wife and three children. Two more—twins named Milton Cramer and Byron Brown—were born on June 27, 1857, following the most severe winter in the territory's history.

The promise of prosperity failed to materialize for Ephraim White and many other immigrants of the period. Unfavorable weather, which ruined potato and wheat crops, combined with a glut of Russian grain in 1857, at the end of the Crimean War, to send the agricultural markets into a tailspin. The larger economy was convulsed by the Panic of 1857. Railroads had overextended their lines into areas whose traffic could not supply an adequate return to share- and bondholders. Rail stock values fell considerably, and many rail companies defaulted on their bonds. Insurance companies failed, banks and businesses went bankrupt, and unemployment shot up. The bubble of debt and speculation driven by westward growth and fueled by railroads burst. The country was living through its third, and worst, economic crisis since 1800.

The outbreak of the Civil War presented Ephraim White with a dilemma. His earlier war record made him a natural candidate for a leadership position in regiments that were mustered soon after Fort Sumter. His convictions lay with the bulk of the state, which supported the Union, as opposed to lower Mississippi River communities nearby, which, by social and economic ties, favored the Confederacy. At the time of Fort Sumter, however, he had a struggling business, no property, six children, and a wife with problematic health who was four months pregnant. The governor of Iowa issued a call for volunteers when early casualties were substantial and it became clear that the war would not be over quickly, as many had hoped. White responded within a month of hearing the call. He signed up with the 22nd Iowa Infantry Volunteers in August 1862 and was elected first lieutenant of Company E, the second-ranking officer in the thirty-man company. The company mustered into the thousand-man 22d Regiment of Iowa Volunteers in September under Col. William M. Stone (later governor of Iowa, 1864–68). The regiment saw combat in the battle of Port Gibson in the spring of 1863 and then supported the siege of Vicksburg. Ephraim White was quickly promoted to captain and then to major, "for distinguished bravery" in connection with the assault on Vicksburg.

The day that Vicksburg surrendered—July 4, 1863—Major White requested a leave of absence due to ill health. It was quickly granted, and he returned home for twenty days to see his family. It would be the last time he saw his wife alive. She died in February 1864 at the age of thirty-six. White received word of her last illness in time to request another leave of absence, but it was refused.

The regiment was sent from Indianola, Texas, where he had eventually received word of his wife's death, to the Shenandoah Valley, in Virginia, under Gen. Philip Sheridan, to repulse Gen. Jubal Early's threats to Washington, D.C. Sheridan was charged by Grant to eliminate the valley threat to Washington once and for all. The 22nd Iowa played important roles in the battles of Winchester, Fisher's Hill, and Cedar Creek. White, now lieutenant colonel, was cited in the combat reports of the battle of Winchester for gallantry under fire. The 22nd Iowa then moved south and were mustered out of service in July 1865. A regimental history noted, with some wonder, the final tally: the 22d "traveled [more than] 8,000 miles, participated in eight general engagements, two sieges and numerous skirmishes, and five great campaigns, in the States of Missouri, Mississippi, Louisiana, Texas and Virginia."

Ephraim White returned to Iowa with a distinguished war record and high rank, but also with ill health (rheumatism and chronic diarrhea), no steady work, and seven children between the ages of four and sixteen. He worked as a farm laborer and relied on neighbors to help with his children. Within a year of returning to Wapello County, he married Nancy Jane Robinson, a neighbor who was eighteen years his junior. A year later, she gave birth to the first of nine children they would have together. Some of their names reflected values rooted in the Civil War. James Getty White was named for a maternal uncle who died at Vicksburg, Charles Sumner White for the abolitionist senator from Massachusetts, and Samuel Kirkwood White for the wartime governor of Iowa. Colonel White's commitment to the cause was manifested also in his energetic activities in the Grand Army of the Republic, the original Union veterans' organization.

The war nonetheless exacted a high cost. Ephraim White told the 1870 census that he was a "farm laborer," but the 1880 census listed him as "disabled." Three years later he applied to the federal government for an invalid's pension, which was granted, and in September he began receiving $16 a month. Two months later, Ephraim White moved his family for the last time. The Agency Camp of the G.A.R. presented White with an inscribed gold-headed cane, and he packed off his family in covered wagons to Audubon County, Iowa, 125 miles away in the southwest corner of the state. Again he was chasing an economic boom. Between 1873 (another panic year) and 1883, the population of Audubon County had grown fivefold, to ten thousand. The principal cause was the completion of a branch of the Chicago and Northwestern Railway, which brought lower east-west freight rates and newly built grain elevators. Rich farmland was still readily available. Ephraim White purchased his first real property, 160 acres northwest of the county seat of Audubon. His last child was born at the end of the following year. By mid-1888 he was bedridden, and he died in March of 1889. His second wife died five years later. Four of the surviving children were still minors, ranging from eight to seventeen years old.

Of Ephraim White's fifteen children, ten spent all or the largest part of their lives in Iowa, including four on family farms in Audubon County. Three spent most of their lives in Colorado, including Alpha Albert White, who journeyed to Ft. Morgan in 1900 at age twenty. There he worked on a sheep ranch for almost four years, not far from the residence of his half sister and her husband (who was also his uncle). He returned to Audubon briefly to be married, on January 27, 1904, to Maude Burger. She was the daughter of immigrants from Rheinbayern, the Rhenish Palatinate in what is now part of Southern Germany. They then relocated to Colorado, first to Pueblo, then to Fort Collins, where two sons were born, Clayton Samuel (on October 11, 1912) and Byron Raymond (on June 8, 1917, at Larimer County Hospital). Al White had abandoned farming and was starting a career in the lumber and fuel business. In 1920, the family moved eleven miles northeast to Wellington (named for a railroad official, not for the victor of Waterloo), where he was the resident manager of the Forest Lumber Company, later the Gould Lumber Company.

At the time, Wellington was a 550-resident hamlet that owed its existence to the Colorado and Southern Railroad and to the Great Western Sugar Refining Company. The dominant industry in the area was farming sugar beets, which bore the apt botanical name *beta vulgaris*. Since 1909, Colorado had been the leading sugar beet producer in the United States. Wellington had begun to take form in 1903, when the C&S branch line was extended from Fort Collins to the Wellington beet dump. Incorporation followed quickly, in 1905, and a depot was built in 1911 to handle passenger traffic between Fort Collins and Waverly, and eventually Cheyenne. In many respects, the town was simply a large annex to the depot: the grid of unpaved and unnamed streets occupied little more than three hundred acres, and a crosstown walk on foot took—and still takes—only fifteen minutes. Al White purchased a tiny five-room, two-bedroom bungalow on a boxcar-sized and -shaped lot that was two blocks from the lumberyard and another block from the depot. A block north of the Whites' house was the main street, unpaved Colorado Highway 1, which had one bank, two drugstores, a grocery or two, the post office, and the occasional rattlesnake. When the Whites arrived, in 1920, the searing local political issue of the day was whether the pool hall's license would be renewed by the town trustees. The nearest movie theater was in Fort Collins.

Wellington, altitude 5,201 feet above sea level, would be like numerous small towns on the high plains of Colorado but for its undisturbed vista of the mountains. Less than twenty miles to the west, the front range of the Rockies established the horizon, and behind them, the Medicine Bow Mountains and the Rabbit Ears Range were dotted with peaks of ten to twelve thousand feet. From Al White's front door, the short walk to the lumberyard looked west, across a flat valley empty but for the odd cottonwood tree, to the terraced rows of mountains that, at least behind the front range, often were snowcapped for most of the year. His boys, like all children along the front range from Cheyenne, Wyoming, to Raton, New Mexico, grew up with a solidly grounded sense of geography: during daylight, there was never any doubt which way was west. The mountains west of Wellington were drained by a series of creeks and streams that fed two of the great tributaries of the South Platte River—the Big Thompson, which flows south of Fort Collins, and the Cache La Poudre, which slices through the northeastern quadrant of that city. At the western edge of Wellington, just beyond the railroad tracks, Boxelder Creek meanders south until it joins the Cache La Poudre at Timnath, five miles east of downtown Fort Collins.

The beauty of the little valley town during the interwar years and the close-knit relationships enjoyed by its residents are evidenced in a detailed set of oral histories collected by the Wellington Public Library. There is an undercurrent, however, in both the oral histories and in subsequent interviews of those who came of age in the 1920s: one consequence of the crisp horizons was isolation from larger worlds. "Fort Collins was a hell of a long walk for a movie," in the words of one of Byron White's boyhood friends. "In the winter, the eastern sky was cold and bleak and empty, and sometimes you wondered if you'd already died." The sparseness of the population and the ruggedness of the country taught fast lessons: "You knew you had to be prepared for anything—storm, animals, snakes, getting lost. Self-reliance really means something in a place that can be that desolate." Others were less lyrical: "I liked growing up there, you bet; but the main thing was to get out."

The small-town calendar of Wellington and of similar towns in the region was dictated by the beet industry. The children of farmers would be absent from school during spring planting in May, and the school district declared an annual two-week holiday in October for the beet harvest. Teachers from elsewhere were shocked to discover that the school year began in September but lasted only three or four weeks until the Beet Holiday. The school schedule was dictated by economic imperatives: school came second to work, and seasonal work required field hands of all ages. Byron White did his first beet work when he was six years old, for $1.50 a day. The standard contractual arrangement between the refining company and the farmer was for the planting of a specified acreage with seed furnished by the company. The grower's payment depended on a formula whose factors were the net sugar content of the beets and the final net return on all sugar sold by the company. Payments were not made until specified dates after delivery of the crop to the refinery. Growers were responsible for contracting with workers on a piece basis for each operation in the cultivation process (thinning, hoeing, and so on).

Beet work wholly lacked romance, and beneath the sweat and grit of the jobs lay larger political issues. Byron White would later observe that the sugar beet industry meant that "the prosperity of the people depended largely on irrigation and the federal policy toward sugar." In Midwestern and European growing regions, rainfall provides adequate water for sugar beets, but the semiarid climate of northeastern Colorado requires intensive irrigation. The Boxelder Valley, where Wellington sits, was honeycombed by a network of reservoirs and irrigation ditches that supplied water to growers under contracts from the local water company. Beets were extremely lucrative compared to other crops: historically, only 25 percent of the arable land in the area, planted with beets, produced 40 percent of value for all cash crops. Eastern Colorado's unquenchable desire for water, propelled by such economic attractions, led to the historic water-diversion projects that brought water across—or through—the Rocky Mountains in both the north (the Colorado–Big Thompson Project, first authorized in 1937) and the south (the Fryingpan-Arkansas Project, first authorized in 1964). Both projects now look economically and environmentally questionable, but just after World War I, the power of water to make semiarid valleys bloom and to double or triple cash returns on land seemed divinely ordained.

Cultivation of sugar beets between the world wars was backbreaking work (it has since become highly mechanized). After the ground was prepared, the beet seeds would be planted in the spring in rows approximately two feet apart. When the seedlings reached four inches in height, they were thinned—the poorer specimens were eliminated, so that the heartiest plants grew eight to ten inches apart in rows. Then came two hoeings to control weeds. At harvest, mature beets were pulled from the ground and topped—the green leafy matter was removed from the bulb. The tops were processed for livestock feed, and the beets were hauled to a dump to be weighed. An acre could sustain thirty thousand beet plants. Every job of tending and harvesting the crop was done by hand. Workers spent hours on their hands and knees or in a stooping position, and the hours were dictated by the arc of daylight. The physical demands of the crop and the low pay for seasonal workers meant that sugar beets utilized more labor than any other commodity on comparable acreage in the United States.

Working conditions in the industry, especially the physically arduous nature of the jobs, were largely invisible to the outside world until 1935, when Hope Williams Sykes published her first novel, *Second Hoeing*. The book depicted life among the Volga German immigrants from Russia who farmed the South Platte River Valley near Fort Collins (Valley City in the novel) and who lived the proverb *'Die Riewe sein seiss, awer die Arweit is' bitter* (the beets are sweet, but the work is bitter). The teenage protagonist at one point muses wearily—"Her arms ached to the bone, and her back was solid pain. Chop, chop, up, down, up, down went her hoe. Only one phrase, going round and round in her brain, gave her comfort: two weeks, and you're through thinning."

The book galvanized revulsion over child labor in the beet fields and won the admiration of reformers, from the *New York Times* to Eleanor Roosevelt. The Sugar Act of 1937 authorized the secretary of agriculture to establish minimum wages for field hands working the crop and to ensure that child labor was not used; in effect, the former practically precluded the latter. By the time of the act, the Volga German children depicted in *Second Hoeing* had been replaced almost completely by what locals called Spanish Americans, thanks to aggressive recruiting in Texas by the Great Western company. The act of 1937 also provided some measure of price relief to growers, especially on family-sized farms, who had watched market prices bottom out in 1933 before achieving some relief under the Jones-Costigan Act of 1934. (Market prices for sugar beets had fallen from a high of $11.88 per ton in 1920 to $4.62 in 1933.)

The one feature of the beet industry where the New Deal failed to make a dent was water policy. The Department of Agriculture had the temerity to suggest early in Roosevelt's administration that the industry was inefficient and that irrigation programs under the Bureau of Reclamation need not be maintained indefinitely. Western senators, led by William E. Borah of Idaho, were powerful allies for the eighty thousand farmers who depended on irrigation for their livelihood, and the reclamation lobby grew as a sophisticated political force in the region. As the decade wore on, the industry discovered a new argument for expansion of reclamation projects in the West: independence from foreign imports during wartime.

During the 1920s, which spanned Byron White's school days, Wellington prospered briefly, then began to decline. A brief oil boom coincided with near decade-high prices for beets, but the boom was over almost as soon it started and beet prices began to slide at the same time. White later recalled:

> In the late '20s and the early '30s the farmers weren't making much money. There was very little money around Wellington, and I suppose you could say by the normal standards of today we were all quite poor, although we didn't necessarily feel poor because everyone was more or less the same. Everybody worked for a living. Everybody. Everybody.

He might have added, "all the time." Byron White worked odd jobs while he was in school—unloading lumber from train or truck, shoveling coal from boxcar to bin, sweeping out the bank building, or swinging a sledgehammer as a summer section hand on the C&S. It is no accident that he grew from a skinny, 103-pound freshman in high school to a powerful 175-pound senior. The unrelenting beet work built stamina and determination as well as physical strength.

When Byron White was in junior high school and his brother, Sam, was almost finished with high school, they rented twenty-five acres of land and contracted to bring in the acreage's beet crop. They hired other boys to help with the blocking and thinning, both hoeings, and the harvesting and topping, but they were not overseers: they worked the fields side by side with their schoolmates, and then, after their hired hands had gone home, the brothers would often have to patrol the irrigation ditches late into the night. To fight off the mosquitoes attracted to the ditches in warm summer evenings, field workers and "ditch riders" smoked cigarettes—to a man—and Byron White did not abandon the forty-plus-year habit until 1973.

Although the stock market crash of 1929 and the ensuing Depression hit Wellington hard, the most important year for the White brothers was 1928. In the fall of that year, Evelyn Schmidt was hired to teach English in the high school, and John V. Bernard was hired to teach mathematics. Bernard also became the high school's first football coach. He had actually come to Wellington in the spring of 1928 as a substitute teacher of sorts. The math teacher and coach had quit abruptly to become the extension agent in Glenwood Springs. Bernard, a senior at Colorado A&M in Fort Collins, was hired to finish the last six weeks of the year. During that period, Sam White, then a sophomore, suggested to Bernard—who had played football at A&M—that he volunteer to coach a team at the high school.

Bernard was rehired for the following year and, with the superintendent's endorsement, convinced the school board to approve fielding a team. The sum of $125 was appropriated to purchase uniforms, but equipment had to be begged and borrowed from high school and college programs in Fort Collins. "The uniforms were secondhand and didn't fit," Bernard later recalled. "The shoes didn't fit. Nothing fit. But, by God, we had a team." Fielding an eleven-man team in a high school whose enrollment during the period, male and female, never exceeded one hundred for all six grades proved to be an annual challenge; only fourteen boys came out the first year. Nonetheless, enthusiasm overcame lackluster play, and the program enjoyed vigorous support until after World War II.

Sam White proved to be a star at quarterback on the first two teams. Byron was "smart, but too small," according to Bernard, to be a starter his freshman year. Injuries—a broken arm one year, a broken shoulder another— retarded his development, but he enjoyed a successful senior year despite the team's losing season. Both Whites also played basketball during the winter and participated in track each spring. Each fall, the school staged a dance to generate funds for the basketball program. At some points, sports and work abutted, as Byron White recalled for an interviewer in 1962:

> One year a fellow named Shorty Shearer and I contracted to harvest beets for a man who had a farm three miles out of town. I remember our walking into town on Saturday for the football game, walking along the railroad tracks. We hadn't practiced for a week or so on account of the beet holiday, but everybody showed up and we still played the game on Saturday.

"It was largely through [John] Bernard that I got so interested in high school sports," White declared during the interview. "He was a very bright fellow, and he always saw that you got your schoolwork done."

White has always been an excessively self-effacing autobiographer; Bernard tells the story somewhat differently. Housing was at a premium in Wellington at the time. Unmarried female teachers lived in a "teacherage," or boardinghouse; men had to fend for themselves. Bernard lived in a room behind the town barbershop his first year. The next two, he lived with the White family and slept on a cot in the boys' bedroom. The boys slept in bunk beds, younger above older. Mrs. White charged Bernard $30 a month for room and board. Bernard, embarrassed at what he viewed to be undercharging, wrote the first and succeeding checks for $35, and there were no further negotiations. Bernard later remembered that he felt like one of the boys when it was time for horseplay, but "when Byron had homework to do, he'd throw me and Sam out of the room, slam the door, and only God would have the nerve to open it before he was done." Bernard lived with the Whites while Byron was in eighth and ninth grades, and Sam was a high school senior or in college. "When Byron worked," according to Bernard, "he worked hard. When he played, he played hard. When he relaxed, he did it alone—you know, listen to music or something."

Hard play included softball two or three nights a week in the summer for the local Elks Club team. Relaxation, besides listening to music on radio, could be swimming in nearby irrigation ditches (and once getting typhoid fever as a result) or what would become a quiet lifelong passion, dry-fly fishing. Al White and his sons took to local streams and rivers, early and often, for rainbow and other trout. Other diversions included spectator sports, especially horse racing at summer fairs. One of Bernard's most vivid memories of Byron White was as spectator, not participant. Not yet a freshman, Byron attended a district basketball play-off game in Longmont, where a local fan loudly ridiculed Wellington's uniforms, which were hand-me-down gray sweat suits. After Wellington won, Byron tapped the fan on the shoulder and asked, "Now what do you think of those sweat suits?"

Like Bernard, Evelyn Schmidt came to Wellington directly from college—in her case, Colorado State College in Greeley, the state teachers college. She was hired in 1928 to teach English, supervise study hall, oversee the drama program, and teach public speaking. Her passion was poetry, her standards were high, and she was cowed by no one. She handed out detentions to the superintendent's children, she gave stiff homework assignments, and she was a stickler for grammar. She also had great initiative. When she arrived at the two-year-old high school building, she discovered the library had space but no books, and no budget to buy them. So she convinced the Fort Collins Public Library to allow her to check out sixty books for six-week periods on her personal card.

One of the books she checked out was Tolstoy's *War and Peace,* which she gave to Sam White during his senior year and told him to provide a full report by the end of the term. Other students were impressed by both teacher and student. "Can you imagine?" one later recollected. "No one in Wellington had ever seen a book that thick, let alone read one." For Miss Schmidt, the assignment was strategic. Sam and Byron "were completely different, night and day," she later recalled. "Sam knew how brilliant he was, right from the start. He had to be challenged, but you could push him as hard as you wished, and he would come back for more." The report on *War and Peace,* she said flatly, was "quite satisfactory." Byron, she said, "had no idea how good he was. He was always challenging himself, always trying to find his limits. He pushed and dug and went further than anybody in school, including his teachers." To challenge him, she gave him and the rest of the class a two-hundred-question short-answer test on the entire syllabus at the end of the year. "He missed one and couldn't believe it," she stated. "We had a little argument, but I had dug my heels in. I was so pleased to show him he wasn't perfect. The next-best score was fifty percent—that is, one hundred wrong, from a genuine straight-A girl."

Evelyn Schmidt found the boys "so different in manner," as well as in self-regard. "Sam was outgoing and open, very loose and easygoing. Byron was very quiet, measuring every single word, showing no emotion, and revealing nothing. I was struck over and over how different they were. I think Byron was, and is, tender, and even shy." She thought Byron was sometimes curt as a defensive measure. "He was always somewhat gruff, even in eighth grade. I think he was abrupt to hide his feelings . . . he struck me as very sentimental under it all. But he never liked to show emotions. I remember one day I was greasing our car—you had to do it yourself in those days—and Byron saw me (our houses were within eyeshot; it *was* a small town), and he came over right away. All he said was, 'Get out of the way; I'll do it.' Other times, he would come over to the house on a Sunday afternoon with two pieces of cake that his mother had just baked. He would say, "Which one do you want?" and we would sit down in my kitchen and eat them together. He was such a joy. He was remarkably tender and instinctively generous but neither wished to acknowledge it nor have it recognized."

Miss Schmidt cut a wide swath through the school during her five-year tenure. Her first year, she began a poetry club, which met Wednesday evenings at her residence. The purpose was to supplement the curriculum, as she later explained. "In order to cover the prescribed curriculum, I did not have time to teach the contemporaries, which I love almost as much as Browning. So I thought I could read one evening a week to fill out the readings." She expected "a small group of girls, but the first night, lo and behold, the whole football team showed up. Coach Bernard said he simply gave up on practice those nights." Sam White (it later turned out) was, in Miss Schmidt's words, "one of the ringleaders."

Despite the contretemps, Bernard admired Miss Schmidt enormously. "She was the most demanding and dynamic English teacher I encountered in my entire career," he said of her—a compliment of some weight from a man who went on from Wellington to earn a doctorate in education and to carve out a nationally recognized career as a rural superintendent of schools. Miss Schmidt left teaching at the end of the 1932–33 school year, "when my last month's pay was a twenty-five-dollar check and a nonnegotiable state warrant." She never lost touch with the Whites, however, and attended Byron White's seventieth-birthday party in Denver. "I never realized at the time how good I had it," she said in retrospect. "Sam and Byron were splendid students. I wish I had complimented their parents at the time. They were the boys' lodestars."

Neither of the Whites' parents had graduated from high school—a fact often cited later to suggest incongruity with the academic records of their children. Byron White would correct the misimpression: "My folks had never gone through high school, but they always put going to school first, ahead of everything. I can't remember when I first thought of going to college. My brother Sam was always going to go to college, and as far as I can remember I was, too." The comparison between the education of the parents and of the children is both patronizing and anachronistic. For turn-of-the-century farm families, a college education was an expensive luxury of dubious utility. Farming promised more immediate and practical returns. Only one of Ephraim Godfrey White's fifteen children, Charles Sumner White, attended college, and he did not receive his bachelor of science degree from Iowa State College in Ames until he was twenty-six. The reason was that, in his own words, he "taught rural school in Audubon County, Iowa, for some years"—earning sufficient money in one year to buy a year of college the next, a cycle that almost doubled the customary time to finish the course. He then did the law course at the Des Moines College of Law, later Drake University, and received his LL.B. in 1904.

Byron White met Charles White for the first time in 1927, and as he later recalled, "I took a great shine to him. My dad was always interested in the law and would have made a fine lawyer himself. He used to like to discuss and argue all kinds of things with my brother and me." John Bernard confirmed the point, with a slight qualification: "Al White was a very bright man and a very deep man, but he was a man of few words. He measured everything, let you know what he thought, no adornment, and that was a compliment."

As to politics, Bernard said, "Al was a dyed-in-the-wool Republican." The die had been cast in the Civil War. The natural choice for the son of a loyal member of the Grand Army of the Republic was the party of Lincoln. Locally, although Al White was active in town politics, party meant little. The mayor and trustees of Wellington were elected under the banner of local parties or caucuses, not under national party affiliations. Al White was elected to a two-year term as town trustee in 1920 in what the local newspaper called "a very quiet election": only twenty-one of two hundred registered voters went to the polls. Two years later, he was elected mayor of Wellington and served the two-year term. He never ran for mayor again. When the Citizens Caucus ticket swept into office in 1930 with a near unanimous vote among the forty-four of 250 registered voters who cast ballots, he received a "scattering of votes" for trustee. That was the extent of his formal political career for the three decades he lived in Wellington, although he occasionally served as a director of the Wellington Chamber of Commerce.

More telling about Al White than party and local political career was his capacity to avoid conflict in a small town. He and his wife were avid tennis players, so much that he blocked and rolled a dirt tennis court in a lot adjacent to their house. Within days, the entire family could be awakened at dawn by the sound of tennis balls hitting the wall of the house. Instead of complaining to the uninvited players, he arranged to have another court built in another location. "You just can't stand on your rights all the time in a small town," Sam White later explained. "Dad understood how to get along with people."

The Whites were anything but outliers in Wellington. They were charter members of the local Odd Fellows and Rebekah Lodge and active members of the Wellington Federated Church. (Catholics and Lutherans attended churches in Fort Collins. The Federated Church was founded in 1915 when both the Congregational and Methodist clergymen left town. The abandoned parishioners, representing a total of five Protestant denominations, formed the Federated Church, which is still active today.) Mrs. White was an excellent bridge player who often anchored the bridge tables at church and high school fund-raising events. Al White was an energetic supporter of the high school, especially its sports teams, and particularly when his sons were playing. His passion for football began, in John Bernard's view, with radio broadcasts of Knute Rockne's Notre Dame games. "We always listened when Rockne's games were on," Bernard remembered. When Bernard started the high school team, in 1928, Al White asked him for books on the finer points of the game. "He didn't want to miss anything or fail to understand the strategic elements of the game," Bernard explained. The interest was a triumph of curiosity over necessity, as Bernard understood, because the Wellington team was often outweighed twenty pounds per man, wholly lacked depth of personnel, and was chronically weak on fundamental skills in the early years of the team.

Al White was able to capitalize on his studied attention to the game when Sam graduated from high school in 1930. As valedictorian of his class at an accredited state high school, Sam was entitled to a four-year, full-tuition academic scholarship to the University of Colorado under a program established by the board of regents. Sam played both football and basketball at CU and earned all-conference honors as a football end. His parents were season-ticket holders for home games.

Four years after Sam left Wellington, Byron graduated from Wellington High School with a "straight A ranking," and the superintendent of schools reported that "so far as he could discover from looking over the school records this was the highest rank ever attained" at the school. Commencement was held on May 18, 1934, and Byron White was named the "most outstanding student in the class." As he acknowledged thirty years later, the availability of the scholarship meant that "you made a noticeable effort to be first. That's how I was able to get to college." The commencement speaker was a Congregational-Unitarian minister imported from Fort Collins, who gave, according to the local paper, "an inspiring message to the students," entitled "Is Life Worth Living?" So the second White was off to the University of Colorado on a full tuition scholarship.

Two weeks after Byron White's commencement, Sam White was awarded a graduate scholarship, which covered tuition and major fees, to pursue research in the Department of Psychology. By the end of their common year at the university both would be accelerating in career directions neither had envisioned in Wellington.

Their values were deeply rooted by then, however, and in later life their moral center of gravity was always Wellington. As Byron White told the *Sports Illustrated* interviewer in 1962, "My parents . . . had a pretty simple prescription for living. You worked hard, did as well as you could and were considerate of other people's feelings." When he was asked two decades later what he had learned in Wellington, his reply was as wryly understated as it was authentic: "Do your work and don't be late for dinner." Sam White would be more blunt. Asked why he held this or that conviction, he would reply, "We learned that in Wellington," as if it were a course in ethics as well as a place.

2

"NO CLIPPINGS"

THE UNIVERSITY of Colorado, in Boulder, was founded in 1876, the same year that Colorado became the thirty-eighth state in the Union. But for half a century it was a university in name only, more a small liberal arts college than a combined undergraduate school and research institution. When the White brothers matriculated, in 1930 and 1934, CU— as it was commonly known—owed its shape, direction, and qualified success to George Norlin, who had taught Greek since 1899 and had been president since 1919. A frontier-bred "symbol [who was] a link between the past and the future," Norlin personified the university and its aspiration. Born in Kansas of Swedish immigrants in 1871, Norlin worked his way through college, went to graduate school at night, and won a graduate scholarship to the University of Chicago, where he became a student of Paul Shorey and an expert in Greek philosophy—eventually writing the introduction to the Loeb Classical Library edition of Isocrates. Norlin faced two challenges as president of the university, an inadequate physical plant and an underdeveloped graduate school. Two years before he became president, he declared that the campus looked more like a "third-rate farm" than a university. A decade later, he was chagrined when the Association of American Universities denied CU admission in 1924 because "graduate study and research in no more than a few departments seem to be, at best, beyond the experimental stage."

For Norlin—perhaps for almost all Western state-university presidents during the period—a common source drove both problems: in a time of economic volatility, the state legislature had neither reliable funds nor, more important, the desire to support higher education much beyond the baccalaureate level. College meant training, and the state was well served by the Agricultural College in Fort Collins and the Colorado School of Mines in Golden. Boulder had an engineering school but otherwise was seen to some extent as a luxury. Norlin acknowledged the comparative advantage of the sister schools in the practical disciplines and consequently tried to build CU's strength in the humanities. But the first half of his two-decade presidency was chronically distracted by the imperative of building and sustaining a medical school, and no year was free from financial anxiety. His budget never enjoyed more than fifty percent state support. The school was always tuition reliant, and the rising tide of students in the Depression decade (enrollment grew from three thousand in 1930 to forty-four hundred in 1939) brought with them less rather than more capacity to pay.

Despite the chronic financial stress, Norlin could measure two enormous achievements during the first decade of his presidency—an architecturally distinguished building plan and a nationally recognized honors program. Utilizing proceeds from a temporary mill levy, the regents approved Norlin's plan to build a series of urgently needed structures, including an arts and sciences building, separate men's and women's gymnasiums, a football stadium, and two new wings on the chemistry building. All were built under the direction of the Philadelphia architectural firm of Klauder and Day, in what came to be called Colorado Style. At a time when campuses were dominated by Georgian and mock-Gothic styles, Charles Klauder's plan utilized local, rough-cut sandstone and red roof tile in the Italian Provincial manner to create a scheme that harmonized with the foothills of the Rockies, two miles away. Two years after the last major building was completed, a new honors program, modeled loosely on the new Swarthmore College program, was introduced. In order to receive Latin honors at graduation, students in the College of Arts and Sciences were required to undertake two hundred hours per year of supervised reading from selected bibliographies. The program was applauded as one of the outstanding honors programs among all state universities in the nation. Only 30 percent of the students were eligible for the program, which routinely had a 60 percent dropout rate and raised complaints from junior faculty of being overworked.

When Norlin began his second decade as president, in 1930 (the same year Sam White matriculated), his reputation, local and national, was near its apogee but deserved to be even greater. In addition to his conspicuous achievements, Norlin had demonstrated quiet courage in one of the state's darkest political hours. Colorado politics in the mid-1920s were briefly dominated by the Ku Klux Klan, which was able to elect its candidates for governor, senator, and various local offices in Denver. Clarence Morley, the Klan-backed governor, promised Norlin all the funding he wanted, "provided the University would dismiss from its staff all Catholics and all Jews." Recounting the episode years later in a private letter, Norlin declared that he "preferred to do without that support." In recognition of his record and his sustained public defense of the humanities, Norlin was appointed as Theodore Roosevelt Professor of American History and Institutions at the University of Berlin for the 1932–33 academic year. He came face-to-face with Adolph Hitler (literally—he lived in the same hotel) and Nazism, both of which he would outspokenly condemn from the time he returned to Boulder in 1933.

For many, Norlin was the model university president and looked it. In appearance, he resembled the postwar George C. Marshall, although he was taller and less severe. The official portrait by Charles Hopkinson, who also painted Oliver Wendell Holmes, Jr., emphasizes his tutorial side and fails to capture his gravity and strength. Norlin favored tweed suits, spoke quietly and correctly, and seemed to bridge the ivory tower and the increasingly distressed world outside with both intelligence and compassion.

The 1930s posed even greater economic and political problems than the 1920s, but Norlin's successes now tended to be more rhetorical than administrative, although his skill with Works Progress Administration officials led to grants and loans for a second wave of building in the mid-1930s. He condemned oppression in Europe and defended students who left the country to fight for the Loyalists in the Spanish Civil War, but his courtly manner was losing traction with the legislature, and his reliance on aging individuals in important positions was a recipe for administrative stagnation. Norlin was famous in the twenties for refusing to enter the legislative chamber in Denver in order to plead for funding (appointments with key legislators were arranged at the University Club). The austere charm of the practice had worn thin as the depression deepened. Reliance on a popular journalism professor to develop alumni relations became more quaint than effective over time. Neither the librarian nor the comptroller was closely managed by the president, and both offices would be embroiled in scandal, minor and major, respectively, by the end of Norlin's tenure.

Even the president's rhetoric began to misfire. In 1932, when popular support for a junior college began to grow in Grand Junction, Norlin's pre-

dictably elitist response won no friends for the university. He called the legislature's funding of two new junior colleges "porkbarrel politics": "While this
has been gratifying to local pride and interest, it has been done against the
judgment of educational leaders, and it has not been in the interest of either
education or economy." In many respects, as the University of Colorado grew
in fact from college to university, Norlin remained an administrator better
suited to the former than the latter, more headmaster than chief executive.

Sam White arrived at Boulder in 1930, at the midpoint of George Norlin's presidency. The university was beginning a growth spurt, but it was still
largely rural in composition and parochial in outlook. More than 90 percent
of the student body were from Colorado. The economic riptide of the Depression would prevent many from graduating in four years. Prohibition was
still the law of the land, and would be until December of 1933; "there wasn't
any spare money around anyway," in the words of one undergraduate. Social
life revolved around the Greeks—members of social fraternities and sororities—and their calendar was organized around intramural sports and intercollegiate athletics. Sam White thrust himself into the center of this world. He
joined a fraternity and played two varsity sports: football, in which he was
named all-conference left end as a senior, and basketball. He maintained an
academic record in the top 10 percent of his class, and, in the words of his senior yearbook, "Everyone proclaim[ed] him a 'good egg.'" In his senior year
he was president of the Associated Students of the University of Colorado, an
office with less significance than meets the eye; he was not elected by the student body. Between 1930 and 1938, officers of the ASUC were chosen by a
joint faculty-administrator committee, because Norlin concluded that popular elections were too subject to electioneering abuses. Sam White was presiding officer of a student council that was chosen by senior faculty and exercised
very modest powers, primarily over social events.

The most significant influence on Sam White's college career, and ultimately his brother's as well, was neither Norlin nor any faculty member but a
fraternity brother—George A. Carlson. A senior when Sam White was a
freshman, Carlson was the son of a former Republican governor of Colorado
and a three-year football letterman. He grew up in Milliken, another sugar
beet town, thirty miles southeast of Wellington. Carlson was president of the
sophomore class and of his fraternity, was active in dramatics, served on the
ASUC board, and worked his way through school as a "hasher" (table waiter
in fraternity and sorority houses). Two months after Sam White arrived on
campus, Carlson was elected to a Rhodes Scholarship, the eighth university
student to be chosen since the scholarships were established, in 1903, and the

third in five years. Carlson went to Hertford College, where he studied ("read," in Oxford terminology) for both the bachelor of arts in jurisprudence and the bachelor of civil law degrees. His tutor was C. H. S. Fifoot. Although Carlson's academic record at Oxford was disappointing, he was widely admired by students and faculty alike. He was active in college affairs and played lacrosse for the university against Cambridge. (Later, he won the Bronze Star, Silver Star, and Purple Heart in the Pacific Theater during World War II before returning to Colorado to complete a law degree en route to private practice in Tulsa, Oklahoma.) Carlson first planted the idea of graduate work overseas in Sam White, and then actively cultivated the thought with letters from Oxford during the three years he spent there, which coincided with White's final three years as an undergraduate.

Although Sam White graduated in 1934, he stayed on a fifth year to pursue graduate study in psychology and to begin premedical course work. He was also looking out for his little brother, whose arrival he had widely and frequently advertised. "If you think I'm good," he would say to anyone who openly admired his football play, "just wait until you see my little brother." His audiences were nonplussed. "I didn't like the remark much the first time I heard it," recalled one fellow student. "And it didn't wear real well with constant repetition." Byron White matriculated at the University of Colorado in September of 1934. Almost thirty years later, he would recall lightly: "By the time I got to college my brother was already very well known, so it was fairly easy for me to get around."

Byron White planned to major in chemistry and intended to go to medical school. He pledged Phi Gamma Delta, following his brother's footsteps. He could not live in the fraternity house until he was initiated, during the second term, so he lived the first term in a rooming house, but he did not miss the fraternal company, as he later explained: "I was 17 then and I'd go out a little, but I didn't go over to the fraternity much. I was waiting on table at a sorority to earn some money, and by the time I was through work at night I wanted to study at home." In addition to hashing at the sorority house, he did odd jobs on the physical plant and for the athletic department. "He was the oldest seventeen-year-old I've ever known," recalled Jerry Scofield, then a senior and eventually a basketball teammate. He and White worked together doing odd manual-labor jobs. When Scofield complained one day about digging a ditch across campus, White rejoined lightly, *Well, I guess we're doing this now so we won't have to do it forever.* White's scholarship covered tuition and fees, approximately $100 per year; the jobs went to defray the $300–500 that room and board cost annually. Fraternity brothers in his class thought of him as a ghost: "He was never in the house that I can remember," according to one. "He went to class, went to football practice, went to his job, and went back to the rooming house to study. We never saw him outside that routine." "He was a brute for study," said another.

Thanks to the personalized publicity supplied by his brother, Byron White came to the freshman football program under an annoying magnifying glass. He was said on campus to have "no clippings," a condescending reference to the fact that he had played only one full season for a small school with a losing record and with an unimposing reputation, unworthy of substantial press coverage. His brother imposed more immediate pressure on him. In addition to the psychology scholarship, Sam had wangled a graduate assistant coaching job for the 1934 football season. *Get your butt down, White,* Sam would bark during practice when the freshman backfield lined up. *Wrong position, White,* and so on—attention that the freshman told his friends he could appreciate but could have done without.

Any doubts about the "little brother" were erased in the second, and final, freshman game of the season. The freshman team served largely as a scrimmaging opponent for the varsity, but twice a year played against opposing schools. In their first game, they handily beat the Colorado State College freshmen, 38-12. The other game would be against stronger competition, the freshmen from Denver University, the school's arch rival in the region and in the Rocky Mountain Conference, which also included Colorado College, Colorado Agricultural College ("Aggies"), Colorado School of Mines, Colorado State College ("Teachers"), Western State College (in Colorado), Montana State University, University of Utah, Utah State College, Brigham Young University, and Wyoming. The CU-DU freshman game was scheduled for November 9, 1934, at DU Stadium. Two days earlier, the buffalo was officially designated as the mascot of all CU sports teams, the result of a contest sponsored by the *Silver & Gold,* the student newspaper. The freshmen naturally became the Baby Buffaloes.

White stole the show, as Harold Nikkel reported in the *Denver Post* on November 10:

> Colorado University's newly christened Baby Buffaloes eked out a lucky 7-0 decision Friday afternoon at the D.U. Stadium over a plucky D.U. frosh eleven when Byron White of Wellington, Colo., slipped off his own right tackle and cut back over the middle to race 32 yards for a touchdown with the generous assistance of some courtesy tackling on the part of two D.U. backs.

White also kicked the point after touchdown. Nikkel reported that White "was easily the best back on the field and carried the entire C.U. offense all afternoon with a classy exhibition of slipping around end and cutting off-tackle." The unsigned *Rocky Mountain News* account was briefer but dubbed White "sensational." Harold Koonce in the *Silver & Gold* called him "stellar." No one attached the label "Whizzer," however. That would not come until ten months later, notwithstanding Leonard Cahn's insistent claim many years later that he christened White immediately after the freshman game with the alliterative nickname that White eventually came to detest. (In 1965 Cahn, then with the *Rocky Mountain News,* asserted that he coined the name "after he ran wild against the DU yearlings," and "printed it the next day," but Cahn did not cover the game for the *Post,* for whom he then worked, and filed no stories about the team in the weeks following the game.) White's performance, impressive as it was, did not make him a star overnight. He was a freshman who had proven himself once against unprepossessing opposition.

Between the fall and winter quarters, Sam White was nominated by the university for a Rhodes Scholarship, which he was awarded in early January. The award carried a £400 annual stipend (approximately $2,000) tenable for three years. He planned to read for a bachelor's degree in physiology, the traditional university course for physicians. News of the award reached the White family in Colorado by telegram from San Francisco, site of the final competition, on January 7, 1935, and made an immediate hometown splash. The *Wellington Sun* put the story at the top of the front page, and "everybody in Wellington knew, just knew, as soon as we heard the news about Sam, that Byron would have to win a Rhodes, too," according to Andrew Mair, a contemporary of both. "I wouldn't call it the greatest sibling rivalry in history, but that wouldn't be far off." Almost sixty years after Sam won a Rhodes Scholarship, a grade school class wrote each member of the Supreme Court of the United States to ask whom they most admired. The answers, with explanations, ranged from John Marshall to Abraham Lincoln to Oliver Wendell Holmes. Byron White's choice: "My brother."

As the academic year wore on, Byron White's daily routine did not change—only the sport, and occasionally the part-time job. When winter quarter arrived, he moved into the fraternity house. Another freshman, Robert Morton from Pueblo, roomed with him that quarter. Morton still remembers his roommate vividly: "He was very quiet and extraordinarily studious. (He actually tried to have study hours enforced! Unheard of.) In a student population that was mostly liberal—strongly in favor of the New Deal, for example—Byron was rather middle of the road, although he kept

most of his opinions to himself. He was quite thoughtful. I found him ideal-
istic in his views, especially about people and how one might expect them to
behave."

Freshmen were eligible to play varsity basketball at the time, and White
not only played but quickly became a starter even though he was still only
seventeen. The game bore little resemblance to its modern descendant. After
each field goal, the teams went to center court for a jump ball to determine
possession. Annual proposals to abandon the jump ball were opposed by
most coaches, who feared that players would become exhausted. The game
was consequently very slow and scores were low: winning scores commonly
ranged in the 25-to-40-point range. The most used shot was a two-handed
set shot, or push shot. Hank Luisetti of Stanford added the one-handed shot
in 1936. (Jump shots were unknown until Kenny Sailors of Wyoming introduced the shot in 1943.) The premium was on precise passing and play development.

The style of play suited White's skills nicely, because he was not naturally
fast on the court and the deliberate pace suited his methodical approach. "He
was the most physical player on the team," Fred Folsom, a teammate for two
years, would later say. "He had an odd build—no shoulders, but arms and legs
like oak posts. He played very hard, and loose balls looked like scrambles for
fumbles when he went after them." Folsom said White was effective due to determination more than finesse. "Byron's two-hand set shot had a flat trajectory, so he had to rely on follow shots and fast breaks for a lot of his points. He
was a bear on defense—all hands and elbows." Art Unger, another teammate,
observed that White's strength was passing and defense: "He wasn't a great
shot, but nobody pushed him around—nobody. He defended his space, and
the other team was on notice. That was the game then."

White's coach freshman year was Earl Harry (Dutch) Clark, a Pueblo native, who was better known as a former football player at Colorado College
and in the National Football League, and to whom White would eventually be
chronically compared. Clark was a controversial selection on the Associated
Press all-America football team of 1928. Critics thought AP sports editor Alan
Gould was a knave or a fool for selecting Clark because no player from the
Rocky Mountain region had ever been so recognized, on the assumption that
the level of competition did not remotely match that of the Ivy League and of
what is now called the Big Ten. Clark played for two seasons with the
Portsmouth Spartans (forerunner of the Detroit Lions), where he was named
all-league quarterback both years. His elusiveness and natural talent won effusive admiration from players and journalists alike. Paltry pay drove him to

coaching, first at Colorado Mines, where he coached three sports during 1933–34, and then to CU. Both football and basketball players admired Clark for his natural ability and modesty, but as Fred Folsom observed sadly, "He was a lousy coach. He simply couldn't teach you to do what he did exquisitely almost by reflex."

Clark had hoped to succeed Navy Bill Saunders as head football coach at Colorado when Saunders abruptly resigned at the end of the 1934 season. Instead, Bernard F. (Bunny) Oakes, head coach at the University of Montana, was named to the job in February 1935. Ten days later Clark signed to play with the Detroit Lions in the National Football League for $6,500. The CU athletic department had tried to keep Clark on as assistant football coach and head basketball coach, but both the $3000 salary offer and the snub in the football job search were too much for him.

Oakes had a grade A coaching résumé for the day. He had played tackle at Illinois during the Red Grange era (he was a senior when Grange was a sophomore). After graduation, he held successive assistant coaching positions under Dana X. Bible at Nebraska and Major Bob Neyland at Tennessee before his four-year tenure at Montana. While at Montana, Oakes published a two-hundred-page monograph, *Football Line Play*, which dissected every aspect of line play, offense and defense, and even detailed an eight-week practice schedule, divided into fifteen-minute increments. The book, especially the fine-tuned practice schedule, carried a clue to Oakes's coaching personality. As wags of the day said, "Bunny was anything but sunny." He was brusque, obsessive about detail, insensitive to the lives of his players outside of athletics, and suspicious both of his opponents and of staff or team members who crossed him or appeared insufficiently enthusiastic about his methods.

Almost as soon as the basketball season ended, spring football began, on March 28; it finished May 4 with a regulation-length intrasquad game. Many experienced players ignored the spring football session, but Byron White did not, and it was his play that spring—not in the freshman game the previous fall—that began to make his name. Spring football had been a fixture for several years, but press coverage had never been more than slight. The spring of 1935 was different, because expectations for the football program were rising. Although the team had achieved five winning seasons and one cochampionship in the past seven years, they had failed to win the conference championship outright and were 1-7 against the University of Utah, their principal rival in the conference after DU. The pressure was on Oakes, who brought the most distinguished football pedigree of any coach in the history of the program, and he knew it. The question, which the spring practice season would begin to clarify, was whether he had the personnel to deliver a championship season, including victories over both Denver and Utah.

Newspapermen from Denver and Boulder monitored the spring drills with unprecedented interest. Oakes initially welcomed the attention but quickly grew nervous with repeated, and unanswerable, questions about team strengths and weaknesses. Almost half of his lettermen were engaged in other sports, and his freshmen were physically impressive but unproven. The final major factor affecting the team's performance was the capacity of the players to adjust to a new coach and a new system. Oakes wisely retained the basic offense that Saunders, and most other coaches of the day, used—the unbalanced single wing.* The only substantial modification Oakes added to the existing offense was a weakside attack, which focused on reverses by the wingback. He also added more trap blocking, effective but difficult to execute.

The press finally quenched its curiosity about the new regime on April 19 in the first of two full-scale intrasquad games. "Byron White, the strong-legged young freshman from Wellington, was the whole show on offense," wrote the *Boulder Daily Camera*. White scored on touchdown runs of 25 and 12 yards and carried the ball on play after play. He was even more impressive in the final game, on May 4. Howard (Ham) Beresford, who had been basketball coach two years prior to Dutch Clark before becoming sports editor of the *Daily Camera*, wrote: "Byron White's 85-yard run to a touchdown after intercepting [a] pass was right up thru the whole [opposing] team . . . zig-zagging[,] straight-arming, shaking tacklers off with his powerful legs for one of the prettiest runs we have seen." The *Rocky Mountain News* put both White and, indirectly, Oakes on the spot. "If you have a pencil handy," began the lead paragraph by Monte, the *News* reporter, "jot down this name: White." According to Monte, "He can carry the mail and needs little help in his carrying. The youngster, it seems he's but a freshman, can go thru a broken field like measles in a crowd. Then he can pass, kick and receive . . . and what is that but an answer to a coach's prayer." Oakes tried to downplay both White and the team ("I'd hate to send these boys against Washington or Washington State. It would be terrible"), but Monte smirked: "And your recorder of these remarks smothered a skeptical, 'Oh, yeah,' behind a polite hand." Both the star—still a month away from his eighteenth birthday—and the coach were now in the local limelight.

---

* Four linemen lined up to the right of the center, two to the left, with the backs lined up in a row at a forty-five-degree angle from the deepest back to the nearest back. The center snapped directly to a back, usually the deep back.

Byron White spent the summer in Boulder working during the day and playing softball in the evening. When term resumed, White returned to the classes-football-work-study routine he had established as a freshman. The high hopes for the football team that had developed during spring practice quickly withered in the face of a brutal early schedule and a rash of illness and injury, which included a serious knee injury after the first game that effectively put White on the shelf for the season. He had initially been injured in practice more than a week before the opening game of the season, on September 28, against the University of Oklahoma at Norman, and did not scrimmage for the entire week before the game, a 3-0 loss in which White played well but briefly. A week before the next game, against the University of Missouri, White injured his knee again in a scrimmage against the freshmen and was briefly hospitalized. He did not even suit up for the Missouri game and did not play in any of the next five games. Although he would see action briefly against Wyoming in the penultimate game of the season, for all practical purposes his season was over before the team returned from Norman, Oklahoma, and the season opener. "Everybody thought I was through," he later recalled.

Two days after the Oklahoma game and four days before the devastating scrimmage injury, on September 30, 1935, the *Denver Post* printed, for the first time, the name that would forever be lashed to him: "Whizzer White is Shifted to Fullback Post," said the one-column headline. The two-paragraph story, which carried no byline or wire-service logo, reported that Oakes had announced "that Byron 'Whizzer' White, sophomore sensation, will start Monday learning the fullback assignment," a strategic decision obviously designed to allow both White and William (Kayo) Lam, the two best backs, to play at the same time. As White told friends later, the season was a double loss: *I couldn't play, and I got rechristened.* On October 4, the name was printed for the first time in the *Silver & Gold,* in a reference to "Byron 'Whiz' White, the sensational understudy of Lam." The *Boulder Daily Camera* climbed on the "Whizzer" wagon and printed the nickname for the first time three weeks after the *Post* and the *Silver & Gold.* No newspaper had used the nickname during White's freshman year, and even the usage by the *Post* and the *Silver & Gold* did not become routine until the basketball season was under way several months later. The *Rocky Mountain News* did not use the tag until White's junior year.

Although Byron White would later say that the nickname must have been coined "by some sportswriter who didn't like me," the genesis of the tag was more complicated than a single moment of spite. White suspected that the author was C. L. (Poss) Parsons, sports editor of the *Denver Post.* Parsons never manifested any animus toward White, nor did he take credit for the nickname. Students recall the name being "in the air" early that fall. Kayo Lam even quipped before the Oklahoma game that "I had to beat out the great Whizzer White" in order to start the opening game of the season.

Whatever the source of the nickname, there is no doubt about the driving force behind its popularization. The *Silver & Gold*, having succeeded in changing the school's mascot, began a campaign in the fall of 1935 to have a player named to an all-American football team. The operation began as a one-man show, pushed by the sports editor, Mark Schreiber, but it soon enveloped the entire staff and became an annual goal with first Lam and then White as the candidates of the year. Thanks to nationally impressive statistics and perhaps, in some measure, Schreiber's efforts, Kayo Lam—who was beginning to lose his own quotation marks—was invited to play in the annual East-West Shrine football game in January. He failed, however, to make any all-American list other than as a fifth-team selection on a minor team. The Lam-for-all-American campaign was doomed from the start. Not that Lam was an empty candidate: in 1935, he set a national rushing record with 1,043 yards on 145 carries and led the nation in total yards (rushing, passing, punt returns, and kickoff returns) with 2,225. Lam was victimized by being located between the coasts and playing in a conference whose quality was still under suspicion, despite Clark and the handful of recent graduates who were playing effectively in the professional ranks.

Two further factors damaged Lam's candidacy. The first, reinforcing suspicions about the region, was that in 1936 CU lost every game except one to out-of-state competition and was outscored by a three-to-one margin in losing to Oklahoma, Missouri, and Kansas—nationally respectable teams from the Big Six Conference. The second was, in the words of a contemporary observer, that "no one saw him play": all-American teams were chosen by panels of coaches and sportswriters still largely concentrated on the East and West Coasts and to a lesser extent on the Gulf. No writer with a national reputation ever saw Lam play. Of the twenty-four all-American teams chosen in 1935, only one player from west of the Missouri River was named to any team— Bobby Grayson, a halfback from Stanford. His career had been chronicled by writers from San Francisco and Los Angeles newspapers, including Braven Dyer of the *Los Angeles Times,* the nationally recognized writer who served on Grantland Rice's board of advisers for the widely respected *Collier's* team. Robert C. (Bob) Zuppke, who coached both Red Grange and Bunny Oakes at the University of Illinois, captured the artifice of all-American voting: "Often an all-American halfback is made by a long run, a weak defense and an inspired writer." Grange enjoyed the most famous nickname in football, "the Galloping Ghost," and Zuppke's players were largely exempt from geographical bias. When the Downtown Athletic Club of New York City inaugurated an award in the fall of 1935 for the outstanding player in the country, the bias was candidly institutionalized: players from west of the Mississippi River were not eligible. The following year, the name of the award was changed to the Heisman Trophy and players nationwide were eligible. From 1936 to 1941, the winners came from Yale two years in a row, Texas Christian University, Iowa, Michigan, and Minnesota. The first Westerner to win was Terry Baker of Oregon State in 1962.

If the *Silver & Gold* was to realize its ambition for a hometown all-American, it needed a new candidate and Zuppke-like luck to overcome the handicap of geography and its attendant consequences. Byron White was the obvious choice, but his football future was uncertain. Throughout the fall of 1935, his knee was subject to constant swelling and he was urged to undergo surgery to correct the condition. He refused. "I decided I wouldn't let them operate, that if I couldn't play athletics then what the hell," he claimed years later. In fact, he was hardly nonchalant about his athletic future. He realized that competition and physical challenge were fundamental parts of his personality, so he took aggressive steps to restore his ability to play. He had the university athletic trainer tape his knee for support every day, and he pushed himself to be in condition to play basketball during the winter. The physical condition required accommodation, as he later explained: "When you have a bum knee like that you develop a protective reaction. Anytime anyone got within 10 yards of me, I'd make damn sure my knee was bent. You can't get hurt as long as it's bent." He started every basketball game during the 1935–36 season, "and by the time basketball was over I knew the knee was O.K." He decided not to play spring football, but "I played baseball, and after the baseball season I put on my football cleats and worked out with the knee."

The academic year ended in multiple triumphs for Byron White. He had rehabilitated his damaged knee; won all-conference honors, largely on the strength of his defensive play, on a basketball team that managed only a 6-8 win-loss record; received the Phi Delta Phi gold medal for the highest grade in inorganic chemistry; lettered on the conference championship baseball team; and finished the year with one of the four straight-A records in the sophomore class in the College of Arts and Sciences. In addition, he had made a decisive change in career direction, as he would later recall: "I started off studying chemistry and mathematics and science, but by the end of my second year I'd switched over to the humanities and economics. I quit chemistry just at the point when you've done all the boring memory work and it begins to get interesting. I have a feeling that if I'd kept on I'd have ended up a doctor." He never explained the reason for changing majors, and those who inquired said the response was inaudible.

White began his junior year with a lot to prove, principally to himself. The new major drew on different intellectual skills than the hard sciences. His fraternity brothers joked that it was a difficult adjustment, because he failed to make a straight-A record for the first time winter quarter. The greater challenge was to make a comeback in football, the game that he found the most challenging and the most stimulating, and to do so he pushed himself harder in practice than any other member of the team. During the summer, he had built up the knee by working as a hod carrier (cement, bricks, and the like) on university construction crews. Despite the self-designed therapy, the knee required a brace, and a technical adjustment to his kicking game, as he later explained: "If I kicked the ball [at] the normal height my knee gave me trouble, so I had to learn how to kick low. It was great for accuracy and kicking into the wind but not much good for getting [tacklers] down under the punts."

Once he adjusted the kicking style, the next challenge was to maximize its utility. Because the low trajectory did not provide enough time for his teammates to cover opposing receivers, he spent extra time practicing to kick out of bounds with precision. Before other players arrived for team practice, he and Art Unger, who played end, would compete to see who could punt out of bounds closest to the ten-yard line and then the five-yard line. "I lost a lot of 'malted milk shake' bets doing that," Unger would recall with a smile many years later.

White also spent extra time working on punt receiving. As he once explained, "Oakes put great store in the punt and the punt return, and he saw no reason why you couldn't play basketball with a football, catch it while you were running at full speed." He spent thirty to forty-five minutes a night after the formal practice had ended working on catching punts at full speed, "learning how to go to the ball at the last possible second." Once he caught the punt, he ran a zigzag pattern downfield and practiced throwing his hip and stiff-arming tackling dummies held by teammates. "I hated that," said Unger. "It was like getting hit by a freight train that was turning a corner."

The stiff-arm part of the regimen was especially lethal. White once dismissed the stiff-arm as simply a way of "keeping me away from" potential tacklers, but those on the receiving end remember more menace. Instead of holding a tackler at bay with his free arm, as many runners did, White waited an extra six inches and then blasted the heel of his hand at his pursuer's fore-

head or the bridge of the nose. Victims called it "White's left jab," and assistant coach Frank Potts said it had the "power and effect of a billy club" and an element of meanness.

For all of the extra practice and all of the calculated skills development, White's teammates uniformly thought his principal asset was determination. Unger, probably the best natural athlete on the squad, had no doubt: "He was a determined man. He had goals and he was going to accomplish them. Everything he did he was going to do to perfection. He was unique. There was never any patty-caking with Byron. You've heard that 'winning isn't the only thing.' Well, that's just stuff; Byron thought it was the only thing. It's win, win, win. He instilled that in everybody who played with him. It was leadership by example—he was *so* competitive. From the first down, he was ready to go all out."

The student newspaper continued to experiment with literary gimmicks to catch the eye of all-American selectors. At first Byron White was "Straight-A White," then "Lord Byron," and finally "the Duke of Wellington." Once the season began, the paper settled on "Whizzer White" by a process of elimination. "Straight-A White" made him sound like a drudge, "Lord Byron" was effete, and "the Duke of Wellington" was clumsy, incongruous, and repetitive (Jim Counter, a three-year backfield letterman, had been called the Duke two years previously, and the editorial board thought a "Duke a year" looked unimaginative at best). "'Byron White'," one editor explained, "was just too dull a name to be inspiring. Maybe if he had been 'Willie' or 'Wes' he wouldn't have needed the nickname. But 'Byron' . . ." The *Rocky Mountain News* finally made the usage unanimous on September 6, 1936, when the paper referred for the first time to "Whizzer White." At the age of nineteen, Byron White was saddled with a name he did not seek, did not like, and could not shake.

The 1936 season put Byron White on the national map, but not because of an artificial public relations campaign or because of a championship season. Colorado was 4-3, was shut out by Oklahoma for the second straight year, and was beaten in the season-ending Denver game by 1 point. White's individual play was often remarkable, however, with the high point coming against Utah in midseason. Colorado lost the opening game of the season 8-0 to Oklahoma, then ground out victories over Mines, Aggies, and Colorado College. A homecoming crowd of eight thousand watched White turn in the most impressive single-game performance in the school's history against Utah. He scored four touchdowns—a 39-yard run off-tackle, punt returns of 38 and 33 yards, and a kickoff return of 88 yards to open the second half. The final touchdown of the day was a 50-yard scoring pass from White to Unger. The

final score was 31-7 and the outcome was never in doubt. Utah made more first downs and amassed more yardage than Colorado, but was beaten all day by the big play. White set school records, which still stand, for punt return yards and average in a single game, 159 and 53, respectively. His punting was acutely precise, even though the field was dusted with snow and footing was unreliable. On Colorado's first possession, which could not penetrate the Utah 40-yard line, White punted 30 yards out of bounds on the Utah 1-foot line, which put the opposition in a corner from which they never recovered. The play was widely regarded as the turning point of the game. Local sports-writers began to suggest that White was the second coming of Dutch Clark.

Some of the luster wore off the following week in what was the confer-ence championship game when Colorado lost 14-13 at Utah State. White missed a point-after-touchdown kick, which would have left the score tied, and even with all sixty band members kneeling in silent prayer, he kicked wide by inches on a 35-yard field goal attempt in the fourth quarter. He rebounded somewhat a week later in the final game of the season, on Thanksgiving, be-fore nearly twenty-eight thousand spectators at Denver University Stadium. All of the action happened in the first period. After Denver scored a touch-down and converted the extra point, White took the ensuing kickoff 2 yards deep in his end zone and ran, by a very indirect route, the length of the field, to make the score 7-6. Exhausted from the run, during which he had to retreat and change direction twice, White asked Unger to kick the extra point. "I blew it and I felt god-awful," Unger would later recall. "But Byron never said a single critical word. 'You did your best,' that was it." The loss meant that Colorado finished fourth in the conference.

By White's own estimation more than twenty-five years later, "I had a pretty good year." But the comparisons to Clark and the burgeoning attention to every facet of his campus life were less than welcome:

> That was when all the publicity started, and I had a little difficulty adjusting to it. I thought it was exaggerated, and besides, it set me off from the other people. As much as anything else, you never felt you were alone anyplace. You couldn't go anywhere without someone wanting to come up and talk to you. But I figured these newspaper people knew what they were doing and it was their job to do it, so I went along as best I could.

White not only disliked the press pestering him incessantly with ques-tions—about his social life, his daily schedule, his career plans, his brother, his parents—but also felt acutely uncomfortable as a celebrity, even at his frater-nity house. "Byron would do anything to avoid postgame parties at the

house," one fellow member remembered. "He drew a discernibly sharp line between those who were established friends and acquaintances and those hail-fellow-well-met swells who simply wanted to patronize celebrity," in Robert Morton's view. "His inaccessibility could sometimes reach the point of rudeness in those circumstances." Morton and others saw White's reactions essentially as a defense mechanism. "You must remember that he was extremely shy," said another fraternity brother, Kenneth C. York. "The university was very small, and Byron couldn't walk across campus after his junior football season without being stopped by people who didn't know him. He had no way to be prepared for what hit him, and I think he found the whole situation very difficult."

Celebrity status was a multiply mixed blessing for White. Whatever the costs, he also began to enjoy nonathletic benefits because of his growing status as a regional athletic star—benefits that he evidently desired. In October 1936, he allowed himself to be placed in candidacy for the largely ceremonial office of junior class president. He was elected over a field of three others. In the spring, he allowed himself to be considered for a position on the multi-member commission of the Associated Students of the University of Colorado. The faculty-administrator Executive Council still controlled selections to the commission, and for the first time in years, no input from students was solicited prior to the new selections. White and nine others were chosen by the council to form the new commission, and the *Silver & Gold* reported that "Byron White was unanimously selected President by the new commissioners."

The commission had limited powers but could make appointments to committees, choose editors of some publications, shape policy for campuswide entertainment, and the like. The only controversy during the commission's tenure was over a new plan for class elections. White and the commission backed a plan providing for elections from slates chosen by representative committees, much like nonpartisan political caucuses, and preferential ballots. The objective of the plan, which the new commission was unable to implement in the following fall term, was to break the political power of the fraternities and sororities, which had swung their weight in the past, sometimes in an ugly fashion, in slating and balloting. Much of the impetus for reform came from the non-Greek students, who were called Barbs (for "barbarians," the antithesis of Greeks), and who formally organized in 1934. The new plan was widely, and accurately, assumed to be a precursor to wresting selection of the ASUC commissioners from Norlin's handpicked Executive Council and returning the process to the student body. By all accounts,

White presided over the weekly Monday night business meetings of the commission with chilly dispatch, as if the meetings were an annoying distraction and, as one commissioner would later remember, "as if he had something better to do. Byron may have been shy, but it could come across as, well, cold." Luther Stringham found White "brisk, businesslike." Other commissioners found him humorless. "I remember teasing him once early in our term about smoking," recalled one commission member. "I asked him, 'What's a big-shot athlete like you doing with a dirty habit like that?' He snapped, 'What's the matter? Haven't you ever had to work a beet field at night?' I grew up in a city, and he knew it. I didn't tease him again."

Discomfort in what passed for public office within the university never translated onto the athletic field. Impatience was limited to politics. "As long as you did your job," according to Art Unger, "Byron never said an unkind word. He was the most team-oriented person I ever played with." During the remainder of his junior year, White won all-conference honors again in basketball and earned his second letter in baseball, as a third baseman. The basketball team missed the conference play-offs by losing to Denver in the final game of the season, and the baseball team won the conference championship by beating the Colorado Aggies in extra innings on the last day of the season. White missed three games of the basketball season with the flu and a chest injury, but the knee held up for the entire year and became, in his own terms, a "factor" rather than a "handicap" for the balance of his career. Over the summer, he honed his skills for the football season, particularly his pinpoint punting and his downfield passing; he set up an old tire at 40 yards and practiced firing passes through its center on the dead run. Expectations were running high for the football team during his senior year, and he would not disappoint anyone.

3

WHIZZERMANIA

W HEN BYRON White opened his copy of the *Silver & Gold* on September 24, 1937, the multiple worlds he had come to inhabit popped up on every page. On page 1, he appeared as president of the student body, offering incoming freshman a welcome he labeled "hearty, if peculiar: It is a welcome of anticipation. It is up to you to do the rest." The balance of the three-paragraph statement seemed, to knowing readers, autobiographically informed:

> Your actions and accomplishments will justify any welcome however warm. And with very little adieu, the University, grown overnight to keep pace with each year's demands, opens to be the testing ground for a completely new crop of hopes, ideals and ambitions. The results will serve as a means to grade the untried talents which you have.
>
> All of which means that you are the backbone and spirit of the Colorado University. You can make of it what you will. Of course the promptings and advice of professors, and upperclassmen should be heeded at times. Perhaps even you can do a little sifting and grading of your own. That would be very commendable.

Turning to page 4, he found his name at the end of a list of five members of the class of 1938 who had straight-A averages for the preceding quarter in the College of Arts and Sciences. He was now in the top 1 percent of his class academically. He had not elected to join the honors program, however, so regardless of his grades during his senior year, he would not graduate with Latin honors. The second section of the newspaper, devoted primarily to sports, was, as one editor put it, the Byron White section. White's name appeared on nearly every page.

The following Tuesday, the paper noted that White had been mentioned in Grantland Rice's Friday night radio broadcast and had been identified as a prospective all-American in Francis Wallace's story in the *Saturday Evening Post,* even though Wallace erroneously referred to White as the "Buzzer." The *Silver & Gold* reported that Rice said, "'Whizzer' White was the ideal moniker for a triple-threat tailback, and he believes the man with that name was going to live up to it." Rice's mention, slight as it was, could not have been more important to the all-American ambitions for White. Grantland Rice, a Phi Beta Kappa graduate of Vanderbilt University, was the acknowledged dean of American sportswriters, the most widely circulated sports columnist in the country, and, more to the point, the selector of the annual *Collier's* magazine all-American team—successor to the Walter Camp team, the original all-star team. At fifty-seven, Rice's influence was enormous, not so much for his expertise as for a charming combination of experience, memorable if florid writing (he christened the Notre Dame "Four Horsemen"), and impeccable manners. Although White had already been singled out as a potential all-American and Rhodes Scholar by the *Illustrated Football Annual,* a whisper from Rice was an alarm bell to the sportswriting guild. Mark Schreiber, who had moved from sports editor of the *Silver & Gold* to become assistant business manager for athletics and director of sports publicity in 1936, could begin to see his student dream coming true.

Enthusiasm for Byron White as all-American became infectious. The local press dropped all pretense of objectivity once the season began. On October 2, Colorado hosted the University of Missouri, a perennial contender for the Big Six championship, but not at its strongest in 1937 nor its sharpest on opening day. When Colorado narrowly won 14-6 in a game that was statistically almost even, the United Press reported that "the dervish White bewildered the Missouri defense, and between his kicks and swirling cutbacks kept the Tigers on the defensive most of the game." Then the predictable comparison popped up: White "tore" through the opposition, including its many substitutes, "in such a way that Colorado fans were comparing him to 'Dutch' Clark, the best footballer ever developed in the area." Notwithstanding the local press's boosterism, White produced objectively impressive achievements throughout the 1937 season, and he constituted a one-man offense. More significant than the flashy play, White called his own number twenty to twenty-five times per game, and his yardage was acquired in short, brutally fought chunks, unless he could break into the clear, usually on an end run. The publicity thus came at a high price physically, and White would "play black and blue," as one teammate later said, all year.

After the Missouri game, Colorado rolled up four straight victories by shutout in Boulder over teams from the Rocky Mountain Conference (Utah State, 33-0, BYU 14-0, Colorado Aggies 47-0, and Colorado Mines, 54-0). White scored at least one touchdown in every game and had a total for the month, counting the Missouri game, of 62 points on eight touchdowns and fourteen extra points—one of the highest totals in the country. As the achievements piled up and the national recognition began to grow, the nagging question recurred whether White and his teammates had been seriously challenged by the competition. That issue would be put to rest, if at all, when CU played its first road game of the year, at Utah on November 6, against the only team in the league that conceivably had equal strength.

Before then, two important nonathletic issues inserted themselves onto Byron White's schedule. The first was an irritation, the second became an obsession. On October 18, White announced, as president of the ASUC commission, that class elections held on October 15 had been declared void, due, in his words, to "political combinations" and other "underhanded activity" in connection with the voting. The reform endorsed by the commission the previous spring had been frustrated. The question was what would replace the voided balloting. Although much of the class officers' work was ceremonial, selection of senior class officers affected senior week activities and commencement activities in the spring. When three weeks elapsed with no further decision by the ASUC, the *Silver & Gold* criticized White for failing to take prompt action to sort out the electoral mess and to enable new officers to be installed in time to plan the events in the spring. The editorial was entitled "What Now, Mr. White?" and was published the day that the football team departed by train for Salt Lake City and what everyone knew was the make-or-break game of the season.

The other issue was personal, but much more consequential, and enough to rattle White from time to time over the next two months. On October 14, the day before the tainted elections, Dr. Walters Farrell Dyde, professor of education, announced that all applications for Rhodes Scholarships were to be submitted to him by October 21. Each scholarship was tenable at Oxford University for two or three years of study and carried the same stipend that Sam White—then in his third year of study there, enjoyed, £500 per annum.

Dyde chaired a university committee composed of five deans who screened applicants and selected "two, three, or four" to be endorsed by the university for competition at the state level. Under the selection plan recently adopted by the Rhodes Trust, each state was entitled to nominate two finalists to a "district" (of six states), where four winners would be chosen from a field of twelve. The university planned to announce its nominees on October 26. The state competition was scheduled for December 15 in Denver, the district competition for December 20 in San Francisco.

In order to apply, White had to prepare a thousand-word essay describing his objectives for Oxford and for his career, and he had to secure letters of recommendation from at least a half dozen referees, a time-consuming enterprise even for those, unlike White, with time-rich schedules. Under the will of Cecil Rhodes that established the scholarships, the criteria for selection were "scholastic attainment," character, leadership, and "fondness for, and success in, manly outdoor sports." Rhodes claimed he sought "no mere bookworm," but "the best man for the world's fight." Questions were beginning to be raised in popular journals about the program and whether it produced cultivated, public-spirited alumni or simply successful trophy hunters. Regardless of the answer, by 1937 the scholarships carried sufficient prestige to make universities seek them for their students and advertise their acquisition as broadly as possible. Every year for a decade, the *New York Times* had printed the list of winners and their nominating schools, and the institutional affiliations served in the public mind, rightly or wrongly, as *Good Housekeeping* seals of approval.

Interviewed by *Sports Illustrated* magazine twenty-five years after the fact, White would say of the Rhodes Scholarship that he "hadn't consciously worked in that direction; in fact, I don't think I thought any more about my grades in college than I had in high school. I guess I just got in the habit of working." Perhaps White, by then Justice White and a self-conscious symbol of the New Frontier, was trying to extol the virtue of hard work for its own sake. Perhaps he was trying to rub the luster off some of his résumé, a function of the aggressive posture of demythification he began to affect in the 1930s— a response to overheated journalists who tried to make him larger than life and who bruised his privacy in the process. Whatever his motivation, all of the contemporary evidence refutes his modest dismissal of the scholarship as an objective. His fraternity brothers, teammates, and fellow commissioners all knew that he had set the scholarship as a goal, if not the primary goal, for his senior year. Letters from his brother, in England, had persistently reinforced the idea. In late October, Sam wrote: "You are to be commended for your great athletic record, but, Byron, I only hope you do not neglect your studies for football." After the Utah game a week later, Byron White told a reporter for the *Rocky Mountain News*, "I would quit football if I thought by playing I would jeopardize my chances for getting the award." Over the next two months, he would admit to several sleepless nights worrying about the competition. According to the *Silver & Gold*, he was one of the first candidates to submit a completed application to Dyde. On October 26, he became one of five nominated by the university committee.

The day Dr. Dyde announced the deadline for filing applications for the Rhodes Scholarship (October 14), Byron White's all-American hopes—or at least the hopes others had for him—took an important turn. Henry M'Lemore, the thirty-one-year-old sports humorist for United Press, began a cross-country tour of the hinterlands to determine whether East Coast–quality football was in fact being played west of the Alleghenies. M'Lemore's column was syndicated in more than three hundred newspapers and emphasized witty writing over reporting or serious analysis. For M'Lemore, the Western tour had multiple benefits: in addition to an all-expenses-paid two-month trip, he could play the urbane swell among the rubes, and at the end of the journey he would be rewarded with a one-week vacation near some of the premier horse racing tracks in the country before watching the Rose Bowl on January 1.

When M'Lemore arrived in Boulder, university officials treated him like a visiting head of state even though the team (accompanied by M'Lemore) was scheduled to leave for Salt Lake City forty-eight hours later. Escorted by Mark Schreiber, M'Lemore was introduced to President Norlin, the business and coaching staff, and two players—White and center Gene Moore—before viewing half of one of Oakes's exhausting three-hour practices. M'Lemore told the *Silver & Gold* he had two immediate impressions: the stadium resembled the Yale Bowl, and he was delighted to discover that an undefeated, untied team respected academics enough to forestall practice until late afternoon instead of "after lunch"—like "all the major schools I have attended on my trip." The primary focus of the stopover, of course, was White, and M'Lemore devoted his column on November 3 to his quarry. "He's in the headlines more than Mr. Roosevelt," M'Lemore wrote, "and declarations that he is the greatest football player in the country are more common than silver dollars." After mentioning that "many critics rate him as better than Earl ('Dutch') Clark," M'Lemore announced that "I came here to look at him and was besieged with stories of his prowess." The stories were mainly old press clippings, and the column rehearsed White's four-touchdown performance the year before against Utah "on a snow-covered field that offered insecure footing." President

Norlin even got into the act. M'Lemore quoted him praising White's busy schedule and academic achievements and concluded with a remarkable anecdote: "Between the halves of the Utah game last year President Norlin said he visited the team's dressing room and found Whizzer stretched out on a rubbing table—studying his calculus." Although M'Lemore wrote as if he were convinced of White's national star quality, he still had doubts, which he aired openly to fellow journalists. His first question to Chester (Red) Nelson of the *Rocky Mountain News* when he arrived in Colorado had been, "What kind of competition is he playing against this year?" Until that question was put to rest, White was more of a curiosity to the Eastern press than a certified national star.

A note of artificial drama accompanied the team's departure for Salt Lake City Thursday evening. That afternoon, the semiannual meeting of Phi Beta Kappa, the national academic honor society, elected seven students on the basis of their records over three years. White was one. Both Norlin and Robert L. Stearns, dean of the Law School and president of the local chapter, wanted White to know of his election (formally, "receive his bid") before the train departed, so Robert F. Tyler, White's predecessor as president of the ASUC, was dispatched to the Boulder train station with the news shortly before the scheduled departure. Tyler breathlessly conveyed the bid to White shortly before the train left for Utah. Friday's newspapers reported White's election, and "Phibetakappatriplethreat" became one word overnight.

When the team arrived in Salt Lake City early Friday morning, it was mobbed by local reporters seeking copy to sustain what had been overheated coverage all week in both Salt Lake City newspapers. (The *Salt Lake City Tribune* meanly, but accurately, labeled a picture of White "Team Photo.") For once, White was relaxed with the press, probably because Oakes had become so testy that the entire team was put at ease by the overbearing coach's pregame jitters. Oakes, who had yelled at Denver reporters earlier in the week for referring to his "wonder team," refused to answer any questions, but according to the *Deseret News,* White "was more amiable. Likeable in fact. He grinned at his coach's irritability and obligingly looked at the birdie." After breakfast, Oakes dispatched the team to its quarters but reminded them not to drink any water other than that imported from Boulder on the team train. He feared local sabotage.

Almost twenty thousand spectators watched the Rocky Mountain Conference championship be determined Saturday afternoon, November 6. Oakes was still obsessed with chicanery by the opposition. When White came off the field after the pregame coin flip, Oakes yelled at him, "Why the hell didn't you grab that coin when they tossed it up? You know they might have run a phony coin in on you!" The game was physically punishing for both sides, and "there was a lot of feeling between the teams," as O. T. Nuttall, White's blocking back, would later recall. More than one unnecessary-roughness penalty was called, and two Utah players were carried from the field on stretchers, including one in the fourth quarter with a compound leg fracture. Both teams had trouble getting started offensively, and there was no score at halftime. Colorado advanced as far as the Utah 23 in the first quarter and the 15 in the second quarter but failed to score. In the second quarter, Utah missed a 28-yard field goal, and minutes later Colorado staged a goal-line stand at the one-foot line. In the second half, Colorado scored first when White kicked a 17-yard field goal on fourth down, but Utah went ahead 7-3 with three minutes left in the period. The third quarter ended with Utah punting on fourth down at its own 48-yard line.

What everyone agreed was the turning point of the game occurred on the first play of the final period. All week Utah had been coached to punt away from White, either by kicking out of bounds or directing high spirals to the opposite side of the field from where White lined up to receive. The strategy worked until the fourth quarter, when Paul Snow's punt was high enough to allow White to camp under it. The height also allowed six of Snow's teammates to converge on White at the Colorado 14-yard line. He retreated 10 yards to his own 5-yard line, and as he would later recall, it seemed as if more than eleven Utah players were on top of him. Paul McDonough, Utah's six-foot-four-inch end, got a hand on White, but he spun away, and in a decision as daring as it was physically demanding, he changed direction, sprinted for the opposite sideline, and charged upfield. Once he turned the corner and broke into the open at the CU 20, he picked up blockers, some of whom were startled to find him still on his feet. With their help, he raced past three converging tacklers who had the angle to knock him out of bounds, and eluded his final pursuer thanks to a crisp block by Joe Antonio at the Utah 30-yard line.

That made the score 10-7 for Colorado. Moments later, White put the game away with a more conventional 57-yard touchdown on a fake inside and end-around run with textbook blocking from every man. The final score was 17-7, and more than one newspaper headline the next day read, "White 17, Utah 7." White's other statistics were extraordinary. He carried twenty-three times for 187 yards (all but 30 of the entire team's rushing yardage), an 8.1-yards-per-carry average. He was 2-for-4 passing. He averaged 25 yards per return on punts, as the *Tribune* put it, "by handling the ball at top speed with courage that only confidence can bring." He averaged 39 yards per punt, including three that went out of bounds inside the Utah 20.

A brief melee broke out after the game when spectators spilled onto the field from the grandstands; a faint attempt was made by a few Colorado fans to capture a set of goalposts, and there were one or two fistfights among drunken fans. Surprisingly, both locker rooms were relatively calm. Both teams were physically spent. Ike Armstrong, the Utah coach, shook hands with each of his players and told the team philosophically, "Congratulations, boys, you just made Whizzer White an all-American." In the Colorado locker room, while White and others were savoring a beer, there was a knock on the door from an unexpected quarter, and what happened next remained indelible in White's memory for fifty years. "I'll always remember that the president of Utah's student body came to our locker room after the game with a piece of the goal post. . . . He gave it to me and I saw someone had painted, 'White 17, Utah 7.'" The memento also contained a crude map of White's cross-country touchdown run.

The focus of postgame news accounts naturally was the long-distance punt return. Many Utah sympathizers who witnessed the plays swore later that White stepped out of bounds as he tightroped the east sidelines. Others, conceding the score, debated how many yards White actually ran, counting his retreat and cross-field run as well as the sprint downfield; the consensus was 140 yards. "It will go down in the books as the greatest run in R.M.C. grid annals," wrote Mack Corbett in Sunday's *Deseret News*. "If it had been made east of the Mississippi, it would doubtless be the greatest feat in the country this season." To Corbett, it "won a grim ball game that had begun to look very doubtful for the Boulder eleven, and stamped the Whizzer as an all-American if ever there was one." Corbett captured the sentiment of those who saw White play that day. As he wrote, "With 18,500 pairs of eyes—some admiring, some critical, but the majority skeptical—fastened on him, Byron White came through."

For those who were neither eyewitnesses nor readers of the Denver and Salt Lake City newspapers, White's feats were barely visible the next day. The *New York Times* carried only a hundred-word story from the Associated Press that mentioned the score but focused on the postgame melee. (As the *Silver & Gold* later said correctly, almost no one among the fourteen hundred members of the special Union Pacific train returning from Salt Lake City realized they had witnessed a riot until they read the wildly exaggerated accounts in Sunday's *Denver Post* and *Rocky Mountain News*.) M'Lemore filed a very brief game story that began, "Byron (Whizzer) White, Colorado University's sensational quarterback, picked up the white man's burden again today and single-handed, carried his team to a 17-to-7 victory over a big and strong Utah eleven."

The world outside the Rocky Mountains obtained a much fuller and more colorful account of White's performance on Monday, November 8, when Henry M'Lemore filed his six-hundred-word column describing the game. It was a letter of recommendation that began:

> As this itinerant observer gets it, the recipe for an all-American backfield man, as endorsed by the leading press box chefs, reads something like this:
>
> Take equal parts of speed, power and savvy. Mix well with ability to kick and pass. Add a generous pinch of endurance, and serve on any field.
>
> If that's right, then Byron (Whizzer) White of Colorado deserves the gold watch, the parchment scroll, the double-breasted sweater and all the other items that a man named on the All-America comes in for.

M'Lemore added statistics about the game, mentioned White's Phi Beta Kappa key, detailed the 97-yard run—so inexplicable that White must have used "mirrors"—and concluded that Utah was no "pushover": had White been on the sidelines, Utah "would have defeated Colorado by a brace of touchdowns."

Henry M'Lemore's vivid, if self-important, essay, which was carried by 412 newspapers across the country, made Byron (Whizzer) White, as he now was, a national figure overnight, and started a journalistic craze. On November 10, French Lane of the *Chicago Tribune* published a lengthy profile of White based on a quick trip by rail to Colorado. Two days later, Harry Cross of the *New York Herald-Tribune* labeled White "the newest galloping ghost about whom the whole country soon will be talking." The story was a stream-lined rewrite of M'Lemore's two dispatches from the Rockies. Cross took artistic liberties with the facts (among other things, he had Norlin visiting the Utah locker room again to find White reading calculus, and he put White on the track team), but he punched the magic button at the end of the brief profile: "folks out that way say that White is even better" than Dutch Clark, who was due in New York Sunday to play for Detroit against the New York Giants.

White was now the household name of the season, and something that might be called Whizzermania was in full swing. Although there were two games left on the schedule, against Colorado College on November 13 and Denver University on Thanksgiving, the twenty-fifth, White's admirers in the Denver press corps were already looking beyond the end of the regular season. In what was apparently an uncoordinated division of labor, the *Denver Post* staff worked behind the scenes to lock down White's all-American status, and the *Rocky Mountain News* staff initiated feelers for invitations to postseason exhibitions or bowl games. Poss Parsons told his press box cronies that he would meet with Alan Gould of the Associated Press in New York near Armistice Day to plump for White. "It was 'Poss' that convinced Alan Gould of Dutch Clark's ability," the *Daily Camera* explained to its readers on the eve of the Colorado College game, "and he hasn't urged a man for All-American honors since then."

White was now the number two scorer in the country. That statistic, combined with all of the groundwork for the previous six weeks—plus the recent rash of national publicity—put all-American honors within reach. Postseason play was a much greater challenge. First, the University of Colorado was on record against postseason play as a matter of policy. When CU and Utah State had tied for the football conference championship in 1935, Parsons suggested a one-game play-off to establish the champion, and Oakes readily agreed, but a faculty committee, closely controlled by Norlin, vetoed the idea. Norlin thought postseason play was inconsistent with the institution's educational mission. On a more practical level, the proposed game was planned for the eve of "closed week" for both schools, the week before pre-Christmas finals. Neither Norlin nor his deans could tolerate the disruption that would be caused by that timing. Even Eastern football powerhouses such as the University of Pittsburgh did not excuse athletes from classes or examinations for athletic events. If the policy could be changed, the question remained, who would take the gamble of inviting a small and essentially unknown school—even with a marquee player—to a showcase game whose success turned entirely on ticket sales?

Chet Nelson, the sports editor of the *Rocky Mountain News,* and Hank Rabun, his senior writer, launched a two-man campaign for a bowl invitation within twenty-four hours of Colorado's victory over Utah. Nelson wrote a lengthy column calling the promotion of the team "and its all-America candidate, the versatile White," a "civic duty," and quoted Henry M'Lemore, who had witnessed all three previous Orange Bowls, as certifying Colorado's worthiness, provided the season ended with no defeats. Rabun called the promoter of the Cotton Bowl, J. Curtis Sanford, whom he knew, and elicited a telegram of interest, which became a news story in Monday's paper. Nelson and Rabun sent Sanford a two-thousand-word letter arguing Colorado's merits and enclosed a complete set of clippings on White and the team, covering the entire season. The Cotton Bowl had only been played once before and was the newest of the New Year's Day games (the Rose Bowl dated from 1902, the

Orange and Sugar from 1935). Sanford promoted the first game as a showcase for Sammy Baugh, the passing star from Texas Christian University, now with the Washington Redskins. The gate was only seventeen thousand, less than half the capacity of the State Fair Park Stadium, but a moral and—barely—financial victory for the oilman-turned-promoter.

CU officials, remembering the corner they had backed into two years before, at first threw cold water on the whole postseason idea and pointed out that closed week was December 6–11, followed by final examinations, December 13–18. The business manager left the door open for a late-December game, "provided the boys would agree to return to practice following final examinations." "The squad itself shows a total disinterest for post-season speculation," publicly because the regular season was not finished and privately because they feared Oakes would turn their Christmas vacation into a lonely, nerve-wracking grind far from home—a worry that had dampened player interest in postseason play two years before.

By the end of the week, the "campaign to gain all-American recognition for White [had] reached state-wide proportions," including newspaper petition drives, as one nationally syndicated football columnist noted. (Years later, when everybody was taking some credit for White's prominence, Poss Parsons would insist that he had ordered his staff to mount a publicity campaign—"at least a story a day about what a great guy White is"—but the staff's actual output does not support the claim; the *News* was much more aggressive promoting White.)

More publicity was on the way. Motion picture coverage of the game against Colorado College was suddenly scheduled by three newsreel organization, Fox-Movietone, Pathé, and MGM. *Life* magazine announced that it would send a photography team to campus the Monday after the Colorado College game to capture White's entire daily routine on film—"getting up in the morning, going to class, studying in the library, going to lunch, dressing for football practice, taking a shower after practice, eating dinner, and finally studying for his next day's classes."

The *Rocky Mountain News* sports section ran White's life story in five installments on consecutive days leading up to the Colorado College game. The series, coauthored by Rabun and Gorman Hogan, was unsurprising—Horatio Alger becomes Frank Merriwell—except for Rabun's first-day interview of White. Rabun talked to White after he finished his hashing job one evening. Rabun portrayed White as genuinely modest, obsessed with study, worried about the Rhodes Scholarship interviews a month away, and reticent to discuss football. The interview struck a nerve when Rabun asked if any of his teammates resented "the publicity being received by the recently-named Phi Beta Kappa. He grew grave. 'If I thought for one moment that such was the attitude of any member of the squad, I'd turn in my uniform tomorrow and never set foot on the field again,' he shot back."

Against Colorado College, White scored three quick touchdowns in ten minutes, and Colorado sailed to a 35-6 victory. The touchdown binge kept White the number two scorer in the country, with 100 points. He still could claim the title, because the leader—Sid White of Brooklyn College, with 113 points—had completed his season.

After the Colorado College game, Colorado officials announced that they had received "overtures" to participate in both the Sun Bowl and the Cotton Bowl on New Year's Day. The *Rocky Mountain News* speculated that an invitation from the Sun Bowl would not be considered but that in any event no decision would be made until after the DU game, on Thanksgiving. The statement was an exercise in principle serving expediency, because in two more weeks Colorado's cachet would probably be substantially increased. Not only would they have finished an undefeated season, but at least one all-American team—selected by Newspaper Enterprise Association—was due to be published by then, and White's expected certification would tie up the team's package in a neat bow. The problem, over which university officials could do nothing, was that the major bowls, including the Cotton, might forswear Colorado for more established national teams with bigger followings.

The off week between the Colorado College game and the season finale against Denver University was an eerie lull with White in the calm eye of the storm. Speculation continued that CU would receive a Cotton Bowl invitation, but the final offers would probably not be issued until after Thanksgiving and perhaps not until two days later, when unbeaten Pittsburgh—ranked number one in the country since early November—finished its season at eighteenth-ranked Duke. The only consequential event in Boulder during the quiet week was the long-delayed senior class elections, which got White and his commission off the hook with the *Silver & Gold*.

The final week of the regular season began with a telegram from Curtis Sanford to the *Rocky Mountain News* stating that Colorado was one of six teams left in contention for Cotton Bowl bids. The others, besides the SWC champion, were Santa Clara, Pitt, Villanova, and Fordham. The CU athletic department announced that two offers to play in a charity game in Los Angeles on December 18 had been rejected because final examinations did not end until the eighteenth. The two-year-old policy was intact, but pressure was building against it. Simultaneously with the announcement by Colorado

officials, the Newspaper Enterprise Association became the first organization
to announce its all-American team, and White was one of four backs named
to the first team. Most all-star teams would not be named until early December, when all schools had completed their regular schedules; the Associated
Press, which had the most electors, was not due to ballot until the day after
Thanksgiving.

Colorado was undefeated and untied but ranked only sixteenth in the
country by the Associated Press. But for the traditional rivalry, the Thanksgiving Day teams were unevenly matched. Denver was 6-2 but had lost to the
same Colorado College team that CU had pummeled ten days earlier. Oakes
still fretted over the risk of an upset, which would tarnish the entire year, so he
closed all practices during the week of the game. Both the press and the team
itself found the decision humorous. "So what was Bunny going to do," one
player wondered, "disguise the Whiz as down marker and pull off a trick
play?" White, needing no trick plays, lived up to his reputation. He accounted
for all of Colorado's scoring in a comfortable 34-7 victory before nearly thirty
thousand fans in Denver. White scored two touchdowns on scrimmage runs
of 51 and 19 yards, threw two short touchdown passes, returned an intercepted pass 46 yards for another touchdown, and kicked 4 extra points. White
played with unusual intensity, even for him. At one point in the third period,
he tackled Denver halfback Charles Loftus, who was thirty pounds lighter,
with a ferocious body slam that triggered a volley of boos from DU supporters. Chet Nelson defended the play as high-spirited in his column the next
day, and Loftus issued a statement two days later that "there wasn't anything
wrong" with the tackle. "White was perfectly justified in tossing me down. I
was still in motion and still inside [the sideline]." (On the next play, White intercepted a pass from Loftus and ran half the length of the field for CU's final
touchdown of the afternoon.)

Colorado won the Rocky Mountain Conference championship, and
White finished the season as the leading scorer in the country, with 122
points. The most remarkable statistic was the one that tended to be forgotten
the fastest, perhaps because it required so long to explain. Although White
was often described for popular purposes as a triple-threat player, the Oakes
offense relied very little on passing, so White's principal threats, in conventional terms, were running and kicking. Yet if one totals what the National
Collegiate Athletic Association classified as all-purpose yards gained—yardage
from rushing, receiving, pass interception returns, punts returns, and kickoff
returns—White had the most accomplished season in NCAA history for a
half century. White set the record for average all-purpose yards per game of

246.3 in the 1937 regular season, a record that lasted until 1988, when Barry Sanders of Oklahoma State averaged 295.5 on his way to the Heisman Trophy as a junior.

The day after the Denver game, President Norlin convened a meeting of the university athletic board to discuss the general question of postseason play and the specific offers on the table. Notwithstanding precedent, resistance to postseason play melted away gradually that night, and Oakes was told to have the team vote in two days on whether to accept any postseason invitations.

The result of the vote was not foreordained. The athletic board had directed Oakes to hold a team meeting Sunday to learn the details of the expected offer and to vote on whether to accept it. The players and the athletic board had different priorities. The board was trying to secure the most prestigious opponent; Norlin, in particular, wanted a university that was academically respectable. The players were more concerned about the question of *any* postseason play than of the identity of their prospective foe. The team's priority was shaped by two facts—the postseason offers were still inchoate, and the idea of another month of practicing under the irritable Oakes was, as one player later put it, "more like a bad job than a sport." Not only were practices physically exhausting, with an unusual proportion of full-contact scrimmaging, but they lasted half again as long as scheduled. Two-hour sessions routinely became three, and players with hashing jobs were constantly late; more than one player lost his job for chronic tardiness.

In addition to extending the unpleasant training regimen, postseason play would deprive the players of family holidays and provide them no rest before the winter quarter started. "Not many families could afford to travel very far for a postseason game," Lou Liley explained later. "Christmas with Bunny was not very attractive. Byron [White] made a little speech about not needing to play anymore, since we'd won the conference and all, but in the end people decided to play." A team that had read all year about the poor reputation nationally of the Rocky Mountain Conference evidently had something to prove. Ironically, the Colorado players were given the opportunity to do so when the Pittsburgh players, weighing precisely the same concerns about postseason play, decided, on the same day that the CU team met, against accepting any postseason invitations. The vote was sixteen to fifteen.

Two days after the team meeting, Colorado formally accepted an invitation to play in the Cotton Bowl against the winner of the Rice–Southern Methodist University game to be played on Saturday, December 4. The acceptance was conveyed theatrically by Gov. Teller Ammons of Colorado, a football enthusiast, in a staged telephone call to Sanford, the promoter.

The next day was bittersweet for Byron White and his enthusiasts. He was named to the first team of the all-American team selected by United Press, but he came in a distant second in voting for the third Heisman Trophy. Clint Frank became the second consecutive Yale University team captain to win the award. He polled 534 points* from sports editors, writers, and radio announcers nationwide (although more than half of the voters were located east of the Mississippi River). White was second, with 264 votes, and Marshall (Biggie) Goldberg of Pitt was next, with 211. On the same day, the Robert W. (Tiny) Maxwell Memorial Football Club announced that Frank had been unanimously chosen as the outstanding college football player of the year. Dick Harlow, the coach of Harvard and a member of the Philadelphia-based club, called Frank the greatest back he had ever seen. Frank had won universal praise, and a great deal of attention, for his courageous running and defensive play with an injured knee in Yale's final game and only defeat of the season, a 13-6 loss to Harvard.

Bunny Oakes refused to allow what he viewed as East Coast–biased honors to tarnish his star. On the day that the Heisman and Maxwell Trophies were announced, he made the ultimate comparison: speaking with the authority of both coach and former teammate, he compared White favorably to Red Grange in an interview with the *Dallas Morning News*. Oakes was in Dallas to scout the Southern Methodist–Rice game on Saturday. Promoters and sports enthusiasts were rooting for SMU, because if Rice lost, Texas Christian University would have the best record in the Southwest Conference, and a Colorado–TCU game would set up the most interesting individual contest of the bowl games—White versus Davey O'Brien, the five-foot-seven-inch, 147-pound quarterback of TCU, who was an excellent passer and leading scorer in the league (and would win the Heisman Trophy in 1938). Rice, on the other hand, had no players on the all-SWC teams announced on December 1, and the only player with any star quality was a sophomore, Ernie Lain, who as yet was more size (212 pounds) and promise than performance. Eastern newspapers such as the *New York World-Telegram* hoped for a White-O'Brien showdown, which would give the Cotton Bowl game a "backfield duel surpassing any other on New Year's Day—one that would claim a huge [radio] audience throughout the nation." "No other bowl teams have been so dependent on the skill of a single back as have Colorado and Texas Christian," the *World-Telegram* declared, but there was a nagging note of caution: "Except for one

---

* Each voter selected three men, and three points were awarded for each first-place designation, two for second, and one for third. Approximately six hundred ballots were cast.

game, however, White's opposition came from the Rocky Mountain area whose quality is unknown hereabouts and in no game was he opposed by a ranking offensive back through whom his quality could be arrived at by direct comparison." The White-O'Brien showdown did not materialize. Rice beat SMU 15-7, led by two touchdowns from Lain, and the complicated formula used by the SWC (involving win-loss records, records against common opponents, and so on) made Rice the league champion.

Less than a week later, the most prestigious all-American team was finally announced, the *Collier's* magazine team, selected by Grantland Rice and his board of advisers. White was a unanimous selection of Rice's eight-man board. Although announcement of the *Collier's* team was, as the *Silver & Gold* put it, "long-awaited," by the time the magazine published Rice's article announcing the team, on December 10, the news was somewhat anticlimactic. White had already been chosen for thirteen other all-American teams. By the end of the month, he would also be named to the first team of five others. The only major teams he did not make were the North American Newspaper Alliance and the All-American Board of Football, popularly known as the Christy Walsh team.

The *New York Daily News* pronounced White a consensus all-American on December 14 because he was named to eight of the ten major teams (AP, UP, INS, *New York World-Telegram, Boston Post, New York Daily News*, Newspaper Enterprise Association (NEA), and *Collier's* all named White; NANA and Walsh did not). Grantland Rice's story in *Collier's* pointed out that White was one of three unanimous selections (Clint Frank and Ben Chapman, the California running back, were the others) and, somewhat self-defensively, noted the inevitable comparison:

> This year Byron "Whizzer" White, a student leader for three years, hit such a dazzling pace that the Rocky Mountain region regards him as superior even to the practically immortal Dutch Clark, when Dutch was in college. He was the nation's leading scorer. He ran, kicked and passed. As a blocker and tackler he was better than most. The entire Colorado attack was molded around him.

Even Rice, who had begun to draw attention to White in late November, was worried that White had never seriously been tested. Privately, other journalists were suspicious of the Whizzer White bandwagon. Shirley Povich, the columnist for the *Washington Post*, was startled when the United Press list— the first of the major all-American teams—came in over the wire: "I frankly couldn't believe it," he recalled many years later. "I even wondered if they [UP]

were trying to build up their client base in the West. White simply never played against real competition. The case for him just wasn't there." Publicly, skeptical sportswriters remained circumspect. Joe Williams, the widely syndicated columnist for the *New York World-Telegram*, was the only writer who addressed the issue directly in a sustained fashion. Williams observed that Frank, White, and Joseph Routt, a lineman at Texas A&M, "swept the election. Every responsible selector picked them. They must be good." The rest of his column examined the premise and wondered aloud whether White was the "sleeper" of 1937, the new Dutch Clark, who had been picked in 1928 "as another of those desirable unknowns that provide an illusion of completeness." Williams agreed that Clark was now recognized as a "remarkable player," if not necessarily "the greatest quarterback of all time," notwithstanding the fact that in college he "played in a Class B league and faced only minor competition. Sometimes the big frog in the small pond is genuinely big."

He concluded:

> Normally, this year's Colorado contribution—Mr. Whizzer White—would qualify as the sleeper of the all-teams despite the fact that he led the nation in scoring points. Statistics of this sort, as a rule, don't mean much. It's simple even for a fair ball-carrier to click off touchdowns against weak defenses.
>
> The Whizzer may be everything a great back should be; he may be more entitled to All-America rating than any other back in the country; but in the rush to get aboard the White band wagon the selectors haven't forgotten Dutch Clark and how magnificently he stood up in later years. This memory made the Whizzer's selection practically unanimous. A majority of the selectors had overlooked the Dutchman, but they were going to be sure they didn't overlook the Whizzer. Not a rational approach to the problem, but probably a correct decision.

The subhead for this section of Williams's column was "An Assist for Dutch Clark." Alan Gould, the AP sports editor who had originally put Dutch Clark on the national map, later observed that "'Dutch' made it relatively easy for 'Whizzer' White to make most everybody's all-America."

The day after the *Collier's* team was announced, the owners of the National Football League met in Chicago. The main purpose was to conduct a draft of college seniors for the 1938 season, that is, for each team in sequence to identify players with whom they would have first negotiating rights for one-season contracts. It was the third draft for the owners. The first was established in 1935, largely to settle the negotiating rights to Jay Berwanger, winner of the first Heisman Trophy and consensus all-American at the University of

Chicago. At the meeting on December 11, 1937, White was selected as the first draft choice of the Pittsburgh Pirates. The *Washington Post* headline read, "Pirates Get 'Buzzer' White." He was not the first overall choice in the draft. In fact, he was passed up by the Cleveland Rams, Philadelphia Eagles, Brooklyn Dodgers, Chicago Cardinals, Green Bay Packers, and Detroit Lions.

For most teams participating in the draft, White was seen as a wasted selection. Exactly a month before, E. A. Batchelor's column in the *Detroit News* speculated that White was a "certainty for the [Rhodes] Scholarship," a "prospect" with "more allure than professional football." Even with the endorsement of Dutch Clark, who had coached White as a freshman in football and basketball, the Lions assumed that White would rather be in England than in the NFL in the fall of 1938. Clint Frank announced that he would not play pro football, if offered, when he accepted the Heisman Trophy earlier in the week. "I entered football as a game, played it as a game, thrilled to it as a game—and I leave it as a game," he told an audience of nine hundred at the Downtown Athletic Club when he received the award. Despite Frank's declaration, the Detroit Lions drafted him, although not until the final round.

The decision by Arthur J. Rooney, Pittsburgh's principal owner, to spend a first-round choice on White surprised many, not only because of his prospects and presumed preference for study at Oxford but also because of lingering questions about his quality in the face of truly national competition. Rooney, always known to press and public as Art, explained to a skeptical interviewer from the Associated Press that he believed a triple-threat player was the best value for his money. He claimed to have been inspired by watching Sammy Baugh in Washington's overwhelming 49-14 win over the New York Giants in the NFL championship game a few days before the draft. "Your chances are better if the player happens to be a man like Baugh, who can do more than one thing," Rooney said. "Watching him against the Giants gave me the idea of going after a fellow like Whizzer White. He could make my ball club."

Others thought Rooney had more complex motives. In the public mind, professional football was a distant second choice to the college game for autumn entertainment, and the teams tended to be ragtag collections whose personnel changed from week to week and whose schedules were changed more often than prizefight cards. "I thought Rooney was trying to bring some class to the league," Shirley Povich later observed. "The idea of a Phi Beta Kappa all-American had family box-office appeal, and Rooney wanted to exploit it." If Rooney offered a high-salary contract, White's gate appeal would only be

enhanced. The problem was that Rooney had lost money on the team four of the five years he owned it, including a reported $21,000 deficit for the 1937 season. Rooney had a reputation as a successful "plunger," an inveterate horse racing gambler, but neither he nor anyone else believed that a successful football team could be financed at the track. Drafting White was the first step in an incomplete multistep plan to boost fan interest and reverse his team's fortunes. Three days after the draft, Rooney was undaunted by White's Oxford ambitions and told a New York sportswriter that "we'll get him anyhow. We'll offer him $10,000 and then see if he'll play. That's a lot of money in Colorado." In fact, Rooney was prepared to offer White $15,000 plus an $800 bonus to play in exhibition games. The figure was twice that enjoyed by any other player in the league, including Sammy Baugh.

There is no evidence that White was anything but bemused by the NFL draft and Rooney's quoted comments. His sights were locked on his most immediate target—the Rhodes Scholarship. The state competition was scheduled for December 15 at the University Club in Denver. There were a total of twelve candidates, from whom two would be chosen to attend the district finals in San Francisco the following week. The University of Colorado fielded five candidates, including White; Denver University, three (including Robert H. McWilliams, later chief justice of Colorado and eventually a federal judge); Colorado College, two (including Leonard vB. Sutton, later chief justice of Colorado); Colorado School of Mines, one; and the United States Naval Academy, one. (Candidates could compete either in their home state or in the state where their college was located.) Peter H. Holme, a prominent, sixty-year-old Denver lawyer, was chairman of the five-man selection committee. The committee nominated White and Edward Pelz—another junior Phi Beta Kappa and class president, and also a track letterman at Colorado College—to the district interviews. The next day, White put himself through a grueling two-hour workout in view of the six-day break in training that his trips to San Francisco and Dallas would cause.

The following day, White left Denver for the district interviews in San Francisco. He went by train, Union Pacific's Pony Express, which departed Denver Friday night and arrived early Sunday morning. He got a ride to the Denver train station from a friend in Boulder and discovered that his departure was a photo opportunity for the Denver newspapers. For the first time in his college career, he lost patience with the press. "Here's the way it is," he said to Gorman Hogan of the *News*. "I don't want all this tied in with the scholarship exams. Members of the committee might think I'm getting the big head or something getting pictures taken every time I turn around." Hogan was unfazed by the testy remarks. The next day the *News* ran two pictures of White—one shaking hands with a friend and the other appearing to study, although the cutline slyly conceded that White was in fact reading a railroad timetable.

For the next day and a half, as the Pony Express rolled westward, White spent almost all of his time reading. He was not studying, because he had already taken early final examinations for the quarter, and the interviews focused on academic interests and objectives generally, not on specific information. As White had told Hogan, "cramming for a Rhodes examination just can't be done."

For the first fifteen years of the Rhodes Scholarships, some cramming had been necessary. All candidates were required to demonstrate knowledge of Greek, like other Oxford applicants, and many plausible candidates lacked the necessary facility with the language. The astronomer Edwin Hubble, for whom the space telescope was named, later admitted to his father that he structured his curriculum for more than one year to prepare himself for the qualifying examinations for Oxford and the Rhodes Scholarship. (Hubble, who had also won election to an uncontested campus office in order to demonstrate his leadership, won in 1910, read for a law degree at Oxford, then returned to the University of Chicago for a doctorate in astronomy.)

The Greek examination was eliminated by Oxford University officials after World War I, so the interviews for which White could not prepare were wholly open ended, usually focused on areas of demonstrated academic interest, career objectives, and questions designed to elicit personality or a sense of humor—some evidence of an effective and engaging personality that was associated with leadership. White was more challenged by such an indeterminate interview than by a two-hundred-question objective test or double-teaming linebackers. The interviews, he said to Chet Nelson of the *Rocky Mountain News* before he left Denver for the West Coast, "[have] me worried. I'm afraid they'll cut me up and ship me back in little pieces when I get to San Francisco."

Sam White had told fellow students at Oxford that the only bad part of the Rhodes selection process was the "personality" questions. He said he was asked to describe his reaction to seeing the Grand Canyon for the first time, a question aimed at eliciting the philosophical and perhaps even the poetic. "Sam said he 'just told the truth,'" a classmate recalled, "and said, 'Now don't that beat all hell!'" No matter how much Sam encouraged Byron to pursue the Rhodes Scholarship, and he did in frequent letters from Oxford, Byron could never strike Sam's pose. "I tried to talk to Byron a few times on that trip to San

Francisco," Pelz remembered later, "but he was quite subdued. He said he just wanted to read, and I respected his privacy." Friends of White in Boulder told a reporter that he had suffered more sleepless nights worrying about the Rhodes interviews than about the entire football season.

White arrived in San Francisco to good news: there were only nine finalists, not the maximum of twelve that could have been named if each state in the district had sent two forward to the finals. Finalists were booked at the Palace Hotel, but White elected to stay at the Y.M.C.A. so he could continue to work out in preparation for the Cotton Bowl. The chairman of the selection committee was Dr. Robert G. Sproul, the distinguished president of the University of California at Berkeley. The interviews were held on Monday, December 20—the same day that the Colorado football team was due to arrive in Fort Worth to prepare for the Cotton Bowl—and were scheduled to conclude by dinner with announcement of the four winners from the district. The committee spent four hours longer than expected. At 11 P.M., the winners were finally announced: John Golay of the University of Southern California, Russell McDonald of the University of Nevada, William McEwan of Utah Agricultural College, and White.

The committee secretary explained diplomatically to wire service reporters that "we encountered great difficulties in arriving at a decision. These are all brilliant young men: I only regret there are not nine awards so each might have received one." For once, the diplomatic line had weight. Two of the five nonwinners were elected the following year by the same committee, Pelz—again nominated from Colorado—and Tom Killefer, who had been president of the student body at Stanford, where he also played baseball. White and Killefer, whose father, Wade (Red) Killefer, had been a major league baseball manager, became lifelong friends as a result of the one-day interviews, their affinity born of intercollegiate sports, fly-fishing, and mutual discretion.

When Killefer succeeded the following year, his Oxford ambitions were thwarted by the war. He went instead to Harvard Law School, where he roomed with Joseph P. Kennedy, Jr. "Byron and I didn't say a lot to each other that day," Killefer later recalled of the 1937 interviews, "but we had a long time to take each other's measure. Byron was extremely quiet but somewhat intimidating. None of us in the room could believe how fully his forearms filled out his suit coat. We all felt like wimps." Pelz and McEwan shared the same memory. Both recalled White saying little, and McEwan said that the prolonged waiting period for the committee's decision was aggravated by the fact that no one felt he had blown the interview. "The questions and conversation were very straightforward," according to McEwan. "We couldn't figure out what was taking them so long."

White expressed similar views to reporters that night. "The oral examination was conducted so that everyone was put at ease," he told the *Rocky Mountain News* by telephone. "Everything was done to help the candidates." White fielded a half dozen uninformed questions (was the test hard? did he flunk any questions?) with half-sentence answers, then announced that he was eager to get to Dallas.

President Norlin abandoned his customary restraint and issued an effusive public statement warmly applauding White, who was the seventh Rhodes Scholar selected from the University of Colorado during his presidency.

Before leaving San Francisco, White sent two telegrams—one to his parents ("Got the scholarship. Am tickled to death. Love, Byron") and one to Bunny Oakes and the team ("Successful examination. Leaving soon as possible. Keeping fit."). His parents actually learned the news from the long-distance telephone operator in Wellington, who declined to pass on the information when the *Rocky Mountain News* called late Monday night because the Whites had retired for the night. The next day they expressed pleasure and pride, but Al White declined to be interviewed at length by the *Rocky Mountain News:* "I guess enough has been said about it all. Byron, you know, isn't so strong for all this publicity. Mrs. White is terribly happy about the appointment, and so am I. I guess that's about all there is to say." A modest man from a modest family nevertheless became the first American Rhodes Scholar to have the news of his election published from coast to coast; papers that carried reports included the *San Francisco Chronicle,* the *Los Angeles Times,* the *New York Times,* the *New York World-Telegram,* and the *Washington Post.*

Byron White had little time to enjoy the realization of his long-held goal. When his travel arrangements were firm, on Tuesday, he wired Oakes: "Leaving San Francisco by plane this evening. Arrive Ft. Worth 8:25 A.M. Wednesday morning. I need a workout." Not only did he need to catch a plane for Colorado's training site at Texas Christian University, in Fort Worth, but sportswriters wanted to know whether he would play professional football or accept the scholarship. White had long ago resolved the issue, but he would be called upon to repeat and explain his choice several times in the next few days. His interview with the Associated Press just before he left San Francisco was typical. He modestly dismissed questions about the details of the interviews ("I can't remember a thing about them") and stated, "I'm happy, I'm satisfied. It took my breath away." But he added quickly that the award "definitely ended any possibility he would turn pro. And he made a startling disclosure: 'I never received any offers.' Previously he had been reported as receiving pro bids." The *Chicago Daily News* got the point: "White Shouts 'No' to Pros; He's a Rhodes Scholar," read the headline over the AP dispatch.

The story evoked one final column on White from Henry M'Lemore, who had been in Los Angeles since December 1, nominally preparing to cover the Rose Bowl but also indulging his passion for horse racing. His column for December 23 began by extolling White's commitment to his studies and his uncommon capacity not to mistake athletic achievement for virtue or ultimate success ("To him the end zone was a touchdown and nothing more"). The balance of the column was a cool analysis of the Cotton Bowl, beginning with the frank contention that "if it were not for White, Colorado never would have gained the honor of a bowl game. Actually, Whizzer White and not Colorado was invited to the bowl." M'Lemore regretted that White did not have better support, an observation that carried authority because of his eyewitness coverage of the Utah game. He predicted that Rice would beat Colorado but that White would be the best player on the field, and ended the column with homage unusual both for its frankness and its genuine note of admiration:

> [The prediction] is hardly a guess at that, because I saw White play and he has what it takes. He can run, he can drive, he can kick and he can pass. Too, he can take it. He will go into that game knowing that not only the eyes of Texas will be upon him, but the eyes of the entire country. Knowing this, he will deliver. He'll do all right at deah ol' Oxford, too.

The same day, a columnist with an even wider circulation than M'Lemore, Bob Considine of the Universal Service Syndicate, quipped: "Who remembers 'way back when it was hot news if a college football player turned pro? . . . Now, as the case of Whizzer White shows, it's hot news when he doesn't."

Not all of the pregame publicity extolled White. The day before the columns were published, the Associated Press moved a story that emphasized incongruities in Colorado: "[They] wear fancy uniforms of silver helmets, gold jerseys and silver pants, but there is nothing 'lady-fingered' about their football." The story said that "no one on the team gets more fun out of bodily collisions with enemy players than White," despite the brace worn to protect the injury sustained as a sophomore, and continued:

> One of his favorite stunts, back in the safety position, is to head an opposing ball carrier into the sideline and bunt him out of bounds with a hip or shoulder backed by the authority of his 185 pounds of big bone and muscle. A

Utah assistant coach swears White's straightarm carries as stiff a jolt as any left hook he ever saw in the prize ring.

Another story recalled that White had been loudly booed as recently as the Denver University finale when he tackled halfback Charles Loftus like a rodeo bulldogger.

The mix of publicity intrigued what the *Dallas Times-Herald* called a "flock of Dallas sports writers and photographers," who were on hand when White's plane, delayed in Tucson, arrived several hours late on Wednesday, December 22. White brushed off the reporters on arrival and added little two days later when he finally consented to what the Associated Press called a "very brief" conversation that left "interviewers reeling":

"How were the exams, Whizzer?"
  "I don't think such things as football and scholarships should be mentioned in the same story," was the reply.
  "Will you play professional football?"
  "I should say not," came the scornful reply.

White may have stiff-armed the press out of frustration with the situation he discovered when he finally arrived in Fort Worth. The team was demoralized by Oakes's training regimen and nearly exhausted after three days of practice in cold, rainy weather. Oakes believed in training hard, regardless of the weather, because game conditions could replicate training conditions. Worried that his team had lost its edge, he tried to restore it by lengthy morning workouts followed each afternoon by full-contact scrimmages for the entire first week in Texas. The strategy backfired terribly. A steady rain Monday was followed by a soaking raining Tuesday, which turned the TCU practice field into a mud flat. Oakes ordered the players to shower with their uniforms on in order to remove the mud before taking their normal showers. "You wouldn't believe how down everybody was," O. T. Nuttall would recall years later. "Bunny was grinding us into the mud, people were getting hurt right and left, and our only hope was that the Whiz would save us when he arrived. We were confident he would protect us."

Byron White respected what Bunny Oakes knew about football and was careful to acknowledge that respect in later interviews. White tactfully omitted that he refused to be intimidated by Oakes. After one game during the 1937 season, White was soaking his bad knee in a whirlpool and reading a textbook when Oakes entered the training room and ridiculed White for not doing something "worthwhile," such as "boning up on players." The calm reply was,

"You take care of the football, coach. I'll take care of the books." Now, in Fort Worth, White had to take care of team morale. A direct confrontation with Oakes would put the coaching staff in an untenable position, so there was no dramatic showdown, but the scrimmages suddenly stopped for two days and the two-a-day practices were replaced by one light practice and one "skull session," or lecture, each day. Oakes reverted to form the following week, however, and held scrimmages in the rain and mud on the Monday, Tuesday, and Wednesday prior to Saturday's game. Now White tried to use humor to defuse the tension. Lou Liley, a reserve end who was outspokenly critical of Oakes, found his team jacket adorned one morning with a new label made of pieces of training tape, courtesy of White: C-O-A-C-H. Despite White's efforts, plenty of damage had been done. Three players were hobbled by injuries sustained during the scrimmaging, but the most dispiriting grace note came on game day: several players discovered that their protective pads were still wet, smelled of mildew, and needed to be wrung out before they took to the field for the game.

In the final week before the game, with Christmas out of the way, press attention intensified. White was irresistible copy. On December 27 he was presented with the Douglas Fairbanks Award as the Most Valuable Player of the 1937 season. The award was sponsored by *Liberty* magazine and was based on ballots sent to fifteen hundred players on one hundred major college teams, who were asked to rank the best player against whom they had played all year and to quantify specific skills. For once, weak competition proved to be a boon: all 131 of White's opponents who were polled rated him the best, the only player unanimously named. Second in the voting was Clark Hinkle, the Vanderbilt center, followed by Clint Frank. The most absurd pregame story was in the *Houston Chronicle*. James Nance, who played end for Rice and, like White, had recently been elected to Phi Beta Kappa, bragged that he was going to take his own key along to "wave it in Whizzer's face." Nance could expect to see White on Colorado's end-around plays and said with mock menace, "I'm going to make a special point of meeting this Whizzer."

Almost a dozen newspapers from Colorado and Texas were covering the game, but the real pressure on White and his teammates came from the national newspapers. Bill Corum of the *New York Journal-American* and Joe Williams of the *World-Telegram* devoted space in their pre-bowl-day columns to White and the lingering question of what size pond he and Colorado belonged in. Williams, calling White the "most talked-of back of the year," pointed out that as the "most celebrated" player on the field he "will be a marked man from the opening gun. . . . The stage is set for the most poignant individual drama of the day. Will the Whizzer stand up?" Williams predicted that "it will take more than the Whizzer to beat Rice": "The Whizzer could be all that everybody says he is and still be stopped if his supporting cast is greatly outmatched. So in a sense Rocky Mountain football is just as much on trial as the All-America status of the Whizzer." Arch Ward, the sports editor of the *Chicago Tribune,* predicted that Colorado would win, but Rice was a 13-point favorite and carried odds of two and a half to one.

Grantland Rice, never too far in front of the field, captured the conventional wisdom and predicted that White would be the best player on the field but that his team would lose to superior manpower. Rice provided a focal point for the pressure on White with a stanza of his self-styled poetry:

> *How good is Colorado, pal—we hear the echoes call?*
> *How good is Byron Whizzer White—when Whizzer takes the ball?*
> *The query rings from east to west—by vales of sun and ice—*
> *We'll tell you more about it, pal—when Whizzer tackles Rice.*

Bunny Oakes felt every bit as much pressure as White but responded defensively. He closed all of his practices to the press, fearing his game plan would be secretly revealed to the opposition. He even moved his final pregame practice to an undisclosed location. When reporters finally tracked him down at the team hotel, his final pregame statement was almost comical in the circumstances. After two weeks of rainy weather and uncertain field conditions, Oakes told the press: "The boys are in perfect—well, not perfect, but good—condition. I like their mental attitude. If it's dry and firm, look for a good game from Colorado."

New Year's Day was dry, bright, and a crisp fifty degrees. For fifteen minutes, Colorado held Rice completely in check and played aggressive, opportunistic football. Joe Antonio recovered a Rice fumble to start a 58-yard scoring drive early in the first quarter. White carried the ball on ten of the next fifteen plays, then threw a 7-yard touchdown pass to Antonio and kicked the extra point, to give Colorado a 7-0 lead. Rice began a sustained drive, and Lain, who had started the game on the bench, entered the game. His first pass was intercepted by White, who ran 47 yards for another touchdown. His second point-after-touchdown kick made the score 14-0. The quarter ended, Rice came to life and scored three touchdowns, and the game was functionally over. Rice added one more touchdown in the third quarter. The final score was 28-14. Lain accounted for all of Rice's touchdowns, passing for three and running for one.

White finished the game with 54 yards on twenty three carries, a 2.3 average, but all of his positive yardage came in the first half. He rushed eighteen times for 56 net yards in the first half. In the second half, he carried five times but gained yardage only once—losing twice and being stopped twice for no gain. White had a tough day against his fellow Phi Beta Kappan: Nance held White to 5 yards net on five carries, including two tackles for no gain and one for a 3-yard loss. He also tackled White for no gain on a punt deep in Colorado territory. Rice dominated Colorado statistically, 20-6 in first downs, 257-87 in rushing, 158-8 in passing (where White was 1-for-5 with two interceptions, compared to Rice's 11-for-20 with two interceptions), and 415-95 total offense. The most telling statistic of the game was probably first noted in the game program: the Rice line outweighed Colorado by ten pounds per man, and the *Houston Post* accurately pointed out that "those 180-pound [CU] tackles were no match" for Rice.

Every newspaper account of the game acknowledged that White had lived up to his reputation despite the lopsided defeat. Several referred only too accurately to Colorado as a "one-man team." Numerous Rice players complimented White. Nance, grinning from ear to ear, said: "White is the best back we have met this season. It was a real pleasure the few times I had to tackle him." The game came as a relief for the Colorado team, whose locker room was reported in high spirits afterward. White complimented Rice and said, "It was a great game. I'd like to play it all over again." Would he now sign a professional football contract? White told the Associated Press that the pro game would "get along without him," despite "reports" that he would be offered $15,000 for one season by Art Rooney.

Bunny Oakes lost more credit with both his team and the press after the Cotton Bowl by denigrating his players ("Those two quick touchdowns ruined us. The boys must have thought it was going to be easy from then on"), giving little credit to Lain, and complaining that his team was "handicapped" by the "warm weather" at game time. What Oakes could not realize was that the Cotton Bowl was the beginning of the end for him at the University of Colorado. Some players talked of quitting football altogether during the train ride home. After a 3-4-1 season in 1938, two starters from the Bowl team—Nuttall and Marty Brill, who had been White's roommate—quit the team and said they would never play again for Oakes. Liley, a two-year letterman, joined the walkout. Oakes nonetheless went 5-3, beat Utah and Denver, and won the conference championship in 1939, but he was fired a few months later after all but a few players signed a petition to the regents condemning his abusive coaching methods and calling for his dismissal. He finished his coaching career at Grinnell College in Iowa.

More than seven thousand fans from Colorado had travelled to Dallas for the Cotton Bowl, and many wondered when they returned whether the trip had been worth it. In financial terms, the university's share of the gate was $26,018.55, which netted $18,342.97 after expenses— more than the entire net income from football for the prior season and within $200 of the season before that. Team morale was deeply wounded, however, and even the code of discretion honored by the players could not hide their feelings completely. Poss Parsons wrote an unusually perceptive column that empathized with what the players had suffered during multiple scrimmages in the mud. "From publicity and financial angles, the game was a great success," Parsons wrote. "At the same time, don't overlook the fact that the players . . . made a supreme sacrifice, giving up their holiday vacation for two weeks of football." Parsons had been the first nine-letter man at the University of Iowa, and he never forgot the players' perspective.

4

THE DECISION

SATURATED BY attention from the press, Byron White avoided the team train home and remained in Dallas briefly to rest after what had been a tumultuous three weeks. He could not stay long, because classes resumed the first week in January, and the basketball team had already finished its Midwestern road trip. When White returned to Boulder, he found himself under the most intense media scrutiny of his career, but not for athletic play. His quarterly academic performance was suddenly meat for the local newspaper: "Despite participation in football and Associated Student activities during the fall quarter," the *Daily Camera* reported on January 15, "Byron 'Whizzer' White completed the period with a straight 'A' average." The daily question he faced from local and occasionally national journalists was, the Rhodes Scholarship or the National Football League? For six months, it was an either/or question, and it was often painted in moral overtones: virtue or expediency? Everyone had advice, and White was surprised to discover that the end of his football career did nothing to diminish public interest in his career plans. Two weeks after the Cotton Bowl, White received a letter from the Southern California Rugby Football Union, pledging assistance in his prospective rugby career in Oxford: "The union congratulates you on winning a coveted Rhodes Scholarship. We hope that this membership card will introduce you to the game at Oxford and to international rugby in

England." The union believed, erroneously, that no American had ever won a place on the Oxford rugby team and hoped the drought was finally over. A few days later, the Denver Elks Lodge presented White with an expensive steamer trunk in "appreciation for his outstanding record as an athlete and scholar" and in anticipation of his overseas shipping needs.

The attention was beginning to draw down White's small reservoir of patience with the public. He regained his starting guard position on a basketball team that otherwise started sophomores, and his play became even more rough and aggressive than in the prior two years. Crowds outside of Boulder booed him when he brutally blocked shots, but opposing players and coaches denied that his play was intentionally dirty. R. M. Muir, who had been elected to a Rhodes Scholarship from the University of Wyoming, tried to chat briefly with White after CU had defeated Wyoming in Boulder early in February, but he regretted the effort: "Although the stress of an exhausting game and his status as a star athlete must be acknowledged, I rarely have encountered so little courtesy as I received from him." Muir had hoped to discuss Oxford and other potentially mutual interests, but the episode put him off: "I never saw him again." The *Silver & Gold* worried that the steady drumbeat of public attention was taking a high toll on White. On February 18, the sports editor's column begged, "Let's declare the season on 'Whizzer' White closed." Decrying a recent Lion's Club affair at which White became the youngest honorary member in the club's history, the column remarked: "That is all very wonderful, but let's call a halt to this jumping on the White bandwagon. . . . we suggest that something be done to stop making 'Whizzer' the foil of every publicity-seeking organization in the region."

The problem for White and his protectors was that exploitation was no longer penny ante or confined to the region. Within days of the *Silver & Gold*'s plea, the ultimate showcase for Whizzer White reached the final planning stages. The Metropolitan Basketball Writers' Association of New York invented a six-team tournament to span St. Patrick's Day week, to be held in Madison Square Garden. It was the first National Invitational Tournament, and it was the only postseason collegiate basketball tournament in the country; the National Collegiate Athletic Association, spurred in part by the NIT, did not begin until 1939. The New York writers were capitalizing on the city's new passion for college basketball doubleheaders at Madison Square Garden, and perhaps its old passion for big names. The Garden had been sold out two nights in a row in late December when Stanford and Hank Luisetti highlighted doubleheaders that pitted local teams such as City College, New York University, and Long Island University against teams from beyond the Alleghenies. The feat of back-to-back gates of eighteen thousand fans startled Tom Meany, the *World-Telegram*'s "Frothy Facts" columnist. "It was not so long ago that the players used to outnumber the customers." The Metro Writers had hoped to repeat the phenomenon in March and worked hard to nail down Luisetti and Stanford, which finished the season 21-3. Luisetti had matinee idol looks, as the New York newspapers called them, and his novel, one-handed set shot added both variety and speed to a game that had been dramatically accelerated with the demise of the jump ball after each basket in 1937. The strategy was to put Luisetti and White in one bracket, give them both byes, and then have them play in a semifinal doubleheader against the winners of first-round games between local teams.

Colorado accepted the invitation on March 3 after a favorable decision by the university Executive Council. None of the hesitancy over postseason play emerged. In fact, the invitation was accepted despite three factors that would have been viewed very unfavorably only three months earlier: the tournament was scheduled during exam week; the identity of the other teams was not yet set; and, unlike the Cotton Bowl, there would be no financial benefit to the university—the Metro Writers and the managers of the Garden were offering no guarantees or percentages, only expenses for ten players, a coach, and a trainer. Norlin was willing to allow the players to take makeup examinations when they returned, and neither of the other considerations made any purchase. No university athletic team had ever competed east of Columbia, Missouri, and the prospect of a New York City showcase for White and his teammates was irresistible to university officials, who had developed a taste for White-generated publicity.

Stanford, having made one trip to Manhattan during the academic year, declined the offer. The Writers turned to Oklahoma State, the Missouri Valley champion, with a 24-2 record. Oklahoma State's coach, Henry Iba, brought a distinguished coaching name and highly disciplined game that emphasized passing, play development, and high-percentage shots. To the extent the tournament had a theory beyond gate maximization, the games would provide a case study for testing the superiority of the different regional styles—the deliberate West versus the run-and-shoot East. The Colorado coach, Forrest (Frosty) Cox, learned his basketball at Kansas University under Dr. Forrest C. (Phog) Allen and was twice all–Big Six, more for his defense than his shooting. Allen changed his offensive style more than once, but he owed his enormous success (almost six hundred victories in thirty-nine years and a winning percentage of 73) to perfect fundamentals, fierce conditioning, and heavy emphasis on defense.

Cox was a model pupil, and his players at Colorado found that they worked much harder under him than under Dutch Clark. White often remarked, according to Art Unger, that "as hard as Bunny worked you, Frosty worked you twice as hard." Cox's NIT team had only one gifted shooter, Jim (Swisher) Schwartz, who won the conference scoring championship two years in a row. Colorado was 10-2 and had tied Utah for the league championship in 1938, thanks to Schwartz's shooting and to White's floor leadership and backup shooting. White and Schwartz were both named to all-conference teams. Cox's team, like Phog Allen's, utilized screens and picks to set up shots, and Schwartz had a reliable hook and set shots from the pivot. The question, too reminiscent of the Cotton Bowl, was whether Colorado could hold its own with the tall and talent-rich Eastern schools.

Once again, a Colorado team lead by Whizzer White was a curiosity on display. This time the press scrutiny would be vastly more intense than it had been even in Dallas and personally more unflattering. The experience would leave White with scars that he would never allow to fade. In a masterpiece of understatement a quarter-century later, he said: "The New York newspapers put out quite a bit of publicity about the team and about me. I figured it the same way I always had—it was their job and they probably knew what they were doing. But I didn't like it, even so." Privately, he was more frank. When an old Colorado friend asked the new Mr. Justice White when his intense distaste of the press began, he replied, "In 1938. In New York."

Before the Manhattan trip, White agreed to accompany Bunny Oakes to Chicago to address 175 alumni of the University of Colorado at a dinner whose announced purpose was "to make our Chicago high-school people Colorado conscious," and each alumnus was encouraged to host a high school student. White and Oakes both spoke briefly; the highlight of the dinner was a thirty-minute film featuring scenes of university life and several scenes from the 1937 football season, including shots from the Cotton Bowl. White was back in Boulder for one week, then off to New York, where the team arrived to a driving storm of publicity on Sunday, March 13. Monday night's card would match Colorado against NYU (which had barely beat Long Island University in one of the first games) and Oklahoma State against the Temple Owls, 24-2 (which had overpowered Bradley, previously 18-2, in the other).

The niceties of regional play carried little interest for the New York sportswriters covering the tournament. Only the *Brooklyn Eagle* spent much time actually analyzing the playing style of the different teams. The *New York Post* knew where its priorities should lie. "Whizzer White Nears Gotham," read the *Post* headline Saturday, and the brief story detailed the upcoming basketball schedule, but the salutation emphasized what was on everybody's mind: "Attention Mr. Art Rooney: Whizzer White will be in town tomorrow."

If White thought he could put the Rhodes/Rooney question out of mind for a few days, he was bitterly mistaken. The Colorado team had barely arrived in New York City when White and Cox were besieged by reporters for a press conference and photography session. The next day, five of the eleven newspapers (the *Times, Herald-Tribune, Journal-American, Daily Mirror, Daily Worker,* and *Brooklyn Eagle*) printed photos of White or of the team. One picture depicted White carrying a basketball tucked football-style into the crook of his right arm. Willard Mullin, the cartoonist for the *World-Telegram* and the *Sporting News,* provided a four-column cartoon of the "The Whizzer of Ahs." A half dozen papers carried bylined stories, all of which focused on White the phenomenon, and the pro football offer in particular.

Two stories got under White's skin immediately. The first, resulting from an impromptu press conference in the lobby of the Lincoln Hotel minutes after the team's arrival, put White in what might be loosely called a false light. Reporters from United Press and the *New York Sun* took a mumbled, off-the-cuff answer to a novel hypothetical question and turned it into headlines. A writer from the *New York Sun* reported that "White said that if he decided to join the Pirates he would like to try out with a major league baseball club next spring. 'I did all right in high school and college baseball, and if I can make the grade I figure I can last longer in big time baseball than in professional football,' he said. 'Besides—there is more money on the diamond if you make good.'" White told his teammates that he never said anything like that and declared that the *Sun,* and others who later picked up on the quotation, were printing "goddamn lies."

The quotation printed in the *Sun* is implausible on several grounds. At the time of the interview, White remained firmly noncommittal about his preference; if anything, he tended to suggest that Oxford was the more likely choice. He also never exaggerated his talent in baseball, which was modest. It is likely that the *Sun* writer took an equivocal response about his baseball play and melded it together with two others factors: a resonant image—famed football star playing baseball in the off season, as Sammy Baugh was trying to do in the St. Louis Cardinal system—and a climate at the moment charged by signings and threatened holdouts by prominent baseball players (Lou Gehrig had just signed for $39,000 after asking more than $41,000, and Joe DiMaggio was reportedly ready to hold out if the Yankees offered no more than $25,000). Putting to one side White's unprecedented rookie season offer of $15,800, professional football players could not expect to make more than $7,500 a year, the salary Dutch Clark expected as player-coach for the Detroit Lions in 1938. White may have been pressed to answer a question such as, "If you sign with the Pirates, would you be willing to consider a baseball contract as well?" Any remotely positive response could easily become a declaration of intent. It is telling that only three of the nearly dozen reporters who cornered White in the lobby of the Lincoln used the baseball angle, and one was the *Daily Worker* reporter, who did not file copy until two days after his colleagues. Had White meant to make a positive declaration, everyone at the press conference would have viewed the statement as big news. The best explanation is that the *Sun* and UP took advantage of a young athlete unskilled in the world of hardball New York sports journalism—and unwittingly made a permanent enemy.

The other story that irritated White appeared in the *Herald-Tribune* and carried an undertone of ridicule that was announced in its eighteen-point-type headline: "Whizzer White, Rhodes Scholar, Stumped by Pro Football Offer." The story began, "To be utterly frank about it, Whizzer White doesn't look like a Whizzer (whatever a whizzer may be). For that matter, he doesn't look like a Rhodes Scholar either." The story said he nonetheless was both, "And right now he is astride the horns of a dilemma—whether to play professional football for a fabulous seasonal salary or cast aside commercialism for the purely academic life of a Yank at Oxford" (a reference to the Robert Taylor–Vivien Leigh film that had just finished a two-week run at the Capitol Theater in Manhattan). The balance of the story discussed the team workout Sunday and then rehearsed a curt interview held in White's Lincoln Hotel room. The *Herald-Tribune* found White physically imposing and impressive during the afternoon workout at the New York Athletic Club. "Oratorically, however," the newsaper reported,

> the Whizzer is somewhat less of a success. He talks quietly and confidently, but yesterday at the Lincoln, where he was resting following the trip from Boulder to New York, White was not exactly garrulous. It is probable that he is a little tired of all the fuss being made over him.
>
> What, for example, did the Whizzer think about things in general and his sporting career in particular?
>
> The Whizzer was noncommittal.
>
> Come, come, Whizzer, you're a national figure, you must have some ideas about what you're going to do about this professional offer from the Pittsburgh Pirates.
>
> The Whizzer opened up a little, but still refused to commit himself definitely.

A photographer interrupted the conversation and "asked the Whizzer to pose informally, something like reading a book or relaxing abed." White did both. More questions, few answers: "Why is he called Whizzer? He didn't know, but a Denver newspaper man had so named him after seeing him perform on the gridiron." Only the belated arrival of Marty Brill, White's roommate, gave the interview a natural stopping point.

The biggest pregame splash for White came in John Kieran's column, "Sports of the Times." Kieran had a taste for poetry and even edited a volume of memorable verse. His columns mixed the lyrical and the topical. Referring to the recent Walt Disney film, he wrote, "The debate now is whether Snow White or Whizzer White has stirred up the bigger commotion in the country." The primary motif of Kieran's column was the suspicion that anyone as highly publicized as White had to be mythical; had he existed, "surely some . . . traveler would have come back this way chanting, with apologies to the late Alfred Lord Tennyson: *'Sole star of all that place and clime/I saw him in his golden prime:/This White of Colorado.'*" When Kieran finally got down to cases in the last third of his column, he erroneously described Colorado as a run-and-shoot-from-the-hip-with-either-hand team with "no such word as 'defense' in their bright lexicon," a shameless crib from the less than accurate advance story in Sunday's *Herald-Tribune*.

The game against NYU came as a relief from the publicity blitz for White and his teammates, although as they jogged down the runway into a Garden holding more than twelve thousand spectators, they could hear distinctive New York accents bellowing, "Whizzah! Whizzah! Whizzah!" The game left more than one observer with "battered nerves," said the *Daily News* following Colorado's 48-47 victory over NYU. Colorado relied on a furious fast break and screens off a double pivot to develop a 26-23 lead at halftime. The game was tied four times in the second half and neither team enjoyed more than a 2-point lead during the last fifteen minutes. With NYU leading 45-44 and only fifty seconds left, White tackled NYU center Irwin Witty for a jump ball. White caught the ball on the rebound off two other players, cast "desperately," according to the *News,* and scored, for a 46-45 CU lead. NYU regained the lead, 47-46, on a long set shot with twenty-five seconds showing on the clock. Don Hendricks took a pass from White, headed down court in front of his own bench, and with CU substitutes screaming, "Shoot," he popped the game-winning basket from 30 feet away with ten seconds left.

The *World-Telegram* wrote

If there was any one man who stood out in this mad melee it was Whizzer White, the Rhodes Scholar and football star who is built on the heroic muscle-rippling lines of an ancient gladiator and is never more cool than when the battle is hottest. White lived up to his press notices last night. He is a superb team player who rarely takes shots at the basket. [He had 8 points on four field goals.] He devotes most of his time to ball handling and setting up plays. He is the type of player who may be depended upon to keep the ball secure once he gets his fingers on it.

Everett Morris of the *Herald-Tribune,* who coincidentally was president of the Metro Writers' Association sponsoring the tournament, said "the great Byron (Whizzer) White proved all the glowing things said about his athletic prowess." Arthur J. Daley of the *Times* swooned over the "great Whizzer White, as mighty a court performer as advance notices said he was." He added that White "was the guiding genius of the team and its steadying influence. The Rhodes Scholar, with a build solid as an oak tree, was all powerful on defense and an excellent shot when he so chose."

Despite what Daley called the "most spectacular fray that the Garden ever has seen," with a "photo-finish [that] supplied a drama-laden struggle with a perfect ending," no one expected Colorado to win the tournament. In the other semifinal game, Temple blew out Oklahoma State 56-44, and with more height if not more speed than Colorado, rated at least a slight favorite in the final game. Still, Temple's 2-out and 3-back zone defense had not been impressive against Oklahoma State. Against Oklahoma State, Temple's best defense had been a frantic offense—twenty-five field goals on 135 shots, an 18.5 percent average. The shooting spotlight would be on Schwartz, Hendricks, and White.

Both Temple and Colorado took the day off between the semifinals and the finals and visited the Empire State Building. A Colorado alumnus who headed the Press Radio Bureau introduced the team to former governor Al Smith and then conducted a guided tour of Rockefeller Center and the National Broadcasting Company studios. It was a heady and hectic schedule, as the *Herald-Tribune* noticed on March 16: "The Colorado boys are having a hard time avoiding being swamped by the felicitations of their ecstatic alumni here, but they are bearing up nobly."

The championship game that night was over soon after the opening tip-off. Temple lead 10-1 after four minutes. By halftime it was 33-18, with the Owls "behaving," according to Everett Morris in the *Herald-Tribune,* "as though they could stretch it whenever they were so minded." Colorado was worn down: Cox used only five players in the first game and did not make his first substitution of the tournament until there were two minutes left in the first half against Temple. The decisive factor, however, was size, as White explained afterward to the *World-Telegram:* "Temple is a good, big team. . . . And a good, big team will lick a good, little team any night of the week." White won admirers with his determined play to the very bitter, 60-36 end. Morris wrote: "Despite the awesome shellacking his team was taking, he kept grinning, diving after the ball, setting adversaries rudely on their haunches, shooting baskets and otherwise having a grand time."

White scored 10 points, one less than the team leader, Jack Harvey. White was 5-for-20 from the floor and Schwartz was only 1-for-12. The most telling statistic of the game was indeed shooting percentage: each team took seventy-seven shots from the field, but Temple made twenty-eight and Colorado made only twelve. Blocked shots led to numerous fast breaks and easy layups for the winners. Don Shields, whom White had been assigned to guard, led Temple with 16 points and was named Most Valuable Player for the tournament, which drew more than forty thousand spectators over three days—including 14,497 on the final night.

A reporter with the Associated Press cornered White after the game for an interview that ran nationwide the following day. White was quoted as saying that he had been through a "tough year: Ever since September the heat's been on. Nine Saturdays of football. You have to be out there trying and it's tough with a lot of people counting on you. Mighty tough." And now, the chronic dilemma—"this pro offer." For the first time, he revealed the growing source of irritation: if the actual choice were not enough of a problem, "there are about 500 people trying to make up my mind." He spelled it out: "People keep telling me to grab the Rhodes Scholarship. Others say, 'Take the money and play pro football.' We'll leave it there." He revealed that Art Rooney had arranged to visit him after the championship game, but cautioned, "I'm pretty sure I won't have a definite answer for him for some time. I have to think this thing out." Then the least informed question of any interview all week: Did he mind losing to Temple? "Mister, you bet I mind. They were a good team, all right, but I hate to lose. Hate it. If I said I didn't I'd be a hypocrite. I hate to lose right down to my heels."

Rooney, perhaps sensing White's dejection after the defeat, decided against paying a call after the game. "I don't have to tell you," Rooney said to the *Journal-American* at the Garden after the games, "that I'm very anxious to see White sign up. He's still undecided. I think it would be for White's best interest to play pro football next fall." Rooney waited until the next day to make the pitch, and for public relations purposes he was joined by a charming collaborator—John Victor McNally, the player-coach of the Pirates, better known by his football name, Johnny Blood. (McNally was a self-styled character who had been inspired by a motion picture marquee for Rudolph Valentino's *Blood and Sand*). The Associated Press staged a photograph of McNally, fountain pen in right hand, giving White a piece of paper while whispering confidentially to him. The photo ran in the *Daily News,* the *Philadelphia Inquirer,* and, in a four-column blowup, in the *Denver Post.* The publicity stunt was designed to put even more pressure on White by suggesting that he was receiving the formal offer for the first time, following his final collegiate basketball game, and could, if he wished, sign on the dotted line now that he had fully expended his football and basketball eligibility. (That assumed, of course, that he was willing to forfeit his final baseball season at CU.)

Rooney was eager to close the deal with White for obvious reasons: the sooner White signed, the sooner Rooney could begin drumming up interest in Pittsburgh for the upcoming season and the sooner he would know the precise range of his financial exposure for his player payroll. White had in fact already seen a copy of the standard player's contract and had asked Walt Franklin, the athletic business manager for the University of Colorado, to examine its coverage and details, including guarantees in case of injury (there were none in the standard form contract used by the NFL), payment schedule, provision for nonleague games, and so on. At this point, White was unwilling to discuss any details publicly, other than the base salary, which was $15,000, twice what Sammy Baugh had made in his 1937 rookie season. After the photo session, White told the Associated Press that he would not have a definitive answer for Rooney until he had conferred with his brother, Sam, who was not due to return from Oxford until "this summer." The *Daily News* reported that McNally had offered a sweetener to the deal—full law school tuition at either Duquesne or the University of Pittsburgh in the off season.

Byron White and his teammates attended a luncheon held by tournament officials, at which they received silver watches for finishing second in the first NIT. That evening they were treated to a dinner by the energetic Colorado alumni group, and the next morning they headed for Washington, D.C., by train to visit the Capitol as guests of the Colorado congressional delegation.

White's arrival at Union Station in Washington meant another press conference. His patience with the press by now was almost wholly spent. The first questioner wanted to know what was on his mind. Getting a summer job, was the reply; "I'm not a rich man, you know." Then White blasted the New York sportswriters: "One thing the eastern sports writers got me wrong on was professional baseball. I'm not a good enough baseball player to think of that. I'm interested in getting a job which will get me thru next summer." What was the highlight of the trip east? "Getting on the train in New York to start home." White declared that he would play baseball again in the spring, which precluded signing any professional contracts for almost three months, although the Associated Press dispatch did not pick up on the point. He also said he would like to play in the charity football game between the NFL champion and a collegiate all-star team—held annually in Chicago and sponsored by the *Chicago Tribune*—one of the premier sports events in the country.

Byron White and his teammates made a whirlwind nine-hour tour of Washington, escorted by Colorado's two senators, Edwin Carl (Big Ed) Johnson, the former Democratic governor, and Alva B. Adams. Breakfast and lunch were provided by the congressional delegation in the Capitol, and White's remarks at the luncheon, covered by the *Washington Post* and the wire services, made national news. The Associated Press said he "stiff-armed questioners on athletic topics, including Colorado congressmen." White continued to imply that he preferred Oxford to Pittsburgh, and for the first time detailed why he was attracted to study overseas: "The tremendously fascinating foreign situation makes that Oxford scholarship very appealing to me right now." But he reiterated that he would not decide until he had conferred with his brother during the summer. Did he agree with isolationism? No, the United States "ought not to try to hide behind the mountains," he replied. "We ought to understand these other nations' problems and take an active lead in world affairs."

When the congressmen tried to ask White about sports, he responded by quizzing them about their views on "'collective security,' 'ideology,' and diplomacy in general." After being pressed several times, White finally addressed athletic issues. He said college athletes should concentrate on one or two sports and not spread themselves too thin; that sports should never distract from "scholastic work"; and that "if they ever pay college athletes for taking part in college it will ruin college sports." His final remark suggested that the publicity bruises of the year, especially those acquired in New York, were still throbbing: "If I ever wrote a book, I might call it 'From Hero to Heel in an Hour and a Half' and show how a college athlete's fair weather friends desert him when he cracks under the pressure of partisans and the press."

Walter Haight, the *Washington Post* sports humorist, spent most of his column considering the incongruity of being assigned to cover a college athlete speaking on Capitol Hill, but buried in his self-focused prose was a prescient observation:

Perhaps the most significant remark he made was "I like Washington very much and I mean to return and spend some time here." There was determination in his eyes which seemed to spell "campaign, politics, House, Senate, and possibly Supreme Court." Inasmuch as he will study law if he takes the pro offer, I may have read his mind.

Byron White surprised his teammates, and perhaps even himself, with his unequivocal comments on foreign policy and international affairs. He had spent much of the year trying not to pin himself down on any opinion, regardless of the topic. Part of the reason was genuine modesty, a conviction that his athletic notoriety provided no warranty for the wisdom of his views, especially with respect to nonathletic issues. Another factor was his anxiety over misquotation, as the story over his professional baseball "ambitions" had recently demonstrated. He had even gone to the length recently of asking a fellow ASUC commissioner to attend an interview by another student who was looking for a big story and who might stretch the quotations to meet the goal.

Yet foreign affairs were a serious concern for Byron White, and for many of his fellow students. Agitation over the Spanish Civil War had finally hit Boulder in early 1938, when two students announced they were leaving school to fight with the Loyalists. The Pueblo American Legion smelled a communist plot, but Norlin defended the students and helped to convince the local Legion post of the students' bona fides. Other students asked the ASUC to sponsor a "peace demonstration" as Europe appeared moving inexorably toward war. A small group of militants wanted a strike, echoing a protest held two years before, but the commission, under White's leadership, underwrote a Peace Convocation, with Dean Stearns as the speaker. Fellow students praised White for helping to mediate conflicting preferences without unduly crediting or discounting any one view.

The risk of war frequently appeared in the columns of the *Silver & Gold*, which even commissioned a poll in February to determine who would fight if war came; 9.2 percent said they would fight overseas, 76.6 percent said they would fight only if the United States were invaded, and 14.2 percent said they would not fight under any circumstances. As the spring wore on, war began to seem more likely. On March 12, the day before White and his teammates arrived for the NIT, the half-page headline of the *New York Daily Mirror* announced, "Hitler Seizes Austria." Hitler's troops had invaded at dawn. The reunification of the German peoples—*Anschluss*—had added 9 million people to the Nazi domain; the question was who would be next. Czechoslovakia, with millions of Germans living in the Sudetenland, was the obvious

target. As White deliberated what to do after he graduated, however, there is no evidence that conditions in Europe shaped his decision one way or the other. The American Congress's reaction to the *Anschluss* was remarkably muted, and optimists on both sides of the Atlantic believed that Hitler could be placated.

Despite student awareness of the grave developments overseas, the immediate, pressing—indeed daily—question for White was "the decision." Every attempt by White to dampen or defer interest in his choice between Pittsburgh and Oxford only served to provide another occasion for someone to help him make up his mind. The Pirates kept up the pressure. The same day that White and his teammates toured Washington, March 18, Johnny Blood—as the newspapers preferred to call him—told the *Denver Post* that he expected White to accept the offer from Rooney. Blood had attempted to allay White's anxieties about the details of the offer by answering a series of questions from Franklin, White's ad hoc legal counsel. According to Blood, Franklin "wanted to find out whether the Pirates really could pay White that kind of money, whether he would be paid if he got hurt, and when he would be expected to [report for] play." Blood conceded that White "doesn't want to throw away" a Rhodes Scholarship worth $6,000 "for anything that might be uncertain"—a concession to rumors constantly trailing NFL teams that many players were paid with IOUs by the end of the season. The tuition sweetener at Pittsburgh law schools seemed to be a signing bonus. After repeating those features of the offer, Blood said he "believed" that his conversation with Franklin had "clear[ed] doubts" in White's mind and that "he would agree to sign soon instead of awaiting return" of his brother "to advise him."

The public courting of the $15,000 man was beginning to strike a jaded press as somewhat contrived. The day after Blood's prediction, the sports editor of the *Washington Star* declared that White's delay in making the Oxford/Pittsburgh decision "smack[ed] faintly of publicity." Mocking the plight of the "Phi Beta Kappa," the editor said: "Each admission of indecision brings a new wave of publicity—all of which leans toward the fact that White may be under strict orders" from Rooney "to play the game to the hilt before announcing that he will accept the measly $15,000." The *Rocky Mountain News* leapt to White's defense on March 27 in an unsigned column, wishing a "hive of bees" upon the *Star* editor and pointing out that "White's position is an awkward one. . . . If he tells the scribes to go soak their noggins, he is immediately tabbed as a heel. . . . If he answers them, he is tabbed as a publicity seeker. . . . So what's a man to do?" What the *Star* editor failed to understand was that Rooney had already

maximized the publicity value of the offer; the longer White delayed, the more skeptics—even White himself—could wonder if Rooney could back up the promise. The incentives for Rooney, which included putting the local publicity machine in high gear and determining the budget, all lay with closing, not prolonging, the issue.

Byron White was on a publicity treadmill that his manners prevented him from leaving but that his dwindling patience with the press made increasingly uncomfortable. Within a week of returning from New York, he was a featured guest at a lunch meeting of the Fort Collins Rotary Club along with Dutch Clark and Glenn Morris, a former three-sport star at Colorado State College and Olympic decathlon champion in 1936. Morris had left his job as a car salesman to compete in the Berlin Olympics and won the third decathlon he had ever entered. Now he had just finished the first in what would be a forgettable two-film career—*Tarzan's Revenge* and *Hold That Co-ed,* both released in 1938.

Each of the three athletes spoke briefly, answered questions, and posed for pictures. The only Denver reporter present was Chet Nelson, sports editor of the *Rocky Mountain News,* an unquenchable Whizzer White fan. He asked Dutch Clark what White should do. "My position is not like that of 'Whizzer' White's, but for $15,000 I would play football on crutches," Clark answered. Nelson was kind enough not to ask White his reaction to Clark's quip, so he settled for a rather bland if nonetheless exclusive interview. Published the next day, March 24, the account was brief and wholly unrevealing. The pro offer? "Let's just skip it right now." Reports by United Press during the NIT that he wanted to play professional baseball? "Entirely erroneous." Would he play for Colorado again during the spring? Yes. Finally warming to his task, White observed that the floor at Madison Square Garden was subpar but that the glass backboards were "quite the stuff." The trip to Washington, D.C.? "Makes one realize that we have a federal government." The most memorable remark came in response to the tritest question. Greatest thrill on the NIT trip? With a smile: "Seeing the Rockies as we neared home."

A week after the luncheon, White made a liar out of himself, evidence that the weight of the decision and the relentless publicity attention were taking their toll. On March 31, he informed Harry Carlson, dean of men and coach of baseball, that he would not play baseball that spring. He gave no explanation to the *Silver & Gold;* privately, he told friends he was worn out and thought perhaps he should take up a recreational sport, such as golf. The widespread suspicion was that what everyone now lightly referred to as "the decision" had tied Byron White in a knot. The *Silver & Gold* declared that

"the 'Whizzer's' decision ended one of the most brilliant athletic careers in university and conference history."

White had won seven letters—three in basketball, two in football, and two in baseball—and was all-conference every time in every sport. His academic record put him at the top of his class. The *Rocky Mountain News* speculated that White quit baseball so that he could sign with Pittsburgh without disrupting the baseball team. No move he took was without implication or free from speculation. He talked to a variety of friends on campus about what he should do, but most felt that his brother—who was not expected to return from Oxford until late July—would be the decisive influence on the decision.

The Pittsburgh newspapers, frustrated with indecision, began to put on the pressure, too, and they found a new twist. The January issue of *Scribner's* magazine had published an essay by Milton McKaye, "What Happens to Our Rhodes Scholars?" McKaye found that 10 percent of living Rhodes alumni were listed in *Who's Who,* that a third were university teachers, a fifth lawyers, 14 percent in business, and only 6 percent in government service. The implication was that Cecil Rhodes's design of "fighting the world's fight" had been sacrificed on an academic altar. Chester L. Smith, sports editor of the *Pittsburgh Press,* concluded that the Rhodes Scholarships were not what they had been cracked up to be: the assumption that recipients combined "the intellectual attainments of the Younger Pitt, the moral fiber of an Eagle Scout and the athletic ability of a Walter Eckersall" was bogus. In addition to denigrating the significance of the scholarship, Smith had two more arguments. The Rhodes Trust was paying only $2,000 a year for three years, and Rooney was offering $15,800 for one year, plus law school tuition and plenty of chances to study in this country. Second,

> Art says he can pay the "Whizzer" for the year in exactly one home game which draws a minimum of 16,500 persons to Forbes Field. There are five home games and six on the road. So if White is anywhere near as good as reports say he is, he'll prove a drawing card, for he never has strutted his stuff this side of the Mississippi.

Chet Nelson noticed the column from the *News*'s sister Scripps-Howard newspaper in Pittsburgh, quoted the arguments in detail, but speculated that there would be no decision until Sam White returned.

On the day Nelson's column was published, April 10, the NFL owners met in Pittsburgh, and Rooney told his colleagues that he had come up with a surefire maneuver to reassure White and to close the deal. He was ready to deposit $15,000 in a Pittsburgh bank to White's credit as a demonstration of the integrity of the offer. Bert Bell, coach of the Philadelphia Eagles team, told a reporter for United Press the next day that White had not signed yet, but that the odds were "100 to 1 or any odds you want" that White would sign before spring training, as soon as Rooney made the deposit. When the story moved on the UP wire, the Denver bureau immediately telephoned White in Boulder and found him "indignant" at being awakened at 1 A.M. and adamant that he neither had signed nor would sign anything in the foreseeable future. He said he would "take that 100 to 1 shot," and added: "I don't know how such a story got out—and I guess I don't care—but I have made no decision on either football or the scholarship and I don't know when I will make the choice."

For the next two months, Byron White dithered. Johnny Blood made one special trip to Boulder, hoping that his charm could play on White's passions for physical challenge and for competition. When that failed, he peppered White with long-distance telephone calls, with equal lack of success. For his part, White received advice about the decision from every corner—campus, town, newspapers, and radio, even the odd politician. The drumbeat of interest reached such a steady level that White seemed to adopt an uncharacteristically wry view of the incessant question about his postgraduation plans. When a local reporter popped the question one more time on May 27, White could play Will Rogers without flinching: "All I know is what I read in the papers."

White finished his studies as the number one member of his class academically in the College of Arts and Sciences, with a 2.968 grade-point average on a three-point scale. He had 180 hours of A and six of B (three each in sociology and public speaking—the latter a gift, said campus wags). He was elected most popular man on campus and received the highest honor for a graduate, designation as "canebearer" at commencement; unlike in previous years, the ballot for the honor, voted on by the students, listed only one name. "His popularity was quite remarkable," Patty Nash, a fellow ASUC commissioner, recalled later. "People admired his achievements and respected his modesty, which was painfully genuine."

Byron White celebrated his twenty-first birthday on June 8, and less than two weeks later he gave himself a present: he decided to decline the offer from Rooney and to go to Oxford. He called a press conference for late Saturday afternoon, June 19, in the lobby of the Brown Palace Hotel. He told the gathered press that he had arranged the announcement to accommodate their deadlines in order to give "all the papers a break because they've been so swell to me." Other than the setting and the staging, the announcement was almost an anticlimax, or at least White tried to make it seem that way—the logical result of a logical process. "I'm going to England," he announced "jauntily," according to Gorman Hogan's account for the *Rocky Mountain News.* He told the press that he had made the decision two nights before on the train back to Boulder from his parents' home in Wellington. No, no one particularly had influenced him. Yes, his brother, Sam, wanted him to go to Oxford, but, no, Sam gave him no advice: "I haven't heard from Sam more than two or three times since I've been considering this thing and about the only thing he wrote me was how hard the studies were there."

For someone whose unvarnished frankness with the press was one of his charms, the press conference produced one answer after another at war with the facts. It was almost as if White responded with accounts of what he wished had transpired rather than what in fact had occurred over the past three months. The decision was entirely his own, he said. "He said he asked for advice, received little." No, he had not thought of applying for a Rhodes Scholarship before last fall. Art Rooney and Johnny Blood had put no pressure on him; they were "swell" and "never tried to hurry me or influence me in making my decision." White noted that he had sent a telegram to Rooney and Blood informing them of his decision. The only news that emerged from the conference was that White announced he wished to play in the annual *Chicago Tribune* all-star game in September, as long as it did not compromise his amateur standing. (He did not want to arrive at Oxford stigmatized as a professional in a world that adored amateurs, especially if he had rejected, not accepted, a lucrative contract.)

Only at the end of the brief conference was there a snap answer, and the question was mindless: "Was it hard for you to turn down the $15,000?"

"Well, what do you think?" White, suddenly the scholarly pauper again, revealed that he would attend summer school and do odd jobs, hashing and working on university construction crews, to earn his passage to England and spending money. When he was asked what Oxford's starting date was, he was forced to confess that he did not know. The answer, which his father knew and supplied to a reporter by telephone, was October 8.

Both Denver newspapers treated the announcement with front-page headlines. Although one member of the Board of Regents was quoted as saying that White had made the wrong choice, local newspapers uniformly applauded White's decision. The *Denver Post*'s unusual front-page opinion box, which performed the function of conventional editorials, hailed White: "It's his own decision—and one that took courage and manliness to make. Byron White, stout fellow!" The *Boulder Daily Camera* congratulated White for his "determination": "Rarely has a poor boy been so tempted and so fortified by intelligence to arrive at a decision." The *Sterling Advocate* applauded the "deliberate choice" for "patient work which should qualify him for service to his fellow man" over "easy fame and easy money. . . . Mr. White appears to have intellectual integrity."

With the die cast, Byron White took the first step to Oxford. He wrote to the student chairman of the committee charged with making arrangements for the new class of American Rhodes scholars to sail together to England in September. His $10 deposit for the third-class passage on the SS *Niew Amsterdam* on September 27 was long overdue. He wrote on June 20 on *Silver & Gold* stationery, enclosing his check and apologizing: "I have delayed quite some time. I do sincerely hope I am still able to obtain the reservation, for I want to sail with the rest of the group." White's belated tender meant that twenty-five of the thirty-two American Rhodes scholars would form the sailing party for 1938.

The summer school of the University of Colorado was not an open scandal, but by the time Byron White settled into his jobs in the summer of 1938 the annual ten-week session was commonly viewed as a venue where study could be avoided without sacrificing academic credit. In August of 1937, the *Topeka (Kansas) Daily Capital* had ridiculed the summer session as a "Country Club of Higher Education" where a beautiful mountain setting provided distraction and recreation each year for more than three thousand registered students, many of them schoolteachers working at a deliberate pace on graduate degrees. The female-to-male ratio ran two to one. Byron White had no trouble landing a hashing job at the Alpha Chi Omega sorority house, which served as one of the housing sources for the summer session. He and a fellow student, Richard W. (Dick) Wright, served and cleared four tables of ten each in the dining room. Outside of meal times, White worked a full eight-hour day doing odd jobs for the campus construction crew. The man who had turned down a $1,000 per week football contract was now working for $5 a day and counting his pennies. Having sent his deposit to secure the sailing reservation, he needed to raise the balance of $93 over the summer. His goal was $400. His brother had traveled all over Europe on a motorcycle during his three-year tenure; his résumé eventually would note thirteen thousand miles in two summers, through France, Belgium, Denmark, Holland, Germany, Norway, Sweden, Austria, Czechoslovakia, and Hungary. Byron White wanted spare cash to supplement his stipend in order to see as much of Europe as possible.

With the decision behind him, White settled into a comfortable routine that mixed thirteen-hour workdays with study of Latin, which would be necessary for the two Roman Law "papers" (courses) he would take at Oxford. White also agreed to make two trips with university officials in late summer to speak to Western slope alumni in Trinidad and in Grand Junction. Since classes began at 8 A.M., tables needed to be set by 7 A.M. Dick Wright remembers the first morning he arrived for work at six-forty-five and found that White had already set the tables. The next morning, Wright was there at six-fifteen and finished the job before White arrived. The third morning, Wright arrived at six-fifteen again, only to find that White had already finished the job. "We struck a truce," Wright said years later, and dining room competition was then limited to seeing who could stack the most plates on his arm while clearing, until the housemother put a stop to the competitive horseplay.

To kill time before breakfast, they played table tennis, but, Wright added, "After the first three or four days, I don't believe I won a set." Wright later discovered that White arose early to work on his Latin and secondarily to be ready for the constant long distance telephone calls from Johnny Blood trying to turn White's focus from Oxford back to Pittsburgh. Afternoon breaks left time for recreation, and Wright initially suggested boxing, in which he was experienced and White was a novice, but after one bout, Wright said, "I rejected any return matches."

Social life was not competitive, according to Wright: "Occasionally in the evening we would go to Stibes Tavern in Boulder Canyon. There was one girl from Texas who had met Byron during the Cotton Bowl in [January] and who had come to Boulder for the summer. Byron wasn't very much interested, so he would ask me to take her friend and double-date. The four of us would sit on benches in a booth, drink beer, and she and I would discuss a wide range of subjects—world and domestic affairs, life, politics. I remember how frustrating it was not to be able to pin him down to a fixed position. He was a master at parrying a question with one of his own. At intervals he would turn to the Texas girl, who was watching him with a worshipful gaze, tap her on the arm with his fist, and say, 'How are you doing?'"

Although White seemed relaxed or at least relieved with the choice he had made, a part of him was eager to accept the challenge of professional football. In a fundamental sense, Pittsburgh and Oxford held an identical attraction: each in its own domain would test White and the limits of his proficiency. During the spring, he spoke often to friends about *finding out what I have and stretching myself,* a reference to Oxford but a notion that applied also to professional athletic competition.

Sam White felt that he owed Oxford a debt for showing him how little he knew, notwithstanding the glittering prizes he had won at home. Oxford took

Sam down a peg or two—not enough for some tastes—but Sam felt nothing but gratitude to the institution. He was especially thankful to his tutors, particularly Sollie Zuckerman, who referred to his pupil as "White, he with the mind like a sieve." Years after the experience, Sam White would say frankly: "Oxford taught me how to read, Oxford taught me how to write, and Oxford taught me how to think clearly. It was as simple as that."

Sam was eager for his brother to have the same opportunity, but he respected his brother's passion for competition. He was also practical. The Pittsburgh offer would easily finance Byron White's legal education and then some, perhaps providing a retirement nest egg for their parents as well. Throughout the Trinity (spring) term 1938 at Oxford, Sam White weighed the pros and cons of his brother's choice. It was not his to make, but his advice, no matter how indirectly offered, would weigh heavily. Many of Sam White's fellow students grew tired of hearing "the decision" weighed. Finally, near the end of term, one fellow student at Hertford, R. Canon (Sam) Clements, suggested matter-of-factly to Sam White that his brother simply should do both—accept the Pittsburgh offer and matriculate one term late, in January of 1939, at Oxford.

Sam Clements's solution was simple but not obvious. The Rhodes trustees historically had been very rigid about declining requests to defer the scholarship. It was understood that a scholar elected in one year would either matriculate that year or forfeit the scholarship. No one had ever asked for a partial deferment, however, at least as far as anyone could remember. There was a further complication. Even if the Rhodes Trust agreed to the one-term deferment, the college that had accepted White would also need to agree to the proposal. The college would be one student light for a third of the year, which had financial consequences. Moreover, both the Rhodes Trust and the college would be seen to be ratifying professionalism, and in sport at that, in preference to scholarship. Perhaps only academics can invest great weight in such evanescent symbolism, but the Oxford culture extolled the amateur's effortless superiority and was death on the man who had to be paid to excel. Recent pay-for-play scandals had dotted the sports pages of London newspapers, quality and tabloid alike, so Byron White's football contract cut a bit too close to the knuckle for the Oxford establishment.

When Sam White, acting in effect as his brother's agent, explored the possibility of a one-term deferral with the Rhodes Trust and with Hertford College—his own college had accepted Byron White as a Rhodes Scholar—he was surprised by the different reactions he received from the two institutions, in the person of their authoritative officers, C. M. R. F. Cruttwell, the principal of Hertford, and C. K. Allen, the warden of Rhodes House and administrator of the Rhodes Scholarships. Cruttwell is now best known in caricature—as Sniggs, the junior dean of Scone College in Evelyn Waugh's *Decline and Fall.* Cruttwell—Crutters to everyone, if never to his face—had been dean of Hertford when Waugh was an undergraduate there. They had rubbed each other the wrong way, to put it lightly, but Waugh took revenge disproportionate in its duration, viciousness, and distortion. Even Waugh's memoirs spend four pages fashioning a vivid and cruel portrait of Cruttwell as repulsive, often drunk, and perhaps sexually attracted to dogs. By the summer of 1938, Cruttwell was fifty years old but seemed older, due to progressively debilitating aftereffects of World War I, including a game leg and open psychic wounds; nonetheless, he had just published the second edition of what is still the definitive military history of the war. Even discounting Waugh's fictional and autobiographical excesses, Cruttwell was curt, frequently coarse, and notoriously rude, but he was also hostile to cant. Cruttwell's response to Sam White was briskly encouraging: *We accepted Byron White for his academic accomplishments, not because of or in spite of his athletic achievements.* The college would be pleased to welcome "White the Younger" in January of 1939.

The warden of Rhodes House was extremely reluctant to make the same accommodation, although the ultimate decision rested with the trustees. The aura of professionalism raised a taint in the minds of the trustees, a taint that would follow White in Oxford and, more important, could conceivably cast the American Rhodes Scholarships in an unfavorable light. As the *Scribner's* magazine article had demonstrated, the entire Rhodes Scholarship program was undergoing detailed, and not very sympathetic, scrutiny. Not only were the post-Oxford performances of the scholars less distinguished than the selection criteria seemed to promise, but the actual operation of the selection committees was open to charges of favoritism and arbitrariness. A professional athlete with a Phi Beta Kappa key could reduce the program to self-parody at an inopportune time. C. K. Allen, an acknowledged master of understatement, referred privately to White's "application" as this "unusual case." The case was sufficiently delicate, or the trustees sufficiently uncertain, that Sam White received no formal response to his brother's application before he left Oxford for good in late July.

Byron White was now in a very awkward position. He had called a press conference to decline a professional football contract in favor of an academic scholarship, enjoyed applause throughout the state for his high-mindedness, and now secretly wished, as he knew the newspapers would say, to have his cake and eat it, too. By mid-July, he did not know whether he was halfway there or back where he had thought he was when he called the June press conference. On July 11, he consented to an interview with the Associated Press in Boulder that was described as an explanation of his preference for Oxford over Pittsburgh. Familiar themes were rehearsed. White explained that he wanted to be a lawyer, that Oxford "doesn't offer a superior legal education," that more study in the United States would be necessary, but that "if I've got anything on the ball, Oxford will bring it out. . . . will accomplish the drawing out process." As to weighing $6,000 worth of scholarship against a $15,000 contract, White said he took the long view: "I'm willing to gamble that I'll come out ahead in choosing Oxford." But there was also a statement that foreshadowed the prospective costs of getting his way with the Rhodes trustees. Had he turned professional and then gone to Oxford one term late, he said, he would have sullied his reputation and foreclosed any opportunity to compete in university athletics: "Over in England they don't regard professional athletes as they do in this country. Pros aren't quite—well, you know. They just aren't thought of quite as well as amateurs." He quickly dissociated himself from that view, and his regret over spurning Pittsburgh sounded genuine:

> I have no prejudice against professional athletes. I'm not that much of a high-hat intellectual, despite what some people have said. I would almost have given my right arm to get in there for a year of professional competition. I would have loved it.
>
> But that is a vain, childish urge. It would have flattered my vanity to be a pro player. I had to disregard that motive and get down to facts.

The thoughtful reader, not knowing of the unanswered application to the Rhodes trustees, could reasonably wonder whether White had convinced himself, let alone his audience, that he had made the right choice.

Two weeks after White gave the interview, his brother returned from three years in England. Sam White arrived in Wellington on July 26 and came to Boulder the next day to visit his brother. Asked by the *Boulder Daily Camera* what he thought of his brother's decision, Sam was, in the newspaper's word, "laconic": "Byron's problem was Byron's problem, and I have no doubt he chose what was best for him." Did he attempt to influence the decision? "All I attempted to do was to present to Byron some idea of what he could expect" if he decided to attend Oxford. "I know it would be useless for me to try to make up Byron's mind for him, because I know he is as 'hard-headed' as I am." The interview degenerated into chat about lacrosse and cricket, which Sam attempted to explain. Byron was asked if he planned to play cricket, but as the *Camera* reporter shrewdly observed, "he stuck to his usual habit of being non-committal when it isn't absolutely necessary to be otherwise." Neither brother let on that the door to professional play was still open at least a crack, and that the question turned on the as yet unexpressed judgment of the eight elderly men—median age sixty-five—who constituted the Rhodes Trust. (One of the trustees was former prime minister Stanley Baldwin.)

The day after the interview with the *Camera*, Byron White's world turned upside down. The Rhodes trustees granted White's request to matriculate in January of 1939. He received word of the decision by cable received in Wellington on Thursday, July 28. Years later, Sam White would explain more than once that the reason the trustees approved the one-term deferral for his brother was fear of bad press in the United States. Sam often claimed that he told C. K. Allen that the American Rhodes Scholarships would get a black eye if they refused a reasonable request from the most warmly publicized recipient of the award in the program's history. Allen explained the decision rather more evenly in a private letter to George Carlson—the ex-Colorado, ex-Hertford Rhodes scholar—on August 2, 1938: "The question of his postponement in the particular circumstances of his case was an unprecedented one for the Trustees, and after some doubt they felt it would be rather harsh to refuse his application."

Whatever moved the Rhodes trustees, their belated decision triggered a barrage of events in rapid-fire order beginning on Friday, July 29. Byron White cabled Johnny Blood and Art Rooney to see if the offer was still open. It was. The following day he sent another cable, requesting permission to play in the *Chicago Tribune* charity all-star game on August 31 against the Washington Redskins in Soldier Field, Chicago. As a courtesy, White contacted the Colorado committee of selection for the Rhodes Scholarships to seek its blessing, although the trustees formally had the ultimate authority over the issue. There were finally no contingencies left by Sunday evening, but it was not until 1 A.M. on August 1 that Byron White was able to telephone Art Rooney to accept the offer to play for one year with the Pirates at a guaranteed salary of $15,800 ($132,000 in 1997 dollars). The final hitch, in the context of all the twists and turns and even U-turns of the previous six months, was absurd: White got the wrong number in Pittsburgh. He had been put through to the local office of Paramount Motion Pictures. Minutes later, Rooney and Blood heard the voice and the answer they had sought since December 11, 1937.

The next day, the Pittsburgh newspapers exulted, but others across the country were more cynical. The *Rocky Mountain News* headline said, "Whizzer Thinks Way to Cash." The *Los Angeles Times* said, "Cash Has a Way of Talking." The *Silver & Gold* said, "Whizzer White Will Eat His Cake and Have It Too." Local boosters were totally forgiving. The Denver Kiwanis Club made Sam and Byron White honorary members, and they were guests of honor at a lunch on August 3, where they were photographed flanking Poss Parsons, the sports editor of the *Denver Post*. The only person who remained phlegmatic throughout the new flurry of headlines was Al White. When asked if he was surprised by his son's change of course, he told the Associated Press to "let the boys tell the story. They have been working on it a long time."

Many of White's putative classmates at Oxford viewed the summer drama with a mixture of amusement, envy, and admiration. Shortly after White's final decision was announced, Frederick Suits, who became the class cutup, wrote Gerald Brown (who organized the sailing party):

> Saw in [the news]paper where White plans to wait until January to come, and, inadvertently, pick up a cool 15 grand while doing so; can't say as I blame him much; that will come in handy to a poor boy who steps out of school with nothing but an Oxonian degree to eat. I'd do the same if I had some way to gather in a few thousand.

Others in the class wondered if he would ever come at all.

Part II

GRADUATE WORK

5

PITTSBURGH: "GOLDEN BOY"

T HE ATHLETIC wedding of Byron White and the Pittsburgh Pirate Football Club, although destined to last only one year, by mutual agreement, was one of the most valued relationships White ever established in his life. The reason was a pair of deep friendships. Years later, White would call Art Rooney "the finest man I have ever known," a uniquely unqualified compliment from someone whose entire public life was committed to discretion and moderation in weighing others. Johnny Blood would float in and out of White's life for nearly fifty years as well and, near death, would evoke an uncharacteristically sentimental expression of affection from the man Blood first called "the kid."

In the summer of 1938, Rooney and Blood were an odd, and somewhat desperate, couple. Rooney had bought the Pittsburgh franchise in 1933 for $2,500 and had never made a dime on his investment. His latest season loss was publicly reported at $21,000, but may have been more. He had trouble building attendance, largely because the University of Pittsburgh was such a powerful hometown draw—home gates routinely ran fifty thousand per game. Rooney was always thinly capitalized, in part because his first real love—as with many of his fellow owners—was horse racing. He had made headlines up and down the East Coast a year before when he hit New York tracks for a killing of at least $250,000; there were no follow-up stories about where the money went.

Paying $15,800 for White was a high-stakes plunge for Rooney, who needed big attendance in his five scheduled home games to meet what was now probably the highest payroll in the league. Other than Frankie Filchock, the rookie Indiana quarterback and Big Ten passing sensation, the offensive roster was not impressive. Blood was listed as thirty-four years old, which the newspapers often referred to as a "conservative estimate," and had been all-league in 1931. Since then, he had played all around the league, and was better known, especially of late, for his off-field enthusiasms than for his on-field capacity. He was a problematic coach, not known for handling players well, and in fact too well known for arriving late—if at all—for games. He still had modest blocking ability, but his speed was largely gone, although he could still outrun some of the backs. Rooney made him the second-highest-paid man on the payroll, at $3,500. With the exception of Clarence (Tuffy) Thompson, the experienced backs were, like their playing coach, past their prime. Late in the season, after the team had absorbed a string of losses, one player would observe: "The Pirate backfield had a ball carrier, two blockers and one old man in the road." Blood was nonetheless good copy—the hard-hitting and hard-drinking relic of the Green Bay Packer glory days who could quote Shakespeare, microeconomic theory, and racing odds with equal accuracy and gusto. White later said, half in truth, that Blood's charm lured him to Pittsburgh as much as Rooney's money: "John didn't actually talk me into signing. It's just that I got so interested in [him that I had] to follow him and see what happened."

To say that Byron White was, again, a one-man team would be an overstatement, but Rooney did nothing to allay the impression; indeed, he marketed the idea. One of his first moves when White agreed to terms was to print more than one thousand three-by-four-foot wall posters with the home schedule superimposed over an action photograph of White and headlined "The World's Greatest Football Player." The stunt embarrassed White, annoyed George Preston Marshall—owner of the Redskins and Sammy Baugh—and made White a target for every opposing player in the league.

Rooney's publicity campaign started even before White arrived to formally sign the contract. Posters were dispatched and interviews supplied at the drop of a hat, but few noticed; the other Pittsburgh Pirates were leading the National League by more than five games with two months left in the season, and local sports fans were beginning to think eagerly about the possibility of a World Series, probably with the New York Yankees. That was bad news for Rooney, not only because his prospective audience was distracted, but also because his team used Forbes Field, too. His first four home games would compete with the end of the season and possibly with the series.

Rooney scheduled White's formal contract signing for August 10, live, during prime time, at the KDKA radio studios. White was due to arrive the evening before. The trip by air was scheduled to take all day, with stops in Chicago and Cleveland, but delays at both stops made White three hours late. White had plenty to read on his journey if he wished. Columnists had been providing nonstop advice for him since his final decision was announced. Denver's ordinarily booster press sounded sober notes of caution. Hank Rabun, who had covered White for three years and had written much of the *Rocky Mountain News*'s multipart life story of White in 1937, warned White on August 3 that the NFL was a tough league, both on the field and off:

> At the moment, we would say that White will have more trouble with the Eastern press than with pro linesmen. That is, of course, unless Byron realizes he is now a professional athlete, and as such, is public property, target of autograph hounds, interviewers and photographers.
>
> White acquired the reputation of being a tactless young man in his relations with the press. While we have always found him to be most congenial in granting interviews and answering even the most personal questions, there are those who insist he is a difficult subject.
>
> One local cameraman frankly told the Whizzer this week that he was contemplating listing his (White's) name at the head of a roll call that included Charles Lindbergh and a host of other celebrities who are always only too happy to offer a cameraman the back of their neck as film subject.
>
> Blood and Rooney may be able to convince Whizzer that publicity is the life blood of professional football, and that every inch of space they can grab in the press means more gate admissions.

Colleges can rely on alumni to fill stadiums, Rabun concluded, but the NFL "is a league built on ballyhoo and which, to a great extent, still depends on a free ride from a friendly press."

In the *Washington Post* on August 3, Shirley Povich gently rained on White's parade. The provocation for his column, or at least its tone, may have been White's somewhat flip reply to the Associated Press two days before when asked if he felt "on the spot" with such a salary: "Well, I've been in tight spots before." Povich's column congratulated White on landing twice the salary that Sammy Baugh had earned the year before without ever proving himself, and warned that opposing players, beginning with the Redskins in the *Chicago Tribune* all-star game, would be laying for him. "I don't mind telling you that they play just a bit different kind of football than the college boys," Povich wrote. "For one thing, they hit awfully hard. They hit the ball carriers awfully hard, especially. And you're apt to get kicked in the face if you are going too well. That comes under the heading of accidents."

Despite the hard-boiled rhetorical pose, Povich was the most scholarly sportswriter of the day now that Paul Gallico had retired to write novels. Povich was genuinely concerned that Rooney had set up a talented but naive young athlete, only recently turned twenty-one, as a target in a league where fists flew in faces and midsections on many tackles and other "accidents" often happened on routine plays. Privately, Povich was convinced, but did not at the time print, that the salary for White had cost Rooney his silent partner—and a fellow gambler—who believed that the twenty-to-one pay disparity between White and the average lineman would wreck team morale. After Rooney died, Povich wrote:

> When [Rooney] founded the Steelers in 1933, he needed the help of a Pitts-burgh friend, Harry Jaffe. This was on a handshake basis; no contract. Good friends, gamblers, are like that. They split when Rooney signed [White to] an unheard-of figure, in an era when such a league-leading player as the Red-skins' Cliff Battles was refused a raise to $2,700 by George Preston Marshall and quit the team. To Rooney, Jaffe said, "Art, you can't pay one ballplayer that much. It won't be fair to all the others." Whereupon, according to the late Bo Bregman, friend of both men, Jaffe conceded his interest in the team to Rooney, no payment asked. Rooney neatly solved all immediate problems by raising player salaries all down the line.

The first question after White's early morning telephone call concerned the *Tribune* all-star game: White had asked permission to play, but the Pirates had refused. White had a rare, guaranteed contract, and would be paid whether he was physically able or not; his lawyer uncle in Audubon, Iowa, had seen to that, although his uncle's partner, Clark Mantz, was primarily respon-sible for providing advice on the matter. (The standard-form player's contract provided for cancellation on forty-eight hours' notice.) Rooney and Blood may have worried that their expensive prize could be seriously injured in a meaningless exhibition game, especially with George Preston Marshall's poorly paid players teeing off on him.

But the publicity value of White's participation for the entire league was too great to allow Rooney the luxury of holding out White. The *Pittsburgh Post-Gazette* reported that a rival owner telephoned Rooney on August 2 and threatened to pull five of his signed players from the game if White was not al-lowed to play. As Povich admonished, "if you think the Pirates are paying you that 15 grand because of your football ability alone, Whizz, you are quite naive.

The Pirates want you because, among other things, you were the hottest thing to graduate from the football camp last season and the Pittsburgh club, a dull, colorless outfit, needs a gate attraction." White meant fans for the entire league. The promoter of the Pittsburgh-Philadelphia game scheduled for September 14 in Buffalo, New York, reported selling $258 in advance tickets the day White's contract was announced. Both the Philadelphia Eagle and the Green Bay Packer officials wired Rooney, very publicly, and congratulated him on his accomplishment. Privately, other owners were angry with Rooney for raising the salary expectations of the players. George Preston Marshall phoned Rooney and sniped, "What are you trying to do?" Rooney blandly explained that he was trying to "bring a little class to the game." George Richards of Detroit, who was as generous as Marshall was tight, also thought that Rooney had made a mistake.

When White finally arrived, three hours late, on August 10, Rooney and Blood must have had their hearts in their throats. Rooney had never met White; Blood had spoken with him in person only twice; and neither had ever seen him play football. Blood was startled when White came out the plane door: "God," he said, "he's wearing cheaters." White wore wire-rimmed glasses to correct astigmatism when reading, but Blood did not know his new star that well. He was afraid that White had a vision problem; White was concerned because he had lost his glasses case somewhere between Chicago and Cleveland. Not an auspicious beginning, thought an otherwise enthusiastic local press corps.

The next day, White signed the contract and was whisked away to the Pirates' training camp in Loretto, Pennsylvania, where he would spend ten days and play two grueling intrasquad games before flying to Chicago to prepare for the all-star game. Before White's arrival, the *Tribune* shamelessly hyped White's participation in the game, and Whizzer versus Slinger stories (referring to the Redskins' Baugh) appeared on an almost daily basis prior to White's arrival from the Pittsburgh camp. Povich arrived a few days before the game and ridiculed the hype, both for exaggerating the qualities of the two stars and for ignoring the other participants.

Byron White proved himself only too human in Chicago. In his first full scrimmage with the All-Stars, he fumbled an easy pass from center on a punt, he squibbed a punt only 15 yards, he threw a pass interception, he had another punt blocked, and he was sacked on his only other pass attempt. "It was a dizzy reception for one of the most publicized backs since Harold (Red) Grange," reported the AP on August 25. "Whether his teammates planned it that way—White had little blocking on any play—not even [coach] Bo

McMillin could be sure." The day before the game, White slipped in the shower on a bar of soap and gashed his forehead. The actual game, played before 74,250 in Soldier Field, was no better than the scrimmage. The All-Stars won 28-16, but White's backup, Cecil Isbell, was the star of the show. "White Makes Poor Showing," read the *Denver Post* headline. White did not play until the second quarter. The friendly *Post* reporter tallied the disappointing performance: "In all, White threw three incomplete passes, had one intercepted and completed none. He didn't carry the ball from scrimmage. He returned one punt for five yards, kicked one for 17 and failed to get off another, and he intercepted a pass." The *Boulder Daily Camera* dug up one of the All-Stars who claimed that White had been disadvantaged in Chicago by two factors—the pro–Big Ten bias of the coaches, who maximized the playing time of their own players, and hostility from jealous teammates, who envied his pro contract and who consequently muffed center snaps to him and blocked poorly for him. White objected to those who supplied unsolicited alibis for him: "I was just terrible." In addition to wounded pride, White suffered a black eye when he was slugged by a Redskins tackler on his only punt return. The *Pittsburgh Post-Gazette* cheerfully reported that as a result White "feels that he is set for the season now."

In fact, White's body absorbed brutal physical punishment all season. His black eye was only the first, and he frequently found himself with a fist in the solar plexus or a knee in the kidneys after being tackled. Professional rules, as opposed to college rules, allowed flying tackles and blocks and, more important, decreed that play was not completed until the ball carrier was physically stopped (as opposed to having one knee touching the ground); the consequence was harsh and emphatic tackling, which often carried over into near beatings. More than twenty years after his professional football career was over, when he was deputy attorney general of the United States, White explained to William Orrick, who was an assistant attorney general, how he coped with the on-field muggings he received early in the season. The occasion for the story was Orrick's request for advice on how he should have handled back-stabbing subordinates while he was working temporarily at the State Department:

> "Well, I know what you mean," [White] said. "That happened to me when I started playing professional football. I was with the [Pirates], and after the whistle was blown, they were kicking me in here and I asked the coach, 'What'll I do?' and he said, 'Wait till you catch one of them out of bounds and after the whistle's blown, then you kick him there and kick him in the

face but be sure you kick them in both places and be sure the whistle's blown and everybody sees you. It'll cost the team twenty-five yards, but I'll be able to keep you for a couple of seasons.'" So Byron said he did just exactly that. He said he did a very good job of it. It did cost the team twenty-five yards, and he said he never had any trouble after that.

White no doubt exaggerated the effectiveness of the tactic in order to preserve the utility of the story; every new team required fresh instruction, and some opponents were incorrigible. In the second game of the regular season, White was stopped cold at the line of scrimmage on an unusually vicious tackle by New York's Alphonse (Tuffy) Leemans, who refused to let go even after the referee's whistle blew. *I just wanted to see what it's like to have $15,000 worth of football player in my hands,* Leemans explained. After the game, Leemans offered White a "no offense" handshake. Other tacklers were not as sporting. In the third game of the season, against the Philadelphia Eagles, the threat to White was relayed through his cohalfback, Tuffy Thompson, and was issued by Bill Hewitt, the Eagles' captain and all-league end. Hewitt was one of the last two players in the league not to wear a helmet and, in the respectful words of Red Grange's memoirs, a "tremendous competitor." Early in the game, Hewitt snarled at Thompson and told him, *You'd better protect your golden boy, because we're going to kick the shit out of him—now or later.* The opportunity did not arise until two months later, when the teams met a second time. White called his own number and headed straight at Hewitt; Thompson (illegally) hooked Hewitt's arm; White stiff-armed the bareheaded defender and was off for a 79-yard touchdown run—his longest of the season. In other games, White was not as successful in preempting brutal play aimed in his direction, but most of the physical wear and tear he suffered was a function of routine play and a punishing schedule.

As much as by any other factor, the 1938 Pittsburgh Pirates were defeated by a schedule over which they quickly lost control and that forced them to play too often with too little rest and with too small a squad, which led to several devastating injuries to important players. Between the August 31 *Tribune* all-star game and September 16, inclusive, White played six games—three exhibition games, and three league games. He redeemed his disappointing debut in Chicago the night after, despite a wearying cross-country plane trip to Providence, Rhode Island, where he rushed for 60 yards on eleven plays and scored one touchdown for a college all-star team, which lost to the Chicago Bears 26-14. Two days later, he joined the Pirates for an exhibition game against St. Rosalia Prep School.

Rooney had expected to open the NFL season the following day, September 4, at Philadelphia, but the baseball Pirates were still clinging to first place in the National League by three and a half games, and Forbes Field was off limits after September 11. The domino effect of other schedules suddenly meant that instead of playing eleven games a week apart, including five home games between September 11 and October 16, Rooney's football Pirates would open the season with three league games in seven days and would end up playing only three home games all season. Rooney had depended on home game attendance, padded by his White-driven publicity campaign, to finance his expensive payroll. Now he was at the mercy of his foes and dependent on the $5,000 minimum guarantee that visiting teams enjoyed under league rules.

Because of the baseball Pirates, Rooney was in a publicity drought. On September 3, he whined to the sports editor of the *Post-Gazette,* "Here I have the highest-priced star in football, Whizzer White, and the biggest payroll club in professional football, tuned up for the start of the season, and all I see you guys in sports writing about is the baseball club." Rooney feared that the first home game, a week away with the New York Giants, would have a poor gate as local sports fans focused on pennants and the World Series to the exclusion of football. The sports editor of the rival *Pittsburgh Press* gave Rooney publicity on September 3 that he could have done without and that sounded the opening note of a discordant song that would play off and on all season: "The tip is out that some of the football Pirates aren't any too fond of Whizzer White on the grounds he's getting too much spondulix. . . . It's hard to imagine anyone being that small to a grand kid." The players ignored the rumor; a like rumor had dogged Red Grange during his rookie season, more than a decade before, and had proved inaccurate, the product of journalistic ingenuity.

Byron White and the football Pirates opened the National Football League season on the road—on September 9, against the Detroit Lions, in Detroit. The vaunted duel between Colorado all-Americans failed to materialize when Dutch Clark was unable to play due to an injured ankle. The Lions won 16-7. White scored Pittsburgh's only touchdown, rushed ten times for 47 yards, and caught one pass for 35 yards. He also misjudged a punt, which hit him in the eye on his own 20-yard line, and he was forced to chase the ball down at his own 3. He played less than half the game. Blood explained weeks later that White had been hospitalized for three days before the game with a "wrenched" back, but no excuses were offered the morning after the game itself. White was interviewed thirty years later by Bob Curran, a sportswriter who was compiling an oral history of professional football's "rag" days (as in "rags to riches"), and described his NFL debut:

> My debut with [Pittsburgh] was unforgettable. At least to me. We were play-
> ing the Lions and when we came onto the field, the fans made some remarks
> about my publicity. The first time I had a chance to run with the ball was on
> a punt return. At the last second I lost the ball in the shadows and it caught
> me in the right eye. The ball bounced away and was recovered by the Lions.
> You can be sure that I received some messages from the stands. For three
> weeks the eye was black.

For someone who spent a lifetime meticulously respecting the facts, White's account is puzzling. His desire for an almost corrosive self-effacement produced a very distorted picture. First, White's first chance to run with the ball came on a running play, the first play from scrimmage in the game. He gained 6 yards. After a penalty, he gained 2, and then on the next play was forced out of bounds for no gain. In the second quarter, he was roughed up so hard on a tackle at the line of scrimmage that Detroit was penalized. He sat out the third quarter. His mishandled punt did not come until the last minutes of the game, and he—not the Lions—recovered. He apparently had trouble see-ing in the University of Detroit Stadium, because a punt in practice the day be-fore hit him in the eye as well. White's memory is a caution about oral history, but more important, it is an index of his intense unease with any accounts of his athletic history that suggest glory; his tendency has been to compromise de-tail in the service of making his public history commonplace. His spotty pro-fessional debut did nothing to diminish his luster with the fans, however—a police cordon was necessary to escort him after the game, when he was beset by "a mob of his admirers who sought his autograph as he left the field."

When the Pirates returned to Pittsburgh the day after the game at De-troit, White finally attended to a piece of unfinished business that had been crowded out of his mind by the crush of attention that preceded the season opener. The American Rhodes Scholar class of 1938 was scheduled to sail from New York on September 27, preceded by the traditional smoker the night before, hosted by previous holders of the award. White had not formally canceled his reserved passage. He was embarrassed by the lapse, which testified to the internal conflict that the decision had caused and to the mixture of re-lief and remorse that came with his signature on the lucrative contract. He was still bothered by the perceived reversal of field, as critics unkindly called his final decision, and his letter of September 10, 1938, to the student chair of the sailing committee suggests a writer calling himself to account:

Your letter reminded me of something I was already powerfully conscious of—that I owe you an apology for not writing much sooner.

The jumble of events which led to a one-term deferment of the scholarship developed and were over very suddenly. I am extremely glad I was able to obtain such a deferment; and it was only by the very decent attitude of officials in England and of a committee in Colorado—to say nothing of other American officers—that permission to enter in January was granted.

There are of course many drawbacks to the course I have taken. I expect to encounter numerous difficulties and be called upon to pay more than one way for having things my way for the time being. But I am willing to face this, for I am not getting paid $15,000 for my football abilities alone. In my position I just could not see neglecting the use of any ability I might have—within bounds of course.

After apologizing for not being able to attend the smoker and asking for his deposit back for the ship passage, he said his plans for January were "quite hazy right now," and continued:

Believe it or not, with the correct attitude one can learn something from professional football life. It's lots of fun in a certain way, requires watching one's physical welfare in an exacting manner. It will afford opportunity to do some necessary studying before January—I hope. At the same time there are many phases of the thing to be avoided.

At any rate, after having my evaluation of Oxford more than confirmed by my brother, I wouldn't pass up going to England for anything less than a broken neck—which, I'm told, isn't so much a fairy story this time of year.

I do hope this reaches you before you leave home. I didn't get your letter until I got back from Detroit today. Thank you kindly for your efforts.

The letter, written in a young, round hand on the stationery of the Hotel Fort Pitt, which Rooney used as team headquarters, is poignant for its self-realization. White assumed that Oxford could be accommodating but unforgiving, and he had already learned uncomfortably that Rooney had hired him as much or more for his gate power as his athletic ability.

The day after White penned his letter, the New York Giants arrived for the home opener, and a disappointing crowd of 17,340 watched the Pirates lose gamely, 27-14. White drew approving reviews from a local press as much relieved that the preseason hype was over as it was impressed with his play. He scored one touchdown, gained 33 yards rushing on ten attempts, caught two passes for 28 yards, and averaged 10 and 20 yards each on punt and kickoff returns, respectively.

The Pirates were now scheduled to play in three days against Philadelphia in Buffalo, New York, but heavy rains allowed a two-day postponement that both sides, especially the exhausted Pirates, welcomed. Thanks to extraordinary pregame coverage and no competition, the game drew 19,749. The *Buffalo Evening News* devoted almost a full page of coverage each day for several days before the game, featuring individual sketches of all the starting players, including personal notes on favorite actors, actresses, and pet peeves. (For White, it was Spencer Tracy, Norma Shearer, and uncomfortable hotel beds.) Philadelphia overpowered the Pirates, 27-7, but White again scored a touchdown and rushed for 44 yards on eleven carries. He also fumbled twice, and one led to Philadelphia's first touchdown. After three games, he had three touchdowns and a 3.5 yards per carry rushing average. He was carrying the ball only ten times a game, however, in large measure because opposing teams were keying on him defensively, which provided opportunities for Thompson and for Frankie Filchock's passing.

White's biggest problem was kick receiving: he had misjudged or fumbled at least one kick in every game, although none had led to a touchdown for the opposition. Nonetheless, Pittsburgh was suddenly 0-3, and Rooney's dreams of competing for the championship had died within a week. He was beginning to float excuses. After the third straight loss, he told the editor of the *Buffalo Evening News:* "My payroll probably is twice as large as any other club in the league, and on paper it's a better team than last season, but there's something wrong."

Harry Keck, the sports editor of the *Pittsburgh Sun-Telegraph* first raised the issue the day after the second game of the season against New York:

> Whizzer White is all right, but his supporting cast isn't. . . . he showed flashes
> of extraordinary skill and speed, but he had little support. He was almost
> alone in most of his tries at carrying the ball and running back kicks and he
> was in and out of the game so often, as was almost everybody else, that the
> lineup was a patchwork most of the afternoon.

Keck suggested that the Pirates change strategy and use White on end runs or off-tackle:

> Too much time was wasted yesterday in trying to get him through a stout for-
> ward wall between the tackles. He is distinctly a runner, not a line-breaker,

and will have to be aided up to and past the scrimmage line, preferably on sweep plays or cutbacks. Then he will be able to run.

Havey Boyle in the *Post-Gazette* had a simpler but less practical suggestion: "faster . . . blockers to match the Whizzer's speed."

A week later, after the Pirates had returned from Buffalo and before they left for New York to play the Brooklyn Dodgers, Keck pinned down Rooney about growing rumors that some players were "laying down" and missing their blocking assignments when White carried the ball, out of jealousy over his contract. Rooney was furious:

> If I find out there's dissension on this I'll tear it apart and wreck it. I'll clean house. I've heard those reports, but I haven't been able to pin down any of them. So far as I can see, the players like the Whizzer and are for him be-cause he came in here unspoiled and a regular fellow and because he wants to play football and is playing it. Every man on this squad is being paid what we think he is worth, and if any of them doesn't think he is getting enough he can quit. But he can't stay on the club and draw his salary and quit on the field.

As to another rumor, that Johnny Blood's job was in jeopardy, Rooney issued a denial more emphatic for its hashed metaphor: "I never change motors in the middle of an ocean. I started the season with Blood and I'll finish with him."

Only the *Pittsburgh Press* made any effort to get to the bottom of the rumor mill, and what their reporters found suggested that Blood was a major part of whatever problem was affecting the winless Pirates. Over the weekend, Blood had released three players—Bill Karcis, a twenty-nine-year-old fullback who had played at Carnegie Tech and had the second-highest salary on the team; Izzy Weinstock, a third-year quarterback from Pitt; and Billy Wilson, a fourth-year end from Gonzaga. None was seeing much playing time. Accord-ing to the *Press*, both Weinstock and Karcis "said every player on the team liked 'Whizzer' White, and that the 'Whizzer's $15,000 salary was not the cause of the trouble." They hinted, however, that Blood's erratic substitution patterns, his own ineffectual blocking, and his "faulty" play calling were dam-aging the team. "I could say plenty, but I won't," was the only statement Wein-stock would make for direct attribution. Karcis, in his eighth year in the league, declared that "any dissension among the players is not caused by Whizzer White. . . . I know the Whizzer is taking these losses pretty hard. He realizes the team is on the spot because of him. He has tried hard to make good. He hates to lose." Another player, demanding anonymity, claimed that the players were for White "100 percent" but were "kicking about Blood's methods of playing White." The concern was that Blood had not developed effective return plays so that White could take advantage of downfield blocking. "Why, the guy is likely to wind up in a hospital instead of Oxford."

Rooney won respect for his integrity and for standing up for Blood, although his denial that Karcis's salary "figure[d] in his release" convinced no one, especially when he was signed by the New York Giants in mid-October. The entire story might never have developed further were it not for another scheduling fluke. The next Pirate game was on September 23 in Brooklyn, and that meant the New York City football debut of Whizzer White, which the New York press treated as if it were a coming-out party. A private dinner was held in White's honor at the Pennsylvania Hotel by Chick Meehan, the promoter and former Manhattan football coach, and attended by every major sportswriter in the city. Consequently, a dozen columns featuring White were published within a day or two before the game. White's self-effacing modesty and unpolished touch with the press charmed the writers and won him the benefit of the doubt when he blamed himself and not his colleagues for the team's poor record and his unspectacular start. The *World-Telegram* pointed out that the "gratuitous raps" on White ignored the facts: according to official league statistics, White was tied for first in scoring, second in rushing, and third in pass receiving. "Omitted from the yardage figures are runbacks of punts and kickoffs"—150 yards on punts and 100 on kickoffs.

Other writers were more frivolous. Bill Corum, recently elected president of the National Professional Football Writers Association, spent a chunk of his column in the *Journal-American* describing White's hands:

> The only thing I know for sure about him is that he has a hand the size of grandma's palmleaf fan. . . . When Chick [Meehan] introduced me to White, I thought my mitt had dropped into the Grand Canyon. To paraphrase the late Texas Guinan, they gave the little boy a great hand. . . . Whizzer must be able to pick up a football between thumb and forefinger like the average man fishes the olive from his Martini. Or his cherry from his Old Fashioned, depending on his taste. What's yours?

Tucked away in the stack of wisecracks was Corum's dismissal of the blocking rumors: "So far he has been going like a house afire," he wrote, referring to White's standings in the league statistics. Jimmy Wood, sports editor of the *Brooklyn Eagle,* was also impressed with White, or at least his hands: "Shaking hands with Whizzer, you feel that he could easily gather in the surplus wheat crop with one hand and heave the potato output over his shoulder with the other. What hands! They look like the business end of a brace of steam shovels."

The question of the team's blocking arose indirectly in a story published in the *World-Telegram,* subheadlined "Whizzer Admits Debt to Blockers," but White addressed the question directly in an interview with his old benefactor, Henry McLemore, still with United Press but no longer affecting an apostrophe:

> White didn't try to hide his indignation when it was mentioned that there were rumors going about that his Pirate teammates were jealous of his publicity and salary, and had not been blocking any too vigorously when he carried the ball.
>
> "That's a lie," he said. "Everybody on the team, from Art Rooney down, has been swell to me. The players give me everything they've got. My failures are my own. I threw away that game to Philadelphia right at the start when I fumbled the ball. But there wasn't one word of criticism, or one dirty look from any of the players."

Most of the column was devoted to White's view that the professional game was much tougher physically than the college game and that the competition was extremely keen. He denied that the NFL was dirtier than college play and insisted (contrary to his own experience), "Knees and fists aren't half as common as they are in college games. The pros hit you so hard they don't have to resort to rough stuff." McLemore asked him if he was as good now as he had been a year ago at Utah.

> I'm smarter. But I'm not as good a ball carrier or kicker or passer. The opposition in pro football has something to do with that, of course. But so has the strain I have been under. You know, I have been exhibited like a freak since I signed with the Pirates. Not that I'm complaining—if I paid a player $15,000 I would exploit him to the hilt, too. It's tough to play your best game when you feel nothing short of a 50-yard run or a 75-yard pass will satisfy the customers.
>
> I find myself pressing all the time in an effort to live up to my reputation. I try not to, but I can't help it. You know that no player ever was as good as my publicity made me out to be. Well, maybe Dutch Clark is. But I'm no Dutch Clark. He's the tops.

White had come close to burying the issue, but he was undone on game day by another old benefactor, Grantland Rice. Rice's column, "The Sportlight," usually avoided pro football, but since his September 23 dispatch focused on an interview with the University of Pittsburgh football coach, Rice added a throwaway observation at the end: "Whizzer White's pro debut so far hasn't been any too big. But the Whizzer has lacked the blocking support needed to move a football anywhere forward and the Pittsburgh team hasn't come to top form." Rice stopped short of crediting the rumors that White had tried to spike in his interview with McLemore, but the passing remark stoked the fire.

Indirectly, White added to the intrigue by having his worst game so far, despite Pittsburgh's 17-3 upset of Brooklyn under the lights at Ebbets Field before a crowd of 21,494. Defense dominated the game for both sides. The AP account called White a "sad figure," with fifteen carries and a net loss of a half yard. Although the *World-Telegram* praised Johnny Blood's play-calling, most of White's rushes were plunges into what the AP called the "savage Brooklyn line." White did not play the entire game; he was benched in the second quarter. In an unrelated and rather comical coincidence, White's worst game coincided with the publication in *Liberty* magazine of an article by Bunny Oakes entitled "One Whizzer White Does Not Make a Winning Team." The article's immodest predicate predictably elicited a snide response from Hank Rabun of the *Rocky Mountain News:* "A Whizzer White helps quite a bit, though, doesn't he, Bunny?"

The Pittsburgh Pirate football club had ten days off between games, but that meant opportunity for another exhibition game nearby, not rest. Rooney scheduled a game with the Boston Shamrocks. After a postponement for rain, the Pirates won 16-6 on Monday, September 26. White played only half of the game, but he threw two long passes to set up two touchdowns, one of which he scored on a 3-yard plunge. The notoriously critical Boston press corps was unimpressed. Harold Kaese of the *Boston Transcript* found White "no ball of fire" but noted that "the Rhodes Scholar won some ohs! however, with a long, low punt that carried 52 yards beyond the scrimmage line."

The same day, White got a plug from a welcome corner. Sammy Baugh's biweekly column in the *Washington Post* was devoted to White, and its burden was that "it's high time somebody came to the defense of 'Whizzer' White." Baugh's column argued that White had been held to unreasonable expectations, forced to play a crippling schedule at the beginning of the season, and had been saddled with a weak supporting cast. (The column was in fact ghostwritten by Shirley Povich, which White eventually discovered. More than forty years later they met at a dinner in Washington, D.C., and White greeted Povich with an affectionate bear hug, which prompted a witness to say, "That's the first time I've ever seen Byron White embrace a sportswriter.")

Shortly after the Pirates returned to New York City to prepare for their October 3 game with the Giants, the rumor mill exploded. On September 28, Gene Ward of the *New York Daily News* published a 650-word column, headlined "A Lone Buccaneer," whose thesis was an insidious question: "Is Whizzer White being jobbed—given the old business by resentful Pittsburgh Pirate teammates?" Ward conceded that the players had no incentive to damage their "meal ticket," but he pointed out that White had been roughed up in early practices, that he was averaging only 2.5 yards per carry (compared to 4 for other backs on the team), and that some players—whom he named—were seen standing around watching during the Brooklyn game as White battered the line for no yardage time after time.

The motivation for the players to go in the tank was twofold, in Ward's view: pure "resentment and jealousy," especially from local-college Pitt and Carnegie Tech players not making anywhere near $15,000 and knowing that White was around for only one year, and second, bitterness among the friends of Karcis and Weinstock, who had been released to "offset" the "ante to White." Ward concluded:

> It doesn't add up to anything with a pleasant odor. . . . Here's a kid with worlds of ability; a strong, eager lad trying to justify his pay. He has those same qualities you find in your Hank Greenbergs and Donald Budges. He has worked as a waiter at the University of Colorado for book money; only recently turned down a cigaret endorsement offer, "because it might harm America's kids." Give him a real chance and he'll sell himself and keep those turnstiles clicking all around the circuit. Here's hoping the Whizzer gets his break.

When the column, which was reprinted in the *Denver Post,* hit the streets, the players reacted with fury. They called a team meeting and sent a telegram to Ward, which he printed the next day, September 29:

> Following repeated stories that Whizzer White has not received full co-operation of the Pittsburgh Pirates, the team held a meeting this morning in the Garden City Hotel. We took this means of assuring Byron that these rumors are entirely false. There are no cliques on the team whatsoever. Moreover, White, though reporting under conditions which tend to breed such rumors, has the full support of every player on the club, all of whom admire him and have confidence in his ability as a great player. Next Monday night at the Polo Grounds, against the Giants, we will demonstrate our support of Byron White.

The cable was signed "Armand Niccolai, Mike Basrak—field captains—Pittsburgh Pirates Football Club." Niccolai was one of the players Ward had fingered in his column as a shirker. Ward was unrepentant: "That's the spirit, boys; we'll be watching."

The *World-Telegram* refused to take the story seriously: "The printed charges that the Pirates were making Whizzer White walk the plank because of jealousy aroused skepticism in well-informed pro grid circles. Proximity to the Pirates-Giants game made it appear designed wholly to help steam up public interest, a maneuver not uncommon in sports promotion." Neither Blood nor Rooney directly addressed the furor, apparently content with the players' telegram and a supportive letter to the *Brooklyn Eagle* by Ned Irish, the promoter for Madison Square Garden, who was now also doing publicity for the Giants football team. Irish explained White's problems as "a lack of practice for White with the team," which was "being corrected this week" by "a double drill" that would be held on September 29 and 30 in preparation for the game on October 3.

White kept his own counsel during what Pittsburgh papers called "the furor." He opened up only for the folks back home. When the Pirates came to Colorado for an Armistice Day game, on November 11, he granted an interview to the sports editor of the *Colorado Springs Evening Telegraph* the day before the game and declared, "You can tell anyone for me that these stories about lack of cooperation are hooey, nothing more." Rooney had tried to defuse the matter a month earlier with a three-page handwritten letter to the *Rocky Mountain News* denying the charges in Ward's column and reassuring anxious Denver fans that White was playing well and receiving full support from his teammates. After the season was over, White spoke only once in any detail about the controversy. In the interview for *Sports Illustrated* in 1962, he said:

> As far as I'm concerned, that was just a figment of some people's imaginations, or maybe some people thought they observed it because we were having a lousy season. I never knew anything about it, and anyway you would never make a yard unless those guys blocked for you. I roomed with Ed Karpowich, who played tackle and end, and I knew he never would have put up with that sort of thing.

Rooney often told the story—which may or may not support its credibility—that one day during an early-season scrimmage after White had been hazed verbally and physically, Karpowich "lifted White off the ground and yelled, 'Don't anybody else touch him—we can't afford to lose this guy.'" Before he died, Johnny Blood told Ray Didinger, who was writing a history of the team, that the rumors were "baloney. Whizzer was our meal ticket. It would have been crazy to sandbag him." Gene Ward had anticipated the point ("Rather like cutting off your nose to spite your face"), but argued that resentment and jealousy trumped economic self-interest. Tuffy Thompson makes a more compelling point. "That sorta stuff [intentionally bad blocking] would have torn the team apart," Thompson stated recently. "Whizzer was such a nice kid and worked so hard that the overwhelming sentiment was for him to do well. If anybody had laid down, we'd have been at each other's throats." Frank Altmar, the team trainer, makes the same argument. The controversy became overwrought in the hothouse atmosphere of the New York City press, where competition often pressured speculation into assertion. Moreover, as the *World-Telegram* was always careful to point out, during the period in question, White was near the top of the league in almost every offensive category, which was remarkable when opposing teams were all keying their defenses on him. In addition, Blood's offense was hardly a model of clockwork coordination. Gene Ward seemed to have second thoughts as the season wore on: on October 16 he published a two-page profile of White that was dotted with inaccuracies—all to White's benefit—and predicted a bright future from "this Byron (Whizzer) White."

There was behind-the-scenes intrigue, but it originated with Art Rooney. The day after the players swore their allegiance to White, Rooney admitted publicly that he had been in serious conversations with Dan Topping, owner of the Brooklyn football franchise, over White. Rooney's public statement said, "We have talked of financial terms but if you want my honest opinion, I believe Whizzer will finish out the season in a Pirate uniform." Three days later, White led the Pirates to a 13-10 upset victory over the New York Giants before almost nineteen thousand at the Polo Grounds. White did not score, but he dazzled the press. His blockers "were banging viciously into the foes," wrote Jack Sell—a White skeptic—in the *Post-Gazette*. White made 75 yards rushing on eighteen plays, a substantial improvement in his average gain per carry, and added 101 yards on punt returns. His rushing yardage came on runs "through the center" as well as "off-the tackles and the flanks," noted the *World-Telegram*. Defensively, he had a critical pass interception late in the game. Rooney announced two days after the game that White would not be sold to Brooklyn. Reports circulated that Rooney asked Topping for a lump-sum cash payment and a promise that White's contract would be assumed by Brooklyn on its terms. The deal never closed, probably because Topping would not make the financial commitment and Rooney was having second thoughts, at least about White. Rooney's genuine affection for White may have been cemented by the extraordinarily game performance against New York, which traded big statistics for a patch of facial scratches and other bodily abrasions and bruises. "He wasn't a pretty sight after the Giant game," one player later recalled. The effort even prompted a letter to the sports editor of the *New York Times* applauding White's play.

Rooney's hopes that the season could be turned around suffered a mixed fate less than a week after the Giant game. With the baseball Pirates knocked out of the pennant race by the Chicago Cubs, Forbes Field was now available, and Brooklyn was scheduled in for an October 9 date—ten days ahead of the revised schedule. Rooney was in a cash flow crisis, and the re-rescheduled Brooklyn game did not help matters. (The schedule was now so contorted that the Pirates would not play another game at home for a month, and that would be their final home game of the year—even though a month would then still be left in the season.) Only 8,372 paying spectators turned out to watch the Pirates beat Brooklyn, 17-7, for their second straight victory. White made enough yards from scrimmage to take over the league lead in rushing, a lead he would hold for the rest of the month, lose in November, and then finally recapture in the final game of the season. For Rooney, however, the only numbers that mattered were head counts of crowds, and they were disastrous. The puny home crowd for Brooklyn yielded only $6,400, and $5,000 went to the visiting team as its guaranteed share. That left Rooney with only $1,400 net to meet the biggest payroll in the league; all but $400 would be needed simply to meet White's weekly draw. (At the end of the year, Rooney would reveal that White was so sensitive to Rooney's plight and so disappointed with his own play that he refused for half of the season to accept his paychecks and absolutely refused to receive any proceeds from exhibition games, contrary to a clause in his contract.)

Other games had produced similarly poor returns. The first game of the season, at Detroit, had been to a near-capacity crowd, but discounted and complimentary tickets had kept Pittsburgh's share to only $5,900. The New York City trip had been a net loss: the Brooklyn game yielded $5,600, and the Giant game—which was played before the smallest Polo Grounds crowd for the Giants in three years—produced only $5,200, just $200 over the minimum guarantee. Rooney was realizing less than half of what he expected and needed to support his payroll. On October 14, Jimmy Powers, the *New York Daily News* columnist, wrote that he suspected that the White-to-Brooklyn negotiations were triggered by an early-season loan from Topping that was being called in, but the speculation was never confirmed. The other data were undisputed, so Karcis's release in September was the first step in what might be called a financial restructuring of the team. By mid-October, Rooney had three players—starting center Mike Basrak, guards George (Bunko) Kakasic and Ted Doyle—laid up with serious injuries, and one, Basrak, would never play again. White's roommate, Ed Karpowich (playing under the less intimidating name of Ed Karp) was out for the season with a broken leg. End Ed (Eggs) Manske, who had scored one touchdown and played well all year, was traded back to the Chicago Bears.

The second Brooklyn game, with the bitterly disappointing small gate, was the last straw. Rooney gutted the team in two days. He sold fullback Scrapper Farrell to Brooklyn, released Paul McDonough (the end from Utah who had almost tackled White in 1937), traded Tom Burnette to Philadelphia for cash and draft rights, and in the most controversial move, sold Frankie Filchock, the rookie quarterback from Indiana, to Washington. Very soon tackle Tony Matisi, a former two-time all-American, was sent to Detroit for sixth-round draft rights. Surveying Rooney's handiwork, the *Pittsburgh Press* headline October 11 read, "'We Haven't Given Up,' Says Rooney After Sale of Stars." By now, Rooney's shamelessness knew no limits. The night the headline ran, the Pirates lost an exhibition game before eleven thousand in Cincinnati. Before the game started, Rooney called the owner of the Cleveland Rams and asked that their game scheduled for October 16 be postponed, due to "bad weather." The Cleveland owner was over a barrel. He agreed to the postponement, but issued a statement saying Rooney's franchise should be canceled by the league. The reason for the postponement was obvious: the game was scheduled for Forbes Field, and the cancellation allowed Rooney to "sidestep" the $5,000 visiting team guarantee due to Cleveland, as the *Plain-Dealer* pointed out. Rooney later admitted: "Well, actually we canceled it because there weren't going to be any customers there." His team was also riddled with injuries and handicapped by the lack of time for his players to recover from the exhibition game. Rooney's charm mollified the Rams, who withdrew their demand for his franchise to be canceled. The game was rescheduled, first to Roanoke, Virginia, then to Chattanooga, Tennessee, and finally to New Orleans in December. Cleveland and Pittsburgh were the two poorest-drawing teams in the league, and they were both looking elsewhere for a big crowd to end seasons that had been frustrating both at the gate and in the win-loss column. Two days after obtaining the cancellation, Rooney released two more players, including Lindy Mayhew, an experienced lineman.

Once Rooney had cleaned house, the Pirates lost their remaining five league games. The team was shut out in three of the five games and scored only one touchdown in each of the other two games. One of the shutouts was a 7-0 defeat by Washington in the final home game, at Forbes Field on November 6; the gate was 12,910, the smallest crowd to see the Redskins play all year, and the visitors' share resulted in a $3,000 loss for Rooney on the day. (Fan interest had undoubtedly been dampened by the college game the day before between Pitt and Carnegie Tech.) Despite the near-empty grandstands, White impressed players on both sides with his fiercely determined play. "He didn't quit, even for one play, all day long, both ways," Sammy Baugh later remembered. "He was no fun to tackle, I'll tell you. Others were faster, but listen, he was a hard man to bring down. A hard man."

To cut his financial losses, Rooney scheduled five exhibition games during the balance of the season, including two games in two days against semi-pro teams at the end of October, and a pair of games against the professional Los Angeles Bulldogs, on November 11 in Colorado Springs, Colorado, and on November 13 in Los Angeles. The Western swing claimed one bizarre "casualty." As Rooney later commented, Johnny Blood took the "scenic route" home from the West Coast. He failed to show up for the game against Philadelphia, which was played in Charleston, West Virginia, on November 20. Blood was in New York watching the Giants play his old team, the Green Bay Packers. One of the Packers asked him why he wasn't with the Pirates. *We aren't playing today,* was the reply. Moments later, the public address system announced the final score, Philadelphia 14, Pittsburgh 7. Rooney was soon denying rumors that Blood would be fired, and he went so far as to rehire him for the 1939 season. Despite all of Rooney's efforts to economize, by the end of the first week of November the team was operating at a $35,000 loss for the year, and rumors were circulating that the franchise would be moved to Jersey City at the end of the season. The roster was down to twenty-one players, including Johnny Blood.

The final game of the season was the controversial appointment with Cleveland, which Rooney had canceled in October when his cash balance hit bottom. Rooney convinced the Rams to move the game to New Orleans, where he believed that local promoters with good political connections could help produce a big gate. When the Pirates arrived in New Orleans, Rooney discovered that there had been little publicity about the game. Trying for a last-minute splash, he took White to meet the local promoter. "I figured [the promoter] might not have heard of me, but everybody had heard of Whizzer White," Rooney later recalled. The local promoter not only had never heard of Rooney, but "he never heard of White either. . . . right there and then I knew I was dead." Only eight thousand showed up to watch Byron White play his final game for the Pittsburgh Pirates. Although the Pirates were guaranteed, win or lose, their worst season since 1934, White had a chance to win the rushing championship. He had led the league in October, fallen as low as seventh in mid-November, climbed back to fourth a week later, and then re- gained the lead by only 32 yards over Tuffy Leemans of the Giants with one game to play. Against Cleveland, White rushed thirteen times for 81 yards and claimed the rushing title by more than 100 yards over Leemans, who gained only 9 yards on the ground against Washington in his final game. White fin- ished with 567 yards on 152 carries, a 3.7 average.

Not only did White win the rushing championship, but he finished what was expected to be his only season in professional football with flair and de- termination. With Pittsburgh trailing a bigger and stronger Cleveland team 13-0 in the closing seconds, White dropped back to pass on first down at his own 47-yard line, met a furious rush from the Rams, sprinted off left end, cut back to his right, and was not stopped until he reached the Cleveland 11-yard line. The field announcer said there was time for only one play. In the words of the AP dispatch, "White drifted back and hurled a liner straight into the arms of [Wilbur] Stortet, substitute right end, who took the ball one-yard from the goal and fell over for a touchdown that one minute before had seemed utterly impossible."

The Pittsburgh Pirates finished in last place with a 2-9 win-loss record. In addition, they played a total of seven exhibition games. The worst statistic from Rooney's standpoint was the home attendance: notwithstanding the publicity campaign and countless speaking appearances by White, the Pirates drew only 38,622 to three games at Forbes Field. Only Cleveland had poorer home attendance.

Byron White's farewell to professional football found its most sentimen- tal note the day after the Cleveland game. He surprised his teammates by per- sonally hosting a farewell dinner for every member of the traveling squad, plus Rooney, two team officials, and the wives of three players who had made the trip to New Orleans. The dinner was held in the Hawaiian Room of the Roo- sevelt Hotel and featured "the biggest steak I had seen since I started playing pro ball," according to Tuffy Thompson. "It was an extremely generous act after a very tough season for everyone. I loved him for doing it, but I never saw him again." (White, allergic in his later years to taking credit for his own kind- ness, told a New Orleans audience in 1995 that he had fond memories of a party "given by the team" at Antoine's.)

After the dinner, White headed home to Wellington via Audubon, Iowa, for a short visit with his uncle Charles. Even the trip home made news. When he stopped in Audubon, he was interviewed by the Hearst organization's International News Service, which coaxed little from him ("Professional football has all the thrill and fun of college football with more competition and less glamour," INS summarized). He had been named to the first team of the all-NFL team by both United Press and the International News Service, and to the second team of the list, selected by the league's coaches. Despite their poor record, the Pirates had two all-pro players on the UP team, White and rookie guard Byron Gentry from USC. Gentry and Nick Niccolai were honorable mentions on the Official All-League team.

Byron White was expected to arrive in Colorado by Saturday, December 10, but that day his brother explained to the Boulder newspaper: "He is with his uncle now, which means that there is no telling when he will get home. I stopped to visit the same uncle on my way home from Oxford, intending to spend only a few hours, and it was three days later when I finally left." As usual, Sam was telling a good story. The day he provided the quotation, Byron White arrived in Cheyenne, Wyoming, and drove the thirty miles to Wellington in a 1939 Plymouth coupe that he had given his parents as an early Christmas present. Shortly after he arrived home, he again was denying rumors, this time that he would again change his mind and forfeit the Rhodes Scholarship in order to play pro football in 1939 with the New York Giants. His denial to the *Denver Post* manifested a hard-earned self-consciousness: even if he received a formal offer from the Giants, he "'didn't think' there was a chance he would give up his Rhodes Scholarship. But he added, in an off-hand manner, 'But then, I used to say a lot of things.'"

In a functional sense, Byron White pronounced his formal benediction on professional football in an interview with the Associated Press, dated December 3. White called the "football wars 'an experience I wouldn't have missed for anything.' But Oxford fits his desire to equip himself with all the academic background possible before stepping out into the law business. He has seen a danger in pro football." White stated:

> Most of the guys are paid comparatively well, but they haven't any future. They've learned that give and take brings immediate results—a well-placed straight-arm—but they cannot seem to become really interested in something that may not bear immediate results for years.
>
> I think I may find it awfully difficult grappling again with problems in a book, instead of those on a football field, but I'm better equipped for having done it.

The AP writer was moved to observe that "football players aren't supposed to talk like that."

That, of course, was the point. Byron White was trying to force his mind and his sensibilities through a cultural racing change, from a world of physical brutality relieved by card games and beer to a highly stylized world of the intellect, full of indeterminate ideas, precise expression, and indirection. The only similarity between the two worlds was that they were both almost exclusively male. White left pro football, for what he thought was the last time, with two friendships that endured over time—with Art Rooney and Johnny Blood. Both friendships had paradoxical elements.

Rooney unhesitatingly exploited White for every cent and every ticket sale he could. The final deal they negotiated apparently had no provision either for endorsement pay for White or even for his approval of products to be endorsed. From time to time, White discovered his likeness in a newspaper advertisement or on a broadside for a product or business that he knew nothing about. In one instance, his name was attached to the endorsement of a local department store. White decided that his compensation would be a new suit of clothes and a topcoat for Paul McDonough, the six-foot-four-inch end, a deal White imposed on the embarrassed merchant, who did not realize that White had not been told of his endorsement. In another, less amusing case, Rooney provided three action photographs of White—kicking, passing, and stationary—that were used in a seven-column advertisement for Chesterfield cigarettes. The ad's concept was that Chesterfield was the "right combination" of "the smoking qualities of the world's best tobaccos in one cigarette," just as White was the multidimensional player ("These action shots of 'Whizzer' White . . . famous All-American football star . . . show what it takes to be a triple-threat man"). White was not quoted, but most tobacco ads featuring athletes at the time did not contain endorsement quotations. The large, almost half-page ad ran on November 7, 1938, in the *Pittsburgh Press* and in the *Pittsburgh Sun-Telegraph*. White was both a cigarette and pipe smoker at the time, but he had received compliments less than two months earlier for refusing to do a national cigarette endorsement, a point mentioned in Gene Ward's troublesome column.

White cannot have enjoyed Rooney's stunts, but none of the exploitation seems to have torn White's affection for the team owner. As White explained bluntly to the *Denver Post* early in the season: "That's just what I get fifteen grand for—to get publicity and bring people in the stadiums." Over the years, White could always be counted on to appear at events honoring Rooney, even after appointment to the Supreme Court. For example, White spoke at the Circus Saints and Sinners Dinner on January 19, 1964, and shared the podium with Vince Lombardi, George Halas, Eddie Arcaro, and Johnny Blood. A few years later, he appeared at the Dapper Dan Dinner, also in Pittsburgh, also honoring Rooney among others. When Rooney died in 1988, White issued a statement: "There is no man in the world I respect more than Art Rooney. I always felt I could rely on his word. Everyone did. He was a man's man."

Byron White's devotion to Art Rooney was a function of two traits that they shared—both passionately hated to lose, and both prized personal loyalty above all other values. White had been with the team only a month when he told the *Denver Post* why he liked his new situation so much: "I'm the worst loser in the world . . . and this is a swell bunch of fellows. They don't make them any better than that fighting Irishman [Johnny Blood] and Art Rooney." Rooney's house was famous for its "two-day rule": for two days after his team lost, none of his five boys was to mention the fact, nor would Rooney watch game films, analyze game statistics, or otherwise postmortem the event. At the same time, Rooney stood up for his players and coaches, even under harsh criticism in the press, and he kept his promises. Even when White got off to what was an unsatisfying start for everyone, Rooney never lost faith in his expensive rookie. No player ever got paid with an IOU or received less than agreed.

Johnny Blood was a tribute to the individual and collective senses of humor of White and Rooney. Only three years younger than Rooney when he became playing coach, and physically not up to par with his players, Blood had lost whatever magical capacity to turn a game around Rooney believed he possessed. Instead, he was a hard-living, roguishly irresponsible manager who could not figure out how to get the most of his players and who occasionally missed practice in order to do "library research" on his latest pet economic theory, as White later recalled with bemusement. Blood was nonetheless urbane without being affected, and beneath the bluster of the self-styled intellectual was a shrewd observer and loyal friend whose verve White admired. In many respects, Rooney and Blood together put fun into football for White at a team level, something he had not enjoyed for the previous three years under the humorless and obsessive Bunny Oakes. As White told the *Denver Post* on his visit home before leaving for Oxford, "Pro ball gets in your blood. I like it a lot. We were constantly on the road, rarely staying in Pittsburgh any length of time. About the only places I missed this year were the northwest and Florida. It seems I traveled thru every other place. It was like being in a circus." When his ringmaster, Johnny Blood, was elected as a charter member of the National Football League Hall of Fame in 1963, he was introduced at the induction ceremonies in Canton, Ohio, by Byron White.

For White and his friends, the 1938 season has always been remembered for three facts: he received the highest annual salary in the league's history, he

won the rushing title in his rookie year, and he was the victim of poor support—by design or incapacity—early in the season. White and every other
player who ever addressed the last issue denied the rumors that blocks were
misplayed due to jealousy or spite early in the season. So did Blood and
Rooney. The statistical evidence for the season sheds little light on the issue,
with the exception of one suggestive fact: after September 29, when the players issued their pledge to White in response to Gene Ward's incendiary column, White's average jumped from 2.2 to 4.5 yards per carry. There was no
difference in the caliber of the competition. The winning percentage of Pittsburgh's first four opponents was identical to the winning percentage of the
final seven—approximately .600. White's final average for the entire season
was 3.7, which was the best on the team. Only three other players gained more
than 100 yards rushing for the year, and their averages were 3.6 (Tuffy
Thompson), 3.0 (fullback Stu Smith), and 2.9 (Frankie Filchock).

Whatever the statistical picture, the standard view of the blocking issue is
that of the *Pro Football Chronicle,* an anecdotal history of the sport: "There
were rumors [White's] envious teammates didn't block hard for him. When
three players were released early in the season, owner Art Rooney publicly denied it was because of team dissension." It is unlikely that White's disappointing debut in the first three games of the season could be explained primarily by
jealousy on the part of some of his blockers. Practice time was negligible, every
opponent keyed its defense on him, and the early-season schedule was physically punishing. Other facts mesh poorly with the standard view. The first
game after the September releases was White's worst performance of the
year—minus ½ yard net rushing in fifteen attempts—yet the Pirates beat
Brooklyn 17-3. The Pirates finished the season with essentially the same interior lineup from tackle to tackle as the lineup that started against Brooklyn
(Mike Basrak, the center and team captain, suffered a season-ending injury in
mid-October). White thus averaged nearly 4 yards per carry for the final seven
games of the season after the game in which he netted minus yardage—all behind the same line. It is possible, of course, that Gene Ward was onto something and that his column and the ensuing controversy proved to be a
powerful motivator for White's front line; it is more likely that the hothouse
world of New York City sports journalism made rumor and guesses into a
brief scandal that can never be dispelled. For Byron White, the allegations of
intrigue were doubly offensive: they implied he needed alibis and they im-
pugned the integrity of men whom he liked and whose acceptance he had
worked very hard and successfully to earn.

6

"A YANK AT OXFORD"

A FEW DAYS before Byron White concluded his first season in the National Football League, the Associated Press moved a story, dated December 3, that ended with a suitably romantic paragraph containing an image that would briefly annoy Byron White almost as much as the nickname to which he now seemed permanently yoked: "He'd play another year or two of pro ball, if he could without passing up old Oxford. But that's over now, he says. The game that brought him fame and riches has served its purpose, so he waves a cheery good-bye and—presto!—becomes a Yank at Oxford."

The reference was to the first film produced by Metro-Goldwyn-Mayer in England pursuant to what was planned to be a multifilm venture between MGM and British talent, both on- and off-screen. The film was designed as a vehicle for recasting Robert Taylor's screen image from sleek matinee idol to he-man, and secondarily to introduce a young English actress named Vivien Leigh. It was a send-up both of American universities, with their growing emphasis on rah-rah athletics, and of Oxford, which was depicted as overflowing with scatty dons, supercilious undergraduates, and befuddled administrators. The few critics who took it seriously, such as Alistair Cooke, found the caricatures cruel, but audiences made the film the top-grossing motion picture of the year in Great Britain and a runaway success in the United States. The film created a genre—one that depicted the clash of cultures created by the inser-

123

tion of a brash and naive American in an English institution sustained by tradition and complacency. Taylor, as the conceited American lout, makes a fool of himself at the outset, fights back in ways that his fellow students both admire and detest, and finally wins both the big boat race and the right girl.

Whatever the details, incongruity was the dominant motif of the film, and at that level, Byron White seemed to personify the Yank at Oxford (although students who knew both Sam and Byron White unkindly viewed the film of that title as Sam's unauthorized biography). Byron White departed for England aboard the *Europa* on January 3, 1939, seen off by a small group of friends and forced with his departing breath to deny rumors that he would spend only one year abroad and then return to play professional football again the following fall. "Football and I have parted," he told the Associated Press at dockside. "I've heard a lot of rumors about my coming back next year to play again for Pittsburgh or for the New York Giants. They're all news to me. I've got to get to work on this scholarship."

While he was at sea, the *Sunday Chronicle* became the first London newspaper to pick up the motion picture angle: "'Whizzer' (Real Yank at Oxford) On Way Here," read the headline. The brief story was more imagination than reporting:

> Listen, Goils. America's Heart Throb No. 1 will soon be here to play a real "Yank at Oxford" drama. He is 21-year old Byron ("Whizzer") White, £3,000-a-year professional all-America football star, now crossing the Atlantic on his way to Oxford University to study law. Oxford students plan to make "Whizzer" feel at home by a reception in the "Yank at Oxford" film tradition. "Byron is going to have a rough time—all because of Robert Taylor and that film," a friend at Rhodes House, Oxford, told the Sunday Chronicle.

The other half of the story reported White's seriousness, his poverty ("son of a beet farmer"; paid college fees "by waiting at table"), and his £3,000 contract with Pittsburgh.

The advance publicity foreshadowed the very public spotlight that greeted White's arrival in Southampton late on January 9. The cultural hazing began at the dock. According to the Associated Press dispatch, British customs officials asked White to spell his name and to explain "where Colorado was. They made him declare his last carton of American cigarettes and in general treated him like a freshman reporting for his first practice." The first question from the press was whether he planned to play rugby for Oxford. "I don't know whether they'll let me play anything," he replied. "I'll just have to let them decide." The response was politic, and White did his best, under obvious strain, to defuse unsympathetic expectations, according to the AP: "Outside of losing his trunk and not being able to get his bags closed after he opened them in customs, Whizzer seemed to enjoy his first rainy night in England." In response to the predictable question of how he would cope without central heating or private—even proximate—bath facilities, he gritted his teeth and said: "I think I'll like it over here, because I'm just a country boy and I'm not very used to modern conveniences anyway."

The so-called quality London daily newspapers ignored White's arrival. The *Daily Herald,* whose reporter caught White on the ship's tender, noted, "Whizzer Slips into Oxford," and the *Daily Express,* who tracked down White aboard ship, headlined, " 'Whizzer' Becomes a Yank at Oxford." The tag was already annoying White. The *Herald's* special correspondent wrote that White "has been called a real life 'Yank at Oxford'—but [he] is determined there shall be nothing of that about him." White refused to discuss his athletic career at the University of Colorado, nor "would he discuss Oxford's new problem: *Will 'Whizzer' play for the University rugby team?"* White tried to dampen the assembled reporters' interest: "I thought I came here to get away from all that publicity stuff. I'm here to study. After all, I'm a beggar at a feast."

The press ambush at Southampton was only the beginning. When White arrived in Oxford, he was badgered into a photography session with the *News-Chronicle.* He was supplied with a cap and gown—standard student issue—plus an old bicycle and a pair of notebooks, and he was depicted riding down the Turl, a street fronting Hertford College. Another shot showed him talking with a coy smile to a "coed," who in fact was a reporter for the *News-Chronicle,* Betty Nolan. Her paper labeled the photo of White on the bicycle, with Nolan trotting at his side, "Another Yank at Oxford." She wrote: "He is six feet one and has flaxen hair and blue eyes. He looks cute in his cap and gown." White was able to end the session only by inviting her to lunch. The local paper, the *Oxford Mail,* ran a copy of the photo the next day. Within a week, the picture was also published in the *New York Daily News,* the *New York Sun* ("A Real Life Yank at Oxford"), the *New York World-Telegram* ("Whizzer Gets New Headgear and a Bike"), the *Denver Post* ("Whizzer White Is Now Yank at Oxford"), and the *Boulder Daily Camera* ("Pigskin to Mortar Board for Whizzer").

White did not realize it at the time, but the photo session was a faux pas. He knew, as he had told the AP a month before, that Oxford "professors" (meaning principally Rhodes Trust officials) "had frowned on his starting school three months late." They also frowned on professionalism. On top of that, the MGM film was hardly good advertising for the Rhodes Scholarship. Ironically, although the film's protagonist—Lee Sheridan—is not identified as a Rhodes Scholar, several critics made that assumption, and the breezy *New York Times* review noted that Sheridan had "accepted Cecil Rhodes' posthumous invitation to Oxford." The review's description of the character ("lung-burstingly Midwestern, perfect Kiwanis material, as cerebral as a well-worn Indian club") ridiculed Oxford-bound American scholar-athletes as a class, irrespective of the auspices of their attendance. The point undoubtedly was not lost on L. S. Amery, the chairman and senior member of the Rhodes Trust, who attended the London premiere of the film as the guest of the new American ambassador, Joseph P. Kennedy, on March 31, 1938.

It is no surprise that the Rhodes trustees were hesitant to accommodate White's application to defer his arrival. In light of the publicity generated by the film, deferral would send precisely the wrong message about the relationship between scholarship and athletics among Rhodes scholars and about the trust's priorities. White added a further embarrassment—he was a professional athlete in a world that esteemed, indeed mythologized, the effortless superiority of the keen amateur and disdained the play-for-pay athlete as ungentlemanly. White was unlucky enough to arrive in England during one of the country's periodic anxiety attacks over how rigid the line between professional and amateur should be drawn. A twenty-four-year old former Cambridge "blue"—a varsity rugby player—was a director of a local professional rugby club, thus compromising his amateur status in the eyes of the Welsh Union, which refused to let him play as an amateur. A lengthy sports column in the *Herald* ridiculed "these crazy sports laws," but the existence of controversy was almost as important to Oxford athletic officials as its proper resolution. White, for a complex of reasons, simply could not compete in the gentlemanly world of Oxbridge sports.

Years later, many of White's contemporaries would reminisce about their first encounter with an English undergraduate. All were awkward in one way or another, and White's experience was no exception. He had been in his rooms at Hertford for a very short time when he was visited by the captain of the university rugby club, who, White later said, "suggested very clearly that they didn't want me to play athletics at Oxford because I was a professional. I would have had to use another dressing room from the amateurs."

While he was still adjusting to the gentle admonition from the rugby captain, he was visited by three fellow American Rhodes scholars, all coincidentally from the Western United States. (White's closest friends at Oxford were from Nevada, Utah, and Montana.) The trio provided a warmer welcome but also a warning. The photo splash a few days before had caused rumbling at Rhodes House, where Warden Allen was said to be displeased with the attention White had drawn to himself. White was suddenly behind a golden eight ball: he was a professional, which was bad enough, but he was also apparently ostentatious, which was bad form. At worst, he was making some in Oxford fear that *A Yank at Oxford* was not fiction but prophesy. White explained, but did not try to excuse, his mistake with the London press as a hangover from his habits in Pittsburgh. He said that Art Rooney told him, *You're being paid to bring people to the games, so you have to accommodate the press even if you don't particularly like it. If they want an interview, give them an interview; if they want your picture, let them take it.* White appreciated Rooney's strategy, but said it came at a high price. The worst part, he said, was after games, when *you're trying to put body and soul back together and some famous sportswriter sticks his drunken nose in your face and starts asking stupid questions.* White vowed to lie low, and the prohibition from playing rugby and other sports came more as a relief than a disappointment. *For the first time, I could be a student and not have to juggle studying, sports, and other activities,* he said to more than one fellow student.

White's vow to settle into a quiet academic routine required finesse as much as discipline. At the end of his second week in Oxford, the *Daily Express* ran a version of the scholar-on-the-bike shot, captioned " 'The Yank' gets a bicycle," observing that White bought a bicycle on his second day "just like the film Yank at Oxford." The same day that the photograph ran—for the last time, as it turned out—White had lunch at Rhodes House with three fellow American Rhodes scholars, and word quickly spread that the warden "had a word" with White afterward, advising him to stay out of the papers. Shortly thereafter, White made a date with a fellow American Rhodes scholar in Hertford, George Piranian, a mathematician from Utah, to play squash at the college's courts, some distance away. White was late and apologetic, Piranian recalled years later. "He said he had finished a tutorial and gone back to his rooms, only to find several reporters from London tabloids awaiting him," Piranian said. "They asked for 'Whizzer White,' and White replied, 'He's my roommate. He just left.' " The reporters were both in violation of college rules, which forbade visitors at that hour, and, lucky for White, ignorant that two-room suites in Hertford College were occupied by one man only.

It was easier for Byron White to make peace with C. K. Allen, the warden of Rhodes House, than with his tutor, C. H. S. Fifoot. Fifoot had succeeded Allen in 1925 as law tutor at Hertford and had established his scholarly reputation in legal history with the publication of *English Law and Its Background* in 1932. He later would be coauthor of the leading treatise on the English law of contract. A small, trim man who was devoted to bicycles and bowler hats, Fifoot was widely regarded as a premier teacher and scholar in a world where tutors tended to be one or the other but not both. White had chosen Hertford as his college not only because his brother had preceded him there but because he was told that Fifoot was the best law tutor in the university. George Carlson, the same ex–Rhodes scholar from Colorado who had encouraged Sam White to apply for the scholarship and to attend Hertford, wrote Byron White in late 1937:

> In support of Mr. Fifoot I have one thing to say—just the thought of my association with him at Oxford makes me feel that I had three very happy and constructive years. When you are five thousand miles from home with almost no one in the immediate vicinity who cares about your activities, it is a mighty pleasant thing to have a capable professor who will make your interests his interests and add the human element to your academic life.

Carlson predicted to Warden Allen that White "and Mr. Fifoot will do well together," and repeated the prediction to White after he had been accepted by Hertford. When White returned from his first tutorial with Fifoot, he told Russell McDonald, a Rhodes scholar from Nevada whom he had met at the district competition in San Francisco, that he was facing "long odds." Fifoot stated bluntly that he feared that White could not adequately prepare the law syllabus in the time remaining before examinations in June of 1940. Counting the term that was already a week old, White had only five terms to learn nine subjects ("papers"), including two in Latin—the Roman law of obligations, actions, and usufruct (based on the *Institutes* of Gaius and Justinian) and the Roman law of sale (based on the *Digest*) in comparison to the English law on sale of goods. Other subjects were contracts, tort, the newly titled Law of Land (based on the Law of Property Act 1925), English legal history (covering real property, contract, tort, and criminal law), international law, jurisprudence, and an elective.

Fifoot's pessimism may seem odd, because the actual workload averaged less than two subjects per term. However, both the Oxford schedule and the Oxford culture worked against White. Terms were only eight weeks long, followed by six-week vacations (or "vacs"); summer (the "long vac") lasted four months. Tutors were thus available only for twenty-four weeks of the academic year, and no teaching was scheduled for the final term before exams, to allow students to review ("revise"). Fifoot would have only four terms to teach nine subjects to White. Moreover, the content of several subjects had recently changed, which made more work for tutor as well as student. The idea had been to put more meat in the law finals, a reform supported by Fifoot, and it would not do for a supporter of the more rigorous curriculum to appear to be presumptuous about a foreign student's capacity to master the new syllabus, especially one who had been absent one term. The new law syllabus attracted six American Rhodes scholars, including White, in the thirty-two-man class of 1939. (Most, like White, read for a second bachelor's degree, with seven reading "PPE"—politics, philosophy, and economics; ten pursued thesis degrees, including six doctorates.)

Faced with Fifoot's worries, Byron White became, in the words of his friend Gerald Brown, "the only Rhodes scholar who ever worked fourteen hours a day on his studies." Brown's remark implied a double anomaly. Most American Rhodes scholars were not obsessive about their academic course, at least until finals loomed. More significantly, the mood pervading Oxford throughout the 1938–39 academic year was one of anxious passion over Hitler's intentions, intensified by near universal disgust for the Munich Agreement of September 1938. According to the memoirs of Philip Kaiser, "No issue aroused the students more than the Munich Agreement," which Neville Chamberlain hoped had bought peace at the price of Sudetenland Czechoslovakia.

The first political challenge to the appeasement policy in general and Munich in particular had been the Oxford by-election, in which the master of Balliol College and retiring vice chancellor of the university, A. D. (Sandy) Lindsay, stood as an independent candidate against Quentin Hogg, the Conservative M.P. Lindsay's challenge to the university's apolitical tradition and to the government was, wrote Kaiser, "the most memorable event in my three years at Oxford." Byron White missed it, of course: the day of the election, which Lindsay lost, White and his Pittsburgh teammates were licking their wounds after a 20-0 drubbing on the road at Green Bay and beginning to prepare for the Washington Redskins—their second home game of the year. Denis Healey, who was then in his final year at Balliol, later captured the simplicity and urgency of Oxford politics in the year of appeasement:

> For the young in those days, politics was a world of simple choices. The enemy was Hitler with concentration camps. The objective was to prevent war by standing up to Hitler. Only the Communist Party [which Healey joined] seemed unambiguously against Hitler. The Chamberlain government was for appeasement, Labour seemed torn between pacifism and a half-hearted support for collective security, and the Liberals did not count.

American students played an active role in the intellectual hothouse of Oxford politics. Philip Kaiser was the head of the Balliol junior common room, in effect the leading undergraduate officer of the college. Howard K. Smith, an American Rhodes scholar from Louisiana, succeeded Healey as president of the Labour Club, which during 1938 and 1939 listed one thousand dues-paying members in a university of five thousand. White played no role in the popular Labour Club, nor for that matter in Conservative or Liberal clubs. Smith later recalled "seeing [White] coming into the hall, attending our meeting, and looking about him at the crowd with evident circumspection as if to say, Am I in the right place? Are these my kind of people? I have the impression that after a while he decided that we zealots—anti-Hitler ones, but still zealots—were not, and I think he left."

White must have felt that he came in late to a strangely costumed drama whose plot was clear to everyone except himself. Beyond the caps and gowns, the streets of central Oxford, where White's small college of 150 students was located, were mixed with workingmen in flat caps and fraying tweed jackets, eccentric dons, and the odd student in white tie and tails coming or going to a formal dinner. As Kaiser later wrote, "Oxford students were fairly homogeneous," coming largely from upper-middle class and aristocratic families, "their elite status already established. An increasing number of scholarship students came from poorer backgrounds, but once in Oxford they tended to 'aristocratize' rapidly." The American Rhodes scholars tended to come from more modest circumstances, and several Rhodes scholars from the West admitted privately to "growing up dirt poor."

For Americans, Oxford provided a standard of living never before enjoyed and not realized again until much later in life. White described a typical day in an interview for the *Boulder Daily Camera* after he had returned from England. He was awakened at 7:30 A.M. by his manservant ("scout"), attended chapel at eight, and then went to a breakfast of "a single course, which not infrequently consists of some one of the excellent English pork products, with an egg or kidneys," and "ended with toast or jam and marmalade." Then,

> The Englishman gives an hour or so after meals to relaxation and should the breakfast be interrupted about ten o'clock for a moment by the exit of someone bent on attending a lecture, he apologizes for such an act as if it were scarcely good form. An appointment with one's tutor is more usual and a more legitimate excuse for leaving.

After a light lunch of cheese and bread, "with perhaps a half pint of bitter beer, . . . everybody scatters to field and track for the exercise that the English climate makes necessary and the English temperament demands." Postgame tea obviously struck White as ironic:

By 4 o'clock every one is back in college tubbed and dressed for tea, which a man serves for himself in his rooms with as many fellows as he has been able to gather in on the field or river. It is in this way that the host, if he has not been able to witness the games[,] may hear the minutest details from the players themselves. Thus the function of the "bleachers" on an American field is performed with a vengeance by the easy-chairs before a common-room fire.

Dinner, in cap and gown, followed at 7 P.M., and afterward, a "meditative Whizzer ran his fingers through his hair as he recalled":

After a quarter of an hour in the store where the fellows go for dessert, they drop off to read or to take coffee in someone's room; with the coffee a glass of port is usually taken. In the evening, when the season permits, the fellows sit out of doors after dinner, smoking and playing bowls. There is no place in which the spring comes more sweetly than in an Oxford garden where the high walls are at once a trap for the firm warm rays of the sun and a barrier to the winds of March.

White never came closer to a poetic touch in describing his experience at Oxford. What Evelyn Waugh found a "respectable but rather dreary little college," architecturally "nondescript," with "ancient but unremarkable buildings," White found cozy and charming. As the future would prove, the afternoon teas and the evening beer sessions would put him in contact with men whom he would either remain close to or call upon years later. For the moment, the incongruity between his recent past and his genteel present proved vastly more enriching than the law course about which he had worried so much for the six months preceding his belated matriculation.

The core of his social life was his college, due to the conventions of the day. Everyone had to be inside the college when the gates closed, at 9:10 P.M. during the week and at midnight on weekends. Students ("members of the University") were barred by university regulations from entering pubs, which naturally led to both ritualized and ad hoc exercises of hide-and-seek on the part of the students and the university officials charged with enforcing the rules ("bulldogs"). Thus, social life was generally either taken on the fly or confined to the walls of the college.

At the fringes of his Oxford experience, White's social life was an odd mixture of the highly stylized and the haphazard. For more than a decade before White arrived at Oxford, Nancy, Lady Astor—an American native and the first woman to take an elected seat in the House of Commons—had entertained American Rhodes scholars and other American students in her

London town house and at Cliveden, her country house in Maidenhead, between London and Oxford. George Bernard Shaw was customarily an add-on for the London drinks parties, which White attended with fellow scholars in the early spring of the year. Shaw, according to Gerald Brown's diary, apparently viewed White as an intriguing curiosity at first but too ironic a conversationalist for sustained repartee. The Astor-Shaw party was a curious grace note to the year of Munich, because both, especially Lady Astor, were closely identified by the public with the appeasement policy, and the "Cliveden set" became synonymous with an aggressive but naive pacifism that made even the government uneasy.

During the frequent and lengthy Oxford vacations, Rhodes House paired with the Dominions Fellowship Trust, a World War I venture, to arrange visits in English country homes for Rhodes Scholars. Or as C. K. Allen put it in the official history of the trust's first half century,

> A large number of Rhodes Scholars enjoyed hospitality in English homes through the good offices of the Dominions Fellowship trust, which grew out of Lady Frances Ryder's organization in the first war and was latterly under the chief direction and wise administration of Miss Macdonald of Sleat, C.B.E. In this way many lasting friendships were formed for which a cloud of witnesses are most grateful to this admirable organization. In pre–[World War II] times some Rhodes Scholars perhaps were a little discomposed by the unaccustomed formality they found in the well-provided English country house; but the second war introduced great changes in economics, in social customs and in understandings of different national types, and I think that both hosts and guests found advantage in the less formal conditions which became general.

Allen's observation is cumulative evidence of the transition through which Oxford and the Rhodes Scholarships were passing with only partial self-awareness. Philip Kaiser was certainly correct that there was a "drastic change in attitude between the pleasure-loving Oxford of the 1920s, so imaginatively evoked by Evelyn Waugh in *Brideshead Revisited,* and the more politically conscious Oxford of the 1930s, which was reacting to the worldwide economic collapse after 1929 and the breakdown of the international political order." (And the dreary war-time austerity of Philip Larkin's *Jill* had definitely not arrived.) English undergraduates who had organized their lives for more than a decade toward admission to Oxford or Cambridge and its attendant pleasures did not in 1939 abandon champagne breakfasts and other self-indulgent pleasures at a stroke in favor of the imperatives of anti-Fascism. Sebastian Flyte may have become a relic of the past, but the new Charles Ryders still had white tie and tails.

Some American Rhodes scholars continued to utilize the services of Miss Macdonald of Sleat as late as the spring of 1939, but White was not one of them. "Dressing for dinner at a country house was not Byron's idea of a vacation," Charles Jelinek would say years later. Instead, White repaired to the south of France with Jelinek, Russell McDonald, and John (Slim) Logan, a Canadian student. White later explained that they "rented the top part of a villa on the French Riviera. I'd spend maybe half or three-quarters of the day on the books, and then we'd horse around the rest of the time." To Jelinek, the vac was exhausting: "Byron would be up at the crack of dawn, out the door, and running up and down a steep hill outside the villa. Then he'd come back for a big breakfast and study until dark. He studied the rest of us into the ground."

Despite the grinding schedule, the Easter vac included an unanticipated benefit. White met John F. Kennedy, son of Joseph P. Kennedy, the American ambassador to Great Britain, while the younger Kennedy was touring the Riviera after a family visit to Val d'Isère in the Rhône-Alpes. John Kennedy was spending the spring semester of his final year at Harvard College nominally assisting his father and researching his senior thesis but actually sightseeing across Europe. Kennedy and White were an odd pairing. White was physically powerful and taciturn, Kennedy was thin—his sister Kathleen (Kick) called him John of Gaunt—and gregarious. Both shared a taste for irony, although Kennedy's was more highly developed and artfully deployed. Yet they both enjoyed high-spirited pleasure, and White would later call Kennedy the "most fun-producing man I ever met."

Joe Kennedy esteemed the Red Granges and Johnny Bloods of the world and had even produced Grange's one feature-length motion picture, *One Minute to Play*. The son, lacking the physical equipment to match the heroic models, liked surrounding himself with rugged football players; during his sophomore year, he roomed with Torbert Macdonald, Harvard's preeminent running back, and the following year he and Macdonald shared a four-room suite with two other first-team football players, Ben Smith and Charlie Houghton. Whizzer White, the most publicized college football player of 1937, was more than a step up, and the unlikely chemistry surprised and pleased both men. Despite their many differences, they shared similarities small and large—they were born within a month of each other, were suspicious of the press (although Kennedy flirted with the idea of journalism as a career), and were intuitively hostile to dogmatic views and conventional wisdom.

John Kennedy and Byron White also arrived late to what some more cynical students of the day called the "end-of-the-world party." While White was playing professional football, Kennedy was at Harvard and then in Palm Beach, Florida, for the Christmas vacation. Both young men missed Joseph P. Kennedy's incongruously undiplomatic behavior during the autumn of 1938 after Munich. Less than three weeks after the Munich Agreement was signed and Chamberlain returned home waving the agreement and proclaiming "peace in our time," the ambassador addressed the Navy League on Trafalgar Day, October 19, 1938, and created a "firestorm." He declared that "it has long been a theory of mine that it is unproductive for both the democratic and dictator countries to widen the divisions now existing between them," and that "there simply is no sense, common or otherwise, in letting these differences grow into unrelenting antagonisms. After all, we have to live together in the same world whether we like it or not."

The speech sounded like a repudiation of Roosevelt's year-old declaration in Chicago that a "quarantine" should be placed around outlaw nations. Reaction was bitter in both the diplomatic and press corps. The ambassador was surprised by the reaction. Roosevelt was furious and cut him out of the foreign policy loop. John Kennedy reassuringly wrote his parents from Harvard that the speech "while it seemed to be unpopular with the Jews etc. was considered to be very good by everyone who wasn't bitterly anti-fascist." Less than three weeks after the speech, a German diplomat was killed in Paris in retaliation for the deportation of Polish Jews from Germany, and the Nazis unleashed *Kristallnacht* in reprisal—the plunder of more than two hundred synagogues, destruction of nearly one thousand Jewish-owned shops, and the arrest of twenty thousand Jews. Roosevelt responded by urging Chamberlain to intervene with Hitler.

At the same time, Ambassador Kennedy visited Oxford for the first time and offhandedly defended his isolationist views to the United States Society, a group composed of most of the Americans students resident in Oxford. Kaiser recalled the performance in his memoirs:

> Foolishly, he had no prepared speech. Instead, he boldly announced that he would make no preliminary remarks and was ready to devote all his time to answering questions. We couldn't resist this opportunity to bloody him. It was no secret that Kennedy strongly supported Chamberlain's appeasement policy and favored Franco in Spain, which most of us deplored. Kennedy arrogantly emphasized his position in his replies to the first few questions, and we reacted by prodding him with one sharp query after another, adding

provocative supplementaries whenever we felt his responses were unsatisfactory.

After twenty minutes of "a rising crescendo of hostility between the students and the speaker," Denis Brogan, the faculty adviser to the society, intervened and sagely adjourned the meeting. Others who witnessed the performance viewed the ambassador with contempt. "I was embarrassed for the country," one later recalled. "Here was our chief representative, casually defending Franco and supporting Chamberlain as if there were no other conceivable view. And sitting at his feet were two of his teenage daughters, loudly chomping gum. It was all tasteless."

Neither White nor John Kennedy was hit by flying debris when the ambassador's improbable diplomatic career blew up in late 1938, because both were far out of range. John Kennedy arrived in England with his father on the *Queen Mary* a few weeks after White reached Oxford in January 1939. One of the Kennedys' traveling companions had been Lord Lothian, who was retiring as secretary of the Rhodes Trust to become ambassador to the United States. While White worked to catch up in his academic work, John Kennedy crisscrossed Europe visiting one capital after another, occasionally purporting to gather information for his father—as Joe Jr. did during the spring in Madrid—and generally making a nuisance of himself to one American embassy after another. The regimen kept him away from England for much of the time, and after the unanticipated rendezvous in the south of France, White and Kennedy did not see each other again until one of the many parties that the ambassador staged for Americans abroad late that spring. The social occasions, including the odd dance in Oxford at Rhodes House, provided the ambassador's oldest girls—Kick, age eighteen, and Eunice, seventeen—with full dance cards of young American men, about whom Kick shamelessly gossiped in letters to friends back home. White, she found, was at a disadvantage in her eyes because he had not "gone to an eastern college." Kick had been voted "most exciting debutante of 1938," and she easily adjusted to the London social world revolving around her.

Dance cards were not a priority for Byron White during the spring of 1939. Nor were international politics, at least at the participatory level of many of his fellow Americans in Oxford. When a majority of the American Rhodes scholars in residence at Oxford cabled President Roosevelt in mid-March urging him "to withhold recognition of the Government of General Franco unless guarantees were given that no reprisals will be carried out against leaders and citizens of Republican Spain," White was not a signatory.

White was equally closed about domestic American politics. Years later, his fellow students could only point to one occasion when he revealed his convictions, a statement memorable for both its singularity and its brevity.

"It was an American party—not an English sherry hour but a real scotch-and-soda party—and the issue was the Works Progress Administration," recalled Charles Jelinek. The question was whether the WPA was a useful program, in terms of both economics and dignity, for its beneficiaries, or was an economically unjustifiable reward for "shovel leaners" whose work breaks exceeded their productivity. Jelinek tended to the shovel-leaners school, and White's reaction was fierce: "What do you expect those men to do? Starve to death?" Others who witnessed the suddenly sharp exchange said that "you could hear a pin drop for a couple of seconds" before the party resumed. Anxiety over playing academic catch-up and what many were beginning to think was a congenital hostility to abstraction had a price. White remained at the periphery of the endless extracurricular conversations that filled the time-rich days of the Oxford student body, especially the politically enthusiastic Americans.

One priority White never abandoned was maintenance of his physical condition. "He had one of the most extraordinary physiques I have ever seen," remarked one American Rhodes scholar. "He looked fit but he was unprepossessing with those sloping shoulders and round wire-rimmed spectacles." But "stripped to athletic shorts for a workout or a squash game, he looked like a Greek god—only made of pale oak, not marble. And when he hit you, by accident or by design, you felt like a locomotive had crashed into you at top speed." Barred from college and university sports teams by his professional status, White turned to informal channels for the physical challenge that was so central to his personality and to his desire to maintain his physical condition. One channel was extraordinarily unorthodox and would have had him on the carpet again had word got out; the other was as unexpected as it was satisfying. During the grim Hilary term, which ran from January to early March, Oxford experienced bitter cold and even a rare snowfall; Yeats died at the end of that January, "in the dead of winter," as Auden would later write. When squash courts were not available, White turned to wrestling with his scout, Beasley. Fellow students could not believe the rumors at first. "Either White challenged him, or vice versa," according to George Piranian, who lived nearby. "They would clear the furniture out of the sitting room and have at it." No other American student had ever crossed class lines so freely, but discretion prevented an incident.

Once spring arrived, White discovered somewhat to his surprise that he was able to indulge his favorite sport—baseball. In college, he had enjoyed

"baseball more than I did any other sport. . . . I was always ready to get out in the sunshine and horse around playing a relaxed game like baseball." During the late 1930s, a small baseball league flourished in the English Midlands, with impetus from Canadians who had immigrated to work in mills in Manchester and Birmingham. In late May, a pickup team of Americans and one Englishman traveled by bus to Cambridge to meet a similar pickup team. Oxford won, 19-3. White impressed Penn Kimball, who played right field, as the "greatest natural athlete I have ever seen." The big series was not against Cambridge, however, but against a team from the Durex Factory in Birmingham, which manufactured condoms. The Durex team, loaded with Canadians, had won fifty-nine straight games going into a two-game series with the Oxford pickup team. The first game was called by darkness with the score tied 3-3. In the next game, the Oxford team prevailed 7-3, with White playing a critical role. The infield for Oxford, which was the heart of the team, consisted of Elvis Stahr at first base, White at second, Philip Kaiser at shortstop, and Robert S. Babcock at third; twenty-five years later, the infield would become secretary of the army, associate justice of the Supreme Court of the United States, ambassador to various countries, and professor cum Vermont state legislator.

The term drifted to a languid end, elegantly struggling to forget the ominous developments in Europe. The university almost parodied itself at the annual Encaenia, at which honorary degrees are conferred. Felix Frankfurter, the Byrne professor of administrative law at Harvard Law School and conspicuous confidant of President Roosevelt, received an honorary degree, introduced by custom in Latin, with a variation on Virgil: *"Felix, qui potuit reorum cognoscere causas."* He was joined honoris causa by P. G. Wodehouse, creator of Jeeves and Bertie Wooster. White developed his own agenda for the four-month summer vacation. He recalled later:

> I borrowed a car from a South African fellow and toured around France and Germany and then settled down for a couple of months in Munich, where I rented a room from an old German woman.
>
> I spent those months studying Roman law and trying to improve my German, reading the newspapers and talking to the Germans. There were a couple of German fellows I horsed around with, and much of the time we would hang around the Hofbrau House, where a lot of American tourists used to go. Most of the young Germans I knew had already been in the army and were subject to recall. Naturally, there was a great deal of debating about war, because it was after the Munich settlement and on everybody's mind. When a

couple of those German guys got recalled, that was a pretty good sign that the war was about to start.

Roman law remained White's bête noire. He had finished tutorial work in three or four papers, more or less, but still had more than half of the curriculum to cover in only two terms. He knew that Fifoot would keep the heat on as soon as Oxford resumed in October—assuming that war did not intervene. Fifoot had high expectations for his students, including his overseas students. One American Rhodes scholar, Robert C. Barnard, had just received first-class honors in the B.C.L. (Bachelor of Civil Law) exams.

White's Munich summer must often have seemed like a double dose of the surreal. White had chosen to read for a degree in jurisprudence because he had been convinced that the English common law was the basis for American law, and because the Oxford degree might save some time on the way to the bar back home. Roman law in Latin was hard to connect to either rationale. Outside of the books, White's daily reading of the German newspapers was a tour of what Dr. Goebbels's Propaganda Ministry allowed or required their editorial desks, and the desks of every other paper in the country, to publish. Foreign papers were proscribed, so the picture of German life and world politics that White acquired from the press was artificial, to say the least. He may have learned more in the beer halls than he did in the books or papers. His dominant memory of the summer, as he recalled years later, was that "the south Germans are a friendly and attractive people, but there was never any doubt that they would fight for Germany if war came."

One evening in early July, White had an unexpected reunion in the Hofbräuhaus with John Kennedy, who was taking a final tour around Europe with Torby Macdonald, gathering materials for his senior thesis. Munich came after France and before Italy and, one last time, Paris. Many American Rhodes scholars made similar trips, and one thought he was witnessing "the sun setting on a golden age that would never recur." Kennedy felt the same: "You had the feeling of an era ending, and everyone had a very good time at the end." The pleasures of Munich almost led Kennedy, White, and Macdonald into harm's way. Macdonald later explained what happened:

> We got along very well, all three of us, so we decided to take a tour of the city [in White's borrowed car] and we went by this monument to some beer hall hero, Worst Hessel [sic] or something, and we slowed down to take a look. They had a flame burning and they started to yell and at that time I didn't know who Worst Hessel was, frankly.

Despite Ambassador Kennedy's admonitions to both his son and to Macdonald not to create an incident or to allow themselves to be baited, they stopped the car and suddenly were faced with rough heckling from some young Germans, who soon escalated to throwing stones and bricks. "So we drove the car away for awhile, and I turned to Jack and said, 'What the hell is wrong with them, what's this all about?' We weren't doing anything, I mean, we weren't agitating people or anything." White, who had unobtrusively clenched his fists in preparation for self-defense before the car retreated, explained that the car they were using had English plates, which was sufficient provocation. Kennedy realized, Macdonald thought for "the first time," that war was unavoidable "if this is the way these people feel."

What Kennedy and Macdonald failed to understand, but what White must have known after several weeks in Munich, was that Horst Wessel was one of the principal heroes of National Socialism, whom Josef Goebbels, Hitler's minister of propaganda, had created almost from whole cloth. Thought to be a pimp for a prostitute during his lifetime, Wessel was turned into a martyr for Nazism when he was murdered by communists in 1930. He conveniently left behind the words and music of a popular tune that he had composed, which soon became the official song of the Nazi Party and a secondary national anthem, after "Deutschland über Alles." Cruising up to the eternal flame for Horst Wessel was insufficiently respectful in the tinderbox tension of midsummer 1939. To paraphrase Roosevelt, the hand that held the dagger was poised over the back of Poland, and German soldiers on leave or subject to recall were in no mood to humor uninformed Americans touring through the heart of Germany in a British automobile.

For the next two months, Kennedy continued his European idyll, with Macdonald at his side for the first part of the journey. He repaired to the German countryside from his near dustup in Munich, then went to Italy and Paris, and drove to the south of France, where his mother had rented a summer residence in Cannes. In mid-August, he went back to Munich, stayed one night to hear *Tannhäuser,* then worked his way to Vienna, Prague, and Berlin. At the end of the month, after touching base in Cannes, he was back through Germany to Czechoslovakia and Poland before returning to Berlin for a briefing at the American embassy. White, during the same period, remained in Munich, working on Roman law and trying to avoid trouble. On August 23, the die seemed to be cast. Germany and the Soviets signed a nonaggression pact in Moscow; a few days later, Great Britain signed a multilevel mutual-assistance agreement with Poland, and the stage seemed to be set for war when, not if, Germany invaded Poland. On August 29, German troops occupied Slovakia, and Byron White cabled his parents in Wellington, Colorado, that he had left Munich for Oxford.

White got out of Germany in the nick of time. On September 1, Hitler sent 1.5 million troops—more than fifty divisions—into Poland under a tissue of pretexts that only underscored the outrage of the invasion. Neville Chamberlain waited two days to declare war. On September 3, he summoned Ambassador Kennedy to 10 Downing Street and previewed the speech he would deliver in the Commons later that day. Joseph Kennedy cabled the secretary of state and then telephoned Franklin Roosevelt with the news, and repeated over and over, "It's the end of the world . . . the end of everything." Later that day, the ambassador escorted his wife, Joe Jr., John, and Kick to the Strangers' Gallery in the House of Commons for ringside seats to hear Chamberlain declare war and announce tearfully, "Everything that I have believed in during my public life has crashed in ruins."

One of the many consequences of the September 3 declaration was that Oxford, which had dawdled earlier in the year over developing air raid plans, was seen as a potential seat of government should London come under heavy air attack. The blitzkrieg in Poland—fast armor combined with heavy air strikes—was a terrifying warning of what might lie ahead. The immediate question was what to do with overseas students. President Roosevelt had declared a limited national emergency on September 8, but that affected only troops already under arms and reservists. The day before, the warden of Rhodes House called a meeting of all Rhodes scholars who were already in Oxford—term did not begin for several weeks—to discuss their options. There was no edict from the Rhodes trustees and no unanimity among the students over what to do. Some insisted on staying, others preferred to stay in Oxford or even to pursue work in other European locations, and many wished to return to the United States and get on with work or graduate school. There were indications, later confirmed, that the university was prepared to conduct all of its operations out of three colleges, leaving the others to government use if necessary. C. K. Allen encouraged Americans who could secure places in graduate schools at home to do so, and reported that the American secretary for the Rhodes Trust, Frank Aydelotte of Swarthmore, was working earnestly to place the sudden evacuees.

White and Gerald Brown left the meeting convinced that they should return home and begin Yale Law School. They had discussed their options for several days, and White had considered several law schools—University of Colorado, University of Michigan, Harvard, and Yale. Robert Maynard Hutchins, president of the University of Chicago and ever the opportunist, had publicly offered full-tuition scholarships to any Rhodes scholar who wished to pursue graduate work there. Brown pushed Yale, where he had spent one year in law school after graduating from USC. He emphasized the generous student-faculty ratio, the quality of the physical plant—including libraries and multisite athletic facilities—and the fact that many students from Oxford would be attending Yale University in one capacity or another.

White, nudged by all of the arguments, decided on Yale. "I want to live the law," White told Brown, and Yale sounded like the place for total immersion—with the Payne-Whitney Gymnasium complex available for good measure. Three other members of the American Rhodes scholar class of 1938 would be there (Brown, J. H. Currie, and Louis Hector), along with three from prior classes (Dyke Brown, Karl Price, and Frank Taplin). "Once we added up everything," Brown said later, "Byron decided to apply to only one law school, Yale." When the meeting at Rhodes House concluded, White and Brown went to lunch at a Chinese restaurant, the Stowaway, to celebrate reaching a decision. After a walk and a short, illicit pub crawl, they attended a second meeting at Rhodes House at 6:30 P.M., to learn of the latest sailing opportunities.

With full-scale war under way, securing passage home was no easy task. The American embassy devoted the bulk of its early-September energies to finding berths on vessels of all descriptions, including tramp steamers and cargo ships. There were thousands of stranded Americans—three thousand tourists and fifteen hundred of the forty-five hundred permanent residents—desperately seeking passage home. Ambassador Kennedy was frantic over the task, and the State Department was impatient with both his effectiveness and his beleaguered attitude. Roosevelt had lost confidence in him six months earlier but kept him in place overseas on the theory that he would do more damage at home chafing from embarrassment than abroad sulking with other diplomats. When a U-boat sank the liner *Athenia* on September 3, tensions rose, and soon merchant mariners were demanding bonuses and war-risk insurance before casting off from Southampton. Gerald Brown took an American steamer, which was scheduled to depart Southampton on September 14. As it turned out, the ship was delayed and Brown did not arrive in New Haven until one day before registration was scheduled to begin. White's passage was on the United States Lines' *Manhattan,* but she was held up for five days in Southampton taking on cargo and coping with blackouts and anxious crew members. Once she left Southampton, she was laid up three more days at Le Verdon, the port for Bordeaux, again taking on cargo. The atmosphere on the ship seesawed, first anxious when passengers and crew were left unprotected in port without gas masks or protective gear, then suddenly relieved under the protection of the American destroyers *Badger* and *Jacob Jones,* which escorted the *Manhattan* in protective convoy onto the high seas beginning September 21.

The *Manhattan* arrived safely in New York City in the early morning of September 30, laden with 1,868 passengers, nearly 650 above normal capacity. The total, according to the *Herald-Tribune,* was "the greatest number to arrive on an American ship since the war began." Among the other passengers besides White were the last three members of the Kennedy family to be evacuated (the others had left earlier)—Jean, eleven, Edward, seven, and Patricia, fifteen—plus Arturo Toscanini, who complained about his accommodations, and Lord Beaverbrook, who complained pointedly about press blackouts in Great Britain and implicitly about American reporters' annoying questions.

With the arrival of the three children, the only Kennedys left in Great Britain were the ambassador, Joe Jr., and John, whom the ambassador had sent to Scotland to assist victims of the *Athenia* sinking. The ambassador was in the twilight of an ignominious diplomatic career. He had cajoled the appointment out of Roosevelt because he held the promise of not becoming an Anglophile and thus not the source of distorted intelligence for the president. His social ambition quickly outstripped his ancestral antipathies, and his enthusiasm for appeasement prompted the joke that Chamberlain was making an extra space in his cabinet for an American. The failure of Munich and the disastrous Trafalgar Day speech cost Kennedy the president's ear but simultaneously freed him to indulge himself and his family. Kick was presented in the 1938 season, Eunice a year later, and the entry fee for each debut bore the same price tag as White's full-year stipend, £2,000. Parties, dances, and a dinner for the king and queen made the embassy a social center in London and the older Kennedy children a toast of society.

Chamberlain clung inexplicably to his appeasement policy until just after Czechoslovakia fell, in mid-March of 1939, but the ambassador, shut off from Roosevelt, had lost his taste for the issue well before then. By the end of March, Harold Ickes recorded in his diary that "Joe Kennedy was having the time of his life." So did Kick and the other girls. Joe Jr. and John were less successful—Joe because he was rough mannered and pushed his way around even among the white-gloved set, John because his charm was mitigated by a ponderous choice of conversation topics. He seemed to be doing his research even in full dress. There was another trait that cast a dark shadow over the clan, a competitive ferocity that seemed bred in the bone to those who felt it. One debutante complained, "It was hell to go to dinner with the Kennedys, as they were fearfully squashing to anyone who was not in their close-knit circle."

The darkest issue, which for years would dog the ambassador as well as his ambitions for his sons, was the ambassador's rather naked anti-Semitism. To those who watched him closely during the last year of peace, Joseph P. Kennedy's views responded to a different chord. Kennedy seemed to be isolationist and hostile to Jewish views in order to serve his tribal interests, primarily his male children and his ambitions for them: if the United States went to war, his sons were at risk, and even victory meant chaos followed by a long, uncertain recovery. Joseph Kennedy had been riding a comet for years, moving from one financial success to another and quitting one public job after another—the Securities and Exchange Commission, the Maritime Commission—at the height of his success. He was flattered at the outset of his ambassadorship by friends who first quietly and then indiscreetly touted him for the Democratic nomination for president in 1940 after Roosevelt finished the customary two terms.

Foreign affairs were Joseph Kennedy's undoing. He was no longer chairman of the board or of the commission, and he had neither knowledge of nor feel for the complexity of European diplomatic history. When cornered, he circled the family wagons while simultaneously talking loosely in terms of larger policy concerns. His harshest critics noted that he was at his most efficient, and flying under his truest colors, after Munich and after Hitler invaded Poland, when he removed his family to the safety of Ireland or the London suburbs. The safe arrival in the United States of the last of the ambassador's small children was thus literally front-page news, although Eunice refused comment to reporters, apparently on her father's orders.

Unlike the Kennedy children, Byron White managed to slip unnoticed into New York City on October 1, perhaps in part because the *New York Times* had carried an erroneous story two weeks earlier reporting that twelve American Rhodes scholars, "their studies at Oxford University interrupted by the war," would soon return to the United States, but that another twelve, "including Byron (Whizzer) White, football star, will stay to continue their work in the 'skeleton' university." White was extremely eager to begin law school and to put professional football, and his storybook athletic career, behind him once and for all. He took every step he could to remain anonymous aboard ship; he avoided the press dockside when the *Manhattan* berthed; and when he arrived in New Haven on Monday, October 2, he paid his $450 tuition for the year in cash, a demonstration, he implied to Oxford friends now at Yale, that he did not need and did not want to be presented with any big-dollar offers to return to the National Football League for the 1939 season.

As Byron White feared, his anonymity lasted less than forty-eight hours. On October 2, the day White registered at Yale, the Associated Press reported that the New York Giants were trying to sign him to a one-year contract. The source of the story was Art Rooney, who "said Tim Mara, president of the Giants, telephoned that he wanted to obtain White's contract, which called for a record $15,000 last year. He said Mara told him White is visiting friends in New Haven, Conn." For the next two weeks, White would fend off one NFL coach or owner after another and try to concentrate on studying law.

7

YALE AND DETROIT

B YRON WHITE went to Oxford seeking intellectual challenge and hoping to have his mind stretched—a man in quest of a map of his own mental topography. Instead, he found a curriculum front-loaded with Roman law and an academic pressure both unanticipated and aggravated by his deferred matriculation. Some contemporaries thought unkindly that White survived Oxford without a scratch, untouched by either the larger world of ideas or the rich culture of England and the Continent in the twilight of a golden age. Yet Oxford provided White with the glimpse of a worldview that he had lacked, and more important—and more permanently—Oxford supplied White with an endowment of human capital that he drew on throughout his life, beginning with his arrival at Yale Law School.

Gerald Brown had urged White to attend Yale by emphasizing the student-faculty ratio and the physical facilities of the institution, and was delighted when White seemed to be persuaded by his sales pitch. Brown's diary recorded curiosity, then anxiety, when the first day, and then week, of classes passed without White's appearance. When White finally reported for classes, steps ahead of National Football League coaches and owners, Brown helped him move into his room in the Sterling Law Buildings and located a boardinghouse (Mrs. Walker's) where cheap, plentiful meals were available. Karl R. Price, another Oxford refugee and a Rhodes scholar from Tennessee, soon joined Brown and White at Mrs. Walker's table. Price, who had just taken his

Oxford law degree, was a third-year student. Brown was a second-year student and White a freshman. As the Dean's Report later noted, "the war situation made it impossible for college graduates who had been awarded Rhodes Scholarships, or had otherwise planned to study abroad, to take advantage of that opportunity, and a number of these men were admitted late in the summer, in addition to the regular quota." In fact, there were seven Rhodes scholars enrolled in 1939–40, and Price's academic plans were not affected by the war. Nonetheless, the usual quota of 120 per class was up—131 in the first year, 126 in the second, and 113 in the third.

The school was in transition on multiple fronts. For two decades, Yale had played a leadership role in the post–World War I professionalization of American legal education. Successive deans, including Robert Maynard Hutchins and Charles Clark, had hired young scholars who were eager to change the theory of both legal scholarship and legal education. By 1930, many would be identified as "American legal realists," but the label suggests more unity of method and conviction than ever existed among those swept into the category. At most, the realists shared premises that they deployed in different directions with different intensity. Any summary is risky, but most would subscribe to three interrelated tenets: (1) Law is not like geometry, with agreed premises and protocols for verification, but is a type of rhetoric. (2) That rhetoric adopts a logical format, but decisions are driven more by social input than by reason. (3) The test of law's utility is not its intellectual cogency or logical clarity, but whether it produces desirable social effects when measured by precise empirical tools. Debates over realism filled scholarly journals for more than a decade but had largely run out of steam a few years before White entered Yale Law School, largely because many so-called realists went off to work in the New Deal and because much of the realists' energy was expended in the classroom—where it began—and thus became invisible to the outside world.

By the fall of 1939, Yale had lost four of the most prominent practitioners of the new orthodoxy to various forms of public service. In 1936, Thurman Arnold became assistant attorney general for the Antitrust Division, and William O. Douglas joined the Securities and Exchange Commission; Abe Fortas joined Douglas, his mentor, at the SEC in 1938 and went to the Interior Department in 1939; and Wesley Sturges, after a brief stint with the Agricultural Adjustment Administration in 1935, took leave to run the Distilled Spirits Institute for a two-year period beginning in 1940.

President Roosevelt inadvertently shook up the faculty dramatically in the spring of 1939 when he appointed Douglas to the Supreme Court and

Charles Clark, who had spearheaded procedural reform, to the United States Court of Appeals for the Second Circuit. Clark's replacement, Ashbel Gulliver, was a genial place holder who became acting dean when internal divisions within the faculty precluded consensus on a permanent replacement. Although the school sustained its generous student-faculty ratio, the intellectual leadership of the institution was up for grabs with Douglas and Clark gone permanently and Arnold not likely to return; as so often happens on divided law school faculties, the fight was between the young Turks and the old Turks.

White was not immediately conscious of the intellectual turf wars that were developing, and in fact by outward appearances Yale University must have seemed eerily like Oxford—a well-furnished bastion for the elite, who expected first-class amenities and were not disappointed. The Payne-Whitney Gymnasium, whose manifold facilities Gerald Brown had detailed for White, was prominently featured in the Yale Law School catalog:

> Equipment for competitive sports is an outstanding feature of the gymnasium. For practice and recreation there are badminton, tennis, basketball, squash, and handball courts, golf galleries, polo cages, rooms for wrestling, fencing and boxing, swimming pools, rowing tanks, a sundeck, and an outdoor running track. Lockers, showers, drying rooms, and dressing rooms are conveniently located.

Yale resembled Oxford in another, but unwelcome, way: White's classmates, like many at Oxford, thought he had a lot to prove. *This isn't Wellington or Colorado,* muttered more than one student under his breath. *Byron White finally is going to learn about the big time.* More than half of the student body were from Ivy League colleges, including the third who were from Yale itself. Half of the students were from the tristate area of New York, New Jersey, and Connecticut. The decor had changed from Oxford, but the academic pressure had, if anything, actually increased. White's response was familiar: he studied fourteen hours a day and found release in the gymnasium, usually on one of Payne-Whitney's basketball courts. The pickup games soon took on a competitive edge that closely matched the classroom.

One of the graduate students who frequented the courts was Clint Frank, the winner of the 1937 Heisman Trophy and a first-class basketball player, who had been forbidden by Yale's football coach, Raymond (Ducky) Pond, to play basketball during the football off season for fear of injury. Witnesses of the frequent pickup games that featured White and Frank on opposite teams retain vivid memories to this day. "I can still hear them," Robert Harry, a classmate of White, has recalled. "Blocking each other's shots, they crashed into each other with incredible brutality." "They took physical competition to a higher, and somewhat frightening, level," remembered another; "I never wanted to play when they were on opposite teams: it would be like getting between Paul Bunyan and Babe the Blue Ox." Gerald Brown tried once, and "felt like I'd been crushed between two steel walls." Frank was smaller and more compact than White, but at least as quick and an equally fierce competitor. His performance in the 1937 Harvard-Yale football game sent usually jaded sportswriters into swoons of admiration, as he played both ways in intense pain and managed several stirring plays—including running down Torby Macdonald from behind to save a touchdown—in a losing cause. Frank later became an advertising executive in his native Chicago.

Byron White missed the first week of classes and arrived midday on Monday of the second week. He quickly issued public denials that he was interested in resuming his professional football career. He told the *New Haven Journal-Courier:*

> My football playing days are over. I'm started on a law career. Don't get me wrong, though. I would like to play football again. . . . anybody who has ever played the game and loves it the way I do wouldn't feel any different, but I am in law school now, and my classes wouldn't permit it. It's just impossible. Yes sir, you can quote me as saying my football playing days are over. I've unpacked my clothes and books and if there is anything I dislike, it's packing and unpacking.

Tim Mara, the owner of the New York Giants, made more than one trip to New Haven trying to change White's mind, as did representatives from other NFL teams. White remained adamant, however; his only concession to his celebrity status in the athletic world was his attendance in late October at the annual fall lunch of the Connecticut Sportswriters' Alliance, at which he consented to a brief interview and "made a very favorable impression."

With the football issue behind him, White turned, again, to catching up with his course work. His class schedule consisted of four basic courses plus two minor courses—a research seminar and an introductory course, emphasizing legal ethics, taught by James Grafton Rogers, who had been dean of the University of Colorado Law School from 1928 to 1935 before returning to his alma mater to be master of Timothy Dwight College and to teach part-time at the Law School. The basic courses were commercial bank credit with Underhill Moore, civil procedure with James William Moore, torts with Harry Shulman, and contracts with the grand old man of the faculty, Arthur Linton Corbin.

The schedule illustrates why it is a mistake to assume that academic institutions have an intellectually homogenous character and how the philosophical division over law and its pedagogy manifested itself to the student. J. W. Moore and Shulman were both in their mid-thirties and had taught at Yale for one and eight years, respectively. Moore was a Montanan who had graduated from the University of Chicago, where he taught for two years before coming to Yale. Shulman was a Harvard graduate and protégé of Felix Frankfurter, a conventional and very liberal scholar who pooh-poohed the realists as peripheral or frivolous. Underhill Moore was a Columbia graduate who was sixty and had taught at Yale for ten years. He was one of the leading realist scholars and a pioneer in developing the social-science, or empirical, strand of realism, which tried to analyze the practical effect of legal rules and processes.

Corbin, sixty-five, was the senior member of the faculty and combined an original mind with impatience for passing enthusiasms. He was often identified as a realist but did not court the designation, disliked the agenda of many of those who did, and remained a stoutly independent, even stubborn, figure. His writings reshaped the law of contracts and pushed the field away from highly abstract theories to market-oriented, pragmatic rules and doctrines. Corbin appealed to White on multiple grounds—he was a Westerner, whose only private practice had been in Colorado (Cripple Creek, 1899–1903); he was an athlete of sorts (first base—still—on the faculty softball team); and he was insistently practical. Only Corbin taught from a standard casebook, the two-year-old second edition of his own work; the others used mimeographed materials almost exclusively, evidence of the intellectual ferment, even turmoil, in which American law churned on the eve of World War II.

Within less than three years prior to White's arrival at Yale, three events of monumental significance had occurred. Any one of them would have constituted an intellectual earthquake on its own, but together they recast the map of American law no less than the Revolution of 1848 wholly redrew the face of Europe. The first event was a pair of decisions decided by the Supreme Court of the United States during October term 1936. In late March 1937, the Court decided, in *West Coast Hotel v. Parrish,* that a state law regulating wages and hours did not violate an employer's property rights under the due process clause of the Fourteenth Amendment. The decision reversed more than three decades of judicial allegiance to laissez-faire, which had invalidated state legislation controlling various aspects of employment, including child labor as well as wages, hours, and working conditions. Two weeks later, by another 5-4 vote and in another opinion by Chief Justice Charles Evans Hughes, the Court, in *NLRB v. Jones-Laughlin,* upheld Congress's power under the commerce clause to regulate labor pursuant to a national statutory regime. The decision swept away generations of close analysis of the precise relationship between the regulated activity and interstate commerce and asserted simply that the court took "judicial notice" that labor was an interstate market.

The two decisions constituted a "switch in time that saved nine"—Prof. Edward S. Corwin's famous quip that, somewhat unfairly, ascribed the Court's change of direction to fear of President Roosevelt's Court-packing plan. Between Roosevelt's landslide reelection in November 1936 and the new congressional session in early March 1937, Roosevelt had suggested legislation to increase the size of the Court by one justice for every justice aged seventy then sitting. He claimed the purpose of the plan was to help an elderly Court—with a median age of more than seventy—to keep pace with its caseload, but no one was fooled: operation of the law would have increased the Court's size to fifteen, and the six new appointments could be counted on to provide the president with a comfortable 10-5 or 9-6 majority for the constitutionality of the New Deal, which had suffered a string of invalidations on constitutional grounds during the previous three years—of the Agricultural Adjustment Act, the National Industrial Recovery Act, the Guffey Coal Act, and others. In every case, the Court—often by a bare majority—had construed the due process clause to prohibit the mechanism chosen by Congress to implement the legislation or had concluded that the commerce clause or the taxing power did not reach the activity in question.

The Court-packing plan divided the country politically, split progressives, who could ordinarily be relied upon by the president, and politicized the academy as no other single issue had in the New Deal. The presidents of Harvard, Yale, and Princeton publicly opposed the proposal, but Charles Clark testified before the Senate Judiciary Committee in support of the plan. No other dean appeared on Roosevelt's side, although Wiley Rutledge, the dean of Iowa, energetically supported the plan. The Yale Law School faculty favored the president's plan by an eleven-to-eight margin, according to the *Yale Daily News,* a position that caused sharp criticism of the school by many alumni, including members of the Yale Corporation, the governing body of the university. When the Court capitulated, a majority of the faculty naturally felt vindicated, both on the merits and against the forces of reaction in the alumni body.

The second major event of the period was also a decision by the Supreme Court. In April of 1938, *Erie Railroad v. Tompkins* held that the Court lacked the constitutional power—and had always lacked the power—to declare general common law in suits brought in federal courts by citizens of different states. The decision was a blockbuster both as to process and as to result. The question had not been briefed or argued; the Court raised the issue *sua sponte* and overruled a precedent, *Swift v. Tyson,* that was a century old. *Swift,* written by Justice Joseph Story, one of the leading nationalists of the early-nineteenth-century Court, had established the Court's power to create ("identify") controlling common law in "diversity" suits (between citizens of different states) and thus to help shape a uniform national commercial law at a time when it was most needed. Justice Louis Brandeis's opinion for the *Erie* court reasoned, in effect, that the Supreme Court had behaved unconstitutionally since 1842, because neither the Constitution nor the controlling legislation authorized such creativity; the most that federal courts could now do was to apply the law of the appropriate state.

Erie thus provided, along with the timely switches from a year before, a second symbolic stake in the heart of loosely reined judicial creativity. (Brandeis, who had dissented in most of the old Court's nullification of the New Deal, had worked hard since his controversial appointment, in 1916, to both model and explicate a modest role for the federal judiciary.) The Court's landmark decisions during the last two terms marked a dramatic institutional change of course, although there were hints that the retreat from aggressive constitutional adjudication was not wholesale: a footnote in an otherwise obscure case, *United States v. Carolene Products,* contained a germ of a new theoretical posture for the Court—passivity toward economic regulation, energetic scrutiny of cases involving freedom of speech, religion, and discrimination.

The third major event raised the prospect that federal judges needed to restructure their entire approach to litigation, as well as to learn to follow the Supreme Court's new, deferential approach to the constitutional powers of co-ordinate branches of the government. The Federal Rules of Civil Procedure, which became effective in 1938, dramatically changed the process of litigation in federal courts, from the content of the complaint to the creation and management of pretrial discovery, and from the nature of relief available to the treatment of the fact-finding function after trial. Getting into court was now simpler; losing on technicalities was less likely; fact finding could be compelled by court order; relief could combine damages and equitable remedies; and fact finding was formally entitled to respect after judgment. To judges schooled, or at least trained, before the turn of the century in the categories of the common law and in the technicalities of code pleading, the new Federal Rules were more revolutionary than any of the Supreme Court's decisions. For many reasons, the rules did not fully take hold for nearly a decade; because most litigation still took place in state courts under local versions of the old regime, all law schools, including Yale, continued to teach the pleading regime that preceded the rules. The new learning had arrived, however, and two of its principal architects were associated with the Yale Law faculty, former dean Clark and J. W. Moore.

Taken together, the three events constituted both a restructuring of many of the basic premises of American public law and an epochal break with the constitutional tradition that had been dominant since the turn of the century. With *West Coast* and *Jones-Laughlin,* the era of *Lochner v. New York* (1905) was over. *Lochner* was a minor case in a string of regulatory due process cases spanning the turn of the century, but it became a symbol of the wicked political instincts of a majority of the Court. *Lochner* held that the due process clause of the Fourteenth Amendment prevented the state of New York from limiting the number of hours that a baker could work in one day. The "liberty" at stake was that of the employer and the baker to fix the terms of their mutual engagement.

The case had comic overtones—the plaintiff's case was argued by a former baker who had gone to law school and declared at oral argument that bakeries were not terribly unsafe, even at long hours. Academic critics, unamused by the result, seized upon Justice Rufus Peckham's majority opinion as proof of the Court's subjectivity and of the incapacity of formal analysis to comprehend political reality. Legal scholars from Walter Wheeler Cook, one of the earliest realists, to Roscoe Pound, dean of the Harvard Law School and a progressive who later came to deride the realists, condemned *Lochner.* They took their tack, if not their text, from Justice Oliver Wendell Holmes, Jr., whose dissent in *Lochner* attacked both the majority's economic theory and its political authority (in contrast to Justice Harlan's long and pedestrian dissent, which argued the merits of bakeries). *Lochner* ignited the realist movement and lasted more than thirty years, outlasting the movement itself.

Ironically, realist scholarship, in all its many forms, did not confront constitutional questions head-on but instead examined the elements of the common law system from the ground up. This was due less to strategic design than to the training and expertise of those who identified themselves with realism—men who were recognized, and middle-aged, authorities in a variety of nonconstitutional-law fields such as jurisprudence (Joseph W. Bingham), conflict of laws (Cook), sales (Karl N. Llewellyn), commercial law (Herman Oliphant), and insurance (Edwin W. Patterson). The Yale realists followed the same pattern. Underhill Moore was a banking expert, and Wesley Sturges was a specialist in credit and in arbitration. Even the younger realists were not constitutional lawyers. William O. Douglas was an expert in corporate law, including reorganization, and Myres McDougal focused on property before he turned to international law.

As a result of the disjunction between animating passions and expertise, realism—in all its shapes, weights, and focal points—permeated the Yale Law School curriculum, however diffusely, in 1939. In its crudest form, the realist message could be reduced to a student mantra recalled by Louis Oberdorfer:

1. Substantive due process is original sin.
2. The authors of the *Lochner* case were evil incarnate.
3. All judges are biased in favor of property or some other anti-social interest.
4. Congressmen and legislators are crooks, fools or both.
5. The only proper way to allocate resources is to create an administrative agency—staffed by experts—such as former Professor Douglas or former Professor Fortas.

Sometimes the more sophisticated version of the message did not get through clearly. By constantly shifting from the general to the particular and back, and by frequently changing focus from method to substance and back, a particular instructor's realist insights could be garbled in the transmission. Gerald Brown found Underhill Moore "brilliant," with "breathtaking synthetic powers"; to Frank Taplin, who had read law for two years at Oxford, Moore's presentations frequently were "gobbledygook."

Despite the critical mass of realists of various stripes, not every faculty member located himself in the realist camp, and some, such as Edwin Borchard, who actually taught constitutional law, seemed to ignore his younger and trendier colleagues. (In a speech to the American Political Science Association several months after the 1937 decisions, Borchard celebrated "the deflation of the due process clause to normal proportions" and approved Justice Cardozo's recent decision in *Palko v. Connecticut:* "Not all the first eight amendments need be regarded as sacred against state limitation.") Others were "old beyond their years," such as Shulman, who acquired Frankfurter's patronage as well as his distaste for realist hyperbole.

Where realism was most clearly manifest was in the structure of the curriculum. Unlike other leading law schools, which confined the first-year curriculum to civil procedure and the standard common law subjects (contracts, torts, and property), Yale intermixed both business law and public law topics in the first year. Byron White and his classmates took commercial bank credit from Underhill Moore in the first semester alongside contracts, torts, and procedure; in the second semester, the curriculum was agency (Business Units I), Constitutional Law I with Borchard (taught from the 1937 second edition of

Walter Dodd's very conventional casebook), property with McDougal, and Public Control of Business I, a course on antitrust policy if not antitrust law, taught primarily by Walton Hale Hamilton, an economist who had been admitted to the Georgia Bar by act of the legislature in recognition of his advisory service and expertise.

Many have assumed or even argued that Byron White's view of law was determined by his exposure to the Yale realists. The claim ignores the diversity of the realists and the influence of the nonbelievers. One journalist even identified Myres McDougal as the infectious agent who turned White into a realist. It is true that White and McDougal enjoyed a warm relationship for many years, beginning with second-semester property, continuing through McDougal's famous seminar, Law, Science and Policy, in the spring of 1946, when White returned to Yale after the war, and rekindled informally over time. Their exchanges in both courses are still vividly remembered by many fellow students, if only for the intensity of the debates and not for their substance. McDougal was a stimulating sparring partner, but not necessarily a dominant influence. Nicholas Katzenbach, who also attended McDougal's seminar in 1946, later recalled White's contribution: "a healthy skepticism—a probing questioning of premises and an insistence on conclusions reached by small and visible steps in a rational process as opposed to giant leaps of faith."

Other evidence suggests that more practical, subtle, and less dogmatic instructors than Myres McDougal had a greater impact on White's thinking. White supplied his own testimony years after the fact when he provided an encomium for Wesley Sturges on the occasion of his retirement from the deanship of the University of Miami Law School. White wrote:

> His classes were intense and consuming experiences, which seemed to be over before they began, stimulating, fast-moving, exhausting and mortifying. His insistent, driving analysis was a kind of classroom surgery which produced exceedingly thin slices of case, principle, and judge, so thin they were transparent to even the dimmest eye.
>
> Learn "the law" we did, or what the cases said it was. But this was a by-product, a rather minimum goal which would never get you a passing grade. Lawyers are hired for many things, but the essence of their engagement, he thought, is to think and understand. And to this end he never for a moment took the pressure off a single student. He did not so much want the student to marvel at the teacher's mind and wisdom—which we did—but to get the student to use his own and to develop his own sense of things. . . . He inoculated with a hardy skepticism and this he hoped would be lasting protection against a flabby mind operating on flabby principle.

Grant Gilmore, a contemporary of White at Yale, echoed the point:

What did Wesley teach us? He taught us, in a way that none of us will ever forget, something—indeed a great deal—about the use and the uses of words. . . . He taught us to be forever on our guard against the slippery generality, the received principle, the authoritative proposition. He taught us to trust no one's judgment except our own—and not to be too sure about that. He taught us to live by our wits. He taught us, in a word, how to be lawyers.

Yet White did not encounter Sturges until after his first year. The most formative influence on his thinking, according to several fellow students, was Arthur Corbin, the senior member of the faculty and White's contracts teacher first semester. "We both loved Corbin, because he put complex theoretical issues in very practical terms and showed you how to think like a lawyer," according to Robert Harry, who sat near White in the front row of Corbin's contracts classroom. Corbin, like Sturges, had no dogmatic program to inculcate, nor did he allow himself to dazzle his class with feats of theoretical dexterity. What he did, in the words of Louis Oberdorfer, was to teach the law of contracts, "case by case, fact by fact," with emphasis on the precise factual context of each dispute. Corbin emphasized that the lawyer's task was first to predict how courts would respond to facts, and then to craft arguments whose factual characterizations and use of precedent would appeal to the relevant tribunal. To predict judicial behavior accurately, Corbin taught his students to see patterns of results regardless of how the outcomes were explained by the courts; "think things, not words," Corbin would quote Holmes while simultaneously ridiculing Holmes's penchant for arid theory and pretty phrases. "Corbin never let you lose sight of the practical stakes involved in theoretical debates," Harry added. Nor did Corbin argue that rules were meaningless or that law was, or should be, purely subjective: his great strength was in demonstrating how formal analysis could be used and abused, and how doctrines develop and die.

His normative message was twofold—doctrine should address practical reality, not theoretical nicety, and no authority should be taken to be final given the potential permutations of human behavior. He said he had no respect for

. . . the "rules" and doctrines and generalizations of men often (if not always) based on quite insufficient life experience and inaccurate observation, but solemnly repeated down the corridors of time. . . . It was only after beginning the teaching of "law" that I fully realized that the meaning and value of any "rule" or generalization are wholly dependent on the specific items of life experience and observation on which they are based.

The passage was published in 1965, but the theme was first aired by Corbin in 1913 and recurs, in a somewhat milder form, in the preface to the first edition of his casebook, in 1921, and appears again in essence in the prefaces to the second edition, in 1937, and the third, ten years later.

Corbin spanned both periods of the legal realist period, chronologically and intellectually. His work in the 1920s and early 1930s coincided with the corrosive realist phase, which belabored the subjectivity and logical fallacies of traditional legal analysis, sometimes pejoratively labeled "formalism." During this period, the realists split into two camps, those who continued as textual critics of law, and those—like Underhill Moore and William O. Douglas—who shifted their focus to empirical studies of the impact of legal rules on society. The second realist period was forced to some extent by the New Deal, which borrowed many law teachers for the alphabet agencies (including ten Yale University faculty members during the first administration) and prompted many to think that much of the battle they had been fighting in the scholarly journals had been won. The triple-witching events of 1937–38 (the 1937 decisions, *Erie,* and the new civil rules) took realism to the next period, which required development of positive doctrines and theories on top of the harshly negative work that had been the staple and the fuel for the movement at its outset. The agenda of second-generation realists, such as Myres McDougal, was to develop mechanisms for "securing certain generally accepted social ends," but the goal was never consummated, in part because of World War II and in part because the quest assumed a greater capacity for consensus than an increasingly pluralistic society could forge. Writing in the fiftieth-anniversary issue of the *Yale Law Journal,* in 1941, McDougal also cautioned, in the wake of the 1937 volte-face by the Supreme Court, that "the judicial institution, indispensable though it may be for the preservation of many of our old and continuing values," may be "utterly helpless" to address "many of our modern, complex problems, requiring as they do for their solution a continuous and informed exercise of highly specialized skills."

Looking back many years later, White declared: "Yale Law School was the most stimulating intellectual experience I had had up to that time." The faculty "had a very exciting approach to the law and its relationship to the world around you. The law was interpreted in relation to the social and economic aspects of our society." And as he told Gerald Brown in Oxford, he lived the law. Brown's diary is dotted with the occasional concert that they attended together in New York or New Haven, but those occasions were rare. Classmates even today recall vividly a rather still figure with abruptly sloping shoulders, sitting erect in the library, frequently with green eyeshade, reading for hour after hour seemingly without a break. "The combination of intensity and concentration was eerie," in Frank Taplin's view. Potter Stewart, a year ahead of White, later remembered him "as a serious-minded, scholarly, and rather taciturn (except when he found himself engaged in lively colloquy with J. W. Moore in his class on Procedure), and extremely likable young man with steel-rimmed eyeglasses."

When the University of Colorado basketball team was invited to play in the third National Invitational Tournament, during White's second semester at Yale, he went to New York City to see his old team, which included several members of the 1938 team, who had been sophomores then and were now seniors. He was asked about the academic competition, and he said, *I've never had it so tough. I just hope I make it.* "It wasn't exactly false modesty," recalled Don Thurman, one of the seniors. "Byron just hated ever to seem bigheaded. We weren't surprised when we heard later that he was top of his class. He was just constitutionally incapable of tooting his own horn."

White had been number two in his class academically at the end of the first semester, but at the end of the year he was awarded the Edgar M. Cullen Prize, "established in 1923 by gift from William B. Davenport, B.A. 1867, in memory of Edgar M. Cullen, formerly Chief Judge of the Court of Appeals of New York" and "awarded to that member of the first-year class who receives the highest grades in his annual examination." (The corresponding prize for second-year students was won by Potter Stewart, B.A. 1937.)

As soon as term ended, in mid-June, Byron White went to New York City to spend a few days as a guest of Tim Mara, the owner of the New York Giants. Mara had stayed in touch with White throughout the year, and the visit reinforced speculation that a deal was in the offing for White's services. Nonetheless, White left New York for Colorado, where he planned to attend both sessions of the summer school at the University of Colorado Law School. Recurrent abdominal pains forced him to modify the plan: he had an appendectomy on June 20. As he entered the hospital for surgery, reporters asked about the rumors linking him with the New York Giants, and his response was tersely familiar: "I haven't heard a thing about it." He was confined for ten days, then returned to Boulder, where he made national news by becoming a waiter again at his old fraternity house. He told the Associated Press, which was incredulous that someone who made more than $15,000 a year before could be a waiter again, that "I waited table for my board when I was in school here. . . . It's a good way to earn your food and you don't make money to go to school."

The life of a summer school student, which White had found so pleasant after he graduated, lasted little more than a month. Unbeknownst to him, Art Rooney—chronically strapped for cash—had sold his contract on August 7 to Freddie Mandel, Jr., the new owner of the Detroit Lions. Mandel had bought the franchise for $225,000 from George A. (Dick) Richards, who had been fined by the league for tampering with the draft rights to Bulldog Turner and consequently quit the league in a pique. Mandel owned department stores in Chicago, where he lived, and wanted more than second- and third-place conference finishes, which is all the Lions had managed since 1936. The franchise had been streaky since moving from Portsmouth to Detroit in 1934. The Lions were second in the Western Conference that year, then won the league championship in 1935. Then began the string of "almost" seasons. Dutch Clark had been the team mainstay during the period—all-NFL from 1934 through 1937. He was less successful as a coach, and he fell out with Richards in 1939, ironically over White, who was so often compared to him. Richards wanted to purchase White from Pittsburgh in 1938 when Rooney quietly let it be known that he would entertain bids for his very expensive rookie. Clark told Richards that White was not needed; Richards disagreed and publicly second-guessed Clark, who resigned at the end of the season. With Richards gone, Mandel was making a move that had been mulled over by the organization for almost two years. Mandel paid Rooney $5,000 for White's contract and promptly telephoned White in Boulder at the Phi Gam house. He asked White to come to Chicago to discuss terms.

White was not surprised by the topic of the call, but he had expected it would come from Tim Mara and not from Mandel. Unlike the lengthy courtship in the spring of 1938, the negotiations with Mandel were brief and not particularly warm. Mandel offered $7,500 with no bonuses or extra compensation. The contract was good for two seasons, apparently at White's option, and Mandel agreed not to disclose White's salary publicly. To ease White's acceptance by the team, Mandel delayed announcement of the agreement for several days so that the new coach, George (Potsy) Clark, could inform the players. The diplomatic courtesy proved unnecessary; the veterans, many of whom had played against White two years before, were either pleased or nonplussed, and the rookies—who had been college sophomores during White's senior year—saw him as simply one more veteran to haze them. White signed the contract with Mandel on August 17, a week after the Rooney-Mandel deal closed. The next day White reported to the Lions' training camp at the Cranbrook School in Bloomfield Hills.

There were immediate repercussions in Pittsburgh. The *Pittsburgh Press* asked testily, "How come Whizzer White signs a Detroit Lions pro football contract for this season?" Art Rooney, playing slightly dumb, claimed he knew nothing about the deal but that, if it was true, "it's just like finding $5,000." Rooney claimed that the Lions had offered Rooney twice as much at the beginning of the 1939 season, when White resolutely refused to leave Yale Law School. The Giants then also tried and failed. Mandel renewed the bidding in July of 1940; White stalled. The Giants asked for time, "contacted White again, and once more were refused." Rooney then told the Lions to go ahead. White "apparently has become interested in continuing his law study at the University of Michigan, and it was this, according to Rooney, that probably" tipped the decision for White.

The *Post-Gazette* was more philosophical than the *Press* about losing White. Havey Boyle, the sports editor, wrote that the $5,000 from Mandel gave Rooney

> about the only break he got out of the sensational contract he gave White to play here in 1938. . . . White gave everything he had while he was a player here, but considering his total cost and upkeep, Rooney, after Whizzer decided to retire to Oxford and pursue his studies, lost interest in White as a member of the local club. . . . Everything here went against White's coming up to expectations. First his publicity value was dulled by his appearance in several exhibition games before the start of the regular season; second, the Pittsburgh [baseball] Pirates were engaged in such a death struggle for the pennant that the football schedule was all gummed up.

Boyle concluded that local fans would follow White's career, out of respect for the "'all out' attitude" he displayed playing for Rooney.

When White was asked why he signed with the Lions, his answer was simple: "The reason I returned to football is because I love to play it." With the accelerating threat of American involvement in war overseas, he may have also thought it was now or never. On top of that, his brother had interrupted his medical schooling in Denver in order to teach, and White later confided to Myres McDougal that the football salary was not a luxury.

White's decision to play with the Lions came at a dual price, both short- and long-term. As an initial matter, he had to finish his course work for the University of Colorado summer school or lose what now looked to be precious credits toward his graduation from Yale—or Michigan, or even CU, for that matter. Teammates recall, to this day, hearing White's portable typewriter clicking away late into the night, often not stopping until 1 A.M., as papers and reading notes were completed. Anyone who came into his room after dinner found him at his desk, green eyeshade in place, riveted to a law book. Special arrangements were made for him to take his final examination in downtown Detroit at the offices of a Yale Law alumnus. The long-term cost to White was that his formal legal education was deprived of continuity and of any opportunity for sustained research and writing.

As it developed, White exercised the option to play a second season in 1941; conscription had already begun to take its toll, and he thought he would be lucky to finish the 1941 season without being called into service. The net result was that White had one full year at Yale Law School, 1939–40, and one semester, spring of 1941, before war changed everyone's plans. (He would complete his legal education with a double session at the University of Colorado School of Law in the summer of 1941, and a semester and a summer in 1946 at Yale after the war.) He was handicapped in the spring of 1941, because many if not most courses lasted all year and he could not enter in midcourse. His curricular choices were circumscribed, and as he later recalled, "I was chosen for the *Law [Journal]*, but I went off to play football and make some money instead." The remark, made almost a quarter century after the fact, may suggest a projected disdain for legal scholarship, but whatever the motivation, White never had substantial writing experience in any of the law schools he attended.

In the steamy days of mid-August 1940, the primary thought in Byron White's mind was making the team—in both a social and an athletic sense. He impressed his new teammates literally from day one. In order to get in shape, he imposed a prepractice on himself—a mile with each lap around the school track paced by a different lineman. "I had never seen anyone work as hard as he did," Bill Radovich remembered years later. "And after practice was over, he was still out there, practicing punt returns—catching them on the fly—or kicking, and always taking extra laps." Lloyd Cardwell, the former Nebraska halfback who George Richards thought was underutilized by Dutch Clark in 1938, paid White the ultimate understated compliment of a hard-nosed world: "He was a real player, not just a name. The man always gave more than a hundred percent." Chuck Hanneman—three-year veteran end, place kicker, and team captain—found White "such a nice guy: you couldn't believe somebody with all that p.r. could be so down-to-earth and generous."

White not only impressed the veterans but discovered instant personal affinities with several teammates. John Wiethe, a guard from Xavier in his second season, was also a law student, "and they hit it off like bread and butter," according to Radovich. When Potsy Clark gave the team a day off in late August, White and Wiethe put themselves through a tough ninety-minute work-out by themselves. Radovich, who one day would figure by name in an an-titrust suit against the league, showed White quiet neighborhood spots where he could unwind and have a beer *without people pestering me with a lot of stu-pid questions.*

White had won over his teammates within a week, but the fans and the press did not come around until after Labor Day and the traditional varsity-freshmen game. Potsy Clark, who had named White as his starting quarter-back at the beginning of the month, feared injury and kept him out of the game until the fourth quarter, when a chant of "We want White" began among the 21,299 fans who had come out to the University of Detroit sta-dium to see the intrasquad exhibition. The next day, the *Detroit Times* said that it took White less than five minutes to convince "the coaches, the owners, and the fans that here was a great player." The inevitable comparison, favor-able to White, was made: "White looks a lot like Dutch [Clark] on the field. He is quick to see the smallest opening in the defense of the opposition. He passes and kicks better than Clark. One of his boots carried more than 70 yards." The headline confirmed the local hope: "White is a Whiz."

Other journalists worried about the hype. A week after the intrasquad game, Charles Ward wrote in the *Free Press:*

> The Whiz received gallons of printer's ink when he was starring at the Uni-versity of Colorado. He received more when he signed to play with the Pitts-burgh Pirates of the National Football League. The result was that the fans expected too much of him. Expecting to see a Superman, they saw a very good football player. But they didn't criticize him as they would a very good football player. They criticized him as a Superman, and naturally White did not measure up to the expectations of some of them. Now the Whiz is in De-troit, and on Sunday a week he will make his bow as a Lion in a game with the Pittsburgh Steelers. . . . His friends are hoping that the fans will not expect to see him reel off 40 or 50 yards every time he carries the ball. If the fans do they will be disappointed. Whizzer is not that kind of football player, and who is?

The Lions lost the home opening game to White's old team, 10-7, and the defeat presaged a season of mediocrity highlighted by two features—White's extraordinary achievements, especially running and kicking, with little offen-sive support, and, in the words of Chuck Hanneman, "the guy's incredible courage—raw guts—in the face of incredible physical poundings week after week."

Detroit finished the season with a 5-5-1 record, never winning or losing more than two games in a row. The victories were over Cleveland (now coached by Dutch Clark), Green Bay, both Chicago teams, and Philadelphia. In retrospect, the most remarkable win was over the Chicago Bears, who eventually defeated Washington 73-0 in the most lopsided championship game in NFL history. Detroit lost to the Bears in Chicago 7-0 in October, then defeated the Bears 17-14 in a mid-November home game. White blamed himself for the loss in October, despite the fact that he played all but five minutes of the game and was the "hero on offense" *(Detroit News)* and played "courageous football" *(Detroit Times)* all afternoon. The team reached the 10-yard line four times without scoring, and White criticized his own play-calling afterward, a rap that Potsy Clark refused to let him take. The judgment of those on and off the field was that the Bears were outplayed for all but the first eighty-six seconds of the game, when they scored the only points of the day. White had a limited role in the November victory. His season was symbolically captured more by Detroit's 21-0 victory over the then-winless Philadelphia Eagles late in the season. He scored two touchdowns and started the third "on a pretty deceptive reverse" with Cardwell receiving the handoff, but he also fumbled three times, twice on punts and once as he was reaching the goal line. Yet his punting, as well as his running and passing, shaped much of the game.

Halfway through the season, White had suffered so many bruises and sprains that his teammates joked about "the mummy"—taped from head to toe for every game. One shoulder was so badly bruised that he could not raise his arm above his head for two games in mid-October. Part of Detroit's problems during the season resulted from injuries to important players—including Hanneman, Cardwell, and Wiethe—which crippled the team's offense. Cotton Price, a rookie from Texas A&M, helped supply some versatility to the backfield late in the season so that defenses could not key on White, but even then the line was dilapidated and the season ended with a humiliating 50-7 loss to Green Bay—the worst in the franchise's seven-year history.

When the season ended in late November, White was the league leader in rushing with 514 yards on 146 carries—34 yards ahead of John Drake, the Cleveland fullback. White had taken the lead in mid-October and never lost it. His yards-per-carry average, which hovered near 3.0 at the end of October, hit 3.5 in early November and remained at that level for the rest of the season. His strong second half of the season helped to secure his second selection on the all-NFL teams chosen by the league, the three wire services, and the *New York Sunday News.* John Wiethe also won all-NFL honors on the same teams, except for United Press, which placed him on its second team. White was the workhorse for a weak offense. He carried the ball more times than anyone else in the league, and he punted more times than all but one other in the league (and his average yards per punt, 41, were fourth best in the NFL; Baugh was the leader with a remarkable 51). Overall, Detroit scored fewer points than any other team in the Western Conference and amassed less total yardage than any other team in the conference except the Chicago Cardinals. Freddie Mandel responded predictably: he fired Potsy Clark.

Byron White needed time to recover from the physical ravages of the season, as well as the emotional letdown of a disappointing third-place finish in a five-team conference, but he had only five weeks. The season ended November 24, and the second semester at Yale Law School began at 8:10 A.M. on January 4. When the season ended, reporters asked White whether he would return for the 1941 season, but he was noncommittal—inclined to believe, according to the *Detroit News,* that "conscription is here to stay" and that he "may decide to volunteer for a year. His plans about next football season are rather vague." Not only was the prospect of American engagement in the European war more likely, but White found the Detroit organization much colder than the slightly wacky, buoyantly precarious operation of Art Rooney and Johnny Blood. Freddie Mandel was as jealous of a nickel as Rooney was generous. For example, after Chuck Hanneman provided the margin of victory against the eventual champion Bears with a field goal early in the game, he thought he was entitled to ask for at least a $25 per game raise after starting for four years, including the most recent year as captain, and scoring 16 points on two field goals and 10 points after touchdown—more than 10 percent of the team's meager point total for the season. Mandel's reply was caustic: "Who the hell do you think you are?!" By the halfway point of the next season, Hanneman, like Potsy Clark, would be gone, released on waivers. Players veered between anger and disbelief over Mandel's salary policies. "It was degrading to argue over a few bucks a game," said one. "But Freddie seemed to think that was good management. What it really was, well, was just arbitrary."

White's curricular opportunities as a second-year student in the spring of 1941 were doubly circumscribed by his ineligibility for courses continuing from the first term (business units–finance; estates–gratuitous transfers) and the unavailability of courses taught only in that term (administrative law; Business Units II–Management; Estates I–Gratuitous Transfers; evidence; labor law; Procedure II–Equitable Remedies; Sales). Since he had declined to join the *Law Journal,* the spring semester of 1941 for Byron White was five quick months of stopgap curricular work and speculation over whether the war in Europe would ensnare the United States and capture him in the process.

On the same day that the semester began, President Roosevelt outlined the lend-lease program and declared the Four Freedoms, and two days later he asked for a defense appropriation of nearly $11 billion for fiscal 1942. Roosevelt was cranking up the pressure to support the European nations that had been besieged by Hitler, especially Great Britain, which had absorbed more than thirty thousand tons of German bombs during the second half of 1940. The lend-lease program, designed to circumvent isolationist congressional strictures, was announced less than three weeks after Roosevelt had suggested for the first time that Britain should receive direct arms aid. The legality of the program was hotly debated, and White's constitutional law professor from the year before, Edwin Borchard, emerged as one of the leading critics of Roosevelt's constitutional authority for lend-lease. Borchard had come to professional maturity as an admirer of, and then an advocate for, the prerogatives of the Senate in foreign affairs. The new constitutional question of the day, now that the authority of the New Deal had been safely established, was whether the judiciary would try to intervene in foreign policy.

The semester ended in mid-June with Nazi troops pouring into Finland in preparation for invasion of the Soviet Union, notwithstanding the nonaggression pact between the two countries and statements, such as the one issued by TASS as White was packing to return again to Colorado, that there was no rift between Germany and the U.S.S.R. Shortly after White returned home, he volunteered for the marine corps in hopes of becoming a fighter pilot, but was rejected because of red-green color blindness.

During the summer of 1941, the Nazi invasion of Russia—Operation Barbarossa—was in full swing, and Byron White was again turning his mind from law school to football. He decided after weighing several options to play football until he was conscripted or some end run could be developed around the navy doctors who had kept him out of the Marine Corps. Exactly thirty days after he flunked the marines' eye test, White reported to the Detroit Lions preseason camp near Detroit. The only good news for the team was that they would again play in Briggs Stadium, the Tiger baseball team's home ground, after a year's exile in the smaller, and less comfortable, University of Detroit stadium.

Other changes were less promising. Potsy Clark had been replaced by Bill Edwards, who had a distinguished record in six years at Western Reserve University but whose strength was discipline and fundamentals; he consequently was at sea in a league where personnel, strategy, and player-management skills were more important. He was a stickler for discipline and imposed a dress code for the team when it traveled. His one concession was to allow the players to continue to play cards and dice on the trains, but only for a nickel a point; White avoided the games and retired, John Noppenberg later recalled, "with two-inch-thick law books to 'relax' with." Edwards was the fourth head coach in as many years for the team, but the discontinuity was mitigated by the wholesale turnover on the roster. Half of the backs were rookies, as were more than 60 percent of the linemen. The average experience was 1.8 years, and only two players had been in the league more than four years—Chuck Hanneman, the team captain, was a six-year veteran, and Lloyd Cardwell had played halfback on the team for five years.

Notwithstanding the host of uncertainties posed by the team's structure, the annual intrasquad game shortly after Labor Day excited the nearly fifteen thousand spectators, who endured muggy heat to witness the rookies defeat the veterans, 21-17. The cause for optimism among the fans and press was the backfield play. Billy Jefferson, a tall rookie halfback from Mississippi State, demonstrated that he could run effectively off-tackle, move well in the open field, and pass as well as anyone on the team. With a trio of veterans—White, Cardwell, and Cotton Price—Jefferson, and another rookie, fullback Milt Peipul (White's roommate), the Lions appeared to have an offense with depth and some versatility. White remained the marquee player, and the *Detroit Times* ran an admiring profile of him shortly before the intrasquad game that emphasized his self-punishing work ethic. "There was the Whizzer, the heralded All-American, the league's leading ground-gainer, undoubtedly the highest paid member of the Lions, still working out 30 minutes after the rest of the team had left the field for the clubhouse." The story reported that White had so impressed the "new leadership" of the team that "they are counting upon him heavily to pull the Lions out of the doldrums in the National League." The leadership was sufficiently positive about White to allow him to fly to Denver—but only for four hours—in order to serve as best man at Sam's wedding. Although Mandel feared that his prize player might be late returning for an exhibition game, he was not.

The offense failed to match preseason expectations. The Lions lost an exhibition game to Pittsburgh 7-0, then opened their regular season with an embarrassing 23-0 defeat at Green Bay. According to the *Detroit Times,* "Although Whizzer White and the rookie, Billy Jefferson, made occasional gains with surprisingly few blockers to aid them, the Lion attack worked mostly in reverse against the overpowering Packer line." The Detroit attack was marred by "fumbles, slipshod execution and little deception." The press quickly turned sour on the rookies and grew impatient with Cotton Price, so the headline before the second league game of the season, accurately reflecting the story, read: "Whizzer White Again Holds Fate of Lions; He's Counted on Against Dodgers in East Sunday." White played brilliantly during the scoreless first half at Ebbets Field. He ran back the opening kickoff 36 yards, then connected on a 13-yard pass play, which put the Lions on the Brooklyn 26-yard line, but a fumble by Peipul on the next play ended the drive. White later kicked his team out of trouble with punts from his own end zone of 44 and 57 yards, and a quick kick of 58 yards that backed up the Dodgers to their own 16-yard line.

Some of the Lions suspected that the press clippings and the first-half performance made White a marked man when the second half began. "I will never forget it as long as I live," Chuck Hanneman recalled years later. "He caught the second-half kickoff and was steaming downfield when he got hit by Bruiser Kinard," the aptly nicknamed 195-pound rookie tackle from Mississippi who eventually was named to the NFL Hall of Fame. "Wow! I have never seen anyone hit so hard. I thought Byron was dead. I thought he had been killed." White was revived with smelling salts and taken off the field, but, the *Detroit Times* reported, "Although he could speak he didn't even know what the score was for several hours after the game." Hanneman said, "The guy had a lot of guts. He knew they [Brooklyn] were laying for him, the way most teams did, and he went back out there every time." White did not play in the balance of the game, which Brooklyn won 14-7, but he was back in action the following week in Chicago for a game against the Cardinals, which ended in a 14-14 tie. White suffered a knee injury in the fourth quarter and had to leave the game, but the *Detroit Times* selected him as its player of the week: "Whizzer White—the one-man football team—had even the Chicago fans cheering him." White set up one touchdown and passed for the other, but he "electrified" the fans with his broken-field running and a 65-yard touchdown pass to Cardwell that was nullified by a holding penalty.

The Lions finally opened their home season two weeks later in mid-October against Cleveland, whom they beat 17-7 for their first league victory of the year. White was slowed by a charley horse that had plagued him for two weeks, but the *Detroit Times* still made him player of the week—as much for his defense as for his offense: "He made brilliant tackles, knocked down many passes and once batted the ball from the hands of a Ram receiver right in the end zone." The win came at a high price: Lloyd Cardwell suffered a broken leg and was lost for the season. In many respects, the game was an ominous turning point. The Lions were humiliated the following week by the Bears 49-0—

the most lopsided defeat in franchise history—and they were beaten badly, 24-6, a week later, at home, by Green Bay. Don Hutson caught six passes for the Packers, more than one with White trying to defend against him. Mandel apparently decided to clean house, or at least to cut his losses. Two days after the Green Bay game, which made Detroit's season record 1-4-1, Mandel asked waivers on Hanneman and Fred Vanzo, the four-year blocking back from Northwestern, as preliminary steps to releasing them outright. The players, Mandel said, had "reached the end of the football trail," and it was time to re-build for the future. Both men were bitter, although Vanzo had been bothered by injuries and in any event was awaiting a duty call from the navy.

In their final road games of the season, the Lions split—beating Cleve-land, the division doormat, 14-0, but losing 20-13 to New York. They re-turned home for the final three games of the year carrying a 2-5-1 record and risking the worst season in franchise history. Edwards, sniped at more behind the scenes by his players than by the press, seemed to quit psychologically. When the Philadelphia Eagles came to town for the first of the remaining three games, he quit in fact—if only for two quarters. With Philadelphia lead-ing 10-7 midway through the third quarter, Wiethe complained to Edwards on the sidelines that play selection needed to be changed and that *we shouldn't be losing to these clowns.* Edwards replied, *I quit. You guys think you're so smart, you run the team.* He then took a seat on the bench, and Wiethe directed Bill Radovich to organize the line and White to organize the backfield. Radovich and White collaborated on an unbalanced line offense, and to frustrate the Eagle defense, which had been keying on White's running, more passes with White as receiver were called. The Lions scored two touchdowns in the final period and pulled out a 21-17 victory—"the most satisfying triumph the Lions have scored this season," according to the *Detroit Times.*

White received disproportionate attention from the *Times,* whose lead paragraph declared, "Whizzer White is the best all-around back in the Na-tional Football League." He scored two touchdowns, including one in the critical fourth-period rally. His running and pass receiving helped to set up the other. The *Times* enthused about White's impact, and the game coverage was dotted with phrases about the Whizzer "whizzing" and "the football miracle man." Mandel, not fully aware of the in-house rebellion that had ignited the comeback, was quoted optimistically about the upcoming game with the champion Chicago Bears. He must have been thinking more of his prospec-tive gate than of his team's chances, because several players were sidelined with injuries and the starting center was a converted back. On game day, nearly thirty thousand spectators materialized on a bitterly cold day—the highest attendance in two years—but the Bears easily disposed of the Lions 24-7. The loss, which dropped the Lions to 3-6-1, clinched the worst win-loss record in team history with one game left to play.

The intervention of the Thanksgiving weekend served not only to provide recovery time for a physically battered squad, but also to adjust the focus of all the players to the end of the season and whatever followed. For White, the future held not Yale Law School again but some branch of the military. He was registered for the draft in Detroit, not Colorado, and local draft board officials told the newspapers that he was likely to be called up in December if certified as physically fit. He was classified 1-A, eligible to be called on November 1. On November 17 (the day after the self-coached comeback against Philadelphia), White reported for his draft physical. The acting chief medical officer of the army examination station held a press conference and pronounced White to be "a perfect specimen." Now the ball was with the naval reserve, with whom White had filed an application a few weeks earlier after he was told that Naval Intelligence might grant a waiver to the requirement for the eye examination.

In the meantime, White waited and passed the time with the public appearances that were so much a part of his game-week routine in both Pittsburgh and Detroit. One appearance, at the annual University of Michigan banquet for high school seniors, provided material for a thoughtful and admiring column by Bob Murphy of the *Detroit Times*. Murphy traveled to and from Ann Arbor with White, and they were together for nearly six hours. Murphy's column on November 27, three days before the season (and career) finale against the Chicago Cardinals, was unusually insightful about its elusive subject. Murphy observed White not only at the banquet but in repose on the round trip and "listened to him talk—although he talks little, except when asked questions." Murphy noted that White was self-consciously unpretentious:

> Although a Rhodes Scholar and a brilliant student, White talks the lingo of the sporting mob when around them. If you care to switch to literature or arts he can carry his part of the conversation as easily as the salesman adds tax to anything you buy these days. But Whizzer White shuns any spot where he might give the wrong impression. Versatile as he is, he refused a sizable sum recently to go on the "Information Please" program. Those who know him best tell me he turned down this money because he didn't want his mates to think he is not "regular."

The burden of Murphy's column was the importance of football to White: "I never knew until this week how much football meant." Murphy wrote that White said it calmly and coldly. It was no publicity aerial bomb intended for the lap of the press. It was strictly a simple statement. But the look on the scholarly man's face, and the way he said it, impressed those listening so much. "I've known for sometime," said Whizzer, "that this final game against the Chicago Cardinals would be the last for me. But now that the hour has arrived, I'm not very happy about it."

Nor was Freddie Mandel. His thirty-third birthday coincided with the final game of the season, and the loss of his best player, combined with the team's dismal win-loss record, made his quarter-million-dollar investment in 1940 look like a bad plunge. Mandel's taste for professional football was turning to ashes (although he would continue to run the franchise during wartime, absorbing huge operating losses, until finally selling at a loss in 1948).

To those on the field and among the 17,051 in the stands at Briggs Stadium on the cold, damp, and dark final day of November 1941, Byron White rose to the occasion with a memorable performance that marked him as more than a talented football player. "He went out a champion," Bill Radovich later declared. Other teammates felt White's customary intensity somehow ratcheted up a few notches for his last bow. The Detroit press corps, always a difficult audience, was unanimous in celebrating the artful completion of White's career, which everyone understood the final game of the 1941 season to be. By game time, White had been notified that Naval Intelligence would waive the eye examination and accept his application to the reserve. He expected to report for training soon. Regardless of the duration of what journalists often euphemistically called the "present emergency," no one—beginning with White himself—expected that he would ever play football again. The Lions handily defeated the Cardinals, 21-3. H. G. Salsinger tabulated White's play—"one of his best performances"—in the *Detroit News:*

First period—Intercepted a forward pass on the Detroit 19 and ran 81 yards for a touchdown.

Second Period—Returned a punt from Detroit's 2-yard line to the Chicago Cardinals' 35, a 63-yard runback.

Third Period—Threw a 23-yard forward pass to End Bill Fisk for Detroit's third touchdown. Got away a 62-yard quick kick.

Fourth Period—Spent most of his time on the bench. Re-entered the game when the Cardinals made a first down on the Detroit 3. Inspired a defense that held the Cardinals' attack and enabled Detroit to take the ball on downs on the 7.

Other press accounts were equally admiring. John Sabo wrote in the *Detroit Free Press:* "Whizzer White, the scholarly producer of touchdowns, bid adieu to professional football Sunday afternoon at Briggs Stadium and, as his farewell gift, he fired the Detroit Lions to their most spectacular performance of the season." According to Lewis H. Walter of the *Detroit Times,*

> Byron (Whizzer) White is marking time today as he awaits the call of the United States Navy to service in the intelligence division for the duration of the war. But the greatest all-around back in football wasn't marking time yesterday as he played his last game. He was strictly on active service as he led the charge of the Detroit Lions to a 21-3 victory over the Chicago Cardinals at Briggs Stadium.

The Associated Press also pegged the story of the game on White's "farewell to professional football." The angle was too obvious to resist. White had been the most publicized college football player in the country three years before, and his outstanding performance with mediocre or worse professional teams only enhanced his stature. Like Ted Williams years later in a different sport, White ended his career memorably, with play that both exceeded his own standard and included a signature feat that provided his fans a singular mental keepsake and his career an exclamation point. For Williams, it was a skyrocketing home run; for White, it was the first-period interception. White appeared to take the pass right out of the Cardinal receiver's hands. The ensuing 81-yard touchdown run electrified the stadium, seized the momentum of the game for the Lions, and provided a quick return on the emotional investment of those who expected White to end his career with a flourish. Drama began and ended the play—from stealing the pass deep in his own territory to breaking free of the final defender "with a mighty twist," according to the *Times,* when he appeared to have been tackled. Captured on newsreels, the play would stay with White for years and provide a vivid image to sailors who met him in the South Pacific, to law students when he returned to Yale after the war, and to law clerks at the Supreme Court of the United States when he began his first professional job. "Everyone had heard of Whizzer White," one of his coclerks with Chief Justice Fred M. Vinson, Francis Allen, later recalled. "The newsreels and the headlines about his last game, especially the long touchdown run with the intercepted pass, made him a permanent celebrity at the time with his contemporaries."

The enduring fame had an ironic touch. White's final game in his final season made him memorable notwithstanding that he failed, unlike in his first two professional seasons, to lead the league in rushing and to be named to the first team of the all-NFL squad. Clarence (Pug) Manders of Brooklyn won the rushing championship with 486 yards on 111 carries, a 4.4 average. White was eighteenth, with 238 yards on eighty-nine carries, a 2.7 average. His place on the all-NFL first team was taken by George (One-Play) McAfee of the Bears, who was second in the league in both rushing and scoring; White was named to the second team. He could not be overlooked, because his performance in other statistical categories kept him among the top individual performers in the league. He led the league in punt returns, both in number of receptions, nineteen, and in total yards, 262; his longest return was 64 yards. He also led in kickoff returns, with eleven for 285 yards—a 25.9 yard average, with his longest run 41 yards. On the defensive side, he was second in punting, with a 41.6-yard average on forty-eight punts, only one short of the leader in total kicks. His longest punt was for 63 yards. Sammy Baugh again led the league with a 48.7-yard average and a 75-yard longest kick. White was the only statistical bright spot for the Detroit Lions, who were at the bottom of the league in total yardage and total offensive plays. The Lions finished third in the Western Division, at 4-6-1, ahead of the Cardinals (3-7-1) and the Cleveland Rams (2-9).

8

THE NAVY

S SOON as his season was finished, on December 1, 1941, Byron White began packing in preparation for returning to Colorado, where he planned to spend Christmas before returning to Yale, where he would await orders to report for training with the navy. He drove to Chicago, spent the night in Evanston with Freddie Mandel, owner of the Detroit Lions, and set out in the morning for Wellington. He later recalled: "I was driving home to Colorado, and as I was driving along the Outer Drive in Chicago I turned on the radio and heard about the attack on Pearl Harbor. I was going to stop and see some friends in Chicago, but when I heard the news I just kept right on driving through to home." Football sank like a stone from White's life and from that of much of the nation. The Chicago Bears defeated the New York Giants 37-9 at Wrigley Field for the league championship on December 21, 1941, but by then men and women were scrambling to support the war effort, and fewer than fourteen thousand fans attended the game.

After Christmas, White bided his time at Yale Law School waiting to be called for basic training by the navy. Finally, he was appointed ensign in the naval reserve on May 6, 1942—listing the Savarine Hotel, in Detroit, as his enlistment residence—and was assigned to Intelligence. He spent twenty weeks in basic and advanced intelligence training at Dartmouth College and New York City, respectively. His first duty posting was to the staff of commander, Third Fleet, in the Southern Pacific Force; he was now lieutenant (junior grade). He reported for duty on July 9, 1943, in Nouméa, New Caledonia (approximately midway between Australia and Fiji). By the time White arrived in the Southwest Pacific, Allied forces had gained the initiative after the disaster of Pearl Harbor and the retreat from the Philippines in March 1942. American carrier forces had inflicted the first decisive defeat over Japanese forces in June of 1942 at the battle of Midway. The victory shifted the balance of power in the Pacific. Japan was forced to build more carriers instead of battleships as planned, to delay plans for further advances in the southwest (New Caledonia, Fiji, and Samoa), and to postpone the offensive already initiated in New Guinea. For the first time, American forces could go on the offensive, and the first step was Guadalcanal, in the southern Solomon Islands. The strategy was to move up the ladder of the Solomons chain toward the Philippines, and eventually Japan, while neutralizing Japanese-held bases along the way. The Guadalcanal campaign lasted almost six months and imposed heavy casualties on both sides, but gave the American forces a critically important air base that allowed them to control the skies, at least during daylight, in the southern Solomons.

White's first duty involved protection of Guadalcanal and the nearby navy installation on Tulagi Island. "Installation" is generous. As the photographs in books on the Solomons campaign illustrate, Tulagi contained a modest makeshift port better suited to motor torpedo boats (MTB, or PT boats) than the larger cruisers that occasionally called. The port, named Sesape, had a floating dry dock, a machinery shed, and a PT tender. Quarters for the troops consisted of Quonsets, thatched huts, and tents. Later students of the location would observe: "The whole base would have fit on the flight deck of the carrier *Enterprise*." Almost as soon as White reported for duty in Nouméa, he was assigned to temporary duty on MTB Flotilla 1, based at Tulagi. He missed, by a matter of weeks, being billeted with his old acquaintance from England, Lt. (j.g.) John F. Kennedy, who had been in Tulagi since April 1943 in command of PT *109*. In late May, Kennedy's base shifted two islands north, to the Russell Islands and even more primitive conditions. The troop movement was in preparation for invasion of New Georgia, one of the next rungs up the Solomons ladder.

The New Georgia campaign was more lengthy and costly than anticipated. The situation was aggravated because the Japanese held two islands to the north of New Georgia—Kolombangara and Vella Lavella—and the larger islands of the central Solomons to the east. The passage between the larger islands and the New Georgia–Kolombangara–Vella string was called New Georgia Sound but known locally as the Slot. Under cover of darkness, the

Japanese would send destroyers loaded with reinforcements, both troops and materiel, down the Slot to relieve their positions; later, the same route would be used for evacuation. The destroyer convoy traveled south from its base at Rabaul, in New Guinea, at 18 knots, then returned north at almost twice the speed. Adm. William F. (Bull) Halsey, the Allied South Pacific commander, accordingly dubbed the convoys the Tokyo Express. One of the jobs of the PT boats, in addition to routine nighttime patrols, was to derail the Tokyo Express whenever possible. That assignment accidentally linked Lieutenants Kennedy and White in what evolved from a chaotic accident into an act of courage and, finally, with some burnishing by a succession of friendly journalists, into an enormous political asset for Kennedy.

By early August, with White still at Tulagi and Kennedy now at a new base, Lumberi, next to Rendova Island, at the north end of the Slot, the New Georgia campaign was reaching a bloody conclusion. The Japanese were retreating inland on New Georgia and would finally be defeated if American destroyers could prevent their reinforcement. The next stop logically under the Allied plan was Kolombangara, next door to New Georgia. On the night of August 1–2, 1943, Kennedy was on patrol with two other PTs in Blackett Strait between Kolombangara and Gizo Island to the southwest, just south of the Slot, under orders to stop the Express. There was no moon; it was pitch black. The Express that night was a four-destroyer convoy—three ships loaded with a total of nine hundred troops and 120 tons of supplies, the fourth a bodyguard. The convoy pushed through the Slot after dark, but encountered uncoordinated torpedo fire from several PTs. More than thirty "fish" were fired unsuccessfully at the convoy. At one point, a searchlight—presumably from one of the enemy destroyers—bathed *109,* and Kennedy quickly took evasive action.

The convoy transferred its cargo in twenty precisely organized minutes at Vila, on Kolombangara, then reversed course at top speed. One of the ship commanders later remembered that the passage, honeycombed with reefs and shoals, was a "weird and treacherous waterway—in peacetime no ship would have ventured here at night in excess of 12 knots, even with all lights burning. We, of course, were running fully blacked out." The risks of American PT patrols produced a "cold sweat . . . on every brow" in the convoy as the Express turned back north through Blackett Strait at more than 30 knots. The column was headed by the *Amagiri,* a two-thousand-ton destroyer. A few miles into the Blackett Strait, the column spotted "a small black object" closing on the *Amagiri* at fifteen hundred meters. No more than ten seconds later, the destroyer sliced away much of the starboard quarter of the object, which was

Kennedy's PT *109*. The captain of one of the other ships, the *Shigure,* recalled later: "The black object melted into the darkness and was gone, with no explosion, no flash, no fire. It was mystifying." As the other three destroyers came upon the wreckage in the *Amagiri's* wake, they all opened fire with machine guns, and the remains of *109* "disappeared into black water as if they had never existed."

Two of the *109's* crew were killed in the crash. Kennedy heroically guided the survivors at night on a four-hour swim to a safe island, unsuccessfully swam more than once to find rescuers, moved his men to a better location, and finally oversaw their recovery, which was initiated and largely engineered by an Australian "coast watcher" located on Kolombangara. The incident was controversial both at the time and years later. Kennedy and his father were seen as glorifying the incident and exaggerating the lieutenant's rescue efforts for political purposes both in the 1946 congressional election and in the 1960 presidential election. Immediately after the accident, the question for navy officials was how Kennedy could have been overtaken by the *Amagiri.* One of Kennedy's fellow PT captains, William F. Liebenow, asked, when the survivors were returned to base, "Jack, how in the world could a Jap destroyer run you down?" Kennedy replied: "Lieb, I actually don't know. It all happened so quickly."

The Intelligence report "Sinking of PT 109 and Subsequent Rescue of Survivors," derived from survivors of *PT 109,* was written by two intelligence officers from MTB Flotilla 1, Lts. (j.g.) B. R. White and J. C. McClure, primarily by White. The five-page, single-spaced report, filed two weeks after the survivors were rescued (but not declassified until 1959), focuses on the plight of the survivors after the crash; only the first page and a half discuss the actual collision. The White Report—as it came to be called—has been criticized on several minor points, but its principal weakness is that it fails to cast light on the most troubling questions about the sinking of the boat. Kennedy's post-collision heroism initially made him a candidate for the Silver Star, but soon, and for years thereafter, the incident was acutely embarrassing to the navy. One Annapolis historian recently wrote:

PT-109 was the *only* patrol craft ever hit by a Japanese destroyer during the Pacific war. That particular night, Kennedy's command was part of a three-boat picket line that was *expecting* Japanese destroyers. When the collision came at 0200 on August 2, two of Kennedy's men were asleep, and two were lying on deck. Visibility was almost one mile. Kennedy was radioed about a bow wake heading toward him; he gave no response. . . . Within the Navy the

loss of *PT-109* was something of a scandal. "Kennedy had the most maneu-
verable vessel in the world," recalled one PT squadron leader. "All that power
and yet this knight in white armor managed to have his PT boat rammed by
a destroyer. Everybody in the fleet laughed about that."

The White Report provides no information to help explain why Kennedy
was taken by surprise and then was unable to elude the *Amagiri*. The report
notes that Kennedy was aware that "action with the enemy was in progress,
and a significant one," but the entire crew apparently was not on full alert—to
say the least. White accounts for the locations of only eight of the thirteen
crewmen. Later it emerged that Lennie Thom, the executive officer, was lying
down on deck, not "standing beside the cockpit" as White reported. Nor does
the report note that up to three others were also probably lying down on deck,
taking advantage of two-hour rest periods Kennedy allowed between watches
on lengthy patrols. The men were undoubtedly tired after patrolling for seven
hours, but their patrols routinely lasted that long. Although Kennedy had his
crew under loose rein even with the enemy thought to be nearby, he nevertheless could have evaded collision had he not been patrolling, according to
White, on only "one engine ahead at idling speed." The other two engines
were not in gear.

The *109* had three 1,350-horsepower engines to propel the two-ton boat;
the craft was capable of making more than 30 knots under normal conditions.
But when the *Amagiri* appeared on *109*'s starboard bow, she was at "200–300
yards distance," White noted. She was closing fast, probably at 30 knots (not
40, as White speculated), or more than fifteen yards per second. Kennedy
knew if he tried to gun the idling engine it would stall. So he began to turn to
starboard "preparatory to firing torpedoes," he told White, but made no more
than thirty degrees when his boat was run over. Indeed, the effect of the
aborted turn, which may have been virtually a reflex, was to put his boat
squarely in the destroyer's path; had he not turned, the ship probably would
have passed the *109* without contact.

White concluded his summary of the circumstances leading to the collision by noting that "scarcely 10 seconds elapsed between time of sighting and
the crash." Kennedy himself later admitted in the flotilla's newsletter that "the
reason he was unable to get out of the way of the Jap destroyer which rammed
him was because only one of his engines was in gear. He strongly advises that,
whenever enemy destroyers are known to be in a patrol area, all engines should
be in gear." Kennedy did not admit that he was practicing 20/20 hindsight.
The reason he cut two of his engines and idled the third was to reduce his

wake and thus diminish his visibility to an enemy vessel. The practice was contrary to Squad Nine policy and effectively made *109* a sitting duck. Kennedy's belated recommendation in the flotilla newsletter was not a revelation but a reiteration of the policy he had been obliged to follow.

At best, the White Report was uneven. It provided a brisk and incomplete account of the circumstances prior to the collision, and a carefully detailed narrative of the rescue efforts. Although the report states that "survivors" were sources, it is not clear how many crewmen were actually interviewed—or how closely—about the precrash period. The report failed to determine the location of all the crew members, and whether they were all awake or alert in battle stations; one whose position was unspecified, Andrew Kirksey, did not survive the collision. The report avoided any analysis of whether Kennedy's starboard turn would have left time for firing any torpedoes, although perhaps it was readily apparent to informed readers that the objective was futile—the lumbering Mark VIII torpedoes, which were originally designed for action in World War I, needed to dive, stabilize, and run out approximately four hundred yards to arm properly. Finally, the report omitted any analysis of the critical issues of Kennedy's cruising speed and engine utilization. Strictly speaking, such analysis was not the function of the report, which was to gather all information available that was relevant to the sinking of the boat.

White did not appear to think that Kennedy's behavior prior to the collision was questionable; the premise of the report seems to mirror Kennedy's perplexed reply to Liebenow. The tone of the report is highly professional, but there are two flat-footed attempts at humor that suggest the author thought the performance of the captain and crew was unexceptional and that levity could brighten the account of an otherwise open-and-shut case. The report explains that the crew designated their first refuge Bird Island "because of the great abundance of droppings from the fine feathered friends." The crew's next island refuge "was slightly larger than their former, offered brush for protection and a few coconuts to eat, and had no Jap tenants." Overall, the report recounts quiet, methodical heroism and sustained efforts in the face of unknown odds with no initial support from search vessels. Kennedy deserves great credit for remaining undaunted after the collision, but the fact remains that two crewmen died in a unique encounter that probably could have been avoided. Had he been in the British navy, he probably would have been court-martialed—the standard practice for captains whose vessels were sunk. The American navy ignored the practice in the case of PT boats, one more example of the famed "expendability" of the plywood crafts. Gen. Douglas

MacArthur, for whom PT boats were prominent props in the Philippines, was quoted by a columnist in 1960 as saying that Kennedy should have been court-martialed, but MacArthur later denied the statement.

Less than a month after White filed the report, his name was back in American newspapers for the first time since he entered the navy. Leif Erickson, an Associated Press reporter who had been previously based in Denver, covered the rescue of the *109* survivors. He filed a story about Kennedy's exploits and, a few days later, on September 5, a brief sketch of White:

> AT A MOTOR TORPEDO BOAT BASE SOMEWHERE IN THE NEW GEORGIA ISLANDS, Sept. 5 (delayed) (AP)—A turn to the right, and take three steps, turn left and walk fifteen more steps, and there in a desk in a sandbagged dugout in the yellow glow of electric lights is one of the most extraordinary young men to gain fame playing football. He is Navy Lt. (j.g.) Byron Raymond White, 26, of Wellington, Colo., commonly known as Whizzer White, a nickname he earnestly dislikes.

After two paragraphs summarizing White's football career and his new job "with the PT boats staff operating against the Japanese in the North Solomons and the New Georgias," Erickson wrote:

> Tall, fair-haired and still evidently very fit physically, White smiles in recalling incidents of the football field, but his interest is in winning the war and going back for his final year of law study. "Football was just a means to an end—education—so far as I was concerned," he said. "I went from college to pro football to make money to pay for schooling."

The final two paragraphs of the story supplied more detail about White's collegiate and professional football career.

Jack Kennedy—as the White Report referred to him—was entitled by navy custom to return Stateside in recognition of losing his boat, but he managed to remain in the Solomons. After recuperating in sick bay on Tulagi, Kennedy picked up a new boat, PT *59*, at Rendova and reported on October 18 to his new base, Lambu Lambu Cove on Vella Lavella Island, just northwest of Kolombangara and only a few miles from the location where *109* went down. The PT boats still had the same job—to sink enemy supply barges and generally harass enemy traffic in the close quarters of the Slot. The futility of the old torpedoes prompted a shift in artillery to multiple machine guns, making the MTBs into speedy eighty-foot plywood-hulled gunboats. In the small world of the Solomons, Lambu Lambu's intelligence officer turned out to be Byron White. For one month, Kennedy and White were stationed at the same base, and the acquaintanceship that began in England and revived after the sinking of the *109* developed into a warm friendship.

"Part of the young JFK," an unfriendly navy historian later wrote, "was sheer rakehell, with women, ships, anything that came along." Kennedy enjoyed racing PT boats and debating social policy afterward in whatever passed for the officers' club, a combination of tastes that White relished. White even went out on patrol with Kennedy from time to time, since the intelligence duties on Vella Lavella often extended no further than to a foot or jeep patrol around the island. On one evening patrol with Kennedy, White tried firing a mounted machine gun on the boat, but the gun's bolt malfunctioned and White was left with a nasty gash in his palm. Two decades later, after more than two years of Kennedy's presidency and after eighteen months on the Supreme Court, White recalled his impressions of Kennedy at Vella Lavella:

> I remember riding in his boat a couple of times—that is, the boat they gave him after he had lost his first boat. As a result of these encounters with the President, I began to get a strong feeling about what kind of fellow he was. He proved himself to be very intelligent in the way he ran his boat, as well as cool and courageous under fire. I concluded he was a pretty solid sort of person.

Kennedy shipped out under doctor's orders on November 18, 1943. White got out of PTs, but unlike Kennedy, stayed in combat. At approximately the same time that Kennedy was leaving for the States, White "hopped a PT boat" (as he later told the story) to introduce himself to Capt. Arleigh Burke, who he had heard was calling nearby. Burke commanded Destroyer Squadron 23—the Little Beavers (named after Red Ryder's cartoon sidekick, who provided the squadron's insignia). Burke was already a well-known figure in the Pacific Theater of Operations. He was regarded as a deft and imaginative tactician who maximized return on his military assets. He was also a colorful figure in a world of dull old men (save Halsey). For White, he had an added attraction: Burke was a native of Boulder, Colorado, who had grown up on a hardscrabble farm south of the young town and never forgot his Western roots, despite twenty years in the navy. Shortly after they met, White received new orders: "Detach from MTB to Staff, ComDesRon 23." For the next four months, White served as an intelligence officer to Burke on the *Charles S. Ausburne,* the flagship of the Little Beavers squadron. It would be White's most satisfying service of the war.

Burke took command of the eight-destroyer squadron on October 23, 1943. He had a promotion as well as a new command—to commodore, a flag rank. The success of the central Solomons campaign caused a shift in American strategy. The initial plan had been for Halsey's Third Fleet to march up the Solomon chain and for Gen. Douglas MacArthur to take the Seventh Fleet through New Guinea so that both forces could converge on the heavily fortified Japanese base at Rabaul on the way to the Philippines and eventually Japan. Halsey decided that it was both unnecessary and too costly to climb the Solomons in sequence, so he began to leapfrog islands lacking strategic importance. Thus, instead of attacking Kolombangara, he elected to strike Bougainville, to the north. One immediate consequence was that the Japanese shut down the Tokyo Express. Kolombangara now needed evacuation, not reinforcement, and that task could be handled by barges, at least under cover of darkness. Burke's new squadron could accordingly ignore the Slot and concentrate on securing forward positions.

DesRon 23 engaged in two important battles during Burke's four-month command, the battle of the Empress Augusta Bay (November 2, 1943) and the battle of Cape St. George (November 26); the latter earned Burke the Navy Cross, the second-highest honor that the service could bestow. Between the battles, Burke acquired a nickname that would enhance his growing reputation with the public. His destroyers were rated at 35 knots, but battle damage and lack of upkeep meant that most could sustain no better than 30 knots. To drive home the point, Burke began the practice of concluding his reports to headquarters with the notation that he was proceeding at a modest 30 knots per hour. When the prospect of new combat developed, Burke reported with enthusiasm that he was now proceeding at 31 knots. That brought a tweak from SOPAC, directing him to action and addressing him as "31-Knot Burke"; the order was signed "Halsey" (although actually written by a subordinate). Reporters immediately picked up the salutation and broadcast it globally. Although 31 knots was a modest pace for a destroyer, nonsailors assumed it was breakneck speed; as Burke's biographer later observed, the public "pictured Burke as a hotshot, hell-for-leather destroyer man, which of course he was. He thus gained worldwide celebrity, well-deserved though based on a misconception." After the war, Byron White told friends in Denver that *the press never worries about facts getting in the way of a good story.*

After the battle of Cape St. George, Burke's squadron spent the weeks between Thanksgiving and the end of the year providing cover to the delivery of supplies and development of the beachhead on Bougainville, less than two hundred miles from Rabaul. White received his promotion to full lieutenant on New Year's Day 1944. After the first of the year, the squadron established a distinguished record against installations on the Bismarck Islands, northwest of Bougainville and adjacent to Rabaul. So successful was the combined operation that Halsey convinced the Joint Chiefs of Staff that Rabaul could safely be bypassed without occupation and that the combined forces should now move even further north toward the Philippines. Aircraft carriers would play the dominant role in the drive north. To answer complaints from aviators that surface sailors at the command level were insufficiently responsive to their operational problems, the navy decided to mix the top echelon of command: a surface commander would have an aviator as a chief of staff, and an aviator who held command would have a surface sailor as chief of staff. In late March of 1944, Burke was relieved of his command of the Little Beavers—which was being absorbed into another unit—and ordered to report as Chief of Staff to ComCarDiv 3, the fast carrier task force of Rear Adm. Marc A. (Pete) Mitscher, whose flag was on the *Lexington*.

The new staffing policy made tactical and strategic sense, but confounded navy culture. The two worlds were wholly different in orientation, right down to their uniform shoe colors—black for surface and brown for air. The clash of cultures sometimes exaggerated personality differences between commanders and chiefs of staff, and the flag plot of the *Lexington* became a famous example. Mitscher enjoyed a reputation for daring, but he was reticent and physically frail—the common joke was that no matter what his age (he was then fifty-seven), he never looked a day over eighty. Burke was robust and outgoing, looked as if he never missed mess, and attracted wisecracks and loyalty in equal measure.

White followed Burke to the *Lexington* and Task Force 58 in May with a new title and no real experience to back it up—air combat intelligence officer (ACIO). His job was to brief and debrief pilots involved in combat operations and reconnaissance activities. The work was done, as one pilot on the ship later remembered, in a room that was "large and rather bare so we could spread the hundreds of 8 x 10 photos in overlapping strips on the deck." The pilot, three years younger than White, recalled that the "Director of Air Intelligence aboard the *Lexington* was a bright young Lieutenant by the name of Byron 'Whizzer' White." "Byron was probably the least anonymous junior officer in the navy," one of his fellow ACIOs, E. Calvert Cheston, later declared. "Everybody had heard of him, but no one could believe how unpretentious and down-to-earth he was. You couldn't get him to talk about his football days. He never brought it up, and if you did, he'd just shrug it off." Cheston cited White for his energy and organizational capacity aboard the *Lexington*, achievements that were important and underrecognized.

Soon White's work with the Little Beavers was recognized with a Bronze Star and a Presidential Unit Citation. His service was also recognized, rather breathlessly, Stateside. On June 1, 1944, ten days after White had joined Burke on the *Lexington,* the *Chicago Daily News* published a lengthy story under the byline of Harry Sheer that recounted the exploits of three of the 450 former National Football League players then in the armed services. All three were alumni of the 1941 Detroit Lions—Capt. Maurice (Footsy) Britt, who lost an arm and won the Congressional Medal of Honor for heroism in Italy, Ens. John R. Tripson, who won the Navy Cross after the North Africa campaign, and

> White . . . of U.S. Navy Intelligence. No one can tell his story yet. Whizzer could have stayed home, but he didn't want it that way. The marines rejected him, but the navy didn't. Soon he became a lieutenant (jg), a PT boat officer and the last picture of him was taken at Vella Lavella in the Central Solomons. The story of Whizzer White is probably the most hush-hush of any to come out of that area.
>
> Alone, equipped with only shorts and the necessaries of self-protection, Lt. White goes in and out of Jap lines, piercing deep into the periphery of Jap front lines. What he does there, what he brings back, no one but a few men know—and they aren't talking.
>
> "He—Byron White is the No. 1 outstanding candidate as THE hero of this war," said a high Navy officer recently, returned from the central Solomons.

The story was baseless, possibly the function of creative gossip that warfare and shore leave produce, especially to a credulous journalist whose regular beat was features, sailing, and sports quizzes. Neither White nor anyone else on Vella Lavella had any need to penetrate enemy lines on foot. The tactical and strategic objectives at the time White was on Vella Lavella were elsewhere, and PT intelligence officers did not need to be expended when surface patrols could provide as much control over remaining Japanese positions as was required. Yet the appetite for stories about White, which he paradoxically stimulated with his fierce reticence, gave Sheer's story more legs than it otherwise might have enjoyed. Every major newspaper in Colorado rehearsed the story. The *Fort Collins Coloradoan* headlined its summary and quotations from the *Daily News* story " 'Whizzer' White Rated Leading Hero of the War."

On July 3, Arthur Daley, the featured sports columnist for the *New York Times,* gave the phony story national prominence. Daley quoted twice from Sheer's story without actually acknowledging the source, then retold White's hinterlands-rags-to-NFL-riches story, briefly summarized the exploits of Britt and Tripson, and concluded:

Whatever Whizzer White has done to become an even greater hero than either of his teammates is one of those hush-hush propositions with which the navy cloaks its intelligence officers. His lone forays behind Japanese lines in the Solomons have been shrouded by utmost secrecy. But he is quite a lad is Whizzer White. And so are the hundreds of other National Football League stalwarts, professional sports' leading contributors to the war. More power to all of them.

When White received a clipping of the column several weeks after publication, he was furious. It was bad enough to repeat Sheer's fantasy, but it was worse to applaud White at the expense of two authentically heroic servicemen and former teammates. White wrote a letter to Daley in which he denounced the story, he told friends later, as "a goddamn lie." (When his friend and classmate Louis Oberdorfer repeated the story fifty years later in a tribute published in the *Yale Law Journal,* Oberdorfer was politely invited to lunch by White and rebuked for reprinting the lie.) Publicly, White dodged comment on the Sheer-Daley story. His only public statement about his war service by the summer of 1944 was made earlier in the spring in response to his medals for work with the Little Beavers: "I just got in on the gravy train. The other guys really deserved the medals. I came into the squadron from a PT job in November after the biggest work was done."

While Harry Sheer was fictionalizing White's war record, the Pacific campaign was building toward a climax. The Joint Chiefs authorized a plan whose objective was American control of the Luzon-China-Formosa triangle by early 1945. The fleet's job was in two sequential parts: first to support the invasion of the Mariana Islands and the Palaus, east of Japan, in June, then to support invasion of the southern Philippines under MacArthur in November. Thanks to cryptoanalysis and to captured secret documents, the Allies knew Japan's plan for defending against the advancing American fleet. By early June 1944, the Allied forces enjoyed superiority in both intelligence and firepower, including ships and aircraft.

One of the first steps in the new American plan was to "capture, occupy and defend" Saipan, Tinian, and Guam in the Marianas, located north of the Solomons and east of the Philippines. The Marianas were important enemy bases, and their control would put B-29 bombers within range of the Japanese mainland. The battle of the Philippine Sea was fought over two days, June 19–20, and resulted in devastating losses of Japanese aircraft as well as the torpedoing of two enemy carriers by U.S. submarines. Mitscher's planes sank a third carrier and damaged two others. Almost three hundred Japanese planes were lost in what Americans came to call the Great Marianas Turkey Shoot. The battle was a turning point, for both the forces and for Arleigh Burke, who finally won the confidence of his taciturn boss. Mitscher now trusted his chief of staff's tactical judgment and even began to open up personally. In rare moments of idle conversation, they discussed a common passion, fishing. Both men were invigorated by the bottom line of the battle in June—the Japanese fleet was in shambles, and the amphibious landings on Saipan were secure.

In September Halsey became fleet commander, and consequently the fleet name changed from Fifth to Third, and Mitscher's task force designation changed from 58 to 38. Halsey was itching to administer the kill to the crippled Japanese fleet, an itch that would prove tactically troublesome and, in the long run, blemish his career. The controversy over Halsey's judgment ensnared many officers in his command, including, at the fringes of the action, Lt. Byron R. White. The trouble arose less than a month after Halsey assumed fleet command in what came to be called the battle of Leyte Gulf, which was actually a series of four actions south of the island of Luzon, October 23–26. It was the greatest naval battle in history: more ships were engaged and more ships were lost with greater tonnage than in any other sea battle, including the battle of Jutland. More than two hundred thousand men participated. When the Leyte battles were over, Japan had effectively lost the Philippines, and with them their supply of natural resources. The battle of Leyte Gulf marked the beginning of the end for the Japanese empire.

The focal point of the battle was Douglas MacArthur's theatrically promised return to the Philippines following successful bombardment of Okinawa, Luzon, and Formosa. MacArthur's beachhead—with more than one hundred thousand troops of the Sixth U.S. Army—was on the island of Leyte. The Japanese plan was to lure Halsey's fast carrier task force (TF38) northeast of Leyte so that two striking forces, from the southwest and the northwest, could converge on the beachhead, expel MacArthur, and inflict as much damage as possible on the skeletal forces left behind. The bait for Halsey was the remains of the Japanese carrier force. Adm. Jizaburo Ozawa commanded the last four carriers in the Japanese fleet more than three hundred miles north of Leyte and hoped that Halsey would be more concerned with eradicating the carrier force than with adequately protecting the Leyte landing forces.

The plan almost worked. After Mitscher had repelled Admiral Takeo Kurita's task force from the southwest on October 24 as it crossed the Subuyan Sea, Halsey—crediting overly optimistic reports of the damage to Kurita—sent TF38 and its escort battleships and cruisers (TF34) north to engage Ozawa, who had just been sighted. Halsey had risen to the bait, but the plan began to go awry when the other half of the Japanese pincer from the south-west, the Southern Force under Vice Adm. Shoji Nishimura, was thwarted by Rear Adm. Thomas C. Kinkaid's Seventh Fleet (composed of battleships and cruisers) at Surigao Strait—the last battle-line engagement in naval history. Unhappily for the U.S. forces, Kurita returned after regrouping and ploughed through the San Bernardino Strait, heading for MacArthur's beachhead on Leyte. All that stood between Kurita's Central Force and the exposed American landing forces was Rear Adm. Clifton Sprague's tiny force of escort (or jeep) carriers and destroyers near Samar Island.

Frantic calls for help to Halsey, now nearly three hundred miles north of the crisis, at first seemed to fall on deaf ears. Then, prodded by an apparently sarcastic query from Adm. Chester Nimitz (Halsey's commander at Pearl Harbor), Halsey peeled off his fast battleships (TF34) under Vice Adm. Willis A. (Chink) Lee and sent them south to help Kinkaid. The decision turned out to be doubly futile. Without Lee, Halsey was unable to deliver the knockout punch to Ozawa, and Lee arrived too late to prevent Kurita's escape. Halsey was sharply criticized for leaving the San Bernardino Strait unprotected, but he declared that his biggest regret—and only mistake—was sending Lee south when he did.

Halsey's most dubious decision, however, was to chase the decoy in the first place and consequently to leave the San Bernardino Strait, and thus MacArthur's position, vulnerable. One of the many oddities of the four-day battle was that Halsey steamed north after Ozawa with no idea of his location after the initial sighting, late in the afternoon of October 24. In the early hours of October 25, a search plane from the light carrier *Independence* reported contact with what was now being called the Northern Force (Ozawa's fleet). Mitscher recommended that the fleet course be changed from northeast to north and that TF34 be formed. Halsey concurred, and the chase was on, although at the modest pace of 16 knots. Dawn broke at 0600 (6 A.M.), but the Northern Force was still nowhere to be found. Mitscher ordered three flight groups into the air—combat air patrol, search planes, and the first strike group. At 0730 there still was no contact—although some staff estimates earlier in the morning had placed Ozawa within eighty-five miles of TF38. After the war, C. Vann Woodward, fresh from Naval Intelligence, explained what happened next:

> Two young intelligence officers on Mitscher's staff, Lieutenants E. Calvert Cheston and Byron R. White, had been insisting on their belief that the Japanese carriers could be to the east of the scheduled search sectors, which

did not extend east of north. They were finally given permission to try out their theory. Instead of launching more search planes, they vectored out a division of four fighters from the combat air patrol.

At 0735 one of the planes spotted the entire Northern Force approximately two hundred miles east of Cape Engaño—the large carrier *Zuikaku,* three light carriers, two converted battleships, three light cruisers, and eight destroyers. Within an hour Mitscher's planes had the Northern Force under sustained attack. The most striking feature of the engagement was how few "bogeys" the enemy put in the air, a fact first attributed to surprise, then, in time, to the actual cause—Ozawa had next to no planes available. Success in the north was immediately tainted by a series of urgent messages from Kincaid requesting help against what first appeared to be the remnant of Kurita's force. Soon it was clear that almost the entire Central Force (four battleships and eight cruisers) was back in the San Bernardino Strait. Halsey ordered Vice Adm. John S. McCain's TF38.1, a subgroup of five carriers and four heavy cruisers, to assist Kincaid, but Halsey continued northward with both his battleships (TF34) and the other subgroups of his carrier force (TF38). Finally, at 1000, Nimitz's pointed dispatch arrived demanding to know where TF34 was, and Halsey sent the missing battleship task force south to aid Kincaid. In a further irony, Kurita broke off the engagement just at the point that the American forces seemed to be exhausted and reaching bottom on ammunition. Kurita thus saved Halsey from himself, and as Woodward wrote after the war, the battle turned on the Shakespearean personalities of its leaders—"an American Hotspur and a Japanese Hamlet."

As Woodward's account detailed for the first time, White and Cheston played a minor but valuable role in what was later called the battle of Cape Engaño (the nearest point of land on Luzon), or the second battle of the Philippine Sea. Mitscher's tactic of sortieing his planes *before* sighting the enemy was designed to give the attack planes a head start on their targets, but the gambit could work only if the targets were quickly found; otherwise the planes would need to return to the carrier to be refueled—a wasteful and potentially dangerous result. By revectoring search planes to the northeast, where Ozawa was quickly located, Cheston and White saved Mitscher hours of fruitless flying and probably changed the calculus of Halsey's eventual decision, at 10 A.M., to peel off his battleships for a run south. Mitscher's action report acknowledges the value of the White-Cheston suggestion. One of the four recommendations at the conclusion of Mitscher's fifty-eight-page report was, "Carrier searches should be made in all directions from which enemy carriers might approach."

In retrospect, both White and Cheston were dismissive of their contributions. "I thought they'd be where they could get some land-based fighter protection," White was later quoted as saying. Cheston viewed the incident as a triumph of persistence more than ingenuity. "We just wanted to pursue the only logical direction we hadn't," he recalled matter-of-factly years later. "The real problem was a combination of personality and command structure. Halsey had functionally displaced Mitscher as tactical commander for the operation, so Mitscher wasn't inclined to push Halsey on anything, and he wasn't interested in seizing the initiative either." Both White and Cheston were dismayed the night of the twenty-fourth, when Burke and Comdr. James Flatley, the staff operations officer, awoke Mitscher and vainly tried to convince him to recommend to Halsey either a reversal of course, from north to south, or at least a detachment to guard the San Bernardino Strait. *Mitscher listened, shrugged, and just went back to sleep in his sea cabin,* White later recalled to friends in Denver.

Halsey probably could not have been swayed anyway. He was set on his course (in every respect), he hated being contradicted—especially with battle impending—and he wasn't about to repeat Adm. Raymond Spruance's mistake of six months earlier, in the first battle of the Philippine Sea, when the enemy carriers were on the ropes but were not knocked out. Kincaid could have protected himself by better reconnaissance of enemy positions and by ascertaining more quickly the extent of his support. Nonetheless, Halsey knew he had misstepped, notwithstanding his consistent, bitter denials for the rest of his life. As Clark G. Reynolds, historian of the fast carriers, has aptly observed, Halsey began his self-defense "immediately"—the night of October 25, in a report to Nimitz and MacArthur that reads like a brief for the defendant in a court of inquiry. Although there was some question whether Halsey should formally answer for his command decisions October 24–25, his vast popularity insulated him from close public scrutiny, and certainly from being relieved of command. The navy tacitly acknowledged his questionable judgment by deferring his promotion to a fifth star until after the war, an unobtrusive but, within the service, unequivocal message that on the ninetieth anniversary of the Charge of the Light Brigade, "someone had blundered."

President Roosevelt was so cheered by the "rout" of the Japanese fleet in the Philippines that he called an impromptu press conference on October 25 to proclaim the news. Although the enemy fleet had not been completely destroyed, the losses were enormous—one large and three medium carriers, three battleships, six heavy and four light cruisers, eleven destroyers, four submarines, 116 aircraft, and more than ten thousand men; the United States lost nine ships, a few planes, and fifteen hundred men. On November 11, Roosevelt was elected to an unprecedented fourth term over New York governor Thomas E. Dewey, who had initially considered making Pearl Harbor a campaign issue before backing off. Byron White arrived home in Wellington on November 7 on thirty-day leave, in time to vote for Roosevelt (a second time). The *Fort Collins Coloradoan* immediately pounced on him for an interview by telephone. The *Coloradoan* found him to be "still the same modest, unassuming hero," who said "that the story of his tour of duty in the Pacific war theater was nothing compared to what many of the fighting men had done." Asked how much the country had changed during his eighteen-month absence, he replied: "The mountains and wonderful Colorado air are the same and that is what I am enjoying the most." Souvenirs?

> He said he didn't bring any souvenirs home from the Pacific because as far as he was concerned there wasn't anything there worth bringing back. He said he was perfectly willing to leave everything in that part of the world just where it was and let the natives have all their south and central Pacific islands.

End of interview. The article rehearsed the *Chicago Daily News* story from early June, but White's only comment about his work—issued at the top of the interview—was that "he was not at liberty to discuss the work he had done."

When White returned to duty on Burke's staff, he was aboard a new ship, the fast carrier *Bunker Hill*, Mitscher's flagship. TF58, as it was now redesignated with its original number, had new objectives as well as a new fleet organization. With the Japanese fleet decimated, the U.S. Navy's principal tasks were threefold: to frustrate Japanese merchant shipping in the East China Sea, to support the invasion of Japanese-held island bases surrounding Japan, and to make pinpoint air strikes on strategic targets in Japan. All three jobs were dangerous, but the second was the most time consuming, and freighted with high-casualty risks. The carriers were particularly vulnerable to the latest Japanese weapon, a tactic that bewildered the Western serviceman—the kamikaze ("divine wind"), or suicide, mission, flown by young poorly trained pilots who would die in the process of inflicting potentially massive damage to American ships. The tactic was introduced in the final stages of the battle of Leyte Gulf and became a grim feature of the rest of the war in the Pacific. The first major engagement for Mitscher's task force was in February in support of the invasion of Iwo Jima, the most famous battle of the war and one of the bloodiest; in one day alone, for example, five Congressional Medals of Honor were awarded in one division. The carriers provided preinvasion bombardment, the heaviest for any single landing in the entire Pacific Theater.

Byron White's last service in harm's way came less than two months after Iwo Jima. On April Fool's Day 1945—which also was Easter Sunday—the Allies began a massive invasion against Okinawa, the island fortress that could serve as the launching pad for the final assault on the home islands of Japan. The island was located 340 miles south of the Japanese mainland and an equal distance from Formosa. The battle, which would last eighty-three days, involved more Allied troops (540,000), more ships (sixteen hundred), and more firepower than the more publicized D-Day invasion of Europe, ten months before. By the time the battle was over, the island would be secured at a cost of more than fifty thousand American casualties, compared to one hundred thousand Japanese and Okinawan militia lost. The suicidal tactics of the Japanese reached their peak on Okinawa, both on land, where the rallying cry was to drown the invader in Japanese blood, and in kamikaze sorties at landing forces and supporting naval positions.

The invasion went forward, inch by bloody inch. The army had difficulty establishing its own airfields on the island, so the navy needed to provide air support for a longer period of time than during other island invasions. The Japanese responded with massed kamikaze attacks, called *kikusui* ("floating chrysanthemums"). Between April 6 and June 22, more than nineteen hundred kamikaze sorties were launched, inflicting unprecedented losses on the Allied naval forces. The strategy meant that Halsey's carriers were under constant alert, beginning the day with general quarters and frequently awaiting attack for forty minutes at a time. Although flight crews were carefully rested at routine periods, the deck crews were not, and by mid-April, Mitscher's staff—including Burke and his principal ACIOs, Cheston and White—had been at sea unrelieved for almost sixty consecutive days. White marveled at Cheston's durability: *The guy lived on coffee and aspirin,* he told friends in Denver after the war, *and could work around the clock.*

On April 11, the divine wind struck the *Bunker Hill* with devastating consequences. The ship was one hundred miles east of Okinawa, serving two functions—direct air support for the Southern Force ashore, and fighter plane cover over the island. At 1002, the flag duty officer notified Mitscher and Burke that a returning support group might be inadvertently providing cover for enemy planes. The report sent a shiver down the spine of Burke, who was superstitiously convinced that 1000 was the prime time for air-to-ship attacks. At 1004, the alert was sounded and the first kamikaze hit the *Bunker Hill.* A five-hundred-pound bomb released by the diving plane blew through the side of the ship and exploded above water. The plane itself hit the flight deck, rammed a group of fighters manned for takeoff, and exploded into flames. A second "Judy" dive-bomber shot past the ship at full throttle, steeply climbed to port, then dropped its bomb—which hit amidships and exploded on the gallery deck—and crashed less than one hundred feet from where Admiral Mitscher stood on the flag bridge. Smoke poured into the flag plot, and Burke ordered all staff out. A third kamikaze was shot down by antiaircraft fire as Burke evacuated the staff. The premium now was on controlling the fires on the flight and gallery decks. The American carriers were more vulnerable to kamikaze attack than their British counterparts, because their flight decks lacked armor. "They were basically nothing more than reinforced plywood," E. Calvert Cheston later emphasized. "That meant that the Zeros and Judies punched right through the flight deck into the hangar and stores, like a multi-ton match in a gasoline and powder magazine." After the war, back in Denver, White would credit Cheston with saving his life: *I was below, and he said, "You better get up here, because it's getting pretty hot!" A few minutes after I made it out, the staff quarters were hit.*

Until rescue efforts began in earnest, none in the flag area knew that the second bomb had killed thirteen of Mitscher's staff. For more than five hours, the crew of the *Bunker Hill* fought to extinguish the fire and to rescue men who were trapped by smoke, either in the ready room of the flight squadron or in other locations. Several weeks later, Arleigh Burke poured compliments on several members of his staff, including White and Cheston, for their work during the lengthy fire-fighting ordeal. "There were some fine stories of bravery came out of that burning, exploding mess with gasoline fires all over the decks," Burke wrote his wife, Bobbie, including "Anderson [who] fought fires in the hangar deck and gradually, by pure guts and will power, brought them under control [and] White and Cheston who also fought fires and brought out suffocated men."

In an interview several days after writing the letter, Burke told the *Rocky Mountain News:*

> White and two other officers were down below when we were hit. They got as far as the hangar deck, where gasoline in planes was burning and ammunition going off in all directions. They led fire-fighting parties and often manned hoses themselves. They did a beautiful job.

Years later Burke wrote a testimonial letter for White that said, in part:

> I remember one time when I saw him use his phenomenal strength to lift a beam in the [*Bunker Hill*] to rescue some people who were pinned under a beam and were about to be killed by fire. He had personal strength and was

outstanding even among people who exhibited strength for nonpersonal reasons.

Cheston later recalled that White seemed oblivious to his own physical safety during the four hours that they personally fought the fires and pulled asphyxiating men from smoke-engulfed positions: "He was absolutely focused on the fires and on the men. A shell would go off or an explosion would occur, but there was Byron—locked in on the man who needed help or on the hose that needed to be manned. I don't think he ever thought about himself. We were all working frantically, but he stayed so cool it was almost unnerving. And he never took a rest."

The *Bunker Hill* was too badly damaged for Mitscher to continue his command there, so Burke organized the evacuation to the destroyer *English*, which began at 1500 and concluded, with Burke the last man off, at 1630. More than three hundred men had been killed, including the thirteen from Mitscher's own staff. Most of the fighter squadron, who had been in the ready room when the second dive-bomber hit, were killed by smoke. Another forty-three crew members were missing, and 264 were wounded. Burke, so generous in praise of others and so modest about himself, received a Silver Star for his work following the attack on the *Bunker Hill*.

Admiral Mitscher now commanded TF58 from the *Enterprise,* a carrier deployed for night work, unlike the *Bunker Hill.* That meant that operation ran from dusk until dawn and that the crew was at general quarters during daylight, which proved to be fortunate for Mitscher and his staff. The strategic question now was how to deploy the task force's air assets. Mitscher thought that his planes could be best utilized near Okinawa for close-support duties; Burke and others, frustrated that they were becoming sitting ducks, urged him to bomb the airfields on Kyushu that spawned the kamikazes. With reluctance, and a big nudge from Admiral Spruance, Mitscher capitulated, and for two days planes from the *Enterprise* sortied against Kyushu. On the morning of May 14, 1945, at 0620, Mitscher was called to the flag bridge with the message that enemy planes had been sighted. The flag bridge on the *Enterprise* was above the ship's bridge, exposed, unlike on the *Bunker Hill,* whose flag bridge enjoyed the protection of the ship's bridge overhead. From the flag bridge, Mitscher and several members of his staff—including Burke, William A. (Gus) Read (who had duty watch), communications officer Frank Dingfelder, and White—watched for the four-plane group of Zeros that had been sighted.

The planes had been sent with orders to "Get the carriers!" in retaliation for the audacious strikes on the home islands. Three of the Zeros were quickly knocked out by antiaircraft fire, but the fourth, piloted by Lt. Tomai Kai, popped from a cloud at fifteen hundred feet and locked a course on the *Enterprise,* scarcely two hundred yards away. At that moment, White raised his left arm and sighted the trajectory of the flight path down his arm. *He's head-on for the bridge,* White said quietly. *We've had it.* Then, at what seemed like the last second, the pilot veered from his fifty-degree dive, nosed directly into the flight deck, and simultaneously released his five-hundred-pound bomb with delayed-action fuse. The bomb went down the elevator well and exploded with a deafening, jolting roar that tossed the elevator roof like a giant cookie sheet into the sea. The plane struck the ship at its most vulnerable location, the rear edge of the forward elevator.

Damage to the ship was substantial, but precautions that could not be taken on the *Bunker Hill* dramatically reduced the *Enterprise's* casualties. Crewmen on deck were wearing flashproof clothing and facial protection; planes were drained of fuel, disarmed, and stowed; fuel hoses were drained and filled with CO_2; compartments below had been made watertight by dogging down the bulkheads. Fire-fighting details were on alert. As a result, the fires were controlled within an hour; only thirteen crewmen were killed and another fifty-eight injured.

Mitscher enhanced his growing legendary reputation for cool bravery when the Zero struck. He refused to obey his operations officer, James Flatley, who yelled, "Hit the deck!" and, unscathed, he told Flatley, when everyone on the flag bridge was upright again, "Tell my task group commanders that if the Japs keep this up they're going to grow hair on my head yet." Mitscher and several members of his staff enjoyed a grisly memento of the attack: the pilot's intact body contained a fistful of calling cards, which Mitscher distributed to several of his staff members.

Although the fire was quickly controlled, the *Enterprise* required extensive repairs and was forced to retire. Mitscher and his staff were transferred to the *Randolph.* For all practical purposes, they were out of the war. Those who attended debriefings after the two kamikaze attacks were startled by how weary Mitscher's staff looked after nearly three months at sea, and shocked at how frail the admiral had become. Two weeks after leaving the *Enterprise,* Mitscher was relieved of command of the fast carriers (which again had the TF number changed, this time from 58 back to its original designation, 38). He and most of his staff flew to Guam, then via Halsey's private plane back to Pearl Harbor en route to the States. Mitscher's biographer later noted: "They held a formation behind the administration building at Pearl Harbor, and awards were presented. It looked very much like a parade of scarecrows," but "they were lucky, for more than two thousand men in Task Force 58 had not lived through the Okinawa campaign."

Byron White arrived back in Wellington at the end of May on rehabilitation leave, then returned to San Francisco to await further orders. While there, he billeted at the cottages located midway up Telegraph Hill on the Greenwich Steps and managed by Valetta Evalyn Heslet; she later became famous for her gardens and her enlightened judgment—and was portrayed fictionally in Armistead Maupin's *Tales of the City.* Also stationed in San Francisco was Lt. Marion Lloyd Stearns, one of the daughters of Robert Stearns, who was dean of the law school while White was an undergraduate and succeeded George Norlin in 1939 as president of the University of Colorado. She was one of the first women in Colorado to enter the WAVES (Women Accepted for Voluntary Emergency Service) when she enlisted, on September 5, 1942, after graduating from Vassar College. White had encountered her father at Pearl Harbor while awaiting transport and agreed to say hello to her when he arrived in San Francisco. The greeting began a romance that would lead to marriage within a year.

After temporary duty in the Bay Area, White was ordered to Washington, where he served on the intelligence staff of the chief of naval operations. The navy did not underestimate his publicity value. In September, for example, he was sent to Chicago to be interviewed on the Columbia Broadcasting System's radio program *The First Line,* on which he discussed recent aspects of the Pacific campaign. Three months later, White wrote his parents that his release from the navy was pending and that he expected to return to Yale Law School in time for the beginning of the second semester, in mid-January of 1946. When rumors in Colorado began to spread, the Associated Press interviewed White's mother by telephone, and the impending discharge became nationwide news—on the sports pages: "He told his parents in a recent letter he hadn't changed his mind about quitting football and going back to Yale to obtain his law degree."

Rumors continued to smolder, however, because White spent almost every Sunday in the fall of 1945 at Griffith Stadium, watching the Redskins, or, when they were on the road, in New York City at the Polo Grounds, watching the Giants. Of the ten game dates that season, all but two had either the Redskins or the Giants—an easy train ride away—playing at home. E. Calvert Cheston, who had served with White in the Pacific on Burke's staff and now shared housing with him in Washington, often tagged along, both to the games and to the postgame visits to the locker room, where White renewed prewar friendships and rivalries. "On those occasions, it was as if Byron had never left the game. They loved him, and he loved them. I think he had a real pang, being in the stands and not on the field."

9

SUPREME COURT:
OCTOBER TERM 1946

L IKE MANY servicemen mustering out after World War II, Byron White was determined to make up for lost time and committed to a personal agenda. He was formally separated from the naval reserve on January 25, 1946. He began classes at Yale Law School, but the interruptions caused by his play for the Detroit Lions meant that he would need both the spring and special summer terms before he could collect his LL.B. Less than a month after leaving the navy, his engagement to Marion Stearns was announced. A June wedding in Boulder was planned. The only remaining question was where to practice law, and on that point, White was uncharacteristically ambivalent. He later recalled:

> Before the war I was reasonably sure I wanted to practice law in New York, because that's where so much of the really significant law is handled. By the time the war was over I wasn't so excited with the idea of living in the East. That was one of the reasons I wanted [to work in Washington for a year]; I wanted a year to think things over.

A clerkship with one of the justices of the Supreme Court of the United States was the most prestigious one-year appointment available, and White had enjoyed Washington during his posting with the chief of naval operations. But there were only ten clerkship positions. Each justice was allotted one clerk, and the chief justice had two (a third position was created in the fall of 1946). By early March 1946, there was only one clerkship position that had not already been filled. The newest member of the Court, Justice Harold H. Burton, was the only justice still interviewing applicants. Two justices were carrying over clerks from previous term. Eugene Gressman (Michigan Law '40) was continuing with Justice Frank Murphy (as he had since October term 1943), and Murray Gartner (Harvard '45) was staying on the payroll of Justice Robert H. Jackson, although Jackson was returning to the Court after a one-year leave of absence as the chief prosecutor at the international military war crime trials in Nuremberg. Justice William O. Douglas hired clerks only from the West Coast, and his selection committee, headed by Prof. Max Radin of the University of California at Berkeley's Boalt Hall, selected Roger Wollenberg from Boalt. Justice Felix Frankfurter, per custom, had hired from Harvard (Louis Henkin); the other clerks would be from Yale (F. Aley Allen with Justice Stanley F. Reed, Louis F. Oberdorfer with Justice Hugo L. Black, and Richard F. Wolfson with Justice Wiley B. Rutledge).

Several members of the Yale Law School faculty were personally close to Justice Black, whose son Hugo Jr. was a first-year student there, and to Justice Douglas, who had taught there. Thanks to the energies of professors Fred Rodell and Walton Hale Hamilton, White secured interviews with Douglas and Burton on Monday, March 18, 1946. White spent a half hour with Douglas in the morning and with Burton after lunch, but to no avail. Although Burton told Fred Rodell he was "most impressed" with White, a job offer was out of the question, for a simple logistical reason that Burton noted in his diary: "'Whizzer' White of Yale Law School and formerly of Colorado and Oxford and the Navy came in about a law clerkship, but probably could not come before October, which makes it practically impossible to consider him." (Two weeks later, Burton interviewed Harris K. Weston of Harvard on the recommendation of James M. Landis, the former dean, and hired him on the spot.)

Rodell pushed hard for White with Douglas, notwithstanding the offer already accepted by Wollenberg. On March 19, the day after White interviewed Burton and Douglas, Rodell wrote Douglas:

> Thanks a lot for talking to Byron White yesterday; he enjoyed it and appreciated it tremendously. My guess would be that I need not add to the praise of him that I've already relayed to you, for he usually needs no outside salesman.

I am one hundred percent with him in hoping that Max Radin's boy—and other Ninth Circuit candidates—break their legs so that you might come around to White for next year. I know that you would never find an abler or nicer gent.

If Burton would not hire White, Rodell went on, there were others "somewhat behind White" who would satisfy Burton and coincidentally achieve another goal—"reduction in the number of Harvard clerks." Rodell, and others close to Black and Douglas, viewed the Harvard-trained clerks as too sympathetic to the views of Felix Frankfurter, their common bête noire: "If we can get Burton to take either White or [Jack] Furman [editor in chief of the *Yale Law Journal*], it would, I know, be a big help to you and Hugo. Can't we sell one of them to Rutledge?"

Rodell's scheme failed, but White's ambitions—and the Law School's— were ironically revived when Chief Justice Harlan Fiske Stone died suddenly on April 22. The vacancy ignited a chain reaction of intrigue within the Court, which culminated in an unprecedented breach of judicial decorum. Jackson, away at Nuremberg, had been promised the chief justiceship by Roosevelt, but Truman's succession to the presidency put off all bets, although Jackson privately hoped that his service at Nuremberg might fortify his candidacy to replace Stone. Word reached Jackson overseas that members of the Court, probably Black and Douglas, were working against his appointment. Truman consulted with retired chief justice Charles Evans Hughes, who privately recommended Jackson. Truman, knowing that Jackson's appointment would cause unpredictable repercussions both inside and outside the Court, instead appointed a crony, Frederick M. Vinson, his secretary of the Treasury.

When Vinson was named, Jackson unleashed a temperamental public statement from Nuremberg excoriating Black for unethical behavior. The statement was not without substance, but it was wholly lacking in judgment and taste, and several newspapers called for both justices to be impeached. Vinson, inevitably identified in the press as a peacemaker, was nominated as the thirteenth chief justice of the United States on June 6. Without missing a beat, Douglas wrote Vinson the next day recommending

White, who comes from Colorado and who is finishing at Yale Law School this summer. You have probably read of him [in] the sport section of the newspapers. He was an All-American football player whose nickname was Whizzer White. He played professional football. He was in the service for a couple of years. He has led his class at Yale Law School for three years. Members of the faculty tell me he is the most outstanding man they have had in a long time. As a matter of fact, he probably will have an all-time scholastic record at Yale Law School. He is a delightful person, of great charm and poise.

Douglas disavowed knowledge of White's plans, but volunteered to "see that he gets down here right away" for an interview if Vinson wished.

Douglas knew his quarry. Vinson was a dignified but down-to-earth man from small-town Kentucky who was a former semipro baseball player and enthusiastic sports fan. White's résumé was the perfect combination for Vinson. The real matchmaker, however, was Karl R. Price, whom White knew at both Oxford and Yale. Price, like Vinson, was a Kentucky native. Vinson hired him as a law clerk from the Treasury, where he was an assistant to the undersecretary. Price convinced White to apply for the job, and suddenly White's career plans seemed to jell overnight, marred only by the death of his favorite uncle, Charles S. White, on May 16 in Audubon, Iowa. (The size of the estate surprised everyone. The crusty small-town lawyer, who privately complained throughout the 1930s about his finances, had assets that eventually were liquidated after 14 years of probate for more than $250,000 and distributed among two dozen relatives, with modest sums to the Whites of Wellington.) Byron White and Marion Stearns were married on June 15 at St. John's Episcopal Church in Boulder, Colorado, and a clerkship seemed to be in the offing. Tradition reigned at the wedding: the same kneeling bench that Marion Stearns's parents had used at their wedding was used again, and Sam White returned his brother's favor by serving as best man. The social pages of the local newspapers reported the ceremony with their customary detailed attention to attire and decor, and the only slip in formal tone appeared in the cutlines to White's picture: "Byron (Whizzer) White."

On August 12 the *Boulder Daily Camera* reported that Vinson had appointed White as one of his law clerks for October term 1946. United Press did not pick up on the story for more than a month, but on September 19 UP reported that the clerkship "was disclosed today." Shortly before starting the new job, White stayed briefly in the Washington suburbs with a college friend, Wes McCune, now a journalist. McCune had just completed a short book on the Supreme Court, tentatively titled *The Nine Young Men.* McCune asked White to read the manuscript, ostensibly to check for errors concerning constitutional law, but also for White's reaction to the portrait of White's new employer. White's reaction to the draft? "Kind of a muffled grunt," McCune later recalled.

A few days later, in the edition dated September 30 but published a week earlier, *Time* magazine ran a one-column photo of a bespectacled White, suit jacket buttoned and two law books crooked under his arm. "Byron ('Whizzer') White, All-America halfback, Rhodes Scholar and Navy hero, who forsook professional football's enticements ($15,000 a season) to study law, got the job most coveted by fledgling barristers. The job: clerk to Fred M. Vinson, Chief Justice of the U.S." The pay, which *Time* did not mention, was $5,116 per year. *Time*'s sister magazine, *Life*, ran a four-photo spread dated the same day under the headline "U.S. Youth Pushes Itself into the News." The bottom two photos were of Mary Ellen Quinn, who won a contest at De-Paul University for the prettiest woman with an I.Q. of at least 120, and Elihu Yale, the twenty-two-year-old ninth-generation descendent of the university's founder. The top two photos were of Whizzer White and John F. Kennedy—the first time that the two men would be yoked together, even accidentally, in the public imagination. The caption under White's picture read:

A 29-year-old All-American halfback from Colorado (1938), Byron ("Whizzer") White was ready to get his Yale Law degree and take over his fine new job as clerk in the office of Chief Justice Fred Vinson, a post regarded as one of the best plums a young lawyer can get. White, shown above beside a portrait of Justice Holmes, spent two years between college and law school playing professional football and serving in the Navy.

The caption under Kennedy read:

The 29-year old son of Joseph P. Kennedy, former U.S. Ambassador to Britain, this month campaigned hotly in Massachusetts' 11th District, where he is Democratic candidate for Congress and where, 50 years ago, his grand-father was a representative. He won nomination last June in a slam-bang fight. A PT-boat skipper during the war, ex-Lieutenant Kennedy was ship-wrecked on a Pacific Island, won Navy and Marine Corps Medal.

Kennedy was accustomed to such attention. John Hersey had published a stirring account of the PT *109* episode in June 1944 in the *New Yorker,* which the *Reader's Digest* reprinted two months later. The *Life* pictorial, appearing two weeks before the congressional election, was more than welcome and a partial nationwide antidote to *Look*'s multipage spread of June 11, which ridiculed his rich-boy candidacy. Despite a Republican sweep in statewide of-fices, Kennedy won the congressional seat with almost 73 percent of the vote.

White, unlike Kennedy, did not welcome the attention from the press. He formally received his law degree in November (although he had started work with Vinson in mid-September), at the end of the "summer" term. He was the first magna cum laude graduate in ten years, since Lloyd Cutler (who later became a prominent Washington lawyer and counsel to Presidents Jimmy Carter and Bill Clinton). Nonetheless, some clerks at the Supreme Court, at least those whom White did not know at Yale, were initially skeptical of his ability. His other coclerk besides Price, Francis A. Allen, later explained: "Everyone had heard of him, of course. There was a famous play in the pros when he grabbed the ball out of his opponent's hands and ran all the way back for a touchdown. It was all over the press. It is hard to overstate how famous he was. That bred skepticism, although I could tell in five minutes of conversation that he was extraordinarily bright. I could not at that time tell how well educated he was, but he quickly disabused anyone who underestimated his native ability. . . . We all expected him to run for public office: he was famous, smart and good-looking. He was a poor public speaker, however, which would handicap him."

Allen and White shared a partners' desk just outside the Supreme Court conference room. For a year, they sat at arm's length—a cozy arrangement dictated by Vinson's insistence on having three law clerks in a space designed for one or two. Allen thus became a forced eavesdropper on nonbusiness calls to White's desk. At the beginning of their term together, Allen learned both how much of a celebrity White was and how little he enjoyed the status. For weeks at the beginning of the term, for example, White received constant telephone calls from Ann Golenpaul, the senior producer of *Information, Please!*, the radio quiz show over which Clifton Fadiman presided, which anchored CBS's Tuesday night schedule from 1938 to 1947, when it moved to the Mutual Network. Fadiman would ask a panel of scholars a series of questions submitted by listeners over a wide variety of topics. Politicians and other celebrities joined regular panelists, principally Franklin P. Adams, John Kiernan, and Oscar Levant, for a weekly quiz that featured witty exchanges, puns, and the occasional cutting riposte. After several telephone invitations, White finally slammed down the phone in frustration after explaining to Golenpaul for the last time why he would not appear on the program: *You're not asking me because of my academic record—all the fellas here have a good one—you're asking me because I was an all-American football player, and I won't do it.* Allen was surprised that White was so adamant, but "he explained to me when I pushed him about it that he was afraid his career would be damaged by appearing to capitalize on his past, especially because it was not a serious enterprise."

White enforced his new self-imposed noncelebrity status rigidly. The only exception was for Vinson himself, and it came reluctantly. Vinson volunteered White—without his knowledge—to speak at one of his sons' prep school sports banquets. When White learned of the obligation, he told Vinson, *I don't want to do this.* Vinson insisted and implored: *You can't make me look bad in front of my son.* "That was that," Allen remembered, "and Byron complied reluctantly." Vinson was a demanding taskmaster who expected six-day weeks and saw no reason to bestow the warm, avuncular attention on his staff that made Black, Frankfurter, and Jackson so popular with their clerks. If a clerk wished to schedule a wedding, he needed to check the conference schedule first; there were no excused absences. If Vinson invited the justices to listen to the Kentucky Derby on his office radio and only Harold Burton showed up, then all three clerks and the administrative assistant to the chief justice were expected to be there—even at 5:45 P.M. on a Saturday in May. If Vinson wanted to chat about football or the World Series, the agenda was not negotiable.

Fred Vinson came to the Supreme Court with a distinguished record in government, the absolute confidence of the president who appointed him, and the wrong skills for the job. He was the son of the town jailer in Louisa, Kentucky, had worked his way through Centre College, and had achieved the highest academic record in the school's history. His career rocketed him from city attorney to Congress, where he became an effective legislative broker and a genial opportunist. He coauthored the Guffey Coal Act (which by custom should have been known as the Guffey-Vinson Act), which the Supreme Court invalidated in *Carter v. Carter Coal* in 1936. He negotiated revisions of the law that passed constitutional muster after he had left Congress. President Roosevelt appointed him to the District of Columbia Court of Appeals in 1937, but he resigned from the court in 1943 to become director of the Office of Economic Stabilization. Vinson later successively became Federal Home Loan administrator and director of the Office of War Mobilization and Reconversion before finally joining the cabinet as President Truman's secretary of the Treasury in July of 1945. Many suspected that his career coasted smoothly because of his unassuming personal skills and his deft management of Sam Rayburn's campaign for the Democratic leadership of the House of Representatives in 1937, for which Rayburn was forever grateful.

Truman thought that Vinson had the capacity to harmonize a badly fractionated Court, which had been embarrassed by deep and snide divisions even before Jackson's tirade from Nuremberg. The president misunderstood the problem, and his appointee was poorly equipped to meet the challenge. Vinson lacked both the taste for the complex work of the Court and the fine-tuned analytical skills to lead some of the ablest and most self-confident men ever to sit on the Court—particularly Black, Frankfurter, Douglas, and Jackson. As an administrator, Vinson had become accustomed to staffing out the close analytical work, a habit that betrayed him in the Court's conferences, which only the justices attended. He was left to homely nostrums, such as, "You can't run the world from this chair"—a response that had no traction in the acrid debates, which constantly veered between detailed technical analysis and larger theoretical perspectives, often based in detailed constitutional history. Vinson's strength was in absorbing large quantities of material and analysis that were provided orally to him—again, a skill essential to a cabinet officer but deeply inadequate for the type and quantity of information that reached the Supreme Court.

Vinson's initial strategy to reduce the Court's conspicuous fractiousness was twofold: to cut down the caseload to more manageable proportions, perhaps in order to reduce opportunities for division, and to minimize dissent, apparently by setting an accommodating example that placed institutional unity over individual declaration. Both strategies failed to appreciate the decision-making dynamics of a small group whose presiding officer is only primus inter pares, and consequently were doomed. Vinson nonetheless stuck to his guns. He voted to grant certiorari, or to note probable jurisdiction, only 114 times during his entire first term. Most justices voted to grant review half again as often, with Murphy the leader of the pack at 209. The Court disposed of 144 cases with full opinion; ninety-two, or 64 percent, were nonunanimous, and twenty-six—almost 20 percent—were by 5-4 vote. The figures for nonunanimous and 5-4 decisions almost exactly matched those for the 1944 term under Stone, the last time that the Court was at full strength. Vinson cast only nine dissenting votes during the term, easily the lowest number for the entire Court; Rutledge cast the most, with thirty; and the median number was twenty-one, shared by Black, Douglas, and Murphy. The number of cases filed continued to grow steadily, from 1,161 to 1,366.

Of particular concern to Vinson was the in *forma pauperis** docket, which had trebled in only five years, from 178 to 528, although only eight cases were granted from that docket during the 1946 term, slightly below the annual average over the past five years. Vinson's principal contribution to the management of the Court's internal affairs was to centralize the preliminary analysis of i.f.p. petitions. One of the main reasons for the addition of a third clerk to the chief justice's office was so that all i.f.p. filings could be read and analyzed by one of the chief justice's clerks. The problem had been that treatment of i.f.p. petitions had been sluggish because there was only one set of papers,

---

* Cases in which the party applying to the Court certifies that he cannot afford to pay the fee for filing his application. Most cases at the time consisted of applications from prisoners seeking review of their convictions after a state or federal court had rejected their initial appeal.

which had to circulate from office to office. Vinson's system loaded the work on his clerks, but the rest of the Court was briefed much more quickly on the content of new filings on the so-called pauper's docket. Karl Price operated as the senior clerk in the chief justice's chambers for the 1946 term, which meant that he assigned cases for preargument bench memoranda, for internal memos on paid certiorari petitions, and for i.f.p. memos to the entire Court.

None of White's bench memos or memos for paid cases exist in the Vinson Papers at the University of Kentucky, but more than 175 memos on i.f.p. filings have survived in the Stanley F. Reed Papers in the same library. The available memos confirm the assessment of White by his coclerk Frank Allen: "I only began to understand his views, which I think were well formed by the time he arrived at the Court, in talking with him about cases and cert petitions. He was a classic New Deal liberal who believed in the affirmative obligations of government and who was skeptical of limits on government power—be it due process requirements in administrative cases or the Fourth Amendment or whatnot. He was very skeptical of judges. Unlike most of the Yale clerks, who were pretty far left without being communists, he was well on the right. He was a lot like Vinson: very smart, very down-to-earth, and very scornful of big theory. Byron always focused on the context of any case and on its details. His broad perspectives were always grounded by the facts of the particular cases."

Allen added that White privately defended Vinson against his in-house critics: "Byron admired Vinson's background. I once said that I knew six law professors who could do the job better than all but three members of the Court. Byron adamantly disagreed: *You must have experience. You need to know how the law affects people, and you need perspective in order to do the job well.*"

White's surviving i.f.p. memos contain no smoking gun that reveals his view of constitutional criminal procedure or the judicial function in a sentence or two. The memos are highly repetitive, reflecting the twice-told-tale nature of the filings and White's surgical identification of the decisive case or fact that would dispose of the case. A substantial share of the i.f.p. filings were legally frivolous. In addition, many petitioners, proceeding *pro se,* either lacked the necessary information to formulate a legal argument or sought relief that was inappropriate or authoritatively precluded by precedent or statute. Numerous cases during the term were disposed of on the authority of *Woods v. Nierstheimer,* which was decided in May of 1946. *Woods* held that Illinois could require prisoners seeking release from state prison because their convictions violated the Fourteenth Amendment to proceed by a *coram nobis* writ as opposed to habeas corpus—more than a technicality, because *coram nobis,* unlike habeas corpus, carried a five-year statute of limitations. Of the 528 i.f.p. filings in the 1946 term, a substantial majority—322, or 61 percent—came from Illinois, usually claims from state prisoners that they had been denied effective assistance of counsel at trial. In no i.f.p. case did White suggest that the Court grant review, a startling statistic until one remembers that the entire Court granted review to only 1.5 percent of i.f.p. filings. Three memos, considered here in chronological order, illustrate the analytical approach, in focus and tone, that White commonly adopted with nonfrivolous i.f.p. filings.

*D*avis v. Smyth, which arose two months after White began work, illustrates the stringent prerequisites to habeas corpus relief that the Supreme Court enforced at the time. On a practical level, the case is one more example of the steady and ugly parade of abusive Southern justice in which black defendants received no better than the appearance of due process of law. Willie Davis was a repeat offender who received an eight-year sentence for felonious assault; he plausibly claimed that he was denied the right to effective assistance of counsel, in violation of *Powell v. Alabama* (the case of the Scottsboro Boys). His lawyer was appointed on the day of the trial, had no opportunity to confer with him, and failed to seek a continuance so that defense witnesses could be called. Years later Davis sought habeas corpus in state court, which was denied by the trial court and the Virginia Supreme Court of Appeals. Davis then went to the federal district court, which denied relief. The federal court of appeals affirmed, following the rule of *White v. Ragen,* the 1945 per curiam decision precluding federal habeas relief unless the denial of relief in the state system had been presented to the Supreme Court of the United States. Davis then started all over again in the Virginia Supreme Court and petitioned for certiorari when he was denied relief without opinion.

White was sympathetic to Davis's claim, and noted that the federal court of appeals "seemed to think, as I do, that petitioner's allegations, taken as true, constituted a violation of his rights to counsel." The Virginia Supreme Court's summary disposition of Davis's claim did not strike White as "complete protection of constitutional rights to counsel," so he recommended that "a response [from the state] should be called for at least." The Court was unmoved, and the petition for certiorari was denied with no dissent. The reason is probably to be found in Justice Reed's cool reaction to White's memo. Reed scribbled a penciled note on the White memo indicating that *Williams v. Kaiser,* decided the year before, refuted White's analysis. That case held that "where the decision of the state court might have been either on a state ground or on a federal ground and the state ground is sufficient to sustain the judgment, the

Court will not undertake to review it." Thus, the petitioner had the burden of showing that the decision below did not rest on a state ground—a burden, of course, that would often be impossible to meet, and that stood as a bar to review in the Supreme Court until 1972, when *California v. Krivda* provided the Court with a remand mechanism to force the state court to identify which ground—state or federal—had been decisive.* White's two-page cert memo, which probably should have flagged the *Williams v. Kaiser* issue, can only be explained as hasty, a rare moment where his concern for the merits overcame his customarily meticulous survey of jurisdictional and prudential bars to relief—a mistake not repeated during the balance of the term.

Trudell v. Mississippi, which arose late in the term, produced the longest of White's i.f.p. memoranda—five careful, closely analyzed pages. The case, actually two petitions by separate defendants, obviously troubled White, but not enough to recommend that the Court grant review. Two black boys, aged fourteen and fifteen, were convicted and sentenced to death for the murder of a farmer for whom they had done day labor. They were arrested the day after the murder nearly one hundred miles from the site of the crime, confessed, were moved to another location, confessed again, and finally returned to a jail near their home. The day after they were indicted, the fourteen-year-old retained counsel; he was convicted a week later. The fifteen-year-old was provided with appointed counsel and convicted the following day. Their convictions were affirmed by the Supreme Court of Mississippi.

Thurgood Marshall of the National Association for the Advancement of Colored People (NAACP) Legal Defense and Education Fund filed petitions for certiorari in both cases, but he had little to work with, and White concluded with little hesitation that "cert should be denied in each case." Neither petitioner had raised a federal question in the state courts. There were vague allegations about a lack of fair trial, but none was tied to the federal Constitution or to Supreme Court precedent. The two most substantial issues were the confession and the effectiveness of counsel, but neither issue as presented was "certworthy"—that is, of sufficient moment under the Court's rules and practices to justify a hearing. Marshall's petition did not claim that the confession was coerced by threats or by violence, only that it was obtained while the petitioner was alone, frightened, and far from home. The appointed counsel had only one day to prepare, but according to White, conducted an active defense.

---

* The Court now presumes that the decision below rests on federal grounds, even though the lower court may cite both state and federal authority. *Michigan v. Long,* 463 U.S. 1032 (1983).

Marshall was in the awkward position of arguing not that governing federal case law was misapplied, but that a novel confession issue and a common "effective assistance of counsel issue" should be addressed for the first time in the Supreme Court—an argument contrary to the Court's rules, practice, and precedent. The only hope was practical, not logical: perhaps the Court could be stirred by the summary nature of the arrest and trial, by the youth of the defendants, or by growing perceptions that Jim Crow infected the entire system of criminal justice in the South. One of the defendants had been referred to by the trial judge as a "colored boy" in front of the jury, which included one man who expressed full-throated enthusiasm before the trial began for imposing the death penalty. The Court denied certiorari, but Marshall got two votes, from Justices Murphy and Rutledge.

Smith v. California, which came down on the penultimate decision day of the term, was a routine but not uninteresting case involving the scope of the Court's "effective assistance of counsel" cases. The petitioner was a nineteen-year-old army sergeant who was indicted for murder, kidnapping, and robbery. He was arraigned on May 9, 1944, counsel was appointed, and he pleaded not guilty. Trial was scheduled for June 16. Four days before trial, on June 12, his relatives retained private counsel. Motion to substitute counsel was made June 14, but was denied. According to White,

> Court was reluctant to bring about a situation in which a continuance would be necessary, stated that the public defender had had ample time to prepare, allowed the private counsel to associate himself with the case, ordered the public defender to remain in the case, and indicated that the latter might withdraw when the trial opened.

On the day of trial, the public defender's motion to withdraw was denied, private counsel's motion for a continuance was denied, and both counsels told the court that they were uncomfortable proceeding. The trial judge postponed trial for three days, the public defender was excused, further continuance was refused, and the trial lasted ten days. The petitioner was convicted and sentenced to life imprisonment. His appeal, alleging denial of a fair trial by the refusal of a continuance, was unsuccessful, although two members of the California Supreme Court dissented on the ground that denial of the continuance was inconsistent with the United States Supreme Court's line of cases beginning with *Powell v. Alabama.*

The petitioner then applied for habeas corpus in the California Supreme Court. The writ was denied without a hearing, but again with the same two justices dissenting. White dispatched the petition from that denial, which was prepared by counsel, with one terse paragraph:

> Petitioner relies upon *Powell,* 287 US 45; *Avery,* 308 US 444; *Mangum,* 237 US 309; *O'Grady,* 312 US 329; *Betts* v. *Brady,* 316 US 455. But I think it would require more aggravated circumstances than are present here to bring this case within those cited. It is not denied that private counsel thought that he could be ready or that he did not conduct a spirited defense. The case does not strike me as one which should be reviewed here.

The Court denied certiorari with no recorded dissents. The case was a poor vehicle to develop *Avery's* ruling, written by Justice Black in 1939, that denial of a continuance to court-appointed counsel who had only three days to prepare for a murder trial did not deprive the defendant of effective assistance of counsel "under the circumstances disclosed." The dissenting opinion in the state supreme court was rhetorically strong but never demonstrated precisely how the trial court's impatience prejudiced the defendant.

Cert memos were the relentless, grinding work of the law clerks, especially in the chief justice's chambers, where all i.f.p. filings, disbarment actions, and motions related to pending cases were processed, but the entire memo workload occupied at most two days of work each week. Work on pending cases and opinion work consumed the rest of the time. Vinson was one of two justices who did none of his own opinion writing; the other was Murphy, whose clerk, Gene Gressman, did all of his writing—barring the odd rider here or there on a working draft. The other seven justices, as their surviving working papers richly demonstrate, did almost all of their own opinion writing, starting with handwritten drafts on long yellow legal pads and proceeding through typed drafts and printed opinions produced in the Court's basement print shop for circulation to the other justices.

The regime provided a heady opportunity for Vinson's clerks, but as with Murphy, did nothing to enhance the intellectual reputation of the chief justice in the eyes of his colleagues. With staffs so small, the justices were on a first-name basis with the law clerks in other chambers, and there were no mysteries about the genesis of anyone's work product. The common wisecrack in the corridors of the Court, among both the justices and their staffs, was that Vinson wrote his best opinions with his hands in his pockets. Vinson was thin-skinned about criticism, from how few cases the Court decided to how little he wrote. Perhaps as a result, his archive retains very little working material and provides only dim illumination of his thinking processes or precisely how he utilized his staff. Only one draft opinion unambiguously written by White survives in the archive of the Vinson Papers—a draft dissent in *Parker v. Fleming,* which arose in midterm, involving the Emergency Price Control Act of 1942.

The issue in *Parker v. Fleming* was whether the Emergency Price Control Act of 1942 provided tenants with administrative and judicial review of eviction notices obtained by their landlords with the permission of the administrator of the Office of Price Administration. The issue was less important than the intracourt context in which it arose and can be understood only in that light.

When Vinson became chief justice, his natural inclination was to heed Felix Frankfurter, whose knowledge of the Court's history and operation was exceeded only by his solicitousness, at least initially, for the new chief justice. Frankfurter's advice, from the largest question of due process to the smallest point of Court procedure, soon evolved from a word to the wise to lectures that sometimes resembled scoldings. The crucible was argued cases. Frankfurter was impatient with Vinson's failure to see issues his way, and what Vinson viewed as disagreement was treated by Frankfurter as one more example of the new chief justice's inadequacy. "I have never seen anything like it," Frank Allen later recalled. "Vinson began the term deferring to Felix and within six weeks couldn't wait to find a case in which he could vote against him."

Black was another matter. "Black was the consummate judicial politician," according to Allen. "He knew when to give in and when to dig in. By midterm, Vinson would just glow when Black was on his side." White, occupying a different position and anything but starry-eyed over the senior associate justice, tended, at least from the middle of the year on, to take Black's writings with a large dose of salt.

Black's work in *Parker v. Fleming* is a case in point. Strictly speaking, certificates of eviction issued by the administrator and contested by the tenants did not authorize evictions; rather, they permitted landlords to seek legal remedies under their lease and local law, free from limitation by the act and complementary laws. The Emergency Court of Appeals, which had jurisdiction over the administrator's action (and over which Vinson had once presided while he was a court of appeals judge), held that the statute did not provide tenants with a remedy against the issuance of the certificates. The court concluded that the act was not designed to provide a private cause of action for tenants facing eviction; instead, the act provided review for those "subject to" the administrator's authority, in this case, the landlord. The act was not structured to provide a vehicle for second-guessing the administrator's judgment on rent levels, nor was it designed to frustrate landlord's recognized legal rights.

Judge Albert Maris wrote for the majority, which also included Judge Calvert Magruder; Judge Thomas F. McAllister filed a lengthy and somewhat rambling dissent. Five justices voted to grant certiorari: Black, Reed, Douglas, Murphy, and Rutledge. The Court's initial vote was a very provisional 6-3 to affirm (with Reed, Douglas, and Rutledge in the minority), and Vinson assigned the opinion to Justice Black on December 20, 1946, two days after argument.

Justice Black's tentative majority opinion was a shock to Vinson. In seven brisk pages, Black concluded that a different provision of the act than that relied upon below required review by the administrator and that the Emergency Court of Appeals had jurisdiction to hear the tenants' complaint. Shortly after Justice Black circulated his opinion, White prepared a Memorandum for the Conference under Vinson's name that scorched Black's analysis in twelve tough, methodical pages. The memorandum unequivocally pounded home one point after another. "The legislative history to me is very clear indeed": the administrator and the lower court were, simply, "correct." Three-plus pages covered the legislative history; three more examined the administrator's practice; several more pages examined case law and the functional consequences of Black's analysis.

As Vinson's argument picks up steam, the tone becomes sharper—"But, says Justice Black," and, "But, so the memorandum says," and finally, on the last page, "I note that there is much heart appeal in the McAllister dissent dealing with veterans, widows, orphans, etc." and other potential evictees, but those sentiments are beside the point because they rest on conjecture: "But I am certain that we will not be controlled by such conjecture." The memo, circulated January 6, 1947, was strong stuff.

Frankfurter agreed immediately: "Amen! Reads to me like a Q. E. D." Burton also agreed, but Vinson simply did not have the votes. When the Court met again in conference on January 11 to consider Justice Black's volte-face, the vote was 5-4 for Black's memorandum—in fact, the five who had originally voted to hear the case in the first place. Vinson had not yet published a dissenting opinion (indeed, he did not during the entire term), and the man who was appointed to pull the Court together was not about to start over an ephemeral squabble about wartime rent control, especially with an opinion that gave no quarter to the other side and whose tone was too reminiscent of the atmosphere that he had been appointed to eliminate. On January 17, Vinson sent a note to Black: "I will not write in this case, but will ask you to mark me as dissenting." The decision came down three days later with the notation "The Chief Justice, Mr. Justice Frankfurter and Mr. Justice Burton dissent." Justice Jackson apparently decided to switch his vote, join Black, and like Vinson, keep quiet.

Another case from the same argument session as *Parker v. Fleming,* whose opinion for the Court was also written by Justice Black, sheds further light on the relationship between Vinson and his "all-American law clerk," as he often called him, as well as on the complex interaction between Vinson and Black. The case, *Jesionowski v. Boston & Maine R.R.,* was one of the many cases during the decade—including five in the 1946 term alone—that involved the Federal Employers Liability Act. The FELA was a pet project for Black, who waged a crusade to establish recoveries for the workingmen, or their survivors, who failed to win relief in the lower courts. Stanley Jesionowski was a brakeman who was killed during an uncoupling operation when a railroad car derailed. His widow sued the employer under the FELA, alleging negligence and *res ipsa loquitur.**

The jury's verdict for her was reversed by the court of appeals, which held that the *res ipsa* doctrine did not apply, because the proximate cause of the accident was not in the exclusive control of the railroad: the defendant himself controlled some of the equipment that was involved. Under classic doctrine, *res ipsa* would lie only when there were no actors other than the defendant in control of the "thing which causes injury." For the court of appeals, Jesionowski was sufficiently in control of some "elements" of the cause of the injury to make the doctrine inapplicable.

Only four justices thought the case was worth hearing: Black, Douglas, Murphy, and Rutledge. Vinson assigned the case to Black, the Court's established FELA champion. His draft opinion, circulated in early January, rehearsed the facts in much more detail than the court of appeals and concluded that the lower court had both read the *res ipsa* doctrine too rigidly and improperly deprived the jury of considering the case on a theory of pure negligence, even though the plaintiff could point to no specific act triggering liability. The opinion follows a well-worn path for Justice Black, both in restoring jury verdicts for plaintiffs under FELA and in extolling the autonomous fact-finding capacity of the jury.

White's memo to Vinson found the draft opinion unacceptably tendentious. He criticized Black's statement of the facts ("not only incomplete but it gives a rather unjustified slant to the situation") and the draft's unqualified

---

* A theory—literally, "the thing speaks for itself"—that relies on the nature of the injury and the control of the defendant over the source of the injury to establish liability, even if the precise cause or negligent act cannot be identified.

breadth ("There is no attempt to limit the case to FELA situations"). To Black's reliance on a "decision which cut through the mass of verbiage built up around the doctrine," White sarcastically observed: "Even with the mass of verbiage cleared away, middle p. 5, the statement there of the meaning of res ipsa seems to ignore the function of the instruction in handling that doctrine." White's memo was concerned less with the proposed result than with the opinion's sweep, and his conclusion pinpointed his concern:

> I get the impression that anytime the jury could find that an injured man's control was not contributory to the accident, then it is permissible to first eliminate this element and then rely on res ipsa. But I should think faith in the jury could be cut off where all the elements in an accident were at the time in control of an employee, through whom, and through him alone, the employer is exercising any control, maintenance or care. In the present case, only one of several factors were under J's control.

White's pointed reference to "faith in the jury"—a staple in Black's jurisprudence—underscored his impatience with what he appeared to view as the Hugo Black technique for deciding at least some types of cases: simple convictions in the service of predictable results. Vinson, still trying to keep peace within the Court and trying to work effectively with Black, ignored White and joined Black's opinion. So did Frankfurter, after exacting some minor changes in language from Black. Reed, Jackson, and Burton dissented without opinion.

Both *Parker v. Fleming* and *Jesionowski v. Boston & Maine* were argued early in the term, in mid-December. The first few months of the term had, to the relief of everyone, been devoid of verbal fireworks or fallout from the Black–Jackson feud the previous summer. Harold Burton noted in his diary, with relief, that Jackson and Black seemed very cordial to each other. The tone of opinions published before Christmas, with the exception of a "stiff" dissent by Justice Reed from an opinion by Vinson in an Indian property rights case, was moderate, and the pace was quickstep: twenty-five cases were disposed of before the calendar year turned.

External appearances were deceptive, however. Vinson was discovering that he was operating in a fishbowl whose ethics precluded responses to personal criticism and rumors, no matter how unfair. He was stung by an item in Leonard Lyons's gossip column on November 1 that reported Vinson was using his longtime administrative assistant, Paul Kelley, to insulate him from the rest of the Court. His heated reaction fell on deaf ears within the Court. A major story on the Court, informed by inside information, was known to

be on the way in January. Even though neither the forum nor the author—
Fortune and Arthur Schlesinger, Jr.—was sensationalist or trivial in the vein
of Lyons or Drew Pearson, most members of the Supreme Court viewed any
press as bad press. More important, whatever temporary equanimity operated at the beginning of the term was beginning to unravel by early December. The reason was the volatile content of the Court's docket. Important
cases, both doctrinally and politically, suddenly galvanized philosophical battle lines within the institution. As the stakes in the cases rose, so did the
rhetoric.

Since the first Monday in October, the Court had heard but not yet decided cases raising several important questions—the extent to which government can examine the validity of religious belief *(United States v. Ballard);* the
constitutionality of the Hatch Act of 1938, which prohibited nonpolicy governmental employees from participating in political activity *(United Public
Workers v. Mitchell);* the scope of pretrial discovery under the Federal Rules of
Civil Procedure of 1938 *(Hickman v. Taylor);* the constitutional validity of
capital punishment after the first execution failed due to a faulty electric chair
(Louisiana ex rel. Francis v. Resweber); and the constitutionality of state-paid
transportation of parochial school students *(Everson v. Board of Education).*

On December 9, the Court turned up the political pressure on itself by
granting certiorari to resolve the legal squabble between the United States and
John L. Lewis, who had taken out his United Mine Workers on strike on November 18 against the government, which had seized control of bituminous
coal mines pursuant to statutory authorization the previous spring. When
Lewis failed to obey the district court's order to return to work, he was hit with
civil and criminal contempt citations and fines of $10,000 personally and
$3.5 million against the union. The dispute drew enormous attention, and
the case tied the Supreme Court in a knot for almost three months, beginning
with contentious conferences over the complicated issues presented even at
the threshold by the unusual petition for certiorari (unusual mainly because it
was filed before judgment in the court of appeals). Oral arguments were not
held until mid-January, and opinion work lasted for two more months, until
March 6, when the injunction and contempts were affirmed but the fine
against the union was reduced. More than 125 pages of opinions in the *United
States Reports* were produced by five separate justices.

Vinson, who earned a reputation for "generous" assignment of opinions
to others during his tenure, assigned the opinion of the Court to himself. During the entire term, he wrote no concurring opinion and no dissenting opinion, and wrote fewer opinions for the Court (thirteen) than any other justice

except Burton (six). The Lewis case, as *UMW* came to be called within the Court, mattered a great deal to Vinson. He was "extremely interested in that case," Karl Price later told the Vinson Oral History Project at the University of Kentucky. The recollection was expressed with loyal understatement. Vinson abandoned the even judicial mien he had tried to hard to cultivate at the beginning of the term; now, he told Frank Murphy, "The chips are down. We've got to help the administration out of this mess." The doctrinal obstacles to Vinson's goal were substantial, and the chief justice assigned White to draft the opinion for the Court. The task was enormous and consuming. The statement of facts alone occupied eight pages in the *U.S. Reports*. Eventually, both Price and Allen were conscripted to help White finish the job as one member of the fragile majority after another suggested emendations to the draft. The final opinion for the Court covered nearly fifty printed pages.

The primary legal issues in the Lewis case were simple but contentious: Did the Norris-LaGuardia Act* divest the district court of jurisdiction to enjoin the strike? Whether or not the injunction was valid, was the lower court empowered to punish violation of its orders by civil or criminal contempt? Did the record below support the level of fines imposed? The answers were no, yes, and yes—although the fine against the union was reduced to $700,000 after lengthy internal wrangling within the Court. The opinion for the Court, wrote John P. Frank, a close if not friendly reader, "is one of those block-buster opinions which smashes its way to its result."

As a technical matter, Frankfurter, the leading expert in the country on the labor injunction, devastated the Court's analysis of the Norris-LaGuardia Act (which he had helped to draft in 1932). Vinson wrote that the act did not apply when the United States was the employer. Frankfurter emphasized that the act was directed at the power of courts in labor disputes, not—as Vinson argued—at the nature of the parties in the dispute. Black, joined by Douglas, concurred in part and dissented in part; they would have made any fines against Lewis and the union conditional and thus discharged upon full compliance with the temporary injunction. Murphy filed a characteristically inflamed opinion, which expressed fear that the decision could justify "breaking any or all strikes in private industries" in the future, as long as the government was willing first to seize the industry in question. Rutledge wrote a dissent that, standing on the shoulders of Frankfurter's treatment of the

---

* Signed into law by Pres. Herbert Hoover in 1932, the act restricted the use of labor injunctions to strikes threatening public safety and—not relevant here—banned yellow dog contracts, which denied workers the right to unionize and required them to agree not to strike.

Norris-LaGuardia Act, patiently picked apart what was left of the opinion of the Court.

The best that could be said in the short run for the Court's decision, as Frank conceded, was that "it broke a strike which, without regard to the merits, had to stop in the nation's interest"—a result that "had to be achieved by some instrumentality." In the long run, the episode helped to lead to a different instrumentality, the Taft-Hartley Act of 1947, which provided for executive authority to stop strikes temporarily (for an eighty-day cooling-off period) upon an essentially unreviewable finding of national emergency.

The decision in the Lewis case churned columnists and editorial writers, maddened the academic allies of Black and Douglas (who saw them as sellouts to political expediency), and put the chief justice permanently on his guard toward the press. He felt especially burned by Drew Pearson, author of the column "Washington Merry-Go-Round" and social confidant of Douglas. Pearson's radio broadcast the day before the Court granted certiorari in December announced that Vinson had "held a very significant conference with President Truman in which he expressed his private opinion that the Supreme Court would uphold the lower court injunction" against the UMW. "The Chief Justice, of course, was only speaking for himself, but his influence on the Court is important and afterward word of the Chief Justice's view was quietly transmitted to the" union. One week later, Pearson retracted the story in language that sounded almost as if it had been dictated by counsel, and he used his broadcast

> to correct an impression I may have conveyed last week that Chief Justice Vinson took any sides in the coal strike case or conferred with anyone in such a way as to indicate he might decide against the miners. The Chief Justice, for whom I have the highest regard, took absolutely no sides, except to express himself very forcefully that the Supreme Court owed it to the nation to try this injunction case in a hurry. That in itself probably has a lot to do with John L. Lewis's calling off the strike.

Pearson triggered the chief justice's ire at least twice more during the term. On May 11, 1947, Pearson "predicted" that the Court would reverse the constructive criminal contempts issued against the publisher and two staff members of the *Corpus Christi Caller-Times* for printing a series of articles and columns attacking a local judge's handling of a forcible detainer case as a travesty of justice. Pearson also said that Jackson and Frankfurter would dissent. The decision, *Craig v. Harney,* was handed down May 19, with the chief justice joining Jackson and Frankfurter in dissent. Justice Douglas wrote the Court's opinion, reaching the outcome Pearson predicted.

On June 23, the final day of the term, Pearson wrote a column lambasting Justice Burton for not writing enough opinions and implying that he was "soldiering"—attending too many diplomatic receptions and not carrying his share of the workload. Every member of the Court except Murphy and Rutledge either called on Burton or wrote a note decrying the injustice of the charge, and one of Harold Ickes's lieutenants telephoned to volunteer a letter of protest. Burton was experienced in public life (he had been mayor of Cleveland before he was elected senator from Ohio) and wisely decided, as he noted in his diary, "not to say anything and to let it drop." The chief justice had even broader experience in government, but he was nevertheless unprepared for sniping criticism to which he could not respond, or for leaked information or stories, which he could not trace and could not stop in any event. At the beginning of the term, Vinson was said to enjoy three topics of conversation with his colleagues—baseball, bridge, and politics. By the end of the term, he had reduced the agenda to baseball and bridge.

Other than the Lewis case, the case in which the chief justice most deeply invested himself was *Harris v. United States,* a search and seizure decision that produced an unexpected alignment of the justices and an unexpected ruling that turned out to have a very short half-life. George Harris was arrested in his small apartment for mail fraud, and the arresting officers conducted an extensive search for stolen checks that had been used as the models for the fraudulent paper. In a sealed envelope marked "Personal Papers," the arresting officers found draft cards and related documents that Harris was not legally authorized to possess. He was then charged with illegal possession of the Selective Service materials, and his motion to suppress the evidence was denied. The Court sustained his conviction and the use of the evidence by a 5-4 vote. Vinson spoke for the Court; the dissenters were Frankfurter, Jackson, Murphy, and Rutledge.

The decision shocked the press and the bar. Since the final days of Prohibition, the Court had held that the Fourth Amendment prohibited searches incident to a lawful arrest from becoming roving expeditions for evidence; a recent qualification to the doctrine, *Davis v. United States,* permitted seizure of contraband or property to which the arrestee had no legal right. Vinson relied on *Davis* to justify the search of Harris's apartment, because possession of the draft cards meant that "a crime was thus being committed in the very presence of the agents conducting the search." The analysis begged the question, as the three dissents (Frankfurter, Murphy, and Jackson) demonstrated. In *Davis,* the materials seized were related to the charges underlying the arrest warrant; the question in *Harris* was whether lawful entry for one reason justified search and seizure of evidence on another, unrelated charge. Justice Murphy, always ready for the rhetorical jugular, thought that the chief justice's unacknowledged extension of *Davis* functionally sustained a "a writ of assistance." The other dissents were more temperate, but not by a large margin. Frankfurter even circulated a memorandum to his colleagues apologizing for speaking "with too much vehemence and intensity" when the Court discussed and voted on the case. The precedent was functionally reversed a year later in *Trupiano v. United States,* when Justice Douglas switched sides and an opinion by Justice Murphy invalidated a search that one of his biographers noted was "more readily justified by precedent than the *Harris* search." *Trupiano* moved Vinson to publish a dissent, his first as chief justice.

Harris is noteworthy for the cast of mind about abuse of power and how its risk should weigh with judges. Jackson's dissent focused on the issue and pointed fingers directly:

> The difficulty with this problem for me is that once the search is allowed to go beyond the person arrested and the objects upon him or in his immediate physical control, I see no practical limit short of that set in the opinion of the Court—and that means to me no limit at all.

Jackson's pique apparently had been set off by the final paragraph of the chief justice's opinion:

> The dangers to fundamental personal rights and interests resulting from excesses of law-enforcement officials committed during the course of criminal investigations are not illusory. The Court has always been alert to protect against such abuse. But we should not permit our knowledge that abuses sometimes occur to give sinister coloration to procedures which are basically reasonable. We conclude that in this case the evidence which formed the basis of petitioner's conviction was obtained without violation of petitioner's rights under the Constitution.

The disagreement between Vinson and Jackson, imperfectly joined to some extent, was a disagreement over presumptions about official behavior and, more particularly, over how much the potential for abuse should shape doctrine—especially where the record under review falls short of the range of abuse that may seem likely. "Byron had great sympathy with Vinson's approach," according to Frank Allen. "*Just because something could go wrong doesn't mean that it will, and it certainly doesn't mean we should rule as if it will, especially if the record doesn't go that far*—that seemed to be the view that he and the chief justice shared. Hypothetical risks did not move either man very far."

October term 1946 was the first postwar term of the Supreme Court with a full bench. Justice Jackson had left for Nuremberg for what he expected to be a brief task, but it occupied him for more than a year and left the Supreme Court understaffed for an entire year. Nine cases were put over from the 1945 to the 1946 term, as the Journal of the Court routinely noted, to be heard "by a full bench." The docket for the 1946 term thus mixed the mop-up work of the war—such as cases involving substantive and jurisdictional issues of price control or prosecutions for treason and other wartime offenses—with emerging issues involving labor and civil liberties. At the time, the Lewis case was seen as a harbinger of the Court's postwar attitude toward control of labor activities, but Congress moved more quickly than the Court. The Taft-Hartley Act effectively erased the board and restarted the game, just at the point that the personnel of the Court underwent a dramatic change—the simultaneous deaths of Justices Murphy and Rutledge, in the summer of 1949, at the conclusion of Vinson's third term as chief justice. The enduring effects of the most contentious constitutional decisions of the 1946 term—*Everson v. Board of Education* and the criminal due process cases *Francis v. Resweber* and *Adamson v. California*—were thus also cast in dramatically different light shortly after they were uttered.

Although the Lewis case drew the most attention during its pendency, the most controversial decision of the term was *Everson,* which engrafted Thomas Jefferson's "wall" between church and state into the establishment clause of the First Amendment and then, nonetheless, held that state payment of Catholic schoolchildren's transportation costs did not breach the wall. The internal tension in Justice Black's opinion for the Court elicited the rude reaction from Justice Jackson that the most fitting precedent for the result was Lord Byron's Julia, who, "'whispering "I will ne'er consent,"—consented.'" The chief justice was solidly on Black's side, if not fully enthusiastic about the opinion. To Vinson, the test was whether the subsidy program discriminated for or against religion; since the state program did not, and because the program benefited education and children, he was comfortable affirming. Only Frankfurter and Rutledge voted to reverse at the outset, but Black's problematic opinion and the forceful dissent by Rutledge brought over Jackson and Burton, so that the final vote was 5-4, which exacerbated the public controversy over the decision.

Within thirteen months, the Court confounded the issue further by invalidating "released time" programs (less than one hour per week of optional religious instruction by sectarian instructors in public school buildings) in *McCollum v. Board of Education.* The programs affected more than 2 million schoolchildren nationwide. The chief justice again assigned the opinion for the Court to Black. Again, the Court was strongly criticized, and the internal divisions grew more bitter. Since so many communities viewed accommodation of religious instruction and secular education as central to their public duties, *Everson* guaranteed that litigation over the establishment clause would visit the Supreme Court's docket for years.

Adamson v. California took a staple of the Court's docket, the constitutional dimension of the criminal justice process at the state level, and reoriented the debate over its foundation with similar consequences for the Court's workload. Although the fundamental case law stretched well back into the nineteenth century, the basic test under the Fourteenth Amendment for the constitutional floor of due process of law in state criminal proceedings was formulated in 1937. Writing for an 8-1 Court, which included Hugo Black in his first term, Justice Benjamin N. Cardozo held in *Palko v. Connecticut* that the due process clause required states to provide only those rights that were "implicit in a scheme of ordered liberty"—which *Palko* held did not include the protection against double jeopardy guaranteed in federal prosecutions by the Fifth Amendment. Since *Palko,* Black had been to Damascus. He had begun to wage a vocal campaign against what he viewed as the indefensibly subjective test of due process utilized not only with respect to criminal procedure in *Palko* but also to the scope and definition of substantive crimes. When *Francis v. Resweber* arrived at the Court early in the 1946 term, Black considered using the case as a vehicle to push his new theory. He even circulated an opinion in the case condemning the continued use of the *Palko* analysis, but when Justice Burton began to pick up support for his rather strong dissent from the Court's rejection of Francis's arguments, Black put the draft away for another day.

He did not have to wait long. Certiorari was granted in *Adamson v. California* on the same day as in *Francis v. Resweber* but argued two months later, in January of 1947. The question in *Adamson* was whether the California practice of allowing prosecutors to comment on the fact that a criminal defendant failed to testify in his own behalf violated due process. At conference, when the Court met to discuss the case after oral argument, Black passed. He would not say that the state practice constituted a requirement of self-incrimination, but he withheld his vote. Weeks later he circulated a dissenting opinion, arguing that the history of the drafting of the Fourteenth Amendment in the Thirty-ninth Congress demonstrated that the congressional advocates of the due process clause believed that it was meant to enforce the first eight amendments of the Constitution against the states.

The opinion was dubious history (although the amendment's sponsor had told the Senate it would do just that), and its logic required impractical results. Black's view would have required a jury trial for every civil case with more than $20 at stake and all criminal prosecutions to proceed by grand jury indictment—consequences that, as Earl Warren told Black years later, would "make the states topsy-turvy." Nonetheless, Black provided a more ascertainable standard than *Palko* and one that sets its own limits, unlike that of the other dissenters in *Adamson,* Murphy and Rutledge; they would not only have incorporated the first eight amendments but would have gone further when "fundamental standards of procedure" were not satisfied. In essence, Murphy and Rutledge thought Black's opinion should be the constitutional floor and not the ceiling for due process of law in state criminal proceedings.

The conflicting approaches of Black and Murphy meant that those who were dissatisfied with *Palko* and its foundational precedent, *Twining v. New Jersey,* had to choose between an argument based on history, whose logic quickly went to impractical extremes, and an argument that continued the subjective development of due process but could not be backed into awkward corners. Academic critics such as John P. Frank were initially less interested in the quality of Justice Black's history or the reach of Justice Murphy's views than in the combined effect of the four dissenting votes in *Adamson:* "the striking aspect of the minority thesis here is not its novelty but the extent of its support. One more vote, and the Bill of Rights *will* be a limitation on the states." As a formal matter, the vote never came, and the deaths of Murphy and Rutledge in 1949 meant that Black no longer had any momentum for his opinion. Charles Fairman's essay in the *Stanford Law Review,* published in 1949, seemed to demolish Black's position as a historical matter, but the achievement of the *Adamson* dissent, as Frank among others noted, was that a critical mass had developed against the *Twining-Palko* test. The chief justice, however, was not part of the new learning. He had no interest in Justice Black's campaign.

The 1946 term ended on June 23, 1947, although the last sulfurous grace note of the contentious year was not sounded until the first day of the following term, October 6, when Justice Jackson filed an extremely belated dissent, filled with barbs and sarcasm, to the second *Securities and Exchange Commission v. Chenery* decision.*

White and his law school friend Louis Oberdorfer finished their clerkships with Vinson and Black, respectively, on the same day near the end of

---

* *Chenery II,* as it came to be known, effectively reversed a 4-3 decision several years earlier and established the standard of judicial review of agency orders, a standard that was deferential to the the agency's expertise. Jackson put it acidly: "The Court's reasoning adds up to this: The Commission must be sustained because of its accumulated experience in solving a problem with which it had never before been confronted."

June. Both were convinced, on the basis of faculty gossip from Yale Law School, that Justice Douglas had been instrumental in promoting their successful applications for clerkships. At the time they applied, Yale had not developed the more structured process for supporting candidates for Supreme Court clerkships that eventually obtained during, and largely thanks to, the deanship of Wesley Sturges; in early 1946, it was every man for himself. White and Oberdorfer felt obliged to Douglas, and they decided to tell him so and to seek career advice before they departed. When they arrived at his chambers, he was dressed for the hiking trails and obviously not long for the building, so they quickly mumbled their thank-yous. As to advice, Douglas looked up briefly from his desk, where he was writing furiously, and said softly, "Go to your roots." Then Douglas looked back at his work and said, "Bye." The clerks were left flat-footed and departed somewhat awkwardly. The advice, rendered with the curt impatience Douglas was now widely known for, was incongruous. He had made his professional career by abandoning his own roots, as attested to by the eventual title of the first volume of his memoirs—*Go East, Young Man.*

With the term over, the other clerks now had to plan the next step in their careers. Two stayed to work another term, Allen with the chief justice and Gressman with Murphy. Most went into private practice. Oberdorfer went to work for a Washington, D.C., law firm, and White headed west to take the Colorado Bar examination and then a job with a small law firm in Denver named Newton, Davis & Henry. Washington firms tried to recruit him, but he confounded them by insisting that he be considered for partner within two years, to which the reply—according to local legend—was, "Certainly not." White's reported response was, "Then I'm not interested."

Byron White never saw Fred Vinson again. The chief justice rewarded White's work with the customary signed formal photograph. On the matting of the Bachrach three-quarter portrait, which makes Vinson look, in the words of a Court wag, like a "tired sheep" with heavy bags under his eyes and his mouth tightly pursed, Vinson wrote: "To Byron 'Whizzer' White, whose future promises to be as brilliant as his past, Fred M. Vinson." Almost a year passed before White wrote Vinson, and the occasion was not social but business—to endorse the clerkship application of someone he knew briefly at Yale, Adam Yarmolinsky. White apologized for not writing sooner and seemed embarrassed in taking so long to report his pleasure with practice in Denver. He closed: "I should like to stop and see you some time and pick up a little more solid wisdom." Vinson's response, obviously written in haste, expressed disappointment at not hearing sooner from one of his favorite clerks: "You waited so long to write that I was beginning to feel that perhaps you had forgotten your Washington associates. I am looking forward to having a chance to sit down and talk with you again." The letter was addressed "Dear Whizzer"—no quotation marks, no apologies for the detested nickname.

Vinson's former clerks staged a reunion dinner for the chief justice in May 1951, two years before Vinson died, and only two of the law clerk alumni failed to attend; White was one of the absentees. After repeated inquiries from the organizers of the affair, White finally explained his silence in a short letter to Newton Minow, one of the former clerks who was planning the dinner: "a tangle on the squash courts put me in the hospital for a back operation and I have only now returned to the office. Unfortunately, I shall be unable to travel as far as Washington for some time. Please convey my regrets, and also my regards to the Chief, as well as to the assembled group." When Vinson died, White did not attend the funeral or the memorial service. He declined to participate, after several plaintive requests from different agents, in the Fred M. Vinson Oral History Project developed by the University of Kentucky Library in the mid-1970s. His stock response, in so many words, was, *What could I say?*

Fred Vinson's clerks liked to tell him that he was "pretty adept at taking brickbats on the chin" over a twenty-five-year career in public affairs, but it was a compliment that generously inverted the truth. Vinson was stung by arrows large and small, and he shut off Yale Law School as a source of staff after Fred Rodell published a caustic attack on Vinson's views and his management of the Court in *Look* magazine. Sturges tried to repair the damage but was unsuccessful. Beginning with October term 1950, Vinson's clerks came from Pennsylvania or Northwestern. Vinson's behavior now seems petulant, but the grounds for the nonphilosophical criticism he suffered—for taking too few cases, for allowing the terms to last too long, and for permitting important decisions to stack up at the end of the term—proved in time to be driven more by institutional dynamics than by factors within the control of the presiding justice. Vinson did not vote like Hugo Black or William O. Douglas, which for the authors of the annual reviews of the Supreme Court's works during the period—Fowler V. Harper, Rodell, and John Frank—was fault enough. One of the least constructive legacies of the postwar period was the highly personalized partisanship of the institution's critics. Fred Vinson was the most prominent victim, and Felix Frankfurter was the most durable target. Neither enjoyed sufficient resources to neutralize the debate, let alone change its terms of discourse. For Byron White, those debates and the changing critical currency about the performance of the institution were now behind him. He was bound west, toward home, his roots, and, he thought, private life on his own terms.

Part III

LAW AND POLITICS

10

DENVER: LAW AND
LOCAL POLITICS

T HE DECISION to practice law in Denver turned out to be easy for
Byron White. As he explained later:

I think one of the reasons I wanted to go back to Denver was that it was growing so rapidly after the war. It seemed like an exciting thing to begin your career in a town that was growing that fast. In a small law firm you would be in
a position to come to grips with a great variety of significant problems that
you might never meet in a larger eastern firm. Also, living in a pleasant envi-
ronment like Denver seemed a little more important to me than it had a few
years earlier. I must have been getting old and soft.

In fact, White had just turned thirty a week before the end of October
term 1946, but he was right about Denver. The city was growing, thanks
largely to the capital investment made by the federal government during and
after World War II. The city's population grew from 322,412 in the 1940 census to more than 400,000 by the end of the decade. Denver had a modest and
stagnant industrial base, resting on a handful of manufacturing concerns such
as Gates Rubber, Coors (brewing), Schwayder Brothers (Samsonite products),
and the various enterprises run by the Boettcher family (Ideal Cement, Great

Western Sugar, and the eponymous brokerage firm). Putting to one side the federal government, which started huge reclamation projects before the war and built major arms and research installations near Denver shortly after the war, there was little indigenous capital development in the area. Real estate and construction were initiated by nonlocal concerns, such as William Zeckendorf's Webb & Knapp from New York, and financed by banks in Chicago, New York, and Detroit. The conservative Denver banking establishment, controlled by old Colorado families who were tight with both interest rates and lending policies, played a passive role in the city's postwar development.

What eventually came to be known as the three-stage process of economic development in the West—agricultural production, industrialization, and services—did not obtain in Colorado or the rest of the Rocky Mountain region. The region "jumped the second stage, the industrialized stage," Ruben Zubrow, professor of economics at the University of Colorado, later observed, "and [went] directly to services." The federal government became the principal service employer. By 1951, Denver had fourteen thousand federal employees, most at the Federal Center, which had been an ordnance plant during the war. The journalist John Gunther, writing soon after the war, listed the historic staples of the Colorado economy ("scenery, beet sugar, gold, molybdenum, livestock, tourists and tuberculosis") but observed that the federal government continued to be a major presence despite the end of the war and that tourism was substantially underdeveloped.

Comfortable insularity struck postwar journalists as Denver's economic hallmark. Gunther found Denver "Olympian, impassive, and inert. It is probably the most self-sufficient, isolated, self-contained and complacent city in the world." Robert L. Perkin, who had been a contemporary of White at the University of Colorado before becoming a distinguished reporter for the *Rocky Mountain News,* wrote in 1949: "Today Denver is the reluctant capital of a region larger than most nations. It is big and beautiful [but] it is also smug, sleek and satisfied . . . disinterested in its own continuing growth, abhorrent of risk-taking, chary of progress."

Legal practice in Denver was just beginning to change when White joined the four-man law firm of Newton, Davis & Henry in August of 1947. Before the war, legal practice in Denver consisted almost entirely of one- and two-man firms. By the autumn of 1947, the one-man firm was a dying breed and almost half of the firms in the city had three to six lawyers. Only four had more than six. The partners in White's new firm were Quigg Newton, age thirty-six—a graduate of Yale and Yale Law School and a former aide to William O. Douglas at the Securities and Exchange Commission—and

Richard M. Davis, thirty-five, and S. Arthur Henry, forty-six, both Harvard Law graduates. The other lawyer was John N. Adams, forty-three, who had attended Western Reserve Law School and practiced in Cleveland for sixteen years before moving to Denver in 1945.

The firm had been founded in 1938, when Newton and Davis left the firm of Lewis & Grant to form their partnership. They had one client, Denver University, whose board of trustees appointed Newton as its secretary a year later. Thanks to Newton's expertise, the firm developed an SEC practice and created the first two mutual funds in the city; labor became a second specialty. White chose the firm in part because of positive chemistry with Davis and in part because the firm was small, responsibility would be substantial from the outset, and the client base included individuals and small businesses as well as larger concerns.

Three months after White's arrival, Newton was elected mayor of Denver on a reform platform that ousted Benjamin F. Stapleton, who had held the office for more than twenty years. Newton's election and the death of James B. Grant of Lewis & Grant triggered the merger of the two firms into a nine-man firm named Lewis, Grant, Newton, Davis & Henry. The new firm's client base was centered on established corporations, principally the Denver National Bank and the various divisions of Ideal Cement Company. The merger made rapid growth, which Newton's smaller firm resisted, inescapable if not necessarily imminent.

Within five years of the merger, the firm went through a major reorganization, of which the principal catalysts were Newton's decision to leave the firm and Robert Stearns's decision to resign as president of the University of Colorado after fourteen years and to join the firm of counsel. Both decisions were announced in September 1952. S. Arthur Henry and John Adams, two of the oldest members of the firm, also decided to leave and to form their own partnership. Suddenly one of the larger firms in Denver was reduced to six partners and known as Lewis, Grant & Davis. (The other partners were Donald S. Graham, Donald S. Stubbs, White, and Donald W. Hoagland.) More manpower was needed, and specialists—in tax and litigation—were the top priority.

White did the recruiting, and went for the first time to what would become for him a reliable well time after time over the next decade—the Yale Law School. To cover tax, he persuaded Howard W. Rea, Yale Law '41, to leave his practice in Washington, D.C., and join the firm. The trial lawyer White tapped was Robert H. Harry, '42, who had been a classmate but whom White had not seen or talked to in twelve years. (The first time the two met, White nailed

Harry in the chest with a 40-yard spiral pass as he crossed the New Haven Green with an armful of legal textbooks. The forewarning was a split second too late, "just like a scene in the movies," Harry later remembered.)

Harry was then at Hughes, Hubbard & Reed in New York City, where he had been for seven years after leaving the navy. He later recalled White's recruiting pitch, which had no soft edges: "He called me one day out of the blue: *Bob, this is Byron. I'd like to come by, as soon as it's convenient.*" A time was set, "and damned if he didn't arrive an hour early. He was so smart: he wanted to see us—the family—the way we were, the way we really lived, not the way we entertained. It was a little awkward at first, but then we all felt very comfortable and it got things off to a great start."

White pulled no punches in selling Denver to Harry: *There isn't much litigation yet, but there will be. And there isn't much to Denver. All the houses are made of brick and look the same; there are only three good restaurants in town; and there are no trees. But it's a good practice and a good life.* Harry joined the firm in 1953 as the eighth partner and practiced with the firm for more than thirty years.

Byron White was a transactional lawyer, almost never seen in either the state or federal courthouses. He tried only a handful of cases, usually minor criminal matters by appointment of the court. He appeared in only four reported cases in the Supreme Court of Colorado (although one preserved a judgment in favor of a client who had been sued for more than $670,000), four in the federal Court of Appeals for the Tenth Circuit, and one in the federal district court in Denver. The only federal case of more than local interest was *Loew's v. Cinema Amusements* in 1954, in which White represented local plaintiffs in a national antitrust suit brought by Thurman Arnold on behalf of independent motion picture theater operators, who were being squeezed by the major producers, who channeled premium films to affiliated exhibitors. The plaintiffs won a $100,000 damage judgment, which was trebled pursuant to the damage provisions of the Sherman Act.

Although White wrote few briefs, his research was legendary in the firm. His partners later said that he was the only lawyer they ever knew who "physically attacked a library," giving new meaning to the phrase "hit the books." "Illegible notes in green ink on an endless series of yellow foolscap pages" would be typed by patient secretaries into compendious memoranda analyzing a case or a legal issue. Robert Harry still remembers one example of White's work, a hundred-page memo analyzing the doctrine of *res ipsa loquitur* in Colorado: "After he left the firm, I'd take it out of my desk from time to time and just shake my head over its depth."

Most of White's practice took place behind closed doors—negotiating real estate deals, structuring financial mechanisms for various commercial transactions, counseling clients, large and small, on antitrust exposure or the effect of the labor laws. He eventually developed specialized knowledge of bankruptcy and some areas of tax law. His clients included not only the Denver National Bank, IBM, and the Boettcher interests, but also small ready-mix concrete firms who faced price-fixing charges, restaurant owners seeking zoning variances, out-of-state corporations seeking to make quiet purchases of industrial sites, real estate companies buying and selling property, and even a new mining company—the Leadville Corporation—which later became a cult stock. One of his clients, Marshall Goldberg, had been an opponent for two years in the National Football League. Biggie Goldberg had been an all-American halfback at the University of Pittsburgh and then played for the Chicago Cardinals, including their 1947 championship team. He then moved into the heavy equipment business and made a fortune buying and refurbishing equipment for manufacturing in both the United States and overseas. "I needed some legal advice for a deal I was putting together in Colorado," Goldberg remembered years later, "and I said to myself, Why not Whizzer White? So I called him, we talked briefly, he took care of the matter, and that was that. Not a lot of reminiscing, even though we both remembered playing under the worst conditions in the history of professional football—the scoreless tie in monsoon rains in Buffalo at the beginning of the 1940 season."

When White returned to Denver, he vowed to shed his past and to build a career on his own professional merit. He made a conscious effort to dissociate himself from professional sports and routinely declined interviews with Denver sportswriters who wanted to chronicle the athletic hero home from the war and from Washington. He told his college friend Ira Rothgerber at the time: "I want to establish my practice, contribute to the community, and keep my name out of the goddamn newspapers." White's community service was enormously energetic and covered multiple fronts. During almost a decade and a half in Denver, he served actively, often holding leadership positions, in a variety of organizations, including the Social Science Foundation at Denver University, Boy Scouts of America, the Urban League, the Denver Welfare Council, YMCA, Denver Chamber of Commerce, Denver and Colorado Bar Associations, the Rhodes Trust, and several charities, principally the United Fund, Camp Chief Ouray for Children, and Rose Memorial Hospital.

Of all the organizations to which he devoted time, the one that most engaged his mind and his passions was the Social Science Foundation, whose board of trustees he joined in the summer of 1953. (Others elected that year

were Walter Paepcke, the founder of the Aspen Institute of Humanistic Studies, and Gordon Wright, chairman of the department of history at the University of Oregon.) The foundation was created in 1923 to create a forum at
Denver University to inform the university and the local community "upon
the major aspects of the great social, industrial and international problems of
the present and future." In practice, the foundation sponsored lectures and
symposia on foreign policy, with emphasis on economic and political issues.
Eventually, the foundation was transformed into the Graduate School of International Studies, but in the mid-1950s it provided one of the few local vehicles for national and international speakers. Denver University may seem an
ironic object for White's energies in the light of his identification with the
University of Colorado, but his father-in-law, Robert Stearns, was a member
of the foundation's advisory board and his mother-in-law was the grand-
daughter of the first chancellor of DU. Denver at midcentury was a city where
family ties created multiple social and business connections.

No matter how hard he tried to stay out of the limelight or to suppress his
fame, he was still Whizzer White to many—clients, courthouse personnel,
and strangers on the street. Even countermen at local lunch spots near his office, such as Shaner's, tried constantly—and fruitlessly—to forget his lunch
bills, out of admiration. He was largely successful in keeping his name out of
the newspapers, but not because the press had lost interest in him. His unremarkable success in passing the Colorado Bar examination required headlines
in Denver. He had not been home four months when the Colorado Jaycees
(Junior Chamber of Commerce) nominated him, more on the basis of his entire public career than for his recent activities, as one of the national organization's ten "outstanding young men of 1947" (the other local nominee was
Newton, but neither won). When he agreed to chair a committee to evaluate
the overall program of the Denver area Boy Scouts a few months later, the
Denver Post finally had an excuse for a new headline. He was so well known,
even in his early thirties, that he attracted cranks who tried to exploit a household name. A man claiming to be Byron (Whizzer) White passed a $225
bogus check at the West Virginia American Legion Convention in early 1949.
Even White's football days were never completely behind him. He was elected
to the National Football Hall of Fame, a creation of the Helms Foundation, in
1952, and he was voted one of the "greatest native athletes" by Colorado
sportswriters in 1953.

White's vow of privacy was not inconsistent with sustaining his passionate attachment to athletics, especially football. In public, he declined to participate in a reunion on Ralph Edwards's new radio program, *This Is Your Life!*,

in 1948, when Edwards gathered former *Collier's* all-American football players to honor Grantland Rice. Only five of the 1937 team selected by Rice agreed to attend the event; Biggie Goldberg was there, but White and Clint Frank were not, and neither replied to the invitations. Rice was "deeply touched" by those who were able to attend, especially Amos Alonzo Stagg and Jim Thorpe, both of whom he had known since the turn of the century, and all four members of the 1923 Notre Dame backfield, whom he had denominated as the Four Horsemen of the Apocalypse—the most famous cliché in sports history.

In private, White was a season-ticket holder for University of Colorado football games and a recruiter for the football program. His loyalty was to Harry Carlson, his former baseball coach and still the director of athletics, a father figure whom White later called the "most influential man on me while I was in school." Bunny Oakes, White's old coach, was gone. Oakes had been fired after the 1939 season; during the controversy that led to his dismissal, White defended Oakes in the press from the "wolves" who were after his head, notwithstanding private distaste for the coach's obsessive tactics. Beginning in 1948, when White's recruiting became active, the head coach was Dallas Ward, who had been an assistant coach for several years under Bernie Bierman at the University of Minnesota. Ward, tracking Bierman, ran a single wing, which put a premium on quick, smart running backs. White focused his recruiting energy on that category. Hugh Burns, an all-city halfback on Denver South High School's 1947 city champion, later recalled White's pitch: "He was extremely warm and solicitous and had me over to dinner at his house a couple of times. He pushed CU pretty hard, but I told him I was interested in Princeton, which I thought was a better school. *You wouldn't be happy there,* he said. *Too many rich boys. Stay here.*"

Burns went to Princeton nonetheless, played football briefly, and did not encounter White again for four years. When he applied for a Rhodes Scholarship, Burns discovered that White had become state secretary for the Rhodes Trust and as such the organizing official for the first step of the competition, whose structure had not changed since White's own candidacy, in 1937. At the reception for candidates, according to Burns, "he thrust out that huge right hand of his and simply said, 'White.'" At the interview, White asked Burns the first question: "Why did you quit football?" Burns thought he had lost on the spot, but his frank explanation—a dangerous concussion early in his college career—satisfied White and the rest of the committee. Burns won a scholarship and, on White's strong recommendation, attended Hertford College to read law because, White told him, "Fifoot is the best law tutor in Oxford."

Athletics—he was both participant and observer—remained central to the way Byron White organized his life. He regularly played squash, which he first learned in England and then mastered at Yale. He picked up golf after several years in Denver, after more than one false start. One of his early golf companions, a scratch golfer who was captain of the golf team at the University of Colorado and a classmate, thought White was frustrated with a game that moved so slowly and took so long to master at a refined level. His favorite recreation, and a lifelong passion providing profound pleasure, was the first sport of his youth—dry-fly fishing. Every summer he took four or five fishing trips, including at least one lasting a week to ten days. His range extended from the Clark Fork in western Montana to the tributaries of the Arkansas and Rio Grande Rivers, but his first love remained his deepest, the waters of the Cache La Poudre, near Fort Collins.

As a spectator, White not only enjoyed sports in which he had participated, but also went out of his way to watch unusually proficient athletes or contests, such as track meets and invitational tournaments, in which individuals and teams at peak levels of preparation put themselves to the test of the keenest competition and of the most focused pressure. He has portrayed his attendance at one event, the annual Amateur Athletic Union state track meet in 1959, as a turning point in his life. He told an interviewer from *Sports Illustrated* in 1962:

> I had a good, satisfactory law practice and a pretty decent life. One day in the summer of 1959 while I was living in Denver, I was driving back from an AAU track meet in Boulder and I got to thinking about the coming presidential campaign. I'd been reading what I could about the various candidates and shuffling through the names of these guys in my mind, I began to feel that Jack Kennedy would be my preference.

In fact, by the time White attended the track meet in June 1959, he had been talking with Kennedy and his political advisers for almost two months about what role—if any—he could or should play in the campaign for president that John F. Kennedy had been planning for almost four years but would not formally announce for another six months. White's ambivalence was not over whom to support but over how effective he could be in more than a grassroots role, a question that raised questions both of his own political judgment and of personal taste: much of his pleasure in Denver derived from rejecting chronic entreaties to run for political office and instead applying his belief in political participation only at retail. As Byron White turned forty-two, he had arrived at a crossroads he had taken measured steps for some time to avoid.

The Democratic Party of Colorado had tried to draft Byron White into elective politics while he was still in the navy and before he was of age to hold any office higher than congressman. In October 1945, a year before the midterm elections, leaders of the self-styled liberal wing of the party floated a clumsy trial balloon in the press seeking to generate a groundswell of support for his candidacy for governor. They quickly discovered that White would not be thirty—as required by the state constitution—in time for the election. The fallback target was the House of Representatives and the Second District, which included Denver and was held by a Republican. White was stationed in Washington, D.C., at the time, and working in the office of the chief of naval operations. He had no interest in elective politics. He had a year left in law school and had not decided where to practice. The party leaders were persistent, and they eventually convinced a reporter for the *Rocky Mountain News* to publicize their efforts by publishing that they had "written several letters to White" but had "received no reply" so far. "Democrats are expected to make several more attempts to get an answer from White before turning their support to another candidate."

Although the draft-White maneuver was both obvious and predictably futile, the liberal Democrats were earnest if not deft. The party had been dominated for more than a decade by Edwin Carl (Big Ed) Johnson, sixty-one, who had homesteaded in northeastern Colorado, served in the statehouse during the 1920s, then moved from lieutenant governor (1931–33) to governor (1933–37), and to the U.S. Senate (since 1937). His party allegiance was strictly on his own terms. He was unenthusiastic about the New Deal, sought to control federal relief programs at the local level, and opposed Roosevelt's candidacy for a third term. His most famous act as governor was his most ignominious: he briefly called out the Colorado National Guard in 1936 to close the southern border of the state to Hispanic migrant workers. Yet Johnson, who called himself "the big dumb Swede," was enormously popular and appealed to conservative elements of both parties. His critics said that he was the only politician in the state who could keep both ears to the ground, but he routinely won election by overwhelming margins. In 1945 Johnson was the only Democrat in the Colorado congressional delegation, although many contended that party made no difference in his case.

The strategy of the liberal upstarts in the Democratic Party, led by Eugene Cervi, the state chairman, was to identify young veterans whose youth and war service could be capitalized to shift the base of the party away from Johnson and those beholden to him. Cervi, in his late thirties, was a newspaperman who started a business journal after the war and served as a local gadfly, annoying the banking and commercial interests that made his publication successful. He was acerbic, volatile, and above all, loud—in both person and print—and Denver lawyers of the day would say, *The only thing certain about Gene Cervi is that sooner or later he would impugn your integrity and call you a son of a bitch—in person or in print.* Cervi's passionate support for White in 1945 eventually became equally passionate antagonism, but neither view ever made any difference to White, his reputation, or his career. Cervi made only one run himself for elective office. In 1948, he challenged Johnson for his Senate seat in the Democratic primary but carried none of Colorado's sixty-three counties and only three Denver precincts. His last attempt to convince White to run for elective office was in 1952. Cervi tried to manufacture a boom for White with a front-page story in his *Journal* that was more wishful thinking than reporting. Cervi wrote that

> White was being groomed as a candidate for governor on the Democratic ticket this week by a group of the party's young political leaders. White himself declined to comment on the movement when questioned by the Journal. Substantial support is building to present his name to the democratic state convention in Golden on June 28. Mr. White has been quietly active in the party since he returned from World War II navy duty overseas.

White's name was not placed in nomination, and Dan Thornton, the Republican incumbent, a rancher from Gunnison via Texas, was reelected.

Byron White was active in Democratic Party politics almost from the moment he arrived in Denver, but most of his work was strictly at the neighborhood level. "Every year after 1947 I worked on someone's committee," he recalled years later. "It might have been a judge, a candidate for state legislature or someone running for local office. I worked at it and I really got to know those people." He quickly became a precinct committeeman, but would not allow himself to be named one of the city's fourteen district captains for several years and then held the office—which was generally a holding pen for those wishing appointments as bailiffs and other low-level public employees—for only a few years. He resigned his captaincy in 1954 when Quigg Newton, his former law partner, ran against John Carroll, the former Denver congressman (1947–51), for the Senate seat held by Johnson, who, weary of Washington, was returning to Colorado to run for governor. Carroll was an ex-policeman who had gone to law school at night and had become a reform district attorney. When he won his congressional seat in 1946, he was one of the few Democrats to unseat a Republican incumbent. Carroll ran for reelection in 1948, and White went door-to-door distributing campaign literature.

The Newton-Carroll race put White in what he thought was an unten-able position, which he later explained: "I didn't feel it was right for me to get involved in that campaign in view of my personal relationships with these men." The primary was, as White lightly acknowledged, "heated," and frac-tured the Democratic Party in Denver. The traditional liberal-labor con-stituencies followed Carroll. Newton enjoyed the support of the so-called bluestocking country club Democrats, who probably would have been Re-publicans but for the unsavory capture of the Denver GOP by the Ku Klux Klan in the mid-1920s, an episode that helped to shape a generation of polit-ical allegiances. The intraparty division helped to elect the Republican candi-date, Gordon Allott, who held the seat for three terms.

In 1955, White was approached by Democratic leaders to run for office in the 1956 elections—mayor of Denver (Newton was retiring after eight years), congressman, or senator—any office. He refused, politely in public, more testily in private. "The trouble with you liberals," he told Lawrence Henry, the Denver County party chairman, "is that you think the only way to contribute to society is to run for office." When White discussed his decision later with one of his partners, Donald Hoagland, he was more pensive. "Well," he said, "I guess *somebody* has to run for the office"—pause—"but not me."

To Ira Rothgerber, White admitted that he did not dismiss the prospect of elective politics entirely, but on balance thought that he and the party were better off without him on a ticket: "I thought I could get elected to office. Once." The cryptic statement had a twofold meaning. White knew that he was too stubborn to compromise on principle or on important policy, and that his convictions were too strong to allow him simply to represent con-stituent interests. In the second place, his name might carry him into office, but his impatience with the press and public speaking was not necessarily ideal for the task. The exchange recalled for Rothgerber the decade-old campus joke—inaccurate but apt—that White's B in public speaking was a gift. After declining any nomination (as it turned out, for the last time), White spent his electoral energies in 1956 supporting John Carroll, who ran again for the Sen-ate and won this time over Dan Thornton. The election marked the best showing by the Colorado Democratic Party since World War II, because in addition to Carroll and two of the four congressional races, a reform Democ-rat, Stephen L. R. McNichols, was elected governor. McNichols had been lieutenant governor and had acquired experience and name recognition when Johnson developed health problems early in his term.

The election of McNichols was also significant because it marked the first time that a Catholic had been elected to statewide office in Colorado. There were other prominent Catholic governors, such as Michael DiSalle of Ohio, David Lawrence of Pennsylvania, and Edmund G. (Pat) Brown of California. Only Brown was from a Western state, but he presided over a deeply divided party and offered an unpromising test case for John F. Kennedy. When Kennedy, who had lost a strategic bid for the vice presidency in 1956, began to develop plans for pursuing the presidency in 1960, Colorado stood out as a propitious site for demonstrating the capacity of an Eastern Catholic to win votes. Kennedy's religion was not well known nationally and did not become a factor until well into 1959, but Kennedy and his advisers knew that the issue would pose a problem sooner or later, so the 1956 gubernatorial vote in Colorado was more than simply noteworthy.

The problem for a Kennedy campaign in Colorado was not religion but invisibility. No one knew him, and party officials who could be expected to play a significant role in the 1960 state convention, where delegates to the national convention would be chosen, tended to favor Adlai Stevenson or, to a much lesser extent, Stuart Symington. The first time Kennedy visited Colorado, to give a speech in Colorado Springs at the Broadmoor Hotel in 1956, was dispiriting. On a four-hour layover, Kennedy sat in the old Denver airport sipping coffee with a former Senate aide, Joe Dolan, who was now practicing law in Denver; no one recognized either man, and according to Dolan, "Kennedy wondered with something less than bemusement where he was and why he was there." Carroll's election to the Senate that fall buoyed Dolan about the possibilities for both the state party and for Kennedy.

In May of 1957, Dolan decided to light the fire from the West. He invited Kennedy, who readily agreed, to attend a reception in Denver. The visit, Dolan wrote Ted Sorensen, Kennedy's principal assistant, "was an unqualified success," complete with substantial radio and television coverage and adequate opportunities to meet party officials despite "the fact that it was opening day of the fishing season." Once the summer and the fishing season were over, Sorensen and Dolan mutually worried about the National Farmers Union, which was headquartered in Denver and showed signs of throwing its support to either Sen. Estes Kefauver or Sen. Hubert Humphrey. Dolan alerted Sorensen to the risk with a pair of newspaper clippings, and on October 1 Sorensen encouraged Dolan to meet with the NFU's "inner circle" and "point out to them" that "although Kennedy is not now a candidate, he may well turn out to be the Democratic nominee in 1960 (or later) whether or not the Farmers union supports him," and that they might not want to antagonize him. Dolan agreed to do what he could with the NFU leaders, but he was also anxious about Senator Carroll, who "damns with faint praise publicly—'a fine *young* man' may be the dubious compliment given while praising others," such as Paul Douglas, Kefauver, and Joe Clark, "more to his liking." Dolan was almost ready to write off Carroll and the NFU, but he was encouraged by support "among rank and file Dems, independents and Republicans." The persistent worry for Dolan was lack of enthusiasm in what he felt should be Kennedy's base: "The biggest stumbling block in my opinion is still the liberal Democrats, rather than religion." Dolan ticked off the liabilities: voting against the censure of Sen. Joseph McCarthy, family support in Massachusetts for McCarthy, and Kennedy's record "against reclamation" and "against the West."

To bolster Kennedy in the West and to shore up his foreign policy credentials, Sorensen began looking for a venue where the senator could deliver a mayor address on foreign affairs. With Dolan's help, the Social Science Foundation issued an invitation to speak in late February of 1958. The occasion had all the ingredients for a major embarrassment. Tickets were available only by stamped, self-addressed envelope, the location was changed at the last minute from a cozy three-hundred-seat auditorium at Denver University to the eight-thousand-seat Civic Auditorium, and Kennedy's private plane from Phoenix was late and buffeted by high winds as it crossed the Continental Divide into Denver. (To settle his nerves, Kennedy ordered a grasshopper—a blend of crème de menthe and cream—at the airport lounge, but only stared at the concoction when it was served.) A curtain was hastily hung behind the lectern to provide a background and to hide what were expected to be oceans of empty seats, but Kennedy drew eighty-two hundred, the largest audience in the foundation's thirty-year history. Dolan introduced White to Kennedy and to Sorensen but—in what he later viewed as a blunder—neglected to invite White to a postaddress reception with Denver district captains of the party.

Kennedy's speech covered a wealth of foreign policy issues—he advocated negotiations with the U.S.S.R. on the Middle East and on arms reduction, and urged more foreign aid for India—but he emphasized that federal aid to education was essential to the country's security:

> A year ago, a speech on foreign affairs would probably not have mentioned education. Today, we cannot avoid it. I do not know whether the Battle of Waterloo was won on the playing fields of Eton. But it is no exaggeration to say that the struggle in which we are now engaged may well be won or lost in the classrooms of America.

In a press conference following the remarks and preceding the meeting with party officials, Kennedy coyly—and charmingly—dodged the question whether he would run for president in 1960. He reiterated the themes of his prepared remarks and added that he viewed a tax cut as a "last step" to avoid an economic "turndown."

The morning after the address, Kennedy had an impromptu breakfast at the home of Lawrence Henry, the county party chairman. Over scrambled eggs, prepared by Henry's mother-in-law, who was the widow of a Pennsylvania congressman, Kennedy asked who should organize Colorado if he ran in 1960. Dolan's advice was, first, not a Catholic (which excluded Henry and Governor McNichols), and not Quigg Newton, now president of the University of Colorado and the most prominent Democrat not then holding office. The Newton-Carroll primary fight still had open wounds, but more important, Newton personified what Kennedy was trying to soft-pedal in the West—Ivy League (indeed, Skull and Bones at Yale), wealthy bluestocking, summer cottage on Cape Cod.

Dolan suggested White: *Should I approach him?* "No," Kennedy replied evenly. "Wait." Dolan was now intrigued with his own idea and did not think he needed to take no for an answer, so he floated his brainstorm to Sorensen in a letter three days after Kennedy's appearance: "Whizzer White looks no more attractive than C. U. President Newton on paper, but in fact Whizzer would help a lot, and Newton would be death (feuds carried over from being Mayor, Carroll-Newton-primary, too much old school tie, etc.)."

The fissures in the state Democratic Party closed somewhat in the 1958 election, when Republicans supported a right-to-work initiative that was defeated by a 60 percent majority in a huge voter turnout that forged a statewide alliance between the AFL-CIO and the National Farmers Union. McNichols was reelected governor, this time to the first four-year term in the state's history, and Democratic control of the General Assembly, which had passed more funding for education and highways, increased substantially. A few months after the midterm elections, John Kennedy theatrically telephoned Joe Dolan from the floor of the Senate and reached Dolan on the floor of the General Assembly—to which he had just been elected—with an agonized question: *Did you see the report in the* Chicago Daily News *that says a poll of delegates to the 1956 Democratic Convention shows I would only get one half vote* [of thirteen full votes] *in the Colorado delegation? What can I do?*

Dolan uncharacteristically urged caution. Stuart Symington was scheduled to speak soon in Denver, and reactions to his appearance would provide an up-to-date gauge of comparative candidate strength. On April 22, 1959, Dolan wrote Sorensen with his report: Symington was a dud, his enthusiasts were disappointed, and Stevenson diehards were discouraged with their pre-

canvass Kennedy's prospects and to review the putative organizational structure for the state campaign, White was presumed by all in the room to be the state chairman for Kennedy.

Any lingering reservations White had about his role for Kennedy were jettisoned less than a week after the Sorensen-Wallace lunch. On June 19 and 20, the seventy-first annual national Amateur Athletic Union (AAU) track meet was held at Folsom Field in Boulder. The best track-and-field athletes in the country would be competing both for AAU honors and to win a place on a team to be selected for the upcoming Pan-American Games. White was walking down the stadium steps returning to his seat after a brief absence and, as he recalled years later at a reunion of former United States attorneys in the Kennedy Administration,

> who was sitting on my left in a little cluster of professors but Richard Nixon. Well, I thought I'd sit down a couple of rows and listen. He had this group of professors' ear and he seemed to know what the records were. Well, riding home, I decided that, well, here I've been deep in local politics ever since I came to Colorado, but I'd never been interested in presidential politics. I thought I'd ought to do that just for fun, because I had some memories of Helen Gahagan Douglas and things like that.

Nixon had defeated Douglas in a battle between members of Congress for a Senate seat from California in 1950, largely by branding her as soft on communism. The *Daily Worker* had labeled her "one of the heroes of the 80th Congress" in 1947; she had voted more than three hundred times with Vito Marcantonio, a New York congressman and communist apologist; and Nixon charged that her support for the State Department's "appeasement" of communism in Asia was one of the causes of the Korean War. Nixon tagged Mrs. Douglas as "the Pink Lady," and the smear tactic worked. As one political journalist later observed: "Nixon won by 600,000 votes but in the process incurred a brutal reputation and a legion of enduring enemies."

Why White would care about Helen Gahagan Douglas's fate is not clear. As a political matter, the Kennedy family had supported Joseph McCarthy, whom John Kennedy had once publicly defended as a "great American patriot" and whose censure in the Senate he would not support. Other Kennedy allies had used tactics identical to those used by Nixon; indeed, Nixon's campaign against Mrs. Douglas was patterned on George Smathers's primary campaign for the Senate the same year in Florida against Claude Pepper, whom Smathers labeled "the Red Pepper." On the other hand, White had a somewhat idealized view of partisan politics and even was uncomfortable providing bus or taxi fare to voters who needed transportation to the polls. "I remember when he was a precinct captain and came to my door with a $10 bill to cover transportation expenses for one local election," Richard Schmidt would later say about an election in the early 1950s. "Byron stood on the doorstep, held the bill at arm's length as if it carried an off aroma, and said, 'Here,' without ever making eye contact. He seemed to think it bordered on corruption."

Perhaps Nixon stimulated White's competitive impulses by suddenly appearing in person. Here was the opponent, personified—the smooth, fluent, and engaging spokesman for a Republican establishment with which White had no sympathy; and here was his natural constituency, a comfortable elite, studiously impractical, with no understanding of the problems facing the common man. Nixon had addressed the National Education Association in Colorado Springs earlier in the day and arrived late, escorted by Senator Gordon Allott—the man who defeated John Carroll in 1954—and saw only the final event, the two-hundred-meter dash. At the medal ceremonies Nixon awarded the team championship to the Southern California Striders, from Los Angeles, and congratulated Al Oerter for setting a new AAU discus record, 186 feet, despite the intermittent rain that afternoon, but he made no public remarks. More significantly, White was now unambivalently committed to running Kennedy's campaign in Colorado, and eager to get to work.

A few days after the AAU meet, Wallace and Sorensen submitted a five-page memorandum to Kennedy that concluded, "We are not as strong as we should be in Colorado," but that ratified the choice of White and Dolan:

> The aim is for a Protestant, well-known Chairman who gets along with all factions of the party, a dependable Secretary [who is] representative of various Congressional districts, interest groups and ethnic groups. Whizzer White seems to be the logical chairman with Joe Dolan the Secretary.

By the time Kennedy received the memorandum, he had already talked with White by telephone and considered the question closed. White and Dolan were already devising an organizational strategy. Dolan would take responsibility for Denver, White for the rest of the state. As a state representative, Dolan was well suited to handle the city, especially with his law partner serving as the county chairman. White was more at home in the rural areas of the state. The fight would be uphill all the way.

11

THE KENNEDY CAMPAIGN

THE MOST powerful Democrats in the state were against Kennedy. Of ten state "political powers" identified in Wallace and Sorensen's memo to Kennedy, only three were publicly known to be for Kennedy (Lawrence Henry, his partner Harold Collins, and Mike Pomponio of North Denver, a restaurant owner who controlled "the largest bloc of Democratic votes in Colorado"); another, Western slope congressman Wayne Aspinall, "has told JFK privately he is for him" but was publicly understood to support Stevenson. Governor McNichols had personal reasons not to support Kennedy. As one of the Catholic governors who hoped to be nominated for vice president, McNichols needed to support anyone but Kennedy, because two Catholics on the ticket would be unthinkable. Joe Dolan and Henry assumed his strategy was to stand as a favorite son when the delegation split over the other candidates. Then he and the other favorite sons could put up a game fight, fall back when no consensus developed, and hope to be picked up by Stevenson or Symington to balance the ticket. The Wallace-Sorensen memo detailed Kennedy's "biggest problem":

opposition of various leaders in Colorado. Governor McNichols is a Catholic who is said to harbor visions of the Vice Presidency—possible with Stevenson but not Kennedy. Former Senator Ed Johnson is for Lyndon Johnson. Denver is the headquarters of the Farmers' Union whose leaders, including

Charles Brannan, lean to Humphrey. E. Palmer Hoyt [editor] of the Denver Post is for Symington. Senator Carroll and National Committeeman George Rock like Stevenson.

Rock, of the Bank of Denver, was nonplussed when Dolan told him in July that a Kennedy-for-president organization was in the final planning stages. Dolan reported to Sorensen:

> Byron White and I had an hour's chat with the National Committeeman yesterday. He said he probably would not get into any effort concerning any presidential candidate but that his estimate of feeling in Colorado was some sentiment for Symington, some for Humphrey and a realization that Kennedy has some substantial strength elsewhere. Many of the delegates, he feels, will have an underlying feeling for Stevenson and if no candidate is nominated on an early ballot they will turn to Stevenson. He indicated in his usual backhand way he still likes Stevenson better than anyone else. Of Kennedy he said "nobody is for him in Colorado except Joe." White corrected this misapprehension by indicating his support for the Senator but we didn't bother to enumerate others to him. "Whizzer" and I share a feeling that he will not help us and he seemed unencouraging about the possibility of "grass roots" efforts in behalf of any candidate. This certainly makes sense for him since he does best if there is no choosing up of sides.

The principal challenge for Dolan and White, other than the top echelon of the party, continued to be exposure of their candidate. In the short run, White was eager to obtain detailed campaign literature from Kennedy's office and discussed the matter by telephone with the senator himself shortly before the meeting with Rock. Dolan wanted pamphlets outlining Kennedy's views on six topics—foreign policy, national defense, monopolies, reclamation, farm policy, and education. The Wallace-Sorensen memo and the White-Dolan team agreed on one strategic objective: Kennedy needed to make more personal appearances throughout the state. His strength was proving to be greatest in states "where he addressed large party gatherings," such as Jefferson-Jackson Day dinners. Dolan had tried unsuccessfully for two years to get Kennedy on a Jefferson-Jackson Day program, so obtaining an invitation to "address a statewide Democratic meeting this fall" seemed more likely to Wallace and Sorensen than to White and Dolan.

With no statewide opportunity available, White and Dolan instead arranged for a multilocation tour, such as Dolan had suggested to Sorensen earlier in the year. Dolan laid out the plan in a letter to Stephen Smith, who was now his contact in the unannounced campaign, while Sorensen was constantly on the road with Kennedy. White was scheduled to speak to the Democratic Club Monday Forum on October 26, "when we will kick off and hope to score on November 28th." The score, to which Dolan's shameless pun referred, was Kennedy's cramped three-day visit to Colorado and Wyoming, now scheduled for November 28–30. The visit would be one of two critical events for the Kennedy campaign in Colorado and for the relationship between White and the candidate. The other—ironically, less important—would be White's work at the state party convention six months later.

When Kennedy's itinerary was distributed to the press, White's prominent role throughout—chairing the lunches and the dinner on the first day, "arranging" the principal meetings on the Western slope the third day—prompted the predictable newspaper story. The headline in the *Rocky Mountain News* read, "Whizzer Carries the Ball for Kennedy." The details were by now familiar to local readers, down to the practiced vagueness about details that White offered about his background. The reporter, Bob Perkin, was a college contemporary of White, and he teased out White's fullest statement about why he was a Democrat, a statement that conveniently buttressed the interests and strengths of his candidate:

> I came from a small town, and we all got pretty well shook up during the '30s. I suppose this was influential in deciding my political affiliation. But it was really nailed down on international issues—the sort of thing we ran into and talked about all the time at Oxford. It seemed plain to me that international issues would dominate our lives, and also would dominate domestic issues. It seemed to me that the Democratic Party had more vision in these areas, and I think it still does.

White conceded that his prominent in-laws were Republicans, and he spoke, uncharacteristically, about his wife's views: "Marion has her own ideas" and "she doesn't like to follow anyone. She leans a little toward being a Democrat."

Kennedy had been scheduled for some time to speak at a lunch of the American Municipal Association on Monday, the thirtieth. That commitment provided the opportunity for plenty of partisan activity sandwiched around the Sunday luncheon address. The centerpiece of the three-day November swing became a dinner in Denver billed as the Metropolitan Denver Democratic Dinner, with Byron R. White as chairman, in the Silver Glade Room of the Cosmopolitan Hotel. "The whole affair was jerry-built," Dolan later explained. "The state chairman and the county chairmen outside of Denver wouldn't do anything for Kennedy, so we convinced the five Denver-area county chairs to sponsor a 'metropolitan' event." Kennedy arrived in Denver the morning of the dinner and went to Boulder for a meeting with local party officials and lunch with known Kennedy supporters. He then attended a football game between the University of Colorado and the Air Force Academy, an event notable for two details: Kennedy and White were photographed together earnestly watching the game, and the photo would occupy a central location in White's office from the day it was hung. The academy cadets, proud of their academic regimen and dismissive of the party-school reputation of their opponents, started a chant at one point that must have startled Kennedy, if he heard it. Derisively referring to CU with the name of a local saloon that had been named for a remote outpost, the cadet wing shouted, "Beat Tulagi Tech!"

The dinner was a financial failure (tickets were $5 each and the hotel took $4.75); the county chairs—who, except for Lawrence Henry, were all for Stevenson—seemed unmoved by Kennedy; and the turnout was disappointing. But the visit achieved its objective: Kennedy met Democrats in Boulder, Denver, Pueblo, Grand Junction, and Cheyenne, Wyoming, and everywhere he went both newspapers and television provided rich coverage and emphasized the warm receptions he received at every stop. Kennedy was also finding his voice in identifying themes for the West—more presidential options under the Taft-Hartley Act for dealing with labor issues (which pleased both sides), a comprehensive reclamation policy (a commitment to the principle, if not particular details), and the unexceptionable planks of more federal aid to education and rational surplus policies for farmers. His main point at every stop, however, was "drift" in foreign policy, nicely captured by a *Denver Post* headline "U.S. Lost World Supremacy to Russians, Says Kennedy." The central image of his dinner speech was loss:

> The Russians beat us into outer space. They beat us around the sun. They beat us to the moon. Half of Indochina has disappeared behind the Iron Curtain. Tibet and Hungary have been crushed. Russia has a long-sought foothold in the Middle East, and even a foothold in Latin America.

Kennedy said that it was "not too late" and that "we can close the gaps and pull ahead" with "everyone's help and sacrifice." The speech tacked between the specific and the general and was well received. For Byron White, the visit was a personal triumph, although he would never acknowledge it in those terms. He was simply doing what he signed up to do. To Joe Dolan, the visit portended more: "We were flying between Denver and Grand Junction, I think, and Byron and Jack were sitting across the aisle from each other. Byron was talking in great detail about local issues, political personalities, and a whole carload of things, and Jack was like blotting paper—absorbing everything White had to say. It was an eerie feeling. He was almost in a swoon. I knew that if JFK won, the Whizzer would go with him—that Jack wanted him, and wanted him badly."

Two weeks after the whirlwind tour, one of the principal obstacles to Kennedy's hopes in Colorado was unexpectedly, and bizarrely, eliminated when George Rock was found dead in a Denver park after what turned out to be a night of carousing. Kennedy's fortunes did not change overnight. In fact, when Kennedy formally announced his candidacy for the presidency, on January 2, 1960, the news hit Denver, in the words of Tom Gavin of the *Rocky Mountain News,* "with the force and impact of a lobbed marshmallow." McNichols and Carroll were noncommittal. Dolan and White used the occasion as an opportunity to announce the opening of local campaign headquarters, and White was quoted as saying, somewhat flatly, that "he's as strong as any other candidate here." Lawrence Henry won a bitter three-ballot election to succeed Rock as national committeeman on January 9—a repudiation of both McNichols and Carroll, who both backed another candidate. White issued a statement assuring that Henry would not play an organizing role for Kennedy in light of his new responsibilities, but privately the Kennedy forces were delighted that one of their people had acceded to the most important national position in the state party. Whatever leverage could have been used against them by an unfriendly committeeman had now been turned around. The state party convention, in Durango, was scheduled for the weekend of June 17, but the Kennedy forces knew that the race would be shaped by two critical primary elections before then—Wisconsin, on April 5, and West Virginia, on May 10.

Between Henry's election and the state convention, White and Dolan would concentrate on developing support for Kennedy in each of the state's four congressional districts. The delegates to the national convention, with forty half votes, would be selected in Durango by congressional district— eight from each of the four districts, plus eight at large. That procedure meant that White needed constantly to be in motion in order to recruit and shore up troops in locations hundreds of miles apart—Greeley (county seat of Weld, the largest farming county, in the Second District); Pueblo and Colorado Springs (both in the Third District); and Grand Junction (heart of the Fourth District, on the Western slope). Outside of Denver, which was Dolan's watch, only Pueblo—with its big labor base in the steel mills—was strongly for Kennedy.

Notwithstanding these challenges, as the Wisconsin and West Virginia primaries grew closer, Dolan asked Robert Kennedy on one of his many trips through Denver whether he wanted "Byron and me to give you some help" in the two key primary states. Kennedy, sitting on a couch in shirtsleeves and concentrating on a fistful of memoranda in one hand, did not even look up from what he was reading. Fluttering the fingers of his free hand, as if he were brushing away a small fly, he muttered quietly, "No, no, no, Joe, that's OK. We'll take care of it." The message was unmistakable—do your job, capitalize on your comparative advantage, and leave the larger projects to the machinery in place. That is not to say that Robert Kennedy—"Bob" to Dolan and White—was either cold or dismissive of the Colorado operation. He respected White's judgment, especially his hardheaded practicality; and White, nine years Kennedy's senior, admired the no-nonsense drive and passionate loyalty he found in the brother of the candidate. White and Robert Kennedy shared a common style and tastes—they were terse, thoughtful, anti-intellectual, stimulated by personal and physical challenge, impatient with routine and structure, and deeply, almost immobilizingly, sentimental about family. They also shared a common sense of humor, touched with irony like John Kennedy's, but not as indirect, and more genuinely self-deprecating, although in a square-, not stoop-shouldered, posture.

Shortly after the senator announced his candidacy, White sent a thank-you letter to Robert Kennedy for the hospitality extended to him when he was in Washington to plan the first steps of the formal campaign: "That was a very pleasant evening at your home and I do wish to thank Ethel and yourself." After reporting Henry's election as national committeeman, White concluded: "We have circled February 8 and hope your schedule still permits planning a swing through Denver on that day. We could certainly get in a couple of hours on the slopes and have a meeting with some key people that evening." More than thirty years later, after he had retired, White tried to put into words the intimacy he felt for Robert Kennedy: "We made several trips around out of Denver and I became tremendously attracted to him. Sometimes you just know you have a bond with another guy—and we did." Like the premature visit to Robert Harry's home, White's first visit to the Kennedy's home at Hickory Hill in McLean, Virginia, reassured him: "after talking to [Ethel] and Bobby and seeing [the] family, I knew I was in the right place."

Byron White also spent time on the campaign trail with Edward M. Kennedy—the twenty-eight-year-old youngest brother, and "Teddy" to everyone. Since October, the youngest Kennedy had been assigned to the

Western states, and he and White saw a great deal of each other from February 1960 through the national convention. Their first task together was the Western States Democratic Conference on the first weekend in February, in Albuquerque. They could have flown, but White suggested that they drive, an opportunity at least for the older man to size up the younger. The meeting was an early opportunity for candidates—declared and presumptive—to develop contacts with politicians from twenty states. Symington did not attend, but Kennedy and Humphrey did, and Lyndon Johnson had plenty of surrogates, including Governor McNichols, who was plumping simultaneously for Johnson and for himself as convention keynote speaker in place of the odds-on choice, thirty-five-year-old Sen. Frank Church of Idaho. McNichols was rebuffed again, at least with respect to his own ambitions. When White and Teddy Kennedy returned to Denver, White announced the formation of the Colorado Kennedy for President Committee, the first committee for any candidate in the state. The committee included prominent Democrats from all over the state and from all spectrums of the party—ranging, as the *News*'s Gavin pointed out, "from union officials to the vice president of one of Denver's largest banks, [and] heavy with top Democratic organizational officials."

Between February and June, White and Dolan watched from the sidelines as the pivotal state primary campaigns in Wisconsin and West Virginia were waged. Both felt out of the line of heavy fire. White even sent a somewhat plaintive two-page letter to Robert Kennedy on April 12, exactly one week after the imposing victory in Wisconsin over Hubert Humphrey, and asked if he could spend a day or two in Colorado and Wyoming at the end of the month shoring up weak areas, but with the proviso that "I'd rather you missed Colorado Springs than lose in West Virginia." He closed with a chilly observation about the renewal in West Virginia of the contest with Humphrey: "Regards to Teddy and best of luck. H.H. can bleed more and longer than any gladiator I've heard about."

The Colorado state convention was six weeks after Kennedy's overwhelming victory over Humphrey on May 10 in the West Virginia primary, which produced Humphrey's withdrawal from the field. In late May, White began to worry that the opposition was catching up. He telephoned Steve Smith and said, as Smith advised Robert Kennedy, that "we will be lucky to get 9 votes out of Colorado and that we need some help in the form of telephone calls from Jack" to the senator's strongest supporters, including Henry, and that "in any case, Teddy should go back out there." Robert Kennedy sent in other Western reinforcements prior to the Colorado convention, one of whom was Congressman Stewart Udall of Arizona, who spent two days campaigning with White. Udall had just pulled off an unexpected upset in his home state by wresting all seventeen of the state votes, bound by unit rule, from the governor, who was a Johnson agent. He later recalled the two-day whirl around Denver, where he was met at the plane by White:

> He took me—his wife had the other car—in an old, battered car and we drove around Denver for two days, in bars and out to homes to see people, talking to delegates or prospective delegates, and trying to persuade them to be for Kennedy. There we were, and within a matter of a year and a half later, I was in the cabinet and he was on the Supreme Court. And here we were, tooting around in an old car, going to bars. It was sort of a fascinating political vignette of the whole American political system.

Both Teddy and Robert Kennedy preceded their brother to Durango, and their presence helped a great deal to firm up wavering convention votes. For example, the blue-collar area of north Denver and Thornton, in Adams County, should have been natural bases for Kennedy, but some political leaders there were initially attracted to Symington or Estes Kefauver. The Ciancio brothers—Don and Frank (Buddy)—ran a restaurant in Thornton that was caught in the cross fire of an intraparty war between the sheriff and the district attorney over gambling allegations, and the dispute threatened to sidetrack attention from the issue of the national ticket. "Then Teddy showed up in Durango, greeted Frank Ciancio like a long-lost brother, and all the ducks began to line up in a row," according to John L. Kane, who was an alternate delegate from Adams County. Kane was appointed chairman of Students for Kennedy by Ira Rothgerber, White's intimate friend from Denver and the chairman of the Colorado citizens committee. "Teddy even rode a bucking bronco; he did anything he could to help," Kane noted.

By the time that Senator Kennedy arrived in Durango, early Saturday morning, June 18, on the second day of the convention, three weeks after White's anxious telephone call to Smith, 80 percent of the delegates to Los Angeles had been selected—those from the First, Second, and Third Congressional Districts had been selected in regional meetings, and those from the Fourth District had been chosen in Durango (which was in the district) the night before. The only delegates left to be chosen were the eight from the state at large, each—as with all delegates—with only a half vote. Kennedy gave a rousing speech, and his forces won five—their entire slate—of the eight seats. As he slumped in exhaustion while waiting for his private plane to arrive at the

Durango airport, he wondered aloud whether the seventeen-hundred-mile trip had been worth the effort for two and a half votes at the convention. Dolan could not resist rubbing it in. He pointed out that he and White had expected to get four delegates, so "all you came for is the difference." Kennedy laughed. "What am I good for, a half a vote?" White chimed in: "But you cheered us all up."

At a press conference in Durango, Kennedy framed the challenge as he looked forward to the national convention, in less than a month: Lyndon Johnson would be his most difficult opponent. Hubert Humphrey had been eliminated by the West Virginia primary, and Adlai Stevenson was being told that he would be improperly evading the primary and state convention process. Stuart Symington, with no organization and little national presence, was not mentioned. Kennedy, whose votes on reclamation had handicapped his candidacy at the outset in the West, also tried again to reassure the region by promising to appoint a Westerner as secretary of the interior. The Denver press—not fully appreciating the magnitude of Udall's achievement in Arizona—immediately speculated that McNichols might be in Kennedy's mind. Kennedy needed 761 delegate votes to win the nomination, and he told the Durango news conference that every vote (he did not say "half vote") counted. The *Denver Post* reporter observed, somewhat myopically: "That is one reason he regards Colorado as a most important pivotal state and is concentrating on trying to get a majority of the state's [twenty-one] delegates."

The Sorensen-Wallace memo a year before had labeled Colorado as an "influential" state, but the attention that Kennedy paid to the state in 1960 may have had less to do with its intrinsic value than with the preconvention message that his muscular state organizations were sending to declared and potential rivals: this is hand-to-hand combat, every yard of beachhead counts, and if you are in the way you will be hurt. One conspicuous casualty in Durango was Big Ed Johnson, who supported his namesake from Texas and failed to win election as a delegate. White denied that the former governor and senator was a target in Durango; he claimed that the Kennedy forces were simply trying to win a majority of the at-large delegates and that Johnson got caught in the cross fire between Kennedy and Stevenson supporters. The explanation contained enough truth to be plausible, but the fact remained that, as Kennedy himself said in Durango, Lyndon Johnson was the principal opponent now, and without a Johnson backer in the delegation—especially an influential one—the Stevenson delegates could be hoped to fall in behind Kennedy in a head-to-head contest between the two senators.

The Kennedy forces had shown their muscle in Durango and emerged with at least 11 of Colorado's 21 votes (eventually the number became 13 ½*), an achievement that earned the grudging admiration of Senator Carroll, who was committed to Stevenson: "Very smooth. They had the horses, and they sure came home. I thought I might be dropped along with Ed Johnson." Others drew an additional lesson from Durango. The *Post* concluded: "'Whizzer' White a Comer in Colorado Politics"—although the question was open whether he would finally agree to run for statewide office or might become attorney general in a Kennedy administration. The night after the final slate was chosen, White and Dolan hosted a celebration party at a local "watering hole," as one of the celebrants later put it, and "everyone was very excited and eager to blow off some steam." Wild Turkey bourbon on the rocks was the beverage of choice, and after the principal host had finished two or three, one of the younger members of the party decided to play follow-the-leader. Dolan lightly interjected a caution: "He's pretty wound up— don't try to keep up with him, kid."

Byron White was a Kennedy delegate to the Democratic National Convention in Los Angeles, but Robert Kennedy asked him and Joe Dolan to come "a week or so" early to help him with delegate challenges, rules issues, or problems with the platform. As it turned out, they arrived only a few days early, there were no substantial questions over the rules, and Robert Kennedy knew more than White and Dolan put together about the practices and rules decisions of past conventions. "Bob would ask a hypothetical question," Dolan would later recall, "and we would scratch our heads, and he would snap, 'Virginia, 1952.' I think he was using us for batting practice." White was the liaison between the candidate and the Colorado delegation, but Robert Kennedy inadvertently prevented him from doing the job. "Every time [White] would try to leave," according to Dolan, "Bob would say, 'Wait a minute, Byron. Stay here. Stick around, stick around.'" Robert Kennedy used White as a tactical sounding board and political compass, testing his reactions to developing situations or weighing options for dealing with different demands or competing priorities. He also used White and Dolan for spot jobs, such as putting delegates who were on the fence together with, in Dolan's words, "outstanding scholars who were publicly for John Kennedy and were at the convention," such as John Kenneth Galbraith and Arthur Schlesinger, Jr.

---

* At the state convention, there were 22 half votes for Kennedy, 9 for Stevenson, 2 for Symington, and 9 uncommitted. In Los Angeles, the final vote was 27 half votes for Kennedy, 11 for Johnson, 2 for Stevenson, and 2 not voting.

Other than the suspense over the outcome, which was diminishing by the minute, the convention was a lark for White, at least by comparison to the constant delegate tending he had done in Durango. As would happen so often in his professional career, his football past came back to life, this time first from delegates rather than from the press—although during the convention the *Denver Post* would note, "Ex–Grid Star 'Whizzer' White Effective Friend of Kennedy." One of the Ohio delegates was John Wiethe, the other law student on the 1940–41 Detroit Lions, now a lawyer in Cincinnati and chairman of the Hamilton County Democratic Central Committee. White and Wiethe were still on the same team, so to speak: the Ohio delegation was solidly for Kennedy, thanks to Gov. Michael DiSalle's early endorsement, three days after the senator formally announced his candidacy. One of the other Lions, now living in southern California, Bill Radovich (now better known for *Radovich v. NFL*), arranged an impromptu postconvention reunion for the two delegates and the other Lion alumni in the area, "which was fun," according to Radovich, "although Byron was awfully pumped up about politics. He kept saying, 'We've got to get this guy elected.' "

John F. Kennedy was nominated on the first ballot, as he wished, in only forty-five minutes, on July 13, 1960, with 806 votes, 45 more than necessary; 13 ½ came from the Colorado delegation. A week later, Senator Kennedy announced that White would serve as national chairman of Citizens for Kennedy, a nonpartisan organization designed to attract active support from independents, Republicans, or others who did not wish to work through their local Democratic organization. Each local committee would be self-financing. When Pierre Salinger, Kennedy's press secretary, announced the appointment, a reporter asked White's religious affiliation. Salinger snapped, "We don't ask about that"; he would consider it a fair question only if Vice Pres. Richard M. Nixon were asked about the religious affiliation of his aides.

The "citizens" concept was copied from similar structures used in the previous presidential election by both parties. In theory such groups provided a mechanism for capturing enthusiastic support that would not be channeled into regular party organizations. In some areas, such as Chicago, the party organization was so strong that it would countenance only token counterorganizations. In New York, on the other hand, the citizens concept was a useful means for mediating the split between Tammany Hall's remnants, led by Carmine DeSapio and state chairman Michael H. Prendergast, and the reform Democrats, led by former senator Herbert H. Lehman and former governor Averill Harriman. In fact, White's first major task as chair was to accompany Robert Kennedy to New York City to reassure the regular Democrats that they could coexist with an independent organization working for Kennedy. White called on Phil Kaiser, his old friend from Oxford, now teaching at American University, to brief him and Kennedy on the problem, since Kaiser had worked for Harriman and knew the topography of the factions in detail. After Robert Kennedy forged a truce between the factions, he and White were off to Philadelphia with Joe Dolan and Fred Dutton—a campaign operative and former executive secretary to Gov. G. Edmund (Pat) Brown of California—to make peace between Sen. Joe Clark, who was a Stevenson loyalist, and Congressman Billy Green, who, in Dolan's words, was "a law unto himself politically." The pace was quick-step and Robert Kennedy took no prisoners. In Joe Dolan's words, "The Kennedys were ferocious: never postmortem, never reminisce—always take the next hill, and the next."

After dealing with the emergencies on the East Coast, Robert Kennedy turned his attention to a tour to stimulate voter registration. He was joined by White, Frank (Topper) Thompson, an ex-congressman from New Jersey, and Lawrence O'Brien, the national campaign director. White asked Kaiser to tag along, because White had picked him to run the Citizens for Kennedy operation in the Midwest. On a plane flight from New York to Chicago, at White's urging, Kaiser confronted Robert Kennedy with a sensitive and unpleasant problem—his father's widely assumed anti-Semitism. Kennedy "defended the old man," Kaiser said later, "but he was very hardheaded about it, in the best sense," and solicited suggestions for muting the criticisms. Kaiser suggested publicizing the ambassador's charitable work with Jewish hospitals and other activities going back for several years, and his plan was implemented, although Norman Vincent Peale's organization, the National Conference of Citizens for Religious Freedom, probably did more to create a useful backlash than Kaiser's direct engagement. In Ted Sorensen's words, "The 'Peale Group' . . . stirred a wave of anger and dismay from coast to coast."

After Chicago, Kennedy and Byron White visited San Francisco to meet with the leaders of the northern California campaign, Thomas Lynch and William H. Orrick. The issue there was whether the split between the regular Democrats and the Tom Braden–led liberal wing of the party would damage the campaign, and whether a Citizens organization could help. Kennedy and White had no chance to debate the question. In Orrick's words,

> We went [into the meeting] with a chip on our shoulder and we got Bob Kennedy and we said, "We're running. . . ." "We want to run the Kennedy-Johnson campaign in northern California, and we don't want any part of this citizens campaign and you've got to decide it. Are you going to let us run it?"

Bob in his customary fashion said, "Yeah." And so we didn't argue with him; we turned on our heels and left and that was the end of it so far as we thought there was any dilution of our authority. We did however, [watch] the citizens campaign very closely but it was really, the one out here [in San Francisco] was just a joke in terms of effective campaigning.

Orrick's tough, blunt style impressed both Kennedy and White, who were also happy to leave well enough alone.

Once the brushfires were extinguished, or at least tamped down, and lines of authority were delineated as clearly as they could be, Byron White's primary job as national chairman of Citizens for Kennedy, eventually Citizens for Kennedy and Johnson, was, as he explained to the *Washington Post,*

to establish state organizations that would supplement and serve the National Committee operations and that would, in no case, be a rival to them. Each state organization would vary in its set-up, he said, to get as many votes as possible from those not committed to the regular Democratic organizations.

The job required energy and tact. Regular party organizations disliked the independent committees for two reasons: they tended to disrupt local priorities and divert resources to the national ticket, and if they became strong enough, they could displace the local organization—which eventually happened, for example, in Cincinnati.

The strategy was simple. Where the local organization was strong, the Citizens committee would work in parallel and simply complement the operation, but where it was weak, the committee would provide primary support. White moved to Washington, D.C., at the beginning of August and set up offices in the Esso Building, at the foot of Capitol Hill, but he spent a great deal of time on the road, vetting candidates for local committee chairmanships and dealing with the odd flare-up between committees and regular organizations. White used only three criteria in selecting his principal local committee chairs: they should not be identified with the regular party organization, they should preferably be non-Catholics, and—most difficult, and to many candidates mysterious—they should inspire his trust.

In addition to organizing local Citizens committees, White had the diplomatic challenge of telling some volunteers either that they were not needed (that is, not wanted) or that they would be better utilized in a different position (that is, at a respectable distance from White or Robert Kennedy's operation as general campaign manager). Joe Dolan, who continued to work closely with White, described them as "amiable foul balls," who had to be shunted off to Businessmen for Kennedy and Johnson or spot or-ganizing work in the Dakotas. From time to time, the travel requirements took on theatrical overtones, literally, depending on local needs, sponsorship, and speaker availability; Joe Dolan still remembers vividly the most unlikely trip, an airborne puddle hop in a DC-3 with stops in Decatur (Illinois), Cincinnati, and Denver, carrying White, Dolan, Arthur Schlesinger, Jr., and actress Angie Dickinson.

White divided supervisory responsibility over the state committees more or less regionally. John Horne, a former administrative assistant to Sen. John Sparkman of Alabama, handled the South. Phil Kaiser was responsible for most of New England and the Great Lakes, particularly his home state of Wis-consin, and the delicate issue—thanks to the Richard J. Daley machine—of Illinois. Luke Harvey Poe, another ex–Rhodes scholar and Kennedy family friend, covered the Middle Atlantic states and worked gingerly between a Cit-izens group and the powerful Byrd machine in his home state of Virginia. Fred Dutton worked more closely with Robert Kennedy than with White but was responsible for the Far West. White took Colorado, New York, and the High Plains. Dolan covered the rest—with emphasis on the industrial and political machine states of Ohio and Pennsylvania. The Citizens committee also helped to coordinate a national voter registration drive, organized by Frank (Topper) Thompson. When White was in town, he worked a fourteen-hour day, capped at 10 P.M. by a drink with whoever else was still around, with Thompson serving as bartender before a late dinner. Often, however, White was on the road, rounding up leaders for the volunteer network or insuring that jurisdictional squabbles did not develop between the committees and the regular party.

By Labor Day or shortly thereafter, the structural organization of the Cit-izens committee was completely in place, area responsibilities were estab-lished, and the communications network was pumping out directives, manuals, and campaign information to local committees. To maximize lead-ership opportunities for the swelling number of enthusiasts, more specialized committees were created—Veterans for Kennedy and Johnson, Senior Citi-zens for Kennedy and Johnson, Businessmen for Kennedy and Johnson, Farmers for Kennedy and Johnson, Students for Kennedy and Johnson, and even Professional Men, Lawyers, Doctors, Scientists, Military Leaders and Mental Health Leaders for Kennedy and Johnson.

The Citizens committees served two basic functions: they provided more and more focused opportunities for volunteer participation in the campaign, and, perhaps most important, they provided multiple avenues for young voters, and even nonvoters, to support a candidate, if not a ticket, when they otherwise might not, due to the closed culture and seniority of the regular organizations. Bill Moyers, Lyndon Johnson's press secretary, drove home the point within a month after the national convention. Writing on August 19 to Pierre Salinger, his counterpart with Kennedy, Moyers said:

> I want to re-emphasize the need for a specific division under Whizzer White to mobilize our ticket, the great bloc of voters being between 21 and 40 years of age. I mentioned to you the comment of the prominent Baptist educator in Oklahoma, who told LBJ and me that "95% of the ministers are vigorously opposed to the ticket, but that their efforts would be counteracted by voters under 40 who (1) are not prejudiced, and (2) who feel that some issues are more important than the religion question, and (3) who are interested in building the kind of future for their country that will enrich their own personal future. What he said in Oklahoma applies in Texas as well, and I am sure throughout the nation. The ticket naturally appeals to the young voters and I feel it is imperative that we move swiftly to enlist their support.

Youth became a drumbeat in the campaign, both in Kennedy's style and in the selection of committee heads, speakers, and priorities for events and the deployment of other resources.

The black vote was a much thornier problem. John F. Kennedy walked a tightrope on civil rights. Early in the year, he carefully supported the growing practice of protesters to sit in at legally or otherwise formally segregated lunch counters and other public accommodations through the South. The civil rights planks of the party platform, driven to approval by Chester Bowles, were strong. They were crafted in an effort to outflank Richard Nixon and the Republican Party, who had dragged their feet on civil rights, especially with tepid support of *Brown v. Board of Education,* the 1954 school desegregation decision. The Republican Party was nonetheless still more appealing to blacks in the South than the segregationist-dominated Democratic Party.

Southern governors and congressional leaders repudiated the Bowles platform, even moderates such as Ernest F. Hollings in South Carolina; they knew that supporting integration below the Mason-Dixon Line was political death. Senator Kennedy made sure that his campaign had a civil rights section, headed by his brother-in-law R. Sargent Shriver and led by Harris Wofford, a lawyer–law professor passionately committed to Martin Luther King and aggressive prosecution of racial justice. At the same time, Kennedy resisted appointing blacks to his political staff with non-civil-rights responsibilities, as being too soon and too cute. White and Robert Kennedy agreed with the candidate's hesitancy, as White's directive two months after the national convention to state and county chairmen of Citizens committees demonstrates:

> As you know, it is important that our nominees have maximum support from all groups in our national community. We hope that you are keeping this in mind in organizing and operating the Citizens organization in your state or county. In addition, we wish to advise you of certain special operations carried on by the Democratic National Committee. In the principal campaign, Congressman Dawson, Vice-chairman of the Democratic national committee, is working with regular Democratic Negro leaders. Mrs. Marjorie Lawson is working with those who wish to participate in an independent campaign like the rest of the Citizens activities.

He closed, after detailing Lawson's authority to deal with state and local chairmen, with something less than a clarion call to action: "We will appreciate your giving this your full cooperation, and making real use of everyone [whom Lawson] can bring into our campaign."

A month after the memorandum, everyone fell off the tightrope. Martin Luther King was arrested with others who sat in at a segregated lunch counter in a prominent downtown Atlanta department store. Instead of the routine processing, he was released, then taken from jail to jail in leg irons, and finally to the state prison, 230 miles away, to serve four months at hard labor for violating probation on a year-old technical traffic violation. Black leaders feared that he would be killed in the prison, and both city and state officials knew that any move to help King would be political suicide. Harris Wofford, acting on his own, began working with the mayor of Atlanta to negotiate King's release, but the deal almost blew up in everyone's face when the mayor, who was not unsympathetic to King, threatened to claim that Senator Kennedy had prompted him to action.

Wofford recovered his balance, went to Shriver, and urged him to convince the candidate to telephone Mrs. King, as a gesture, token to be sure, of sympathy and support. Shriver did an end run around Kennedy's road handlers, and the candidate placed the call. Robert Kennedy "scorched" Wofford and Shriver, calling them "bomb-throwers" who had cost his brother the election. The candidate, whose reflex was always to calm his trigger-happy brother, managed to explain the upside, moral and political, to the call. Early the next morning, the candidate placed another call, this time designed to free King and not simply to soothe his family. He awakened Gov. Ernest Vandiver at 6:30 A.M. and asked what could be done to get King out of prison and what everyone knew was a high-risk position and a political powder keg.

Vandiver consulted with his advisers, including his forty-two-year-old chief of staff, Griffin B. Bell, and telephoned his brother-in-law, Robert Russell, a nephew of Sen. Richard Russell and a Democratic national committeeman from Georgia. He called the clerk of the state Senate, who was the closest friend of Judge Oscar Mitchell—the judge who had canceled King's probation and ordered him to prison. Once the bail order was arranged, Vandiver tried to get back to the candidate but was unable to find him, so instead he telephoned Robert Kennedy, whom he tracked down in New York City. From a pay phone on Long Island, Robert Kennedy put a call through to Mitchell, expressing his interest, as a lawyer and as a citizen, in seeing that King be allowed to post bail for the offense. Mitchell replied that he agreed. In fact, Mitchell had already decided to grant bail, but he did not reveal his decision to Kennedy, because the telephone call would serve as useful political cover for Vandiver and his allies when King was freed: it would appear that Kennedy, not Vandiver and others behind the scenes, had sprung King.

King's release, accompanied by the candidate's compassionate telephone call to Mrs. King, was one of the two or three most "celebrated incidents" of the campaign and a pivotal moment for the Democratic ticket, which appeared to be losing votes rapidly among black voters to Nixon and Henry Cabot Lodge. Ironically, after the election, Robert Kennedy's telephone call was severely criticized in the left-wing press, especially the *Nation*, which raked Kennedy over the call for "improper," ex parte interference with the judicial process. The criticism contains a double dose of irreality. King was certainly in serious, perhaps life-threatening, danger, and any injury, let alone his death, would cause a full-scale riot, so his release on bond—not unusual for either the sit-in or the traffic violation—was hardly a distortion of the system. Second, trial judges, especially in the South at the time, were accustomed to conversations about their rulings on public issues (Mitchell did not admonish Robert Kennedy for contacting him without notifying opposing counsel, but, in the best Southern custom, thanked him for his interest). Robert Kennedy's telephone call went without notice to county officials for only a few hours, until the story broke nationwide. Nonetheless, journals such as the *Nation* and law professors of all stripes put Robert Kennedy under a microscope. One of the part-time academics who upbraided Kennedy was Harris Wofford, who used the incident in his legal ethics class at Notre Dame after the election.

The curricular choice turned out to be a disaster for Wofford in ways he never foresaw. During the transition period, when Wofford was jockeying against long odds to become assistant attorney general for the Civil Rights Division, one of Robert Kennedy's aides tried to advance Wofford's cause by putting Wofford and White (who by then was deputy attorney general), together for a drink. Let Wofford tell his rueful tale:

> The encounter was disastrous. Just back from teaching a weekly Notre Dame law course on professional responsibility, I told how I had spent the entire session on the propriety of Bob Kennedy's call to the Georgia judge requesting Martin Luther King's release from jail. The class was divided on the question of whether he should be disbarred for such behind-the-scenes intervention in a matter before the court. White asked me what I thought. Still in a bantering mood and citing the Canons of Professional Ethics of the American Bar Association, I said I agreed with the majority of the students: reprimand, yes; disbarment, no. White was not amused. He commented sourly, "You might be interested to know that I recommended to Bob that he call that judge."

Wofford was a lawyer who simply did not understand his tribunal, to the extent that he thought of the social encounter that way. An academic postmortem based on arid assumptions that bore little relation to the actual stakes of King's imprisonment would be the last perspective that would have moved Byron White. Whatever suspicion White had of Wofford as a "bomb-thrower," to use Robert Kennedy's term, or a "zealot"—White's preferred epithet for those who prized reflexive convictions over unsentimental pragmatism—the encounter confirmed his worst views. White prized his own pragmatism as much as Wofford prized his own rectitude, but White did not mistake one for the other; that, as much as any other difference, defined the gulf between the two men. The tactical disagreement over the telephone call was subordinate to the strategic question of the government's role in advancing civil rights. Robert Kennedy and Byron White shared a common conclusion on the issue, at least at the beginning of the administration: the political volatility of the issue meant that legislation, especially from a Congress controlled by Southern Democrats at the high-water mark of the seniority system, was a nonstarter, and that executive action and litigation, carefully developed, were the only practical routes with any possibility of success.

King was released from Reidsville state prison three weeks before the election. Despite the long-term importance of the incident, White had what appeared to be graver worries at the time. The Republican ticket was picking up steam, and the Kennedy campaign worried over Nixon's track record and capacity for a bare-knuckled closing push. On October 18, White issued an urgent memorandum to all Citizens for Kennedy and Johnson chairmen directing them to issue statements, prepared in Washington three times a week, called "Correction Please," because "Vice President Nixon is now grossly distorting the facts and substance of so many matters" in the campaign. The bulletins had the double effect of blunting Nixon's statements and galvanizing the local chairmen and supporters for the final push.

The paper-thin victory by John Kennedy is a story recounted many times. Little more than a hundred thousand popular votes separated the candidates, and two of Kennedy's largest Electoral College victories, Illinois and Texas, depended on five thousand and twenty-eight thousand votes, respectively. Kennedy went to bed in the early hours of the morning after his election not knowing who had won. Byron White returned to Colorado satisfied that he had done his duty. He told Phil Kaiser, *That's enough. I'm going back to Denver to practice law.* Joe Dolan had no doubt that White was only on a layover. "I told him, "Byron, you're gonna get a call," Dolan remembered. *Nah, hell, what could I do?* was the dismissive reaction. Denver newspapers continued speculation, which they had presumptuously started in Durango, that White would be in the cabinet, probably as attorney general, perhaps as secretary of the interior.

The more interesting question to many was which direction the new administration would take on the heels of the precarious victory. John Kane remembers a conversation at Saliman's Grill in Denver around the time of the election in which the question was raised in the company of White, Dolan, and Tom Sharp, a former president of the student body at the University of Colorado and a Phi Gam—like White and Kane—who was working as Ira Rothgerber's office manager. *What we need,* one of the younger men proclaimed, *is a liberal administration after the hibernation of the Eisenhower years.* To White, the statement was nonsense: *I've never understood what people mean when they say that—'liberal.' Labels mean nothing. They don't make policy and they don't decide practical problems.*

12

KENNEDY JUSTICE

ORGANIZING JUSTICE

THE ROUTE for Byron White to the deputy attorney general's office in the United States Department of Justice began, indirectly, on a golf course in Palm Beach, Florida. On November 15, 1960, Pres.-elect John F. Kennedy played eighteen holes of golf with Gov. Abraham Ribicoff of Connecticut, who had been the first major public figure to endorse Kennedy's candidacy. During their round, Kennedy offered the attorney generalship to Ribicoff, who declined. Ribicoff's ambition was to succeed Justice Felix Frankfurter, whose health was thought to be in decline, on the Supreme Court of the United States. According to Robert Kennedy, Ribicoff thought, crudely but accurately, that his fortunes would not be aided by the specter of "a Jew" who was "putting Negro children in White Protestant schools in the South"—especially "at the instruction of a Catholic." Another golf game three days later, this time with William H. Lawrence of the *New York Times,* produced a story in the *Times* on November 19 that Robert Kennedy was under "serious consideration" for attorney general, a prospect that the *Times* criticized the following week in a sarcastic editorial that ridiculed Kennedy's inexperience. Robert Novak rued the prospect in the *Wall Street Journal,* and Alexander M. Bickel of the Yale Law School wrote archly in the *New Republic* that "on the record, Robert F. Kennedy is not fit for public office."

By the first of December, the president-elect had settled on Adlai Stevenson for attorney general and Paul A. Freund of the Harvard Law School for solicitor general, but neither wanted to fill the positions chosen for them. Robert Kennedy preferred a position in the Defense Department, but the possibility became moot when Robert McNamara was recruited by Sargent Shriver to be secretary of defense, and one of McNamara's conditions for taking the job was that no one who had worked in the campaign would receive an appointment in the department. Robert Kennedy's strongest advocate for the attorney generalship was his father. Both brothers dithered about the appointment, but the man with the power of appointment came to rest first, and in the end Robert Kennedy had little choice.

At approximately the same time that the president-elect was coming to terms with the idea of having his brother as attorney general, Byron White visited Washington, D.C., ostensibly on business. When White emerged from a meeting at the president-elect's Georgetown residence, Kennedy said to the knot of reporters who were now staking out the location: "I have nothing to say, except that I have asked my friend to come to Washington and work on my team. He is taking the matter under consideration in the light of his own responsibilities." Kennedy would not be more specific, and White stammered noncommittal responses to every question he heard before taking a taxi to the Esso Building, where the transition team was headquartered. The press speculated that White would be attorney general or solicitor general, or would serve "in some defense capacity." A few hours after White visited the president-elect, Estes Kefauver, also thought to be a candidate to run the Department of Justice, made the pilgrimage to Georgetown. Kefauver, who had beaten Kennedy for the vice presidential nomination in 1956, had survived a bruising primary election campaign before winning reelection to the Senate by a landslide in November. He worked hard for Kennedy's election—spending thirty-eight days on the road in sixteen states—and his stature in the Southeast and the party was so high that some speculation was already putting him on a hypothetical short list for the Supreme Court. Kefauver was a maverick, however, and more interested in convincing Kennedy to pursue an aggressive antitrust policy than in serving in the administration.

The path was clear for Robert Kennedy to be attorney general, although he had not yet convinced himself to take the job and he wanted to consult more personal advisers, such as William O. Douglas and Clark Clifford, before making a decision. For White, the president-elect had three positions in mind: secretary of the army, secretary of the air force, or, when and if Robert Kennedy saw the light, deputy attorney general. The cost of service for White was high. An open-ended leave of absence would not necessarily be welcomed by the other ten partners in his twenty-man law firm; he had already been away for four months. His family would need to move to Washington, away from their nearby extended family, a price he was hesitant to impose on his wife and two small children. But the bond with the president's brother decided the issue, and Robert Kennedy's conspicuous visits to the incumbent attorney general and to Justice Douglas began to force the pace of decision.

The day after the *Washington Post* guessed—accurately, as it turned out—that Robert Kennedy had been offered the attorney generalship, he called White from Hickory Hill and asked him formally to be his deputy. The conversation, as recalled by John Seigenthaler, one of Kennedy's aides, reveals a delicate indirectness unusual in Robert Kennedy, which suggests a deep respect and a bond that went both ways.

[Robert Kennedy said to White,] "I talked to the President today, and I'm going to be Attorney General, and I was wondering what your plans are." Byron said something to the effect, "I don't know. I haven't made any decisions." Bob said, "Well, you know, of course, that you could be secretary of one of the branches of the armed forces if you like, and I thought as another possibility you might like to be Deputy Attorney General." He said, "I don't know how you feel about that, and I certainly don't want to impose my decision on you, if you would rather have the other spot or still some other spot than that. But I have great respect for your judgment. I don't think anybody I could have would be of greater assistance to me, and I want to make it clear that if you'd like to be Deputy Attorney General, I would like to have you. Maybe you want to think about it for awhile and make up your mind. I don't have to have a decision immediately." So Byron said, "I imagine there will be some heat over where you are." Bob said, "Yes, I'm sure there will be some heat over where I am." And Byron said, "I don't need to wait to make up my decision. I'd rather be there where there's some action rather than take a job in which I probably wouldn't be doing very much. So I'd like to come." Bob said to him, "Well, don't you want to think it over?" And he said, "No, I don't need to think it over. Count me in." Then he said, "Well, I'm glad to hear you say that because I'm going to need an excellent staff, and I'm going to have to rely heavily on you." And he did rely heavily on him.

Both appointments were announced by the president-elect at a news conference the next day, December 16, and the Kennedy brothers promptly left together to spend the weekend in Palm Beach. James Clayton's coverage of the appointment in the *Washington Post* spent as much time on White's athletic career as on his legal career. Clayton could not resist a final sentence, which came to be characteristic of the press's obsession with the incongruous résumé of the new deputy attorney general: "The appointment spoils one of Washington's best punch lines on Kennedy appointments—that White had been offered the job of touch football coach for the White House team."

The task of staffing the Department of Justice at the assistant attorney general level fell largely to White. The only appointment that the president insisted upon was Archibald Cox, a professor of labor law at Harvard Law School, as solicitor general. Cox had advised Kennedy on amendments to the Landrum-Griffin Act when he was the junior senator from Massachusetts and had provided research and advice during the campaign. The solicitor general was the third-ranking official in the Department of Justice hierarchy. The next level was composed of the thirteen assistant attorneys general (AAGs), who were the chief operating officers of their respective divisions.

White took ten days to get his Denver affairs in order, then immediately after Christmas went to Washington to begin the job of putting together the department. His first stop was Louis Oberdorfer, his law school classmate and fellow clerk at the Supreme Court in October term 1946. Oberdorfer, who was in private practice in Washington, was an Alabama native and had clerked for Justice Hugo L. Black, who selected as many clerks with an Alabama-Yale résumé as he could. White exacted a commitment from Oberdorfer to work in the department, but no job was specified and Oberdorfer had not even met Robert Kennedy. White emphasized that he wanted to bring into government the best lawyers—those with the greatest skill and the most demanding practical experience—for the department. Campaign activity was not a criterion; ability and trustworthiness were decisive.

For himself, White's first personal staffing decision was to hire Joe Dolan as assistant deputy attorney general. Dolan had hoped to be United States attorney for Colorado, but Sen. John Carroll would not accept him, so Dolan set his sights on working for Robert Kennedy as one of his "upstairs assistants." White instead made him his right-hand man. Dolan had extensive experience on Capitol Hill; he had been chief counsel to the House Select Committee Investigating Lobbying and Campaign Finance in 1950, and then, six years later, assistant counsel to the Special Senate Committee Investigating Lobbying and Campaign Finance, working for Senator Kennedy. White's "other right-hand man" eventually was William Geoghegan, whom White had met in Cincinnati during the campaign and whom he chose to direct Citizens committee work there in the ill-fated Ohio campaign. (Geoghegan had known Jean Kennedy Smith in college but had never met White, although as a thirteen-year-old boy he had watched White play for the Pittsburgh Pirates against the Cincinnati Bengals in an exhibition game in October 1938.)

Robert Kennedy chose John Seigenthaler as his administrative assistant. He was one of many journalists who caught Kennedy's attention in the mid-1950s with investigations of labor racketeering and whom Kennedy drafted into the service of the labor rackets committee under Sen. John McClellan of Arkansas and eventually onto his own staff. Others included William Lambert and Wallace Turner in Portland, Oregon, Pierre Salinger in San Francisco, Clark Mollenhoff in Washington, and Edwin Guthman in Seattle. Guthman became Kennedy's special assistant for public information. The experience in labor investigations produced one other appointment in the department: Herbert J. (Jack) Miller, a Washington attorney and a Republican, had been counsel to the board of monitors appointed to implement a consent decree that ended a lawsuit against the Teamsters Union, and Kennedy named him assistant attorney general in charge of the Criminal Division.

There were six other major appointments at the assistant attorney general level: Tax, Civil, Office of Legal Counsel, Civil Rights, Antitrust, and Lands. Oberdorfer was originally considered for a position as a political assistant to Kennedy, but his experience and organizational skills made him more suited to run the Tax Division, and he was appointed there when White vetoed the initial recommendation from Sargent Shriver's famous "talent hunt." After Oberdorfer, White went to work on the Civil Division. A Washington friend telephoned William Orrick, who was vacationing in Santa Barbara on New Year's Day, and suggested he work for the administration. Orrick hesitated, then came to Washington hoping to become secretary of the army. He agreed to take an undersecretaryship to Elvis Stahr, and paid a courtesy call on White, who had called him in early January with an unenticing invitation: "I wish you'd come back. We'd like to look you over." With an undersecretaryship under his belt, Orrick went to White, who told him, "We'd like to have you in the Civil Division." Orrick said he had a job, but White suggested they see Robert Kennedy. The attorney general–designate was bare-knuckled with Orrick, in contrast to his halting conversation with White. White told Kennedy that Orrick already had a job in the administration. According to Orrick,

Bob was looking out the window then and I don't know if he even shook hands with me. He said, "How'd you get a job?" I said, "I went over and asked for it." "Well," he said, "that's impossible." "Well," I said, "it isn't impossible and I got it." And it rather irked me that he didn't believe me. He said, "Well, we want you." "Well," I said, "I'm very flattered but I just told Byron I'd like to think about it." "Well," he said, "think about it." And he said, "Take your time." And I said, "Well, thanks a lot." He said, "You're the only man in Washington that has two jobs in this administration."

Orrick began to relax, but Kennedy drove home the spike: "Take all the time you want but could you let me know tomorrow morning?" Orrick agreed. It was after 8 P.M. when he left Kennedy and White. He accepted the offer to run the Civil Division the next morning.

The Office of Legal Counsel (OLC), White told Dolan, was the "balance wheel" of the department. Formally, the office's responsibility was to "prepare formal opinions for the Attorney General," "render legal advice and provide informal opinions to the various agencies," assist the attorney general "in his capacity as legal advisor to the president and to the cabinet," and review all executive orders and proclamations. White hoped that the office would be staffed by the lawyers' lawyers of the department, who could provide fast and technically airtight advice on breaking issues, long-term projects, and the work product of potential nominees for judicial office. In a political crunch, OLC should remind the relevant departmental officers what the law required, not what was plausible or defensibly expedient.

The position of assistant attorney general for OLC was critically important in White's view, and to fill it he dipped again, and not for the last time, into the Yale Law School alumni directory. He called Nicholas deB. Katzenbach, whom he knew at Yale after the war (Katzenbach was editor in chief of the *Yale Law Journal* in 1946–47 before going to Oxford as a Rhodes scholar). Now on the faculty of the University of Chicago Law School, Katzenbach was in Switzerland doing research on international legal organizations, so White called him there in mid-January. Katzenbach came highly recommended by John W. Douglas, who had been his Princeton classmate and roommate and was practicing law in Washington after a clerkship with Justice Harold Burton. Douglas (who later replaced Orrick as head of the Civil Division) was well known to the Kennedys through Bob Wallace, who had worked for Douglas's father, the senior senator from Illinois.

That left Antitrust, Lands, and Civil Rights. The most watched, and certainly the most controversial, appointment would be Civil Rights, and Kennedy and White took their time. Before they were ready to settle on that volatile position, the Shriver talent hunt produced two assistant attorneys general for whom White had little enthusiasm at the outset. Edwin Guthman later conceded in his memoirs that "politics figured to any extent only in" two appointments: the White House recommended Lee Loevinger, a member of the Supreme Court of Minnesota, to head the Antitrust Division, and Ramsey Clark to head the Lands Division, which dealt with issues of natural resources as well as public lands. Loevinger was an ally of Hubert Humphrey, although Humphrey went to great lengths to deny that he was insisting on the appointment. Clark was the son of Justice Tom C. Clark of the Supreme Court and was recommended by the speaker of the House of Representatives, Sam Rayburn, although no one doubted that the vice president had signed off on Rayburn's endorsement of Clark.

The appointed pair were opposites in many respects. Loevinger, at forty-eight, was the second-oldest member of the upper echelon of the department (Cox was forty-nine) and had no administrative experience to speak of; Clark was the youngest AAG, at thirty-three, and had a deliberate, laconic style that seemed inconsistent with the high-energy, shirtsleeves-rolled-up style of the others. Clark turned out to be one of Kennedy's favorites, thanks to creative innovation and hard work, and Loevinger, after what many criticized as a lackadaisical tenure, left the department to become a member of the Federal Communications Commission in 1963.

The obvious candidate for the Civil Rights Division was also the most controversial, Harris Wofford. Black groups and civil liberties organizations—expecting high-profile, aggressive enforcement of existing civil rights laws and advocacy of much stronger new ones—supported him with quiet enthusiasm. Adam Yarmolinsky, whom White had recommended to Vinson for a clerkship in 1948, was a dark horse candidate and went to Phil Kaiser to put in a good word for himself with White. Wofford's default candidate, if he failed to get the appointment for himself, was a fellow lawyer at the Washington firm of Covington & Burling—Burke Marshall, another Yale Law graduate and, at thirty-eight, already enjoying a distinguished reputation in the antitrust bar. No one has improved on Guthman's explanation of why White and Kennedy rejected Wofford. They knew that the department

> would be at the center of federal action, bearing the greatest responsibility and receiving the greatest amount of criticism and opposition [and] they felt that the only proper course for the department would be to proceed in strict accordance with the law, avoiding any appearance of pitting one social point of view against another. They decided that someone who had been in the forefront of any rights or racial cause might be handicapped by ideology or past associations with civil rights enforcement.

The premium was on a lawyer with first-class analytical skills and substantial experience in theorizing and organizing major litigation on multiple fronts.

Marshall fit the bill, was no less sensitive to civil rights than Wofford, yet was not identified like Wofford as a crusader. Marshall also had an unprepossessing presence—complete with quavering voice and anxious appearance—that was disarming to the uninformed. White encouraged Kennedy to interview Marshall on the strength of endorsements by several Washington lawyers, including Wofford. Kennedy eventually liked Marshall enormously, although their initial interview together seemed to Marshall to be a disaster, and department lore quickly denoted it as the longest thirty minutes in which two high-strung men said the least to each other with the greatest consequences.

Kennedy and White retained two AAGs from prior administrations, but for different reasons. White decided to keep Salvatore A. (Sal) Andretta, the career administrative assistant attorney general, to ensure continuity and a professionalized objectivity about budgeting and fund accounting within the department. White and Kennedy agreed on another holdover for cynical but nonetheless progressive reasons. They endorsed the reappointment of J. Walter Yeagley as head of the Internal Security Division, which enforced the Smith Act of 1940 and the Internal Security Act of 1950. "Byron thought it was the perfect place for bipartisanship," according to Joe Dolan. Who could complain about the department's posture on subversives if a Republican was on watch?

Robert Kennedy planned to recommend disbanding the division in due course. In the meantime, he reorganized the lines of authority for departmental and interdepartmental committees chaired by Yeagley and J. Edgar Hoover of the Federal Bureau of Investigation so that both reported to him. This made the attorney general responsible for internal security in the entire executive branch—a power that the attorney general logically should always have enjoyed but in fact never had until Kennedy. Yeagley was a member of Kennedy's team in name only: his office was in a different building than "Main DOJ," at Tenth and Constitution Avenues, and Yeagley never participated in Kennedy's kitchen cabinet meetings of the other AAGs. Robert Kennedy may have cut his professional teeth under Sen. Joseph McCarthy of Wisconsin during the twilight of the Red Scare (as minority counsel to McCarthy's Permanent Subcommittee on Investigations of the Senate Government Operations Committee in 1954), but one of his first steps as attorney general was to defang the Department of Justice's internal security apparatus.

By mid-February, all of the AAGs were in place and Marshall had survived a rough hazing from Sen. James O. Eastland, chairman of the Senate Judiciary Committee, at his confirmation hearing. White's work was aptly summarized by his father-in-law, Robert L. Stearns, in one of his periodic letters to his extended family. "Byron's work at the moment," Stearns wrote on Valentine's Day 1961, "seems to be in operating and maintaining a high-class employment agency." For every appointment, White and Kennedy picked from a handful to dozens of suggestions.

The most persistent, and highest-ranking, referee during the transition was Justice William O. Douglas, who had known Kennedy since he was a law student and himself was a protégé of Kennedy's father. The day before the inauguration, Douglas scribbled a two-sentence note on small Supreme Court memo pad paper endorsing Ramsey Clark. The note, signed "Bill," was addressed "Dear Whizzer." Earlier, Douglas had promoted John P. Frank, a former Hugo Black clerk who had practiced for years in Phoenix after leaving the Yale Law faculty, for solicitor general. In Frank's case, Douglas wrote Kennedy directly and pointed out, somewhat curiously, that Frank had been active in "promoting Byron White" for the deanship of the Yale Law School when Wesley Sturges resigned in 1954. On another occasion, through an intermediary, Douglas sent a note, again from a Court notepad, with a negative recommendation: "Please tell Bobbie that Phil Elman, who is itching to be an ass't atty general, is Felix's personal mouthpiece," which Douglas apparently assumed would be viewed as the mark of Cain.

White, working fourteen-hour days putting together the department, also filled out his own staff. In addition to Dolan and Geoghegan, he hired, at Kennedy's suggestion, John R. Reilly as a special assistant to head the Executive Office for United States Attorneys. Reilly was a former trial attorney in the Antitrust Division's Chicago office and he had worked for Lawrence O'Brien as an administrative assistant during the campaign. For the first several months of the new administration, Robert Kennedy paid more attention to appointing the ninety-one United States attorneys than he did to filling the eleven vacancies in the federal judiciary that greeted the administration on inauguration day. Kennedy was more concerned with the attorneys than with the judges, because he felt that local prosecutors had a more immediate effect on politics than did judicial appointments. The federal district attorneys had to be installed immediately; the judicial vacancies could remain on hold a while longer. In any event, as Joe Dolan later remarked, political reality inverted Article II of the Constitution: *judges were appointed by the Democratic senators of the relevant state, by and with the advice and consent of the president,* so the short-term priority was clear.

Eventually, White and Dolan would handle the judicial selection work in the department and the ticklish diplomacy with the senators involved. Within a month of the inauguration, the quality of the upper echelon of the

Department of Justice had begun to win over the principal skeptics. The *New York Times Magazine* published an admiring article that noted the objections to Robert Kennedy's appointment but also applauded the quality of his staff and his energetic engagement in every facet of the department's work. Alexander Bickel, who had been so unequivocally opposed to Kennedy's appointment, recanted: "It was the most brilliantly staffed department we had seen in a long, long time, and that was very impressive. One immediately had the sense of a fellow who wasn't afraid of having able people around him and indeed of a fellow who had a vision of public service that would have done anyone proud."

Byron White discovered that another task in his unofficial brief was dealing with the press, and he enjoyed interviews no more now than he had two decades before when he first faced the chore. His interview in mid-January with Miriam Ottenberg, the Pulitzer Prize–winning reporter who covered the department for the *Washington Star,* reveals an understandable impatience with the predictable journalistic gambit—the "contradictory career" of football star and "corporation lawyer": "'What's contradictory about that?' asked the soft-spoken, bespectacled attorney. 'I just liked to play football. I don't see any inconsistency between doing well scholastically and playing football.'" He defended his claim by reference to "the Greeks" and paraphrased Isocrates, in an echo of George Norlin from his college days, that admiration for athletic achievement was not wholly to be derided. Ottenberg found White elusive, if not evasive, about his own career and his plans at the department:

> Between answering telephone calls at his borrowed office in the Justice Department, he explained some of the reasons [for joining the administration]—but only when pressed. Conversationally, he's as adept at broken-field running as he was as the leading ground gainer for the Detroit Lions two decades ago.

White saved the best verbal change of field for the last question: Is he a liberal?

"Well," said Mr. White with a grin, "if resistance to change makes one a conservative, I'm not a conservative."

Shortly after granting the interview, White was hospitalized at Georgetown University Hospital with a duodenal ulcer, which provided the peg for another interview, this time with Dave Brady of the *Washington Post* sports department. White was much more at ease with Brady and even discussed his football playing detail with some verve, a topic he generally brushed off. He even spoke with admiration about Johnny Blood, his playing coach with Pittsburgh. At one point, Brady wrote, White snapped "into the intercom or squawkbox, 'Is the great Johnny Blood in town?' he asked with a roguish grin. Blood wasn't."

The question, as Brady apparently did not realize, was hardly hypothetical. Blood had recently visited Washington to see his cousin, John Doar, who was the first assistant in the Civil Rights Division. In fact, when Doar had left Wisconsin the summer before to take a job that no one else seemed to want, he had left his family behind until he could find appropriate housing in Washington. When he did, Johnny Blood drove Doar's family to their new home. Doar had spent part of his summer in 1938 as the water boy and general gofer, at the age of sixteen, at Pittsburgh's summer training camp in Loretto, Pennsylvania, and had roomed with Ted Doyle, the big rookie tackle from Nebraska. Twenty-four years later, Doar recalled White with admiration and remembered the dispute in the press about team dissension over White's contract—a story, in his view, lacking any discernible evidence.

Robert Kennedy did not know of the Blood-White connection and was startled the first time he encountered Johnny Blood, a sports hero of his youth, in the deputy attorney general's office, chatting warmly with Doar and White. The conversation moved into the attorney general's office, which was decorated with a football on the fireplace mantel and children's drawings taped haphazardly on the wood-paneled walls.

The sinewy vigor of the Justice Department was portrayed in an Associated Press story that the *New York Times* headlined "Attorney General Finds Football Is Useful in Tackling Problems":

> Visitors had been curious about the football sitting on the fireplace mantel of Mr. Kennedy's fifth-floor office in the Justice Building. He and Deputy Attorney General Byron R. White, it develops, toss the pigskin to and fro while deliberating matters of the law. . . . The story has gone around that a Justice Department employee was startled one evening shortly after Jan. 20 when he saw two persons moving about the building.
>
> "Anything I can do for you?" he asked suspiciously.
>
> "Yes," replied the younger of the two strangers. "I'm Bob Kennedy and this is Mr. White. We're looking for the gym."

The story was a welcome advertisement for the muscular vitality of the administration, and it had the concomitant virtue of being accurate. Robert Kennedy and Byron White headed a corps of physically tough men—many of whom were combat veterans of World War II—who enjoyed the square-jawed, challenging decisiveness of the new leadership style in the department. Kennedy Justice was not the home of poets or fey intellectuals. White provided a double benefit for the image-conscious administration: his "distinguished credentials" in football, as the AP story put it, and his Rhodes Scholarship. A *New York Times Magazine* article concluded that the raft of Rhodes scholar alumni entering government (fifteen and counting) meant that the president was trying to "stamp his Administration" with the qualities esteemed by Cecil Rhodes—"literary and scholastic attainments, fondness for and success in manly outdoor sports, moral force of character and instincts to lead." With no extra effort on his part, White had become a conspicuous emblem of the New Frontier.

White's ulcer flared up again in mid-February, but he initially did not require hospitalization. As his father-in-law informed the family, White simply canceled evening engagements, because, in the words of Marion White, "most of the hostesses in the nation's capital do not serve Cream of Wheat for a dinner diet." The regimen was not successful and White was back in Georgetown Hospital again, ironically on the eve of the first major crisis of the administration. On April 17, exiles invaded Cuba with American tactical and materiel support. The object was to overthrow the Castro government, but the operation, which became known for its launching site—the Bay of Pigs—was a fiasco. More than one thousand invaders were taken prisoner, and the administration had worldwide political egg all over its face.

White left the hospital and worked harder than ever as Robert Kennedy spent big chunks of time at the White House helping the president through one of the three of four "major" crises of the administration. During the week of the crisis, White was visited by E. Calvert Cheston, with whom he had served under Arleigh Burke in the South Pacific. White told Cheston: *I've never worked so hard in my life. I'm doing two jobs, because Bob is at the White House most of the time.* The regimen did not last long, but both Kennedy and White discovered that, despite the strain, White could do double duty for short stretches of time when the president needed his brother's counsel. As it turned out, the Bay of Pigs was a prelude to a longer, more publicly visible and trying episode that erupted less than a month later—the Freedom Rides of racially integrated public buses through the South, beginning more or less peacefully in the upper South and, after one bus was firebombed in eastern Alabama, causing full-fledged riots in Birmingham and Montgomery.

The story of the Freedom Rides has been told many times and from many perspectives, including the riders themselves, the Department of Justice, the federal district judge who issued the injunction against the Ku Klux Klan (after the first riot in Birmingham, Alabama, on Mother's Day 1961), and even the FBI informant inside the Klan. The Freedom Rides were the baptism by fire for both the "movement"—as it was called—and the Kennedy administration, and Byron White was Robert Kennedy's point man in Alabama. The five days that White spent in Alabama in May of 1961 constituted—after the recruitment of the assistant attorneys general—one of the three most significant episodes during his career in the Department of Justice. The other was the ongoing process of selecting judges for the vacancies on the federal bench, which multiplied threefold during May when Congress passed the Omnibus Judgeship Act of 1961. The act created seventy-three new judgeships and brought the total of vacancies in the federal judiciary to more than one hundred.

The Freedom Rides taught the administration, including White, a grim lesson about the enforcement of civil rights in the South. The judicial appointments, especially in the South, soon became the target of severe criticism; friends and allies of the administration believed that political expediency had triumphed over principle and conviction, revealing that the department had neither. The criticism of the department has been both skewed and unrealistic, and the fuller picture of the judicial selection process demonstrates a largely admirable record, at least outside of the South, notwithstanding a process that was chronically ad hoc and fluidly structured, to say the least. Both episodes repay close attention, particularly for what they reveal about the political context in which the Department of Justice operated and how Robert Kennedy and White negotiated that world.

THE FREEDOM RIDES

The black vote in the 1960 election was a mixed blessing for John F. Kennedy. His campaign appearances with black congressional leaders, his endorsement of sit-ins at segregated lunch counters, and his symbolic concern for Martin Luther King's plight in Georgia raised hopes among blacks that civil rights would be a high priority in the new administration. At the same time, Kennedy knew that he could not appear to be beholden to a constituency that would be political poison in Southern states, where some of his strongest supporters—such as John Patterson in Alabama and Ernest Vandiver in Georgia—campaigned on segregationist platforms. Worse, the Senate was firmly controlled by Southern senators, who chaired important committees, publicly equated black activists with communists, and relied on the filibuster to forestall unwanted legislation. The black vote was thus simultaneously a source of and a brake on political power. Caught between these opposing political forces, Kennedy had focused his campaign on foreign policy and defense, and emphasized a missile gap with the Soviet Union and a manpower shortage in the military. To establish his leadership credentials overseas, he hoped for an early summit conference with Nikita Khrushchev, the Soviet leader, but he entered secret negotiations for the meeting with an albatross around his neck—the Bay of Pigs incident. With more than a thousand prisoners still held in Cuba as a result of the aborted invasion, Kennedy was still paying the price months after the event for inadequate planning and slapdash action. He wished no more embarrassments prior to taking the diplomatic center stage before the world press corps.

All of the political forces, whose pressure had been building since the inauguration, converged in May 1961. A busload of black and white passengers left Washington, D.C., on May 4, bound for New Orleans, Louisiana, under the auspices of the Congress of Racial Equality, determined to test the segregative practices in terminals and on buses in Virginia, the Carolinas, Georgia, Alabama, and Mississippi. Two days later, Robert Kennedy gave his first speech on civil rights to a Law Day audience at the University of Georgia, which had been desegregated by two black students, Charlayne Hunter and Hamilton Holmes, only months before. Kennedy gave no quarter to what he feared would be a hostile audience, promised sternly to enforce the law, and, to his surprise, received a standing ovation from an audience that included only one black: Miss Hunter had received press credentials from a black newspaper.

On May 10, Louis Martin, deputy chairman of the Democratic National Committee and a respected black leader, sent a pointed three-page memorandum to Ted Sorensen, and a copy to Robert Kennedy, complaining that civil rights legislation introduced by Sen. Joe Clark and Congressman Emanuel Celler the day before lacked a message from the president. Martin argued that the omission could have substantial political costs with Northern black voters in upcoming elections and pointed out that the argument that appeared to govern the president's posture—that executive action was now more productive than legislative initiatives, that legislatively "the time is not right"—might not sell: "Most Negroes know that the time has never been ripe and perhaps feel that the time will never be ripe." Martin concluded with an ominous observation:

> Most important of all I think it should be noted that no small group of Negro leaders nor White Civil Rights experts can exercise a "control" over the Negro electorate. Once the masses become excited over some issue they will just as quickly denounce a leader as praise him. Negro leaders are quite expendable because the pressure for social change comes from the bottom of Negro life.

It can be shown for example that a single speech of a Negro leader which may be interpreted as "appeasement" can almost cost him his leadership role. The sharp edge of Negro resentment over racial discrimination can cut like a knife inside the ghetto.

There were sharp edges on the other side, too, and they began to lacerate the Freedom Rides once the buses crossed the state line into Alabama. On May 14—Mother's Day—thugs burned a bus in Anniston, Alabama, and Freedom Riders were severely beaten when the other bus arrived in Birmingham. For fifteen minutes, a thousand-man mob of whites beat and pummeled the bus's integrated ridership before local police arrived. Events quickly began to cascade on Monday, May 15. The Kennedys sent John Seigenthaler to Alabama, both as the president's personal representative and as Robert Kennedy's aide, to arrange safe passage out of the state for the injured riders. A new integrated group, which Southern newspapers contemptuously labeled "testers" (of segregation laws) or "mixers," left Nashville for Birmingham the next day. Finally, a U.S.–Soviet summit was rumored for early June.

When the Nashville bus arrived in Birmingham, Eugene (Bull) Connor, the Birmingham police commissioner, slapped the passengers into "protective custody." That evening in Washington, Louis Oberdorfer hosted a dinner at his home for an old friend from Birmingham and Byron White. The Birmingham resident, a lawyer, announced that he was worried about his family's safety and was eager to return home. For the first time, the gravity of the situation registered on the leadership of the Department of Justice. Robert Kennedy later admitted that he did not know about the Freedom Rides until he read of the Mother's Day incident in the newspapers. Burke Marshall, who undoubtedly received a press release from CORE about the trip, was recovering at home from the mumps. White had just been released from the hospital after another ulcer attack. There had been no contingency planning within the department for the safety of the Freedom Riders, because there was no information that they were in danger and officials most likely to monitor the situation were temporarily out of commission. Now, over coffee and dessert in the Maryland suburbs, White and Oberdorfer began debating the most appropriate mechanism to deal with future "strikes" by local Alabama police, which is the way Oberdorfer characterized the police paralysis in Birmingham on Mother's Day. White, a World War II combat veteran like most of the AAGs, immediately thought, "Well, we will probably have to use soldiers." Oberdorfer, the Alabama native who understood the costly symbolism of President Eisenhower's deployment of an occupying federal force to Little

Rock in 1957, suggested using federal marshals. White objected: "Where are you going to get marshals?" The brainstorming session produced another option—deputizing a contingent of District of Columbia policemen as federal marshals—but the only action at the end of the dinner debate was a telephone call from White to put a local platoon of federal marshals on standby for travel to Birmingham if necessary.

The following day, May 17, the attorney general, White, and Burke Marshall went to the White House at 8:30 A.M. to brief the president, who received them in his pajamas in the family quarters and listened while his soft-boiled eggs became cold. There were no preliminaries, no small talk. "As you know," Robert Kennedy began, "the situation is getting worse in Alabama." The problem was that the bus had reached Birmingham and there was no prospect that the passengers, who had been arrested, would be able to leave soon, or that a bus could safely make the 140-mile trip to Montgomery. The key question that morning was how much visible federal authority should be used to unstick the risky moral cavalcade. Troops were discussed, but ruled out: Little Rock, and campaign condemnation of Eisenhower's inept handling of the crisis three years before, precluded the option, although no one in the department actually advocated mobilization. White's plan for an ad hoc force of marshals was informally ratified; it was to be composed of local deputy marshals, prison guards from the Bureau of Prisons, Border Patrol inspectors from the Immigration and Naturalization Service, and agents from the Treasury's Bureau of Alcohol, Tobacco and Firearms. All but the latter were under the authority of the Department of Justice and, thus, the direction of the attorney general; Oberdorfer, as head of the Tax Division, worked out arrangements with Treasury to utilize the ATF agents. It was a characteristic solution for the Kennedys—imaginative, improvised outside of channels, and with high upside and downside risks for identical reasons.

Two days after the White House meeting, the Kennedy-Khrushchev summit was announced for early June in Vienna, and Seigenthaler reported back to Washington that he had an agreement with Governor Patterson, essentially for a safe conduct for the Freedom Riders, and the bus would leave the next morning with a highway patrol escort for Montgomery. The next morning, as Guthman put it, "All hell brok[e] loose." As Doar watched from a nearby window and reported back on an open line to Robert Kennedy's office, a mob attacked the bus in Montgomery with bloodier consequences than the Birmingham attack. Seigenthaler was mugged with a lead pipe and left lying in the street for twenty-five minutes while an FBI agent stood by dutifully taking detailed notes. Kennedy was furious and ordered Oberdorfer to "take those marshals and go down there." Oberdorfer left Kennedy's office, encountered a pale White, still recovering from his ulcer, and second-guessed both himself and the attorney general: "I am from Alabama. I am Jewish. This thing will be very controversial." White agreed immediately: "We'll both go."

White promptly departed for Montgomery with Oberdorfer, Joe Dolan, and a departmental secretary. Although they would billet at Maxwell Air Force Base, near Montgomery, they did not travel by military aircraft; they used the private Gulfstream of Najeeb Halaby, administrator of the Federal Aviation Administration and Yale Law classmate of Oberdorfer and White. The flight was a white-knuckle trip, but not because of weather. Until an injunction against the Klan enjoining future violence could be secured from Judge Frank M. Johnson, the federal district judge in Montgomery, White and his team were worried over the legal authority for their utilization of the eclectic collection of deputy marshals. One of Oberdorfer's staff piled law reports and other research books on the flight.

There were several questions: Did 10 U.S.C. §333, which authorized the president to use "other such means"—means other than federal troops—"to suppress, in a State, any insurrection, domestic violence, unlawful combination, or conspiracy," authorize deputizing various federal agents to protect the flow of interstate commerce? (Southern papers routinely referred to the statute as an untested relic of the Grant era, further emphasizing the Reconstruction era overtones to the federal involvement.) Was *In Re Debs,* in which the federal government had asserted its inherent authority to keep the mails moving with the help of troops in the face of a strike in 1895, a safe fallback, or a controversial escalation of the constitutional stakes of the controversy? What if Martin Luther King arrived as planned on Sunday and delivered a sermon in the Reverend Ralph David Abernathy's First Baptist Church and the church was attacked by the Klan—did any of the sources of authority constitutionally justify federal protection of a church meeting?

As he had in Denver, White attacked the books almost physically and dictated memos and portions of briefs in the Gulfstream's cabin. Although Doar was on the ground and preparing the supporting papers for the application for a temporary restraining order against the Klan—actually, two Klan factions—White needed to be ready on the larger fronts, which raised the most tender political issues of constitutional authority for his team. At one point, Oberdorfer was seized by a thought unrelated to their research. Thinking, as he had for some time, that White would eventually succeed Robert Kennedy as attorney general, Oberdorfer remarked: "Byron, if this thing is a fiasco, which it may be, bringing in a disorganized group like this, and we get clobbered, or somebody else gets killed, if it goes wrong at all, you'll never be confirmed for anything by the Senate again." Oberdorfer was thinking of Senator Eastland. White "sort of grinned at that."

There were no smiles when White arrived at Maxwell Field at 8 P.M. He immediately held a press conference, at which he tried to minimize his own presence. He anticipated no further violence, which would be the responsibility of local officials to control. Yes, we have legal authority to be here. No, we have no comment on the handling of the bus's arrival today. "White hedged when he was asked if the primary reason the marshals are being brought here was based on assaults by white mobs on Negroes," wrote the *Montgomery Advertiser*. "He admitted the civil rights issue was involved, but relegated it below protecting interstate bus travel." The paper noted accurately that White was accompanied by twenty U.S. marshals in civilian clothes with yellow armbands stenciled with their identification, but the paper also reported, erroneously, that the team used a "military plane." White hoped to have 150 deputies on the ground by Monday morning and a total of five hundred by Tuesday. The ATF agents "streamed in[to]" Montgomery, as the local newspapers put it, by the private cars they used in their fieldwork, which largely consisted of rousting the operators of illegal whiskey stills.

Sunday was the day of reckoning for the task force. White was still not at full strength physically and went to bed earlier than the rest of the team, but everyone was up at 5:30 A.M. to reconnoiter. After Birmingham, the FBI's intelligence capacity had been thoroughly discredited, so marshals were deployed into the streets to size up the situation. The town was quiet until midday, when word spread like an atomic chain reaction that Martin Luther King was flying into Montgomery that afternoon. Nearly fifty marshals were sent to meet him and escort him to the Reverend Abernathy's residence. Governor Patterson, who had been elusive with both Kennedys the week before, was suddenly available to meet White. The summit conference turned into a showcase for a forty-five-minute diatribe by Patterson for his political constituents. White later said, with great restraint, that "there were strong words spoken strongly." As the transcript of the meeting (see Appendix A) demonstrates, Patterson tried to badger White, to discredit his authority, and to undermine his integrity. In return, White was firm, uncompromising, and evasive when necessary. The stalemate achieved Patterson's objective if not White's, which meant that the resolution would be in the streets, which it soon was. Despite that result, Robert Kennedy never forgot how steely White was in the face of Patterson's bombast; if possible, White rose in the attorney general's estimation.

Sitting on a bunk at Maxwell Field, looking physically drawn but with a set jaw, White looked up at John Doar, who had secured the injunction against the Klan factions from Johnson, and said quietly, "This is how you are measured. This will test us." The injunction was a double-edged sword: it provided undoubted authority for the use of the marshals, but its federal imprimatur was also a symbolic provocation locally. When King arrived at Abernathy's church to preach his sermon, night was falling, and the federal contingent feared for the worst. White remained at Maxwell Field. He dispatched two of the most experienced Border Patrol officers in the makeshift force and told them:

> I want you fellows to go down to the church in your car. I want one of you to stay in your car and stay on the radio and the other of you to step out of the car and look around. I don't want you to do anything but look and tell me what you see. No matter what happens, that's what you do.

When the officers reported at nightfall that a mob was forming, White directed the marshals at Maxwell to prepare to deploy downtown. That order presented its own logistical problem, since by their terms of engagement the marshals were debarred from using military vehicles. The General Services Administration could not locate enough vehicles that day to move the force, so White was left with post office trucks. There were plenty of postal vehicles, but the hitch with them was that postal regulations, which the local authorities said needed to be strictly enforced, required that only postal employees drive the vehicles. So, near 8 P.M., White ordered his convoy of postal trucks to head to the church. The first few vehicles jackrabbited out of their places—but with no marshals aboard. White slapped himself on the forehead and muttered, "My God, another Cuba." When he recovered his composure, and his sense of irony, he turned to Joe Dolan, and asked, "I wonder which side they'll take."

The marshals arrived at the church and discovered that a car had been burned and that a large mob was moving on the church. The marshals formed a skirmish line between the mob and the church. Tear gas and nightsticks turned back the mob twice, but White's judgment was that they could not hold the line much longer. In Washington, Robert Kennedy directed that the troops on alert at Fort Benning, Georgia, be prepared to scramble to Montgomery. At what seemed like the last minute to everyone, the state police, under the direction of Floyd Mann, arrived sometime after 10 P.M., and the standby alert at Fort Benning was canceled. "Floyd Mann literally came in like the courageous town sheriff—which is just about what he was—with gun

Byron White photographed the day before a home game near the end of his final football season at the University of Colorado. *(NFL Properties)*

Sam White, in his second year of medical school, and Byron White, halfway through the first year of Yale Law School, in December 1939. *(Boulder Daily Camera)*

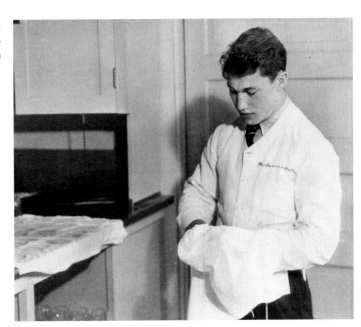

Preparing to "hash" at the Phi Gamma Delta House, November 1937. *(UPI/Corbis-Bettman)*

Studying economics, to please a national photographer, November 1937. *(UPI/Corbis-Bettman)*

Clayton Samuel White, president of the student body at the University of Colorado, in 1934. *(Boulder Daily Camera)*

Providing New York City photographers a display of athleticism, March 14, 1938, prior to the first game of the inaugural National Invitational Basketball Tournament. *(UPI/Corbis-Bettman)*

The mob of press and fans after the first game of the NIT, Madison Square Garden, 1938. *(AP/Wide World Photo)*

Johnny Blood enticing
White to sign with the
Pittsburgh Pirate football
club, March 17, 1938,
after the final game of the
National Invitational
Basketball Tournament.
(AP/Wide World Photo)

Johnny Blood, White, and Art Rooney, August 10, 1938, prior to White's signing
of the most lucrative single-season contract in National Football League history.
(NFL Photos)

On the bench with the Detroit Lions, and on leave from Yale Law School. *(Private Collection)*

White intercepts a pass from Dick Tuckey, Sammy Baugh's replacement as quarterback for the Washington Redskins, and makes a 7-yard return, pursued by the intended receiver, Charlie Malone. It was White's only distinguished play of the night. The College All-Stars won, 28–16, before 74,250 at Soldier Field in Chicago, August 31, 1938. *(UPI/Corbis-Bettman)*

Obliging the *News-Chronicle* upon his arrival at Oxford, with encouragement from a "coed" (in fact, a reporter for the newspaper, Betty Nolan). *(AP/Wide World Photo)*

Flirting with Nolan for the camera. *(AP/Wide World Photo)*

Walking along the High Street, Oxford, with Gerald Brown. *(New York Times/Archive Photos)*

White (44) makes a flying tackle on Herman "Country" Hodges of the Brooklyn Dodgers, who had just caught a pass from Ace Parker in the first game of the 1941 season at Ebbets Field, New York. *(UPI/Corbis-Bettman)*

Lt. (j.g.) Byron R. White, Solomon Islands, October 29, 1943. *(AP/Wide World Photo)*

Marion Lloyd Stearns and Byron R. White,
St. Johns Episcopal Church, Boulder,
Colorado, June 15, 1946.
(AP/Wide World Photo)

Posing on the front steps of the Supreme
Court, September 19, 1945,
at the beginning of his clerkship.
(AP/Wide World Photo)

John F. Kennedy arriving in Denver, November 28, 1959, en route to Boulder for a football game at the beginning of a weekend political trip through Colorado. *(UPI/Corbis-Bettman)*

President-elect Kennedy and White on the steps of Kennedy's Georgetown residence, December 7, 1960, after Kennedy announced, "I have asked my friend to come to Washington and work on my team." *(UPI/Corbis-Bettman)*

The attorney general and deputy attorney general in a rare moment of repose, 1961.
(Copyright Henri Cartier-Bresson, Magnum Photos)

White and Gov. John Patterson of Alabama, May 21, 1961. *(AP/Wide World Photo)*

All alone, leaving the Alabama State capitol after the meeting with Patterson. *(AP/Wide World Photo)*

Confirmation hearings, April 11, 1962. *(UPI/Corbis-Bettman)*

Obliging photographers, April 16, 1962, prior to being sworn in as an associate justice. *(UPI/Corbis-Bettman)*

The Supreme Court, October term 1971. *Front row (l to r):* Potter Stewart, William O. Douglas, Warren E. Burger, William J. Brennan, and White. *Back row:* Lewis F. Powell, Jr., Thurgood Marshall, Harry A. Blackmun, and William H. Rehnquist. *(Photo by Robert S. Oakes, Collection of the Supreme Court of the United States)*

The Supreme Court, October term 1981. *Front row (l to r):* Thurgood Marshall, William J. Brennan, Warren E. Burger, White, and Harry A. Blackmun. *Back row:* John Paul Stevens, Lewis F. Powell, Jr., William H. Rehnquist, and Sandra Day O'Connor. *(Photo by Robert S. Oakes, Collection of the Supreme Court of the United States)*

The Supreme Court, October term 1991. *Front row (l to r):* John Paul Stevens, White, William H. Rehnquist, Harry A. Blackmun, and Sandra Day O'Connor. *Back row:* David H. Souter, Antonin Scalia, Anthony M. Kennedy, and Clarence Thomas. *(Photo by Joseph H. Bailey, National Geographic, Collection of the Supreme Court of the United States)*

Newton C. Estes attacking White, July 16, 1982, in Salt Lake City, Utah (photo taken from television monitor). *(AP/Wide World Photo)*

Visiting University of Colorado Heritage Center in April 1993 and exhibit, including his football game uniform from 1937. *(Photographic Department, University of Colorado)*

drawn, and stopped the mob," Joe Dolan later said. Mann telephoned White's command post at Maxwell Field and asked him to "commit any reserves." "We have committed all we have," White replied; "they are at your disposal."

Patterson, who had argued with Robert Kennedy, contradictorily, that he needed no federal help and that he could not guarantee Martin Luther King's safety, had declared martial law. Behind Mann and his police was a seventy-five-man contingent of the Alabama National Guard under the direction of Maj. Gen. Henry V. Graham, state adjutant general and commander of the guard. When Graham's force was spotted, it elicited a poignantly mistaken re-action. The Freedom Riders and worshipers in the church assumed, erro-neously, that federal soldiers had been mobilized to save them. At 2 A.M., when he was convinced that Graham had secured the area, White ordered the marshals back to Maxwell Field. In total, the marshals, who had been orga-nized and deployed in less than twenty-four hours from throughout the re-gion, were in the field no more than fifteen hours. After Sunday and early Monday morning, they were not in the streets again until a week later, when some of them provided evidence before Judge Johnson on compliance with the injunction.

By daybreak Monday, despite their plans and desires, the Freedom Riders were a spent force. Both the leadership and the Department of Justice had lost patience with each other. Robert Kennedy thought that the riders were creat-ing an undue risk to themselves and others, and that they were risking long-term political damage to their own cause, damage that would have disastrous collateral consequences to the administration. Kennedy also began to fear even greater violence in Mississippi. Mississippi attorney general J. P. Cole-man, Ross Barnett's predecessor as governor of Mississippi, warned Burke Marshall that the riders were in grave danger and that Barnett could not be trusted to protect them. Behind the scenes, Robert Kennedy cut a deal with Barnett, whom he did not trust, and Senator Eastland, whom he did. Missis-sippi state officials would insure the riders' safety in return for being able to jail them as soon as they disembarked from the bus in Jackson. The compromise gave Kennedy safety for the passengers and allowed Barnett to claim that he had stood firm against the "testers"—with minimized long-term political damage to everyone.

White's job was to deliver the bad news to the protesters. He held a press conference in which he stated, much to the displeasure of the riders, that ar-rest of "Freedom Riders by local authorities would not be cause for interven-tion by U.S. marshals": "That would be a matter between the Freedom Riders and local officials," White said. "I'm sure they would be represented by com-

petent counsel." White added that the force of marshals on its way to Montgomery would not augment but relieve those who were already in place and
stand by to assist General Graham only if necessary: "General Graham said he
thought he had capability of maintaining law and order in Montgomery. We
think he has the capability. He indicated we might be able to help at some
time." Asked whether the riders would be escorted through Mississippi to
New Orleans, White said matter-of-factly, "There have been no incidents in
Mississippi which would demand our presence," but added that "anyone has
the right to travel freely on interstate buses."

The policy announced at the press conference outside of Maxwell made
White a villain to the Freedom Riders and a grudgingly admired figure to the
local press, as the *Alabama Journal's* perceptive thumbnail sketch suggests:

> White is about six feet tall, stands somewhat stoop-shouldered, and has the
> massive hands of an athlete. Once noted for his shock of bush brown hair, he
> is now balding and his hair is turning gray.
>
> He speaks in such a soft, halting voice that it gives one the impression he
> might be shy. His conversation is punctuated by pauses as he composes pre-
> cise sentences. His phrases are clear and firm. Rarely does he show emotion.
>
> He has a ready smile, which reveals oversized, sparkling teeth, untar-
> nished, although he is a heavy smoker of filter cigarets. He can become airy
> but unpretentious when he talks about the federal government's role in the
> protection of such constitutional guarantees as freedom of assembly, freedom
> of speech, and freedom of movement.

The observations appeared at the end of the story; White's athletic career provided the lead and much of the first half.

After the press conference, White flew to Washington to consult with
Robert Kennedy, and then returned on Tuesday, May 23, to Montgomery,
where he announced that he was keeping intact his 550-man force (the *Alabama Journal* repeatedly insisted it was 666, apparently to suggest diabolical
connotations). The next day, Robert Kennedy announced that all but one hundred of the deputy marshals would be released from duty. Within two days,
only the hundred-man standby contingent was still in place, and everyone
from Washington had returned there except William H. Orrick, the assistant
attorney general in charge of the Civil Division, who had been conscripted into
service in another of Robert Kennedy's on-the-spot staffing decisions. Within a
few days, Judge Johnson issued a sweeping injunction that calmed the situation
by appearing to threaten everyone equally if violence erupted again—"Police,
Klan, Mixers," as the *Montgomery Advertiser* headline put it.

Although the White-Kennedy posture seemed both cold and surprisingly accommodating to the very officials who had set their teeth on edge only days before, the Department of Justice had in fact achieved a strategic retreat. Patterson's declaration of martial law, and Graham's consequent assumption of responsibility for law and order in Montgomery, allowed the state to repudiate the federal intervention and almost looked like what Orville Faubus—still governor of Arkansas—had called "interposition," after John C. Calhoun, only three years before. Nonetheless, the Patterson-Graham assertion of authority had returned the situation to local control, made local authorities responsible for preventing mob action, and prevented federal authorities from becoming a long-term presence for as long as elements of the movement asserted their civil rights on hostile ground. Both national and local newspapers condemned the violence, and the international reaction was severe. United Nations diplomats, especially from Africa and Asia, deplored the situation. Moscow Radio called the riots "the worst examples of savagery" and even went on to question the moral authority of the Peace Corps in light of the ugly reality of Southern society. The president's summit with Khrushchev was less than two weeks away.

The Justice Department's handling of the Freedom Rides was dramatic, amateurish, and portentous. Although John Doar was a holdover from the prior administration, Burke Marshall had been confirmed only ninety days before the Mother's Day riot. The Civil Rights Division's only experience with Southern intransigence over race had been in New Orleans, where federal marshals had been used more or less without incident to begin enforcement of federal judge J. Skelly Wright's school desegregation decree. Kennedy had gone to the length of retaining the Republican U.S. attorney in New Orleans until the situation was resolved, after a well-publicized strategy meeting less than three weeks after the inauguration, which was attended by White, Marshall, and two White House aides, Wofford and Richard Goodwin, the assistant special counsel to the president. No one in the department was prepared for what happened in Alabama. By sending White and two assistant attorneys general to the scene, Robert Kennedy immediately upped the political ante and made one of two outcomes inevitable: mobilization of federal paratroopers and a grim replay of Little Rock (which both Kennedys had previously criticized as inept), or the strategic retreat that in fact occurred. For an administration that prided itself on multiple options, the high-profile treatment of the Freedom Rides reduced the options to polar extremes. "Well," Burke Marshall admitted ruefully many years later, "I suppose we didn't really know what we were doing at that point. It was too new and events broke too fast." Marshall drew two principal lessons from the Freedom Rides experience: every physical confrontation between black and white crossing the segregation line could be met by deadly violence, and, as a source of intelligence about mob plans, "the FBI was worthless to us in the South," as Birmingham sadly demonstrated.

To meet the first problem, Marshall and others crisscrossed the South during the summer of 1961, meeting with local officials in every location where school desegregation was planned for the fall and looking for ways to avoid violent confrontation. White took steps to make sure that the department was not caught off guard again by risks of violence. He sent a memorandum to Burke Marshall on June 26 asking to be advised from time to time on trouble spots in the South where U.S. marshals might be needed to prevent violence. Marshall briefed White by memo periodically, both on "situations where we should be prepared to consider the use of marshals" and on impending initiatives by the movement, such as a voter registration drive planned for Mississippi by the Student Nonviolent Coordinating Committee (SNCC). The Department of Justice, as its top officials all agreed, was learning as it went.

The FBI presented a more difficult challenge because the nature and scope of the problem remained unclear for some time. Marshall did not discover until the summer of 1964 that the FBI regularly used paid informants inside the Ku Klux Klan, some of whom participated in violence against civil rights demonstrators. Only in 1975 did it emerge that an FBI operative inside the Klan, Gary Thomas Rowe, had been a liaison between the Klan and the Birmingham police and had participated energetically in the Mother's Day riot. (Rowe was also in the car that carried the murderer of Mrs. Viola Liuzzo, the Detroit volunteer killed in Mississippi in 1965.) Marshall and White eventually were required to provide depositions in a federal lawsuit filed by injured Freedom Riders against the United States in 1977. In June of 1961, the most Marshall was able to wring out of the FBI was a change in procedure that allowed agents to provide information directly to him without funneling a formal request through the director's office. The bureau also agreed to provide information on impending violence in advance, when it was developed, which it had sternly refused to do before.

The FBI's standpat policy—*we are an investigative agency, not a law enforcement agency*—had been made risible in Montgomery when Seigenthaler lay bleeding while an agent took notes. What could not be changed as quickly was J. Edgar Hoover's shadow Department of Justice structure for protecting the bureau's prerogatives. Hoover assigned an individual assistant director for each assistant attorney general; the resulting organization provided prompt attention to departmental queries but maintained centralized control over information developed by the bureau. At an even more pervasive level, Hoover had established a thirty-year tradition, which became a culture bred in the institution's bones, of meshing with cooperative local law enforcement bodies and then protecting both them and itself from scrutiny or accountability to transitory political administrations. The Freedom Rides were, in a sense, the beginning of the end of that culture, an end that did not finally occur until the director's death, a decade later.

What would not end for some time was resistance throughout most of the Southern social structure to compulsory desegregation, especially in the public schools. The Freedom Rides were one of the first opportunities that the worst elements of Southern society had to confront the symbolism of *Brown v. Board of Education,* in which the Supreme Court held in 1954 that state-imposed racial segregation in public schools was unconstitutional. The Court's decision was highly problematic from an enforcement standpoint because it seemed so sudden and so sweeping, although the Court temporized for a year before equivocally ordering local federal judges to determine what compliance meant in their respective jurisdictions. The second *Brown* decision set the pace for compliance: time was obviously not of the essence, and the Court signaled that each locality required a tailor-made desegregation plan. Little Rock, two years after the second *Brown* decision, had been the first test of how much desegregation, and at what pace, was minimally necessary. The violent resistance to even a token high school integration plan sent another signal: despite the Supreme Court's ostentatious unanimity in the Little Rock case (all nine justices signed the opinion of the Court), the final result after the Court spoke so dramatically in the constitutional showdown was that the high school was subsequently closed for an entire year due to violence and the governor's use of new statutory power to close public schools.

The lessons of Little Rock were not lost on the Klan in Alabama when, after the Supreme Court held in *Boynton v. Virginia,* a month before the 1960 election, that the Interstate Commerce Act prohibited interstate bus facilities from being racially segregated, the Freedom Riders decided to force the issue in a test of will for the courts and the new administration. The previous Justice Department, mirroring the passivity of the White House, had not moved energetically to implement *Brown.* The Civil Rights Division had a small staff and no agenda. Harold (Ace) Tyler, head of the division, had not been able to attract anyone to the first assistant's position until July 1960, when he telephoned John Doar, then struggling in a small-town Wisconsin practice, and hired him sight unseen. Senator Eastland was attracted to Robert Kennedy for the same reason that Governor Patterson was: Kennedy had made life unpleasant for some labor unions while he worked for the McClellan Committee. If Kennedy could simply match his predecessor's litigation record—no civil rights suits had been filed in Mississippi during either term of the Eisenhower administration—they would get along just fine, or so Eastland implied when he and Kennedy first met to talk substantively after the election. Robert Kennedy's deal with Eastland to end the Freedom Rides meant all bets were off with both sides. Kennedy had signaled to Eastland that he would not lie down on race, but he had also made clear to the movement that the department would not be a national civil rights police force. With both sides now wary, the attorney general needed to decide which tactics and strategies to use in the new political world of rising expectations and simmering resentments.

The movement's tactics had caught the administration off guard, with inadequate intelligence, no strategy, and no indication that the odds could be improved. The attorney general's tactics, once the heat was off, thanks to the devil's bargain in Mississippi, focused on two fronts. Through Burke Marshall, he quietly urged the Interstate Commerce Commission to issue regulations that effectively implemented *Boynton;* the commission was nominally independent, although the department worked closely with the commission's latest Democratic appointee, which the Southern press quickly pointed out. With more fanfare, Robert Kennedy struggled to generate positive headlines to deflect the crisis aura of the Freedom Rides and to boost the spirits of the riders and their political supporters. He predicted over the Voice of America that "a Negro can achieve the same position my brother has," although perhaps not for forty years. Even his feeble optimism made front-page news—a welcome relief from overheated criticism that he bungled the situation by failing to shut down the riders (conservative columnist David Lawrence) or that he instigated, perhaps even planned, the whole affair (several Southern newspapers). Other members of the department worked hard behind the scenes to repatriate the Bay of Pigs invaders who were still held in Cuba; at one point in Alabama, White told Dolan that achieving the prisoners' release would be *extremely welcome—anytime, but especially now.*

It did not take long for the political heat on racial issues to rise in Washington. Simultaneously with the Freedom Rides, White was hit with a request from Senator Eastland, chairman of the Judiciary Committee, for the department's formal recommendation of two legislative proposals to extend the duration of the Civil Rights Commission, which had been established by the

Civil Rights Act of 1957 over bitter resistance from Southern congressmen. White's endorsement was terse and designed to be rhetorically flameproof:

> Apart from the commission there is no Federal executive agency charged with a continuing responsibility for gathering information calculated to assist in the guaranteeing of the protection of constitutional rights. Its field of operation is exceptionally important and extensive, and certainly deserving of continuance on a permanent basis.

The letter, sent to Eastland on May 29, was not publicly revealed until June 16, when Sen. Kenneth Keating, the liberal Republican from New York, released a summary of its contents, apparently in an effort to make the administration go public with its views. When Eastland released the full text of the letter, White conceded that the committee had the prerogative to do so but that the department did not customarily make public its legislative opinion letters. The White House refused to comment on the letter, and White would not even go so far as to label the letter "administration policy." He said lamely that the letter "adds up to an endorsement of the legislation."

The administration was obviously walking on eggshells with the Southern Democrats in the Senate. A few days after the White letter was released, Robert Kennedy appeared before a subcommittee of the Senate Appropriations Committee to defend his department's requested $294,239,900 budget. In fact, the hearing quickly became an oversight review of the Freedom Rides. Kennedy was sternly criticized by his old boss, Sen. John McClellan of Arkansas, who declared that the purpose of the rides was to "provoke, irritate and agitate," and that the $225,000 cost of shipping the marshals to Alabama was unjustified. Sen. Allen J. Ellender of Louisiana told Kennedy that the Freedom Riders were "deserving of their reception and got exactly what was to be expected." Kennedy held his ground: "Whether you like them or not they had a right to travel, and when the law broke down, I believe that anybody would have done exactly what I did."

To some extent, the hearing provided the opportunity for both sides to vindicate their known positions for the benefit of their constituents. In terms of impact, the real action was before the Interstate Commerce Commission, which had ordered a thirty-day period for public comment on proposed rules to prohibit segregation in interstate bus facilities. The administration was buying time and doing an end run around the Southern-controlled Congress. Robert Kennedy, White, and Burke Marshall were banking on the adoption of detailed, formal regulations, capable of federal enforcement, both to satisfy the protest movement in the short run and, in the long run, to provide the noncontroversial predicate for federal superintendence of the field. The administration and the segregationist resistance were flip sides of each other strategically: each bus terminal that remained segregated and each school district that delayed integration one more semester was a battle won for the forces of reaction, and conversely, each school district that was desegregated without violent incident and each Interstate Commerce Commission regulation that delegitimized Jim Crow in public facilities denied the inevitability of what smugly was called the Southern way of life. Although Northern newspapers provided only spot coverage of the ICC initiative, the impact—both direct and symbolic—was not lost on anyone in the South, as the *Birmingham News,* among others, immediately pointed out, under a dark front-page headline, "What RFK's ICC drive means in Dixie."

13

KENNEDY JUDGES

O THER THAN what collectively was called civil rights, the two most important issues that Robert F. Kennedy faced as attorney general were organized crime and judicial selection. Kennedy had made his name and had won political allies by his ruthless pursuit of corruption in labor unions, particularly the Teamsters, and no one expected him to let up at the Justice Department. Although Byron White was a constant sounding board for Jack Miller, head of the Criminal Division, and William G. Hundley, head of the Organized Crime Task Force, Robert Kennedy assigned himself the primary oversight of initiatives against organized crime and labor union racketeering—especially by his personal bête noire, James R. Hoffa, president of the Teamsters. Judicial selection was different. Kennedy placed White in charge of all judicial nominations. In addition, White's small office was responsible for recommending U.S. attorneys for each of the nearly one hundred federal districts, although Kennedy devoted much of his time at the outset to reviewing those recommendations personally; soon John Reilly was appointed as the U. S. attorneys' liaison with the department, although his role was often viewed, both within and without the building, as more shop steward than supervisor.

The issues related to judicial appointments were framed exactly one month after John Kennedy's inauguration, at the midyear meeting of the House of Delegates of the American Bar Association in Chicago. There were only eleven vacancies in the federal courts on inauguration day, but the total was expected quickly to reach more than one hundred with the impending passage of a proposed judgeship bill, which had been stalled, during a Republican administration, by Democratic congressmen a few months before the 1960 election. In addition, several retirements had been postponed, for personal or partisan reasons, until after the inauguration.

Bernard G. Segal of Philadelphia, chairman of the ABA's eleven-man Standing Committee on the Federal Judiciary, which screened candidates for judicial office and advised the president through the Justice Department, spoke in support of the screening mechanism and of nonpartisan nominations. The committee's screening function had been established during the Truman administration and maintained by his successor. During the last two years of the Eisenhower administration, a two-step procedure had been developed: informal screening, followed by formal rating. The committee had rigid views with respect to judges' qualifications (courtroom experience, at least for trial judges, and fifteen years of practice, but no appointees over age sixty-four) and to its own authority (it assumed that no appointment would be made over its strong objection). Segal, speaking to an audience of more than a thousand, including more than 250 delegates, emphasized a third priority. He referred to nonpartisan nominations as "ideal," but said that "if nonpartisanship is not yet available, then bipartisanship in appointments would certainly create a wholesome atmosphere around the whole issue of judicial appointments." With eight years of Republican appointments following two decades of Democrats in the White House, the federal judiciary was almost perfectly balanced between the parties in terms of the judges' declared affiliations at the time of taking office.

White, recently discharged from the hospital after his initial ulcer attack, made his first major public appearance at the ABA meetings, and was non-committal in response to Segal's plea: the attorney general "fully understands the enormity of the task that will have to be performed in 1961 and in the years thereafter." White's principal purpose was not to engage Segal or any other advocate for a particular policy that day, but to promise that "our work" would be "characterized by a great deal of energy and a great deal of dedication and a great deal of vigor." The House of Delegates endorsed passage of the judgeship bill, and appointments in which politics did not play a "paramount" role in the nominee's qualifications. On other issues, the delegates took less progressive positions. They approved a resolution urging that the "inherent evil of communism" be taught in public schools, and defeated a bill sponsored by Sen. Paul Douglas of Illinois advocating disclosure of all finance charges on installment purchases, mortgages, and small loans. Douglas's bill had been prompted by the suicide of a Chicago man who had been overwhelmed by installment debt whose terms he did not fully appreciate.

The Kennedy administration quickly found a convenient way to blunt the ABA's clamor for bipartisanship: they resubmitted the names of three recess appointments made by Eisenhower. Two were readily confirmed, Andrew J. Caffrey in the District of Massachusetts and C. Nils Tavares in Hawaii. A third, John Feikens in the Eastern District of Michigan, never received the courtesy of a hearing before Eastland's committee, and his commission accordingly expired when the Senate adjourned on September 27, 1961. Feikens had been GOP state chairman when Patrick V. McNamara, a Democrat, had been first elected senator, by only a percentage point, in 1954; McNamara's reelection in 1960 meant, in Joe Dolan's phrase, that "the knives were out," and one spiked Feikens's nomination—although Richard Nixon later succeeded in appointing Feikens in 1970. The Caffrey appointment, which went through in early August of 1961, caused a permanent rift of some depth between the Irish Mafia in the White House—led by Kenny O'Donnell, the president's appointments secretary—and the Department of Justice. "I think Kenny soured on Byron over Caffrey," Dolan later observed. After Caffrey and Tavares, President Kennedy named no more Republicans while White was deputy attorney general. He appointed a total of eleven Republicans during his tenure.

When President Kennedy signed the Omnibus Judgeship Act on May 19, he declared grandly:

> I want for our courts individuals with respected professional skill, incorruptible character, firm judicial temperament, the rare inner quality to know when to temper justice with mercy, and the intellectual capacity to protect and illuminate the Constitution and our historic values.

Once the appointments began, however, critics attacked one nomination after another, especially at the district court level in the Deep South. Victor Navasky found "no aspect of Robert Kennedy's Attorney Generalship" to be "more vulnerable to criticism," and Alexander Bickel declared that the administration's admirable record of appointing blacks throughout government service was "more than offset" by appointments of Southern judges "totally out of sympathy with the Supreme Court cases on equal protection." A doctoral dissertation in 1968 by Mary M. Curzan concluded that the Kennedy administration acted passively on judicial appointments, failed to develop a "mechanism" like Shriver's executive talent hunt to "widen its choices," and "sacrificed its control over the appointment process in the South in the hope of building support for its legislative program"—points that Navasky later reasserted.

The criticisms peaked in intensity a decade after the appointments were made but now seem ahistorical and uninformed. White and Robert Kennedy used virtually every assistant attorney general as a recruiter of potential names for judicial appointments. The AAGs relied on their own networks and constantly fed information back and forth to one another. In terms of sheer volume, "Kennedy Justice," as Navasky derisively referred to the department, vetted and cleared more judicial appointments in two years than the entire administrations of Presidents Harding, Coolidge, and Hoover did in more than a decade. No president before Kennedy had ever been faced with so many judicial vacancies in his first term, let alone his first year. By the standards of evaluation employed by the American Bar Association, the quality of the Kennedy appointees was almost identical to that of Eisenhower's. The ABA was more hindrance than help to the Kennedy administration, however, and its dogmatic definitions of quality had multiple costs: they prevented more progressive appointments from being made, retarded the appointment of several men and women who eventually became respected judges, and, perhaps worst of all, papered over grave problems of belief and temperament and thus deprived the department of ammunition against problematic nominations.

It is true that the department acquiesced in some senatorial suggestions, particularly in the South, that proved distasteful and in a few cases even disgraceful, but those decisions were produced less by design, as Navasky and others charged, than by the frank realization in the administration that it was politically outgunned. One other criticism needs to be mentioned, if only in passing, to show how frustration with the selection process could cloud otherwise lucid thinking. Alexander Bickel argued that the Kennedys should either have left positions vacant or convinced the chief justice of the United States to use his statutory powers to assign judges from other locales to work temporarily in needy districts where only unacceptable candidates were available: "It was such an assigned judge from one of the Dakotas who was sitting in Little Rock at the time of the trouble there. This was surely a usable counterpressure to the senatorial veto." For once, Bickel—the most practical of constitutional theorists—was being naive. The fact that Judge Ronald N. Davies was from North Dakota inadvertently cast a political cloud over *Cooper v. Aaron*, the Little Rock school case, and symbolized carpetbagging occupation. A Congress that could consider restricting the jurisdiction of the Supreme Court might have little compunction over taking the lesser step of repealing the chief justice's intercircuit assignment powers. Even without statutory nullification, the rulings of a "foreign" judge would be no more durable than the length of his temporary assignment.

The political reality of the constitutional "advise and consent" power, and the counterproductive nature of the alliance with the ABA, were vividly demonstrated with the very first nomination that President Kennedy sent to the Senate under the Omnibus Act—William Harold Cox, for a new position in the Southern District of Mississippi. Cox's name was suggested to White and Dolan when they paid a courtesy call on Senator Eastland, who mistakenly addressed White as "Buzzer." Eastland was a close friend of Cox, who had supported Eastland's senatorial campaigns, especially in primaries, where it counted. They were not college roommates, as the NAACP and many others thought. Cox, almost sixty, was a highly successful corporate lawyer in Jackson who affected a rather formal manner and who, unlike many white lawyers in Mississippi at the time, was not a member of the White Citizens' Council, which was to the Klan what Sinn Fein was to the Irish Republican Army.

When White and Dolan met with Eastland to develop information on Cox, Eastland stonewalled them: "I ain't gonna tell you a thing, boys. You find out for yourselves." What the department discovered through its own back channels was not reassuring. Lou Oberdorfer learned from one of his contacts in Mississippi that former governor J. P. Coleman, who had provided Robert Kennedy sound intelligence during the Freedom Rides, "thought Cox would make a poor judge because he is lacking in judicial temperament." A lawyer in Jackson reported to the same contact that Cox operated "in the background in the Citizens' Council." The ABA's background screening, conducted by Leon Jaworski of Bernard Segal's committee, produced nothing exceptionable in more than two dozen interviews.

Only when Segal personally interviewed Cox in Jackson did an alarm go off with respect to Cox's views on race. Robert Kennedy personally interviewed Cox, more intensively than any other candidate during his tenure, and was left uneasy. Thinking that Cox could be neutralized on a multimember appellate court that was developing an admirable record for implementing the Supreme Court's new jurisprudence on race, Kennedy directed White to ask Eastland if Cox would take an appointment on the Fifth Circuit Court of Appeals, which covered Texas, Louisiana, Mississippi, Alabama, Georgia, and Florida. There were two seats allocated to the Fifth Circuit under the Omnibus Act, and the department was still deliberating with the White House over which states should enjoy the patronage. Georgia and Alabama were the leading contenders, although Texas and Florida generated more appeals. Eastland actually telephoned Cox in Jackson from the attorney general's office, but Cox understood where the immediate power resided and disdained interest in the appellate court. On the basis of his professional standing and experience, the ABA rated Cox "exceptionally well qualified," its highest rating and one of only six awarded during the first nine months of the administration among thirty-three nominations.

Cox was nominated for the district court in Jackson, Mississippi, in June 1961 and was confirmed by the end of the month. Within a year, Cox proved himself to be a shameless racist—referring in open court to black voters as "a bunch of chimpanzees"—and a master of delay, refusing to hold hearings, make findings, issue final orders, and so on. Bickel called his behavior in voting rights cases "out of Kafka." Even Eastland was eventually embarrassed by Cox and tried years later, without success, to convince him to take senior status.

The ABA was less credulous in the instances of the other two district court appointments that were most severely criticized by Professor Bickel and others—E. Gordon West in the Eastern District of Louisiana (New Orleans) and Clarence Allgood in the Northern District of Alabama (Birmingham). Both were rated "not qualified" by the ABA. The department decided not to abandon the nominations of West and Allgood for two reasons. First, the record against both men was so weak and so subjective that the political fight with the supporting senators (Russell Long and Lister Hill, respectively) would have been more costly than productive. Second, Kennedy and White had other candidates who were screened as not qualified by the ABA whom they were eager to nominate, because they were convinced that the ABA standards were less than perfect measures of quality.

West, a former law partner of Sen. Russell Long of Louisiana, later became another master of delay in school desegregation cases and earned the sternest rebuke that the Fifth Circuit Court of Appeals ever administered to a sitting judge, after he stalled for more than two years the enforcement of a mandate from the court of appeals in a school desegregation case. He had tipped his hand earlier by condemning *Brown v. Board of Education* as "one of the truly regrettable decisions of all time," whose "only real accomplishment to date [1963] has been to bring discontent and chaos to many previously peaceful communities, without bringing any real attendant benefits to anyone." Unlike Cox, whose identity with Eastland put Robert Kennedy and White on their guard, West "didn't have a history," as Burke Marshall later recalled: "everyone we talked to" in New Orleans "thought he'd be all right." Louis Oberdorfer later admitted that he and the department relied too heavily in the South on contacts whose judgment they trusted. West's appointment had one collateral benefit for all its costs—due to complicated negotiations with the Louisiana senators, West's nomination paved the way for the appointment of a distinguished moderate judge, Robert A. Ainsworth.

The vetting net for judges in the South and elsewhere consisted of every political appointee in the department who knew someone trustworthy in the relevant jurisdiction. White took care of the Tenth Circuit (Oklahoma, Kansas, Colorado, Wyoming, New Mexico, Utah); William Orrick covered California and the rest of the Ninth Circuit (Alaska, Hawaii, Washington, Idaho, Montana, Nevada, Arizona); Ramsey Clark could conduct shuttle diplomacy between Vice President Johnson and Robert Kennedy; Geoghegan was useful for Ohio; Oberdorfer, the Birmingham native, worked extensively on candidates in Alabama and to a lesser extent in Florida, where his law school classmate Louis Hector practiced; and Marshall worked on all potential candidates throughout the South.

Oberdorfer took the lead in investigating Clarence Allgood, who was a protégé of Senator Hill and had done political work for Hill and Hugo Black before Black was appointed to the Supreme Court. Allgood's problem was not necessarily his racial views—he was supported by various local black leaders in Birmingham—but his credentials. He had been a referee in bankruptcy since 1937 and had taken a law degree at night in 1941 after referees were required to have legal training. He had never practiced law, never had a client, and never tried a case. When Oberdorfer told Senator Hill that the department would not endorse Allgood's nomination, and thus that his name would never reach the White House, "Hill was adamant about it," according to Oberdorfer. "He had never heard of such a thing as the president refusing to appoint a judge that a senator had recommended and it was a point of personal honor for him. He was just very upset about it."

Instead of digging in, White and Robert Kennedy decided to take a second look at Allgood, and White assigned Oberdorfer to make "a more extensive check of the qualifications of Clarence Allgood," as the first of Oberdorfer's three lengthy memoranda to White in August of 1961 stated. The results of the investigation were again inconclusive. Some lawyers found Allgood's nomination "inconceivable" and others thought that he lacked the "ability (because of lack of training and experience) to reason along conceptual lines." Most lawyers were disposed to the nomination, and one emphasized that Allgood was well read, both within and without the law, and that "ABA people who have not been in bankruptcy court do not realize the multitude of questions which come up in bankruptcy proceedings, from evidence to every substantive field of law."

What turned Oberdorfer were the evaluations of the other two sitting judges in the Northern District, Harlan H. Grooms, a sixty-year-old Eisenhower appointee, and Seybourn H. Lynne, fifty-four, whom Truman had appointed in 1945. Both firmly endorsed Allgood, but the recommendations may have had multiple motivations. Oberdorfer apparently never considered that a sitting judge would be unlikely to speak ill of someone with whom he could end up sitting for decades. Allgood could be seen as an aging retainer from the old Black–Hill political crowd, or as a rags-to-riches story of someone who began life with no privileges and was saddled with a handicap that would have defeated many lesser men: both of his legs were amputated when he tried to jump a freight train as a little boy. Judge Grooms underscored Allgood's "grit" in overcoming the physical limitation. Oberdorfer was moved even more by Lynne, whom he trusted implicitly and who mentioned that Allgood "is one of the most prolific readers of books he knows. He reads 'in every direction' from the classics to *Advise and Consent*."

Three years after the fact, Oberdorfer reflected on why he decided to support Allgood's nomination:

> People began to tell me that Allgood, while he wasn't a superlative lawyer, was a man of intellectual curiosity and he reads books and he had a lot of common sense and he was close to the people, had a lot of human understanding. What is a federal judge anyway? He is not a supreme court judge. He has got to deal with sentencing people who steal cars and who do things like that, presiding over a jury, and understanding the community.

When Senator Hill decided to pay a personal call on the president to insist on Allgood's nomination, the debate was moot. All that was left for the administration was to save face and, as in the case of West, to convince the ABA to upgrade its rating of Allgood from not qualified to qualified. White put Oberdorfer in the deputy's conference room with orders to persuade "Bernie Segal that the bar was wrong in saying that Allgood wasn't qualified." After the conference, Segal "got somebody to go back and recheck Allgood and they said Allgood was qualified. Allgood became the judge." He became number one on Professor Bickel's list of infamous Kennedy appointees when he summarily refused to enjoin the expulsion of more than one thousand black public school students by the Birmingham Board of Education for participating in mass marches in early May of 1963. Bickel ridiculed Allgood's résumé and chided the administration for naming someone with such a crabbed and reactionary view of his duty: "Senatorial pressure is no excuse. The matter is too important; it reaches too far into the future." Bickel was correct on at least one point: Allgood served for twenty-nine years and two months before taking his own life at the age of eighty-nine, in 1991. Allgood maintained a reputation for hard work throughout his career, which included a substantial contribution to the drafting of Chapter 13 of the Bankruptcy Code.

The ABA was willing to rerate West and Allgood when it was clear that the nominations would be made anyway and when the case against both was subjective to some extent. Segal's committee was immovable in several other instances, three of which illustrate the cost of the ABA's dogmatism. The department was "desperate to appoint as many blacks to the bench as we could," according to Dolan, but the ABA committee stood in the way of what Dolan and White thought was one of their best candidates, A. Leon Higginbotham of Philadelphia. The Omnibus Act added three judgeships to the Eastern District of Pennsylvania. Higginbotham was a Yale Law School graduate with experience in private practice, the Department of Justice, and the Pennsylvania Human Relations Commission. He was an ideal candidate in many respects, but he was only thirty-three years old, and the ABA therefore would not rate him qualified. Instead of fighting the age bar, Robert Kennedy suggested to his brother that Higginbotham be appointed to the Federal Trade Commission as a springboard to the federal judiciary. Higginbotham was named to the FTC in 1962 and to the federal district court in Philadelphia the following year.

In Texas, Sarah Tilghman Hughes had the opposite problem. She had reached age sixty-five in August of 1961, and the ABA's ironclad rule was that no one older than sixty-four would be rated qualified. At first Robert Kennedy declined to send her name to the ABA for screening, on the ground that he had refused a similar request about another possible nominee from his old boss, Senator McClellan, but Vice President Johnson insisted, and the president prevailed on his brother to make an exception to his practice of complying with the ABA guideline. White was not in favor of compromising the ABA's age bar, but he yielded to Robert Kennedy as Robert Kennedy yielded to the president. Hughes, who had been a Texas state court judge for twenty-six years, was confirmed in October 1961, despite a rating of not qualified from the ABA. She later became famous when she swore in Lyndon Johnson as president aboard *Air Force One* in Dallas on November 22, 1963; she carried a full load of cases for more than a decade after her appointment and did not fully retire until 1975.

The final example of the ABA's rigidity is James R. Browning, who was suggested for a seat on the Ninth Circuit when Judge Walter L. Pope, a 1949 Truman appointee, took senior status. Pope was from Montana, and Lee Metcalf, junior senator to Mike Mansfield, the majority leader, was the first to suggest a nominee to the department. Browning was Metcalf's first and only choice, but the ABA opposed him on the ground of age—he was forty-three—and of limited experience. Browning, who had been clerk of the Supreme Court of the United States since 1958, had spent most of his career as a litigator with the Department of Justice, first in the Antitrust Division and later in the Civil Division. White interviewed Browning, was impressed with his intelligence as well as his career record, and "we hung in against the ABA," in Dolan's words. Browning went on to a distinguished career on the Ninth Circuit, including a lengthy term as chief judge.

In three other cases in which the "not qualified" rating stuck, the team of White and Dolan shared the ABA committee's reservations in varying degrees. Emanuel Celler, chairman of the House Judiciary Committee, welcomed the return of a Democrat to the White House with a long list of legislative initiatives and personnel priorities, along with the expectation that his agenda would receive high priority. One item near the top of his agenda was the appointment of Irving Ben Cooper to one of the Omnibus Act positions in the Southern District of New York. With no Democratic senators in New York, Celler was entitled to some voice on appointments, although he made no suggestions for any of the other seven judicial vacancies in the state. Celler gently mentioned his preference for Cooper the first time he met White; like Eastland, Celler mistakenly referred to White as "Buzzer" at their first meeting.

Cooper was rated not qualified by the ABA due to anxieties about his hair-trigger temper. The ABA also raised questions about the extent of his trial experience. He was nominated nonetheless and caused the only contentious confirmation hearing during the first year of the administration when the ABA decided to make him a test case of its judgment. Once the ABA threw down the gauntlet, the amiably persistent Celler's pride was on the line, and the department backed him up. "We could have found somebody much less controversial," admitted William Geoghegan; "Celler was never a very demanding person in terms of political patronage but this was something he really wanted and we had, of course, a great deal of our legislation" headed to Celler's committee. Cooper was eventually confirmed and became notorious for his irascibility on the bench.

White hesitated much more on two other vacancies, one, under the Omnibus Act, in Massachusetts and the other, in Oklahoma, resulting from a traffic death in June 1960. The first vacancy pitted the Kennedy family against itself. The Ambassador—as Joseph P. Kennedy was still generally referred to—wanted one of his longtime retainers, Francis X. Morrissey, to be appointed to the federal district court in Boston. Morrissey was a Boston municipal court judge who had served the Kennedys for decades—including as a campaign secretary during John Kennedy's first congressional campaign, in 1946—but his legal credentials were thin. He had failed the bar examination several times, and in fact, the FBI could not verify the law degree that he had claimed in the Martindale-Hubbell *Law Directory*. Robert Kennedy was extremely sensitive to Morrissey's case and even lost his temper with Anthony Lewis of the *New York Times*—terminating an interview and roughly inviting Lewis to leave his office—when Morrissey's qualifications were questioned. White did not want to endorse Morrissey, nor did he wish to cross Robert Kennedy on a matter that was so explosive for him. The final compromise was to send not one but three names to the White House for the position—a pointed, if still implicit, signal that the department, which had supported many controversial cases, viewed its integrity to be in jeopardy. The president declined to name Morrissey, but in deference to his father, named no one else to the position either.

The Oklahoma vacancy caused the most turmoil within the department and raised the greatest doubts in both the attorney general's and the deputy attorney general's offices about the prospective nominee. To fill the position, which was a "roving" assignment covering all three federal districts in Oklahoma, Sen. Robert S. Kerr sent the name of Luther L. Bohanon, a fifty-nine-year-old lawyer with the self-styled reputation as a maverick, but a well-connected maverick. He was a former law partner of Alfred P. Murrah, who had been named to the federal district and circuit courts by President Roosevelt, and he was also a close friend of Kerr's brother, Aubrey, who recommended Bohanon's appointment. As John Seigenthaler later recalled, Bohanon's potential nomination stirred "a tremendous amount of controversy in the Oklahoma City bar" and a "spate" of mail to the department. The complaints conformed to the standardized ABA categories—injudicious temperament, inadequate courtroom experience, too old—but also included darker rumors and innuendoes about sharp practice and hard bargains. The ABA committee rated Bohanon not qualified, and White and Geoghegan were dispatched to deliver the bad news to Kerr.

Kerr did not expect and saw no need to entertain the message. He had just won reelection for a third term in the Senate, although he personally estimated that his support of Kennedy cost him seventy-five thousand votes in hard-line-Baptist Oklahoma. With Johnson promoted to vice president, Kerr was widely regarded as the most powerful, and most ruthless, man in the Senate. He was also the pivotal Democratic member of the Senate Finance Committee, whose chair, Harry F. Byrd of Virginia, detested the Kennedys and would not lift a finger to support any legislation proposed by the administration. Kerr was also on the Public Works and Appropriations Committee. He was thus central to the president's 1961 legislative package, including six major bills in particular—concerning highways, temporary increase in the debt limit, changes in Social Security Aid to Dependent Children, expansion of unemployment compensation, funding for the space program, and air and water pollution.

To White's revelation of the department's decision not to forward Bohanon's name to the White House, Kerr replied: "Young men, I was here a long time before you came. I'm going to be here a long time after you go. I stand by my recommendation." When the department stuck to its guns, the president's tax legislation began to bog down in the Senate. When Bobby Baker, secretary to the Senate majority, went to Kerr to determine the senator's priorities, he was told: "Tell [the president] to get his dumb fuckin' brother to quit opposing my friend."

In July, Robert Kennedy sent John Seigenthaler and William Geoghegan to Oklahoma City for an on-site review of Bohanon and his career. In one week they interviewed nearly one hundred lawyers. Seigenthaler thought much of the objection to Bohanon was based on jealousy or politics. Kerr and the young governor, J. Howard Edmondson, were bitter foes, and Edmondson's allies opposed Kerr's prerogatives. "So when I came back," Seigenthaler later recalled,

> I said, "I don't think it would be a mistake to name this guy. I think you should name him and live with it. The Bar Association won't like it. I don't think he's a crook, and I don't think he's dishonest. I think he's obviously a successful lawyer. If I were you, I'd take him."

Geoghegan, who noted that the earlier FBI investigation "frankly didn't confirm what most of the people objecting to the appointment had to say about" Bohanon, remained opposed to the nomination and wrote a lengthy memorandum to Robert Kennedy detailing his views. Kerr tried to recruit Edmondson into Bohanon's camp, and even Judge Murrah got into the act: when Murrah encountered Joe Dolan at a meeting held in the Supreme Court building that summer, he drawled, gently but firmly, *Now don't you crucify my good friend Luther Bohanon.*

The end game began August 9 when the *Daily Oklahoman,* the state's largest newspaper, reported that "Kerr's political plum was slowly becoming a prune." The loss of face was too much for Kerr, who announced that if the president named anyone else, he would oppose the nomination. The Justice Department closed its files on Bohanon on August 10, when Lou Oberdorfer sent a detailed two-page memo to White analyzing six-year-old allegations that Bohanon had made a false statement in a brief for a client in connection with a criminal tax matter. Oberdorfer rehearsed the IRS files on the matter and concluded that at worst Bohanon had made a good faith mistake and that in any event the government had not relied on the statement. Oberdorfer's memo concluded: "Except on the theory that 'Where there's smoke, there's fire,' I do not believe that this incident *alone* constitutes grounds for the disqualification of a candidate for judicial office."

A few days later, on August 16, Kerr sent Rex Hawks, the United States marshal for the Western District of Oklahoma, to White as his personal representative to determine whether there were any final obstacles to the outstanding Oklahoma appointments—including his own. White replied that there would be no problem obtaining a quick resolution of the outstanding issues— U.S. attorneys, marshals (including Hawks himself), and the like—as long as Kerr supplied a different recommendation for the judicial vacancy. When Hawks reported back to Kerr late that afternoon, Kerr calmly called the White House and demanded an appointment immediately with the president. The next day, the White House issued a press release announcing that the president planned to nominate Bohanon for the fourteen-month vacancy.

The day that Bohanon's nomination formally reached the Senate included two moments that captured the stakes and spirit of the debate over the appointment. On Capitol Hill, the Senate passed the controversial Foreign Assistance Act of 1961 with energetic support from Kerr. Standard operating procedure in the Department of Justice was for the deputy attorney general's office to prepare a letter of endorsement and a résumé of the appointee to be signed on behalf of the attorney general and forwarded to the White House; there, the president would make the formal nomination. When Joe Dolan presented White with the letter and résumé on Bohanon, White very deliberately tore the papers in half and said softly, "Let them do it themselves."

Luther Bohanon was confirmed in less than two weeks. The Bohanon appointment marked one of the many divisions between the Kennedys during the first year of the administration. For Robert Kennedy, a fight against senatorial prerogative was necessary at various points to prevent being steamrolled as time wore on and more vacancies emerged or unfilled positions under the Omnibus Act became tempting targets for the raw end of patronage. For President Kennedy, Kerr's political support was much more important than the fate of one older judge in Oklahoma. Robert Kennedy came to appreciate his brother's judgment in time. In 1964, he reflected on the Bohanon affair:

> The President of the United States is attempting to obtain the passage of important legislation in many, many fields, and the appointment of a judge who is recommended by the chairman of a committee or a key figure on a committee can make the whole difference on his legislative program.
>
> He said, in effect, that the legislation was important for the entire country and the judge was important only for one state.
>
> So you really have to balance it off. It sounds terrible. And you know, you should stand fast on principle. You stand fast on principle: Kerr doesn't get his judge and you don't get any tax legislation. And they play it as tough and as mean as that. He played it as tough and as mean as that.

For Byron White—"a hard-headed, aggressive purist," according to Ramsey Clark—the political compromise was highly distasteful. White's role in the Department of Justice as broker over judicial nominations was thus incongruous in the light of his personal tastes; his impact on judicial appointments was in any event enormous.

Three more instances illustrate the imprint White made as the administration sustained the average pace of nominating and shepherding the confirmation process of one federal judge per week for the first two years of the Kennedy presidency. When Democratic senators or leaders in a state could not agree on one name for a vacancy, White would hit the road and meet with local officials and bar leaders to find an appropriate candidate whose nomination could obtain undivided support. For instance, White went to Ohio when the two Democratic senators in Ohio and Gov. Michael V. DiSalle, who had been so important to President Kennedy's campaign, could not agree on a nominee for an Omnibus Act position in the Northern District of Ohio. The appointment was planned for Youngstown, a daunting challenge, as Joe Dolan later observed: "Ohio was a tough political state, and Youngstown was murder."

The solution was a thirty-nine-year-old local trial court judge, Frank J. Battisti, who grew up in a working-class area of Youngstown, was a tail gunner in northern France during World War II, and then attended Harvard Law School. White was immediately attracted to Battisti after watching him preside in the Mahoning County Common Pleas Court and warmed to him further when he discovered that he was a passionate dry-fly fisherman. In fact, Battisti had spent a month fishing in Colorado after graduating from law school, trying to decide between a career in the priesthood and working as a lawyer for the Catholic Church. Despite his youth, Battisti was rated qualified by the ABA because of his judicial experience and was confirmed less than a month after nomination.

Several months later, White again was charged to mediate a conflict over a nomination, this time between Dennis Chavez and Clinton Anderson in New Mexico over a vacancy on the Tenth Circuit Court of Appeals. White went to New Mexico but he knew what he was looking for. Oliver Seth was a forty-seven-year-old lawyer in Santa Fe with an extensive practice, and more to the point, he had been White's roommate briefly at Yale Law School during the 1939–40 academic year, White's first and Seth's last. Seth, as White later said at his memorial service, was "the most acceptable lawyer in the state," and it was "impossible for anyone to object to him." Seth's appointment sailed through the Senate in June 1962, after White had left the department, but as he told a colleague, "I guess my fingerprints are all over it." (Ironically, the one appointment he wanted to see made more than any other—of Ira Rothgerber for the new position under the Omnibus Act in Colorado—never occurred. Although White strongly recommended Rothgerber and even had a memo prepared to initiate the routine FBI check, the nomination went to William E. Doyle, who was named and confirmed in September 1961 at the behest of Sen. John Carroll, who also happened to be married to Doyle's sister.)

White did not always make the road trips himself. In one important matter, the nomination of James B. Parsons, he sent Joe Dolan instead. When the Kennedy administration took office, there was only one black judge in the federal judiciary—William H. Hastie, fifty-six, who had been appointed to the Third Circuit Court of Appeals by President Truman in 1948. Shortly after the nomination of William Harold Cox was sent to the Senate, President Kennedy nominated three blacks: Thurgood Marshall for the Second Circuit, and two judges for the district court—Wade McCree for the Eastern District of Michigan and Parsons for the Northern District of Illinois. As it turned out, Eastland held Marshall hostage for the first session of the Eighty-seventh Congress, so President Kennedy named him to a recess appointment. Marshall later received a full appointment and was finally confirmed by the Senate almost a year after his name first went to Capitol Hill. (Eastland was later quoted as saying infamously to Robert Kennedy, "Tell your brother that if he will give me Harold Cox I will give him the nigger," an apparent reference to Marshall.) Over time the Kennedys appointed a total of ten blacks to the federal courts.

James B. Parsons became, at age fifty, the first black in history to be confirmed to a federal trial court judgeship, on August 30, 1961—two months after Cox and one month before McCree. Parsons had been suggested to the department by Thomas R. McMillen, a Republican and former Rhodes scholar now practicing in Chicago, who was from Parsons's hometown of Decatur in downstate Illinois. The Decatur connection meant that Parsons was personally vetted by Dolan in more than one sense. Dolan spent two days in Chicago watching Parsons conduct trial work in the old Superior Court of Cook County, where he had been sitting for a year after nine years in the U.S. Attorney's Office following graduation from the University of Chicago Law School. White and Dolan, wary of Eastland on the race issue, were concerned to have as much evidence as possible to support their nomination; "and we didn't think the fact that my mother-in-law knew Parsons as a boy and vouched for him would carry much weight," Dolan remarked later. The department had overexerted itself. The ABA rated Parsons "well qualified," given his age (he had taught music for several years before attending law school), trial experience, and judicial office. In fact, notwithstanding suggestions about the dark influence of the Daley machine over the Kennedys, almost all of the Kennedy appointees in Chicago were highly rated. Roger J. Kiley and Luther M. Swygert for the Seventh Circuit and Hubert L. Will for the district court were all rated well qualified. Although all were nominally suggested by Sen. Paul Douglas, the state's only Democratic senator, Mayor Daley was, in Dolan's words, "no more than two steps behind" each nomination.

Besides Dolan, the most important players on Byron White's judge-vetting team were Oberdorfer and Orrick. Oberdorfer later regretted his failure to learn more about senatorial choices or to turn up better candidates in Mississippi and Alabama, but the political cards were stacked against him and the department in both jurisdictions. He was much more successful in Florida, which his Judge Book—as he called his extensive files on judicial candidates from Virginia to Florida to Louisiana—demonstrates. The first candidates that surfaced for the four positions open in the Florida district courts in the spring of 1961 were unprepossessing, but with arm-twisting from the department, the final nominees were distinguished, and two, William A. McRae and David Dyer, both deserved the "exceptionally well qualified" ratings they received from the ABA. The other jurisdiction where the appointments were of high caliber was the Northern District of California, which was the bailiwick of Orrick, although much of his job was to monitor the preferences of the Democratic senator, Clair Engle, and the governor, Edmund G. (Pat) Brown, both of whom had been elected for the first time in 1958. The other Ninth Circuit vacancy in 1961 besides the Montana seat opened by Pope's retirement was a California seat created by a retirement.

Engle was inclined to name either James M. Carter or Louis M. Goodman, both federal district judges, for the vacancy. Both had been recommended by Justice Douglas, who was constantly peppering Robert Kennedy with suggestions for judicial nominations. The sentiment was to nominate someone from the San Francisco area, which eliminated Carter, but Goodman was sixty-nine and in failing health (he would die in September). The compromise was Ben. C. Duniway, who had an extremely distinguished academic record, two years of experience on the state district court of appeal, and a gilt-edged endorsement from Orrick, which White received shortly after Engle's formal submission to the department. Duniway was nominated and took office three months after Engle first discussed the nomination with White in June. In short order, there were three vacancies on the district court in San Francisco, and Duniway suggested one of the eventual nominees, Stanley A. Weigel, who, as a nominal Republican (he often worked for Democrats and in fact attended the inauguration), further aided the administration's target of 10 percent non-Democratic appointments.

The other San Francisco appointment (a third went to Sacramento) went to Alfonso J. Zirpoli, who was one of many candidates suggested by Paul (Red) Fay, the president's old PT boat buddy and now undersecretary of the navy. More important, Zirpoli had a distinguished record in the U.S. Attorney's Office in San Francisco and had created a program of legal services for indigents while he was in private practice. At one point early in the administration, he had been invited by Orrick on Robert Kennedy's behalf to be U. S. attorney, but he declined, and Cecil Poole, who had worked for Governor Brown, became the first black U.S. attorney in the country. Zirpoli's only competition for the judgeship in the end was Governor Brown's brother, Harold. Even before the nomination was made and while Harold Brown's name was still in contention, Zirpoli met with White in Washington while he was on other business, and White breezily introduced Zirpoli to Sal Andretta, the administrative AAG, as "the next Italian judge."

Zirpoli's nomination, and that of the Sacramento nominee, Thomas J. McBride, went to the Senate on September 14, 1961, and both were confirmed one week later as Congress steamed toward adjournment two weeks later. The administration took advantage of the Senate's formal absence to make seventeen recess appointments on October 5, 1961. Under Article II, § 2 of the Constitution, the president is empowered "to fill up all Vacancies that may happen during the recess of the senate, by granting Commissions which shall expire at the end of their next Session." The Kennedy administration used recess appointments twenty-eight times, in nearly 20 percent of their successful nominations, but most were used to expedite staffing in backlogged jurisdictions rather than to end-run recalcitrant senators. For example, four of the recess appointments made on October 5 were for New York City, where the vacancies were exacerbating the backlog and where there were no Democratic senators whose prerogatives were implicated.

Four of the nominations were used to buy time in order to defuse controversy. Thurgood Marshall in the Second Circuit and two nominees for the civil rights hot spot of the Fifth Circuit—Walter P. Gewin (Alabama) and Griffin B. Bell (Georgia)—were among the October 5 appointments. On December 15, 1961, a retirement on the District of Columbia Circuit allowed a recess appointment to go to J. Skelly Wright, the district judge who had ordered New Orleans schools desegregated and thus infuriated Sen. Russell Long, who was up for reelection in 1962. Long had told Robert Kennedy that he could not win if Skelly Wright were named to the Fifth Circuit. Robert Kennedy made the final decision on the recess appointments at the appellate level, although Bell was the only candidate of the four whom he knew personally. (Bell had been instrumental in the 1960 campaign in Georgia, had helped to keep the political lid on the state after the controversial phone call to Martin Luther King's wife, and had stood by the attorney general on the podium in Athens when Kennedy made his Law Day speech—despite Kennedy's suggestion that Bell might want to "leave the state" rather than be seen with him.) Indeed, Bell's was one of only two nominations that Robert Kennedy personally insisted upon during the first year; for six months, "every time we went over the list of potential Fifth Circuit appointments," recalled Dolan, "when we got to Georgia, Bob would say 'Griff Bell,' wave his hand impatiently, and move us on." The other was of Irving R. Kaufman for the Second Circuit, who was named in mid-September 1961 and confirmed a week later, shortly before the Senate adjourned.

The purpose of the Omnibus Act was to relieve court backlogs, so the premium for the department was to fill vacancies quickly. Recess appointments were convenient for the department, which was under growing pressure as the year wore on to fill the legion of vacancies, which was growing steadily due to retirements. Recess appointees naturally saw their good fortune as potentially hollow, as John Feikens's experience demonstrated. White nonetheless was often clipped in presenting recess offers. Harrison Winter later revealed how White offered him a judicial nomination to the district court in Maryland in November 1961. After White delivered the good news, Winter, weighing the risks, asked for time to consider his answer. White responded with Robert Kennedy–like impatience: "I have another commission with a different name all ready to be issued if you don't accept." Winter complied. Maryland had no Democratic senators, and Winter was suggested by Joseph D. Tydings. In Ramsey Clark's estimation, Byron White was a "tough-minded, strong-minded, extremely high-standard guy." On judges, he was "all business and merit . . . perhaps a little bit abrasive in the handling of the amenities, but a guy who carried such respect for a variety of reasons—football among them—that he could do it."

During Byron White's tenure as deputy attorney general, there were 141 vacancies in the federal judiciary, sixty-eight created by death or retirement and seventy-three by the Omnibus Judgeship Act of 1961. White's office generated thirteen hundred files of persons suggested or formally recommended to fill those positions, of which 670 were sufficiently serious to be sent on to the ABA for formal or informal rating. The net result was 111 nominations (including nine term appointments to local and Article I courts), sixty-two under the act and forty-nine in response to attrition. The Senate confirmed fifty-seven and forty-one, respectively—a total of ninety-eight appointments in roughly fifteen months. The work, thanks to the act, was heavily front-loaded in the first year of the administration, when seventy-three judges were confirmed.

Notwithstanding the remarkable pace—on average more than one nomination per week during White's tour of duty—localities with outstanding vacancies grew impatient as the second year of the administration began. The Massachusetts seat, chronically rumored for the unqualified Morrissey, was more a curiosity than a frustration in Boston, but the four vacancies in the Southern District of New York handicapped and annoyed the New York City bar, and White went to the unusual extreme, at least for him, of granting an interview to the *New York Times* to defend the department. He revealed that eighteen lawyers had "turned down" appointments or invitations to be considered, but he promised at least one appointment would be made soon to what the *Times* pointed out was a "lifetime" position "at $22,500 a year."

The interview raised an old chestnut that was beginning to warm up again—appointments for Republicans. There had been rumors that some of the turndowns had been Republicans, but White "declined to discuss the subject of offers to Republicans," perhaps because he knew that in two weeks the House of Delegates of the ABA would be pointedly criticizing him and the department at the annual midwinter meetings in Chicago for not nominating more Republicans. Bernard Segal presented the standing committee's report, which criticized the administration on two counts, for nominating eighty-two Democrats and only three Republicans (all Eisenhower recess appointees) and for nominating seven whom the committee had rated unqualified. White, "in an unscheduled appearance," defended the department on both issues. He explained that the department relied on its own investigations as well as those by Segal's committee, elliptically suggesting that the ABA standards were too rigid and artificial. As to bipartisanship in appointments, which Segal was rehearsing from exactly a year before, White took the offensive. He saw nothing "odious" in what the committee called an "imbalance" in judicial appointments: the selection of judges was "a political process in the best sense of those words," and "the central question in choosing them was ability, not politics."

Despite recurrent disagreements over bipartisanship and the ratings of individual candidates, Bernard Segal developed an extremely close and warm working relationship with White. He fretted when the administration and his committee got bad press over the pace of nominations or over particular choices, tried to encourage more favorable coverage, and constantly promised to process names more quickly. Telephone calls between Segal and White often lasted an hour or more, and sometimes were resumed after both had gone home for the evening. "Bernie Segal just fell in love with Byron," Joe Dolan later reflected. "He thought he walked on water." At one point late in the first year of the administration, Segal's infatuation with White prompted him to promise that he would "get you elected" to the American College of Trial Lawyers. White, uncomfortable with gushing and disdainful of artificial honors, was scornful—and disingenuous: *Why, Bernie, I've never even tried a case. I'm just an office lawyer.* Segal dropped the idea, but his regard for White only deepened.

Years after the fact, some critics of the Kennedy judicial appointments argued that poor or malicious judges were approved, in Jack Bass's words, because of White's faith "in the integrity of lawyers. White apparently felt that a professionally respected and competent lawyer, if appointed to the federal judiciary, would carry out the laws as a matter of professional integrity, regardless of personal belief or philosophy." There is no evidence that White was that naive, only—as everyone involved in the process agreed—that the administration enjoyed little political capital in its first year, in which more than half of the judges were appointed. The Department of Justice had an extremely mixed record on judicial appointments in the South for many reasons, but blind faith in the integrity of "respected and competent" lawyers was not one. The department's review process was precariously ad hoc, the quality of its intelligence sources was uneven, and the relative political strength of the Southern senators was not uniform.

Two larger points are worth considering. First, it is remarkable that there were not more problem appointees in the Deep South, especially along the so-called Black Belt, from Savannah to Shreveport. The Southern judges so widely admired in the early 1960s were, with the exception of Judge Richard T. Rives in Montgomery (a Truman appointee), all Eisenhower appointees— Elbert P. Tuttle in Atlanta, John Minor Wisdom in New Orleans, John R. Brown in Houston, and Frank Johnson in Montgomery. They were alumni of a minority political party that included both blacks and whites and bore no fealty to the Jim Crow regime of the Democratic establishment. Prominent Democrats, on the other hand, were white men born at the turn of the century, often with grandfathers who had fought for the Confederacy and who preached the sin of Reconstruction to their children and grandchildren. For these middle-aged establishment lawyers, the sea change promised by *Brown v. Board of Education* was beyond comprehension and, at the same time, empty so far.

Second, no one could predict how the Supreme Court would develop that promise over the next several years. The Court gave little guidance to the inferior courts in *Brown II* in 1955, and the noble blank fired in *Cooper v. Aaron* three years later added nothing. To some extent, the Supreme Court's open-ended decrees in *Brown* provided lower courts with a blank check that could be written in any amount, large or small. Many options were open in 1961—neighborhood schools (which the NAACP had initially advocated in 1955), freedom of choice regardless of previous race-based attendance zones, one-grade-per-year desegregation (which still proved to be too much in Little Rock), and so on. Federal district judges in the South—whom Jack Peltason aptly dubbed the "fifty-eight lonely men"—bore a heavier burden, in terms of doctrinal ambiguity and social-political pressure, than was reasonable, regardless of who appointed them. No one should have been surprised that some of the first judicial appointments in the South since *Brown* would test the boundaries of the new order until both the Supreme Court and the courts of appeals unequivocally clarified the lines of compliance and detailed precisely what the Constitution required.

As the Freedom Rides demonstrated, the social protest movement that produced *Brown* was propelled by deeper and broader ambitions than racially neutral schools. The fundamental problem for everyone affected by the decision was that it was doctrinally empty, a conclusion in search of an explanatory theory. *Brown* was a breach few were truly equipped to enter, and aging judges—trained in the niceties of legal distinctions and the imperatives of orderly procedure—did not necessarily enjoy a comparative advantage over anyone else in their communities. The social and political order of the country, particularly in the South, was being reengineered in the name of legal analysis, and predicting the future was hazardous, to say the least. The uncertainties faced by the Department of Justice in guessing how men of one world would adapt to a new role and to extraordinary pressures is nakedly exemplified by Louis Oberdorfer's notes on the background check of one potential nominee in the Deep South who was in fact appointed in mid-1961 and who performed admirably by anyone's lights: "Fairly competent. As good a lawyer as there is in that area. Active politically. Campaigns in that area. Was active for Kennedy. Can't tell how he would do on race. High type fellow. Would do what ct. of appeals says. Not a racist." Other abstracts of appointees with substantially different records once they ascended the bench sound similar.

Although the crisis that resulted from the Freedom Rides and the incessant, endless work of processing judicial candidates were the most important tasks that Byron White addressed at the Department of Justice, his brief tenure also included acting as a central clearinghouse for the development of departmental policies, serving—in the words of the transition memorandum—as "liaison for the department with congress and other Governmental Departments and agencies," and preparing "reports on pending legislation in response to requests by the Congress." Legislative histories and court reports are dotted with White's testimony and formal opinion letters. Occasionally even the newspapers paid attention to his positions for the administration on legislation, such as his strong letter supporting bills that would give states great leeway in using wiretaps in criminal investigations.

White's rare intrusions into constitutional policymaking at the department have been carefully portrayed, from encouraging Archibald Cox to file a brief amicus curiae in the great 1962 reapportionment case, *Baker v. Carr,* to cautioning the president against a reflexive use of executive privilege. His most important contributions to the operation of the department may now be almost invisible, particularly due to the operational style of the department. AAGs communicated more by conversations after regular hours or by quick conferences in the hallway or behind closed doors than by memorandum. Lost with little tangible trace are Byron White's countless day-to-day shirt-sleeve decisions—plus his refocusing of meetings, his providing a sounding board for AAGs from Jack Miller to Burke Marshall, his prodding Robert Kennedy to bring a prosecution for which he had no taste, his pressing colleague and subordinate alike to push the analysis harder and further, his knowing where to allocate resources—all wrapped in a tightly coiled mixture of idealism and cold pragmatism.

Given how crowded his formal agenda was and how Robert Kennedy's spot-assignment style often put him in ad hoc planning situations he had not anticipated, White seemed always to be available from 7 A.M. until well after most senior officials had left the building. He was so busy that he retained only two of the many civic commitments in Colorado that he had enjoyed prior to the election, the chairmanship of the board of trustees of the Social Science Foundation at Denver University, and membership on the board of trustees of the Aspen Institute. The foundation had been his principal commitment since 1953, when he was elected to the board; since 1958, he had served as its chairman. He planned to return to Colorado for almost the entire final week of March 1962 to preside over foundation meetings, receive an award from a local service club, and visit his aging parents, who now lived in Fort Collins.

The trip could not have come at a worse time. Several days before his departure, he learned that Justice Charles E. Whittaker had suddenly resigned and that the president thus had his first opportunity to appoint someone to the Supreme Court of the United States. Although both the White House and the Department of Justice would be independently preparing background materials on potential appointees, White was understandably frustrated to be absent during the most important judicial selection of the fourteen-month-old administration.

14

"THE IDEAL
NEW FRONTIER JUDGE"

I N A N administration that had appointed more than a hundred federal judges in little more than one year in office, John and Robert Kennedy were remarkably unprepared for the first vacancy on the Supreme Court of the United States that occurred during their watch. There had been rumors at the end of the previous term of the Court, in the summer of 1961, that Hugo L. Black, seventy-five, might soon retire, and that Felix Frankfurter, seventy-eight, known to be in failing health, was considering retirement as well. A Chattanooga newspaper even speculated that Estes Kefauver, the senior senator from Tennessee, would be named to replace Black, a baseless rumor that embarrassed both men and prompted Kefauver to issue a public denial. The first vacancy for the Kennedys turned out to be neither Black nor Frankfurter but the most obscure member of the Court, Charles E. Whittaker, who in 1958 had been President Eisenhower's third appointment to the Court.

How the vacancy was filled is a story that has been told many times, with many taking credit for influencing the outcome and several taking credit for suggesting the final nominee. Robert Kennedy provided different accounts to favored journalists at the time, and then later for the Kennedy Library Oral History Program. What in fact happened is now reasonably clear and differs in two principal respects from the standard accounts. First, the Kennedys had more than three weeks, not just a few days, to consider their options; there was ample time for research and deliberation. But second, for all of the energy expended in two offices of the Department of Justice—the Deputy Attorney General's Office and the Office of Legal Counsel—the president knew his own mind from the outset, and the only question was whether any information or argument would dislodge him from his initial preference. Both Kennedys would later discuss lists of candidates considered, but only Robert Kennedy thought seriously of more than one candidate, and the accounts of lists and debates have suggested more deliberation, at least in the White House, than in fact occurred. In the words of Myer (Mike) Feldman, deputy counsel to the president, "Byron White was a foregone conclusion. For the second vacancy [Arthur Goldberg, in place of Frankfurter], we actually generated a list, which the department went over, and then we worked it over again." For the first vacancy, "the president had one name in mind from day one."

Charles Evans Whittaker was a Kansas City, Missouri, Republican whom President Eisenhower had appointed, largely on his brother Arthur's recommendation, first to the federal district court, then to the Court of Appeals for the Eighth Circuit. In 1957, when Justice Stanley F. Reed retired after two decades on the Supreme Court, Eisenhower promoted Whittaker again. He turned out to be one of the most unprepossessing members of the Court during the modern era. His opinion output was annually the lowest on the Court, and his work the most labored. On March 6, 1962, a few weeks after his sixty-first birthday, he checked in to Walter Reed Army Hospital, suffering from physical and mental exhaustion. He had done no Court work since February 1.

The press was unaware of Whittaker's condition or hospitalization, but Robert Kennedy, fresh from an extended overseas trip, had visited Justice William O. Douglas at the Court on March 5 and probably learned of Whittaker's plight then. Within days, the attorney general contacted Emanuel Celler and James O. Eastland, chairmen, respectively, of the House and Senate Judiciary Committees, to confer on the situation. Both had strong views on Supreme Court vacancies. Celler recommended Robert C. Weaver, the black administrator whom the president had been unable to appoint to a cabinet-level housing post he wished to establish. Eastland had been one of the leaders in the token but menacing fight by Southern segregationists against Potter Stewart's confirmation to the Court in 1958 and could be expected to resist, by muscle or guile, a nomination he deemed too liberal. The nomination of Thurgood Marshall to the Second Circuit Court of Appeals, which began with a recess appointment in September 1961, had not yet been calendared for a hearing before Eastland's committee (and would not be for another six months).

On March 15, a few days after Robert Kennedy spoke simultaneously with Celler and Eastland, Chief Justice Earl Warren called on Whittaker at Walter Reed to assess his condition. Warren knew immediately that Whittaker was incapacitated and began steps to accomplish his formal retirement on grounds of disability. The first step was to convene a medical board at the hospital to advise the chief justice as to Whittaker's capacity to continue his duties. The second step, assuming that the board found Whittaker incapacitated, was to prepare a letter from the justice to the president, with a covering letter of confirmation from the chief justice, formally retiring pursuant to §372(a) of the judicial code.

Once the three-man board's anticipated conclusion had been approved by the chief medical officer of the hospital, Warren telephoned the White House to inform the president. The agreed effective date of the retirement was April 1, which gave the president up to two weeks to pick a successor before Whittaker's letter need be publicly acknowledged. Whittaker's state of mind is captured not in the formal documents sent to the president but in a draft statement that Whittaker dictated but that, undoubtedly thanks to Warren's counsel, was not used:

> Having become overtired from continued concentration on the Court work, I entered Walter Reed Hospital on March 6th for rest, observation and tests.
>
> The doctors have found no organic trouble, but advise me that my return to the Court would unduly jeopardize my future health. Accordingly, I have advised the President that I wish to retire from active service on the Supreme Court in accordance with the provisions of the law.

No statement—from Whittaker, Warren, or anyone else—was issued at the time.

Now that Whittaker's retirement was official, the scramble was on within the White House and the Department of Justice to advise the president. There were no prefabricated lists, long or short. The president met with Ted Sorensen, counsel to the president, and Mike Feldman, Sorensen's deputy, and it was agreed that Sorensen would generate a list of possible nominees to be reviewed later. Shortly after the meeting, Abraham Ribicoff (secretary of Health, Education and Welfare), having seen the Supreme Court up close and the cabinet from the inside, took himself out of contention and refocused his ambitions on elective politics.

At the Department of Justice, the advisory process ran along two channels. In the formal channel, Robert Kennedy directed Byron White to have his office prepare a comprehensive list of candidates with detailed evaluations. White told Joe Dolan to scour every category—federal appellate and trial judges, state supreme court justices, bar leaders, and political figures; in due course, Dolan was expected to discuss the project with Bernard Segal, still the chairman of the American Bar Association's Standing Committee on the Federal Judiciary, which would expect to issue a formal rating of the final nominee. White assigned Nicholas Katzenbach's Office of Legal Counsel the labor-intensive job of reading and critically evaluating the written opinions of any judge who made the short list. The second channel was personal to Robert Kennedy, who was making his own inquiries and keeping his own counsel. The two channels would merge when necessary.

Although later oral histories suggest that the department's review process did not begin until late March, Nicholas Katzenbach was ready to report directly to the attorney general on March 18, two days after Whittaker's letter was sent to the president, and coincidentally, a day after the chief justice and the attorney general had been featured guests at the annual white-tie dinner of the Gridiron Club at the Statler Hilton Hotel. Katzenbach's nine-page memo to Robert Kennedy focused on one candidate, William H. Hastie, who was Robert Kennedy's provisional preference to replace Whittaker. Hastie, age fifty-seven, was a Phi Beta Kappa graduate of Amherst College and an editor of the *Harvard Law Review,* class of 1930. He spent his early career as a government lawyer and law school teacher and dean. In 1946 he was appointed governor of the Virgin Islands, and in 1948, after actively campaigning for Harry Truman, was appointed to the Court of Appeals for the Third Circuit—the first black ever named to an Article III judgeship. With impeccable academic credentials and more than a decade on a respected federal appellate court, Hastie was a compelling candidate for the Supreme Court.

Hastie's name had been urged on John F. Kennedy even before the inauguration. Harris Wofford, who with Sargent Shriver had been Kennedy's principal campaign aide on civil rights, sent the president-elect a thirty-one-page memorandum on December 30, 1960, detailing sixteen initiatives for the administration to undertake in 1961. Under "14. *Breakthrough in Government Employment of Negroes.*" Wofford stated: "A Negro should also get an early Federal District Judgeship in New York City. When the time comes Judge William Hastie of the Third Circuit Court of Appeals should get most serious consideration for appointment to the Supreme Court." Katzenbach was much less enthusiastic. Although his memo to Robert Kennedy is not available for research, his views are not in doubt. He recalled in 1964 that "most of the work we [OLC] did was with respect to Hastie," although others suggested by more than one source were Roger Traynor (California Supreme Court, age sixty-two), Walter V. Schaefer (Illinois Supreme Court, age fifty-seven) and Paul Freund, age fifty-four, a chaired professor of constitutional law at Harvard Law School.

> We made a whole review of every opinion that Hastie had written. . . . we went through [Hastie's opinions], and then we wrote a long memorandum with respect to Hastie [only]. There had been some—Byron had been concerned about some left-wing connections that Hastie had had in his early career, and these really ended up being nothing of any importance at all. A review of the opinions indicated a somewhat pedestrian turn of mind. They were good, competent opinions, there was very little that you could find in them, in my judgment that was brilliant at all. And this was possibly in part the problem of the circuit he was in. There were no interesting opinions, by and large.

Katzenbach was clearly unimpressed with Hastie's work product, but he was extremely impressed with Traynor's, and that presented its own problem. Traynor's opinions, in Katzenbach's view, were "right in the tradition of Justice Black," that is, manifesting an aggressive concept of the judicial role and generous solicitude for freedom of speech, including for those of suspect loyalty. The problem for the president was that he would be identified with Traynor's views and assumed to be endorsing them—a serious political issue in the eyes of Red baiters in the Senate, of whom Eastland was primus inter pares.

The day after Katzenbach sent his memo to Kennedy, the attorney general scheduled an impromptu appointment with Chief Justice Warren to solicit advice on the nomination in general and on Hastie in particular. The interview left Kennedy surprised by what he heard and chastened over consulting the chief justice. Warren "was violently opposed to having Hastie on the Court," Kennedy later recalled. "He said, 'He's not a liberal, and he'll be opposed to all the measures that we are interested in, and he just would be completely unsatisfactory.'" Kennedy also asked about Paul Freund, and Warren opposed him as well. Kennedy then spoke with his old friend Justice Douglas by telephone, and Douglas declared that Hastie would be "just one more vote for Frankfurter."

While Robert Kennedy was taking soundings on Hastie, at the other end of Pennsylvania Avenue his brother was doing the same with his own staff. Ted Sorensen produced a list of nineteen names on March 21. Six were "Members of the Administration and the Senate": Arthur Goldberg (age fifty-three),

Nicholas Katzenbach (forty), Byron White (forty-four), Adlai Stevenson (sixty-two), H. H. Fowler (fifty-three), and Archibald Cox (forty-nine). Four were federal judges (Hastie; Henry J. Friendly, fifty-eight, of New York; George T. Washington, fifty-three; and David Bazelon, fifty-two—the last two from the Court of Appeals for the District of Columbia), and three were state court judges (Roger Traynor, sixty-two, of California; Stanley Fuld, fifty-nine, of New York; and Walter V. Schaefer, fifty-seven, of Illinois). Paul Freund topped the list of "Members of the Bar and Academic Community." Others were Bethuel M. Webster (sixty-one), Clark Clifford (fifty-five), Herbert Wechsler (fifty-two), Edward Levi (University of Chicago dean, fifty), and Whitney North Seymour (sixty-one). Most were Democrats—and so identified on the list. The exceptions were Friendly, Traynor, Webster, Seymour, and Levi. Regardless of the list, Hastie remained the focus of staff attention at both ends of Pennsylvania Avenue.

The White House staff worried that appointing a black was politically "too obvious." The president asked one of the listed candidates, Washington lawyer Clark M. Clifford, for advice, hoping to learn from the mistakes that caused Clifford's mentor, Harry Truman, to make undistinguished appointments to the Court; Clifford seconded the White House staff. "I thought it would be a mistake for him to reach out just to put a Negro on the bench," Clifford later said. When the brothers met to compare their findings, Robert Kennedy argued against the obviousness point, but Katzenbach's memo had already tainted Hastie with the president.

The question then was whether there was an alternative. The president kept White's name out of the discussion as his hole card while other names began to be killed off along with Hastie's. Clifford and Katzenbach both liked Paul Freund, but Freund had turned down the president when asked to be solicitor general, and Robert Kennedy did not like the symbolism of yet another Harvard faculty member in high office—along with Archibald Cox at Justice, McGeorge Bundy as national security adviser, and Arthur M. Schlesinger Jr. as special assistant to the president. Two strikes and, to the president, Freund was out. Arthur Goldberg was a possibility, but the president felt he needed him more in the cabinet now than on the Supreme Court, especially with the steel contract negotiations still up in the air. The president also believed that there would be time for Goldberg and others—perhaps four appointments—if he served two full terms. None of the others on the emerging final list from the department generated any interest in either of the Kennedys—Traynor, Schaefer, Leon Jaworski (Houston lawyer, age fifty-six), Edward Levi, (a Katzenbach suggestion).

Time was now beginning to run against the president. Too many people knew that Whittaker's resignation was in the president's hands, and the president himself had other issues weighing down his mind. On March 22, he sat through a punishing four-hour lunch in the White House with J. Edgar Hoover, director of the Federal Bureau of Investigation, who revealed in lurid detail how much the bureau knew about the president's sexual liaison with Judith Campbell, whom an FBI memo archly designated as an "Associate of Hoodlums" because she doubled as a mistress for Sam Giancana, a Chicago mobster. That afternoon, Kennedy placed the last of seventy telephone calls to Campbell through the White House switchboard. Publicly, the issue of the day was whether the steel industry would reach a new contract with labor and avert what was predicted to be an economically debilitating strike. Goldberg was effectively on call to mediate if the parties came to impasse. To fortify himself for the impending week during which the Court question would be resolved and other issues would probably not—such as his stalled Medicare Bill and the steel negotiations—the president flew to Palm Springs, California, for the weekend.

Byron White had been the president's first choice all along and now became the focal point of the search. Propitiously, he left town for his long-planned trip to Colorado. His absence allowed Katzenbach, who now favored White, to move White's name more formally into the deliberations at both ends of Pennsylvania Avenue. The problem was Robert Kennedy. He did not think of White—the muscular, energetic man of action with whom he went skiing and played basketball—as a judge in a cloister; and whether he would admit it or not, Kennedy had come to rely on White so implicitly to run the department in his absence that it would be unthinkable for White to be gone. As it turned out, portraying White as a crutch to Robert Kennedy was precisely the reverse psychology necessary to cancel his resistance to White's candidacy. Katzenbach later recalled his telephone call to White in Colorado inquiring about his interest in Whittaker's seat:

> I said we had a lot of people on the list and we haven't got you and I'd like to put you on the list. There was a long pause, and he said, "Well, I think the President can do much better than that." And I said, "Well, the geography is very good." And he said, "Well, I think the President can do much better than this, and I would rather not be put on the list." I said, "Do you really want me to scratch you off entirely?" And he said, "Well, I wouldn't be unhappy if you scratched me off entirely. Go ahead."

Receiving this "slightly ambiguous answer," Katzenbach "left him on. I think if I had pushed him any further, he would have said, 'Yes, scratch me off entirely.' So I didn't want to do that because at that point he had become my candidate."

White was now not only on the department's list but at the top. The question, made pressing by his equivocal response to Katzenbach, was whether he would accept the nomination if it were offered. On March 27, after taking an urgent telephone call from the president, Robert Kennedy called White in Colorado, "to find out whether he really wanted to do it," according to Kennedy.

> And he was not very enthusiastic about it, really. I don't remember specifically his words, but they were rather interesting: I don't think he liked to retire from active life so quickly. But I talked to him on the basis of the fact that who knew what was going to happen in the future? If you knew definitely that he could be around for five years and then be appointed in 1967, then that was fine. But you never knew that. The time to do it was at the time you could. It was really on that basis that he accepted the appointment.

White spoke to the president from Denver late in the afternoon on March 28, after presiding over the Social Science Foundation board meeting, and cleared the way for the president to go forward. White's mind now needed to turn to his schedule for the balance of the week—meeting with the U.S. attorney for Colorado and receiving the Pueblo Sertoma Club's American Way of Life Award on Thursday, then addressing the Manufacturers Association of Colorado on Friday morning before a final meeting of the foundation board. In between appointments, he granted an interview to the *Denver Post* in which he defended the administration's controversial wiretapping bill on the ground, in part, that "the right of citizens to freedom from organized crime is a right that champions of civil rights sometimes overlook."

On Thursday, March 29, the president held a thirty-minute press conference at midday, at which he announced Justice Whittaker's retirement, promised a prompt nomination, and evaded questions as to what qualifications he would use in making the decision. He refused to comment on speculation that Ribicoff would be named. In the afternoon, Chief Justice Warren issued a statement reporting that Whittaker "has advised us that he has worked to the point of physical exhaustion, and that any further resumption of his rigorous duties here would seriously impair his health." A modified version of Justice Whittaker's prepared statement, first drafted two weeks earlier, was also released to the press. That night, White accepted the Sertoma Club award and told his audience, "Washington, D.C., is not America. It is here." He also said, "Our real gold reserve is not Ft. Knox. It is our people. In America's struggle between tyranny and freedom, it is the courage and ability of the people and their activities that will win the battle." In addition to the plaque memorializing the club's award, White was given a miniature gold frying pan, which symbolized the Fryingpan-Arkansas Reclamation Project—vital to agricultural development interests in the area and currently in jeopardy before the House Rules Committee. White said he supported the project and expected its passage.

The next morning, the question of Justice Whittaker's successor seemed to be wide open to the public, but in fact it was reaching closure at the White House. White, interviewed by both Denver newspapers, denied any inside knowledge of the search, including rumors published by the Associate Press that he was on a short list (along with Hastie, Freund, Thurgood Marshall, and Eugene V. Rostow of Yale). "About all I can say," White told the *Denver Post*, "is that it will be filled by a lawyer and by a man." UPI speculated that Goldberg, Cox, Freund, and Ralph Bunche at the United Nations were the principal candidates. In the *Washington Post*, James E. Clayton identified the top four candidates as Freund, Friendly, Schaefer, and Traynor. The second tier was White, Cox, Goldberg, Hastie, Erwin N. Griswold (dean of Harvard Law School, age fifty-seven), and Rostow. In the *New York Times*, Anthony Lewis implicitly handicapped the field in the following order: Hastie, Freund, Goldberg, White, Ribicoff, Levi, Cox, and Kefauver. James Reston's *Times* editorial-page column, after reviewing the record of the Warren Court and its frequently controversial and close decisions, recommended "a distinguished, detached, personally unprovocative scholar who can help minimize the personal and philosophical divisions that have developed in the court during the past few years." His models were Charles Evans Hughes and "Cardoza [*sic*]."

While speculation boiled in the press, the president was holding a final meeting in the Oval Office to discuss the appointment, which he was now eager to make at once. Sen. Richard B. Russell of Georgia had telephoned the president and advised him that any nominee other than an acceptable conservative would prompt a conspicuous visit from a delegation of Southern senators, which he would lead, to make their case. Against the backdrop of intensifying press speculation and Russell's warning, Kennedy prepared to listen to the presentation from—sitting across from him, left to right—the attorney general, Joe Dolan, and Katzenbach. Robert Kennedy still took Hastie seriously, still believed that a black on the Supreme Court would help the country immeasurably overseas, but had cooled on him due to criticism in every quarter he encountered—the department, the White House, and even the Court itself. The attorney general had also been convinced by Katzenbach that the ABA would give White its highest rating, which was a definite advantage. Finally, Katzenbach used Robert Kennedy's vanity against itself with the following argument:

> I really think Byron White would be the best person to appoint to this job, but you have just lost John Seigenthaler as Administrative Assistant [to a newspaper editorship], and I think it would be very, very tough on you to lose Byron White just a couple of weeks later, because these are really two people closest to you and the Justice Department to lose. And I think that's a legitimate consideration, and you ought to consider it before recommending Byron.

According to Katzenbach, "I think that was the argument that probably got Byron the job because [Robert Kennedy] said, 'I'm not going to stand in Byron's way. I can handle the Justice Department without Byron White.'"

By the end of the week, among the White House staff, Hastie had faded and nominally reappeared, and Freund had enjoyed a brief reemergence thanks to Sorensen and McGeorge Bundy. The morning of the final meeting, Sorensen produced a hasty one-page memorandum advocating Freund's nomination. The memo, in its entirety, read:

> The ages of the eight remaining judges are 71, 76, 79, 63, 62, 62, 56 and 47. (Whittaker, at 61, was the third-youngest member).
>
> Of the three oldest members two are liberal politicians (Warren and Black) and could be more easily replaced by same. One is a Jew and former Harvard professor (Frankfurter). Warren, of course, is Chief Justice.
>
> You cannot appoint both Hastie and Weaver to HEW without appearing to be guilty of reverse racism.
>
> The first appointment should be hailed by all for his judicial mien—not known primarily as a politician—not subject to confirmation delays because of controversial associations.
>
> If a politician is to be chosen, Goldberg is the ablest; and George Meany could accept Leonard Woodcock with at least as much grace as he accepted Goldberg.
>
> Recommendation: Appoint the highly respected Freund from St. Louis;* save Goldberg for the vacancy of Chief Justice; save Hastie for the next vacancy before 1964.

> * Also a Jew and Harvard Professor, but one will presumably retire.

Across the top of the memo, Sorensen added by hand: "Note: I put Byron's name on the attached list,† too. It did not come up among any of those con-

† The list dated March 21, 1962, summarized above.

sulted. When Clark Clifford saw it on the list, he opposed, saying bar would regard Byron as primarily political, too brief in his present job."

Bundy pressed Freund's case more urgently in his March 30 memorandum for the president:

The best and most confidential advice from Cambridge is that Paul Freund would have voted with the *majority* in the Tennessee reapportionment case, and might even have carried Frankfurter with him.

Freund is a great scholar—but not a closet scholar; a Brandeis in conviction, but a Cardozo in temperament.

He is a deeply amusing as well as a cultivated man—a genuine wit—he could become a close personal help to you, with his detachment, his high personal style, and his regard for you.

Of all the men you might choose, he is the most likely to be a great judge—and he is ripe for appointment now.

Sorensen and Bundy were obviously coming to the same conclusion from different angles. To Sorensen, Freund was unexceptionably distinguished, politically costless, and probably fireproof in the Senate. To Bundy, who in another contemporary memo to the president referred to Frankfurter as "a man I love," Freund was the modern Frankfurter and a model judge (although his speculation about Freund's influence on Frankfurter in *Baker v. Carr,* the Tennessee reapportionment case, was probably wishful thinking at best). Both of the president's men were projecting their own priorities onto the president, who privately had not swerved from his first inclination—to name someone he knew well, admired enormously, and trusted at a level of friendship that surpassed abstract philosophy.

In any event, Sorensen and Bundy did not have the last word: the final staff presentation to the president was being made by the Department of Justice and not by Sorensen or anyone else in the White House. The attorney general and Katzenbach were now both on White's side, and Dolan was White's original and least inhibited cheerleader. Dolan's function at the final meeting with the president—whether Dolan himself fully realized it or not—was to provide emphasis for the developing consensus and for the choice the president personally desired all along.

The meeting began, and the now familiar bidding was reviewed. (The night before, Dolan had impishly confided to White by telephone that the decision *was down to a black or white choice*). The president decided to provoke Dolan: "Joe, I understand you want Byron White."

"No, that's not right, I just think he should be seriously considered."

"Maybe," the president tested him, "I should name Hastie."

"You can't do that," Dolan protested energetically. "You'll blow everything we have going on the Hill. Hastie would be an absolute political disaster!"

The president smiled thinly and said he would decide "today—it will be Hastie or White."

After returning to the department, Katzenbach left Washington for a promised weekend in Williamsburg with his son. The president decided after lunch to name White, preferably that day. He telephoned Dolan in Katzenbach's absence and told him to contact Bernard Segal to obtain, if possible, an on-the-spot commitment to rate White "exceptionally well qualified." Segal, jealous of his prerogatives, especially with Kennedy's first appointment to the Supreme Court, initially resisted, and even suggested that the president change his mind until the standing committee could meet to advise him formally. He was in a weak position, however, and he knew it. There was no formal agreement or understanding that Supreme Court nominees would be screened by his committee, and in any event Segal himself had suggested White as "a strong candidate" to Dolan during one lengthy telephone call earlier in the week that had lasted until 3 A.M. as candidates were reviewed in chatty detail.

The attorney general now pressed Segal and agreed to delay the announcement of the nomination for only two hours so that the committee could "meet" by conference call. In return for the brief concession, by 6 P.M. Eastern time the Kennedys had secured the rating they wanted plus a warm official endorsement to boot. The press release from the ABA committee, which would be issued simultaneously with the president's announcement, was strong if also a bit clubby and defensive at the margins:

> Ordinarily our committee might hesitate to accord this rating to a lawyer of Mr. White's comparative youth when appointment to the Supreme Court of the United States is concerned. However, our committee has worked closely with Mr. White for more than a year and we have had an unusual opportunity to observe him under a variety of circumstances. We have developed a high regard for his rugged adherence to principle, his sense of fairness, his intellectual capacity, his even temperament, his soundness as a lawyer.

All that was left was to locate White and receive his assent to the nomination. He had driven much of the night through a blinding snowstorm but arrived only thirty minutes late for his breakfast talk to the business group, who had unfriendly views of the administration's antitrust policy. He then went to Denver University for the meeting of the foundation board. At approximately

4 P.M. Mountain time, a university secretary "peeked around a door, tiptoed past a crowded table and handed a piece of paper" to White that read, "Telephone call. Urgent." At the other end was Ted Sorensen. Minutes later, the president was on the line. Arthur Schlesinger recalled the exchange:

> "Well, Byron," Kennedy said, "we've decided to go ahead on you." There was a moment's silence, and the President said, "We want to get the announcement out in twenty minutes, so we need an answer right away." Another silence, and the President said, "All right, we'll go ahead."

Kennedy privately told Ben Bradlee of *Newsweek* the next day that White "wasn't very enthusiastic" about the offer, because "he honestly hated to leave the Justice Department." For the president, that reluctance was "another plus in his favor. He's the ideal New Frontier judge."

The president then turned to Schlesinger and told him to draft a statement explaining his choice. The attorney general told Schlesinger to emphasize "that White was no mere professor or scholar but had actually seen 'life'—in the Navy, in private practice, in politics, even on the football field." Schlesinger's statement accordingly underscored that White had "excelled in everything he has attempted—in his academic life, in his military service, in his career before the Bar, and in the federal government." The announcement of the nomination, hastily arranged and delivered to only a handful of reporters, lasted exactly three minutes.

Marion White, who had stayed behind in Washington while her husband was in Colorado, telephoned the president at seven-fifteen to thank him after talking to her husband. At approximately the same moment, Martin Luther King and Wyatt Tee Walker—who had not heard of the nomination—conferred by telephone to decide whether they should mount a public campaign in support of Judge Hastie for the Whittaker vacancy; their conversation, overheard by an FBI wiretap, was transcribed and forwarded to the White House. After dinner, the president directed an aide at 10:50 P.M. to obtain a copy of an early edition of the *Washington Post* to see how the nomination played.

The *Post*'s banner headline coverage must have satisfied the president, especially the second subhead, which noted, "Kennedy's Choice Widely Praised by Lawmakers." Senator Eastland predicted that White would be "an able Supreme Court justice" and declared his support for the nomination. Sen. Mike Mansfield, the majority leader from Montana, praised White somewhat parochially as "the right man in the right place for the right job and from the right section of the country." Sen. Everett Dirksen of Illinois, the minority leader, doubted White would have any confirmation problem and called him "one of those solid people who takes a very good look before reaching a decision and then stands by it." Chief Justice Warren, apparently unconcerned over intervening at the margins of a political issue, decided to make his own statement. He called the appointment "splendid," and said: "It was a very fine appointment. He is a man of great ability. He has a wonderful background for this post and is a fine man." The newspaper headlines, pointing to football and the navy as well as to the Justice Department, highlighted the glamour of the nomination. The Associated Press photo library provided dashing pictures of White playing college football, riding the bicycle at Oxford in cap and gown, and clad in pith helmet under a South Pacific jungle canopy. Editorial page cartoonists immediately depicted footballs flying toward the front entrance to the Supreme Court building.

Most editorials applauded the nomination. The *New York Herald-Tribune* praised a "truly first-rate choice," and the *Washington Star* thought White "excellent," but there were off-key notes as well, particularly from syndicated columnists. David Lawrence lashed the president for passing over experienced judges to appoint a "political henchman and a friend of long standing" with "no judicial experience whatsoever," and for not consulting Congress or bar leaders. Lawrence also criticized the ABA committee for short-circuiting its own evaluation process. Doris Fleeson, a columnist for the *Washington Star* for two decades, saw the nomination of the "cautious and plodding" White as "strictly personal" to the president—evidence that he "was simply not ready to re-make the Court in his political image." James Reston, writing from Washington in the *New York Times,* speculated that White would be more "liberal" than Whittaker and would be inclined to vote with the "Warren-Black-Douglas-Brennan group," but "beyond that nobody here is willing to guess very much about what either Mr. White or Mr. Kennedy will do in the future."

Reston's *Times* was the only major newspaper sharply critical of White's nomination. Declaring that "the ideal justice should be a student of life as well as of the law, a man of intellect and compassion and—because the Court must be a teacher—ability to articulate," the *Times* decided, "on the basis of his public life and career," that White "has not yet measured up to these standards." With experience limited mainly to private practice, "he has not yet achieved the scholarly legal distinction that would justify hailing his appointment as a great and inevitable one." Conceding his ability and the respect of his colleagues, the *Times* concluded, with seeming resignation, that "he embarks on one of the loneliest and most exacting of jobs." The *New Republic* was unimpressed, leading its editorial with the observation that "the appoint-ment of a Supreme Court Justice is always something of a shot in the dark." After reviewing his career, the magazine quoted a "colleague" (probably Frankfurter) as predicting "that Mr. White is likely to be found 'a bit to the left of Mr. Justice Potter.'" (With no "[*sic*]" after the reference to Potter Stewart, it is unclear whether the magazine was embarrassing White's unnamed colleague or itself.) The editorial concluded that White "fits thoroughly adequate tradi-tions." The president had succeeded in securing widespread popular and po-litical approval for his nomination, and the captiousness of the intellectual class was both to be expected and discounted. John Kennedy had a friend whom he trusted and who was emblematic of the vigorous tone of his admin-istration, and nothing else really mattered to him.

Local coverage in Colorado newspapers, with one unsurprising excep-tion, hailed the appointment with pride and, in some quarters, as manifest destiny. White's father-in-law, Robert L. Stearns, the retired president of the University of Colorado and of the Boettcher Foundation, said, "It's the logical outcome of his own ability and legal training"—a sentiment that infected many of the stories and editorials published in the state over the weekend the nomination was announced. Asked if he was proud of his son, Al White, the justice-designate's eighty-two-year old father, was no more tolerant of obvious questions from reporters than he had been twenty-five years earlier: "You shouldn't have to ask that. Of course I am." A reporter for the *Rocky Mountain News* tried to determine, in 650 words, the shaping influences on Byron White's life, but his parents responded too matter-of-factly for dramatic effect. Al White attributed his sons' success to their "industriousness." Religious in-fluence? Connection with organized religion was said to be "practically non existent," but "'we read Unity (a magazine of religious thoughts and Bible texts) and we read the Bible each day,' the father said." Books? "I can't remem-ber him doing much reading until he got into college," reflected his mother.

Reporters looking for background color on the new justice found a richer lode in the justice's brother, now director of research for the Lovelace Founda-tion for Medical Education and Research in Albuquerque, New Mexico. He rehearsed tales of brotherly sugar-beet-raising projects, field-hand work, and the like. The contrast between the "rich boy" president and the Horatio Alger of the beet fields was irresistible to Roscoe Fleming of the *Denver Post* and other columnists.

The only cool note locally came, predictably, from Gene Cervi in his *Journal.* Acknowledging that "most of Colorado is bursting with pride at the appointment," Cervi's signed editorial declared:

As professional dissenters, particularly in the wake of the praise heaped on the new justice, we tried to think of something that would knock his halo at least slightly askew. We couldn't do it. . . .

We believe on one hand that he will be a qualified or limited Liberal in its modern sense, that is, in the sense that President Kennedy is a Liberal. His unique position of being the swing man on 4-to-4 decisions is not lost on him even for a moment. They say he is fair—whatever that means. We know he is tough. Nonetheless, we could believe on the other hand, that he will interpret the Constitution coldly, dispassionately, ever mindful of the separation of governmental powers. This, of course, would place him with the Conservatives, and it's possible he may one day give his former boss, the President, some unexpected decisions. Let's face it. At this point he's an enigma in these terms. . . .

In the much publicized list of his many accomplishments, there is one thing he hasn't done. He hasn't been a conspicuous loser on any significant issue and the time to decide whether he could be a good loser is past. His climb to the citadel has ended in joyous triumph. He's inside—for life. Now, the true measure of the man will be taken by history.

Will he be celebrated for majority opinions or will he be distinguished for stirring dissents?

Ever since Durango, when the White-Dolan forces overwhelmed the residual support for Adlai Stevenson in the Democratic state convention, Cervi—a faithful Stevenson man—had viewed White as "vindictive," a "lousy winner," and Kennedy a conservative collaborator. Cervi's editorial, fueled to some extent by a grudge but perspicacious all the same, prevented the Colorado press coverage from being an unqualified celebration.

Byron White's nomination formally arrived at the Senate on April 4, 1962, and confirmation hearings were scheduled for April 11. Between the announcement of his nomination and the Senate hearings and vote, two puzzles—one visible, the other hidden—attached to the president's decision. The public puzzle was foreshadowed in the Fleeson and Reston columns: what were White's philosophical views of the judicial role and the place of the Court in the American polity, or, put much more crudely, in the popular fashion of journalists of the day, was he a "liberal"—at least in the Warren-Black-Douglas-Brennan mold? Two reporters asked the nominee directly and learned as much as anyone who had ever asked the question of him in such terms. Miriam Ottenberg, who put the question to White shortly after he became deputy attorney general, repeated the question in the judicial context by telephone the night of his nomination and was told, "The proof will be in the judging." The *Fort Collins Coloradoan,* functionally White's hometown newspaper, did no better. Asked whether he would classify himself as a liberal or a conservative," he replied, "I guess we'll just have to let the record speak for itself." Tom Gavin, now of the *Denver Post,* had the luxury of interviewing White in person. He was told more, but not much. Gavin, a blunt and wisecracking writer who was also a determined reporter, asked White if "he will be a liberal or conservative justice."

"I never know what people mean by those words," he said.

Well, then, which Supreme Court justices have you particularly admired?

"There have been a lot of good justices. Mr. Justice (Oliver Wendell) Holmes was a great justice. He was a great student of the law." (There's no hint there. While Holmes wrote a number of opinions considered liberal, he authored as many others which could be termed conservative.)

Did President Kennedy discuss your mutual views on the high court before announcing your nomination?

"We had a good talk."

Yes, but did he say anything in particular?

"I won't quote the President. You'll have to ask him."

What about the Court's recent ruling on legislative reapportionment? Did you agree with the majority opinion?

"I really can't comment on any question relating to the Court," White said.

Gavin observed that White's "reserve made him almost an oddity in the administration of President Kennedy, where compulsive rhetoric flourishes as a new art form."

Byron White was indulging in the luxury of necessity. He never had any use for the reductionistic categorization and "thinking by labels," as he sometimes called it, manifested in the journalists' questions. Now, the political deference to the confirmation process and the dignity of the Court allowed him to be evasive or silent as he wished. The question remains to what extent President Kennedy considered White's legal views and indeed to what extent he cared. Nicholas Katzenbach later said that Kennedy took a personal interest in his Supreme Court appointments, not because he worried about their judicial philosophy but because they would be more personally identified with him than lower court appointees would. That made White a natural in the eyes of Katzenbach, who suspected that there would be more public attention and scrutiny of Kennedy's first appointment than of any subsequent ones. Therefore, Katzenbach thought that the first appointment ought to be somebody who in some way was identified with the President's views. On most of these issues, I don't think the President really had a view very strongly, and I don't think Byron had a view very strongly on most of these issues. But I felt that, were that true, it ought to be somebody, then, closely identified with the President.

On that ground—which Sorensen had raised in his last-minute memo—the White House counsel's office agreed with Katzenbach that White was a very sensible choice.

Both the White House and the Justice Department made sure the press got the point, as the *New York Times*'s explanation of the appointment three days after it was made demonstrates: "In picking" between White and Freund, "President Kennedy took the man he knew better. White House aides said the basic reason for the President's choice was his intimate knowledge of Mr. White's philosophy and abilities, and his respect for them."

How precisely were White's judicial views, as opposed to his political views, considered? "Not in any detail," according to Sorensen much later. "Look," Mike Feldman also explained much later, "he was with us in the campaign, he had a good relationship with the president, and we just assumed that took care of the matter." Burke Marshall is more pointed. "I can only remember one judicial appointment where the question of judicial philosophy was raised at all," Marshall later recalled. "Bob worried that Frank Shea might be soft on criminals if he became a judge. Outside of the Southern judges and civil rights, that was the extent of discussions about future behavior. Absolutely."

Two strands of the Kennedy brothers' thinking intertwined to shut off sustained consideration of a potential nominee's judicial views. First, the president, in Katzenbach's phrase, did not see "the Supreme Court as being a really co-equal branch" of government. John Kennedy paid little attention to the work of the Court, did not see its decisions as a major factor in the nation's political economy, and did not wish to tarry over niceties of judicial philosophy. Desegregation of public schools, First Amendment protection for suspected communists, and prayer in public school were all political problems to President Kennedy more than products of philosophical division within the Court. The only legal issue that seems to have stirred him personally during his first-year-plus in office—in terms of contemplating a legislative or legal initiative—was government financial aid to parochial schools, which he flirted with, but abandoned for political reasons.

The other strand was the Kennedys' mutual hostility to dogmatic thinking and their impatience with theory and abstraction. They derided what they saw as overheated partisans of both right and left—in the administration slang of the day, "reactionaries" and "honkers." Robert Kennedy spoke well of Byron White's steady navigation between extremes to Katzenbach after the nomination: "He said, 'Well, Byron ought to be good because he's got so much sense,' which I think Bobby generally use[d] in the sense of blunting doctrinaire ideas with some kind of practical pragmatism." Harris Wofford, who qualified as one of the administration's honkers, put the president's non-ideological tastes in a less admiring light, but one that White found both admirable and compatible: "I think John Kennedy's central principle in politics, as far as I was able to distill it, was his desire to see the maximum intelligence brought to bear on public problems. He had no ideology and, if anything was put off by too far-reaching ideas." The remark to Ben Bradlee—that White's hesitancy to join the Court made him the "ideal New Frontier judge"—bespeaks the president's taste for irony and his admiration for diffidence toward judicial as opposed to political power.

Byron White's reluctance was no pose. The private puzzle prompted by the nomination is why White wanted the job in the first place. When Robert Kennedy first called him in Denver a few days before the nomination to see if he really wanted the position, his immediate response was, *Now why would the president want to do something like that?* His hesitancy with the president when the offer was actually made was equally authentic. Almost as soon as he had accepted the nomination he suffered a case of buyer's remorse. When he returned to Washington on April Fool's Day 1962, he found William Geoghegan in his office. To enthusiastic congratulations, White responded: *I guess they want to put me out to pasture early.* Geoghegan still remembers vividly a tableau between nomination and confirmation: "Byron's back was acting up and he would just lie on the long couch in my office, on his back, flipping a football up in the air—perfect vertical spirals—asking, more to himself than to me, *Should I be doing this? Is this really the right decision? Can I really contribute?*"

The same man who felt that he could be elected to office in Colorado only "once" now wondered whether he was suited by temperament and comparative advantage to be effective and satisfied in a world he knew only too well from his days as a law clerk to Chief Justice Vinson. He would be sitting with two justices his friends had clerked for fifteen years before—Hugo L. Black and William O. Douglas; a third, Felix Frankfurter, was ill, and doubts were growing daily that he would return to the bench. Unlike the Department of Justice, whose teamwork and camaraderie he relished, the Supreme Court was a collection of nine individuals answering only to themselves and defining their own philosophical and institutional objectives. He knew from his clerkship that the skilled and rapid writers, such as Black and Douglas, could have greater impact than otherwise able lawyers, and his writing was neither fluid nor elegant. "He wrote a lot like he played," according to his former partner Donald Hoagland, who knew him well and admired him deeply. "Not pretty, not graceful, but he got the job done and didn't leave anything standing in his wake." One of his closest friends thought at the time that White never would have sought the appointment on his own, that if pushed by Katzenbach he would have issued a Sherman statement, but that once the process began to focus on him, *he was flattered and, like most lawyers, he just couldn't resist. I mean, it was the Supreme Court after all.*

White did not permit himself to muse for very long. On Monday, April 2, he paid a call on Chief Justice Warren at Warren's invitation and spent a half hour with him. That day, the Court, apparently confident of White's confirmation, restored a dozen previously argued cases to its calendar for reargument the following term, only three with enduring interest—*Kennedy v. Mendoza-Martinez, Gibson v. Florida Legislative Investigation Committee,* and *Townsend v. Sain.* A day later, the Court entertained two visitors whose presence prompted small headlines. Marion White, whom the *Post* had so far denominated "Mrs. 'Whizzer'" in the "For and About Women" section of the paper, was spotted in the box seats reserved for guests of justices, sitting behind none other than Mr. Justice Whittaker, who had been discharged from Walter Reed on March 26 and was making his first appearance at the Court in a month, as well as his first since his retirement took effect.

While the confirmation hearings were pending, newspaper columnists across the country dug into their morgue files and rehearsed memories of White's glorious past or interviewed middle-aged football warriors whose playing days suddenly acquired a new luster. Arthur J. Rooney, still the owner of the Pittsburgh franchise, said, "President Kennedy couldn't have appointed a greater man." Rooney had seen White less than a month before in Philadelphia at the banquet of the Maxwell Club, which had selected Clint Frank over White as its outstanding college player of the year in 1937. Columnists tended to extol White's dual success in the classroom and on the playing field (Lloyd Larson of the *Milwaukee Sentinel*) or bask in White's reflected glory: "Over here in the all brawn and no brains section of the newspaper, which is the sports department, there is a new kind of respectability prevailing" (John Steadman, sports editor, the *Baltimore American*). Shirley Povich of the *Washington Post,* who had covered White in the National Football League, said it better: "For every professional football player whose nose has been ground into the dirt or whose calling has been scorned as primitive by politer society, there now must be a glow of pride. One of their boys has made it all the way to the Supreme Court of the United States." Arthur Daley of the *New York Times,* whom White had privately rebuked for popularizing a bogus story about White's war record, wrote a column echoing Povich two weeks later. This time he omitted the phony tale of the South Pacific, but he did repeat the dubious story of the indifferent blocking that was used to explain White's sluggish start in the 1938 season. The stack of clippings was testimony to the durable purchase of the alliterative nickname that Daley conceded the "painfully modest hero grew to dislike. He may have trouble living it down, however. He was no fringe performer. He was a great star, a real Whizzer."

Byron White's confirmation hearings were held on April 11, and over time their lighthearted expeditiousness became a source of fond nostalgia for many, especially the journalist David Brinkley, who often recalled how quickly White's hearings were completed. The entire proceedings before the Senate Judiciary Committee lasted only ninety minutes, although most of the time was consumed with Bernard Segal's oral presentation of the ABA committee's report, extended by Sen. Sam J. Ervin's complaint that the ABA awarded its highest ratings without insisting on any judicial service. "Frankly," Ervin told Segal, "I would be just a little bit happier if he had been a judge for about 10 years." White was accompanied at the hearing by Joe Dolan and by Ethel Kennedy, wife of the attorney general. The *Washington Post* noted that before he began his own testimony, "White, a reticent man, sat quietly, doodling on a pad and smoking cigarettes as Senators and lawyers praised his ability." There was no written record to review, since White had given only six speeches as deputy attorney general and none touched on judicial review or allied issues.

The gravity of the hearings was evidenced by the fact that chairman Eastland attended for only five minutes before leaving and turning the gavel over to Senator Carroll from Colorado until the final two minutes and the brief executive session. The tone is captured by the statement of Sen. Phillip Hart—the conscience of the Senate, or at least of the Committee—that "this is the first appointment of a player of the Detroit Lions to the Supreme Court." In addition to Segal's, a presentation was made on behalf of the Colorado Bar Association, which, like the ABA, considered White "exceptionally well qualified." The CBA report was presented by Hugh A. Burns, whom White had tried to recruit for the University of Colorado football program fifteen years earlier. Burns, now a prominent Denver lawyer, was in Washington on other business and was asked by the president of the state bar to present its report.

Almost lost in the perfunctory hearing were a pair of statements by White—one on the record, the other not—that sounded innocuous but stemmed from deeply earnest convictions. Halfway through White's brief appearance, which lasted, as Brinkley always insisted, exactly eleven minutes, Sen. Edward V. Long of Missouri asked the nominee on the record to comment on the notion that the Supreme Court "legislate[s]." White replied:

> I think it is clear under the Constitution that legislative power is not vested in the Supreme Court. It is vested in the Congress; and I feel the major instrument for changing the laws in this country is the Congress of the United States. The business of the Congress is that of changing the law.

Off the hearing record, after the proceedings were adjourned, a Washington journalist approached White and asked him to define the constitutional role of the Supreme Court. According to Burns, who was standing next to him, White replied coldly, "To decide cases." Burns later said that he would never forget the exchange: "The statement was both a brush-off and a statement of philosophy; you could tell by the way he said it that it carried a fundamental belief for him." After a five-minute executive session, the committee unanimously approved White's nomination.

The nomination moved to the floor that afternoon. Sen. Richard B. Russell made a brief speech, saying that he supported the nomination but urged the president to fill the next vacancy on the Court with a "genuine conservative constitutionalist," because there were 40 to 50 million conservatives in the country who deserved representation on the Court. Under Senate rules, the nomination should have lain over for twenty-four hours after the hearing, but Sen. John Carroll of Colorado successfully moved for unanimous consent to suspend the rules, and the Senate then proceeded to confirm White by voice vote as the ninety-third man to sit on the Supreme Court of the United States.

Part IV

THE SUPREME COURT

15

THE WARREN COURT:
WHITE, J., DISSENTING

ON APRIL 16, 1962—five days after confirmation—Byron White
was formally sworn in as an associate justice of the Supreme Court
at ceremonies in the courtroom. Chief Justice Warren had administered the constitutional oath, prior to the public ceremony, in the justices'
conference room, with three retired justices (Reed, Burton, and Whittaker)
and every member of the Court in attendance except Frankfurter, who had
suffered a serious stroke on April 5. The public ceremonies were attended by
the president and the attorney general, who both shook hands with White
after he took the constitutional oath of office before the clerk of the Court.
Seated in the audience along with Mrs. White and her eight-year-old son were
witnesses to history from a cross section of White's life, including numerous
Justice Department officials, led by the solicitor general and Joe Dolan; Secretary of the Interior Stewart Udall; Secretary of Labor Arthur Goldberg; Colorado congressmen Byron Rogers of Denver and J. Edgar Chenoweth of
Trinidad; Dr. and Mrs. Stearns; Dr. and Mrs. Sam White; former law firm
partner Donald Hoagland; Freddie Mandel, former owner of the Detroit
Lions, who had flown in from Hawaii; John V. McNally—Johnny Blood—
who had flown in from Minneapolis at White's invitation; and two members
of the *Washington Post* sports department—Shirley Povich and Dave Brady.

In the midst of the momentous and very public professional transition, the Whites followed through with a private transition that they had planned for some months before the appointment suddenly occurred. After renting in the District of Columbia for more than a year, they closed, on April 12, on a newly built house in McLean, Virginia, on a three-quarter-acre lot at the end of a cul-de-sac populated by professionals from the nearby Central Intelligence Agency. The location was six miles from the Supreme Court and only a mile from Hickory Hill, home of the Robert Kennedys. Although Byron White jealously protected his private life and treated journalists who wished to investigate his hearth like burglars, Mrs. White agreed to a request from the *Denver Post* to do a feature story, complete with six photographs, on "Justice White's New Home." The building itself was a modest four-bedroom, antique-brick split level with eighteen hundred finished square feet. The primary attraction of the property, said Mrs. White, was the lot:

> The lawns are wide and there is a heavily wooded hillside sloping down to a small creek behind. A split-rail fence ("The kind you see in the ghost towns of Colorado," says Mrs. White) separates the lawn from the woods which are thick with sycamore, dogwood, pine, oak and elm. . . . The Whites believe one nice thing about living in the country is that it helps give the children a feeling for the out-of-doors. . . . "The children love the woods in back of the house," says Mrs. White. "It's full of snakes and poison ivy, but they love it, and it's really marvelous for them."

The purchase price of the house was $42,501, secured by a twenty-five-year mortgage of $32,200 at 5.75 percent, which required a monthly payment of $202.86. The property would always be the family's principal asset and a potential source for financing college for the children, now eight and four years old. As a Supreme Court justice, White's salary would be $35,000, a raise from the $21,000 he made as deputy attorney general but still less than the partner's share he enjoyed for the previous few years at his law firm in Denver.

The guided tour of the new family residence was one of the last glimpses the press enjoyed of Byron White's private life. The Supreme Court of the United States provided White with a welcome perquisite—the luxury of controlling public appearances, and especially relations with the media, on his own terms. No longer would he need to submit to the press as part of his official responsibilities. He could, and did, refuse interviews with impunity. Not that he granted none; indeed, during his first six months on the Court, he granted multiple-day interviews to three freelance journalists who produced both discerning and revealing portraits. The location of the articles inadvertently carried a hint of self-parody: *Sports Illustrated, Sport,* and *True: The Man's Magazine.* All three focused primarily on his athletic experiences, although only the *Sport* profile is largely restricted to his athletic career. The only sustained newspaper interview he gave after being nominated was to the *New York Herald-Tribune's* Robert J. Donovan, perhaps not coincidentally the author of the best-selling account of PT *109.* As time went on, the *Washington Post,* the *New York Times,* and the *Wall Street Journal* would seek interviews in vain, sometimes even without acknowledgment of the request. At the same time, Mr. Justice White would occasionally attend the White House Correspondents' Dinner and grant interviews to the *Boulder Daily Camera,* the *Wellington–Fort Collins Triangle Review,* the *Colorado Daily* (the campus newspaper at the University of Colorado), and other publications tied closely to his roots. Journalists in the New York–Washington corridor could be forgiven for wondering what imp of the perverse dictated the justice's public relations policy, to the extent it could be called that.

The most pressing challenge for the new justice was, of course, neither changing residences nor parrying the press but preparing for the last session of oral arguments for October term 1961. He inherited, for all practical purposes, Justice Whittaker's files, his secretary, and his law clerk, Larry Gunnels. From the Department of Justice, he brought a driver-messenger, David Hall, and a second law clerk, Richard H. Stern, a 1959 cum laude graduate of Yale Law School who coincidentally had an application with Whittaker pending at the time of the sudden retirement. Even before he was confirmed, White was receiving clerkship applications for the following term, October 1962. He hired Ronald Blanc, who had learned of White's appointment from a newspaper box while visiting Washington in early April and telephoned the Department of Justice to arrange an interview. White agreed to see Blanc because they had met at a Boettcher scholars' reception in Denver while Blanc was attending the University of Colorado before going to the New York University School of Law; Blanc would work with Stern, who would stay for the full October term 1962 as well as the last two months of the 1961 term. (A complete list of White's clerks is set out in Appendix D.) White participated in the oral argument and decision of sixteen cases between mid-April and the end of June 1962, and wrote three opinions for the Court—one involving a jury verdict in an antitrust case and two involving construction of §301 of the Labor Management Relations Act.

Much more significant, he published one dissenting opinion, which in retrospect could properly be viewed as the overture for a number of themes in his jurisprudence. Any question as to whether White would sign on to what the press routinely called the "Warren-Black-Douglas-Brennan liberal group" was quickly and roughly resolved. The case was *Robinson v. California,* which turned on whether criminalizing the status of being addicted to narcotics violated the due process clause of the Fourteenth Amendment. The specific question was whether the clause imported—or incorporated—notions embodied in the Eighth Amendment prohibiting "cruel and unusual punishment." (In fact, *Robinson* was a novel case. Previous decisions examined the nature of the penalty; here, the question was the nature of the "crime.") A majority of the Court ruled that the statute was unconstitutional because it punished a status and not an act; Justice Douglas added a concurring opinion to emphasize his view that addiction was a disease, not a crime, and the Constitution required its treatment as such.

White's dissent, only seventeen hundred words long, set a pattern for his writing, both rhetorically and substantively. He began by accusing the majority of misstating the issue in the case and consequently reaching the constitutional question gratuitously. He found ample evidence that Robinson was being convicted for habitual use, including—by his own admission—shooting up eight days before his arrest, although there was no independent evidence of the precise time and location of the usage. Nor did White "find any indications in this record that California would apply [the statute in question] to the case of the helpless addict." After suggesting an unintended logical consequence of the majority's opinion—that invalidating addiction implicitly required invalidating the usage that led to the addiction—White declared that the Court had "cast serious doubt upon the power of any State to forbid the use of narcotics under threat of criminal punishment." His concluding paragraph bristled with sarcasm and accusations of the majority's presumptuousness:

> Finally, I deem this application of "cruel and unusual punishment" so novel that I suspect the Court was hard put to find a way to ascribe to the Framers of the Constitution the result reached today rather than its own notions of ordered liberty. If this case involved economic regulation, the present Court's allergy to substantive due process would surely save the statute and prevent the Court from imposing its own philosophical predilections upon state legislatures or Congress. I fail to see why the Court deems it more appropriate to write into the Constitution its own abstract notions of how best to handle the narcotics problem, for it obviously cannot match either the States or Congress in expert understanding.
>
> I respectfully dissent.

The opinion, initially drafted by Dick Stern and lightly reworked by White, contained coded verbal knives directed at the ribs of two members of the majority, Douglas and especially Black, who had made himself the point man, especially after World War II, of a crusade against the notion of economic "substantive due process"—the invalidation on constitutional grounds of legislation not because it relied on arbitrary procedures but because of its policy judgments. The symbolic totem of the doctrine was *Lochner v. New York,* which held in 1905 that a law regulating maximum hours for bakers violated the "liberty" of the employer and employee to exercise their mutual "freedom of contract." The Court repudiated the doctrine in 1937, and Black wrote one opinion after another decrying any evidence he saw of its resuscitation. *Robinson* did not make the hit list, nominally because it involved personal rather than economic liberty; moreover, the decision marked the first time that the Court had held that the "cruel and unusual punishment" component of the Eighth Amendment applied against the states through the due process clause of the Fourteenth Amendment. The Court had assumed as much without needing to reach the question in *Louisiana ex rel. Francis v. Resweber* (the bungled electrocution), when White was a law clerk to Vinson; the application of the Eighth Amendment to the states in *Robinson* marked a further victory for Black in his holy war to incorporate the Bill of Rights in the Fourteenth Amendment's due process clause, which began in earnest with his losing battle in *Adamson v. California,* decided the same term as *Resweber.* (In 1942, Black raised the issue for the first time in *Betts v. Brady,* when he argued in dissent that the Sixth Amendment "right to counsel" required states to provide indigent criminal defendants with lawyers.) It is no surprise that early in White's first few weeks on the Court one of his clerks overheard him complain alone to himself in his office that *the same issues that were here in 1947 are still here, and Hugo still runs the Court.*

When White was appointed, the press noted, but did not explore, the fact that he was the first former law clerk to be named to the Court. What impact did his staff experience almost sixteen years before have on his views about issues coming before the Court or about how he should operate? No one asked and he did not say, but the casual remark about the durability of issues from the 1940s suggests that he was not starting from scratch in some areas—particularly the law governing federal review by habeas corpus of state court criminal convictions. As a law clerk, he did not find federal courts to be appropriate vehicles for superintending state criminal justice systems, and he believed that police behavior should be understood by practical considerations and not by dogmatic presumptions. The same views provided White with a confident voice when he addressed the criminal justice issues that shaped much of the Court's docket during his first several terms. "I think he had a warm but complex relationship with Justice Douglas early on," Rex Lee later speculated. "Justice White remembered him as a powerfully energetic figure within the Court in the forties and he admired his robustness, but he wasn't quite sure how to deal with him at first as a colleague. That problem didn't last long, though." Lee and others thought White drew few lessons about interpersonal dynamics on the Court from his clerking days. *Every time someone new joins the Court, it's a different instrument,* he often said.

White's first dissent—in fact the only dissenting vote he cast in his first, partial term on the Court—was largely ignored in the press coverage of the final day of the 1961 term because it was properly overshadowed by the most controversial decision since *Brown.* The *Washington Evening Star's* banner headline proclaimed, "High Court Bans School Prayer." With neither Frankfurter nor White participating, the Court ruled 6-1 that New York's twenty-two-word compulsory prayer violated the establishment clause of the First Amendment, applied to the states again through the due process clause of the Fourteenth Amendment. Black wrote for the Court, and only Stewart dissented. The case was argued April 3, while Frankfurter was ill, two weeks before White took office. The decision, *Engel v. Vitale,* plus *Baker v. Carr* (which held that allegations of legislative malapportionment presented constitutional questions capable of judicial answer), made the 1961 term, in the words of a *New York Times* headline, one of the "Most Significant in its History." Trying to discern where White would "put his weight in a delicately balanced court," Anthony Lewis decided that the single dissent provided "too little to draw solid conclusions about his views," but noted that the opinion "at least suggests that the new Justice is going to be no sentimentalist in dealing with criminals"—perhaps even indicating a broader view "that judges should be wary of novel doctrine and slow to impose new restraints on government."

The delicate balance tilted sharply at the end of the summer when Justice Frankfurter, having suffered two heart attacks since his stroke in early April, retired and was replaced by Arthur L. Goldberg, the secretary of labor. Goldberg, age fifty-four, made the Court the youngest—mean age just shy of sixty—in twenty years and marked the beginning of what David Currie, the leading doctrinal historian of the institution, has called "the real Warren Court": "From the moment Arthur Goldberg took Frankfurter's place in 1962 there was a dramatic shift, for the new Justice joined [Warren, Black, Douglas, and Brennan] to form a dependable majority for greater protection of civil liberties and fair procedures"—especially for those caught in state criminal justice systems.

During the first term they sat together, White and Goldberg were on the opposite side of nine of thirteen 5-4 decisions issued by the Court. In one of those cases, they spoke for opposite sides. Goldberg wrote the Court's opinion in *Gastellum-Quinones v. Kennedy, Attorney-General,* which held that there was insufficient evidence to establish that the petitioner was a "meaningful member" of the Communist Party, and thus he was not liable to deportation, despite the testimony of two witnesses and no rebuttal evidence. White's sharp dissent first pointed out that the issue in the case was whether the petitioner was entitled to reopen the deportation proceedings, not the issue that the Court actually decided; second, he argued that the administrative decision was supported by substantial evidence, which should preclude further review under the Court's cases.

As the term wore on, in one case after another, White published dissents pointing out that the Court was deciding issues not presented; failed to defer either to Congress or an administrative agency when it was appropriate; or reached the correct decision but wrote so broadly that legitimate state interests would be prejudiced in future cases. He also wrote a strong opinion establishing his commitment to a generous reading of national power in the face of arguably conflicting state regulation. At the same time, White's opinions for the Court during his first full term fell into the workaday category that Potter Stewart later called "dogs"—

cases where you knew, right from the moment you started to work on it, it would add nothing to the jurisprudence of the United States at all. You had to do the best you could, but it was a "nothing" case, except extremely hard and arduous. Every term there are cases like that.

By that standard, October term 1962 howled for Byron White. Warren distributed opinion work very evenly. No one wrote fewer than eleven opinions for the Court, and Black and White each wrote thirteen. None of White's majority opinions was memorable. Five involved labor law, three tax, and one each admiralty, federal jurisdiction, the Federal Employers' Liability Act, the amenability of national banks to suit, and abuse of discretion by the Interstate Commerce Commission.

Twenty years later, White told Chief Justice Warren's biographer, putting it mildly, that "I wasn't exactly in his inner circle." Nonetheless, he also said that Warren's assignment of opinions was "fair":

I think it is very fair for a Chief Justice to assign opinions to the people who (a) are on his side; (b) will do the job the way the Chief Justice would best like it done, and I think that's part of the prerogatives of the Chief Justice—[to as-sign to the justice who] would more accurately or better reflect the sentiment that he would like to see reflected.

Privately, White told close friends later that he did not receive what could be called a plum assignment until December 1963, when Warren assigned him to write *Jackson v. Denno,* which involved the constitutionality of proce-dures used in New York to determine voluntariness of confessions, and which again had him butting heads with Hugo Black. Until then, he wrote what many saw as unnecessarily exhaustive opinions in routine cases of little lasting significance.

Outside the Court, he was feted—for his past. As James Clayton of the *Post* wrote, "During the winter [of October term 1962] White's career as a star football player was recalled again and again": as a member of the twenty-five-man Silver Anniversary All-America team chosen by *Sports Illustrated,* and with the Gold Medal of the National Football Foundation, the Distinguished Citizen Award of the Maryland "M" Club, and the Mr. Sam Award of the Dis-trict of Columbia Touchdown Club as "the government official who had con-tributed most to the status of athletics in 1962." The only respite during the winter celebration was, of course, physical: the Whites and the Robert Kennedys went skiing in Colorado after the first of the year. White's academic career would not be similarly honored for more than two years. Hertford Col-lege elected White an Honorary Fellow in May of 1965, a courtesy inasmuch as he attended Oxford for only two terms, never took an examination, and never was recognized for his academic work beyond the Rhodes Scholarship, which was awarded before he matriculated.

Jackson v. Denno helped Byron White to focus his priorities for the bal-ance of the 1963 term and the next several terms. The issue that he staked out as his own was the self-incrimination clause of the Fifth Amendment, applied to the states for the first time as a formal matter in *Malloy v. Hogan,* June 15, 1964. He dissented in *Malloy* and in other cases that granted relief under the clause directly *(Murphy v. Waterfront Commission)* or in conjunction with the Sixth Amendment right to counsel *(Massiah v. United States* and *Escobedo v. Illinois).* White's opinion for the Court in *Jackson v. Denno* declined to grant relief to the defendant, but at the same time introduced a fundamental princi-ple in White's jurisprudence, which he would develop further a decade later—that the content of a constitutionally protected right must be decided by an unbiased decision maker. In New York, after a threshold examination by the trial judge (whether in no circumstances the confession could be held valid), the trial jury decided as a matter of fact both on voluntariness and on guilt. White's draft opinion for the Court concluded that the process did not provide a reliable measure of the voluntariness of the confession, because the evidence of the crime and other evidence of the defendant's guilt could taint the jury's assessment of voluntariness, or the evidence of the confession—even if found to be involuntary—might be impossible for the jury to ignore.

Black objected in uncompromising terms to White's approach, basically for two reasons: Black's undiluted faith in the jury, which manifested itself in several areas, and White's emphasis on procedural "fairness," which to Black was code for substantive due process. ("'Fairness' used in [this] context," he wrote White angrily after receiving an early draft of the opinion, "implies that we are relying on the loose definition of 'due process' as meaning anything that is offensive to this Court's sense of decency or the basic principles of 'fundamental fairness in the English speaking world.'") White tried to answer Black with a patient three-page, single-spaced letter, but Black remained adamant, and *Jackson v. Denno* came down as a sprawling treatise on voluntariness, complete with a state-by-state appendix on methods of determining the issue, with asides on the nature of a fair hearing and the reliability of confessions. The decision invalidated practices in almost two dozen jurisdictions—fifteen states, the District of Columbia, Puerto Rico, and six federal circuits. Justices joining Black in dissent were Clark, Harlan, and Stewart.

What split White from his customary allies in questions of constitutional criminal procedure was the mechanism for deciding the voluntariness of the confession, and thus the constitutionality of any conviction that might rest on it. For White, the risk of biased fact finders, inconsistent decisions depending on juror whim, and arbitrary resolution of constitutional rights was too much to accept, so he swallowed his anxieties about disturbing established state procedures. The *Harvard Law Review* sided with Black: "A state criminal procedure may be held to violate due process not only when it is repugnant to 'the concept of ordered liberty' or 'shocks the conscience,' but also when it is less fair than alternate procedures"; this was a snide way of pointing out that White's decisive reasons—reliability and untainted decision making—were no more constitutionally compelled than the new rules governing self-incrimination to which he objected so vigorously in other cases the same term. The decision kept White and Black at odds over due process in criminal procedure for years, and the ramifications of the decision "plague[d]" the Court for years: "The rule, desirable or not, created little difficulty of administration for future trials," observed Philip B. Kurland. "It played havoc, however, with cases already tried under a different rule."

October term 1964 provided a respite for White and the Court from the Fifth and Sixth Amendment issues. At the end of the term, Arthur Goldberg resigned to replace Adlai Stevenson as ambassador to the United Nations, and Abe Fortas took his place. October term 1965 produced the Court's most controversial decision since White's first few months on the Court and triggered White's most furious and sustained dissent. Chief Justice Warren's opinion in *Miranda v. Arizona* required the now-famous warnings to be given, but Philip B. Kurland was right when he wrote later that the opinion was "overrated"— "by those who approved it no less than by those who condemned it"—and the public furor was less over the content of the warnings than about "the time when they must be made": as soon as custodial interrogation began. White's dissent, which canvassed the history of self-incrimination and of the Fifth Amendment in extraordinary detail, ended on a raw note that was widely quoted at the time:

> In some unknown number of cases the Court's rule will return a killer, a rapist or other criminal to the streets and to the environment which produced him, to repeat his crime whenever it pleases him. As a consequence, there will not be a gain, but a loss, in human dignity. The real concern is not the unfortunate consequences of this new decision on the criminal law as an abstract, disembodied series of authoritative proscriptions, but the impact on those who rely on the public authority for protection and who without it can only engage in violent self-help with guns, knives and the help of their neighbors similarly inclined. There is, of course, a saving factor: the next victims are uncertain, unnamed and unrepresented in this case.

Although the Supreme Court's revolution in criminal justice produced a score of controversial decisions during the period of "the real Warren Court," *Miranda* produced more rancor both without and within the Court than any other. Feelings ran so high that three of the *Miranda* dissenters refused until the last minute to join Justice Brennan's opinion for the Court in *Schmerber v. California,* which gratuitously quoted *Miranda. Schmerber* rejected a claim that blood samples taken against the wishes of a defendant in custody violated the Fifth Amendment. Brennan's attempt to "soften the impact of *Miranda*" succeeded only in antagonizing three of its four dissenters—Harlan, Stewart, and White. They refused to sign on to his opinion until the last minute.

Miranda was a watershed for White. He thought the decision was as unwise as it was constitutionally unwarranted. He even went to the extent of publicly criticizing the decision, in fact the whole line of criminal justice decisions beginning with *Mapp v. Ohio,* which held in 1961 that the due process clause of the Fourteenth Amendment imposed on the states the rule for federal courts, established in *Weeks v. United States* in 1914, that illegally seized evidence be excluded from trial. At a speech in Denver before the National District Attorneys Association Foundation, two months after *Miranda* was issued, White said:

> Neither the language nor the history of the Fourth Amendment, which forbids unreasonable searches and provides for warrants only on probable cause, requires or even strongly suggests that illegally seized evidence is inadmissible in the court of a criminal trial. But neither do they preclude such a holding. And in the Mapp decision the court decided that evidence taken in violation of the Fourth Amendment could not be admitted at the trial. This was contrary to its previous interpretation of the same constitutional language.

He added that "neither the text of the amendment nor its history either compelled or precluded the result reached in that case."

What guides the Court? According to the *Denver Post* account of the address, which is the only surviving evidence of what was said, White

> said the framers of the Constitution didn't intend to give a single meaning to some of the provisions in the Bill of Rights. He said they consciously used vague language with the hope it would be appropriate in the 19th and 20th centuries, as well as the 18th. . . . Questions raised by these controversial cases, Justice White said, raise important issues of public policy "which must be decided in terms of the long-range aims of the community."

With historical practices repudiated and contrary precedents swept aside by the *Mapp-Massiah-Malloy-Escobedo-Miranda* juggernaut, White's appeal to a public policy looking to the future had a naked candor that charmed some of his listeners but left them with no theoretical weapons with which to resist the tide or to suggest a doctrinal counterrevolution. Perhaps realizing the intellectual barrenness of the critique, he changed tack a year later in a speech to the Conference of Chief Justices in Honolulu. Instead of attacking the lines of cases, he emphasized their limits—especially *Miranda's*. He pointed out that the decision failed to answer five questions, which would be critical over time: When does "custody" begin? Can evidence discovered on the basis of a confession given without *Miranda* warnings, such as weapons or corpus delecti, be used in evidence? Can tainted confessions be used "for such secondary purposes as to indict the defendant, contradict his testimony, assist the judge in sentencing or support a parole revocation?" Does *Miranda* apply at noncustodial situations such as psychiatric interviews or conversations with juvenile officers? And most important: What evidence demonstrates "voluntarily, knowingly and intelligently" waiving the right to silence and to counsel?

Fred Graham of the *New York Times,* who covered the speech, thought White "realized that the aging liberal majority of the Warren Court could not remain intact much longer" and implied that White was self-consciously providing a tactical agenda for minimizing *Miranda*'s impact. An address to state court judges charged with implementing a decision is a paradoxical occasion to attack that decision and to suggest its limits. White's motivation is suggested by his private views at the time, which were much more direct and emphatic. To a college classmate, now practicing law in Colorado, who visited him in Washington during this period, White said, *The trouble with these liberals up here is that they think they have all the answers to social problems like crime and race, and what's worse, they're putting them into the Constitution.*

At the end of the term, Justice Harlan delivered remarks at the dedication of the new American Bar Center in Chicago, and White later told Ira Rothgerber that "Harlan said it better than I could." Harlan's brief talk began:

> One of the current notions that holds subtle capacity for serious mischief is a view of the judicial function that seems increasingly coming into vogue. This is that all deficiencies in our society which have failed of correction by other means should find a cure in the courts. The principal theme of these remarks will be to challenge the validity of that thesis from the three principal standpoints that are most frequently heard in its support. These are: doubt whether the federal system is any longer adequate to meet the needs of modern American society; impatience with the slowness of political solutions generally; and an urge for quick and uncompromising panaceas for all things that call for reform. I venture to say at the outset that this cosmic view of the place of the judiciary is not only inconsistent with the principles of American democratic society but ultimately threatens the integrity of the judicial system itself.

Byron White's strategic approach to the Warren Court's constitutionalization of state criminal procedure was, as his speech in Honolulu suggested, to circumscribe the reach of *Miranda* and its predecessors. Tactically, he used the techniques of conventional legal analysis with a meticulous vengeance. He would concede, for example, that a case properly raised the privilege against self-incrimination, but he would argue that the determination of "incrimination" ought to be left to the trial judge, and then he would go on to demonstrate that incrimination was illusory on the facts in issue (*Malloy v. Hogan,* 1964). Or he would write separately to emphasize that the immunity from federal prosecution required in return for testimony compelled in state proceedings was limited to "use" and not "transactional" immunity (*Murphy v. Waterfront Commission*, 1964).* Or, pursuing views he had started to develop at the Department of Justice, he would strike a nondogmatic compromise on wiretapping: he would insist on strict standing† requirements before wiretaps could be challenged in court, but when taps were shown to be illegal, he would permit those with standing to review material improperly overheard to be examined in detail—a decision (*Alderman v. United States*, 1969) that the Nixon administration sought to have modified by inappropriate means before convincing Congress to do the job aboveboard.

Finally, White would temper the requirements of constitutional principles when they were applied in novel contexts, a technique that he would perfect in several areas during his career. Two examples: (1) White wrote in the *Camara* and *See* cases that the Fourth Amendment applied to administrative searches conducted under housing and fire laws, but that warrants could be issued without a showing of probable cause. (2) In a twist on the incorporation doctrine, he would find that a provision of the Constitution binding the federal government applied against the states as well, but not necessarily with the identical content or standards as in the federal context. The principal example during the Warren Court period was *Duncan v. Louisiana* (1968), which applied the Sixth Amendment right to trial by jury to the states but reserved the question whether "petty offenses"—not defined or specified—required juries.

Duncan drew a dissent from Justice Harlan, as had *Jackson v. Denno*. Such defections from his customary ally led many to label White as "unpredictable" and even brought him to account in his own family. When his father died, in February 1966 at the age of eighty-six, White jotted a note to Harlan thanking him for his note of condolence "about my Dad. I might say that he thought I should listen to you a little more and did not mind saying so." But Byron White did not have the patience to write Harlan's methodical, measured essays on constitutionalism and statutory construction. White's strength, which he barely muted as a judge, was adversarial: his opinions marshaled all of the arguments and all of the historical data and marched re-

---

* "Use" immunity means that the evidence given may not be used in a subsequent prosecution. "Transactional" immunity is much broader: the witness is immunized not only for what he actually says but for the underlying events he reveals.

† "Standing" is a technical term that means that the person asserting a claim has actually suffered himself and is not simply making a complaint that either everyone could make or that someone else—more directly injured by the act complained of—should make.

lentlessly forward. Harlan weighed opposing arguments and White destroyed them. The opposing styles inverted the saying of Zeno the Stoic that rhetoric is an open palm and logic is a closed fist. Harlan's carefully reasoned and evenly toned opinions were more enticing and ultimately convincing than White's relentless tours de force or the bluster of dissents such as *Miranda* and *Escobedo*.

White's rhetoric was naturally more restrained when he spoke for the majority of the Court, and over time he managed to land a handful of important assignments, during the last three or four years of the Warren Court, including a labor decision of enduring importance, a handful of major if transitory decisions involving race, and *Board of Education v. Allen,* holding that states were permitted to provide secular textbooks as well as transportation to parochial school students—a reaffirmation of Black's twenty-year-old opinion in *Everson v. Board of Education* that state neutrality to religion need not penalize nonsectarian activities conducted by religious institutions.

White also wrote the landmark opinion upholding the Federal Communications Commission's "fairness doctrine" despite serious theoretical problems under the First Amendment *(Red Lion Communications v. Federal Communications Commission).* Under the doctrine, the FCC required broadcasters to provide a right of reply to persons who had been "attacked" during the discussion of a controversial issue. The opinion, later severely criticized in professional journals, drew rave reviews within the Court: "truly superb" (Brennan), written "with great wisdom and skill" (Harlan), "very thorough and thoughtful" (Stewart). Five years after *Red Lion,* the Court would hold unconstitutional a similar state law applying to newspapers. The difference between the two cases was that the print media historically enjoyed editorial autonomy, but the broadcast media was controlled by a statute dating to the first New Deal; many critics argued that the distinction begged the constitutional question.

White's most notorious opinion in the area of civil rights during the period was *Reitman v. Mulkey* in 1968, in which he wrote for a sharply divided Court—with Black, Clark, Harlan, and Stewart dissenting—that a California constitutional amendment repealing fair-housing laws violated the equal protection clause of the Fourteenth Amendment. The basis for the decision was that the state court had found that repeal "authorized" and "encouraged" private segregation, and the Court found no reason to overturn that finding. David Currie called *Reitman* the "most distressing" of a series of decisions "during the later Warren years in attributing racially discriminatory actions to the states." Noting that any repeal would produce the result condemned by the Court in the guise of simply not disturbing lower-court findings of fact, Currie wrote:

> Though the opinion expressly disclaimed any intention of outlawing mere repeal, it flailed ineffectively in search of a distinction. Not long afterward the Court explained with some plausibility that imposing special procedural obstacles to the enactment of laws limiting private discrimination placed the potential beneficiaries of such laws at a disadvantage.

The subsequent decision *Hunter v. Erickson* in 1969 was also written by Justice White and invalidated a city charter provision that required referenda on fair-housing ordinances.

The brace of cases is a curious episode in White's career. *Reitman* was subjected to searching criticism in two of the leading commentaries on the Court for that year, Charles Black's Foreword in the *Harvard Law Review* and the lead article in the *Supreme Court Review.* The essays welcomed the result but not the opinion. White privately dismissed the critiques to friends in Denver, because in his view the case was "One Indian walking single file." Yet two years later *Reitman* had acquired a theoretical tribe that provided the basis for later decisions invalidating antibusing referenda in Seattle and an antigay initiative in Colorado (*Romer v. Evans* in 1996), plus a trial court injunction of California's anti-affirmative-action Proposition 209 in 1996.

Byron White's service on the Warren Court will not be remembered for his opinions for the Court. He had few notable assignments from Warren, or from Black on those rare occasions when Warren was in the minority on a significant case. White's seven terms with Warren were a period of reflection and refinement of views, at least beyond the criminal justice area, where his views were rather fixed when he arrived and only hardened with experience. In fact, White privately became fond of quoting Justice Douglas's remark—which Douglas attributed to Chief Justice Charles Evans Hughes—that "it takes five years to go around the track once," meaning that several terms of experience are required before a new justice understands how discrete cases fit into the Court's larger responsibilities for superintending its jurisprudence and how an individual member of the Court can best husband his own resources and interests. During his first several terms on the Court, for all the ferocity he showed on the bench during oral argument, he was often incongruously tentative in deliberation on pending cases. He occasionally circulated opinions in minor cases that he later withdrew, perhaps "after stewing around" and having "further thought."

Notwithstanding White's claims to later law clerks that "I never agonized over a case in my life," Rex Lee "was frankly surprised by how much he agonized over cases the year I worked with him" (October term 1963): "His instinctive views in many areas seemed to reflect his experience in the Department of Justice—antitrust, crime, labor, intellectual property. The Court's cases forced him to work through one field after another. In retrospect, I can now see that his views in some areas began to recrystallize during that period. He would openly reflect with us about his experiences and how they affected his views."

The cases that absorbed the Court's attention that term were the sit-in cases, involving the criminal trespass arrests of black students who refused to move from racially segregated restaurants and lunch counters. It was the second term in a row with major sit-in cases. The year before, White had tied himself in a knot debating over how to respond to Warren's proposed opinion for the Court; three months after Warren's first circulated draft opinion, White wrote to him, "I am still stewing about the sit-in cases and I hope that you will bear with me until perhaps next week."

In the principal case, *Bell v. Maryland,* the Court dodged the constitutional issues by deciding that a city ordinance passed *subsequent* to the arrest, convictions, and final appeals of the trespassers nonetheless entitled the defendants to relief from their convictions. Brennan's opinion for the majority manufactured a bogus theory that avoided the Constitution in order to prevent the Court from intruding symbolically into the ongoing debate over what became the Civil Rights Act of 1964 ten days after the decision was issued. Black, who originally had drafted an opinion for the Court, wound up in dissent when Brennan's nonconstitutional ground for vacating the convictions appealed to Clark. Harlan and White joined Black's opinion. White drafted his own two-page dissent but withdrew it four days before the decision was handed down.

The draft is revealing about White's thinking at the time, both with respect to the Court's role and to the function of the separate opinion. The constitutional issue, which the Court dodged but Black addressed, was whether police enforcement of a private businessman's customer preferences via the trespass laws constituted "state action" triggering the Fourteenth Amendment; by its terms and as authoritatively construed in 1883, the amendment's due process and equal protection clauses apply only to states and their subdivisions, not to private parties. After walking step by step through the analytical consequences of the arrest at the proprietor's request, White reached the "nub of my reasons for joining the dissent in this case":

> I would unhesitatingly strike down discriminatory action where the state is
> shown to be substantially involved. *Robinson v. Florida, ante; Peterson v. City*

of Greenville, 373 U.S. 244; *Lombard v. Louisiana*, 373 U.S. 267. But none of the theories advanced by petitioners or by the United States convinces me that such is the case here. It is private conduct which is at the core of this case. I strongly object to the notion that the Fourteenth Amendment regulates private choice and that individual action is forbidden by the Constitution if thought by this Court to be irrational or unwise. Powers like this have historically been legislative powers, exercised by elected representatives after arriving at some consensus that specified behavior is inimical and must be controlled by the State. I find nothing in § 1 of the Fourteenth Amendment in the way of public accommodations or fair employment provisions which justifies action by this Court. These are legislative tasks which, in my opinion, are within the constitutional powers of the Congress and of the legislatures. They fall outside of ours.

The quoted passage, which represents half of the dissenting statement, reveals a new judge feeling his way, in very personal terms, for the limits of his role and the appropriate manner to declare it. The statement in the end was too personal and added too little to Black's forceful and sustained opinion for White to indulge his vanity by publishing it. Nonetheless, he had declared himself to his colleagues and to himself. Even on the question of racial discrimination, which he had personally faced down in Alabama, he remained convinced that courts could go only so far to overcome the attitude and institutions underlying racism, a judgment that rested both on personal experience and on his reading of the text and history of the Fourteenth Amendment.

Despite strong opinions for the Court in cases such as *Reitman v. Mulkey* and *Hunter v. Erickson*, among others, White worried over whether the Court's ingenuity outstripped its capacity on the race question. He told Ira Rothgerber many years later that he "agonized—for a long, long time" over whether to join *Green v. New Kent County Board of Education* in 1968, which prohibited a Virginia public school system from relying on an ineffectual "freedom of choice" plan to satisfy a desegregation suit. The plan had little effect on the two high schools in the system, which remained overwhelmingly all-white and all-black three years after the plan was implemented. Brennan's opinion found that the plan was an inadequate remedy under *Brown v. Board of Education II* because it failed to eradicate the "effects" of the prior segregated system. Under the guise of remedy, the Court redefined the right in *Brown:* the right was not to be free from school attendance assignments based on race, but to attend racially integrated schools—at least where state-imposed racial segregation existed as of the date of the first ruling in *Brown*. The Court's step in *Green* committed the Court to measuring the success of *Brown* numerically, and numbers would most likely change only by transporting students. *Green* more or less made busing inevitable. At a deeper level, *Green* committed the Court to superintending social change, not simply dismantling legal superstructures. For White, sooner rather than later the individual had to be accountable for his own choices and his own fortune. *Green* made black students in Jim Crow jurisdictions wards of the state in some respects, and racial balance might not even be the end for the Court. However deep White's reservations about *Green,* however, he would not be the first justice to break unanimity in school desegregation cases since *Brown* itself was decided, on May 17, 1954. That string would not be broken until after Warren retired.

The 1963 term also included a case in another constitutional area that haunted White and would throughout his tenure on the Court. *New York Times v. Sullivan* rewrote the law of defamation in constitutional terms, at least for public figures and perhaps for public issues, although the Court quickly divided in succeeding terms over its scope. The basic rule announced by the decision was that the First Amendment precluded libel judgments against publishers unless the falsehood was the product of "actual malice"—a statement made "with knowledge that it was false or with reckless disregard of whether it was false or not." "I think Justice White had deep reservations about *Times v. Sullivan,*" Rex Lee recalled years later. "He kicked himself for joining Justice Brennan's opinion so quickly." White joined Brennan's draft opinion for the Court four days after it was circulated; only the chief justice joined faster. "He seemed to worry about the scope of the rule and common law metaphor ['actual malice'] that it was based on. The whole thing was a bit of a pig in a poke. No one was quite sure what it actually meant beyond the facts of the case." In subsequent terms, White played an active role trying to prevent the *Sullivan* rule from swallowing the entire law of defamation.

Byron White's career on the Warren Court required a dexterity in public relations that he did not fully welcome but that he developed by necessity. In every year but one from 1962 to 1969 he received or presented an award connected with his athletic past. After receiving the gold medal from the college football Hall of Fame in 1962, which required a speech to fifteen hundred black-tied diners at the Waldorf-Astoria, he presented Johnny Blood the following year at the inauguration of the National Football League Hall of Fame in Canton, Ohio. From the first inductions, presentation came to be regarded as a sentimental message by the honoree about the bonds of friendship and teamwork romantically associated with the game, and White's brief introductory statement—shorter and less openly emotional than any other—reciprocated:

> John has devoted a good many years of his life to the game of football, including 15 wonderful years in the National Football League. Not only was John a magnificent player and a brilliant entertainer but he had the rarest of all qualities namely, giving his greatest performances when greatest was required. This, of course, is the hallmark, historically, of the great athlete and it is also one of the major tests which time applies to the deeds of men. John, you and your performances have survived the test of time and they will continue to do so.

In successive years, White was elected a charter member of the Colorado Sports Hall of Fame, in 1965 (with Jack Dempsey and Dutch Clark); was selected to speak about Walt Kiesling—his former teammate and assistant coach at Pittsburgh—when Kiesling was inducted posthumously into the NFL Hall of Fame, in 1966; was honored by the NFL Players Association, in 1967, which named its annual Byron "Whizzer" White Humanitarian Award "to the player who serves his team, community and country in the spirit of Byron 'Whizzer' White"; and was named, in 1968, the winner of the National Collegiate Athletic Association's Theodore Roosevelt Award (the "Teddy"), given to "a distinguished citizen of national reputation and outstanding accomplishment" who earned a varsity athletic letter in college. During the last six months of the Warren Court, he participated in three sports awards: he was honored as one of the Top Sports Stars in the Nation at the thirty-third annual Dapper Dan Banquet, sponsored by the *Pittsburgh Post-Gazette;* named to the All-Time Rocky Mountain–Southwest football team, sponsored by the Football Writers Association of America and the Western Athletic Conference, in celebration of the centennial of college football; and selected to present Art Rooney with a lifetime service award at the annual New York Pro Football Writers Dinner in New York.

The Warren Court, as it would always be called, formally ended June 23, 1969, when Earl Warren retired and Warren E. Burger succeeded him. White and Warren enjoyed a warm affinity during the seven terms and two months they sat together, even if White did not count himself in Warren's inner circle on the Court. Both were large men of substantial physical presence, firm warm handshakes, and devotion to plain talk. They shared a passion for spectator sports, and White enjoyed the chief justice's annual private trek by train to the Army-Navy game in Philadelphia, although he did not always make the trip. Only Justice Douglas, the Western elitist in hiking boots, was closer to

White during Warren's reign. Yet the day of Warren's retirement, there was no sentiment from White in his note to the man who had come to personify to the public the Supreme Court of the United States:

> Farewell and best wishes to both you and Mrs. Warren. For me it has been a great experience serving with you.
>
> I regret I cannot be on hand this Sunday for the gathering in your honor at the Lincoln Memorial [since the judges of] the 10th Circuit Conference have me by the neck.
>
> Have a good summer.
>
> Sincerely,
> Byron

Warren's departure was only a retirement, which perhaps explains the almost routine tone of the message. The deaths of his mother, of John Kennedy, and of Robert Kennedy, were the truly painful losses for Byron White during the era that closed on June 23, 1969. Rex Lee remembered more than thirty years later, "as if it were yesterday," driving White to Hickory Hill on November 22, 1963. "He didn't say a word. He sat next to me, hard as stone, and ashen." When they arrived at the estate, White walked with Robert Kennedy, his arm clasped firmly around the attorney general's shoulders, and tried to console him. Minutes later, it was Kennedy trying to leaven the grim mood of others who had arrived to mourn. The death of Robert Kennedy, a year before Warren retired, preceded as it was by the announcement of irreparable brain damage and hours of anxiety, deeply affected White, as Lance Liebman suggested in his tribute on the occasion of White's own retirement. Ira Rothgerber thought that Robert Kennedy's assassination, or the cumulative losses at that point, caused White to reexamine whether he *was in the best place to make the best contribution* to society that he could, and others shared that view. Over the next several years, the question would recur, sometimes in earnest and sometimes, thanks to others, virtually as farce.

16

OCTOBER TERM 1971

YRON WHITE was a stickler for the details of jurisdiction—the precise scope of the Court's power in a particular case—and he tended to read issues more narrowly than many of his colleagues. Both tendencies served larger goals of limiting the Court to its proper role. To appreciate his general approach, it is necessary to examine cases and terms in some detail. Three nonrandom terms, spanning his career, serve that function—October terms 1971, 1981, and 1991. In each, the content of the cases and the rhythm of the term help to depict the judge in action. The function of a judge, as White often reiterated, is to decide cases, not to write essays or to create theories. Term by term, his views developed, and in some areas he had second thoughts. Studying three terms helps to provide a broader context for White's career. Outside the Court, he remained a semiheroic figure to many—the model scholar-athlete, the intellectually rigorous man of action. Hero worship produced consequences both predictable (one hall of fame after another) and bizarre (an ad hoc draft movement for the 1972 presidential nomination).

Three terms provide only a snapshot of life inside and outside the Court, however. It is difficult to appreciate the sheer mass of work accomplished in thirty-one years of adjudication. During his tenure on the Supreme Court of the United States, White wrote 1,275 opinions—495 opinions of the Court, 249 concurring opinions, and 572 dissents (354 from decisions on the merits or as to jurisdiction, 218 from denials of certiorari). Regardless of whether he filed an opinion in a particular case, White was never a marginal figure after Warren's retirement.

A premature assessment of Byron White's career and impact on the Supreme Court was written by Nathan Lewin in the *New Republic* in 1984. Lewin declared, both in sorrow and in anger, that White was fulfilling the role on the Burger Court that William J. Brennan had served on the Warren Court—as the guiding intellectual influence of the institution. He noted, "A rough measure of a Supreme Court justice's success in affecting the outcome of cases is the number of dissenting votes he casts," but he added, "A more discriminating gauge is how frequently he or she is on the prevailing side on an issue decided by a margin of only one or two votes." By that measure, White was a central figure on the Court for most of his tenure. During his career, White participated in more than four thousand cases. He participated in more 5–4 decisions, 807, than any other justice in the history of the Court except William Brennan, who was in 893. White was in the majority in 526, or 65 percent of the time; Brennan was in the majority 44.6 percent of the time. Lewis Powell's figure was 68.7 percent. All three justices sat during a period in which the portion of decisions by a bare majority hovered near 20 percent each term.

Byron White defined himself by the votes he cast and by the opinions he wrote, but he did not view his written work as occasions for literary indulgence. Putting to one side the occasional puzzling concurrence or dissent, most of White's opinions are precise, methodical, and impatient to finish the job. The style reflects the character of the man. There are few lapidary lines or memorable turns of phrase. Yet his opinions, particularly in cases where he thought doctrinal clarity or intellectual honesty were not otherwise fully served, bear an urgent authenticity that testify to the importance he had to the institution.

The Warren Court, and the earthquake in constitutional activity with which it was identified, did not expire on June 23, 1969, when Warren retired. The transition was not complete until thirty months later, when Lewis F. Powell and William H. Rehnquist were sworn in to replace Hugo Black and John Harlan, who both retired prior to the beginning of October term 1971. Powell and Rehnquist joined two other appointees of Richard M. Nixon, Warren E. Burger (Earl Warren's successor), and Harry A. Blackmun, who replaced Abe Fortas after two other nominations were defeated in the Senate. The embarrassment of Fortas's resignation in disgrace was compounded by President Nixon's public search—shamelessly focused on the bottom of the legal barrel—for judges who would implement his campaign pledge to turn around the Court on crime and pornography. Powell and Rehnquist both received the ABA's highest rating after a baker's dozen of mediocre candidates were discarded, several after strategic public leaks to the press by sources within the ABA screening committee. Both were roughed up in their confirmation hearings—Powell for his memberships in whites-only clubs and his extensive stockholdings, Rehnquist for his doctrinaire views and political work—but both were comfortably confirmed. Powell and Rehnquist sat for only half of the 1971 term, participating in less than half the cases decided after full briefing and oral argument. They agreed with each other more than 75 percent of the time, however, which prompted Philip B. Kurland to observe in the *Supreme Court Review* that the "Minnesota Twins [Burger and Blackmun] have expanded into the Nixon quartet."

Whatever the ultimate effect of the four appointments made by Nixon, the early returns suggested that, with the exception of an aftershock or two, the Warren era had finally subsided. Prof. Alan M. Dershowitz even reported that civil rights organizations were planning for "lean years ahead" after their "run of victories" since 1962. One striking index of the immediate impact of the new appointees was Byron White himself: he had moved from the fringe to the dead center of the Court. The statistical array at the end of the 1971 term was startling. During the decade of the 1960s, White was a fixture on the periphery with the Warren Court. He found himself in the majority on 5-4 decisions in less than half the cases that Earl Warren presided over in the Supreme Court of the United States. For the 1971 term, he was in the majority in eighteen of nineteen cases decided by a 5-4 vote; Potter Stewart joined the Nixon quartet in the nineteenth case. White also wrote more majority or plurality opinions for the Court than any other justice during the term, nineteen, and fewer dissents, six, than anyone except Powell, who wrote two. White was assigned to write two other majority opinions—*Sierra Club v. Morton* and *United States v. United States District Court*—but they were among the half dozen misassignments made by Burger during the course of the term, a function more often of blunder than of design, although there were cases of both.*

---

* The chief justice was obliged by tradition to tally tentative votes and to assign opinions—as long as he was in the majority—to his colleagues. Burger's assignments often perplexed his colleagues early in his chief justiceship, and surviving conference notes suggest that he often misunderstood qualifications or emphases made by others. As a result, it was uncommon but not rare for him to assign an opinion to someone whose analysis of a case was singular—such as White in *U. S. District Court*. On occasion, colleagues would suspect that Burger manipulated his own vote in order to retain an assignment that properly belonged to another.

The solidity of the Nixon quartet provoked Kurland to label the 1971 term "the year of the Stewart-White Court." The arithmetic of the term suggests one more point beyond the new philosophical divides that seemed to be emerging. Despite being reduced to seven members for the first three months, the Court decided more cases on the merits than in any term since 1925, when the Judges Act made the Court's jurisdiction discretionary in all but a handful of categories of cases. By the end of the term, Chief Justice Burger would create a blue ribbon commission to examine and recommend remedies to what was conventionally viewed as a serious problem of overwork, an issue about which White would express forceful views over time.

Despite the number and variety of important cases that came to the Court during the term—including abortion, the death penalty, freedom of the press, procedural due process, and pornography—there was also a dog's breakfast of routine cases as well, and White drew the assignment on several: a patent case from the shrimping industry, a Federal Trade Commission case, a case sustaining the jurisdiction of the Federal Power Commission and deferring to the agency's fact finding, an admiralty case deferring to state jurisdiction over a longshoreman's injury on a pier, and two labor cases deferring to the National Labor Relations Board, one of which settled an important question of a takeover employer's obligations under a continuing collective bargaining agreement *(National Labor Relations Board v. Burns Int'l Security Services)*. During the term, Burger also assigned White to a number of internal committees of the Court, perhaps on the theory that the busiest man does the best job. In addition, with the departures of Tom Clark (replaced by Thurgood Marshall in 1967) as well as Black and Harlan, White was now fifth in seniority on the Court after Burger (ex officio), Douglas, Brennan, and Stewart. During the term, White served on committees to present the Court's budget to the pertinent subcommittee of the House of Representatives, to oversee "physical changes in the Court Chambers" (including reconfiguration of the bench from a straight line to a semicircle), to search for a new Court librarian, to interview candidates for Court legal officer, and to investigate whether a pool of law clerks should be established to provide a common memorandum on petitions for writs of certiorari.

On top of all of the work inside the Court—which put White in his chambers from 7 A.M. until 6 P.M. daily, with a long half day on Saturday—the term coincided with a bizarre White for President campaign, with the redoubtable Johnny Blood as self-styled publicity manager, quietly supported along the East Coast by a handful of friends who went so far as to organize a campaign steering committee. The "candidate" disclaimed interest in the job, as well as in the directorship of the Federal Bureau of Investigation, for which the unquenchable Washington rumor mill also had him slated.

Despite his newfound position at the Court's philosophical center, Byron White adopted neither new positions nor new techniques to express them. He remained an incrementalist, deciding issues a case at a time, and he perfected an opinion style that was intentionally opaque and self-effacing. As he had from his first three months on the Court, he avoided constitutional grounds for deciding a case where statutory grounds were available, and he avoided the sweeping statement or the multipart test as if he were allergic to them. Two cases demonstrate these fundamental tenets of White's judicial posture, *Peters v. Kiff* and *United States v. United States District Court.*

Peters is a minor but telling example. The question was whether a white defendant could obtain a new trial because blacks were systematically and intentionally excluded from the trial jury. Three justices, whose spokesman was Thurgood Marshall, concluded that the Fourteenth Amendment required invalidation of the verdict, without a showing of prejudice in fact to the defendant and regardless of whether race was even an issue in the case. White, speaking for himself plus Brennan and Powell, rested their vote for a new trial on the federal statute prohibiting race in jury selection, which dated to Reconstruction and which the Court had upheld shortly thereafter. White quoted the governing statute—18 U.S.C. §243—and declared that "by this unambiguous provision . . . Congress put cases involving exclusions from jury service on the grounds of race in a class by themselves." He then quoted a case decided during the term he clerked for Vinson: "For us the majestic generalities of the Fourteenth Amendment are thus reduced to a concrete statutory command." The balance of the three-page opinion concluded that the race of the defendant is irrelevant to the operation of the statute. *Peters* was what had become a typical White opinion: point one, point two, point three—all resting on statute and case law—no tests and no personalized cast on the relevant terrain of authority.

White wrote the same type of opinion, although necessarily at greater length, in the *United States District Court* case. The case raised the question whether the president, acting through the attorney general, could tap telephones to detect threats to domestic security without obtaining judicial authorization. The Court held unanimously that he could not, although White—unlike his colleagues—rested his conclusion on the pertinent statute and not on the Constitution. Again, White was anxious that a broad constitutional ruling—cast, as Justice Powell would often do, in terms of "balancing" competing interests—was being decided on the basis of a paper-thin record: one affidavit, some materials submitted *in camera* to the district court, and a pretrial hearing. "My own conclusion," he wrote, "is that, as long as nonconstitutional, statutory grounds for excluding the evidence or fruits have not been disposed of, it is improvident to reach the constitutional issue."

When constitutional issues could not be avoided, White reiterated a strategic approach he developed during the Warren era: simply because a provision of the Constitution applied to the states, that did not mean that federal standards needed to be incorporated wholesale. Three opinions for the Court during the term reprise the strategy first developed in *Duncan v. Louisiana* in 1968 (the Sixth Amendment right to jury trial applies against the states, but not necessarily for petty offenses) and *Williams v. Florida* in 1970 (the *Duncan* right is satisfied by six-man juries as well as the traditional twelve). Two of the cases were fallout from *Duncan* and *Williams—Johnson v. Louisiana* and *Apodaca v. Oregon*. A third, *Lindsey v. Normet*, was a challenge, based on both due process and equal protection, to the Oregon Forcible Entry and Wrongful Detainer Statute. The statute provided for trial six days after an eviction notice unless the tenant posted security; the statute also precluded the tenant from defending nonpayment of the rent due to the landlord's failure to maintain the premises.

White's opinion for the Court in *Lindsey* brought to the surface the views he uttered privately about the Warren Court's penchant for constitutionalizing social problems. To the tenants' claim that the statute unconstitutionally impinged a "fundamental interest," White's opinion replied:

> We do not denigrate the importance of decent, safe and sanitary housing. But the Constitution does not provide judicial remedies for every social and economic ill. We are unable to perceive in that document any constitutional guarantee of access to dwellings of a particular quality, or any recognition of the right of a tenant to occupy the real property of his landlord beyond the term of his lease without the payment of rent or otherwise contrary to the terms of the relevant agreement. Absent constitutional mandate, the assurance of adequate housing and the definition of landlord-tenant relationships are legislative, not judicial functions. Nor should we forget that the Constitution expressly protects against confiscation of private property or the income therefrom.

White spoke only for a plurality in *Apodaca,* which upheld nonunanimous jury verdicts in state criminal cases. (*Johnson,* with White speaking for a 5-4 Court, applied the same rule to cases that arose before *Duncan.*) Professor

Kurland remarked with characteristic tartness that "the essential difficulty" of the plurality position in *Apodaca* "lies in the proposition that a page of reason is worth a volume of history." White acknowledged that the eighteenth-century common law required unanimity in jury verdicts, but pointed out that the drafters of the Sixth Amendment abandoned express insistence on unanimity in favor of ambiguity; ergo, unanimity was now not necessary. (In fact, unanimity was a postconstitutional development.) Finally, ran the argument, the function—a favorite emphasis of White—of the jury was "well secured" by majority verdicts.

The *Apodaca–Johnson* argument reveals White at his most tendentious. To prevent wholesale incorporation of the Bill of Rights from imposing costly and novel obligations on the states, White was willing to sin against his own lights in multiple respects. He treats the Constitution, which he was fond of saying was not to be construed "like a deed" setting forth its "precise metes and bounds," as if it were an ambiguous statute whose meaning could be illuminated, at least negatively, by legislative history; he analyzes history at a level of generality that ignores contemporary functional understanding, but then relies on its function in "contemporary society" with no factual foundation to support his confidence.

A month later, in *Branzburg v. Hayes,* he would reject a journalist's claim that the Constitution afforded him a privilege not to divulge sources to a grand jury because there was no evidence that being forced to testify would hamstring the newsgathering function. White emphasized in *Branzburg* that another function—the system of law enforcement—was also at stake; thus, in light of the competing interests and the lack of evidence that the privilege was necessary to newsmen, invention of another constitutional right was not warranted:

> Neither are we now convinced that a virtually impenetrable constitutional shield, beyond legislative or judicial control, should be forged to protect a private system of informers operated by the press to report on criminal conduct, a system that would be unaccountable to the public, would pose a threat to the citizen's justifiable expectations of privacy, and would equally protect well-intentioned informants and those who for pay or otherwise betray their trust to their employer or associates.

Branzburg was reviled by the press when it was handed down and has been subjected to a great deal of thoughtful criticism, but one point deserves emphasis, because it reaffirms White's consistency and evenhandedness in cases involving the press. Beginning with *Estes v. Texas* in 1965, White refused to be doctrinaire in measuring novel claims by the press. Dissenting from the reversal of a conviction because a trial was televised, White wrote in *Estes*:

> The opinion of the Court in effect precludes further opportunity for intelligent assessment of the probable hazards imposed by the use of cameras at criminal trials. Serious threats to constitutional rights in some instances justify a prophylactic rule dispensing with the necessity of showing specific prejudice in a particular case [such as *Jackson v. Denno*]. But these are instances in which there has been ample experience on which to base an informed judgment. Here, although our experience is inadequate and our judgment correspondingly infirm, the Court discourages further meaningful study of the use of television at criminal trials.

Faced with the choice between an allegation of prejudice with no empirical basis and a documented effect that could be weighed and assessed—almost cross-examined—White almost never chose the hypothetical. White's consistency on this point in the press cases underscores his disingenuousness in the run of jury cases beginning with *Duncan* and continuing through the 1971 term. His comfortable assumption in *Apodaca* and its companion case that a nonunanimous jury would effectively serve the same function of a unanimous jury and would not undermine the reasonable-doubt standard of proof applicable in criminal cases sets a constitutional standard that obviously "precludes further opportunity for intelligent assessment of the probable hazards imposed by" the nonunanimity rule; the evils of wholesale incorporation apparently outweighed reliance on faith rather than fact.

Although Byron White and others wrote opinions closing the doors on novel constitutional rights throughout the term, the new Court was not absolutely hostile to innovative exercises of judicial power. The paradoxical legacy of the 1971 term is that it provided the centerpiece evidence for later judgments that the Burger Court constituted a "counter-revolution that wasn't." The three most significant examples of judicial audacity during the term were *Eisenstadt v. Baird,* which extended constitutional protection to the use of contraceptives by couples whether they were married or not; *Morrissey v. Brewer,* which held the due process clause applicable to parole revocation proceedings and implicitly to much of the penal process; and *Furman v. Georgia,* which invalidated the death penalty as then implemented and in effect imposed a moratorium on capital punishment while states decided how to respond to the five opinions supporting the judgment. White, who had established himself as a skeptic toward expansive development of constitutional

rights, surprisingly concurred in all three decisions and even wrote brief concurring opinions in both *Eisenstadt* and *Furman*.

A year before, he had concurred in Justice Harlan's opinion for a six-man
majority in *McGautha v. California* holding that unfettered jury discretion
over the death penalty did not violate due process of law. Now he seemed to
have second thoughts. Although White agreed that the due process clause did
not prevent a trial jury from exercising its discretion in death cases, he was
now moved by the utterly arbitrary decision-making process in all three
cases—a process unstructured, unaccountable, and inevitably inconsistent
from case to case. A defendant never knew where he stood once he was caught
in the maw of the system, and for White even criminal defendants were entitled to know the stakes in preparing their cases. The votes did not come easy,
however, because he had an abiding—some thought romantic—belief in the
good faith of public officials. He refused, in the apt phrase of Prof. Kate Stith,
to insist "on perfection from police, prosecutors and others charged with
achieving criminal justice." When arbitrary behavior became chronic, and
empty standards or their absence made consistency impossible and review im-
practicable, White was willing to intervene.

None of his votes against structural arbitrariness is explained in so many
words by his opinions—although he comes close in his brief statement in the
capital punishment cases. That reticence is one of the troubling features of
White's judicial record and more than any other factor makes his jurisprudence opaque. For someone who was widely admired by his colleagues for the
force and clarity of his arguments in conference, White wrote opinions that
were often densely presented and no better than implicit about their theoretical premises. To some extent, he went out of his way to be obscure. For example, one of his clerks during the 1971 term prepared the first draft of an
opinion in a major case and received an unexpected compliment that turned
out surprisingly to be doubled edged: "You write very well," White told the
clerk. "Justice Jackson had that problem, too." The implication, not developed in the ensuing critique of the draft, was that Jackson relied too often on
memorable images and turns of phrase in place of meticulous respect for careful reasoning or for the Court's case law. The function of the opinion, White
made clear to the clerk, was not to draw attention to its own elegance but to
get the job done precisely and unobtrusively. Tactics for self-effacement went
to inelegant extremes: sentences written by White in the passive voice and
converted into punchy, active sentences drafted by law clerks were reedited by
the justice back into the often cumbersome passive voice. Tests, especially presented in multipart form (such as the "three-prong *Lemon* test" or the "least

drastic means test") were verboten. The emphasis was to be on the Court's case law, not on tests, quotations, or history.

White found most constitutional history outside the case law inconclusive. The works of Thomas Jefferson were banned from White's opinions in *United States v. Gravel*, which extended the protection of the speech and debate clause to Senate aides performing legislative functions, and in *United States v. Brewster*, in which he dissented from a ruling that the clause was no defense to a criminal bribery charge. *If we quote Jefferson*, White told his clerks, *so will the other side. And both will be right, because Jefferson was on both sides of a lot of issues. So Jefferson is out.* White stuck to his guns in both cases, but others did not. Although history was banished from his opinions, White was not absolutely hostile to the craft. While the internal deliberations over *Brewster* boiled, White presented each of his clerks the identical Christmas present—a copy of Bernard Bailyn's *The Ideological Origins of the American Revolution*. (The gift was presented without sentiment, inscribed simply, "Dec. 23, 1971, From Justice White.") When White discussed the book later with its recipients, he seemed to be impressed without being moved by Bailyn's work. "I had the impression that the justice admired the scholarship but thought Bailyn went out the same door he came in," one of the clerks recalled later. (As for instant history, such as journalism in hardback form, White had even less patience. When Victor Navasky published his highly critical study of Robert Kennedy's attorney generalship, *Kennedy Justice*, in the fall of 1971, White remarked: "If Navasky is right, we might as well have all stayed home.")

The ideal opinion for White tracked the English model. "He was very taken with the English appellate system," the clerk remembered. "'Look at their opinions,' he said once; 'they develop naturally out of the precedent and resolve the case without a lot of fuss. They stick to the cases.'" It would be wrong to conclude that White routinely tried to mimic the English style— that is, self-consciously personal instead of oracular in voice, tied tightly to authority, and detailing no more of the record than necessary. White's opinions at this stage of his career varied in style, although his separate opinions—especially his short concurring or dissenting statements—were beginning to be more pointed and personal in their expression of his convictions. At bottom, opinions were to be modest, no matter how aggressively argued, because they were secondary to the judgment. "An opinion is just another argument," he told his '71 term clerks, "an argument to the future. It may explain the decision in the case, but it is a claim and a claim only." White was proud of his written work and, one of his clerks that term thought, "bitterly disappointed that academics didn't perceive better what he was trying to do."

White's questioning in oral argument was occasionally almost as puzzling as his opinions. While other members of the Court went straight to the merits of a case, White often focused on threshold questions of jurisdiction (whether a court has power to decide a case or an issue), standing (whether the person raising an issue is the proper one to do so), and—especially during the 1970s—abstention (whether a federal court should let a state court decide a case first before asserting its power). Lawyers arguing before the Court found White to be aggressive and insistent, sometimes quickly nailing the weak link of their argument, at other times amusing himself by asking how a tangential case bore on a peripheral point of their position. All that united what one advocate called "the dual instinct for the jugular and the capillary" was White's drive to pin down each position, limit the scope of a claim, reduce issues where practicable, and extract concessions if possible. The method, first in oral argument and then in both conference room and opinion, was designed to achieve an almost English definition of the judicial role—to decide the narrowest issue presented by the record with the least pretentious opinion, unless the Court reached further, at which point all bets were off. David Kendall, one of the clerks during the 1971 term, later described White as an "inductive reasoner. With each case, he spreads a deck of cards with every conceivable factual variation. He tries to resolve those variations, narrowing them, and work inductively to what the rule in the case should be." The give-and-take had a competitive format but not a competitive ethos: "He wasn't invested in an argument; you could hit him with a chair, intellectually speaking, [and] he could be convinced."

White's incisiveness in oral argument is illustrated by his exchange in the first argument of *Roe v. Wade* on December 13, 1971, when he pinned down the plaintiff's lawyer, twenty-nine-year-old Sarah Weddington, on the source of her claim that the Constitution precluded states from prohibiting abortions, except "for the purpose of saving the life of the mother." Eight months earlier in *United States v. Vuitch*, the Court had upheld, against a claim of vagueness, a District of Columbia law prohibiting abortions except where a mother's life or health was in danger. After forcing Weddington to concede that her argument was the same regardless of the time in the pregnancy that the abortion was sought, White asked:

> What about whatever clause of the Constitution you rest on—Ninth Amendment, due process, the general pattern penumbra—that take you right up to the time of birth?

Weddington: It is our position that the freedom involved is that of a woman to determine whether or not to continue a pregnancy. Obviously I have a much more difficult time saying that the State has no interest in late pregnancy.

White: Why? Why is that?

Weddington: I think that's more the emotional response to a late pregnancy, rather than it is any constitutional—

White: Emotional response by whom?

Weddington: I guess by persons considering the issue outside the legal context, I think, as far as the State—

White: Well, do you or don't you say that the constitutional—

Weddington: I would say the constitutional—

White:—right you insist on reaches up to the time of birth, or—

Weddington: The Constitution, as I read it . . . attaches protection to the person at the time of birth. Those persons born are citizens. The enumeration clause, we count those people who are born, the Constitution, as I see it, gives protection to people after birth.

When the Court met in conference three days later to vote on the case, White was the only unequivocal vote to uphold both the Texas and Georgia statutes at issue. Despite Chief Justice Burger's hesitant vote to join White in upholding the Georgia statute, Burger assigned both opinions to Harry Blackmun, who came out the other way. The assignment provoked Douglas to fury at Burger, which started with internal memoranda but eventually spilled into the *Washington Post* when the cases were set over for reargument in the next term. A major reason for putting the cases over was the chilly reception that Blackmun's draft opinions received even from those on his side, favoring invalidation of the law.

Blackmun circulated opinions on May 18 in *Roe* (the Texas case) and in *Doe* on May 25, and on May 29 White circulated a sharp, terse three-page dissent in *Roe* that attacked Blackmun's conclusion that the Texas statute was vague—as the three-judge court below had concluded. White's argument was simple and based on fresh precedent, *Vuitch:*

If a standard which refers to the "health" of the mother, a referent which necessarily entails the resolution of perplexing questions about the interrelationship of physical, emotional, and mental well-being, is not impermissibly vague, a statutory standard which focuses only on "saving the life" of the mother would appear to be *a fortiori* acceptable.

White added that if "called upon to reconsider this Court's decision in *Vuitch,* I would reaffirm it and would not, therefore, void the Texas statute on vagueness grounds." He concluded that no Texas doctor would fail to understand the reach of the state statute.*

White's narrow and technically oriented argument may have been aimed at buying time late in the term so that he could pick up a wavering vote or raise a knotty issue that could be revisited if the cases were reargued in the fall. The draft became moot two days after it was circulated. A flurry of memos crossed in the marble halls of the Court, and the cases were set for reargument—with Burger, White, and Blackmun himself leading the way against the reasoned demurral of William Brennan and the anger of Douglas, who drafted but did not generally circulate a four-page statement condemning Burger and his colleagues "for allowing the consensus of the Court to be manipulated for unworthy objectives." Brennan talked Douglas out of publishing the statement, but the *Washington Post* printed a well-informed account of the story a month later. Douglas had tried to portray Burger as sabotaging a settled—or settling—majority of the Court by asking for more argument and more deliberation, but his harsh accusations were unfair. The author of the putative majority opinion (Blackmun) was not satisfied with his work, nor was another member of the majority (Stewart); Brennan and Douglas were the only members of the Court who thought more time for deliberation was unnecessary. Burger had undermined his own leadership during the term with several bungled assignments, but his efforts to obtain reargument in *Roe v. Wade* hardly justified Douglas's tirade.

Reargument only hardened White in his position. His questions at reargument on October 11, 1972, looked less to precedent and more to the emotional policy issues at stake. He asked Weddington if the case involved "weighing one life against another" and whether, if the fetus were a person for constitutional purposes, the state could justify "choos[ing] to kill the innocent one." Blackmun circulated his draft opinions, which he had worked on over the summer, forty days after reargument. White waited until January 11 to circulate his dissent in both cases, now reduced to two pages, stripped of technical points, and dripping with indignation. It would be his most quoted opinion as a justice and his least lawyerly, although he could have traced the intellectual pedigree of his position directly to his dissent in *Robinson v. Cali-*

---

* The District of Columbia code provision at issue provided: "Whoever, by means of any instrument, medicine, drug or other means whatever, procures or produces, or attempts to procure or produce an abortion or miscarriage on any woman, unless the same were done as necessary for the preservation of the mother's life or health and under the direction of a competent licensed practitioner or medicine, shall be imprisoned in the penitentiary not less than one year or not more than ten years."

fornia: the wages of *Robinson's* free-form approach to due process of law was the majority opinion in *Roe v. Wade.* His opening paragraph cited reasons why "recurring pregnancies" posing "no danger whatsoever to the life or health of the mother but are nevertheless unwanted" are terminated—convenience, family planning, economics, dislike of children, the embarrassment of illegitimacy, etc." Then a remarkably insensitive sentence—and one that would tear old friendships and even, twenty years later, cause a former colleague to refuse to participate in a *Festschrift* in his honor at retirement:

> The common claim before us is that for any one of such reasons, or for no reason at all, and without asserting or claiming any threat to life or health, any woman is entitled to an abortion at her request if she is able to find a medical advisor willing to undertake the procedure.

"Or for no reason at all" suggested to many that the man who prided himself on mastery of empirical data relevant to his cases and sensitive to the effect of rule on reality was, at best, uninformed. White may have intended to describe the unfettered operation of the rule, which his statement accurately did, but his language sounded to many readers as if he were describing a pregnant woman's state of mind. "I couldn't believe he wrote that," an old friend who was a lawyer said later. "He sounded so callous about the choice a woman faces." There is no evidence that White ever tried to clarify the point privately, although he told several law clerks late in his career that if he had been a legislator he would "have been pro-choice."

White's objection was not to abortion but to its judicial—and constitutional—genesis. Years after the decision, he would confide to Ira Rothgerber that he viewed *Roe v. Wade* as the *only illegitimate decision the Court rendered during my tenure. In every other case, there was something in the Constitution you could point to for support. There, nothing.* The confidential declaration was hardly a revelation. The heart of the six-paragraph opinion was the third, and the author's voice was unmistakable:

> With all due respect, I dissent. I find nothing in the language or history of the Constitution to support the Court's judgment. The Court simply fashions and announces a new constitutional right for pregnant mothers and, with scarcely any reason or authority for its action, invests that right with sufficient substance to override most existing state abortion statutes. The upshot is that the people and legislatures of the 50 States are constitutionally disentitled to weigh the relative importance of the continued existence and development of the fetus, on the one hand, against a spectrum of possible impact on

the mother, on the other hand. As an exercise of raw judicial power, the Court perhaps has authority to do what it does today; but in my view its judgment is an improvident and extravagant exercise of the power of judicial review that the Constitution extends to this Court.

He cited *Vuitch* in the penultimate paragraph of the opinion, but the force of his remarks rests less on doctrine than on the fundamental limits of judicial review: the Court, with "no constitutional warrant," has usurped the political processes and imposed choices "on the people and legislatures of the States."

In succeeding terms, White would never vote to support the right identified in *Roe* and *Doe*. Unlike all other areas, in which several years of reaffirmation settled doctrine and dictated his acceptance of a line of authority even where he had dissented at first, abortion was an exception. An illegitimate decision was entitled to no respect. Nor was the doctrine fit for internal debate. Clerk after clerk, year after year, recalls spirited debate over every issue on the docket except one: "When he got to an abortion case," one clerk from the mid-1980s recalled, "he would get a sheepish look on his face and just turn over the file folder which contained his notes and our memos. The message was clear: there was nothing to talk about." The last time he was tempted to write about abortion was in 1989, when state regulations of the procedure were in issue; he debated with himself at length but finally decided not to write anything.

The abortion cases were at the center of a growing constitutional area that touched Byron White deeply but for which his previous experiences provided few soundings. During the 1971 term, several evolving constitutional questions about family relationships were heard by the Court, including child custody laws and compulsory school attendance laws, as well as laws regulating contraceptive devices and abortion. White voted to hear all of the cases that the Court took presenting these questions. In one case—*Stanley v. Illinois*—he even succeeded in turning around the Court.

Stanley was brought by an unmarried father who lost custody of his two minor children when their mother died. Illinois courts upheld the statutory presumption that unwed fathers were unfit to raise their minor children but did not make the same presumption about unmarried mothers. The Court granted certiorari to decide whether the procedure and its presumption were valid, as White tendentiously framed the issue, "in light of the fact that Illinois allows married fathers—whether divorced, widowed, or separated—and mothers—even if unwed—the benefit of the presumption that they are fit to raise their children." After argument Justice Brennan was assigned to draft a per curiam opinion dismissing the petition as improvidently granted because the constitutional issue—whether the statutory scheme violated the equal protection clause—had not been appropriately presented in the lower courts. White dashed off a ten-page dissent, which he circulated a few days after Brennan's draft, and the Court soon voted 5-2 to reverse on the basis of White's opinion. White's success in turning around the Court was one of three instances during the term in which he wrote an opinion that drew enough support to change the tentative result voted by the conference (the others were *Burns*—the labor case—and *United States v. Biswell,* which upheld a warrantless regulatory search pursuant to federal gun laws).

The achievement was not without some irony. The persuasive force of his opinion in *Stanley* lay in his statement of the facts: unwed fathers seeking to retain custody of their children faced hurdles—often insurmountable in fact—that unwed mothers did not. His statement of the issue, already quoted, stacked the analytical deck. The irony of the opinion lay in the case law that White relied on to support his conclusion that the asymmetry of presumptions violated the due process clause—*Meyer v. Nebraska,* the 1923 decision upholding the constitutional right to learn German in public schools, and *Skinner v. Oklahoma,* the 1942 opinion by Douglas vindicating the right not to be punished by sterilization for repeat property crimes. White's *Stanley* opinion stated:

> The integrity of the family unit has found protection in the Due Process Clause of the Fourteenth Amendment, Meyer v. Nebraska, *supra,* 262 U.S. at 399, the Equal Protection Clause of the Fourteenth Amendment, Skinner v. Oklahoma, *supra,* 316 U.S., at 541, and the Ninth Amendment, Griswold v. Connecticut, 381 U.S. 479, 496 (1965) (Goldberg, J., concurring).

Those decisions had established the importance of the unmarried father's interest. *Bell v. Burson,* which decided the previous term that due process required a hearing before terminating a motor vehicle driver's license, provided the entire doctrinal foundation for the decision. All four cases were relied upon by Justice Blackmun in his tentative draft opinions in the abortion cases, which were circulated within the Court two weeks after *Stanley* was handed down. (Even after reargument, Blackmun's opinion in *Roe v. Wade* leaned heavily on *Meyer* and another decision from the period, *Pierce v. Society of Sisters,* securing the constitutional right of parents to send their children to nonpublic schools, to establish the "liberty" component of the due process clause analysis.) *Meyer v. Nebraska* thus supported both *Stanley* and *Roe v. Wade.*

White and Blackmun were on opposing sides in both *Stanley* and *Roe*. The precedent had a somewhat plastic content, capable of taking different judges in different directions, depending on the issue. For White, it was a predicate to further analysis under the equal protection clause. For Blackmun, it did more: it resolved the ultimate question in *Roe v. Wade*, an analytical stretch that was uniformly condemned by scholarly critics of the decision.

White's vote with the majority during his third full term on the Court in *Griswold v. Connecticut* (to protect access by married couples to contraceptives) looked incongruous after his dissent in *Roe v. Wade*, but it rested on the same foundation as his equally insistent position in *Stanley v. Illinois*—profound, almost preconstitutional respect for the marriage relationship and the family unit. At bottom, as important as he valued the link between the parent or parents and the child in these cases, he manifested particular concern for the children themselves. His comments during the Court's conference vote on *Wisconsin v. Yoder*, which ultimately invalidated a state compulsory-school-attendance law for Amish youth of high school age, focused neither on the question of religious freedom nor on the state's countervailing interests but on the students: "[There is] little talk of [the] interests of the children. Rights of children have independent standing. They are not competent to make [the] decisions [the] Amish want." When *Yoder* was issued in mid-May 1972, White filed a brief concurring opinion, which Brennan and Stewart joined, that emphasized the limited scope of the decision. "Cases such as this one inevitably call for a delicate balancing of important but conflicting interests," he began and explained that he concurred because "I cannot say that the State's interest in requiring two more years of compulsory education in the ninth and tenth grades outweighs the importance of the concededly sincere Amish religious practice to survival of that sect." White emphasized that the Amish were not claiming to be exempt from all schooling or from meeting state educational requirements, and he went out of his way to point out testimony "in the record that many children desert the Amish faith when they come of age"—evidence that many Amish children would consequently be victimized if they were deprived of the secular training provided by the state at the elementary level.

For White, *Wisconsin v. Yoder* was a case about sectarian children preparing for multiple societies, as much as or more than about what the majority grandly called the "demands of the religion clauses." The case, and particularly how he cast the issue, underscored an inconsistency in White's jurisprudence: the stickler for law, with little patience for social engineering, could vote and speak like a legislator in areas touching the family—such as *Yoder*,

Griswold, and *Stanley.* The sanctity of the family structure, as he conceived it, was central to Byron White as a judge.

As well as the cases that were resolved during the 1971 term, there were several, in addition to the abortion cases, that could not be resolved by the time the Court rose for the summer on June 29. In two instances, White played a central but externally invisible role. In one case, *Gibson v. Berryhill,* he circulated a dissent from the Court's proposed summary disposition affirming a federal three-judge court's injunction. At the time, state judicial or quasi-judicial proceedings could be enjoined by special courts composed of three federal judges if they concluded that the state proceedings violated the Constitution. The lower court's order in *Gibson* prevented the Alabama State Board of Optometry from conducting a hearing to determine whether certain optometrists were conducting their trade illegally. The decision was one of many during the period that, stripped of their technicality, presented the fundamental issue of federal government: when is it constitutionally appropriate for the national court system to interfere with properly constituted adjudicative exercises of state government?

White was deeply concerned by the question, but his memorandum to his colleagues focused exclusively on technical issues. Although only four pages of typescript, the dissent was vintage White. He blasted away at the disposition (1) for being inconsistent with a recent state supreme court decision upholding the board's procedures, (2) for circumventing the federal anti-injunction act (28 U.S.C. §2283), (3) for concluding that *Younger v. Harris* did not apply to civil proceedings—a conclusion that White thought dubious—and, in any event, (4) for deciding an issue possibly raised in an argued but undecided case, *Mitchum v. Foster:* "Presented, thus, with a conflict between a three-judge court and a state supreme court, with an important consideration as to the implementation of §2283 and with substantial and unresolved *Younger* issues, I dissent from affirmance without argument or opinion. At the very least we should await our decision in *Mitchum.*" The circulation stopped the Court in its tracks. The Court noted probable jurisdiction in the case a week after *Mitchum* was decided, and White wrote the Court's opinion the following term vacating and remanding the lower court's injunction.

The episode was a minor skirmish in the long road between *Dombrowski v. Pfister* in 1965 and *Hicks v. Miranda* a decade later, in which the Court decided when it was appropriate for federal courts to enjoin criminal, civil, "quasi-criminal," and administrative proceedings. White recognized the practical and doctrinal importance of *Gibson,* however, and his meticulous attention to jurisdiction—especially as it affected federal-state relations—compelled him not to let the case slip through the cracks. The case was also important to him because it was within the class of cases that Congress required the Court to approve or reverse (mandatory jurisdiction by appeal). The vestiges of the Court's mandatory jurisdiction often were treated too casually under Burger's administration, a pattern that troubled White and that he worked to minimize.

In another typescript circulated a week after the draft dissent in *Gibson v. Berryhill,* White threw a monkey wrench in a draft memorandum prepared by the chief justice, designed to solve the intractable problem of providing a workable definition of obscenity for the lower courts. The chief justice's draft, known by the lead case of *United States v. 12 200-Feet Reels of Super 8mm Film,* was highly rhetorical, failed its objective, and broke some doctrinal china in the process. White's dense four-hundred-word dissenting statement pointed out a "transparently erroneous" characterization of a year-old case on point and then explained how either the chief justice's memorandum had to be changed, the year-old precedent repudiated, or "prevailing overbreadth" doctrine reconsidered—awkward in light of a major decision on point, three weeks away from being issued. Justice Blackmun soon expressed agreement with White, Burger backpedaled, others joined the fray, and the cases were put over for reargument in the following term.

A final example of White's review of circulating opinions drafted by others is trivial but for the fact that the papers of his colleagues contain countless examples of such "fly-specking" by him. In his proposed opinion for the Court in *Morrissey v. Brewer,* the chief justice dropped a footnote suggesting the utility of state-provided legal assistants for parolees wishing to challenge threatened revocation. White joined Burger's opinion, "with the suggestion, however, that you eliminate or modify the last sentence of footnote 17 in view of the fact that the circuits are in conflict on the question and we once granted a case to decide the issue." The passage was dropped. In each example, White acted quickly (within two days in *Morrissey*), went straight to the substantive issue with no wasted words, and forged tight arguments with high impact. To some extent, the internally circulated memoranda reveal White at his best and at his most valuable to the institution. The examples could be multiplied in term after term, generally in cases with more doctrinal intricacy or complicated records than the three that occurred during the 1971 term and for which documentary evidence survives.

White's internal memos, prepared for the eyes of his colleagues only, may be his best—the judge as pure legal analyst. They are clear, sharp, and forceful, and they display strengths of both synthesis and analysis in areas of technical complexity. Perhaps most important, they understand doctrine from the standpoint of both judge and justice, from below and above: Which issue is unresolved? How does this doctrine affect that line of cases? Should one issue be resolved by reconsidering another? Once the internal debate was over, White's concurring or dissenting opinions too often were self-indulgent; they became rhetorically personalized statements, at least in cases with high public profile and low technical content—instances of *having my say,* a phrase he often used about his opinions, usually in highly contentious areas where state-craft and political theory bore more heavily on the outcome than did conventional legal analysis. The opinions for the Court, on the other hand, generally adopted a faceless, restless style that resolved the case and drew as little attention to themselves as possible. The exception was when he had the opportunity to rationalize a muddled line of authority, especially where he could draw down his own intellectual inventory—prior concurring or dissenting opinions; then the new opinions brush away arguments like annoying houseflies and nail down the doctrine as tightly as possible.

There is no example of the final category of opinion during the 1971 term, but *Colten v. Kentucky* at the end of term represents a bridge between a first strike and a final blow to the worst excesses of the "vagueness/overbreadth" doctrines then in vogue. The twin doctrines invalidated laws when they were expressed in such general terms that either (*a*) a potential defendant would not know that his actions were covered (vagueness) or (*b*) both constitutionally protected and unprotected activity could be covered (overbreadth). (A feature of the overbreadth doctrine provided that anyone arrested could have the law invalidated for its potential application to innocent behavior regardless of his or her own circumstances.) The Supreme Court used the vagueness and overbreadth doctrines during the 1960s like an all-purpose utility man to dispose of statutes or investigations—particularly in cases involving loyalty oaths and freedom of association—that it deemed unsavory, as even a friendly critic conceded. Unfriendly critics, less charitable about the Court's tendentiousness, redubbed the doctrine the "vague-for-voidness cases."

White viewed the Court's cases just as critically, to the point that he would even resist using the word "vagueness" when he disagreed with decisions that employed the doctrine. White first tried to rein in the doctrine's unruly horses in *Baggett v. Bullitt* during his second full term on the Court, and the project became so consuming that both of his clerks, Rex Lee and Lee Albert, worked with White on the project. "The case, really the vagueness part, just consumed the chambers for what seemed like months," Lee later recalled. "He tried to straighten everything out all at once, and it just didn't work." The goal was to craft a standard for trial judges to test whether the law in question put the average person on notice of whether he risked prosecution. Colloquially, according to Lee, White called it the "'any fool should know' standard." After failing to make any real headway in *Baggett v. Bullitt,* White finally made progress in a different Court several years later with a dissent in *Coates v. City of Cincinnati,* in October term 1970, which used the vagueness tactic to overturn a conviction for "annoying" sidewalk passersby. In *Colten* during the 1971 term, White spoke for a seven-man majority that affirmed a conviction for "disorderly conduct" after the defendant refused to leave the scene of a congested traffic-ticketing scene. The opinion of the Court explained that the

> root of the vagueness doctrine is a rough idea of fairness. It is not a principle designed to convert into a constitutional dilemma the practical difficulties in drawing criminal statutes both general enough to take into account a variety of human conduct and sufficiently specific to provide fair warning that certain kinds of conduct are prohibited. We agree with the Kentucky court when it said: "We believe that citizens who desire to obey the statute will have no difficulty in understanding it. . . ."

White's opinion also rejected Colten's overbreadth argument by emphasizing that the state court had provided an interpretation of the statute that narrowed its scope and thus eliminated the overbreadth vice. The 1971 term would be remembered for a more famous vagueness decision—*Papachristou v. City of Jacksonville*—Justice Douglas's poetic opinion relying on Vachel Lindsay and Henry David Thoreau to invalidate a Jacksonville vagrancy ordinance that included among its definition of vagrants "rogues and vagabonds, or dissolute persons who go about begging," "common drunkards," "common night walkers," "habitual loafers," and "persons wandering or strolling around from place to place without any lawful purpose or object." (Douglas found that the final two categories had been celebrated in song and verse throughout the nation's history.)

Colten set the stage for *Broadrick v. Oklahoma* two years later, in 1973, in which White finally succeeded in cutting the overbreadth doctrine down to size. Speaking for a bare majority, he reviewed the development and application of the doctrine in painstaking detail and concluded that

> where conduct and not merely speech is involved, we believe that the overbreadth of a statute must not only be real, but substantial as well, judged in relation to the statute's plainly legitimate sweep. It is our view that [the statute in question] is not substantially overbroad and that whatever over-

breadth may exist should be cured through case-by-case analysis of the fact situations to which its sanctions, assertedly, may not be applied.

The overbreadth doctrine thus became the "substantial overbreadth" doctrine, vastly more limited in scope than before and now unlikely to excuse prohibitable behavior under a statute capable of being applied both properly and improperly. *Broadrick* was one of White's most significant achievements and resulted from the author's signature strategy, which stretched over several terms: a long, slow build-up of case-by-case analysis culminating in a recapitulation that redefines, and narrows, as it restates. The opinion is not lyrically or stylishly turned, but effective to its purpose.

No matter how hard he tried to cordon off his athletic past, his former identity remained inescapable. A few months before the 1971 term began, he was elected to the Washington Touchdown Club Hall of Fame, and his photograph—in judicial robes—appeared alongside headlines of "TD Hall." A life-size oil portrait, copied from a photograph of him punting during his senior year in college, was installed at the club. On one occasion during the term, he even came face-to-face with his past, although the newspapers did not realize it. On March 21, 1972, the Court heard oral arguments in *M/S Bremen v. Zapata Off-Shore Company.* Zapata owned a drilling rig that was damaged while being towed across the Gulf of Mexico by the *Bremen* in a storm. The parties had negotiated a choice-of-forum clause, which provided for disputes arising under the contract to be heard in London. Zapata nonetheless sued in a Florida federal court, which declined to enforce the clause. The court of appeals en banc affirmed over a powerful dissent by Judge John Minor Wisdom, the most distinguished scholar on his court. The Supreme Court held that the clause was valid and remanded the case. The chief justice spoke for the Court; Douglas dissented; White filed a two-sentence concurring opinion, reflecting views he stated at the Court's conference to emphasize that issues remained open on remand and implicitly that the Court had not ruled absolutely against Zapata.

In a sense, it was White's second nod in the case. Zapata's case was argued by James K. Nance of the Baker & Botts firm in Houston. White's clerks were oblivious to Nance's significance, and White himself said nothing to them about him. Harry Blackmun, who sat to White's left on the bench, prided himself on appreciating the larger contexts of oral arguments, as he later explained to an interviewer:

A number of years ago, there was an attorney from Houston—a very nice-looking, big fellow—who presented his argument. White asked him a couple of questions and, as he concluded, I noticed—I'm sure Byron White didn't think that I would—that they looked at each other and, almost imperceptibly, nodded. The case was concluded and I leaned over and I said,

"What does that nod mean, Mr. Justice?"

And he said "[Mr. Nance] played against me in [the Cotton Bowl], and he played end. I've never had a more uncomfortable, battering afternoon in my life than he gave me. He just beat me up." What happened was, the nod was one of mutual respect between these two old gridiron antagonists.

White and Nance had both been named to the 1962 Silver All-America team named by *Sports Illustrated* to honor college football players from the 1937 season who had distinguished themselves after graduation. Nance had been an honor graduate of the University of Texas School of Law, served in World War II, and developed an admiralty and natural resources practice that numbered George Bush among his clients. The *Bremen* was his only argument in the Supreme Court. At the time he did not know how well White remembered the cool New Year's Day in Dallas thirty-four years earlier when he held White to 5 yards net on five carries, including two tackles for no gain and one for a 3-yard loss.

Less than two months after the de facto Cotton Bowl reunion, White was back in both the sports pages and the political pages. On May 10, 1972, two months before the Democratic National Convention in Miami Beach, Charles C. Mottley held a hastily scheduled press conference at the National Press Club in Washington to announce the formation of a "committee to draft Supreme Court Justice Byron R. White as a Democratic Presidential nominee." Mottley, a Virginia delegate to the convention, explained that the signatures of fifty delegates from at least three different states were necessary to put White's name in nomination. Other answers from Mottley suggested that the draft movement was rather ad hoc. White had not been contacted, and by Court custom could not participate in partisan activities, but the makeshift White-for-President committee frequently reiterated that Charles Evans Hughes had resigned from the Court in 1916 to accept a draft nomination as the Republican Party candidate for president.

How well did Mottley know White? *Never met him,* Mottley conceded, but "I have several friends who have met Justice White and they think he'd make a great President. I do, too." Although the press conference was unprepossessing, the committee—which claimed six members—included at least two who were busy making telephone calls soliciting support for the draft, Louis Oberdorfer and John Doar. White's former law clerks who were solicited were incredulous. He had been rumored to be under consideration in 1965 to succeed Ford Frick as commissioner of baseball and again recently to replace J. Edgar Hoover as director of the FBI, but none of the ex-clerks believed that White in fact was ready to leave the Court.

White had fueled speculation about the FBI job when he attended Hoover's funeral on May 5, a few days before the "Draft White" press conference. The chief justice had postponed the Court's weekly conference for three hours to accommodate justices who wished to accept the bureau's invitation to attend the services at the National Presbyterian Church across town. Burger and White were the only members of the Court to attend the funeral. White consequently became a topic of front-page news and editorial-page speculation, but no one in the White House viewed White as a candidate for Hoover's office. White habitually bore witness at swearing-ins, ambassadorial installations, retirement luncheons, and funerals—from Hoover's to Walter Lippman's—but his attendance was to bear witness, not to make a strategic statement.

No one inside the Court took the rumors or the draft movement seriously. The chief justice arranged a luncheon toast "with our usual product of the Rhine Valley" the day before White's fifty-fifth birthday; on the day itself, White's clerks surprised him with a lunch at Chez François, where the rumors were the butt of a quick joke before the subject changed. The whole affair would have been a tempest in a teacup had it not been for the dashing reappearance of Johnny Blood. Blood was now sixty-two and "retired," but in fact he was from a family of independent means and could enjoy his role as a self-styled "former self-taught professor of economics" whose principal work was a 250-page unpublished monograph, "Spend Yourself Rich." As one of the pioneers of professional football, whose career began in 1925, he was, as some of his old teammates quipped, "forgotten but not gone." He had been the subject of a penetrating portrait, both measured and moving, in *Sports Illustrated* a year after White's appointment to the Court, but there were now fewer and fewer fans or sportswriters who remembered his play. His heyday was 1929–31, and his game bore little resemblance to the glamorous spectacles now licensed by the National Football League. White's record salary of $15,800 now seemed primitive compared to Joe Namath's $400,000 contract—even for those capable of applying the Department of Labor inflation formula to adjust the figures to constant dollars. Yet Johnny Blood was undaunted. Like the firehouse dog rallying for one more run, he began a cross-country tour in late May to plump White's candidacy for president of the United States.

The first stop on the east-to-west campaign was, naturally enough, Pittsburgh, where White and Blood were first allied. Blood's pitch was based on White's character: "Look at Byron White's record: it's impeccable." What are his politics? "He's what everybody thinks he is. We know him from the opinions he has written. His politics are his life, his character." From Pittsburgh, Blood went to Chicago, where he buttonholed Dave Condon, the *Chicago Tribune* sports columnist and author of "In the Wake of the News," one of the oldest sports columns in the country. Now Blood had a slogan: "The dark horse is White!" After a telephone interview with Arthur Daley, the aging columnist for the *New York Times,* Blood was interviewed by Bud Collins of the *Boston Globe,* who wanted to know White's position on the draft movement: "The subject is undiscussable," Blood reported.

With the convention now only three weeks away and the movement looking more and more like a one-man fantasy, Blood headed for Denver—White's home base—before looping back to take his cause to Miami itself. In Denver, he spoke to Bob Collins of the *Rocky Mountain News* but discovered that Collins was more interested in him than in White. By telephone, Blood spoke with a columnist in San Francisco and then visited Jim Murray, the *Los Angeles Times's* featured sports columnist. On his way to Miami, he swung through St. Louis and talked with Bob Broeg, the nationally syndicated sports editor of the *St. Louis Post-Dispatch.* By now, Blood had more slogans: "White for the White House" and "It's time to get our man off the bench and into the ball game." Broeg had the courtesy not to patronize Johnny Blood's odyssey, but it was Murray—the most accomplished writer of the lot—who provided the most vivid sense of the enterprise:

> A man of independent means, Johnny Blood now stumps the country for Byron White, laying blocks just as he did in the old days. He leaves leaflets, tearsheets, testimonials, which you stare at fascinated as he leafs through them with his broken knuckles, acquired, no doubt, in railroad yard fights.
>
> When he's through, he leaves abruptly. He suggests a tiger who has just eaten.

By the time Johnny Blood arrived in Miami, the draft movement was dead, but as one committee member close to the whole affair remarked, "The party was just beginning." White's name was not entered in nomination and the whole affair looked like a bad idea from a dinner party that unwisely was not forgotten the next morning.

When the 1971 term ended on June 29, 1972, Byron White was the focal point of attention. The *New York Times* made him its Man in the News—

because he had "suddenly become the unpredictable 'swing' member of the Supreme Court": "Sometimes Justice White sides with the liberals, holdovers from the Warren Court. Sometimes he sides with the conservatives, appointees of Richard Nixon. Whichever way he moves, the result is a 5 to 4 vote. Washington loves it." After rehearsing the votes and ruling in the three major decisions of the last day of the term—the death penalty, *Branzburg v. Hayes,* and the speech and debate clause cases—the story retold the standard biography, with one sustained sideswipe at his "barbed quips about technicalities" in oral argument, "unadorned" opinions and "bluntness"—"a little too blunt, a little too straightforward, a man more concerned with legal details than legal thought."

The profile was deftly written and fixed White in the popular mind as a justice of unpredictable and indeterminate philosophy. The portrait was no deeper than a cartoon, leaving the impression of someone mired in detail and careening from one intellectual pew to another. One former clerk, Lance Liebman, tried to provide multiple dimensions to White's thinking at the beginning of the next term in a shrewd essay in the *New York Times Magazine.* His argument was organized around a pair of questions: "Is he on the fence between opposing ideologies? Or is he walking a path of his own that happens to intersect now with one group, now with the other?" The essay carefully developed the latter as the proper inquiry and suggested broad outlines of the path; unfortunately, the headline betrayed the nuance of the text and confirmed the image that had been set at the end of the term: "Swing Man on the Supreme Court." The conventional wisdom was now firmly established in thirty-six-point type. By early August the *Boulder Daily Camera* headlined a lengthy profile by the Associated Press "White Acts a 'Swing Man' for Supreme Court." The AP profile sketched White's position between the "four liberal holdovers" of the Warren "era" and the four Nixon appointees, "all conservatives," and proclaimed—in what read like a criticism—that it was "difficult to pin a label on White's judicial philosophy."

The publicity, as usual, was unwelcome to White. He disdained the attention and preferred the anonymity he enjoyed during what now was routinely called the Warren era. There were also signs that he was restless on the Court despite his growing impact. Not long after the end of term, Potter Stewart encountered one of White's old friends and raised the question of whether White was at rest on the Court: *What's the matter with Byron? He's been saying a lot of crazy thing lately.* For the balance of the decade, White would occasionally flirt with the idea of leaving the Court. Halfway through Jimmy Carter's single term as president, White asked one of his friends in

Washington whether he thought Carter would be reelected in 1980. After answering the question, the friend asked if the inquiry was of purely academic interest: "No," was the measured answer, followed quickly by, "Not necessarily . . . maybe," and a grunt. When Carter failed to be reelected, White's oblique references to his friends about "doing something else" or "getting a life after the Court" dropped completely from his conversation. The most decisive choice he made off the bench during the 1970s, according to one of his friends with a cutting sense of humor, was to quit smoking. That happened in 1973, after a false start the term before when the pressure of the death penalty cases interrupted his resolve to break a forty-plus-year habit.

17

OCTOBER TERM 1981

A S BYRON White prepared for his twentieth full term, beginning the first Monday in October 1981, he enjoyed a paradoxical reputation. Inside the Court, he remained extremely influential, if more with respect to results than to doctrinal development; his effect on the Court's agenda as well as its direction had never been greater. Outside the Court, he was derided by both academics and journalists as both a knave and a fool. Their bile was concentrated by a trio of decisions, beginning with *Branzburg v. Hayes* (declining to find a testimonial privilege for journalists in the First Amendment) during the 1971 term. Then, in *Zurcher v. Stanford Daily* in the spring of 1978, White had written for a 5-3 majority (Brennan not participating) that the First Amendment did not prohibit reasonable searches of newsrooms pursuant to specific warrants. A year later, in *Herbert v. Lando,* White's opinion for the Court had refused to allow the First Amendment to prevent a reasonable discovery request in a libel suit for outtakes and other unpublished editorial material.

Zurcher prompted a pompous "Letter to the Whizzer" from James Reston, which began, "One day, if you have time, I wish you'd come down to the Times and tell us how to deal with the practical problems of gathering the news in Washington under the latest majority opinion of the Supreme Court of the United States." He declared that "if your majority judgment, Justice White, had been in place as the law at the time of the Watergate break-in, Mr. Nixon would probably have been able to cover up the whole political and moral mess." Reston concluded with the same apocalyptic prediction that the press lawyers in *Branzburg* relied on six years earlier: sources of "information, fearing exposure, will dry up." Anthony Lewis's column a few days later was more measured but still sharply critical. Lewis quoted from White's majority opinion, that the requirement for specificity in warrants, " 'properly applied, policed, and observed,' should prevent rummaging 'at large' " in newspaper files, but concluded that it was "doubtful" the "cautionary words . . . would have much effect." Prof. Alan Dershowitz of Harvard termed *Zurcher* "a naive refusal to recognize the importance of the press in this country."

When *Herbert* was handed down, "controversy boiled like surf around the Supreme Court," in George Will's frothy image, and any measure of civil criticism was now jettisoned. (The decision had been leaked to ABC News, which rekindled White's loathing for the press, although his demeanor on the bench when the decision was eventually announced was said to bear a "sporting, if chilly, grin" directed at the enterprising ABC correspondent.) Images of journalists being involuntarily psychoanalyzed and of "thought police" were hustled into play, and Charles McCabe of the *San Francisco Chronicle* decried White as a "jock . . . named by a jock" to the Supreme Court: "17 years after his appointment, the former All-American is known chiefly as the Javert of the American press," who "has pursued our editors and publishers with the cold fury of the pursuer of Jean Valjean."

Even legal scholars got into the name-calling act. Prof. Robert Cover concluded a 1979 op-ed piece, which displayed uncharacteristically cruel humor, by writing that White and Jackie Jensen, the college football player turned major league outfielder, were both "better as running backs." The most positive academic review of White's work at this point was by Monroe E. Price of UCLA, who titled an essay for the *National Law Journal* "White: A Justice of Studied Unpredictability." The phrase indelibly stained White's public image and connoted arbitrariness, but Price claimed only that White was not doctrinaire, focused carefully on the record, and could write both *Red Lion* (upholding the authority of the Federal Communications Commission against claims that its power violated the First Amendment) and *Midwest Video* (holding that the FCC exceeded its legislative authority in mandating cable access). Price concluded that White was not a "swing vote." Instead, his work reflected a "determined effort by White to assert his deeply felt convictions and maintain the sense that judges should not be pre-programmed and easily predictable, that their views and values evolve and that they must, therefore, maintain only a tentative and analytical approach to certain of the largest questions in the society."

White's reputation among academics suffered primarily because his opinions bore none of the theoretical sensitivity or elegance of John Marshall Harlan's and because he was on the wrong side of the conventional wisdom about reproductive rights, as the issue in *Roe v. Wade* and its related case law was coming to be called. Although White continued to write aggressive opinions and cast votes to relieve intentional racial discrimination, he had drawn the line in a 1976 case that refused to find a Fourteenth Amendment violation absent evidence of purposive behavior *(Washington v. Davis)*. The opinion elicited disappointed cries in several scholarly quarters but spoke for a unanimous Court on the constitutional issue. In the allied field of affirmative action, White voted with the angels of fashionable opinion to uphold the quota program at the University of California at Davis Medical School. Privately he had deep anxieties, which he expressed internally to his colleagues, that any race-sensitive program "in the end would often make race the determinative factor in administering a seemingly neutral set of qualifications." He was responsible, thanks to a memorandum to his colleagues the day before deliberation in the case, for the eleventh-hour attention that all of the opinions paid to the statutory as opposed to the constitutional ground for decision. Many of the Court's internal working papers in the case were published in 1988 by Prof. Bernard Schwartz, and White's role in the case—again, seeking to avoid a constitutional basis for decision where a statutory basis would be less indelible—was fully documented.

The criticism was a source more of pride or amusement than of pain to White. He had spent much of the last half century of his life not caring what others thought of him, especially in print. On the other hand, he began the October 1981 term still wounded by the press, or more precisely by two reporters from the *Washington Post*, Bob Woodward and Scott Armstrong, who published an exposé of the Court entitled *The Brethren* in December of 1979. A measured retrospective by Linda Greenhouse, the *New York Times* correspondent, at the end of the 1979 term, during which the book was released, observed: "The Supreme Court term began last Oct. 1 in an atmosphere of tense anticipation over impending publication of a book about the Court that was said to contain numerous embarrassing and potentially damaging revelations." In fact, she noted, the justices were depicted "as ordinary mortals given to playing office politics," but there was no "evidence that members of the Court had acted corruptly or abused power."

The book nonetheless provoked a tidal wave of criticism and outrage in the profession. Lawyers publicly worried whether the brethren would be able to speak to one another, let alone to work effectively. Some decried the "trea-

son of the clerks," since the book claimed that more than 170 law clerks, spanning the seven terms covered, had been interviewed for the book. White was
offended and hurt by the book, which retailed backstairs gossip and internal
Court documents in the same leering tone. The image of the institution was
damaged, the mystique of the decision-making process was shattered, and the
net effect, worst of all in White's view, was that respect for the Court was
eroded.

On top of the institutional issues generated by the book, White brought
his own tightly locked baggage to the episode. He had once been a law clerk
himself. His boss, Chief Justice Vinson, was often said to write his best opinions with his hands jammed in his pockets, but even decades after his clerkship White would not discuss Vinson or their working relationship. On the
public record, White dismissed his influence on Vinson. "I don't think anything I ever did or said influenced my Justice," White told *Smithsonian* magazine three decades after the fact. "The only time Byron ever came close to an
indiscretion about his [clerkship] year," Ira Rothgerber remembered, "was
when he once shamelessly admitted that he did some of the spadework for
Bruce's Juices"—an antitrust opinion by Justice Jackson. "That was it. And he
never explained what he did."

White told his clerks for the 1979 term that he would not read the book,
but he assigned them each to read a portion so that he could be told if there
were specific examples of vote trading or irrational behavior that were recounted. After the assignment was completed, White said no more to his staff
about "the book," and for several years he left an impression of unrequited
rage with all those who touched on the issue with him. He was also the old
Naval Intelligence officer again, trying to determine quietly which of his own
former clerks had spoken to the authors; there was no retaliation planned or
executed, only private complaint. The only active measures he took were to
speak less candidly with his own staff and not to have lunch with clerks from
other chambers. Publicly, White demonstrated to the press that clerks would
still be readily hired in the post-*Brethren* era; in July 1980 he became "the first
of his colleagues," according to a press report, to hire clerks for the October
1981 term.

Ironically, regardless of whatever indiscretions were committed by former Court employees, the driving engine behind the project, and the principal source for much of the detailed material that gave the book its resonance,
was not a clerk but a justice—Potter Stewart. The authors claimed at the
time of publication that five justices had been interviewed on background for
the book, but Woodward waited until four years after Stewart died in 1985

to reveal the scope of his involvement, which Woodward claimed began with initiation of the idea and continued with generous cooperation during the project. A second cooperating justice was Lewis F. Powell, who admitted to his biographer years later that he had spoken with Woodward, but denied any indiscretion.

None of Stewart's or Powell's complicity in the book was publicly known in the summer of 1981. The book was topical again because several months earlier Avon had released a paperback edition, which had been as high as third on the *New York Times* best-seller list but was out of the top ten by Easter. Woodward's editorial judgment, and his comfort with anonymous sources, took an embarrassing turn in the spring of 1981 shortly after *The Brethren* disappeared from the paperback top ten. A Pulitzer Prize awarded to the *Washington Post* for the story of an eight-year heroin addict who shot up in the presence of a *Post* reporter, Janet Cooke, was canceled when the *Post* discovered that the child was fictional; Woodward was one of the editors who oversaw Cooke's work. Many journalists were moved to reexamine their views of anonymous sources, and Anthony Lewis even argued that the episode confirmed the wisdom of *Branzburg*.

The question of the Court's image was not reopened until shortly before Christmas 1981, after the term began, when bound galleys of memoirs written by John Erlichman claimed that Warren Burger had discussed pending cases with President Nixon on more than one occasion—a profound ethical breach if true. During the balance of the decade, as more evidence of indiscreet judicial behavior came to light (including Felix Frankfurter's indiscretions with his former clerk Philip Elman and Abe Fortas's revelations of conference discussions to the FBI), the furor over *The Brethren* receded; if the justices could not keep their own counsel, their valets could hardly be blamed for not following a good example, or so the rationalization ran. Perhaps more than anything else, however, Bernard Schwartz's series of books published in the 1980s, documenting one controversial case after another, settled once and for all the question of whether the Court's internal linen could be laundered in public. All relied on internal court papers, apparently even including Justice Brennan's "term histories," written annually by his outgoing law clerks, and describing some decisions that were less than a decade old. The question was not if but when the Court's secrets would go public.

The success of *The Brethren* in paperback, combined with Bob Woodward's partial fall from grace over the canceled Pulitzer Prize during the spring of 1981, made many journalists and lawyers wonder whether any member of the Supreme Court would finally speak directly to the questions surrounding the book once the term ended in July. When none did, speculation refocused on August and the American Bar Association Convention in New Orleans, but the spare comments of the justices who attended—White, Powell, and Stevens—were "so Delphic that they have left some of those in their audiences asking what they were really getting at." The first public statement by a member of the Court about the book was by Harry Blackmun two months after the term began. In a television interview with Daniel Schorr—only the second by a sitting justice—Blackmun said "maybe" the book "served a purpose," if it made the Court's work accessible to laymen.

What was foremost on the minds of the justices was Potter Stewart's retirement and his replacement by Sandra Day O'Connor, an Arizona state court judge and former legislator. O'Connor had been nominated in July at the close of the term, and her hearings were scheduled for September. Justice Powell alluded to her impending arrival by remarking in New Orleans that "several of us have bought new suits. And there is even a rumor that some changes may be made in the court's plumbing," to which the *Washington Post* appended the parenthetical note "(laughter)." For Justice White, the issue was not wardrobe or remodeling but title. He abhorred the title "Madam Justice," so he asked Jean Dubofsky of the Colorado Supreme Court how to finesse the problem and she suggested dropping "Mr." or its like from the Court's stylistic protocol. In fact, the suggestion was made several months before O'Connor was nominated, since, as Justice William Rehnquist later wrote, White was convinced that "in the very near future a woman justice was bound to be appointed, [and] we ought to avoid the embarrassment of having to change the style of designating the author of the opinion at that time by doing it before the event." On September 26, Justice O'Connor—no "Mrs." or "Madam"—became the 102d appointee to the Court and its first woman.

The Court opened the 1981 term with 109 cases on the docket for oral argument. The caseload of applications for review (petitions for certiorari and jurisdictional statements) now hovered near five thousand, compared to approximately twenty-eight hundred when White joined the Court and thirty-six hundred a decade before. The Court's capacity to manage its caseload and to perform its function as what Paul Freund famously called the "umpire of the federal system" was increasingly under scrutiny, as it had been since Warren Burger summoned a commission to study the problem early in his tenure; at the end of the 1981 term, the controversy would again intensify. As he had from the beginning, White would row the laboring oar in the debate.

For the first time in several years, there was no case involving either abortion or affirmative action on the argument calendar. Race remained the most nettlesome issue, its volatility intensified by the turnover in administration from Jimmy Carter to Ronald Reagan. The change manifested itself immediately in one symbolically important case that the Court had agreed to hear. The Department of Justice under President Carter had intervened on behalf of undocumented alien children in Texas who had been denied tuition-free public schooling, but now under President Reagan the Department expressed no views on the local school boards' policy (*Plyler v. Doe*). In other significant respects, the new administration made little difference to the government's position before the Court.

Potentially the most important case accepted on the first day of term was *Immigration and Naturalization Service v. Chadha,* which presented the question whether legislative vetoes violated the constitutional principle of separation of powers. The legislative scheme at issue in *Chadha* provided that an order by the attorney general canceling deportation could be nullified by the resolution of one house of Congress. A Kenyan student who had overstayed his visa faced deportation until INS suspended the proceedings to consider his claims of hardship. The House of Representatives passed a resolution of disapproval, which had the effect of canceling the suspension, and he filed suit. He claimed that under the Constitution one house of Congress could not take binding action by itself. The House and Senate were confined, ran the argument, to agreeing on legislation and forwarding it to the president to be signed into law or vetoed; no step in the process could be sidestepped without violating the Constitution. The Court of Appeals for the Ninth Circuit invalidated the House resolution. The Department of Justice—saying the case raised issues that "go to the very heart of the assignment of powers under our constitutional system"—urged the Supreme Court to give its imprimatur to the lower court's ruling. The legislative veto existed in more than 150 laws enacted since 1932, the most politically sensitive at the moment involving congressional power to block foreign arms sales such as Reagan's proposed sale of five radar-equipped Airborne Warning and Control System (AWACS) aircraft to Saudi Arabia.

By the time the term drew to another belated close, on Friday, July 2, the Court had disposed of 167 cases with full opinion but had been unable to reach a decision in the legislative veto case. White wrote nineteen opinions for the Court, two more than any other justice. He also issued fifteen dissents from denial of certiorari, an unusual practice for any member of the Court until the early 1970s but a common practice for White beginning in 1969. Complaining that the Court bypassed too many lower-court decisions meriting review, he published forty-three dissents from denial of certiorari between

October term 1970 and 1980, inclusive; the high-water mark was 1979, when he published thirteen. Despite two changes in Court personnel (John Paul Stevens for William O. Douglas in 1975 and O'Connor for Stewart), White remained at the center of the Court, as he had a decade earlier. The Court decided thirty-one cases by a vote of 5-4. White was in the majority in nineteen of those decisions. The Court's divisions were hardly routine: the 5-4 divisions were made up by twelve different combinations of justices, and every justice except Burger wrote at least two opinions for a bare majority.

Although White's opinions for the Court may have been institutionally more important, his separate opinions—concurring and dissenting—were more telling about White's deployment of his energies and his own convictions. White wrote dissenting opinions in more than half of the twelve cases in which he was in a four-man minority. The opinions touched a wide range of issues—presidential immunity to civil suit for acts at the "outer perimeter" of his official duties (*Nixon v. Fitzgerald*), sovereign immunity and the Eleventh Amendment, federal criminal law, retroactivity, labor union campaign contributions, double jeopardy (*Tibbs v. Florida,* which Brennan told White was "an excellent and persuasive dissent"), and regulation of charitable organizations. Significantly, four of the dissents objected to the majority's use, or misuse, of precedent, and another disputed the factual predicate for applying the decisive doctrine. *Nixon* was a significant constitutional decision and a testament to the small world of Washington, D.C. Nixon's case for absolute immunity was argued by Jack Miller, White's former colleague in the Justice Department; Miller won, notwithstanding a scathing dissent from White, who rejected for the second time what he saw as Richard Nixon's attempt to set his public office above the law.

The term also found White writing against type. In *United States v. Ross,* the author of *Chambers v. Maroney* (which held that an impounded automobile could be searched without a warrant) objected when the Court expanded the scope of constitutionally permissible automobile searches to include the entire vehicle and all containers in which the object being sought could be found. His dissent was based on stare decisis, and his opinion, in its entirety, illustrates both an emerging concern and an elliptic style that provided new fodder for his critics:

> I would not overrule *Robbins v. California*, 453 U.S. 420 (1981). For the reasons stated by Justice Stewart in that case, I would affirm the judgment of the Court of Appeals. I also agree with much of Justice Marshall's dissent in this case.

Robbins had been decided exactly one year to the day before by a 5-4 vote in a plurality opinion by Justice Stewart joined by White, William Brennan, and Thurgood Marshall. The decision held that police could search unopened containers in vehicles that they had stopped. Lewis Powell cast the deciding vote but rested his opinion on a flexible standard ("reasonable expectation" of privacy, derived from *Katz v. United States*) instead of the plurality's "bright-line" rule. *Ross* was written by Justice Stevens, who was one of the *Robbins* dissenters. The balance of the new majority consisted of the other *Robbins* dissenters, Blackmun and William Rehnquist, plus Chief Justice Burger (who concurred in the judgment in *Robbins*), Justice O'Connor, and Justice Powell, who explained his change of heart on the need for "specific guidance to police and courts in this recurring situation." White resisted chiding Powell for changing his mind and resolving the confusion for which he was responsible by declining to join Stewart's opinion, but he also declined to explain his conviction about the importance of stare decisis, notwithstanding his strong views on the importance of fidelity to precedent and the consequent murkiness of his abrupt dissenting statement.

As the decade wore on, and as four new justices came to be appointed to the Court within ten years, White would find himself more frequently objecting to precedents being overruled by bare majorities or within a short period of time after being decided, or—for him, the worst case—the overruling of a well-settled precedent dating from the Warren Court era. (Those who recalled his stinging dissents from that period failed to understand that he accepted decisions—even those in which he dissented—as time passed, all the more so when the precedent became a decade old.) As he would later often point out at judicial conferences or occasional speeches, he even "extended" the *Miranda* rules in *Edwards v. Arizona,* at the end of the 1980 term, which held that once a suspect requests a lawyer, not only must all interrogation stop but it cannot resume "until counsel has been made available" to the suspect. (*Edwards* was reconfirmed a decade later in *Minnick v. Mississippi,* written by Justice Anthony Kennedy thanks to an assignment by Justice White.) The only decision immune from precedential protection in White's jurisprudence remained *Roe v. Wade.*

White's aversion to creating new constitutional rights, especially on the basis of a thin factual record, was reconfirmed in one of the most closely watched cases of the term, *Board of Education, Island Trees v. Pico.* A Long Island, New York, school board rejected the recommendation of a committee of parents and school staff that it had appointed, and ordered removal from the junior and senior high school libraries of certain books—termed by the board "anti-American, anti-Christian and -Semitic and just plain filthy." Students sued the board to have the order rescinded. The trial court rejected the students' claims, but the court of appeals concluded that they were entitled to have their case tried—in effect rejecting the board's claim to unfettered autonomy over decisions to remove books from school libraries.

The Supreme Court granted certiorari with four votes—the bare minimum—and it does not stretch the imagination to speculate that all four (Burger, Powell, Rehnquist, and O'Connor) were hostile to the appellate court's solicitude to the students' claims. The record was unclear on the board's actual motivation for removing the nine books in question—*The Fixer* by Bernard Malamud, *Slaughterhouse Five* by Kurt Vonnegut, *The Naked Ape* by Desmond Morris, *Down These Mean Streets* by Piri Thomas, *Soul on Ice* by Eldridge Cleaver, *A Hero Ain't Nothing But a Sandwich* by Alice Childress, *Go Ask Alice* by Anonymous, *The Best Short Stories by Negro Writers,* edited by Langston Hughes, and *Black Boy* by Richard Wright. Counsel for the students characterized the case as based on a First Amendment "right to read" but had trouble mooring their theory to any line of authority. The constitutional standard, according to counsel, turned on the school board's "motivation," to which the board's counsel replied, "If all that is required is an allegation of impure motivation, the courts are going to be inundated."

When the Court met in conference to discuss the case, the justices split into two hard-line camps, with Blackmun and White in the middle. Blackmun observed that *Pico* was "a dangerous case to be carefully handled." White said he wished that the record could be expanded, because his view turned on whether the board had acted to suppress "vulgarity" or to suppress offensive ideas; according to Brennan's conference notes, White said, "If [vulgarity] had been found to be [the] reason [for the board's decision, he] would probably reverse." White and Blackmun tentatively voted with Brennan, Marshall, and Stevens to affirm. Brennan's draft opinion took two months to prepare and was circulated to White—the most tentative member of the majority—in advance of the rest of the Court.

White's response, a patient and thoughtful letter, warrants extensive quotation for two reasons. The text illustrates in a precise context the anxieties of an entire career over making precipitous constitutional law, especially in novel situations. Second, although White tended to be frank in separate opinions about his reasons for casting his vote one way or the other, his final opinion in *Pico* rested—or unfairly hid behind, in Justice Rehnquist's view— two classic justifications for avoiding premature constitutional decisions: *Kennedy v. Silas Mason* in 1948 and *Dombrowski v. Eastland* in 1967. White first explained his vote:

As your draft is presently written, I doubt I could join it, at least without seeing what might be written on the other side. If the others voting to affirm see no objections with your draft, however, I surely have no objections to your circulating at this time.

I voted to affirm primarily because I do not usually think it worthwhile to overturn a court of appeals that disagrees with a district court's conclusion that there is no bona fide factual issue foreclosing summary judgment. Although the prevailing opinions in the court of appeals are not too informative, the factual issue appears to me to be the reasons [sic] for the school board's ordering the books to be removed from the library. Until one knows that, the identity and scope of the constitutional issue are obscure.

Then White explained his reservations about Brennan's proposed constitutional rule:

You deem it essential, however, to provide a First Amendment standard for the district court to use on remand. You propose as the proper constitutional benchmark the intention to suppress constitutionally protected ideas with which the school board disagrees, or the intention to impose a political or ideological orthodoxy upon the students of the junior and senior high schools. I am frank to say that I scarcely know what a "political or ideological orthodoxy" is, and it would take years to find out. The removal of any book based on its content could be challenged on this basis.

As for intending to suppress constitutionally protected ideas, if you mean constitutionally protected from removal from a school library, we are back at ground zero and the district court is on its own. But if you mean constitutionally protected in the marketplace, then I suppose anything short of obscenity is protected. No book, however vulgar, could be removed from the school library unless it were obscene under prevailing standards. For myself, had the court of appeals agreed with the district court that the books had been removed because they were vulgar, had agreed that they were vulgar, but nevertheless held that they could not be removed, I would have to vote to reverse. I doubt that you would have so voted.

I also doubt that the standard you propose for the school library in which a student could independently browse could be so easily isolated from the question of what books may be used in the school curriculum or for assigned outside reading.

With all of that, Bill, you have written an interesting opinion in a difficult case, an opinion that may command a majority and that (hence?) may grow upon me with more mature consideration.

Brennan's response employed, for him, a practiced tactic. He told White that they were not "really that far apart," revised his draft to meet White's concerns about distinctions in motivations, and wrapped the package in references to a time-honored precedent—here, Justice Robert Jackson's eloquent treatment of children in *West Virginia Board of Education v. Barnette* in 1943. The new draft remained unchanged on these points and appears as the final two paragraphs of part II (A) (2) of Brennan's published opinion.

Stevens joined Brennan's opinion, but White waited to see what others would say. Chief Justice Burger circulated a steaming dissent in early June, which O'Connor quickly joined, then Marshall joined Brennan, and Powell announced that he would file his own dissent. The Court was split 3-3 with White, Blackmun, and Rehnquist not yet voting. White decided to circulate his draft dissent (which did not substantially change before publication) and concurred only in the Court's judgment of affirmance: "We should not decide constitutional questions until it is necessary to do so, or at least until there is better reason to address them than are evident here"—especially "in a largely uncharted field." Rehnquist circulated his dissent and then Blackmun finally provided the fifth vote to support the judgment of affirmance on June 23, when he informed his colleagues that he joined all of Brennan's opinion except one subpart.

The decision was announced two days later, replete with caustic attacks by the dissent on the plurality opinion and accompanied by a seven-page appendix from Justice Powell cataloguing and repeating the offensive passages contained in the removed books. The *Wall Street Journal* soon noted the increasingly vitriolic language in the Court's opinions, of which *Pico* was the prize example. The salient feature of the decision, however, was that White's position had prevented the Supreme Court from making a novel constitutional ruling in a complicated and emotionally charged area where the motivations and implications of the defendants were both ambiguous and not necessarily representative. Justice Rehnquist chided White for confounding the Rule of Four* and holding eight members of the Court hostage to his anxieties over the state of the record, but the broadside—presented in a footnote—was more a sideswipe than a telling blow. Neither certiorari practice nor what might be called "imprudential" considerations should compel what

---

* Since 1925, the Supreme Court has followed an internal policy of hearing cases at the behest of four justices. The purpose of the policy, which was revealed during testimony by members of the Court about the Judges Bill of 1925, is to insure that a majority could not secretly control the Court's docket. Thus, except in exceptional circumstances, cases will be heard on the vote of a maximum minority of the Court.

could objectively be characterized as the premature creation of a novel constitutional doctrine.

When Powell finally circulated his dissenting opinion the day before Blackmun cast the last vote in the case, he admitted that "11 years on the Richmond School Board and eight years on the Virginia Board of Education" had not made him "enthusiastic" about "your opinion," but he appended what appears to have been intended as a cheerful handwritten postscript: "At least this has not been a dull term!" He may have been referring to the coarse language reprinted in his appendix; or he may have been referring to the combination of the appendix and the record in *Ferber v. New York*—the child pornography case.

For Byron White, the term was hardly dull, although not for the reasons to which Powell seemed, without genuine relish, to be referring. White was the author of *Ferber,* the unanimous decision that held that the First Amendment did not invalidate a New York statute prohibiting the knowing promotion of sexual performance by a person under age sixteen. The vote was an achievement for White. In a term marked by one close division after another—and growing rhetorical tension near the end of the term—he achieved unanimity after the Court had tentatively voted only 5-4 to reverse the lower court's invalidation of the law. White's position in conference was narrow and technical: the court of appeals "wholly ignored" the limiting definition of "sexual performance" and "gave the provision far wider meaning than" written. The ticklish doctrinal problem was whether, even as narrowed, the statute was "substantially overbroad" under White's formula in *Broadrick v. Oklahoma.* Justice Brennan impishly wrote a note to himself that White's challenge was to draft an opinion finding no substantial overbreadth and still not "deterring National Geographic." Those who had voted to affirm the lower court decided not to dissent once they saw White's opinion, and two even praised his work (Stevens: "a stronger and more persuasive opinion than I thought possible"; and Brennan: "right both on the merits and the overbreadth question"). Brennan, Stevens, and O'Connor nonetheless filed separate opinions, and four concurred in the judgment only (Brennan, Marshall, Blackmun, and Stevens). Prof. Frederick Schauer pointed out that the decision was one of very few cases "since 1919 in which not a single justice dissented from a holding that an act of communication was unprotected by the First Amendment," but he applauded White's novel analysis: by carving out a separate category for child pornography instead of trying to square the ruling with conventional doctrine, White avoided diluting doctrine that protected speech or expanding categories that did not.

Due to its subject matter and to the fact that it was announced the last day of term, *Ferber* received a great deal of attention, but so did two other decisions that White announced that day and the day before—*Enmund v. Florida,* which held that the death penalty for aiding and abetting murder was disproportionate and therefore violated the Eighth Amendment, and *Rodgers v. Lodge,* which held that the system of at-large elections in Burke County, Georgia, violated the Fourteenth Amendment. *Enmund* was a 5-4 decision that found White hewing to Eighth Amendment precedent, principally his own plurality opinion in *Coker v. Georgia,* over two dissents, in 1977, which invalidated death for rape. *Rodgers* was a 6-3 decision that was important because it upheld findings of intentional discrimination based on indirect evidence. Justice Powell's dissent viewed the result as a misapplication of *Mobile v. Bolden,* which declined the year before to invalidate at-large voting systems unless they were maintained for a discriminatory purpose. White had dissented in *Mobile.* His opinion in *Rogers* is a tour de force that demonstrates that a precedent can be expanded by simply applying it with heavy attention to the particular facts of the present case and equally heavy emphasis on the findings of lower courts. The *New York Times* thought that *Rodgers* would have "relatively little practical significance," since Congress had recently amended the Voting Rights Act of 1965 to eliminate the requirement of intentional discrimination. White's opinion in *Rodgers* nonetheless demonstrated that the Fourteenth Amendment intent requirement outside of voting rights cases was not to be woodenly applied.

The case also demonstrated, if only to a handful of people, the compassion that Byron White worked so hard to keep from public attention. A few days before the oral argument, Herman Lodge, the named plaintiff, telephoned the marshal's office at the Supreme Court to insure that he and his busload of supporters would have seats in the courtroom. He was told that there were no reserved seats. Distraught, he then called Nina Totenberg, a reporter who had covered his case for months, and asked for her help. She telephoned White and explained Lodge's plight. "He listened, and sort of grunted, but was noncommittal," Totenberg later recalled. When Lodge contacted the Court again, he was advised that space had been allotted to his group, but there was no explanation for the change in policy or its application.

Rogers v. Lodge was one of several cases that knotted the Court during the spring. One of the most important, and time-consuming, opinions produced in White's chambers for the Court during the term was *Edgar v. MITE,* which involved state antitakeover statutes, the Williams Act, and the dormant commerce clause. The case produced six opinions and complicated, and unstable, divisions between the justices, and five years later the ruling was effectively "gutted" by *CTS Corp. v. Dynamic Corp. of America*. During the 1981 Term, however, *MITE* was a focal point in White's chambers for months.

The most important cases of the term, in terms of both doctrine and statecraft, were the two cases that touched on what White would soon label the "advent and triumph of the administrative state"—*Chadha* and *Northern Pipeline Construction Co v. Marathon Pipe Line Co.* The cases represented flip sides of the issue: *Chadha* presented Congress trying to harness administrative discretion, and *Marathon* presented Congress creating a quasi-judicial bureaucracy. The issue in *Marathon* was the constitutionality of authorizing bankruptcy judges, who unlike other federal judges lacked life tenure or security of income, to decide common law claims in the course of adjudicating the bankrupt estate. What was anticipated as a two-part lesson in separation of powers washed out, however, when the Court decided after oral argument in *Chadha* to hear the case again the following term—a maneuver initiated by an anxious memorandum from Lewis Powell about severability (whether part of a statute could be invalidated without invalidating the whole), which for him put "this worrisome case" in an entirely new light. Although the case was left in suspended animation, the public was on notice that feelings within the Court ran high: Justices Blackmun and Brennan noted on the record their dissent from the order of reargument. In fact, the vote in March to order reargument had been 5-4, but the chief justice neglected to prepare the order until Blackmun, obviously frustrated over what he viewed as wasted effort for all concerned, sent a letter to Burger on June 25.

Marathon was argued in April but not issued until June 28. The Court invalidated the act that was at issue, but was unable to produce an opinion supported by five justices; Justice Brennan spoke for four, and Justices Rehnquist and O'Connor concurred on narrower grounds. The bottom line was clear, however: judges without life tenure could not constitutionally do the job assigned to them by Congress. Due to the magnitude of the decision's impact, the Court stayed its judgment for ninety days so that Congress could repair the system. White filed a lengthy opinion, twenty-five pages, for himself and two others, which was adamant and even sarcastic at times about Justice Brennan's analysis for the plurality. All the standard White arguments were marshaled, condemning "abstract theory that has little to do with the reality of bankruptcy proceedings," criticizing the failure to understand the flexible approach developed by Congress over time to deal with different jurisdictional issues, and warning that invalidation of the act requires overruling a "large number of our precedents." When all of the intellectual close-order drill was done, the soul of the opinion revealed, or reaffirmed, itself in the final sentence: "For all of these reasons, I would defer to the congressional judgment."

In all of the cases during the ensuing decade involving constitutional challenges to innovative governmental structures created by Congress, White deferred to the legislative judgment and voted to sustain the mechanism under attack: legislative vetoes (*Chadha*, 1983), the comptroller general as budget-deficit policeman (*Bowsher v. Synar*, 1986), independent counsels appointed by a special court (*Morrison v. Olson*, 1988), and federal criminal sentencing guidelines promulgated by a hybrid judge/nonjudge commission answerable to the president (*Mistretta v. United States*, 1989). White began in dissent, but by the time the last two cases were decided, Justice Antonin Scalia—who was appointed by President Reagan in 1986— was the only dissenter.

INS v. Chadha, issued two-thirds of the way through White's career, has been accorded the status, at least by his friends, of the epitome of his judicial philosophy. Judge Oberdorfer points to the *Chadha* dissent and says, *There you will find Byron White, the judge.* White's delivery of the opinion suggested that the case betokened a personal crucible. Linda Greenhouse's account for the *New York Times* pointed out the "rare moments of drama in the Courtroom" produced by *Chadha's* announcement. After the chief justice, who wrote the opinion for the Court, announced the judgment,

> White said it had been many years since he had read an oral dissent aloud. "But this is probably the most important case the Court has handed down in many years," he said, calling the decision a "destructive action" that was "clearly wrong and unnecessarily broad."

After a moment of silence, Burger—who never read or even summarized his own opinions—spoke at some length without notes about the "difficult and important case" and the need to honor the judgments of the "draftsmen in Philadelphia" who forged the Constitution. Burger's majority opinion took the straightforward tack that the Constitution did not contemplate lawmaking by only one house of Congress, or lawmaking without an opportunity for the president to issue a veto and force a supermajority in both houses. White, advocating a flexible approach to separation of powers, argued (1) that the effect of the veto was as if one house had rejected a private bill proposed by the executive, and (2) that it was no worse for Congress to delegate authority to one of its own houses than for Congress to delegate authority to an executive agency of its own creation. In sum, the legislative veto to White was a counterbalance to Congress's chronic delegation of power to executive authorities;

by checking executive action, Congress was preventing the executive delegates from unchecked action.

The majority opinion was condemned by some, such as Prof. Bernard Schwartz, for stripping Congress of a vital tool for exercising what Woodrow Wilson called "vigilant oversight of administration." Dean Jesse Choper of Boalt Hall thought the issue of "constitutional questions concerning the respective powers of Congress and the President" should be "remitted" for "their final resolution" to the "interplay of the national political process" and should not be adjudicated at all. Prof. Donald Elliott, then of Yale, found Burger's majority opinion unsatisfactorily "formalistic"; he thought White's views, initially appealing, to rest on a "murky" concept of administrative lawmaking and to provide an incomplete response to the mechanical clarity of the majority. Privately, Burger conceded to the other members of the majority that "Byron has a forceful dissent in this case." To Prof. David Currie, the preeminent modern formalist, White's arguments were no more persuasive than his vehemence. Currie pointed out obvious holes in White's analogies: the veto is not akin to a one-house rejection of a private bill submitted by the president (because the attorney general's suspension order was not a proposal but had the force of law), nor is the veto like congressional delegation to administrative agencies (standards are more specific and details are supplied by an executive, not a legislative body). Currie concluded his critique: "There was a more fundamental difficulty with both of Justice White's arguments, however. The Constitution is not to be judicially amended by arguing that what the framers did not authorize is no more dangerous than what they did."

Prof. Allan Ides, a more sympathetic critic, admired White's sophisticated analysis of the administrative state and the emphasis on "how the underlying transaction—the legislative veto—functioned within the real world structure of government." But for all the "intellectual appeal of White's *Chadha* dissent, there is a nagging sense that something is not quite right." The problem lies in one of the last quarters where one would expect to look. As Ides put it: "White's appraisal of legislative vetoes was itself somewhat formalistic"—it "*assumed* that legislative vetoes operate both to assist the administrative state and to protect the values inherent in separation of powers." Chief Justice Burger was less credulous and did not blink at what Ides aptly called "the somewhat seedy operation of legislative vetoes in the context of deportation." Although Congress produced literature supporting the utility of the veto, a study lacking in self-interest concluded that White's assumptions about both the potent efficacy and constructive policy effects of the veto were unfounded. Jessica Korn's careful study of the veto in action, published in 1996, argued forcefully that the legislative veto was "inconsequential" and that invalidation of the veto "made it easier for members of Congress to pass laws containing substantive policy prescriptions" while accommodating the discretionary power necessary to the executive.

Why would White, devotee of functional analysis of the administrative state, be so academic about how legislative vetoes really work? The answer may lie at the foundation of his attitudes about judicial review. Prior to the run of separation of powers cases that began with *Marathon* and *Chadha*, the most disturbing issues to come to the Court, besides all of the cases federalizing criminal procedure, were *Roe v. Wade* and *Buckley v. Valeo*, the 1976 case that raised a welter of constitutional challenges to the Federal Election Campaign Act, passed in the wake of the Watergate scandal. White dissented famously when state prohibitions on most abortions were invalidated, and he argued three years later in *Buckley* that Congress could limit both contributions to and spending on candidates for public office. The Court upheld the limitations on contributions, but not on spending. White wrote a strong opinion stating his views, and privately he was even more adamant. Not long after the term in which *Buckley* was decided, White had an earnest conversation with Ira Rothgerber in which he was unusually candid without being indiscreet. "Judges have an exaggerated view of their role in our polity," White said, rather formally, to Rothgerber. Referring to the litigation over the Federal Election Campaign Act, White became heated, according to Rothgerber, who said he had seldom seen White express himself so openly. "I will never forget what he said," Rothgerber later recalled. White continued: "It can't be like the old Court was in 1937: 'The First Amendment, therefore!' Congress has the authority, not five or six judges."

The power to regulate elections was a deep concern for White, who viewed the process from the ground up, whether from his extensive precinct experience as a young lawyer in Denver or from his state and national work for John Kennedy in 1960; the master of reality respected the record but relied on the autobiographical. The electoral process and the hurly-burly of partisan politics were to him the keystone of the constitutional design and ultimate fount of legitimate social policy. Once he staked his claim in *Buckley,* he was dug in as a defender of electoral regulatory schemes and the agencies created to administer them. Two cases during the 1981 term illustrated White's commitment. In *Federal Election Commission v. Democratic Senatorial Campaign Committee*—his first opinion assignment of the term—he wrote for a unanimous Court, which deferred to the judgment of the commission that state committees could designate national senatorial campaign committees as their agents for making expenditures allowed under the Federal Election Campaign Act of 1971. More important, he filed a solo dissent when the Court invalidated a limitation on committees formed to support or oppose local referenda (*Citizens against Rent Control v. City of Berkeley*). "The result here," he wrote after canvassing the Court's post-*Buckley* jurisprudence on regulating elections, "illustrates that the *Buckley* framework is most problematical and strengthens my belief that there is a proper role for carefully drafted limitations on expenditures. . . . Even under *Buckley*," he added for good measure, "the Berkeley ordinance represents such a negligible intrusion on expression and association that the measure should be upheld." He closed with a mock concession:

> Perhaps, as I have said, neither the city of Berkeley nor the State of California can "prove" that elections have been or can be unfairly won by special interest groups spending large sums of money, but there is a widespread conviction in legislative halls, as well as among citizens, that the danger is real. I regret that the Court continues to disregard that hazard.

He would make the same point again and again until he retired.

In addition to the regular opinion work, White continued for the tenth term in a row to publish numerous dissents from denials of certiorari. (Some of his provisional dissents were not published, of course, because he was able to convince a fourth justice to vote in favor of reviewing a case, as in *Connick v. Myers*, an important First Amendment case on employee speech rights; O'Connor, "persuaded" by White, was the decisive vote to grant.) During the course of the term, White filed fifteen "dissents from denial," as they came to be called, the most since he began the practice on a routine basis in the 1972 term. Within a half decade, White would produce up to forty dissents from denial a year, mostly on the ground that the Court—or the federal system in general—was failing its constitutional obligation by allowing conflicting legal rules on federal issues to exist in different jurisdictions throughout the country.

Two sustained studies, one by Michael J. Broyde, a third-year law student at New York University, in 1987, and a later one, by Prof. Arthur Hellman of the University of Pittsburgh, in 1995, argued persuasively that there was more smoke than fire in White's dissents. Many of the cases identified by White as conflicts in fact were not, others involved minor issues, and still others had technical obstacles or problems that would make their disposition by the Supreme Court problematic. In short, a careful analysis of the data did not demonstrate that, based on White's evidence, "intolerable" conflicts were routinely going uncorrected. At a more fundamental level, none of White's arguments ever went in detail beyond the premise that federal rules should be uniform in all jurisdictions. As Judge Richard A. Posner argued in his study of the federal court system, unless one entity is subjected to conflicting rules by different jurisdictions, it is not clear as a matter of principle why conflicts are unacceptable, let alone grounds for either increasing the Supreme Court's caseload by 22 percent or creating a new tier of appellate review or specialized tribunal. As long as an individual or corporation is on reasonable notice of the rule in the relevant jurisdiction, it is hard to see what prejudice is suffered. (White seemed eventually to realize the quixotic nature of his position: a year or two before he retired, he told his clerks after a Court conference, *Luckily we didn't get four votes for those lousy cases we circulated dissents from denial on.*)

White's dissents from denial, and the debate they generated over whether a new national court of appeals was needed, created a bang at the end of the 1981 term with strong views expressed by Justices Stevens, Brennan, Marshall, and White over both workload and caseload. Ultimately, the debate ended with a whimper. After White retired from the Court in 1993, dissents from denial, as Hellman noted, all but dropped from the *U.S. Reports,* and after Harry Blackmun retired a year later, the Court's plenary docket fell to forty-year lows—half of what the Court had been hearing with full briefing and oral argument at the time White was urging a 20 percent increase. David M. O'Brien at the University of Virginia recently demonstrated that the "incredible shrinking" plenary docket was substantially affected by the retirement of the two most active voters to grant certiorari.

The 1981 term was an odd time for White to be pushing the Court to hear more cases, because the justices were having trouble smoothly processing what they had. *Chadha* went three months after a vote to reargue before the appropriate order was issued. Divisions became embarrassingly intricate, with *Edgar v. MITE* the topper ("JUSTICE WHITE delivered an opinion, Parts I, II, and V-B of which are the opinion of the Court"). And the Court granted certiorari in *Illinois v. Gates* to decide on the validity of a search warrant issued on the basis of an affidavit, denied the state's motion to enlarge the question to include whether there should be a good faith exception to the exclusionary rule, heard arguments on the validity of the affidavit, ordered reargument on the good faith question over three dissents, and finally disposed of the case without reaching the good faith question—with "apologies to all"; the majority nonetheless overruled a firmly established rule from the Warren Court (the *Aguilar-Spinelli* test) and held that the validity of search warrants depended on the "totality of the circumstances." White let loose a blistering twenty-nine-page concurrence in the judgment, objecting to the interment of *Aguilar-Spinelli* but urging—as he had since *Stone v. Powell* in 1976—that the good faith exception be adopted. He acidly noted that the Court's handling of the case "may be hard for the country to understand." One year later, White got his chance to decide his issue squarely, but instead he wrote for a 6-3 majority on narrower grounds—holding in *United States v. Leon* that judicial errors would not require the exclusion of evidence seized by police who executed a warrant they had no reason to suspect was invalid. Although referred to as a "good faith" exception to the exclusionary rule, "reasonable mistake" would probably be a more accurate description.

The 1981 term provided distractions both expected and unexpected beyond the cases themselves and the endless but now sharper debate over the Supreme Court's docket. For the first time since the rumors in 1968, 1970, and again in 1972 that he would replace J. Edgar Hoover as director of the Federal Bureau of Investigation, White was said to be considering retirement. The unsubstantiated, one-sentence rumor in a mid-April edition *U.S. News & World Report* elicited no response from White when he was asked for confirmation or denial. He would reach age sixty-five near the end of term and was eligible to retire at full pay. The press noted that there were now three ex-justices who all led active lives, and two even practiced law with regularity—Abe Fortas, seventy-one, and Arthur Goldberg, seventy-three, although Goldberg was now as much gentlemen farmer as senior lawyer. The third, Potter Stewart, sixty-seven, was the only one of the three who had retired and not resigned, so he still sat regularly on federal courts of appeals. If White needed models for post-Court life, he did not need to look far, but there was no hard evidence that he was in fact looking at all.

A month after the speculation was published, the justices submitted their fourth annual financial disclosure statements pursuant to the Ethics in Government Act of 1978. The law, one of the principal legislative legacies of the Carter Administration, was designed to reassure the public that high-ranking members of the three branches of government were not in the pocket of private interests. The first reports under the act were required in 1979, and the members of the Supreme Court complied notwithstanding an injunction issued by a federal district judge in New Orleans, who accepted the arguments of several of his colleagues that disclosure of assets would make judges targets for kidnappers and terrorists. In fact, as *U.S. News* cheerfully pointed out, the opposite was the case: "Fresh disclosures show that White House hopefuls are well-heeled, while Supreme Court Justices are a lot poorer than many expected."

The fourth set of reports, which was submitted as required by law on May 17, 1982, showed that three members of the Court (Powell, O'Connor, and Burger) were most likely millionaires—they were required to report their assets, exclusive of salary and principal residence, and their investment income only within very broad ranges. White ranked number seven in wealth as defined by the law, with assets between $31,000 and $105,000, and investment income between $2,000 and $6,000. Brennan and Marshall both ranked lower, and Marshall reported no investment income. All three, unlike the other members of the Court (who reported investment income twice that of White and Brennan), appeared to be living solely on their federal paychecks. With the exception of Powell and Burger, the other members then on the Court—chastened by the flimsiest allegations of financial conflicts of interest raised in Clement Haynsworth's 1970 confirmation hearings—had reduced their assets to "government bonds or notes, real estate or bank savings."

The most bizarre incident in Byron White's judicial career occurred two weeks and one day after the term ended in early July. Summers for White meant travel west to see family, including his children and his wife's extended family, and to explore trout streams—either old favorites near his hometown or spots from Montana to Arkansas. Every summer included a month in Colorado. He had agreed this summer to speak at a morning meeting of the Utah Bar Association in Salt Lake City. What developed, in the words of Fred Graham of CBS News, who was an eyewitness, was the "most vivid example I ever saw of how poorly the public understands the Supreme Court." White had just been introduced when a heavyset man rushed the dais from the audience and began pummeling White with his right first. White ducked his head, and, according to Graham, bore a "long-suffering scowl, giving every impression that he could have risen up and flattened the man if it had been appropriate." As Newton C. Estes, age fifty-seven, flailed, he shouted: "Filth! Pornography! Dirty Pictures!" It later developed, as his wife explained, that Estes—who moved from Memphis to "liberate" his daughter from a school-busing plan—was a "patriot to his fingertips" who hoped "to strike a blow against obscenity and some of the other dastardly things the Supreme Court has done." The irony was that White was among the least sympathetic members of the Court toward pornography; in fact, *Ferber* was less than three weeks old.

After three punches, a half dozen thunderstruck members of the audience finally charged the podium areas to assist White, but Estes was actually subdued by Judge Monroe McKay of the Tenth Circuit and two television reporters. After briefly rubbing his cheek, White began his thirty-minute survey of the Court's recently completed term, but not before mentioning that he had been "hit harder than that when I came to Utah to play football." In Graham's view, White then "droned through a lecture that was not in the same class with the pre-speech fisticuffs." After the speech, reporters asked White to comment on the incident. His response was offhand: "I regret the incident earlier in the day, but I think everything went off pretty well. I thought it was unfortunate, but I knew what was happening." Pause. "If someone hadn't grabbed him, I probably would have."

Within days the incident escalated from absurdity to farce. A radio talk-show host in nearby Bountiful, Utah, contending that Estes would not be facing jail if White were not a judge, started a legal defense fund. Another host at the same station was so offended by his colleague's campaign that he began a petition drive to have Estes prosecuted "to the fullest extent of the law," but he and his family soon received death threats. The fund collected less than $100 and its creator conceded that Estes "punched the wrong guy, since Justice White has been pretty conservative on the pornography issue." He added, "But if John Hinckley can get off, I think Newton Estes should have the same opportunity." The president of the Utah State Bar then weighed in, but only to denounce the "extremely rude, extremely aggressive and extremely disruptive" behavior of local television cameramen covering the incident. Estes, a construction project estimator, faced a three-year prison sentence and $5,000 fine if found guilty. He hoped to use his trial as a forum for his complaints about the profanity and "filth" that "flowed into our living room" through broadcast television, but the federal district judge ruled that his opinions about the Court were irrelevant, and the jury took only two hours to return a guilty verdict. The judge told Estes his behavior was "ridiculous," and sentenced him to ten days in jail and two years' probation.

The incident bordered on the ridiculous, but raised disturbing questions about security for members of the Court. Estes had sent a letter to all nine members of the Court on January 28, 1981, threatening "direct action" because of policy excesses with respect to obscenity, busing, and defense spending. (Estes later told the press he was spurred to attack White after his wife's "ears and sensibilities were assaulted" when she watched *Capricorn I* over local broadcast television on April 24, 1982.) Three years after the incident in Utah, what was apparently a stray bullet struck a picture window in Harry Blackmun's condominium in Rosslyn, Virginia, and revived the concerns over security for the justices. White, presenting the Court's budget in 1985 shortly after the shooting incident, requested chauffeured automobiles for each justice as a security precaution; the request was rejected.

As for Estes, six years after he assaulted White, he pleaded guilty to molesting an eleven-year-old girl who did housekeeping for him and received a five-years-to-life prison sentence. He then began a series of unsuccessful lawsuits against the prison warden and other state officials. In one (historical) sense, Estes was lucky. The last person to assault a Supreme Court justice had been shot to death by a federal marshal doing double duty as a bodyguard, but that was in 1889. The incident—involving Justice Stephen J. Field, his estranged colleague David Terry, and an overzealous marshal named David Neagle—led to a significant decision by the Supreme Court in the law of executive power and of federal habeas corpus, *In Re Neagle*. "Even in his feuds," observed Robert G. McCloskey, "Field spawned constitutional law." After three punches, the closest that Newton C. Estes got to the Supreme Court was a series of denied certiorari petitions arising from his frivolous lawsuits against the Utah prison authorities.

A year after the Estes incident, White became unwittingly enmeshed in what would become a tinpot scandal two years after he retired. He accepted appointment to a committee to select a winner annually for an award for "distinguished service to justice" by a federal judge, named in honor of Edward J. Devitt, and sponsored by the West Publishing Company, one of the largest publishers in the country of court opinions and casebooks. The committee meetings to review candidates for the award were held in resorts, with all expenses paid by the company. Meetings during the first two years were in Palm Springs, California, which allowed the Whites to socialize with Johnny Blood and his wife while attending the meetings.

In 1995, the *Minneapolis Star-Tribune* ran stories totaling nearly ten thousand words detailing the service of White and six other justices who enjoyed travel at West's expense but did not recuse themselves from the occasional case in which West had an interest before the court. Experts on legal ethics were divided on whether the participation by the justices was improper, although even those who were concerned by the reported facts thought that the members of the Court had acted unwisely but not improperly, much less illegally. The *Star-Tribune's* case, launched against a hometown industry with a large workforce and thus a high readership base, was tainted somewhat by the flow of self-serving facsimiles sent by the newspaper to prominent journalists on the East Coast, attempting to drum up interest in the series of stories. The *New York Times* was so unimpressed with the ratio of words to substance in the *Star-Tribune* series that it declined to cover the story itself.

Two years after the first Palm Springs meeting, Johnny Blood died at the age of eighty-two. When the end was near, expressions of support were solicited from old friends. Byron White dropped a note that was later published in the old football player's memorial service. No more openly sentimental document will be found in White's career:

> John, old friend,
>
> I wish I could be there to see you again. Our friendship has meant a lot to me. I treasure it, there are so many good memories. Marion sends her love to you. She would like to be there. Goodbye, John, and save a place for me.
>
>> Byron

Less than a week after the letter was written, Johnny Blood was dead. "I think the justice had more pure affection for Johnny Blood McNally than anybody else he encountered in football," said Rex Lee. "The other thing that is important is that the justice was at his best when things were the worst." Lee himself had a recurrence of cancer in 1987, "and the justice telephoned me every day when I was hospitalized in Washington. He didn't want anyone to know it then, and he tried to hide the concern in his voice, but I was deeply touched and strengthened by his concern." Others facing grave injury or illness—such as Floyd Haskell, the former senator from Colorado, or Andy Schultz, who clerked for White in October term 1985—had similar stories to tell. "Look," said Rex Lee, "Justice White had a hard side—everybody knows about that. But you don't know him unless you know the other side, and he works pretty hard to conceal it."

18

OCTOBER TERM 1991

BYRON WHITE'S thirtieth full term on the Supreme Court of the United States was shaped in the public mind and to a lesser extent within the Court by the retirement of Thurgood Marshall, the appointment of Clarence Thomas, and at the end of the term, what appeared at the time to be the final showdown on *Roe v. Wade.* White played only a cameo role in all three events. His influence within the Court remained enormous, although there were growing signs that he was beginning to circumscribe his own impact more often and consequently that he, too, was considering when to follow in Marshall's footsteps. Change had been the hallmark of White's third decade on the Court. Since the end of the 1980 term, almost half the institution had turned over: Sandra Day O'Connor for Potter Stewart in 1981, Antonin Scalia for the vacancy caused when William Rehnquist was elevated to chief justice in place of Warren Burger in 1986, Anthony M. Kennedy for Lewis Powell in 1987, and David H. Souter for William Brennan in 1990. During White's second decade on the Court, by comparison, there had been only one change between the end of the 1970 term and the end of the 1980 term—John Paul Stevens for William O. Douglas in 1975.

Speaking to the annual judicial conference of the Tenth Circuit in July of 1991, White stated that "the big news around the Court is the departure of a Justice, just like it was last year." After reviewing the decisions of the term— which he did in a flat, black-letter fashion—he reflected on the consequence

407

of the changes. "Every time a new justice arrives on the Court, the Court's a different instrument. . . . And it's perfectly obvious from time to time that a case is being decided in a way quite different than it would have been decided if his predecessor were still sitting there." Nonetheless he distinguished degrees of change. Speaking as the "only Justice left from the sixties," he said he didn't "think the 1990 Court is as different from the 1960 Court as the 1940 and '50 Court was different from the 1920 and '30 Court. I think the Roosevelt Revolution changed the Court more than the Court has ever changed between 1962 and now."

Some in the audience thought they were listening to the next retiree beginning to review his experiences and career in retrospect. Those who knew him well saw telltale signs of a growing desire to "come home"—notably, several openly sentimental visits to Colorado, especially a visit to his old high school (now a junior high school) in 1984, an appearance at the Wellington High School Alumni Association's dinner honoring his quarter century on the Supreme Court in 1987, and an appearance at the halftime of a University of Colorado football game, which included a reunion of the 1938 Cotton Bowl team—an event attended by seventeen surviving players and three coaches.

The rumor mill had it both ways. The silver anniversary reunion of his law clerks in the spring of 1987 prompted Tony Mauro of *Legal Times* to suggest that White—"robust and still playing basketball at the Court gymnasium at age 69"—would not retire, since he had a "fair chance of beating William O. Douglas's record of 36 years of service." A few months later, the perennial rumor that White would become director of the Federal Bureau of Investigation resurfaced, but this time United Press International noted only that White "was reported to have been considered, but not contacted about the post." A year later, the *National Law Journal* speculated that White was ready to "leave the high court," because he was "increasingly bored with the work, annoyed with the relatively low pay, and eager to spend more time with his grandchildren." The report also stated that "a source" said that in 1986 White "was prepared to step down and even had a resume prepared to send to a Denver firm he might want to practice with." The retirements of Burger in 1986 and Powell in 1987 scotched White's planning, according to the report, but there is no evidence substantiating any aspect of the story.

Whatever thoughts Byron White had about retirement were cabined by two ground rules he had set for himself. First, he would not retire during an election year, and thus indirectly create a political issue during a presidential campaign. Second, if someone else wished or was compelled to retire, he would not create a second vacancy at the same time for fear that the Court's efficiency would be substantially hampered by absorbing two new members at once—especially if confirmation hearings continued to follow the highly partisan model that attended Robert Bork's nomination to replace Powell in 1987. Under White's self-imposed constraints, since 1985 his only window of opportunity to retire during the six-year period was 1989, which would have created the third vacancy in four years.

On the other hand, he could not and would not wait forever. In the first place, he had no desire, he told close friends in Denver, to set a record regardless of his level of effectiveness; a deeper reason, some thought, was his fear that his tenure would be seen as vain and the inevitable comparison of judicial records and athletic records would prompt ridicule of the institution. Ironically, White had surpassed the tenure of Oliver Wendell Holmes, Jr., in May 1991 without anyone in the press taking note; at that point, only eleven justices had served longer than White, and he would pass number eleven—William Johnson (thirty years, four months: 1804–34)—shortly after the end of the 1991 term. In the second place, White recalled with pain the last eleven months before the retirement of William O. Douglas, whose competence was doubted daily and whose incapacity froze the Court at a time when it was under statutory pressure to decide *Buckley v. Valeo* (the Federal Election Campaign Act case), and he vowed never to place the Court in a similar corner. So far, White's health was undiminished. Chronic back problems when he practiced law in Denver had required surgery, which had been successful, although the prognosis was that he would eventually develop a potentially painful condition—spinal stenosis—that would require more surgery.

For someone who was now chronically suspected of harboring retirement plans, White showed no signs of pulling in his horns at the end of the 1990 term. He was at his best and worst in *Arizona v. Fulminante,* which raised questions of coerced confessions and what to do about them in state criminal trials. With the chief justice in the minority from the outset, the case was one of eleven during the term in which White—as senior associate justice in the majority—assigned the opinions of the Court, five of which he kept for himself. His discussion of the case at the Tenth Circuit conference, while discreetly incomplete, illustrates his manner of explaining his work to a well-informed audience:

> The issue in *Fulminante* was whether a confession that had been admitted was coerced. That was the first issue. Secondly, if it was, does harmless error apply? And if it does, was it harmless? Well, *Fulminante* produced two major-

ity opinions, just like another case did in the last term. I wrote a majority opinion that held the confession was coerced and it was error to admit it. And I thought that the harmless error rule didn't apply at all, but the majority— the majority opinion written by Justice Rehnquist held that the harmless error rule does apply and that [admitting the coerced confession into evidence] was harmless. So, in deciding that the harmless error rule applied, a good many prior cases were overruled.

He then argued that the decision by the Rehnquist majority was not of great moment:

I don't think you should overreact to [the] decision: you can say simply [that it was] an extension of the *Chapman* [*v. California*] rule, that the harmless error rule applies to constitutional violations as well as to non-constitutional violations. . . . And since *Chapman* we have applied the harmless error rule to all sorts of constitutional violations in a criminal trial, but always we said there are some constitutional violations that can never be harmless error: for instance, the failure to furnish an attorney. And we had always included in that category the introduction of coerced confessions, but the majority just thought there was no difference between that kind of an evidentiary error than some others, such as, say, the introduction of illegally seized evidence. Well, I just thought that police should never be excused from coercing a confession and having it even remotely ratified by sustaining the conviction. But I don't think that this portends any great trend to eliminate exclusionary rules under the Fourth Amendment or anything else. I think we are being quite true to the rule under the Fourth Amendment that we exclude the evidence to deter illegal conduct.

One of White's former law clerks who was now practicing in Albuquerque, New Mexico, Andy Schultz, asked White pointedly why he "chose to read your rather stinging dissent from the bench." White responded that opinions were read or summarized at length from the bench "in the 60s," but that the practice had been abandoned. He said the longest he ever spoke from the bench was "in the Act of State case" (*Banco National de Cuba v. Sabbatino*): "I was the sole dissenter and I felt very strongly about that case, and I spoke for about 15 minutes." Although few now detailed their views on days when opinions were announced, White said reading large chunks of his opinion in *Fulminante* was not "anything new, but it did indicate that I had a head of steam up. (Laughter)." White did not admit to the judicial conference what he confirmed to the *Legal Times* the day of the announcement: the last time "he had said more than a sentence or two about an opinion of his from the bench" was *INS v. Chadha*—eight years earlier.

What White withheld from both the circuit conference and the *Legal Times* was how close he came to prevailing on both points in *Fulminante*. There were at least six votes to affirm the Arizona Supreme Court's reversal of Oreste Fulminante's conviction and death sentence for murdering his eleven-year-old stepdaughter. The lower court had found that the confession had been coerced and that Supreme Court precedent precluded application of the harmless error rule. White's draft opinion for the Court affirming the judgment as well as the lower court's conclusions on both issues was met by a forceful dissent from Chief Justice Rehnquist. The chief justice argued that the confession was not in fact coerced and that the harmless error rule should apply in any event. White's majority began to fall apart. He tried to accommodate Justice Scalia. In fact, the last paragraph of Part II of White's opinion was Scalia's price for agreeing that the confession was coerced: White adopted Scalia's proposed language agreeing with the lower court, on a "close" question, that the confession was coerced by a "credible threat of physical violence."

White was inflexible with Sandra Day O'Connor, and he consequently lost his majority on the question of the applicability of the harmless error rule. Not long after White circulated his draft opinion, O'Connor wrote White:

> As I indicated at conference, I am willing to agree that coerced confessions are not subject to harmless error analysis. I would like to make clear, however, that our holding is limited to genuinely coerced confessions—that is, confessions motivated by fear or force. A confession can be involuntary without being coerced, such as a confession obtained without adequate Miranda warnings. I hope the opinion can make such a distinction.

But it did not. After weeks of wrangling back and forth, Justice Scalia embraced Chief Justice Rehnquist's distinction between trial errors (to which harmless error applies) and systemic error (to which it does not) and joined that portion of the chief justice's opinion qualifying the *Chapman* rule. Two days later, O'Connor notified Rehnquist that despite her initial vote to affirm, "like Nino [Scalia] I am persuaded that admission of an *involuntary* confession can be, and should be, analyzed under the harmless error doctrine" (emphasis added). Two years later, when White retired, *Fulminante* was cited by one journalist as a prime example of White's self-defeating stubbornness in dealing with his colleagues, although no source is supplied for the claim that White "preferred to vote quickly and to stand his ground . . . instead of trying to persuade his colleagues." The six-month internal debate over *Fulminante* reveals White as accommodating on some points and not on others, and other members of the Court withholding and changing votes depending on further deliberation.

The postretirement slant on *Fulminante* illustrates that White continued to remain a favorite target of the press, regardless of the evidence, and perhaps in part because he continued to refuse to view the First Amendment through the eyes of journalists. Two decisions at the end of the 1990 term reinforced the climate of mutual antipathy. In *Masson v. New Yorker Magazine,* White wrote a separate opinion declaring a "knowingly false attribution" of a quotation by a journalist was enough to place a defamation case before a jury, as opposed to a standard requiring "material alteration" of a quotation. A few days later, in *Cohen v. Cowles Media,* White wrote for a 5-4 majority that held that a source who had been promised confidentiality by a newspaper could enforce the promise even when the publisher claimed that revealing his identity was an editorial decision protected by the First Amendment. White wrote that the First Amendment claim was "constitutionally insignificant" and that contract law "requires those who make promises to keep them."

Three terms earlier, White had written for a 6-2 majority in *California v. Greenwood* (argued before Justice Kennedy took his seat) that the Fourth Amendment did not prohibit the warrantless search and seizure of garbage left for collection outside the curtilage of a home. The press responded to all three of these decisions with open disdain, but *Greenwood* struck a nerve. Justice Brennan's dissent predicted that "members of our society will be shocked to learn that the Court, the ultimate guarantor of liberty, deems unreasonable our expectation that the aspects of our private lives that are concealed safely in a trash bag will not become public." Justice White responded with a smug footnote that later proved to be joined to a politically tin ear: "Given that the dissenters are among the minority of judges whose views are contrary to ours, we are distinctly unimpressed with the dissent's prediction that 'society will be shocked to learn' of today's decision." The exchange, uncharacteristically abrasive for the two justices involved, carried a sulfuric aroma of law clerk prose unchecked.

In any event, the Brennan prediction proved to be more in tune with popular reaction, at least within the mainstream press. Editorials in the *Washington Post* and *New York Times* lashed the decision. Nat Hentoff devoted a column to arguing against the opinion with the help of quotations from Prof. Yale Kamisar of Michigan and Justice Brennan's dissent, and Tom Wicker of the *New York Times* said the decision was the product of the "bitterest legacy of the Kennedy Administration, Justice Byron White." Tom

Gavin of the *Denver Post,* who had covered White's career on and off for thirty years, wrote angrily:

> Is it possible to trade in a Supreme Court justice? If so, I'd like to offer Byron White. Yeah, the Whizzer. Our very own, home-grown, All-American, Rhodes Scholar, Colorado *wunderkind.* Anything of value will be considered. An engine from a '37 Buick. A bushel of buttered popcorn. A person in touch with individual dignity and privacy. Yes, someone who values privacy would be nice.

As if White's rulings were not bad enough, Stuart Taylor of the *American Lawyer* raked White over the coals for his demeanor in an unusually sarcastic column. Writing a year after *Greenwood,* Taylor painted White as a "sour," unpleasant bully with contempt for lawyers and spectators alike: "He scowls at people who call him 'Whizzer' and glowers at people who don't. White won't give the time of day to the tourists who stand in line to hear their Supreme Court expounding the law of the land." After paraphrasing a typically terse announcement by White of an opinion for the Court, Taylor concluded that the "unspoken message" was, "'You want to know what the case was about, maggots? Then go downstairs and stand in line for a copy of the opinion.'" In Taylor's judgment, White would be better suited running "one of those boot camps where they rehabilitate young toughs by grinding their noses in the dirt. . . . He'd probably like that more than being a justice anyway."

Despite what was becoming an annual roasting at the end of the term by one or more journalists, White's central position on what was now routinely called the Rehnquist Court was acknowledged by several academic observers, from Burt Neuborne of New York University and Michael McConnell of the University of Chicago in 1988 to Jesse Choper of the University of California at Berkeley at the end of the 1990 term. "That the Chief Justice has assigned a number of important cases to him suggests that he holds White in high regard," McConnell observed at the end of the 1987 term, which included opinions for the Court by White in *Greenwood, Hazelwood School District v. Kuhlmeir* (upholding broad discretion by public school officials over the content of student newspapers), and *DeBartolo Corp. v. Florida Gulf Coast Building Council* (upholding "secondary handbilling"—leafleting employers who do business with companies against whom unions have a grievance). "This was a White term," Neuborne was quoted as saying. Three years later, Choper viewed White as a "moderating influence" on a Court that seemed to be perpetually, in McConnell's phrase, "on the threshold of a conservative working majority."

Byron White had grown accustomed to derision in the press and grudging respect from the academy, although he affected indifference to both, but he was condemned at the beginning of October term 1991 by criticism from an unanticipated quarter—a papier-mâché artist. Lee Brozgold created death masks, laminated with newspaper stories and quotations from public speeches and official statements, for an exhibit called *40 Patriots/Countless Americans*. White's death mask was one, as were the Reagans', the Bushes', and Frank Sinatra's. Brozgold explained that the "whole thesis of this exhibit is that these people . . . are opposed to recognizing the rights of what I call common Americans" and "should be dead. They are dead. They are the old order." He cautioned that "these masks are intended to be funny," but he was condemned by Phyllis Schlafly of the Eagle Forum and the Reverend Donald Wildmon of the American Family Association. Schlafly and Wildmon tried to use Brozgold as cumulative evidence of the political tendentiousness of the National Endowment of the Arts, which had provided grant money to a theater that exhibited the work. Brozgold pointed out that he had received no money from the NEA to support the project, and, on the merits of the work, declared: "Metaphor is my business. My choice of the death head to represent right-wing sociopolitical icons is simply my way of saying that I think their vision for America is archaic, and it has got to go." The Supreme Court police force, on alert since the assault on White and the stray shot at the Blackmun residence a couple of years later, was not amused, but White seemed utterly oblivious to the dispute.

At the Tenth Circuit conference in July, Byron White said offhandedly that "it wouldn't be strange if we ended up with just eight justices for a term." He recalled the 1969 term, when Harry Blackmun was not confirmed to replace Abe Fortas until "May, so we went a whole term with eight justices, which wasn't too bad an experience. After all, we just had a lot of ties, that's all. (Laughter)." The first Monday in October arrived, the Court was reduced to eight justices, and the vacancy was no longer a laughing matter. Although Thurgood Marshall had conditioned his retirement on confirmation of his successor, he felt he could not appropriately sit and hear cases, then retire when—and if—Clarence Thomas was confirmed. Over the weekend on the eve of the statutory first day of term, Thomas had been accused of sexual harassment by a former subordinate at the Equal Employment Opportunity Commission. After a day of heated debate on the floor of the Senate, the scheduled vote on Thomas's nomination was postponed in order to hear testimony on the harassment charge. The resulting exchange of testimony the following weekend by the former employee, Anita Hill, and Thomas, became a cause célèbre that severely jeopardized the nomination. Thomas was confirmed on October 15 by a vote of 52-48—the highest number of negative votes ever against a successful nominee to the Supreme Court. When it was all over, among the nostalgic reflections on the tawdry affair were those of David Brinkley and William F. Buckley, who recalled that White's hearings lasted only a few minutes and were devoid of "This is Your Life melodrama."

Once Thomas was confirmed, early during the second week of the term, the appointment took on elements of low comedy and dubious taste. At every stage, White remained in the background as much as possible. He said nothing to anyone during the confirmation process about Thomas, perhaps because he had learned his lesson with the nomination of Robert Bork. Two months after the Bork nomination and one day after the confirmation hearings began, White had attended a cocktail party held by *USA Today* and attended by Pres. Ronald Reagan among others. Reagan spotted White and said that he thought Bork had done well in his first day of hearings. "He's up against bush leaguers," Reagan said to White. White's political antennae should have warned him of danger, but before he could leave he encountered John McLaughlin, the television talk show host. McLaughlin asked, "What would you think of Judge Bork on the Court?" White replied absently: "It would be all right with me." McLaughlin asked, "Can I quote you?" White replied, "Do whatever you want to."

McLaughlin waited five days and rehearsed the conversation on his Sunday program, *One on One*. In the highly charged atmosphere of the Bork hearings, the idle comment was low-grade dynamite. The statement was immediately called an "endorsement," and the Court's public information officer, Toni House, quickly tried to control the embarrassment by labeling the statement "informal": "I wouldn't regard it as a public endorsement." Bork's supporters in the Senate immediately emphasized White's "unusual step" of endorsing Judge Bork's candidacy. White's careless remark was quickly forgotten in the rhetorical turmoil of the nomination, which was defeated in the Senate 58-42 ten days after the last reference in the Senate to the "endorsement" and almost a month after it was uttered. White was privately furious, both with himself and with the press, and told friends in Colorado, *I shouldn't have said anything, and then I couldn't say anything*. The Souter and Thomas nominations found White silent in public and private.

Thomas's confirmation raised two immediate questions: When and where would he be sworn in? And if he was sworn in at the Court, would television coverage of the swearing-in be permitted? The second question, completely within the control of the Court, was answered quickly. Led by

O'Connor and Souter (who was even more hostile to television coverage than White), the Court informed counsel for media wishing to televise, broadcast, and photograph within the courtroom that a "majority" of the Court did "not wish to enlarge the present coverage of Court proceedings in the manner in which you request." The Thomas-Hill exchange played no part in the justices' decision, which was made in late September before the sexual harassment charge was made.

The Court seemed less concerned over allowing cameras in the courtroom than with eliminating tandem ceremonies, first at the White House and then at the Court. Blackmun wrote to his colleagues that the White House ceremony had begun during the Reagan administration, was unnecessary, and symbolically enmeshed the Court in the political side of the appointment process. "I refused to attend the White House ceremony the last time," he pointed out, "and I shall not attend this time, if there is one." Blackmun's fears were richly borne out. The White House staged what Helen Thomas of UPI described as "one of the most elaborate ceremonies ever staged at the White House for such an occasion." The event, attended by more than one thousand invitees, was held one day after the death of Chief Justice Rehnquist's wife. The Court was privately in mourning and resisted having the ceremony then instead of November 1, when the next conference was scheduled. The White House insisted both on the timing and on the finality of the occasion; President Bush wanted to be able to refer to "Mr. Justice Thomas" at the end of the day. The Court drew the line, and White, as senior associate justice, stood in for the chief justice and subtly delivered the message. Before administering the constitutional oath required of all federal officers, White said:

> The swearing-in of a Supreme Court Justice is undoubtedly a very serious affair. But it's also a very exciting one and I'm quite glad to be here to stand in for the Chief Justice, who unfortunately, could not be here because of the death of his wife, Natalie Cornell Rehnquist. We called her "Nan." We dearly loved her and we shall miss her very much.
>
> Judge Thomas, this will not be the first time you've taken an oath that is ordinarily given to federal officers. And when at 10:00 on November 1st, you take the judicial oath that is required by statute, you will become the 106th justice to sit on the Supreme Court, and we look forward to that day.

Three days after the ceremony, with the chief justice still in mourning, White announced Mrs. Rehnquist's death from the bench and the Court awaited November 1 for the final oath to be taken by Thomas. Mrs. Rehnquist's funeral was two days later. The morning after the funeral, Thomas telephoned the chief justice and asked to be sworn in immediately. The press speculated that he feared further revelations about his past and sought the full constitutional protection of office. Thomas explained that he wished to put his staff and himself on the Court's payroll as soon as possible; the next oral argument session was less than a week away. Rehnquist acquiesced and administered the judicial oath in private, without even notifying other members of the Court who were then in the building. The press concluded that Thomas had been rushed into office "with unseemly haste."

Clarence Thomas now had what A. E. Dick Howard of the University of Virginia called a place of "great repose" in which to reflect on his "fevered journey," but the solace lay in insulation from the media and the public, not in the ease or the leisurely pace of the work. His first two argument sessions were watched closely within and without the Court, but Thomas revealed nothing in the courtroom. He asked very few questions during the November and December sessions. Each session produced a case of more than passing mutual interest to Thomas and White. In the November session, on Thomas's first day of oral arguments, the Court heard *Foucha v. Louisiana,* which challenged the constitutionality of a state statute that authorized the continued confinement of someone who had been acquitted of a crime by reason of insanity but who a hospital review committee now found had no evidence of mental illness and should be discharged. The vote in conference to invalidate the statute was lopsided, with Rehnquist in dissent, so White assigned the opinion of the Court to himself.

He had worked on the assignment for little more than two weeks when he received a note from Thomas announcing that he was changing his vote from reversal to affirmance—the first time in thirty years that White could recall losing a vote from his proposed opinion for the Court before the draft circulated. In the end, *Foucha* bubbled within the Court for more than six months, largely because Justice Thomas did not produce his dissent for more than three months after White first distributed his draft for the Court. In May the decision came down as a fractured 5-4 decision holding that the statute violated the acquitted defendant's due process rights. Thomas, joined by the chief justice and Justice Scalia, filed one of two dissenting opinions.

The December session of arguments put Justice Thomas back in a familiar and unwelcome spotlight. The legal question in *Franklin v. Gwinnett County Public Schools* was whether monetary damages could be recovered for sexual harassment of a student by a teacher under Title IX of the Education Amendments of 1972. The *Washington Post* pointed out the symbolic stakes: "The case has drawn attention in part because it is the first sexual harassment case to come to the Court since the arrival of Justice Clarence Thomas, whose confirmation was jeopardized by an allegation that he sexually harassed" a subordinate. "Thomas was the only justice who did not ask a question" during oral argument.

The Court had decided twelve years earlier in *Cannon v. University of Chicago* that private causes of action were contemplated by Title IX, but that decision occurred under what Justice Scalia would derisively call the ancien régime, and only two members of the majority were left on the Court—Justice Stevens, who wrote for the Court then, and Justice Rehnquist; Justice White had written a dissenting opinion, and Justice Blackmun had also been in the minority. The Bush administration supported the lower court and argued that remedies under Title IX were limited to depriving the offending school system of federal funds.

At the conference on *Franklin,* the Court was divided down the middle on which rule to adopt for implied causes of action under Title IX—what was referred to as the traditional *Bell v. Hood* rule, that "any available remedy," including monetary damages, is presumed to be available to redress violations of legal rights, or a more limited rule, recognizing that categorical limitations on the scope of remedial relief are appropriate in cases of implied rights of action. There were only four votes for the traditional rule—White, Blackmun, Stevens, and O'Connor. Scalia, Kennedy, and Souter favored a more limited rationale for reversing the court of appeals ruling that only equitable relief was available for violations of Title IX. Rehnquist and probably Thomas would dissent, so White enjoyed the assignment power, and after some hesitation, kept the opinion for himself.

When White sat down with his law clerk to outline the structure of the opinion, it was apparent that precedent controlled his view of the case. Although he had dissented in *Cannon,* it was now not only good law within the Court but had been effectively approved by subsequent congressional legislation. He was strongly committed to the general rule and said somewhat laconically that he did not care if he obtained only four votes for the view, because it was correct. Nonetheless, he developed a strategy for securing a majority of the Court for the rule. For Scalia and Souter, the draft opinion emphasized the historical lineage of the *Bell v. Hood* rule, starting with the early nineteenth century and even including an earlier English case; for Kennedy, the draft examined legislative materials spanning two decades to demonstrate that Congress had no intention as a general principle to limit remedies for statutory causes of action. The entire package had to be prepared by the law clerk pursuant to White's precepts for opinion writing, in force since the early

1980s: *Write a page a day for no more than twelve days. Do not create or apply any "tests"—simply resolve the case on the basis of precedent. Cite no law review articles.* (One clerk from the mid-1980s, a former editor in chief of an Ivy League law review, did not share White's judicial views but agreed with the taboo on law review articles: "By then, they were all about Hegel—or worse—and not about law.")

The twelve-day time limit was White's response to Chief Justice Rehnquist's Report Card—the periodic table listing each justice and providing a tabular display of opinions "assigned not circulated," "in circulation," "announced," the "total assigned," and "outstanding dissents or separate writings in which a majority opinion is circulating." The Report Card was an internal disciplinary, or shaming, device used by the chief justice to prod opinions from his colleagues. White and O'Connor were consistently the most expeditious and productive writers on the Court during the early 1990s. In addition to the other strictures on opinion writing, White added his own protocols for separate opinions. Concurring and dissenting opinions took priority over majority opinions, so that others writing for the Court were not held up by "vanity" writings. In addition, White tended to circulate separate opinions by seniority, such that a dissent from a Blackmun opinion circulated before one for a Scalia opinion but after one for the chief justice.

The *Franklin* draft succeeded in obtaining six votes. Justice Scalia filed a curiously self-contradictory opinion, joined by Rehnquist and Thomas, which concurred in the judgment. Scalia complained about the entire concept of implied causes of action, let alone the availability of damage relief, but still conceded that Congress had approved both the action and the remedy under Title IX five years earlier. Perhaps because the case had been overwatched, the opinion for the Court was overread in some quarters. The *New York Times* read White's opinion as adopting an "impatient, almost scolding tone toward the Administration"—a characterization that startled White and his staff and was merited on neither objective nor subjective grounds.

Clerks in other chambers occasionally referred, in admiration or frustration, to the "White Court"—implying that major doctrinal change needed to go through White directly or indirectly, that he was capable of persuading doubtful votes to join his or other opinions that avoided extremes, and at a very minimum, that he exerted unmatched influence in setting the size and pace of the Court's plenary docket. The designation was exaggerated, of course, because no one justice exerted singularly dominant influence over the Court at the time. White's achievements tended to be more case-focused than theoretical and not always predictable, a function more of his incrementalism and attention to detail than his charm or doctrinal ingenuity. It is true that other members of the Court tried to use him from time to time as a broker not for votes but for changes in the circulating opinions of others, but his success rate in that role was not high—it was a role for which he was not well suited and that he did not enjoy.

A case in point during the 1991 term was *Burson v. Freeman,* which presented the question of the extent to which states could constitutionally regulate electioneering and related activity in the immediate vicinity of a polling place. Justice Blackmun's draft opinion for the Court—very similar to what was ultimately published—was an apologetic application of standard First Amendment doctrine. He treated the question as if the state were telling people what they could say almost anywhere, then found that the state had constitutionally acceptable reasons—but just barely—for the regulatory regime. Justice Scalia was appalled by the reasoning and treatment of the Court's case law and telephoned White to urge him to work with Blackmun on an alternate theory reaching the same result but relying on White's "nonpublic forum" analysis in *Perry Education Association v. Perry Local Educators' Association* in 1983. White did not view his duty to include protecting his own opinions, so he left the task to Scalia, who tried but failed and published his unsuccessful effort as a concurrence in the judgment. White joined Blackmun's opinion, but since Thomas had not yet joined the Court when the case was heard, the vote was 5-3, and Scalia's opinion turned Blackmun's convoluted exercise into a four-person plurality.

White's hefty internal impact in close cases is better illustrated during the 1991 term by *Jacobson v. United States,* the case of the fifty-six-year-old Nebraska farmer who was convicted of one count of obtaining child pornography. In 1984, Keith Jacobson had legally purchased two magazines containing photographs of nude teen and preteen boys. Shortly thereafter, following enactment of the Child Protection Act of 1984, agents of the Postal and Customs Services used five fictitious organizations for twenty-eight months to induce Jacobson to purchase material unlawful under the act. He pleaded entrapment but was convicted. The Court of Appeals for the Eighth Circuit, after a panel reversed the conviction, affirmed en banc. Troubled by the government's behavior, White successfully pushed for the Court to grant Jacobson's petition for certiorari; his preliminary view of the record was that Jacobson had been harassed by federal agents run amok.

At oral argument in the Supreme Court, several justices worried aloud that Jacobson's version of entrapment would undermine routine undercover sting operations now commonly used by law enforcement agencies. Justice

O'Connor pointed to the example of fake pawn shops used to snare thieves trying to peddle stolen goods. White "differentiated between a pawn shop sting operation—'that's a passive government action'—and 'targeting a person and pursuing' him" for more than two years. The vote at conference was 7-2 to affirm Jacobson's conviction, with White and Stevens dissenting. The case was assigned to Justice O'Connor.

"Talk is cheap," White often told his clerks. "All the persuasion around here is done on paper." Or, as he told the Eighth Circuit judicial conference in 1993, "I've always said that the meat is cut in writing rather than talk around the conference table." White produced a powerful dissent that picked up Justices Blackmun and Thomas rather readily. Then two months went by before Justice Souter switched his vote and provided White with a majority. The "join" came with a price—several items of dicta about entrapment that were neither necessary nor even useful—but White accommodated Souter, and the decision was issued exactly five months after oral argument. Jacobson was vindicated, although he had lost his job as a school bus driver, suffered humiliation in the small Nebraska town near his home, and been forced to sell forty acres of his family farm to defray his legal expenses.

Jacobson was handed down approximately ten days before White celebrated his thirtieth anniversary on the Supreme Court. He was out of town on the actual day—April 16—but when the Court again sat on April 21, the chief justice took note of the milestone and turned to White, whose dry response to the courtroom audience was, "You may hold your applause." Although he feigned annoyance at his annual reunion of law clerks and discounted the significance of the anniversary, he seemed to reflect more openly about his judicial career with both his current clerks and with friends in Denver than in recent years. He was too modest as well as too impatient to deliver himself of a sustained, reflective personal accounting. The judgments trickled out in moments of repose at work, or over a private lunch in Denver, or after a day of fly-fishing on a river in the Rockies. His reflections were less about personalities or momentous cases than about regrets over his own performance.

There were two major areas in which White was dissatisfied with his work, defamation and "employment discrimination." He admitted, not for the first time, that he regretted joining *New York Times v. Sullivan,* and he contended that *no one on either side was happy about the way the doctrine had evolved from that decision.* He had called for a complete reevaluation of the *New York Times* rule in an opinion concurring in the judgment to *Dun & Bradstreet v. Greenmoss Builders* in 1985, a case he helped to force to reargument. His separate opinion declared:

I remain convinced that *Gertz** was erroneously decided. I have also become convinced that the Court struck an improvident balance in [*New York Times*]. In a country like ours, [adequate information] about their government is of transcendent importance [to the people]. That flow of intelligence deserves full First Amendment protection. Criticism and assessment of the performance of public officials and of government in general are not subject to penalties imposed by law. But these First Amendment values are not at all served by circulating false statements of fact about public officials. On the contrary, erroneous information frustrates these values. They are even more disserved when the statements falsely impugn the honesty of those men and women and hence lessen the confidence in government.

To substitute for *New York Times,* White suggested that the constitutional standard focus on the amount of damages rather than the standard of liability. As long as punitive or presumed damages were capped or prohibited

and the common law standard of liability [was] retained, the defamed public official, upon proving falsity, could at least have had a judgment to that effect. The public official should not have been required to satisfy the actual malice standard where he sought no damages but only to clear his name. In this way, both First Amendment and reputational interests would have been far better served. [The] necessary breathing room for speakers can be ensured by limitations on recoverable damages; it does not also require depriving many public figures of any room to vindicate their reputations sullied by false statements of fact. [It] is difficult to argue that the United States did not have a free and vigorous press before the rule in *New York Times* was announced.

Now, more than a half decade later, White remained wedded to his position in *Dun & Bradstreet.* To those who thought his model unworkable, he pointed to Judge Abraham Sofaer's handling of the trial of Ariel Sharon's defamation suit against *Time* magazine. Judge Sofaer refused to let *Time* magazine off the hook before trial, but encouraged the magazine to inquire "thoroughly into the sources behind its story" and encouraged both parties not to "permit the trial to distract them from further, good-faith efforts to resolve

---

* In 1974, *Gertz v. Robert Welch* held that people claiming that they had been defamed who were not public officials or "public figures" did not need to meet the stringent standards of *New York Times v. Sullivan* in order to recover damages. As long as liability was based on some fault on the part of the publsher and no punitive or exemplary damages were available under state law, the Court concluded that the First Amendment had not been violated. White filed a lengthy, and at times bitter, dissent, which complained that the Court had no justification for displacing centuries of common law defamation doctrine in the name of the First Amendment.

their differences." The goal was to allow Sharon to repair his reputation as appropriate and *Time* to avoid the enormous costs of litigation, let alone damages. Both White and Sofaer sought to escape what they saw as the either/or trap of the *New York Times v. Sullivan* rule.

His other major regret, besides his hasty acceptance of *New York Times,* was his unsteady record on affirmative action. "I wish I had been more consistent in the employment discrimination area," was the way he would put it. White began as a friend of affirmative action, whether challenged on constitutional or statutory grounds. He went along with university programs setting aside places in professional schools for racial minority students whose objective credentials did not match those of white applicants (*Regents of the University of California v. Bakke*). He also signed on to Justice Brennan's opinion for the Court in *United Steelworkers v. Weber* in 1979, which upheld a voluntary program that set aside half of the positions in an in-plant training program for minorities; the program was attacked by a white worker under Title VII of the Civil Rights Act of 1964. By 1987, White argued that *Weber* should be overruled. He explained his change of mind in a dissent in *Johnson v. Transportation Agency* in 1987, a 5-4 decision that upheld a flexible affirmative action plan designed to benefit women:

> My understanding of *Weber* was, and is, that the employer's plan did not violate Title VII [of the Civil Rights Act of 1964] because it was designed to remedy intentional and systematic exclusion of blacks by the employer and the unions from certain job categories. That is how I understand the phrase "traditionally segregated jobs" we used in that case. The Court now interprets it to mean nothing more than a manifest imbalance between one identifiable group and another in the employer's labor force. As so interpreted, that case, as well as today's decision, as Justice Scalia so well demonstrates, is a perversion of Title VII.

Privately, White conceded that the anxieties he had when *Bakke* arose—that affirmative action would devolve into academic admissions and employment decisions driven by race—had become manifest by the mid-1980s. *Wygant v. Jackson Board of Education* in 1986 had been a turning point. The case involved a school board's policy to grant preferential protection against layoffs to some of its racial minority employees. A white teacher who was laid off despite having more seniority than some retained black teachers sued the board and claimed the policy violated the equal protection clause. White joined a plurality that held that the policy was unconstitutional. His concurrence in the judgment stated: "Whatever the legitimacy of hiring goals or quotas may be, the discharge of white teachers to make room for blacks, none of whom has been shown to be a victim of any racial discrimination, is quite a different matter." He put it more bluntly afterward to a friend in Denver: "You just can't take an innocent man's job away. You can't call that a remedy."

White offered no other clues to his thinking over the decades on the issue. After his intellectual trip to Damascus in *Wygant* and in *Johnson,* his views were put to the acid test in *Metro Broadcasting v. Federal Communications Commission* in 1990. FCC policies favoring minority ownership were challenged as unconstitutional. After hesitating for weeks, White cast the fifth vote to reject the challenge and to uphold the policies. The decisive factor for White was that the policies had the imprimatur of Congress, and that was enough to sustain the policies, as it had been for him in 1980 when congressionally mandated racial preference programs were first sustained by the Court in *Fullilove v. Klutznick.* Nonetheless, without Congress in the picture, White found racial preference or set-aside programs invalid under either the Constitution or federal employment discrimination laws.

Stuart Taylor, an unsympathetic but discerning critic, wrote after White retired that the record "strongly suggest[ed] that [White] thought affirmative-action preferences, originally advanced as a last-ditch remedy for cases of hard-core discrimination against blacks, had evolved into dangerous engines of reverse discrimination and racial quotas." When White visited the University of Kansas in 1996 to deliver a lecture and answer public questions, he strongly implied that he agreed with the Court's 1995 decision in *Adarand Contractors v. Pena,* which held that financial incentives under a federal program to benefit minority contractors would hardly ever pass constitutional muster. His answer is notable because from *Fullilove* to *Metro Broadcasting,* White had voted to uphold federally sponsored affirmative action programs; either his discomfort with set-aside programs had extended across the board or the tenuous congressional imprint on the program in question—it ran through two agencies, the Department of Transportation and the Small Business Administration—undermined its legitimacy for him.

The intersection of race and the equal protection clause occurred in two cases during the 1991 term. Both turned on *Green v. County Board,* the 1968 decision repudiating freedom-of-choice plans as a solution to formerly de jure segregated public school systems. In *Freeman v. Pitts,* the Court approved partial withdrawal of federal judicial supervision of a large suburban school system that had operated under a consent decree for nearly a quarter century. The school district was represented by Rex Lee, who was appearing before the Court for the fifty-sixth time (he was scheduled to argue again during the term, but the case was settled). His oral argument was one of two during the term by a former White clerk; the other was in *Quill Corp. v. North Dakota,* which was argued by Nicholas J. Spaeth, the attorney general of North Dakota. Lee's argument won high marks from all who saw it, but Spaeth's earned the Worst Sartorial Strategy During a Supreme Court Argument Award in Tony Mauro's year-end review for *Legal Times.* Spaeth wore a tie, given him by Justice White, that featured miniature buffaloes. "Spaeth referred to the tie during his argument, joking that he'd worn it because he particularly needed Justice White's vote" to overrule a precedent that frustrated his position. "The justices did not laugh, and Kennedy asked him glaringly, 'Do you have any better reasons?' Spaeth lost the case," although he won White's vote. The issue in the case was whether an out-of-state retailer could be required to collect a state-use tax on sales to customers within the state. The Court held that the commerce clause of the Constitution precluded the state from collecting the tax. Three justices agreed with Justice White that the clause did not handcuff the state's tax collector.

The other segregation case was *United States v. Fordice*—known for most of its career in the federal courts as *United States v. Mabus,* for Kirk Fordice's predecessor as governor of Mississippi, Ray Mabus. The basic question in *Fordice* was whether a state university system, segregated by race as a matter of law until 1962, had satisfied its obligation to desegregate by providing racially open admissions among the formerly white and black units of the system. In doctrinal terms, the question was whether the obligations of *Green* applied at the university as well as the kindergarten-to-twelfth-grade levels. No one seriously doubted the continuing vitality of *Green,* but its mechanical application to the post-high-school level posed the risk that historically black colleges would be eradicated in the name of integration or doctrinal symmetry. Neither objective commanded enthusiasm among the justices, and the consequences of requiring compliance with *Green*—in a world with less optimism and fewer resources than in 1968—were extremely uncertain. The Court of Appeals for the Fifth Circuit, impressed by what it construed as good faith by the state, held that the duty to desegregate had been satisfied because "Mississippi has adopted and implemented race neutral policies for operating its colleges and universities and . . . all students have real freedom of choice to attend the college or university they wish."

The *Fordice* case demonstrates the accuracy of Justice Robert H. Jackson's observation: "The fact is that the Court functions less as one deliberative body than as nine, each Justice working largely in isolation except as he chooses to seek consultation with others. These working methods tend to cultivate a highly individualistic rather than a group viewpoint." When the justices met in conference to vote on whether to sustain the Fifth Circuit, there was no consensus on the appropriate outcome or analysis—"nine different takes," according to one clerk in another chamber. The chief justice assigned the case to White and told him lightly to "figure it out." The record alone occupied twenty-eight boxes of exhibits, testimony, and court records. The case and the assignment were unusually important to White, and he took his time with the opinion, allowing himself the singular luxury during the term of being posted on the chief justice's Report Card—twice—as delinquent with an assigned opinion for the Court.

White did not circulate a draft in *Fordice* until February 17, three months after oral argument. Justice Stevens notified White three days later that he would join the opinion, then a long silence set in. Justice Blackmun provided a third vote for the opinion a month after it circulated. Justice O'Connor had reservations about White's formulation of the standard of liability, wrote a letter detailing her concerns in early March, and then visited White to discuss her concerns but did not commit herself pro or con on his opinion. Others— including the chief justice and Justice Blackmun—expressed worries over the precise terms of the grounds for reversing the court of appeals, beyond the conclusion that freedom of choice did not go far enough, but in the end White was able to secure a majority with studied ambiguity—"If policies traceable to the *de jure* system are still in force and have discriminatory effects, those policies too must be reformed to the extent practicable and consistent with sound educational policies." Which policies were tainted and how they should be remedied were not identified by the Court and could not be without further proceedings in the lower courts. The case continued to bubble throughout the spring, with the chief justice signing on and then Justice Scalia finally weighing in on May 19 with a snide dissenting opinion that should have provoked final votes from the fence-sitters (O'Connor, Kennedy, Souter, and Thomas) but did not.

The end of May came and *Mabus* stood at 4-1 to reverse the court of appeals judgment that the governor and legislature had done all that was necessary to desegregate the state university system. The justices filed their annual financial disclosure statements pursuant to the Ethics in Government Act. White's assets were listed, in the ranges provided by the act's regulations, at between $165,000 and $414,000, which placed him seventh in wealth among the justices. Justices Thomas and Souter listed assets at half that level, and only Justices O'Connor and Stevens remained millionaires. White's asset value had improved marginally from the year before, but had in fact been stable for the past half decade. The only sharp move in family assets was reported in 1986, when Mrs. White received $89,500 from her mother's estate. White's annual outside income during the period appeared to hover in the $10,000 range, including one or two annual speaking fees in mid-decade. Although the first mortgage on his residence was paid off in May 1987, the disclosure statements made clear that Byron White was at least in this respect one more federal employee who lived on his paycheck.

On June 1, there were still forty cases argued but not yet decided by the Court, and the pressure to circulate opinions was growing markedly in almost every chamber except those of White and the chief justice. White's clerks arranged a midmonth expedition with the Whites to see the Orioles play the Yankees at Camden Yards. The game was scheduled at the last minute, and the best tickets available were in the upper-deck seats in left field. Early in the game, an usher—alerted to the justice's presence by the Supreme Court police escort—invited the justice on behalf of the owner, Eli Jacobs, to relocate his party to the owner's box seats. White politely declined, not wishing to be seen as throwing his weight around and in fact more comfortable not to be on further display. The game was worth the trip: the Orioles won 5-4 with a bases-loaded single in the bottom of the ninth after losing a 4-2 lead in the top of the inning to a two-run home run.

With the arrival of June, the logjam in *Mabus* began to break. Justice Thomas visited White on June 5 to discuss, for the first time, his views of the case, and he left White's chambers with a promise to join the proposed opinion for the Court as long as one sentence—referring to the historical context of racially segregated colleges—was omitted from the circulating draft. White made numerous changes in his opinion and recirculated it a few days later, but Thomas did not immediately keep his promise. White's majority finally galvanized on June 16 when Justices O'Connor and Kennedy provided the fifth and sixth votes for the opinion. Thomas and Souter followed shortly. Scalia held fast to his dissent, and on June 26 the Court ruled 8-1 that the state of Mississippi needed to do more to dismantle the effects of its historically segregated university system. The plaintiffs were pleased: "A great day for America," said the lawyer who first sued the state over the disparities between white and black state colleges in Mississippi. James Cheek, former president of Howard University and a member of the White House Initiative on Historical Black Colleges and Universities, was more properly equivocal: "A positive victory, all right, but no inkling of the remedies."

The Mabus caper—as White later referred to *Fordice*—was symptomatic of the operation of the highly staffed Supreme Court in the early 1990s. Little time was spent in actual deliberation and discussion of the issues; a great deal of time was spent negotiating between the justices and their staffs over minor shadings of wording that had little effect on the outcome or impact of the ruling; and the issuance of the decision was held up as one justice after another (O'Connor and Thomas, both concurring, and Scalia, dissenting) took time to spell out disagreements over nuance, scope, or the practical effect of the decision. Thomas's concurring opinion was widely noted, because he was the only black member of the Court and because he wrote that "it would be ironic, to say the least, if the institutions that sustained Blacks during segregation were themselves destroyed in an effort to combat its vestiges." White's opinion certainly carried no implication that so dire a result was contemplated or expected by the Court. Thomas's statement underscored that litigation was a perilous mechanism for improving the quality of historically black institutions without destroying their identity and their distinctive value in the process. All the justices were sensitive to the risk but had difficulty depicting it in the doctrinal language available to them. Cases from the days of uncompromising precedent insisting on complete integration as the only solution to de jure segregated systems fit poorly with the facts of *Mabus*.

Three days after *Fordice* was handed down, the term ended dramatically with two decisions, *Lucas v. South Carolina Coastal Council,* which involved the scope of the state power over the use of private property, and *Planned Parenthood of Southeastern Pennsylvania v. Casey,* which had been closely watched to see if Justice Thomas would provide the fifth vote to overrule *Roe v. Wade*. Four justices—Chief Justice Rehnquist, White, Kennedy, and Scalia—were on record that the decision should be overruled. The Court had granted certiorari in *Casey* on January 21, 1992, and heard argument on April 22. The order granting certiorari was expressly limited to whether the court of appeals erred in upholding or invalidating specific provisions of the Pennsylvania Abortion Control Act. The state wanted the Court to address the question whether *Roe* should be overruled, but Justice Souter convinced his colleagues to rephrase the questions solely in terms of the specific provisions of the statute reviewed below. Only four—the bare minimum—voted to hear the case: White, Stevens, Scalia, and Souter. Rehnquist and Kennedy voted to deny, and Blackmun passed.

At oral argument on April 22, White was uncustomarily silent. He asked only two questions, in an effort to trap Kenneth Starr, the solicitor general, into defining the constitutional standard that governed state regulation of the abortion decision. The conference vote on April 24 produced the predictable result—five votes (Rehnquist, White, Scalia, Kennedy, and Thomas) to uphold all of the challenged aspects of the Pennsylvania law. During the first week in June, the result was turned upside down by a sixty-one-page opinion issued jointly under the names of Justices O'Connor, Kennedy, and Souter reaffirming *Roe. v. Wade* and reiterating O'Connor's "undue influence" test for the constitutionality of regulations on abortion. The key man was Kennedy, who changed his vote and joined what was quickly called the "troika" to reaffirm the fundamental right to abortion services. Kennedy's decision triggered hard feelings between some chambers; Justice Scalia's staff canceled a group outing with the Kennedy staff to see the Orioles play at Camden Yards when Scalia suddenly refused to go. Scalia turned his energies to a scabrous twenty-five-page dissent accusing the plurality of membership in an "Imperial Judiciary" and of fidelity to the judicial arrogance of the majority in *Dred Scott*. White joined both Scalia's dissent and that of the chief justice. More remarkable than the unexpected joint opinion or the unusually vitriolic opinion of Justice Scalia was the statement filed by Justice Blackmun, the aging author of *Roe v. Wade*. At the end of his twenty-page concurrence, which described the joint opinion as an "act of personal courage and constitutional principle," Blackmun wrote:

> The distance between [the majority and the minority] is short—the distance is but a single vote.
>
> I am 83 years old. I cannot remain on this Court forever, and when I do step down, the confirmation process for my successor well may focus on the issue before us today. That, I regret, may be exactly where the choice between the two worlds will be made.

Partisans, who of course did not need the hint, had placards in place across the street from the Supreme Court piazza within days which proclaimed, "Pro-Choice! Pro-Clinton!"

White wrote nothing in *Casey* or in *Lee v. Wiseman*, another major June decision. *Lee* held that invocations and benedictions at public school graduations violated the establishment clause, and White was one of four dissenters. The only prominent decision at the end of term, other than *Fordice*, in which White filed an opinion was *R.A.V. v. City of St. Paul*, in which the Court invalidated a conviction for burning a cross on a black family's lawn that was based on an ordinance prohibiting the display of a symbol that one knows or has reason to know "arouses anger, alarm or resentment in others on the basis of race, color, creed, religion or gender." White was initially assigned the opinion, but "lost his court"—in the internal slang of the building—to Justice Scalia. Scalia's opinion for the Court noted that the state court had construed the ordinance to reach only "fighting words," but concluded that the ordinance even as construed was unconstitutional because its proscriptions were content-based and were fatally "underinclusive." White filed an opinion concurring only in the judgment, which was endorsed by three other members of the Court. He argued that the case should have been resolved on conventional "overbreadth grounds," because even with a narrowing construction the ordinance reached categories of both unprotected and protected speech.

White's "sharply worded separate opinion," in the words of Prof. Akhil Amar of Yale, joining the "judgment, but not the folly of the [majority] opinion," was full of sound and fury, and uncharacteristically testy language—"untried," "[in]judicious," "transparently wrong," "misguided," "ad hoc," "radical," "confusing," "inexplicable," "doctrinaire," and "mischievous at best." Amar pointed out that the nine justices were much closer analytically than their collective Sturm und Drang in R.A.V. would suggest, and that the difference between what he called the Scalia Five and the White Four was that "the White Four may simply have more tolerance for minority-protective laws, especially where no 'innocent whites' are made to pay the price, but only those who engage in 'evil and worthless' harassment of racial groups." Amar saw the analytical foundation for White's opinion in the Reconstruction amendments, particularly the solicitude of the Thirteenth Amendment for the emancipated slaves and their need to be freed from the "badges and indicia" of that servitude.

The point is apt but even more deeply rooted than Amar claimed. More than twenty years earlier, in *Palmer v. Thompson*, White had argued vigorously in dissent that one of the Reconstruction amendments—the Thirteenth— prohibited a municipality from closing all of its public swimming pools instead of complying with an integration order. The case is a classic. Justice Black's opinion for the Court found no violation of the equal protection clause because both races were in fact treated alike (no pools for any means no pools for all), but White replied that animus against blacks, detailed in the record, established a constitutional violation that required remedy—although the nature of the remedy, which also seemed to trouble Justice Black, was problematic. When Ira Rothgerber read *R.A.V.*, he thought, not for the first time, that claims by the fourth estate that Byron White had changed during his career on the Court were "products of failures to read what he wrote, or maybe to remember what he said." White's views in *R.A.V.* may have been consistent, but the opinion, as Professor Amar gently insisted, failed to provide clear lines of distinction between its views and those of the majority— other than epithetical rhetoric about overbreadth.

As he had now for so many terms, White focused his opinion work primarily on opinions for the Court. He wrote sixteen during the term, more than any other justice (O'Connor had fifteen); he also wrote the fewest concurring opinions (two—tied with the chief justice), and only two justices filed fewer dissents. In the fourteen cases decided by a bare majority, White was in the majority in eight, wrote three, and assigned one other. The Court, freed since 1988 by Congress from almost any vestiges of mandatory jurisdiction, trimmed its plenary calendar back to 114 cases—down at least 30 percent from the levels for most of White's career and notwithstanding eighteen signed opinions dissenting from denial of certiorari during the term. For a term, in Stuart Taylor's phrase, in which the Supreme Court seemed "poised to bulldoze forests of precedents in a militant march to the political and jurisprudential right," October term 1991 confirmed once again that the Court acts by accretion and not avulsion, and that precedent only gains in strength over time. The Court's behavior deeply disappointed the political right, exemplified by Gary Bauer of the Family Research Council: "Of great concern to us is the emergence on the Court of a wimp bloc who are quickly becoming an embarrassment to the presidents who appointed them."

Bauer's angry remark raised the specter, in an election year, of retirements from the Supreme Court. Justice Blackmun had already highlighted the issue, with dubious taste, in his separate opinion in Casey. Attention focused on both Blackmun and White, the two senior members of the Court in service, with twenty-three and thirty years respectively, and in age, eighty-three and seventy-five. White caused a low flicker of speculation when it became known that his law clerks would be all males for the first time since October term 1976. "He's going to spend his last term the way he spent the first half of his career on the Court—in a men's club," one less than admiring former clerk privately predicted. In fact, White said nothing to staff or close friends about his retirement thoughts, whatever they were, as the '91 term concluded.

19

"THE END OF THE RIDE"

YRON WHITE told his friend of more than a half century, Tom
Killefer, that he knew that he had made the right decision to retire
from the Supreme Court of the United States when he discovered the
following summer that he "could not easily tie a number 18 Adams on a standard tippit." Experts call the Adams the Big Mac of mayflies; White, with
growing self-deprecation, was implying that he may have overstayed both the
Court and the river. Yet when he joined a small party of fishing companions
not long after the conclusion of the 1991 term, "there wasn't even a hint that
he was thinking about retiring," according to one member of the party. The
rendezvous, held by then for more than twenty consecutive years, occurred at
the same location and included, more or less, the same fishermen. The party
was organized by Nicholas R. Petry, part-time cattle rancher and full-time
head of a Denver construction company, and a fraternity brother of White at
the University of Colorado. Others who joined the group from time to time
over the years included Eddie Carlson, the Seattle entrepreneur who turned
Westin Hotels into an international chain and also conceived the space nee-
dle; Beverly Dolan, who built a collection of small companies into Textron,
the international conglomerate; James K. Dobbs, Sr., founder of the Dobbs
House food services company; James Hoak, Sr., of St. Regis Paper; Barney
White, the justice's son; and Neil Armstrong, the astronaut-turned-interna-
tional-businessman. The location suited the tastes for privacy of men chroni-

cally in the public eye—a private ranch on the Encampment River west of the Medicine Bow Mountains in southern Wyoming, just across the state line from Colorado and coincidentally not far from where White grew up. White used the annual occasion not to reveal his private reflections but to explore ideas about politics, social policy, and popular culture. "You never knew what *he* thought," according to Petry. "He was like a lawyer or law professor, first taking one side, then another, trying to test or explore a particular point of view." One of the few topics that was not mooted during the summer of 1992 was retirement. "Not one word," Petry recalled firmly.

If White had decided to retire, there is no setting where he would have been more likely to drop a hint or to measure reactions to the decision. "He seemed more relaxed there than anywhere else," in Petry's view. "He loved the physical exercise, the companionship, the fact that the law was thousands of miles away in every respect—and the privacy." Even in a state where the governor boasts that more than 25 percent of the population fish, the Encampment–North Platte system is largely isolated from the public. There are only two miles of roadway adjacent to the North Platte, which intersects the Encampment just below Saratoga, Wyoming.

Burke Marshall, whom White had chosen to run the Civil Rights Division of the Kennedy Justice Department, still remembers a fishing trip with White in Wyoming many years ago. "He was more at ease than I have ever seen him," Marshall remembered, "and I was struck by his patience, even tenderness, for what seemed like hours in teaching my daughter Josie how to cast." Norman Maclean's novella *A River Runs Through It* was published about the time that the annual Wyoming expedition began, and White predictably received more than one copy from friends, who found the poetic final page evocative:

> Now I am too old to be much of a fisherman, and now of course I usually fish the big waters alone, although some friends think I shouldn't. Like many fly fishermen in western Montana where the summer days are almost Arctic in length, I often do not start fishing until the cool of the evening. There in the Arctic half-light of the canyon, all existence fades to a being with my soul and the sounds of the Big Blackfoot River and a four-count rhythm and the hope that a fish will rise.

Unlike the narrator, who was "haunted by waters" and by memories of his brother's tragic early death and lost promise, White found the south-to-north running waters of the Encampment–North Platte system to be soothing—the passion of a lifetime, exercised near the original source, and enjoyed in solitude.

When the 1992 term began a scant month before the presidential election, speculation about retirement from the Court focused naturally on Harry Blackmun, who had publicly emphasized his mortality three months earlier in *Planned Parenthood v. Casey*. Blackmun celebrated his eighty-fourth birthday on November 12—an anniversary with eerie connotation having nothing to do with Blackmun himself. Since 1981, five justices had retired from the Court and only one (Brennan in 1990) had been as old as Blackmun now was. Marshall (eighty-three), Powell (seventy-eight), Burger (seventy-nine), and Stewart (sixty-six) had all been younger. Before that, Douglas had been seventy-six. The lessons of Stewart and Douglas were ominous to White. Stewart, who had been a year ahead of White at Yale Law School, retired in apparent good health, planning to travel, enjoy his family, and write a book. He complained in the first term following his retirement that "I haven't had all the leisure time I've been looking forward to enjoying." Within four years he was dead. Douglas had suffered a debilitating stroke on New Year's Eve 1974 and tried to return to duty at the beginning of the 1975 term after recuperating for the balance of the 1974 term. On the bench he appeared to be half crippled, unable to remain alert, and incapable of speaking clearly or coherently; later reports suggested he was mentally incompetent and physically incontinent.

Douglas's condition prompted the other eight justices to meet in conference on October 17, 1975, to consider how to handle the situation. In the words of Justice Powell's authorized biographer, they "reached an extraordinary—and very private—decision. They took away his vote." The justices "agreed that no case would be decided five-four with Douglas in the majority." The policy could be invisibly enforced by simply ordering reargument in any case in which Douglas held the decisive vote. The decision to strip Douglas of his power was rationalized by history, although the precedents were in fact distinguishable: Justices Grier and Field had been persuaded to retire in the nineteenth century, as had Justice McKenna and probably Justice Holmes since World War I. In none of the cases, however, were the elderly justices involuntarily deprived of their votes, although there is some question in McKenna's case, and Chief Justice Hughes assigned Holmes only easy opinions at the end of his career.

White was the only member of the rump Court who disagreed with the decision. In his view, his colleagues had conducted a secret—and constitutionally unauthorized—impeachment, and he said so in no uncertain terms in a letter to Chief Justice Burger, which he circulated by hand to each of the seven justices who endorsed the policy. He viewed the letter as so sensitive that he told his clerks of its contents but did not show them copies. (The entire text of the twelve-hundred-word letter is set out as Appendix B.) White's fundamental point was that the Constitution "nowhere provides that a Justice's colleagues may deprive him of his office by refusing to permit him to function as a Justice." The only remedy was

> to invite Congress to take appropriate action. If it is an impeachable offense for an incompetent Justice to purport to sit as a judge, is it not the task of Congress, rather than the Court, to undertake proceedings to determine the issue of competence? If it is not an impeachable offense, may the Court nevertheless conclude that a Justice is incompetent and forbid him to perform his duties?

White urged the other justices to announce the decision—being "plainly a matter of great importance. . . . I do hope the majority is prepared to make formal disclosure of the action it has taken." White duly acknowledged his "highest regard" for the seven justices who made the decision, but he concluded: "Yet history teaches that nothing can more readily bring the Court and its constitutional functions into disrepute than the Court's failure to recognize the limits of its own powers." No public announcement was ever made. Three weeks after White's letter, Douglas sent a letter of retirement, drafted by old friends Abe Fortas and Clark Clifford, to the president and notified the chief justice. The chief justice informed his colleagues after a brief birthday toast to Blackmun in one of the Court's private dining rooms. During the interim between the decision to nullify decisive votes by Douglas and his retirement, no cases were put over for reargument.

The incident was first reported in *The Brethren* in 1979, which said that the "decision to cut Douglas out was informal, and it was treated as a deep family secret." It was suppressed at the time, notwithstanding White's plea, and was not confirmed until the Powell biography was published in 1994. Other members of the Court were evidently embarrassed by their action, or at least by White's characterization of it. The October 20 letter to the chief justice is absent from both the William J. Brennan Papers and the Thurgood Marshall Papers at the Library of Congress, and Powell's biographer excuses the complicity of his subject by explaining that "Powell followed the lead of his senior colleagues." The irony is that the rump Court's action was not necessary (Douglas cast no decisive votes during the period), and in fact it is not clear that voting to rehear cases usurps the impeachment power—as long as at least five members of the Court vote do so, regardless of their motivation. Conferring without Douglas present was improper and insulting but did not necessarily constitute a constitutional rupture. White's reputation for constitutional fastidiousness with respect to the Supreme Court as an institution is richly illustrated by his letter about the Douglas affair, although his concern from the cool vantage point of hindsight looks somewhat overwrought.

The issue is vexing, however, and touches fundamental questions about the exercise of power by judges, especially when that power is exercised invisibly—without the usual public disciplines of written and oral argument. White knew as a formal matter that five votes could reset any case for reargument regardless of the reason or reasons. He was worried about the motivation and the scope of the rump Court's decision. After all, a judge can vote for any reason he wishes to report, too, but logrolling—privately trading a vote in one case for a vote in another—is properly viewed as anathema to the judicial process. Even when the formal niceties are observed on the surface, the process can be perverted by improper motivation—for casting or withholding votes. For White, stripping Douglas of his vote was a perilous step into the breach. Douglas's condition threatened the integrity of the Court, but so did the response of White's colleagues. The rump Court decided to protect both Douglas and its own stature by keeping the problem quiet. White resisted as a matter of principle and apparently made his colleagues acutely uncomfortable as a result. Even a decade and a half later, the lingering memory of Douglas overstaying his capacity and propelling the Court into a crisis mentality must have caused White and every other justice who experienced it to wince at its recollection.

When Bill Clinton was elected a month after the 1992 term began, the speculation about retirements at the Supreme Court intensified but the focus did not change. Blackmun began to fuel the rumors after the first of the year with broad hints about impending "change" at the Court. White hit the public eye on January 20, 1993, when he swore in Vice President Albert Gore at the inaugural ceremony. Retired justice Thurgood Marshall had been scheduled for the duty, but he was hospitalized, and White—as the only Democratic appointee on the Court—was a late substitute. (Marshall died four days after the inauguration.) February came and went, and in early March Joan Biskupic of the *Washington Post* learned that neither White nor Blackmun had hired clerks for the October 1993 term. White had wrapped up his hiring for the current term on February 7, 1992; by that measure, he was now a month late. On Sunday, March 7, Biskupic reported that White "apparently is considering stepping down." Citing no sources, she also wrote that White "has said that since he came in with a Democratic administration, it would be fitting to retire under a Democratic administration." Less than a week after the story ran, Blackmun, continuing to flirt with the press, told an audience at the New England College of Law that he and White were the most likely candidates to retire soon. That was enough for White, who began to inform close friends of his decision. He told Ira Rothgerber by telephone, "Ira, I hate to confirm anything, *anything*, published in the *Washington Post*, but I have in fact decided to retire."

On Friday morning, March 19, 1993—coincidentally a "triple-witching" date for the financial markets—Ron Klain, a former law clerk to White now working in the White House counsel's office, picked up a letter from the justice's chambers at the Court and delivered it to President Clinton. White had contacted Klain the night before and asked him to drop by the chambers in the morning. Clinton announced that White's letter informed him "that he intends to retire at the end of the current Supreme Court term." The president's reaction to the news stutter-stepped. In the morning, on his way to Andrews Air Force Base, Clinton said with obvious admiration—for both pre-Court biography and extended judicial service—"He has had a truly remarkable life." Clinton also said that he spoke with White by telephone and "he said he wanted to give me this much notice so that hopefully I could announce my intentions to nominate someone and all the hearings could conclude in time to prepare someone to serve at the beginning of the October Term of the Court"—unlike the recent experience with Justices Souter and Thomas, confirmed too late to begin the term on time due to their predecessors' surprise retirements on the last day of October terms 1989 and 1990. Unstated by either Clinton or White was the fact that the president had no firm advance warning of White's retirement.

The president's formal written tribute, issued later in the day, was more restrained, as UPI pointed out: the statement "lacked any praise for the Associate Justice's past decisions." The statement described White as a "living example of the American dream fulfilled," and concluded, "We are all fortunate that he devoted the great portion of his life to public service." White's positions in *Roe v. Wade* (abortion) and *Bowers v. Hardwick* (gay rights) were inconsistent with Clinton's politics and apparently precluded specific praise for the justice's judicial career. (A year later, when Harry Blackmun finally announced his decision to retire, the president effusively celebrated him and even arranged a press conference for him at the White House. Blackmun quoted White on the occasion: "Byron White, a year ago, put it well, I thought, when he said, 'It's been a great ride.' It has been." The difference in treatment on the two occasions was palpable and politically driven, a fact that was said to amuse White.)

At 9 A.M., shortly after White's letter of retirement had been delivered to the White House, the justice released a brief statement through the Court's public information office:

> I have today notified the president that I have decided to retire from active service as an associate justice, effective at the time the Court rises for its summer recess.
>
> It has been an interesting and exciting experience to serve on the Court. But after 31 years, Marion and I think that someone else should be permitted to have a like experience.
>
> For the time being we shall remain in Washington, and I shall likely move to the new Thurgood Marshall Federal Judiciary Building. I also expect that from time to time I will sit as an appellate judge on the Courts of Appeals.

Public tributes from active and retired members of the Court, which became a routine practice at retirement during Burger's chief justiceship, were largely muted. Greg Henderson of UPI observed that "many of the statements released through the Supreme Court reflected White's no-nonsense, hardworking reputation, and contained less emotion than those heard at the 1990 retirement of Justice William Brennan and the 1991 retirement of Justice Thurgood Marshall." Justice John Paul Stevens was the singular exception to the rule. Stevens first met White in the South Pacific during World War II; almost twenty years later, Stevens was interviewed by him for the assistant attorney generalship of the Antitrust Division. Justice Stevens reported a "feeling of personal loss, for he is an extremely close friend. I have known and admired him for about 50 years, and the better I know him the more I admire him. He is a great individual and a great team player."

Overlooked by the press, who perhaps were distracted by the opportunity for a Democratic nomination to the Court for the first time since 1967, was White's joint assignment of responsibility for his decision: "Marion and I . . ." No other justice had ever named his wife in announcing his decision to retire. The Whites' friends read the statement as more than a formality or a courtesy: it was a subtle recognition by the justice of a relationship that had thrived for almost a half century with sometimes daunting energy and intensity. Marion Lloyd Stearns had grown up in the president's house at the University of Colorado and was accustomed to white gloves and proper social events, but she was also a fiercely competitive tennis player in her youth and—under her husband's tutelage—later became a spirited enthusiast for dry-fly fishing. Family photographs spanning White's tenure on the Court frequently depict the entire family wearing waders and fishing creels. Marion

White took a proprietary interest in her husband's law clerks—recording marriages and births, encouraging the unmarried to settle down, and offering advice on the proper balance between career and family. "She has been an extremely important force in his life," observed a close friend of both who insisted on anonymity lest he incur "the wrath of Byron White." Marion "softened his edges—or some of them—and they made an engaging pair on the tennis court or at the dinner table. She can also make a mean martini—vodka with a Bombay Gin float, no vermouth." Another mutual friend says, "She has strong views. Some times she reinforces the best in him and other times I suspect she files her own amicus curiae brief." Mrs. White's actual influence on the justice is veiled behind the iron curtain of privacy that they both prize and mutually sustain.

During his final three months on the Court, White impressed many as having had a burden lifted from his shoulders, and he even appeared playful during his last round of oral arguments. At White's final oral argument session, Michael E. Tigar, age fifty-two, confessed that he had forgotten a fact in the capital case he was presenting; White, age seventy-five, remarked lightly, "You'll understand that when you get a little older." The jocularity continued through his final day on the bench. On June 28, 1993, in the traditional public exchange of letters between the retiring justice and his colleagues, White wrote:

> Since I remain a federal judge and will likely sit on Courts of Appeals from time to time, it will be necessary for me to follow the Court's work. No longer will I be able to agree or dissent from a Court's opinion. Hence, like any other Court of Appeals judge, I hope the Court's mandates will be clear, crisp, and leave those of us below with as little room as possible for disagreement about their meaning.

The plea was issued with an ironic twinkle of the eye. "Minutes later," wrote Tony Mauro in *Legal Times,* "the Court announced one of the most splintered opinions of the term, the double-jeopardy case of *United States v. Dixon,* which generated six opinions and dissents—including one by White—spread over 86 pages of text." White, who concurred in the judgment in part and dissented in part, was one of the culprits responsible for leaving Justice Scalia to announce the judgment of the Court and the opinion of the Court "with respect to Parts I, II, and IV, and an opinion with respect to Parts III and V, in which Justice Kennedy join[ed]." A month later at the Eighth Circuit judicial conference, held in Colorado Springs, Colorado, White was asked pointedly by a federal appellate judge whether he thought the Supreme

Court had done its job when it issued decisions that failed to "command at least five votes" and thus left the law on the point uncertain. White replied:

> The public ought to be glad that in some cases that there is only a judgment and not a Court opinion that's laying down a broad rule in a very touchy area where the Court might live to regret it. Judgments are there and they are bound to be much narrower than Court opinions. I think it has allowed the Court to creep along rather than take some giant steps you might regret.

More than one lower court judge in the audience thought White's response proved too much. What may have been a virtue in the "very touchy area" of schoolbook censorship—in which, for example, White deprived Justice Brennan of a five-person opinion in the *Pico* case in 1982—was much less welcome by judges obliged to decipher the newest complexity in the Court's double jeopardy jurisprudence. The juxtaposition of White's plea for clarity and his behavior in *Dixon* reinforced those who found him unpredictable or simply perverse. His remarks at the Eighth Circuit conference, which stemmed from more fundamental convictions about the role of the Court, were largely ignored—another contrary remark from someone who was now last year's news.

The postmortems on White's judicial career in the press reflected the editorial predilections of the editors. The *Wall Street Journal* celebrated White for his "old-fashioned liberal jurisprudence," which respected the authority of the legislatures and the legitimacy of the pace of social change they achieved. The *New York Times* was relieved that White's retirement meant *Roe v. Wade* was safe. Beyond that, the *Times* acknowledged that White "was one of the more remarkable people to serve on the Court," but added:

> In three momentous decades on the Court, however, he turned out to be more a witness than a moving force. On the bench he has been a caustic questioner but an enigmatic judge whose philosophy has defied tracing even by legal scholars. He espoused the doctrine of judicial restraint, arguing for less Court interference with the political branches of government, yet several times he so misinterpreted Congress's meaning that new laws had to be passed. He was strong for civil rights in areas like education and voting but not where jobs were at stake.

Both judgments—that White was both passive and aggressively hypocritical—are curious. White was so much a moving force in the First Amendment, especially the fields of libel and privacy, that the *Times* in years past had condemned both his views and his impact, from reporter-shield laws

(*Branzburg v. Hayes*) to the execution of search warrants in newsrooms (*Zurcher v. Stanford Daily*) to the scope of discovery in defamation (*Herbert v. Lando*). The amendment's overbreadth (*Broadrick v. Oklahoma*) and public forum doctrines (*Perry Education Association v. Perry Local Educators Association*) were both remodeled by White. The scope of the exclusionary rule, especially as it related to automobile searches, bore White's stamp, and he was the architect of the "good faith" exception to the rule, even if William Rehnquist deserves more credit for its actual adoption. Until his last few terms, he was also the Court's resident expert on voting rights as well as the more arcane fields of Indian tribal law and original jurisdiction. He was also a leading authority—if not always uniformly admired for his clarity and consistency—on antitrust law and the law of collective bargaining.

The *Times* editorial's claim that White "misinterpreted Congress' meaning" so much that "several" decisions had to be statutorily reversed is at best a half-truth. Four decisions in which White spoke for the Court were reversed or at least modified by Congress: *Alyeska Pipeline Service Co v. Wilderness Society*, modified in part by the Attorneys Fees Civil Rights Act of 1976; *Zurcher v. Stanford Daily*, modified by Public Law 96-440; *Grove City v. Bell*, overruled by the Civil Rights Restoration Act of 1987 (enacted over President Reagan's veto); and *Wards Cove Packing Co. v. Atonio*, overruled by the Civil Rights Act of 1991. In all but *Zurcher*, White's opinions for the Court rejected not unequivocal congressional dictates but a flotilla of case law built on judicial inferences or implications about legislation.

Columnists and magazine writers were no less tendentious than the editorialists. Jeffrey Rosen, the legal affairs editor of the *New Republic*, wrote a scathing profile of White that managed to denigrate White's work product and to patronize him at the same time. The article acknowledged White's technical proficiency but concluded that he was uninterested in methodically delineating a constitutional philosophy. Rosen, born two years after White was appointed to the Supreme Court, recalled his own unsuccessful interview for a clerkship in which White "unleashed a string of hilarious questions" about nonprofessional matters ("What do you do for exercise? How's your health? Are you married?"). The article was a self-regarding hatchet job, but it also accurately emphasized White's opaque writing style and occasionally flip concurring opinions (the most damning example: "I agree with the conclusion reached by Justice Brennan . . . although I do not agree with much of his reasoning. Accordingly, I would affirm"). Rosen's article—a mixture of quotations from law professors, unsourced internal Court gossip, and prescription for how to select a successor—provoked predictably loyal defenses from former White clerks.

And from Prof. Mary Ann Glendon of Harvard, Rosen's essay received a crisp spanking. She observed that the "topsy-turvy world of legal journalism" awarded "no plaudits . . . for the ordinary heroism"—exemplified by White—of "demonstrating impartiality, interpretive skill, and responsibility toward authoritative sources in the regular administration of justice." Rejecting Rosen's conclusions Glendon said:

> What made White hard to classify, of course, were the very qualities that made him an able and conscientious judge—his independence and his faithfulness to a modest conception of the judicial role. His "vision," implicit in nearly every one of his opinions, was not that difficult to discern. As summed up by a former clerk, it was one "in which the democratic process predominates over the judicial; and the role of the Court or any individual justice is not to promote particular ideologies, but to decide cases in a pragmatic way that permits the political branches to shoulder primary responsibility for governing our society. . . . The purpose of an opinion . . . is quite simply to decide the case in an intellectually and analytically sound manner." Though White's competence, independence, and integrity did not make for lively copy, he was a model of modern neoclassical judging.

After an initial burst of editorials and the odd column, White and his career disappeared quickly from the popular press. Gov. Robert P. Casey of Pennsylvania noted the phenomenon in his Pope John XXIII Lecture at Catholic University a year later. Casey, best known nationally as a pro-life Democrat who was denied a speaking role at the 1992 party convention, compared the "mainstream media" treatment of those in the majority in *Roe v. Wade* and those who dissented:

> We see no admiring profiles about [the dissenters]. No accolades, no encomia, no newfound respect. In some cases, outright, virulent hostility. Take Justice Byron White, in particular. Truly a storybook figure: Whizzer White, All-American football hero at the University of Colorado, appointed by President Kennedy, Rhodes Scholar, three decades on the Supreme Court. You would be hard-pressed to find a career, or profile, more worthy of praise. But when he stepped down last year, hardly a word appeared on the subject of his retirement. The media seemed to find only one thing praiseworthy, and that was the fact that he was ending his career. . . . in the real world, he surrendered any expectation, forever, of positive press coverage the moment he decided in *Roe v. Wade* that the majority was engaged in an act, as he called it, of "raw judicial power."

Casey overstated his argument, but not by much. Even Calvin Trillin, writing in *The Nation*, captured in verse the popular salience of White's retirement:

Adieu, Whizzer

We'll bid adieu to Justice Whizzer White,
A running back who moved well to his right,
And thank him for the courtesy of staying
Until a Democrat could get the job of saying
Just who among our learned lawyers might
Deserve to take the place of Whizzer White.
(Apparently, he thought that only fair,
Because the Democrats had put him there.)
We count his loyalty to team a boon:
The other side might well select a loon.

20

SERVICE AS LEGACY

THE MOST dreary aspect of Byron White's decision to retire was the empty investigation made by several journalists into the nature of White's "liberalism." Had he been appointed by Dwight Eisenhower or Lyndon Johnson, the question never would have been raised, but White was the last connective tissue to John Kennedy, the New Frontier, and its optimism about the capacity of government that energized many during the early 1960s. As White arrived home at the end of the day he retired, ABC News stuck a microphone through his car window and asked him whether he was a "conservative" or a "centrist." White replied: "Being a conservative or a centrist is all in the minds of the speaker. It just depends on what you think—and if you think I'm one, you're right, but other people might think I'm something else and they're right." To the *New Republic*'s Jeffrey Rosen, the answer was laughable and confirmed that White was a "perfect cipher" who "was uninterested in articulating a constitutional vision." White's nine-second answer to ABC hardly sustains, or even relates to, such a broad indictment, but perhaps that was not actually the point. In any event, those who had followed White's career recognized the authenticity of the response, which had been uniform since he was first asked the question in Washington more than three decades earlier.

Other journalists persisted in thinking that John Kennedy "nominated Byron White, thinking he was a Warren Court liberal," only to be disappointed. Even Justice Lewis F. Powell, Jr., who served with White for sixteen terms, assumed in 1987 that White's "conservative drift" would have "disappointed President Kennedy." Stuart Taylor of *Legal Times,* who tended to portray White as the judicial equivalent of a snapping turtle, addressed the issue more thoughtfully than anyone else. His retrospective of White's career provided the sharpest antidote to lazy assumptions about Kennedy's expectations and White's public policy convictions:

> The thumbnail sketch that has taken hold in commentary about Justice Byron White over the years goes something like this: Started as a Kennedy Democrat when appointed to the Supreme Court in 1962, moved to the right, ended as a crusty Rehnquistian conservative. . . . Crusty he is, with a vengeance. [But his ideology has not] changed much, if at all. He never was the kind of liberal that the Kennedy name has come to stand for. (Nor was JFK, for that matter.) And he is not really a full-dress Rehnquistian conservative now, except on a bunch of high-profile issues that have come to dominate headlines about the Court over the past two decades.

Others later developed sustained analyses echoing Taylor, principally William Nelson of New York University School of Law and Kate Stith of the Yale Law School—both ex-clerks of White. Stith's remark to the *New York Times* the day White retired is apt: "Civil rights, federal power, those were the salient issues at the time" he was appointed. "Eventually, the Court changed, society changed, the issues changed. Byron White didn't change." Byron White and John Kennedy were tough on crime, tough on communists, friendly to organized labor, and shared a growing conviction that federal intervention was necessary if racial equality was to be more than a pious objective. Shortly after White retired, his friend Ira Rothgerber—also an admirer of John Kennedy—observed that there "are two schools of thought about Byron White, one that he hasn't changed in terms of personality or character in sixty years, the other that Washington brought out the best and worst in him. I'm foursquare in the first school."

When the law journals probed for the headwaters of White's views, they concentrated on two sources: the legal realism he encountered at Yale Law School after the constitutional revolution of 1937, and the New Deal constitutionalism he embraced in both college and law school and that he appeared to manifest in his allegiance to a broad view of federal power, deference to congressional judgments and prerogatives, and skepticism of encompassing judicial wisdom. The realist theory is enticing but lacks much explanatory power. Realism at Yale ranged from Arthur Corbin's incremental emphasis to

Underhill Moore's empirical work to Myres McDougal's "legal science." If the many tastes of realism that flourished at Yale Law School during White's tenure had special purchase on his imagination, Wesley Sturges and especially Arthur Corbin are the most likely candidates. Sturges and Corbin showed how judicial power can and does work, and both emphasized the context of each case and what Justice Holmes called the "interstitial" nature of legal development. White could write opinions that were "fact-intensive" and insistent on the congruence between theory and fact, as Allan Ides demonstrated in a brief essay about three of White's "relatively obscure" opinions.

But for all of White's emphasis as a justice on how laws or doctrines "function" in fact, some of his most important opinions are quite formalistic. *Miranda v. Arizona* speaks authentically of the constable's dilemmas, but other important opinions do not pursue the underlying facts with the same zeal. *Roe v. Wade* demonstrates little understanding of the choice a pregnant woman faces and addresses the constitutional issue at an abstract level. *INS v. Chadha* exhibits a sophisticated understanding of the modern administrative state but ignores the unsavory aspects of the legislative veto in action and seems unwilling to weigh competing concerns at comparable levels of care. *Bowers v. Hardwick* deals with the sensitive issues in the case on an arid level of generality and makes little effort to deal with nagging doctrinal questions. Without stretching the capacity of anachronism too far, few realists would subscribe to White's treatment of the underlying factual foundations in *Roe, Chadha,* or *Bowers.* At some point, of course, the facts are overwhelmed by the march of doctrine, but the decisive issues in all three cases were hardly foreclosed by prior case law. The highest common factor between White and the American legal realists would be what Jerome Frank called "rule skepticism," which Vincent Blasi of the Columbia Law School linked to White at his retirement without using the label: "I think the most interesting thing about him is his disdain for ideological enthusiasms. He is the ultimate legal realist. He cares less than any modern justice for symbolic arguments or ideals or rights in the abstract."

The New Deal provides no better explanation for the roots of Byron White's convictions, because it was a sprawling political movement—not a stable philosophical construct—and it counted members as disparate as Henry Wallace on the far left and reactionary Southern senators dedicated to Bilboism. Moreover, the ambitions of the first New Deal were jarred badly by the Roosevelt recession of 1937 and the political fallout of the failed Court-packing plan, which combined to force substantial retrenchment by the administration. There are nonetheless chords from both New Deals that resonate insistently throughout White's judicial career—primarily his unswerving nationalism and his belief that judges should be wary of making social policy, particularly in comprehensive terms, without clear congressional authorization. *Buckley v. Valeo* and *Chadha* stand as exemplars of White's refusal—as he put it to Ira Rothgerber about *Buckley*—to say, "The First Amendment, therefore!" (that is, the statute is unconstitutional).

On other occasions, publicly and privately, White worried about the ratio of power between the number of justices—particularly in a bare majority—and their effect, both geographically and temporally. "This is a very small organization for the freight it carries," he wrote to his colleagues on his final day at the Court, a remark equally pertinent to the size of the caseload and quantum of power enjoyed by five votes. (Harry Blackmun repeated the phrase a year later on the occasion of his own collegial farewell.) Privately, White told Rothgerber after William O. Douglas retired in 1975 that *it was too bad that Alexander Bickel died, because he would have made a good appointment to the Court.* Bickel's emphasis on the "countermajoritarian difficulty" of judicial review, particularly in *The Least Dangerous Branch,* was particularly compelling to White, as was Bickel's practical and unpretentious presentation.

White prided himself on lack of pretense and prized the virtue in others, which makes his famous hostility to his famous nickname somewhat incongruous. If he in fact cares so little about artifice, why has he spent more than a half century scowling at those who by cheek or by accident refer to him as Whizzer White? The antinickname pose is so well known that it has dominated the definition of his public personality. Casual journalism routinely mentions it; public relations files at his alma mater caution, "Justice White does *not* like the nickname 'Whizzer'"; and Justice Blackmun delighted audiences at judicial conferences with the mock-confidential tip not to "call him Whizzer." At the beginning of White's career in Washington, Jack Foster, the editor of the *Rocky Mountain News* in Denver, wrote a column charitably, if vainly, suggesting that "we should discontinue referring to [the] Deputy Attorney General" as "Whizzer," out of respect for White's wishes and for the sake of the dignity of both man and office. Had White cared less about the point, the name might have faded, but he did care, and the name became a weapon in the hands of satirists and scholars who wanted their criticism of his judicial work to annoy or wound.

Why, then, did he bother? Rex Lee's explanation is a starting point: "perhaps because he does not want to be remembered principally as a football player." It is true that from the moment he left Yale Law School, White tried to seal off his athletic past and to redefine himself simply as a lawyer. While he practiced in Denver, he was largely able to do so, or at least to keep the nostalgic press at bay by pleading the privacy due a private citizen. The Kennedy campaign changed all that and revived the glamour that had been dormant for two decades. When he came to Washington in 1961, his antipathy to football lore and the nickname that neatly packaged it resurfaced, first hesitantly and then with a vengeance. When John Tripson, one of his ex-teammates from Detroit, paid a call at the Justice Department early in the Kennedy administration, he greeted White with the customary, "Hi, Whizzer." The sheepish reply was, "Geez, don't call me that here." Tripson took the response, issued in good humor but firmly, as a signal that White did not want to mix business with pleasure. That impulse may help to explain why White found so distasteful the screening of old newsreels of his playing days at a twenty-fifth-anniversary reunion of law clerks several years later. The two worlds were not allowed to intersect, except on his terms. His enjoyment of athletics as a spectator, especially football, was unobtrusive, at least until he retired. The press construed White's newly unveiled enthusiasm for athletics after his retirement as a personal glasnost, but White quickly reestablished the cordon around his personal world. When he and his friend George Cannon visited the Denver Broncos' summer training camp in Greeley, Colorado, in early August of 1995, a *Denver Post* sportswriter approached him for an interview. White, irritated, agreed, on one condition: "You have 60 seconds. Sixty."

In a sense, the nickname—imposed by sportswriters when Byron White was still a teenager—was an invasion of his privacy, which he construed broadly and defended belligerently. "Byron would have been just as happy—I think he might have preferred—if he played with twenty-one other players in an empty stadium—no fans, no coaches, no referees," reflected one of his college teammates, Art Unger. "Football was like all sports for him—a personal challenge, a thing to test his own limits. He really hated the stuff that happened before and after the whistle." He was a role model before he understood the implications of the obligation. His choice, at age twenty-one, whether to accept a lucrative pro football contract or a less lucrative Rhodes Scholarship was monitored by newspapers and wire services nationwide, and his initial decision to attend Oxford was viewed by the press as imbued with moral significance. After White discovered belatedly that he could accept both, it is hardly surprising that he always emphasized afterward that if he could only have selected one, "I would have chosen Oxford."

Regardless of his decision, however, he was a hero to many whom he never knew. Young scholar-athletes who were forced to defend twin passions suddenly had a lodestar. "Frankly, he was my hero when I was a kid," admitted one man who later became a leading scholar of the New Deal. Men who are now senior professors, from the University of Chicago to the University of Colorado and the University of California at Berkeley, would privately say the same. Bill Gleason, the Chicago author, recalled seeing White play for Detroit against the Chicago Cardinals in 1940 and found him to be one of those "few persons" who "exceed expectations" and "are better than their buildup, larger than life. . . . When we were kids, playing tackle in the 'prairie' next to Mrs. Shaw's house or playing in the street, we argued about the privilege of being the Whizzer." The only grace note of football in the 1930s that White missed having was his own bubble-gum trading card. That gap was closed in 1955 when the Topps Company issued a "Whizzer White—Halfback" card in its College All-Americans series, which included the likes of Jim Thorpe, the Four Horsemen, and Knute Rockne. The card, number 24 in the series, is priced at up to $150 today in mint condition.

The steepest price of indulging his competitive pleasures came from the press, with whom he never felt comfortable and with whom he never fully made peace after the Cotton Bowl and the National Invitational Basketball Tournament in 1938. "He was anathema to the press," recalled Edwin O. Guthman, who was press spokesman for the Kennedy Justice Department, when White retired. "I think it dated back to those sports pages references to 'Whizzer' in his college days." Murray Kempton, the columnist for *Newsday* and other publications, considered the press's impact on White—twice, in fact, first in 1979 for the *National Review:*

> There appears to be a marked but generally unremarked note of the autobiographical in those opinions of Supreme Court Justice Byron White that have set so many of us journalists wailing as from the Lubyanka. . . . His glow as a judge may be a modest one; but he was an incandescent tailback at the University of Colorado and with the Pittsburgh Steelers [*sic*]. He thus bears scars and cannot be blamed for still vividly resenting those awful Sunday afternoons when he stood in chilling locker rooms, his head ringing, his senses numbed, and his bruises bared while the writers had at him about why he zigged when he might more politicly have zagged. The dressing room enforces a mutual degradation upon the sports journalist and the beef he prods; and Justice White can be pardoned if the memories of so many offenses to his dignity impede his respect for the dignity of the calling whose members inflicted them.

Kempton nonetheless "welcome[d]" the "new life that Justice White's resentments have breathed into the law of libel," due to the risk of "egregious errors" escaping liability under the lenient net of *New York Times v. Sullivan.*

There is more than a germ of truth to Kempton's suspicion, but the effect of the past did not dictate the doctrine of the present. In each of the cases that provoked wailing in the fourth estate—*Branzburg v. Hayes, Zurcher v. Stanford Daily,* and *Herbert v. Lando*—practical interest defeated hypothetical risks, and doctrinal structure was logically applied. If Kempton had been onto something, one would have expected a different result in *Cox Broadcasting Corporation v. Cohn* in 1975. The Cohn family sued Cox Broadcasting when it published, in violation of Georgia law, the name of a murdered rape victim. The media claimed its invasion of privacy—clumsy, gratuitous, and of no conceivable social utility—was protected by the First Amendment against civil liability. White drew a bright line for the Court that vindicated the press claim, because the information had been lawfully acquired from the public record. No one on the Supreme Court cherished or guarded his privacy more zealously than Byron White, but for those who viewed White as the scourge of the press, the Cohn family's case presents an inconvenient case of judicial detachment.

The *Cox* decision is all the more striking from someone who admits, "selfish[ly]," that one reason he has resisted telecasting oral arguments in the Supreme Court was his wish to retain his anonymity in public. White's "resentments" were ignited by journalists who put words in his mouth—a problem more in his athletic days than during his governmental career—or who invaded his privacy, particularly that of his family. History began to repeat itself intergenerationally when White's daughter, Nancy, qualified for the 1980 American Olympic field hockey team. In-depth interviews and prying questions—about grades, career ambitions, social life—had a historical ring to them, although she said that she knew little about her father's athletic career: "There are still things I find out in the paper and say 'I didn't know you did that.' He's a very humble person." Like his own parents, he expected his daughter to make athletics a secondary priority. "I don't think he ever put a whole lot of emphasis on athletics. His main concern was developing strength in whatever I did. The first thing he always asks is about school." Nancy White was listed as a starter on the national team for the 1980 Olympics and her father planned to be a spectator, but Pres. Jimmy Carter canceled American participation in retaliation for the Soviet invasion of Afghanistan and both Whites were bitterly disappointed. When Byron White referred derisively in *California v. Greenwood* to "snoops," many in the press assumed that he was referring, with some feeling, to them.

White's hostility to armchair experts seems in fact to have been more profound if less pronounced for legal academics than for sportswriters and other journalists. There are few direct clues, although the rough way he bit off the word "professors" in his remarks to a reunion in 1994 of United States attorneys from the Kennedy administration is a chilling hint. White's twin sins to the academy were confounding doctrine and occasionally writing obscurely. Prof. Kate Stith, a former clerk and sympathetic critic, has written: "To the distress of those who would have preferred greater elaboration or a philosophical vision, [White] approached the judicial task in a lawyerly and pragmatic fashion—though sometimes in curiously cryptic opinions." Another former clerk and sympathetic critic points out that on occasion White's opinions bear an oddly "schizophrenic" quality, the result of careful analysis and strong views double-yoked together: "If you read *Smith v. Goguen*—one of the early flag desecration cases—you find the first half is an excellent analysis of the free speech issue and the second is a very exercised rant which is topped with a confusing analogy. In cases like that, the justice had two things to say but they didn't fit together very well."

Near the end of his career, one word captured the attention of lawyer and scholar alike who flooded the law reviews with critiques of White's opinion for the Court in *Bowers v. Hardwick*. In *Bowers,* White spoke for a five-person majority that rejected the claim that the due process clause of the Fourteenth Amendment prohibited a state from criminalizing consensual homosexual activity between adults in private. The opinion briskly dispatches the claim in less than ten pages. Near the end of the opinion, after surveying the lengthy history of state prohibitions of homosexual conduct, White wrote: "Against this background, to claim that a right to engage in such conduct is 'deeply rooted in this nation's history and tradition' or 'implicit in the concept of ordered liberty' is, at best, facetious." The adjective, almost as much as the result, convinced many critics that the majority, particularly the author, were "vituperatively homophobic" as well as reactionary.

For better or worse, White was more concerned about the decision than the opinion. He had been the moving force to convince the Court to hear the case. When the petition for certiorari was first discussed in early October 1985, there were three votes to grant certiorari (Burger, White, and Rehnquist), one short of the necessary number. White asked for the case to be relisted—the standard procedure for delaying a vote so that a draft dissent from denial of certiorari could be prepared and circulated. White's dissent from denial of certiorari circulated on October 17. When White's dissent from denial circulated, one of Justice Brennan's clerks suggested that he add his name to White's internal opinion. Justice Brennan had initially voted to deny certiorari the first time that the case came up in conference. Somewhat absentmindedly, Brennan quickly agreed, due to the conflict in the circuits on the issue, and sent a memo to his colleagues informing them that he had joined White's dissent from denial. He immediately was besieged by Blackmun, who feared that if the Court granted certiorari, a majority would not only refuse to protect homosexual conduct but would also undermine *Roe v. Wade* in the process.

Brennan was in a dilemma of multiple dimensions: he appeared to be flip-flopping and risked losing face with his colleagues; Blackmun's pessimism over the case and its larger consequences was compelling; and yet he disagreed with the lower court and feared that waiting any longer would only mean that the conservative revolution symbolically led by Ronald Reagan would make the atmosphere for the petitioner's argument worse. So he changed his vote to deny. It was too late: Thurgood Marshall, taking his cue from Brennan's precipitous "join" of White's internal dissent, had already provided the fourth vote to grant certiorari. He could not change his vote, too, without looking as if he were in lockstep with Brennan. Certiorari was granted November 4, 1985. *Bowers v. Hardwick* came to the Supreme Court as much by misadventure as by measured deliberation.

The case was argued on the last day of March 1986, and the tentative vote was 5-4 to affirm and uphold the right. Justice Powell, who had been in the majority, switched his vote on April 8, a week after the conference vote, and the chief justice assigned the opinion for the Court to White. The case was an opportunity for White to develop two doctrinal points about which he cared strongly and had written about in some detail. The first was that the Court's *Griswold-Eisenstadt* line of cases did not, as he insisted and as Justice Brennan had conceded in *Carey v. Population Services,* entirely preclude the states from regulating sexual conduct among adults. The second was the point he first made in *Roe v. Wade,* had begun to elaborate in *Moore v. City of East Cleveland,* and elaborated more recently in *Thornburgh v. American College of Obstetricians and Gynecologists*—that the Court's legitimacy was strained to the breaking point by redefining the scope of fundamental rights without clear authority from the Constitution.

With the end-of-term writing load building, White assigned the draft opinion to one of his law clerks under the now standard twelve pages/twelve days deadline. The clerk did not view the task as heroic but worked feverishly to prepare an opinion that broke as little doctrinal china as possible on the way to the result White required. Twelve days after receiving the assignment, he presented his lengthy draft opinion to White, who replied that he *got tired of waiting and did it last night.* White's draft was circulated within the Court the next day, April 21. The terse opinion betrays the impatience with which the author met and ultimately discharged his own assignment. What could have been the culminating expression of long-standing convictions and obviously profound concerns—suggested previously in *Carey, Moore,* and *Thornburgh*—impressed many as an intellectual hit-and-run incident.

The heart of the opinion deserves close attention. After narrowly reading the cases said to support "a right of privacy that extends to homosexual sodomy" and finding that the weight of history—which precedent made relevant—was also against the claimed right, White wrote:

> Nor are we inclined to take a more expansive view of our authority to discover new fundamental rights imbedded in the Due Process Clause. The Court is most vulnerable and comes nearest to illegitimacy when it deals with judge-made constitutional law having little or no cognizable roots in the language or design of the Constitution. That this is so was painfully demonstrated by the face-off between the Executive and the Court in the 1930's. There should be, therefore, great resistance to expand the substantive reach of those Clauses, particularly if it requires redefining the category of rights deemed to be fundamental. Otherwise, the judiciary necessarily takes to itself further authority to govern the country without express constitutional authority. The claimed right pressed on us today falls far short of overcoming this resistance.

Unlike so many modern Supreme Court opinions, the words are absolutely authentic to the author—down to the ice hockey metaphor awkwardly employed to evoke the constitutional and political conflict between Pres. Franklin D. Roosevelt and the Supreme Court over the constitutionality of the New Deal in 1937. The diction should not distract from two points. First, the legitimacy of judicial review—which White worried about in the abortion cases, the death penalty cases, the campaign financing cases, the legislative veto case, and so on—was central to the "claimed right," and no deft manipulation of precedent could gloss over the fact. Second, White added without elaborating a point that some political scientists and lawyers had argued for years: when the Supreme Court tests the tensile strength of its legitimacy, it not only threatens principle but jeopardizes its own political authority. A Court that weakens itself by overreaching its power invites retaliation by Congress, not only by reversing statutory decisions legislatively but by restricting the Court's power to hear issues or cases. Even worse, the Court's capacity to persuade—its only real power, as Paul Freund liked to emphasize—is likely to be diminished. The loss is likely to be across the boards, at both the center and periphery of its power. The point was important, not expressly acknowledged before by any opinion for the Court, and central to the growing debate over the role of the Court and proper basis for construing the Constitution. White contented himself with making the point with a single word—"vulnerable."

Readers more concerned with the tone or the outcome of the opinion tended to overlook the point, perhaps because it was telegraphed and not developed. "The opinion was judicial modesty with a vengeance," in the words of Rex Lee. One of White's early law clerks once asked White why he did not spell out his views in more detail, especially when he felt strongly about them. *Why should I? The point is there. It doesn't need any window dressing.* White's opinions never aspired beyond plain, workmanlike prose. His former coclerk, Frank Allen, saw rhetorical patterns in 1946 that repeated themselves throughout White's judicial career. "He wrote to get the job done, no more," said Allen. "And he was not an intellectual, despite his obvious gifts and capacity." If Oliver Wendell Holmes, Jr., and Hugo Black would be famous for their reading lists, Byron White would not. When White was asked in 1968 by the *Rocky Mountain News* what he read for pleasure, he replied: "I get rather satiated with reading. History, sociology, economics—these are all work-related subjects. I don't do much reading at home except for newspapers and some news magazines." To the extent that he allowed himself leisure reading, his tastes ran to mystery and suspense novels—Ian Fleming at the beginning of his career and Tony Hillerman toward the end. He also enjoyed Daniel Boorstin's popular histories.

His only recorded fan letter to an author was not to a professional writer or historian but to James J. Fahey, the Waltham, Massachusetts, garbage truck driver who described his experiences as a seaman first class aboard the light cruiser *Montpelier* in *Pacific War Diary 1942–1945,* which Houghton Mifflin published on the recommendation of the naval historian Samuel Eliot Morison. The early part of Fahey's tour of the South Pacific included stops at Tulagi and other bases in common with White, as well as service in 31-Knot Burke's task force. "I think his chief extracurricular intellectual exercise was the *New York Times* crossword puzzle, which he has done every day—and quickly—as long as I've known him," according to Rex Lee.

By discounting what both the press and the academy thought of his work, and by focusing his energies more on efficiently dispatching his caseload than creating a memorable written work product, Byron White guaranteed that his retirement would nonplus many, especially those who had rhapsodized two and three years before when Justices Marshall and Brennan left the Court.

James Lileks of the Newhouse News Service provided the coda for Governor Casey's later complaint about the press's inattention to White's impact on the Court during his career: "Byron White: not a household name. For many people, hearing about White's resignation from the Supreme Court was like meeting a strange man coming up the basement steps who says, 'I guess I'll be going now. Thanks for 30 years of shelter.'" In the academy, White's version of judicial modesty did not measure up at Yale Law School, whose Bruce Ackerman would called White the "banalization of Holmes," a justice with "the arduous sincerity of a man out of his depth."

For White, the antilegacy suited his tastes. "I don't have a 'doctrinal legacy,'" he said with a mixture of pride and impatience to one friend in Denver a year after he retired. "I shouldn't." White was mildly uncomfortable with the fuss created in 1994 by the renaming of the old Post Office Building and Courthouse, pursuant to act of Congress, as the Byron R. White Courthouse. He was unenthusiastic about the flattering portrait that adorned the foyer of the building, and his fierce modesty drew the line at providing photographs or personal mementos for the specially produced exhibition case placed under the portrait: after three years, the case—valued at more than $7,000 and built without screws or nails and with a beveled crystal glass cover—was empty because the justice was "too busy" to provide artifacts to be displayed in it. White's demeanor at the ceremony officially renaming the courthouse suggested a carefully crafted air of incongruity—the legendary local figure as ordinary civil servant.

Many thought that he went to some length to underscore that he was not possessed of special wisdom or insight, that he was simply an ordinary lawyer with an awful responsibility. A professor of law who witnessed White speak publicly several times thought he abstracted all of the "hope and glory" from the law and made his office "sound like he was the manager of a dry goods store." Even in appearance he could adopt a plain aspect, neither suggesting nor expecting the treatment reserved for powerful figures who no longer exercised authority but were to be accorded the appropriate accoutrements of a distinguished career. Surveying the scene on the platform for President Clinton's second inauguration, Mary McGrory of the *Washington Post* observed: "Retired Justice Byron White, brooding at the edge of the stand in the dank air, looked like an unhappy ice fisherman." In a rare moment of vanity, White once admitted to a law clerk late in his career that he wished he had "had a face that made a natural smile, but I don't." The physiological, combined with his natural intensity, which tended to exaggerate the harshness of his face, may have been often misread, especially by unsympathetic observers.

Not long before the courthouse ceremony, White appeared in Denver for the annual banquet of the Colorado Sports Hall of Fame, of which he was now the last surviving charter member. He held a brief meeting with reporters—it could hardly be classified as a press conference: "questions about legal matters or past or present judicial proceedings were declared off limits." He did admit publicly for the first time that he had never had judicial ambitions as a lawyer in Denver or Washington: "I always thought it would be horrible to be a judge." He said that he loved politics, which, noted the *Rocky Mountain News*, "judges at high levels must give up. He never relished the notion of watching whom he associated with, what he did in his spare time or how he lived every bit of his life." But "'I said, "I'll give it a try",'" and, "'I gave it a try for 31 years.'"

Judicial office had paradoxical consequences for White: he was insulated from direct contact with the press, except on his own terms, and free to carry out his duties in his own fashion, but he was always in the public eye, and his private life—including social contacts, financial investments, and family activities—were always potential sources of scrutiny and controversy. When he told old friends in Denver after he retired that "maybe I never should have left," the complaint was not even halfhearted but reflective of decades of annoying attention to the constraints of office. At the same time, he always told his law clerks how valuable and rewarding he thought public service was, and his admiration for his "alumni" who entered public service was always genuine and often vigorously expressed.

Another perspective on White's public service comes from an old friend. His identity is less important than his credentials for measuring his subject: he has known Byron White for more than a half century, and they have socialized together, done philanthropic work together in Denver more than thirty years ago, and fished the waters of the northern Rockies together. He is not a lawyer, and his disinterest in legal theory is genuine.

Asked for his most indelible impression of his life-long friend's career, he says: "You know, I'm not much interested in his legal views, not that we have ever talked that much about them. But I guess I think of him now [May 1996] as someone who sacrificed a lot, at least in terms of wordly things, to be a public servant. He could have made a mint in Denver and lived a quiet life. But he has lived modestly—in the same little house in Washington for thirty years— and put in six and a half long days a week being a judge. I think of his legacy as service, with great dedication and nothing in it for himself. I mean, he was famous as a young man, you know."

When White finally consented to his first substantive interview about his career, in 1996, he was asked by Denver's *Rocky Mountain News* about the effect of "pivotal" justices. His reply: "I think this notion of blocs and extra-persuasive justices is just not accurate." (The entire interview is set out as Appendix C.) Some justices, such as Lewis Powell, were acutely conscious of how their impact would be judged by history. Powell even remarked when he reluctantly accepted appointment that he worried at his age, then sixty-three, that he would not be able to make his mark on the institution. White, having tasted fame early, declined to think in those terms. One of his clerks during the 1991 term, David Frederick, wrote after White's retirement:

> Being non-ideological and non-doctrinaire is clearly very important to White, just as is being his own person and not worrying about his place in history. He recognizes that being a justice who believes in a more limited Constitution is not the way to gain historical notoriety. Whether it's because he gained such fame as a young man in sports or whether it's just his natural disposition, I think he cares a lot more about doing what he thinks is right than whether it will make him a famous figure in history.

Another clerk, from his first few years on the Court, observed: "The 'Whizzer White' thing is such a shame—something that the media just couldn't let go. He was so much more than that . . . so much more than the incongruity even."

For Byron White, the other side of fame was self-effacing duty, the compass that guided his public life. Where was true North? For any visitor to his chambers in the Supreme Court, the answer was in plain sight. Above his desk hung an oil painting of a western panorama—an empty dirt road leading through an irrigated field and heading toward a snowy mountain range. The painting does not claim to represent a specific view of the Rockies from the high plains, although if you stood on the corner of Second and Garfield Streets in Wellington, Colorado, painting and vista might merge in your imagination. The painting suggests the loneliness, the power of the elements, and—implicitly—the self-reliance that is necessary, and sometimes inadequate, in the barren terrain.

Appendix A

White-Patterson Meeting

Unofficial and edited transcript of a conference between Deputy Attorney General Byron R. White and Gov. John Patterson of Alabama, May 21, 1961, in Montgomery, Alabama, as produced by United Press International.

Patterson: I asked Mr. [Macdonald] Gallion, our Attorney General, to be present this morning while we discussed this matter. To begin with I will turn the conference over to you to hear what you want to say to us. And what you are doing here?

White: Well, Governor, Mr. Kennedy, Mr. Robert Kennedy, the Attorney General, suggested that I chat with you and communicate with you when we got down here to let you know that we were here. Mr. Kennedy, after I left Washington, after having some conversations with him, formalized his instructions to me and I thought that I could communicate those to you.

He directed me to come to Alabama and he said, you are directed to enlist the support and supervise the U.S. Marshals in Alabama. And such deputies as I deem necessary to give all persons in the State of Alabama the rights guaranteed them by Constitution and laws of the U.S. without limitation of your authority you are under you are specifically authorized:

1. To protect any passenger vehicle traveling in interstate commerce.
2. Protect any person who exercises his constitutional rights to freedom of speech or assembly.

This, Governor, are my instructions and we are here hoping that we can work with the state and local law enforcement officials to help prevent any recurrence of violence or other unpleasant circumstances such as has by accident or otherwise occurred here in your state during the last week. It was the judgment of the Attorney General and the constituted authorities in Washington that at this time it would be wise for all of us including the State of Alabama that the federal government showed itself here and made its interest in this situation known.

We are here for that purpose. We have assembled some federal officers who will act as deputy U.S. marshals. . . . I'm sure that none of us here from Washington are at all delighted to be here. We much prefer that we did not think it was necessary to come and we would be quite happy if our stay here was very brief. We do hope that we can work with the local authorities and our efforts will be directed to this end.

Patterson: First, I would like to know if you could tell me what specific federal statute you are relying upon to bring in federal marshals into Alabama in this matter. Can you give me that information?

White: Yes, we are relying on a number of things, on [unintelligible] section 333. . . .

Patterson: You point to a section or clause in the Federal Constitution to back up your action in this matter? You are aware that Section 4 of Article 4 of the Constitution provides that in case of civil disturbances that the federal government shall send in federal law enforcement officers or troops only when requested by the legislature or the Governor?

Now how many men do you have here and how long do you propose to remain here?

White: Well we have now, Governor, they are still arriving. And I think that about an hour ago there were somewhat over 200 here. And they are still arriving. And I would think that there may be around 400.

Patterson: Could you tell me what you specifically intend to do? And what those men specifically intend to do while they are here?

White: One thing that they will do is attempt to maintain the integrity of the interstate bus system in the event that it is threatened by violence and another thing that they will do is to protect the other federally guaranteed rights here that are threatened.

New Voice: You stated that your people are watching the movement of this type of individual to try to determine in advance if they are coming into Alabama. Where have you taken any action and do you intend to take any to encourage these people who are coming here to stir up trouble not to come and stay at home? Have you taken any action to try to discourage their coming into Alabama for this purpose and to try to make them stay at home or try to get the ones in Alabama to go home? Have you done anything to discourage them coming here and do you intend to do something?

White: We have, Governor, attempted to. We have not nor do we have the right to attempt to prevent people from traveling interstate. We would like very much if provocative incidents were avoided and provocative situations were avoided.

Patterson: Couldn't you publicly ask these students to stay at college and tend to their lessons and their business and to not come into the State of Alabama for the purpose of getting embroiled in fights? Couldn't the government of the U.S. ask those student to stay at home and mind their own business? Couldn't you do that?

White: Well, there are people in this federal union that have the right to move among the states and while we do, no, we are certainly far from encouraging provocative movements.

Patterson: You understand that these people who are coming in here, Mr. White, are not cooperative with our policemen. The policeman says you stay here and he leaves. If the policeman says don't you go there he goes. It is very difficult for a police officer to deal with people who are not cooperative with law enforcement agencies who are trying to protect them.

Understand that. These people are trained not to obey, they are trained to agitate.

New Voice: Mr. White, let me say this. The CORE organization is under an injunction of the state not to make entry into the state to travel on the so-called freedom rides in order to present a breach of peace. We have a record of experience that there have been three trips, four now into Alabama . . . they had notice of it and yet they came on. Now can we expect cooperation from the federal government in the enforcement of our judicial processes in this state?

Gallion: In the first place you said that you wanted to cooperate in every way. Can the U.S. government relay this information to them? First that they abide by the judicial processes of the State of Alabama.

White: Of course, Mr. Attorney General, we are not custodians of the CORE group [interrupted].

Patterson: Let me ask you this, if they go to a restaurant in a municipality having a municipal ordinance against integrated restaurant facilities do you intend to see that they are escorted to such restaurants? To violate that city ordinance? Do you intend to do that?

White: We've made no determination about this, Governor, we have no intention at all at this point.

Patterson: I am interested in enforcing our laws and identifying those people who are coming into Alabama causing a breach of the peace. Can you furnish us with the files of the FBI and wherever else the government might have the files on certain named people, and we'll give you their names as to the Communist activities or associates with Communist organizations, for us to copy those files if we give you the name of those people?

White: No, we would not guarantee that you could get that information. If we had it, Governor, these are confidential files of the FBI [interruption].

Patterson: Mr. White, if you know in advance that a person is a known Communist with a record of having been involved in riots in other states in New York and places like that. With a record like that, then leads us into enforcing the law and taking precautionary measures when you know he is coming to Alabama . . .

White: Well, Governor, one of the things I think has occurred in the last week is that the law enforcement officers here and the newspapers and everyone knew that there were journeys going on in the state and there was some notice of it. There was no secret for example that the students or riders who were attacked were on their way from Birmingham.

New Voice: . . . In your spirit of cooperation, as you say in law enforcement, if you come in contact with any of these rioters on the bus yesterday is it then your intention for the U.S. Marshall knowing they are subject to arrest to turn them over to state authorities?

White: I do not know what the answer is to that, sir [garbled]. I have not anticipated that marshals would come in contact with these people as I told you.

New Voice: Just what is your estimate of the situation here at this time: as far as maintenance of law and order is concerned. Mr. White, can you tell us what your estimate of the situation in Montgomery is at this time?

White: It appears quite peaceful.

Patterson: Now I would like at this time—I know you are in a hurry—very briefly state to you what the position of the State of Alabama is in relation to this matter and particularly federal intervention in this matter. Of course we are enforcing the law here in this state. We will continue to enforce the law. We have adequate state forces. We do not need any assistance from federal government to do it. We have not asked for any assistance and we don't want the assistance from the federal government in this matter, and we do not believe that the U.S. has any legal constitutional right to come in here with federal marshals to do what they are proposing to do, and I think that your presence is unwarranted and it will only further complicate and aggravate the situation and worsen federal-state relations. And we consider the position of the state that the federal people have been sent in here for this purpose, are interlopers and unwelcome in the State of Alabama. And I think that your presence under these conditions constitute an encroachment on the rights of the people of the State of Alabama. I think your support and encouragement of the outside agitators has brought on the difficulties that we have experienced. And I think and now you send the forces here ostensibly to quell a disturbance that you have helped create. I think that any further encouragement to these agitators is only going to worsen the situation and make our job of law enforcement more difficult. In conclusion I want to tell you this—we are certainly going to do everything we can to enforce the rights of this state and prevent encroachment by the federal government for our constitutional rights as we see them. And I want to request while you are in the State of Alabama that you confine your activities to the federal jurisdiction and not get involved or encroach upon any of the states rights or state functions and I want you to be especially careful that none of the U.S. marshals or federal agents who are in Alabama violate any of our state laws. Because if any of the federal people, U.S. marshals and others, violate any of our state laws, then we will arrest them and prosecute them as we would anybody else. I would hate to see that occur because that would worsen federal-state relations that are already at a very low ebb. That is just about as clear as I can express the position of the Governor of this state and the State of Alabama at this time . . .

Letter of October 20, 1975

Text of a letter from Justice Byron R. White to the chief justice, dated October 20, 1975. Copy located in Lewis F. Powell, Jr., Papers, Washington & Lee University, Lexington, Virginia.

Dear Mr. Chief Justice:

I should like to register my protest against the decision of the Court not to assign the writing of any opinions to Mr. Justice Douglas. As I understand it from deliberations in conference, there are one or more Justices who are doubtful about the competence of Mr. Justice Douglas that they would not join any opinion purportedly authored by him. At the very least, they would not hand down any judgment arrived at by a 5-4 vote where Mr. Justice Douglas is in the majority. There may be various shadings of opinion among the seven Justices but the ultimate action was not to make any assignments of opinions to Mr. Justice Douglas. That decision, made in the absence of Mr. Justice Douglas, was supported by seven Justices. It is clear that the ground for the action was the assumed incompetence of the justice.

On the assumption that there have been no developments since last Friday to make this unnecessary, I shall state briefly why I disagreed and still disagree with the Court's action. Prior to this time, on every occasion in which I have dissented from action taken by the Court's majority, I have thought the decision being made, although wrong in my view, was within the powers assigned to the Court by the Constitution. In this instance, the action voted by the Court exceeds its powers and perverts the constitutional design.

The Constitution provides that federal judges, including Supreme Court Justices, "shall hold their Offices during good behaviour." That document—our basic charter binding us all—allows the impeachment of judges by Congress; but it nowhere provides that a Justice's colleagues may deprive him of his office by refusing to permit him to function as a Justice.

If there is sufficient doubt about Justice Douglas' mental abilities that he should have no assignments of opinions and if his vote should not be counted in 5-4 cases when he is one of the five, I fail to see how his vote should be counted or considered in any case or why we should listen to him in conference at all. In any event, the decision of the Court precludes the effective performance of his judicial functions by Mr. Justice Douglas and the Court's majority has wrongfully assumed that it has the power to do so.

If Congress were to provide by statute that Supreme Court Justices could be removed from office whenever an official commission, acting on medical advice, concluded that a Justice is no longer capable of carrying on his duties, surely there would be substantial questions about the constitutionality of such legislation. But Congress has taken no such action; nor has it purported to vest power in the Court to unseat a Justice for any reason. The Court nevertheless asserts the right to disregard Justice Douglas in any case vote where it will determine the outcome. How does the Court plan to answer the petitioner who would otherwise have a judgment in his favor, who claims that the vote of each sitting Justice should be counted until and unless he is impeached by proper authorities and who inquires where the Court derived the power to reduce its size to eight Justices?

Even if the Court had the authority to do what seven Justices now purport to do, it did not, as far as I know, discuss the matter with Mr. Justice Douglas prior to voting to relieve him of a major part of his judicial duties, did not seek his views about his own health or attempt to obtain from him current medical opinions on that subject.

Mr. Justice Douglas undoubtedly has severe ailments. I do not discount the difficulties that his condition presents for his colleagues. It would be better for everyone, including Mr. Justice Douglas, if he would now retire. Although he has made some noble efforts—very likely far more than others would have made—there remain serious problems that would best be resolved by his early retirement. But Mr. Justice Douglas has a different view. He listens to oral arguments, appears in conference and casts his vote on argued cases. He thus not only asserts his own competence to sit but has not suggested that he is planning to retire.

Based on my own observations and assuming that we have power to pass on the competence of a fellow justices, I am not convinced, as each of my seven colleagues seems to be, that there is such doubt about the condition of Mr. Justice Douglas that I should refuse to join any opinion that he might write. And, as I have said, as long as he insists on acting as a Justice and participating in our deliberations, I cannot discover the constitutional power to treat him other than as a Justice, as I have for more than thirteen years.

The Constitution opted for the independence of each federal judge, including his freedom from removal by his colleagues. I am convinced that it would have been better had retirement been required at a specified age and that a constitutional amendment to that effect should be proposed and adopted. But so far the Constitution has struck a different balance, and I will not presume to depart from it in this instance.

If the Court is convinced that Justice Douglas should not continue to function as a Justice, the Court should say so publicly and invite Congress to take appropriate action. If it is an impeachable offense for an incompetent Justice to purport to sit as a judge, is it not the task of Congress, rather than this Court, to undertake proceedings to determine the issue of competence? If it is not an impeachable offense, may the Court nevertheless conclude that a Justice is incompetent and forbid him to perform his duties?

This leads to a final point. The Court's action is plainly a matter of great importance to the functioning of the Court in the immediate future. It is a matter of substantial significance to both litigants and the public. The decision should be publicly announced; and I do hope the majority is prepared to make formal disclosure of the action that it has taken.

Knowing that my seven colleagues, for whom I have the highest regard, hold different views, I speak with great deference. Yet history teaches that nothing can more readily bring the Court and its constitutional functions into disrepute than the Court's failure to recognize the limits of its own powers. I therefore hasten to repeat in writing the views that I orally stated at our latest conference.

Sincerely,

Byron

The Chief Justice

Copies to: Mr. Justice Brennan
            Mr. Justice Stewart
            Mr. Justice Marshall
            Mr. Justice Blackmun
            Mr. Justice Powell
            Mr. Justice Rehnquist

June 1996 Interview

Edited transcript of an interview conducted by Clifford May and published in the Rocky Mountain News *on June 30, 1996 (page 69A).*

May: Why is it not a good idea to let voters go to the polls and elect their judges?

White: When you have head-to-head elections sponsored by political parties, the judges really have to campaign, they have to spend some money, and they have to raise money. And they keep raising it from lawyers who very likely are going to appear before them, or from special-interest groups who regularly use the courts to further their causes.

May: That helps lead me to a larger question having to do with the impartiality of judges and the difference between judges and politicians. You're arguing that a judge who has to campaign becomes a kind of a politician rather than a disinterested interpreter and defender of the law. But critics of the judiciary charge that many judges act like politicians anyway, that they don't so much interpret existing law as amend and create new law. Do you see any grounds for such criticism?

White: That's just words. The Constitution is an amazingly short document. And some of the language in it is really not self-explanatory at all. And every time you construe that language you are, in a sense, making constitutional law.

May: Are you, in a sense, re-writing the Constitution? In other words, is it an infinitely flexible document?

White: No, not infinitely. You're not going to get me into an argument like this because if you want to go and find out what the Constitution means, you're going to have to go into constitutional law case books and read an awful lot of cases. And it's by reading those cases that you will understand, for example, what an unreasonable search and seizure is or what freedom of speech is.

May: Many people think that the split on the court, now and at other times, is essentially a liberal/conservative split. Is that a fair way to look at it, or is the division rather between those justices who are judicial activists on the one hand and those who try not to impose personal policy preferences?

White: Nothing is that simple. I don't think you can characterize any one of them in the way you did.

May: Can you give me a different way to characterize what goes on?

White: It depends on the case. Everybody—everybody—has to pay attention to the text of a statute or of the Constitution. But anybody who says that you can take the majestic language of the Constitution and say, "I can read it and know exactly what it means," is way beyond my ken.

May: We're now in a presidential campaign season. How much of a difference will it make whether a Republican or Democrat picks the next one or two Supreme Court justices?

White: Well, every time a new justice comes to the Supreme Court, it's a different court. You sit there and for two or three years you say to yourself: "This person is voting much differently than his predecessor." I think it makes a lot of difference who is appointing. It's quite proper under the Constitution for the president to nominate people he thinks will act the way he thinks a Supreme Court justice ought to act. But at the same time, the Constitution says the Senate may advise and consent, and they don't need to consent.

May: I know you don't want to get into abortion as an issue, but my next question is related to what we've been discussing. There are those who would argue—as the majority decision in *Roe vs. Wade* does argue—that the Constitution speaks on this issue and says that there is a right to privacy which implies what have been called reproductive rights. I know you dissented from that view. There are also those who say, "No, the Constitution speaks on the other side, that the fetus has a right to live." And finally, there are those who say, "You know, the Constitution doesn't speak to this issue one way or another—therefore, it should be left to the people and their various legislatures to decide."

White: No question about that, but case after case is decided by a 5-to-4 vote. The justices have different views on what the words of the Constitution mean and what those words allow judges to do.

May: I don't mean to beat this into the ground, but is there in your view no point at which judges may be criticized for becoming essentially politicians with life tenure, politicians wearing robes, rather than people who defend the law as written whether they agree with the law or not?

White: I've heard judges described that way, especially by people who don't agree with what they're doing in certain cases. Even I have been called that. Can you imagine that?

May: Hard to imagine.

White: Anyway, that's what some people say. Doesn't bother me a bit.

May: But is it an unfair criticism in all cases, or are there cases where a judge doesn't understand his role? Has any justice you've ever served with misunderstood, in your view?

White: Never. Never. Thirteen new justices came on the bench while I was there, and nobody, as far as I know, ever thought he was a legislator or acted like a legislator.

May: You were 31 years on the Supreme Court. Did you see changes in the concept of the court, in the concept of constitutional interpretation over that time?

White: Not a great deal in general. But, as I say, every time a new justice came on, you could count on cases being decided differently than they would have been before. But in terms of function, I don't see much difference.

May: To what extent are the personalities pivotal? In other words, you may disagree with a particular justice on many issues, but he may have a personality that is extremely forceful. And there may be alliances, and I would assume friendships form, and maybe some justices don't get along so well with others. How does the personal aspect fit in?

White: I never got really angry with any of the justices. And I think this notion of blocs and extra-persuasive justices is just not accurate.

May: You mentioned that it often comes down to a 5-to-4 decision. Right now, if it's a 5-to-4 decision, I can pretty much tell you who is on one side and who is on the other side. It looks again, to an outsider, that there's a pretty clear split in this particular court, with one or two people sort of in the middle or swaying back and forth. Is that fair to say?

White: Yes, there may be. And at one time I was called the swing justice. That's the way the court changes and certainly this 5-to-4 split, if you want to call it that, is not the same 5-to-4 split that there was on cases 10 years ago.

May: When you are the swing justice is there particular pressure or attention paid to you? Is there an effort either in conversation or in your writing to say, "Now let me address you on this particular point because I know your vote is going to be decisive."

White: No. Most of the meat of the Supreme Court is cut in the writing of opinions. We meet in conference and take tentative votes. And you know from very short conversations explaining those votes roughly what everyone has in mind. But the writing is what really cuts, and if you're assigned to write a majority opinion, you try to write a majority opinion that will get the votes of everybody who voted that way.

May: And if you're writing the dissent are you writing for the other justices or are you writing for posterity, so that later on people will say, "You know, he was clearly right on this. He knew this way back when."

White: Well, every term that I was on that court, the case was assigned based on the conference vote. And every term there would be one or two cases where that was not the final result because of a dissent.

May: Because the dissent was so persuasive and so strongly argued?

White: Well, I don't know if it was or not, but I've had cases taken away from me and it's just that some justice had changed his mind. I didn't think the dissent was very persuasive myself at all.

May: I'm thinking about one of your dissents that people are talking about now. What you said in that dissent is being argued again: That was *Miranda vs.*

Arizona, in which you said that requiring a police officer to say to a citizen in connection to a crime, "You have the right to remain silent," is tantamount to making that police officer say, "Don't cooperate with us, the police."

White: I thought *Miranda* was wrong. I still do, but it's the law. It's become the law and I wrote opinions that if *Miranda* was going to be the law there should be clarification of what the officers' responsibilities were. If you kept refusing to accept a majority opinion as the law every time you disagreed with it, the law would be in a shambles.

May: I'm not arguing that we should refuse to accept the law. The law is the law. But that doesn't mean one can't say "This is a bad law," or "This law should be changed," or "We've experimented with this and it didn't work out the way we thought."

White: Well, that happens, because, you know, the Supreme Court has overruled itself well over a hundred times. And it's because they thought they were just wrong. But usually the people who decide a mistake was made are not the same people who made the decision.

May: In a recent case in New York, Judge Harold Baer found no probable cause when suspects ran from the police, leaving behind duffel bags that contained drugs. He was very harshly criticized by both Bob Dole and President Clinton. He eventually reversed himself after further evidence was brought to him. The question is whether his judicial independence was infringed, as some have charged, or whether he should have changed his mind, whether he did so not because of political pressure but because he realized from the criticism that he had indeed made a mistake.

White: I have no idea what he thought, but I can tell you one thing, that judicial decisions are fair game for criticism. You criticize them all the time, I bet, and so do your colleagues in the media. So do law review professors; so do the people who lose the case. Judges are not above criticism, and that is not what judicial independence means. What judicial independence means to me is that once a judge gets on the bench, he is free to make honest decisions about cases in accordance with the law of the land and without feeling obligated to or under the thumb of anybody. He's not going to do what the president tells him to, he's not going to do what the legislature tells him to or any powerful interest group.

May: But does the president, for example, step across a boundary he shouldn't if he suggests that a Harold Baer should resign because he doesn't understand the law? Or if Bob Dole suggests, as he did, that Harold Baer should be impeached? After all, he committed no crimes or misdemeanors.

White: I won't answer those questions, but Article 3 of the Constitution says that federal judges are appointed for their good behavior.

May: When a congressman gets a lot of letters from constituents about an issue, he tends to respond to that. When there's a march on the capitol, politicians respond to that. When there's a march on the Supreme Court, or you suddenly get a lot of letters, how easy is it to resist that pressure?

White: It's easy. Because there are two sides to these cases, you know. Almost all decent cases have two rational sides. You have dissents from rational justices.

May: Sometimes, don't you have to make a decision where you think from a public policy point of view that this is not a good idea, but that's what the law says and it's up to Congress to change the law if people want a different result?

White: All the time. And if Congress doesn't like it, it can change the law or amend it. This happens every single session of Congress.

May: And the more difficult cases are the constitutional cases because though the Constitution can be amended, it's a difficult process.

White: That's exactly it. But the government and private parties are not averse to coming and suggesting to you, "Your Honors, this past decision was wrong and we suggest you overrule it."

May: Final question. When you retired three years ago you said you'd be in Washington for a while but that you intended to come back to Colorado. Will you eventually?

White: Oh, I'm sure.

1970   William E. Nelson (New York University; Weinfeld—SDNY) A
        Allan A. Ryan, Jr. (Minnesota) O
        Philip M. Soper (Harvard) A

1971   Richard J. Danzig (Yale) G
        David E. Kendall (Yale) PP
        James E. Scarboro (Colorado; Arraj—CO) PP

1972   Rhesa Barksdale (Mississippi) J
        Robert B. Barnett (Chicago; Wisdom—CA5) PP
        Richard L. Hoffman (Columbia) O
        Richard J. Urowsky (Yale; hired by Justice Reed, retired) PP

1973   Pierce O'Donnell (Georgetown; Hufstedler—CA9) PP
        Hal S. Scott (Chicago; Leventhal—CADC) A
        Jonathan D. Varat (Pennsylvania; Mansfield—CA2) A

1974   James T. Malysiak (Yale; Renfrew—N.D.CA) PP
        John W. Nields Jr. (Penn) PP
        Larry L. Simms (Boston University; Oakes—CA2) PP

1975   Robert L. Dietz (Harvard; hired by Justice Douglas) PP
        Dennis J. Hutchinson (Oxford, University of Texas at Austin;
        Tuttle—CA5; later clerked for Justice Douglas) A
        Nields
        Randy Nelson (Colorado; Robb—CADC) PP

1976   Gil Kujovich (Harvard; Hufstedler—CA9; shared with Justice
        Stewart) A
        Robert W. Loewen (University of Southern California; Ely—CA9) PP
        Nields
        John W. Spiegel (Yale) PP

1977   Tom J. Campbell (Harvard; MacKinnon—CADC) G
        Charles G. Cole (Harvard; Leventhal—CADC) PP
        S. Elizabeth Gibson (University of North Carolina; Craven—CA4) A
        Jeffrey Glekel (Yale; Weinfeld—SDNY) PP

1978   David Burman (Georgetown; Robinson—CADC) PP
        Gary Sasso (Penn; Robinson—CADC) PP
        Nicholas J. Spaeth (Stanford; Bright—CA8) PP
        Kate Stith-Cabranes (Harvard; McGowan—CADC) A

1979   Peter J. Kalis (Yale) PP
        Geoffrey P. Miller (Columbia; McGowan—CADC) A
        Robert V. Percival (Stanford; Hufstedler—CA9) A
        Benna Ruth Solomon (Georgia; Oakes—CA2) G

1980   Allan Ides (Loyola-Marymount; Haynsworth—CA4) A
        Paul W. Kahn (Yale) A

Thomas B. Metzloff (Harvard; Ainsworth—CA5) A
Andrea L. Peterson (Boalt Hall; Renfrew—N.D.CA) A

1981   Ellen Aprill (Georgetown; Butzner—CA4) A
Robert B. Bell (Stanford; Flannery—D.DC) PP
Kahn
Stuart Singer (Harvard) PP

1982   Bernard W. Bell (Stanford; Kearse—CA2) A
Patricia A. Dean (Georgetown; Tamm—CADC) PP
William T. D'Zurilla (Tulane; Tate—CA5) PP
Singer

1983   Kingsley Browne (Denver; Rovira—CO.S.Ct.) A
Michael E. Herz (Chicago; Campbell—CA1) A
Richard I. Werder, Jr. (Michigan; Edwards—CADC) PP
Kevin J. Worthen (Brigham Young University; Wilkey—CADC) A

1984   Dean Gloster (UCLA; Kennedy—CA9) PP
Herz
Scott L. Nelson (Harvard) PP
Natalie Wexler (Penn; Rubin—CA5) O

1985   Samuel Dimon (Michigan) PP
Nelson
Andrew G. Schultz (New Mexico; Rubin—CA5) PP
Palma Strand (Stanford; Wright—CADC) O

1986   David Burcham (Loyola-Marymount; Aldisert—CA3) A
Dimon
Mary Gabrielle Sprague (Yale; Carrigan—D.CO) PP
Richard A. Westfall (Denver; McWilliams—CA10) G

1987   Albert Boro (Boalt Hall; Cummings—CA7) PP
Richard A. Cordray (Chicago; Bork—CADC; later clerked for
Justice Kennedy) PP
Ronald Klain (Harvard) G
Barbara McDowell (Yale; Cabranes—D.CT; Winter—CA2) PP

1988   Christopher R. Drahozal (Iowa; Clark—CA5) A
Stephen Higginson (Yale; Wald—CADC) G
Klain
Laura Miller (Yale) PP

1989   Jonathan Bunge (Chicago; Buckley—CADC) G
Stephen R. McAllister (Kansas; Posner—CA7; later clerked for
Justice Thomas) A
Paul R. Q. Wolfson (Yale) G
Lisa Burget Wright (Georgetown; Keeton—D.Mass.) O

1990   Curtis Bradley (Harvard; Ebel—CA10) A
            Kathryn Webb Bradley (Maryland; Smalkin—D.MD) PP
            Martin Flaherty (Columbia; Gibbons—CA3) A
            McAllister

1991   Charles Eskridge (Pepperdine; Clark—CA5) PP
            David Frederick (Texas; Sneed—CA9) G
            Jeffrey F. Pryce (Yale) G
            Susan A. Weber (SUNY-Buffalo; Sprouse—CA4) PP

1992   John C. P. Goldberg (New York University; Weinstein—EDNY) A
            Robert Malley (Harvard; Nelson—CA9) G
            David D. Meyer (Michigan; Edwards—CADC) A
            Pryce

1993   Neil Gorsuch (Harvard; Sentelle—CADC) PP

1994   Stuart Delery (Yale; Tjoflat—CA11) PP

1995   Philip Weiser (New York University; Ebel—CA10) G

1996   John L. Flynn (Georgetown; Becker—CA3) PP

1997   Benjamin A. Powell (Columbia; Walker—CA2) C

Legend

A—academic (28)
C—current clerk
D—deceased (1)
G—government (12)
J—judge (4)
O—other (public interest, nonlegal, miscellaneous) (6)
PP—private practice (46)
R—retired (1)

Prior Clerking Experience
    None—32
    Federal appellate—55
    Federal trial—10
    Federal trial and appellate—1
    State supreme court—1

NOTES

Notes are provided to supply sources for quotations that are not obvious from their context. Newspaper and wire service dispatches are dated in the text in most instances, and no further information is required to find the original source; where the date or the publication is not obvious, I have supplied the missing information here. Quoted statements made to me are not treated further in the notes; quotations not attributed in the text are identified in the notes, except when the statements were made to me on condition of anonymity. When quotations from published works are cited in the notes by the name of the author and page number only, full bibliographical information is detailed under Sources. Full citations for cases mentioned in the text are provided in the Case Index; cites for quotations within those cases are provided only for substantial excerpts warranting block quotes.

Abbreviations

NAMES

John F. Kennedy—JFK
Robert F. Kennedy—RFK

PUBLICATIONS

Associated Press—AP
Boulder Daily Camera—BDC
Brigham Young University Law Review—BYULR
Denver Post—DP
Detroit Free Press—DFP
Detroit News—DN
Detroit Times—DT

Fort Collins Coloradoan—FC

Harvard Law Review—HLR

Legal Times of Washington—LTW

Los Angeles Times—LAT

Montgomery Advertiser—MA

New Republic—TNR

New York Herald-Tribune—NYHT

New York Times—NYT

Pittsburgh Press—PP

Rocky Mountain News—RMN

Supreme Court Review—SCR

University of Chicago Law Review—UCHILR

University of Colorado Law Review—UCOLR

Washington Evening Star—WES

Washington Post—WP

Wellington Sun—WS

Yale Law Journal—YLJ

ARCHIVES

Hugo L. Black Papers, Library of Congress—HLBLC

William J. Brennan Papers, Library of Congress—WJBLC

Tom C. Clark Papers, University of Texas at Austin—TCCUT

William O. Douglas Papers, Library of Congress—WODLC

John M. Harlan Papers, Princeton—JMHP

Thurgood Marshall Papers, Library of Congress—TMLC

Stanley F. Reed Papers, University of Kentucky—SFRUK

Frederick M. Vinson Papers, University of Kentucky—FMVUK

Earl Warren Papers, Library of Congress—EWLC

FREQUENTLY CITED SOURCES

Bakal, Carl, "New Man on the Big Bench," *True,* July 1962—Bakal

Currie, David P., *The Constitution in the Supreme Court: The Second Century, 1888–1986*—Currie

Guthman, Edwin O., and Jeffrey Shulman, eds., *Robert F. Kennedy in His Own Words*—Guthman & Shulman

Hamilton, Nigel, *JFK: Reckless Youth*—Hamilton

Navasky, Victor S., *Kennedy Justice*—Navasky

Schlesinger, Arthur M., Jr., *Robert Kennedy and His Times*—Schlesinger

Strober, Gerald S. and Deborah H., *"Let Us Begin Anew"*—Strobers

Wright, Alfred, "A Modest All-American Who Sits on the Highest Bench," *Sports Illustrated,* Dec. 10, 1962—Wright

Note: "Conference" in Supreme Court documents refers to the Court's internal name for itself.

PROLOGUE

1. *"I was":* Geoghegan interview; *LAT,* Aug. 7, 1978. Others claim to have witnessed identical exchanges elsewhere: Joe Dolan in Denver, 1959 (Dolan interview); John A. Reilly in Detroit, 1961 (*Boston Globe,* Mar. 20, 1993).

2. *"I have":* Rothgerber interview. At the 1996 Tenth Circuit judicial conference at Snowmass, Colo., Justice White was asked whether he planned to write his autobiography, and he said "absolutely not."

2. *Brandeis:* Paul A. Freund, Introduction to Alexander M. Bickel, *The Unpublished Opinions of Justice Brandeis,* xv.

2. *"What could we talk about?":* Greenhouse, O'Brien, Wermeil interviews.

2. *University of Kentucky Library:* Anderson interview.

2. *John F. Kennedy Library:* Nigel Hamilton's remark—"White has declined all requests by serious historians for interviews relating to JFK" (Hamilton, 832 n. 270)—is essentially accurate. After cooperating with William Manchester on *The Death of a President,* apparently at the Kennedy family's request, White confined his interviews to authors of a few works on the Supreme Court, plus Jack Bass, for his biography of Judge Frank M. Johnson, who was involved in the Freedom Rides. (See Chapter 12.) Privately, according to friends in Colorado, he derided "Kennedy hounds" who *were out to make a buck* on gossip about the dead brothers.

2. *Fort Collins, Colorado, Public Library:* When Charlene Tresner, local history coordinator for the Fort Collins Public Library, wrote White in 1979 asking that he consent to a sixty-minute audiotaped interview for the library's Larimer County Collection, he replied: "I have a good many requests such as your inquiry about making a tape. I can't do them all and hence do none. I shall continue to adhere to this policy." White to Tresner, Mar. 14, 1979, Larimer County Collection, FCPL.

2. *donated his judicial papers: Library of Congress Information Bulletin,* June 28, 1993, 26. The detailed contents of the collection have not been publicly disclosed, but they are believed to contain no conference notes, intracourt memoranda, staff work, or personal correspondence. The bulk of the archive is probably printed opinion drafts. The archive is open for research with the permission of Justice White during his lifetime, but he is not granting permission to anyone as of this writing; at his death, the archive is closed for ten years.

3. *"Don't ever call":* Barkley and other interviews.

3. *"walked out of":* Bob Cohn with Mark Miller, "Clinton Gets a Supreme Chance," *Newsweek,* Mar. 29, 1993.

4. *no interviews would be granted:* Tu interview.

5. *at least by him:* When Chief Justice Rehnquist purported to speak for a majority of the Supreme Court in 1993 to condemn the opening of Justice Thurgood Marshall's Papers for research less than two years after his retirement, White released a public statement dissociating himself from Rehnquist's claim: "Whatever may be the reason for Justice Marshall's papers now being open to the public, I regret exceedingly what has happened. As presently advised, however, I do not subscribe to the Chief Justice's May 25 letter." Tony

Mauro, "The Supreme Court and the Cult of Secrecy," in Rodney Smolla, ed., *A Year in the Life of the Supreme Court,* 266. See also Robert Ritter, "Court split on Marshall papers," *Quill,* Oct. 1993; Dennis J. Hutchinson, "The Papers of Thurgood Marshall," *Appellate Law Review* 6 (1994): 72.

5. *"You are on your own":* White to author, June 17, 1993.

6. *"He is on his own":* White to a former clerk, Apr. 29, 1993.

7. *"judges do and must legislate": Southern Pacific v. Jensen,* 244 U.S. 205, 220 (1917) (Holmes, J., dissenting).

CHAPTER 1. WELLINGTON

11. *"in poverty and amid the rugged hills":* Charles Sumner White, *Ephriam Godfrey White and His Descendants,* 2.

12. *"for distinguished bravery":* Quoted in Pamela A. Stewart, ed., *The Whites: Soldiers to Statesmen,* 20.

13. *the 22d "traveled":* Quoted ibid., 23.

13. *"farm laborer":* Ibid., 24.

13. *"disabled":* Ibid., 26.

14. *two-bedroom bungalow:* The house still stands at what is now 3727 Roosevelt Avenue, on the southeast corner of Second Street and Roosevelt. The lot is three times as deep as it is wide. For a photograph of the house, see Ralph Moore, "Remembering Whizzer White," *DP,* Apr. 4, 1962.

16. *"the prosperity of the people":* Wright, 84, 86.

17. Die Riewe sein seiss: Hope Williams Sykes, *Second Hoeing,* xvii (from the Introduction by Timothy J. Kloberdanz). For an updated and very different fictional treatment of beet country on the Colorado plains, see Laura Hendrie, *Stygo.*

17. *"Her arms ached":* Sykes, 95.

17. *Sugar Act of 1937:* 50 Stat. 903 (1937), codified at 7 U.S.C. §§1100–1131 (expired Dec. 31, 1937).

17. *Jones-Costigan Act:* Sugar Stabilization Act of 1934, 48 Stat. 670 (1934).

18. *"In the late '20s":* Wright, 86.

19. *"One year a fellow":* Ibid., 89.

20. *"when Byron had homework":* For an earlier version of the same vignette, see Ralph Moore, "Remembering Whizzer White," *DP,* Apr. 4, 1962.

20. *"Can you imagine?":* Andrew Mair interview.

22. *nationally recognized career:* See John V. Bernard, "Our Best High Schools: Science in the Small School—Green River, Wyoming," *Atlantic,* Apr. 1965.

22. *"My folks had never gone":* Wright, 86.

22. *"taught rural school":* Charles Sumner White, *Ephriam Godfrey White and His Descendants,* 34.

22. *"I took a great shine":* Wright, 89.

23. *"a very quiet election": WS,* Apr. 8, 1920.

23. *"scattering of votes": WS,* Apr. 3, 1930.

24. *"straight A ranking": WS,* May 24, 1934.

24. *"most outstanding":* Ibid.

24. *"you made a noticeable effort":* Wright, 89.

24. *"an inspiring message": WS,* May 24, 1934.

24. *"Do your work":* Gus Peth, "White, Mair Visit Old School," *Wellington News,* Aug. 9, 1984.

CHAPTER 2. "NO CLIPPINGS"

25. *"symbol [who was] a link"*: Frederick S. Allen and others, *The University of Colorado, 1876–1976*, 84 (cited below as "Allen").

25. *"graduate study and research"*: Ibid., 93.

27. *"provided the University would dismiss"*: Norlin to J. S. Boggs, Feb. 4, 1939, President's Office Files, Norlin Library, quoted in Allen, 280 n. 94. See generally Kenneth T. Jackson, *The Ku Klux Klan in the City, 1915–1930*. See also Don Zylstra, "When the Ku Klux Klan Ran Denver," *Sunday DP,* Jan. 5, 1958 (Roundup section); Lee Casey, "When the Klan Controlled Colorado," *RMN,* June 17-18-19, 1946.

27. *The official portrait:* See William E. (Bud) Davis, *Glory Colorado!,* 422. Hopkinson also painted Presidents Eliot, Lowell, and Conant of Harvard.

28. *"porkbarrel politics"*: Quoted in Allen, 111.

29. *"By the time I got to college"*: Wright, 89.

29. *"I was 17"*: Ibid.

31. *"after he ran wild"*: *RMN,* Feb. 9, 1965.

35. *"Everybody thought I was through"*: Wright, 90.

35. *"by some sportswriter"*: White made the statement during a public appearance at the University of Kansas in 1995.

35. *White suspected: DP,* Jan. 30, 1994.

36. *"I had to beat out"*: Nuttall interview.

36. *"Often an all-American halfback"*: Fred Russell, *"I'll Go Quietly,"* 17.

37. *"I decided I wouldn't let them operate and by the time basketball was over"*: Wright, 90.

37. *"I started off studying chemistry"*: Ibid., 89.

38. *"If I kicked the ball / Oakes put great store"*: Ibid., 90.

38. *"keeping me away from / power and effect"*: Jack Newcombe, "Whizzer White," *Sport,* Dec. 1962, 76.

39. *meanness:* Potts quoted in Ray Didinger, *The Pittsburgh Steelers,* 147.

39. *"'Byron White,'" one editor explained:* McCune interview.

40. *"I had a pretty good year"*: Wright, 90.

40. *"Byron would do anything"*: Thurman interview.

41. *"Byron White was unanimously selected"*: May 11, 1937.

CHAPTER 3. WHIZZERMANIA

44. *"Buzzer"*: Francis Wallace, "Pigskin Preview," *Saturday Evening Post,* Sept. 25, 1937, 65.

45. *"play black and blue"*: Nuttall interview.

46. *"scholastic attainment"*: Lord Elton, ed., *The First Fifty Years of the Rhodes Trust and the Rhodes Scholarships,* 20–23. The genesis of the scheme is detailed in Robert I. Rotberg, *The Founder,* 663ff.

46. *"hadn't consciously worked"*: Wright, 90.

46. *"You are to be commended"*: Quoted in *RMN,* Dec. 21, 1937.

47. *"after lunch"*: *Silver & Gold,* Nov. 5, 1937.

48. *"What kind of competition"*: *RMN,* Nov. 3, 1937.

48. *"Why the hell"*: Nuttall interview.

50. *"Congratulations, boys"*: Gehrke interview.

50. *"I'll always remember": DP,* Jan. 30, 1994.

50. *very brief game story:* Reprinted in full in Jack Newcombe, ed., *The Fireside Book of Football,* 201–2.

53. *"The squad itself shows a total disinterest": RMN,* Nov. 8, 1937.

53. *"campaign to gain all-American recognition": DT,* Nov. 11, 1937.

53. *"at least a story a day":* Bill Hosokawa, *Thunder in the Rockies,* 189.

53. *"getting up in the morning": Silver & Gold,* Nov. 19, 1937.

54. *" 'If I thought' ": RMN,* Nov. 10, 1937.

55. *"So what was Bunny going to do?":* Nuttall interview.

56. *"more like a bad job":* Liley interview.

57. *"backfield duel": New York World-Telegram,* Dec. 3, 1937.

58. *"long-awaited":* Dec. 10, 1937.

58. *"This year Byron 'Whizzer' White": Collier's,* Dec. 18, 1937, reprinted as "The Grantland Rice All-America Team of 1937," in Dave Camerer, ed., *The Best of Grantland Rice,* p. 203.

59. *"swept the election": New York World-Telegram,* Dec. 5, 1937.

59. *" 'Dutch' made it relatively easy": DP,* Mar. 15, 1938.

60. *"I entered football as a game": Brooklyn Eagle,* Dec. 8, 1937.

60. *"Your chances are better":* Dec. 12, 1937.

61. *"we'll get him anyhow":* Pro Football Hall of Fame clipping file, Dec. 14, 1937.

61. *"Here's the way it is": RMN,* Dec. 18, 1937.

62. *"[have] me worried": RMN,* Dec. 18, 1937.

62. *"Sam said":* Martin Wagner interview.

63. *more sleepless nights: BDC,* Dec. 21, 1937.

64. *"Leaving San Francisco":* AP, Dec. 22, 1937.

64. *"I can't remember":* Ibid.

65. *"White Shouts 'No' ":* Dec. 22, 1937.

67. *"You take care of the football, coach": WP,* June 29, 1962 (AP dispatch, derived from "Byron White's Priority List," column by Harry Farrar in different editions of *DP* earlier in the week).

67. *"wave it in Whizzer's face":* Dec. 30, 1937.

67. *"most talked-of back of the year": New York World-Telegram,* Dec. 30, 1937.

68. "How good is Colorado": Dec. 14, 1937.

68. *"The boys are in perfect": NYT,* Jan. 1, 1938.

69. *"those 180-pound [CU] tackles":* Jan. 2, 1938 (Bruce Layer column).

69. *"Those two quick touchdowns":* AP, Jan. 1, 1938.

70. *In financial terms:* President's Office Files (Athletics), Norlin Library.

CHAPTER 4. THE DECISION

71. *"The union congratulates you": BDC,* Jan. 14, 1938.

72. *The union believed, erroneously:* Three Americans had won "blues" (the equivalent of American varsity letters, awarded for playing against Cambridge): Donald G. Herring (1909), Alan C. Valentine (1923–25), and F. L. (Ted) Hovde (1931)—the latter two eventually becoming university presidents. See Lord Elton, ed., *The First Fifty Years of the Rhodes Trust and the Rhodes Scholarships,* 264–65.

72. *"appreciation for his outstanding record": BDC,* Jan. 19, 1938.

73. *"It was not so long ago":* Dec. 30, 1937.

74. *"The New York newspapers"*: Wright, 90.

74. *"to make our Chicago high-school people"*: *Silver & Gold*, Mar. 4, 1938.

75. *"The Whizzer of Ahs"*: *New York World-Telegram*, Mar. 14, 1938.

75. *"White said that if he decided"*: Mar. 13, 1938. United Press carried a briefer account on the same day, as did the *Daily Worker* two days later.

76. *"Whizzer White, Rhodes Scholar, Stumped"*: Mar. 14, 1938.

77. *"The debate is now whether"*: *NYT*, Mar. 14, 1938.

77. *"Whizzah! Whizzah! Whizzah!"*: Thurman interview.

82. *The risk of war*: William E. (Bud) Davis, *Glory Colorado!*, 415.

88. *"Country Club of Higher Education"*: Quoted ibid., 423.

91. *"application"*: Allen to George Carlson, Aug. 2, 1938, courtesy of Sir Anthony Kenny, warden of Rhodes House.

93. *"The question of his postponement"*: Ibid.

94. *"Saw in [the news]paper"*: Frederick R. Suits to Gerald Brown, Aug.5, 1938, courtesy of Gerald Brown.

CHAPTER 5. PITTSBURGH: "GOLDEN BOY"

97. *"the finest man I have ever known"*: *LAT*, Aug. 30, 1988.

98. *"The Pirate backfield had a ball carrier"*: *DP*, Nov. 15, 1938 (Poss Parsons column).

98. *"John didn't actually talk"*: *New Haven Journal-Courier*, June 28, 1971.

100. *"When [Rooney] founded the Steelers"*: *WP*, Aug. 26, 1988 (Shirley Povich column); Povich interview.

101. *"What are you trying to do?"*: Myron Cope, *The Game That Was* (cited below as "Cope"), 129.

101. *"God," he said*: *Pittsburgh Post-Gazette*, Sept. 6, 1963.

102. *Camera dug up one*: *BDC*, Sept. 8, 1938.

102. *"I was just terrible"*: *DP*, Sept. 10, 1938.

102. *"Well, I know what you mean"*: William H. Orrick Oral History (JFKL), 61.

103. *I just wanted*: Of the many versions of this story, the statement that sounds most authentic is recounted by Bakal, 100. Leemans was eventually elected to the Pro Football Hall of Fame but was probably most famous for the coincidence of Tuffy Leemans Day at the Polo Grounds and the radio announcement of the attack on Pearl Harbor, which interrupted the game, played Dec. 7, 1941.

105. *"My debut"*: Bob Curran, *Pro Football's Rag Days*, 189.

105. *"a mob of his admirers"*: International News Service, Sept. 10, 1938.

106. *"Your letter reminded me"*: White to Gerald Brown, Sept. 10, 1938, courtesy of Gerald Brown.

108. *"If I find out there's dissension"*: *PP*, Sept. 20, 1938.

108. *"said every player on the team"*: *PP*, Sept. 19, 1938.

109. *"The only thing I know for sure"*: *New York Journal-American*, Sept. 22, 1938 (Corum column).

110. *"White didn't try to hide his indignation"*: Sept. 22, 1938.

111. *"One Whizzer White"*: Oakes, *Liberty*, Oct. 15, 1938 (publication preceded the cover date by two weeks).

111. *"A Whizzer White helps quite a bit"*: *RMN*, Oct. 5, 1938.

113. *"As far as I'm concerned"*: Wright, 91.

113. *"lifted White off the ground"*: *Baltimore Sun*, June 26, 1971.

114. *"We have talked of financial terms":* Pittsburgh Post-Gazette, Sept. 30, 1938.

115. *"He wasn't a pretty sight":* Thompson interview.

115. *At the end of the year:* WP, Nov. 6, 1938 (Shirley Povich column).

116. *"bad weather."*. . . *"Well, actually we canceled it":* Cope, 133.

117. We aren't playing today: Richard Whittingham, *What a Game They Played,* 166, is the standard account, although the incident occurred in New York, not Chicago as he reports.

117. *Despite all of Rooney's efforts:* WP, Nov. 7, 1938 (Povich column).

117. *"I figured [the promoter]":* Cope, 134.

119. *"Professional football has all the thrill":* Dec. 9, 1938.

119. *"'didn't think' there was a chance":* DP, Dec. 11, 1938.

120. *endorsement of a local department store:* Gehrke interview.

120. *"That's just what I get":* DP, Sept. 10, 1938.

121. *"There is no man": Chicago Tribune,* United Press International, Aug. 28, 1988.

121. *"I'm the worst loser":* DP, Sept. 10, 1938.

121. *"library research":* Ray Didinger, *The Pittsburgh Steelers,* 149.

121. *"Pro ball gets in your blood":* DP, Dec. 11, 1938.

121. *"There were rumors":* Daly and O'Donnell, *The Pro Football Chronicle,* 49.

CHAPTER 6. "A YANK AT OXFORD"

124. *"Listen, Goils":* Jan. 8, 1939.

125. *"Whizzer Slips into Oxford":* Jan. 11, 1939.

125. *"'Whizzer' Becomes a Yank at Oxford":* Jan. 11, 1939.

125. *"I thought I came":* Jack Newcombe, "Whizzer White," *Sport,* Dec. 1962, 77.

125. *"He is six feet one":* Jan. 12, 1939.

125. *"A Real Life Yank at Oxford":* Jan. 18, 1939.

125. *"Whizzer Gets New Headgear":* Jan. 18, 1939.

125. *"Whizzer White Is Now":* Jan. 18, 1939.

125. *"Pigskin to Mortar Board":* Jan. 19, 1939.

126. *"accepted Cecil Rhodes'": NYT,* Feb. 25, 1938.

126. *"these crazy sports laws":* Jan. 18, 1939.

126. *"suggested very clearly":* Wright, 91.

127. You're being paid: McEwan interview.

127. For the first time: McEwan interview.

127. *"'The Yank' gets a bicycle":* Jan. 20, 1939.

127. *"had a word":* Jelinek interview.

128. *"In support of Mr. Fifoot":* Carlson to C. K. Allen, Dec. 17, 1937, courtesy of Sir Anthony Kenny, warden of Rhodes House.

128. *"long odds":* Jelinek interview.

129. *"No issue / the most memorable":* Kaiser, *Journeying Far and Wide* (cited below as "Kaiser"), 95.

129. *"For the young in those days":* Healey, *The Time of My Life,* 34.

130. *"Oxford students were fairly homogeneous":* Kaiser, 45.

130. *"growing up dirt poor":* Piranian interview.

130. *"a single course":* Undated clipping, Byron White File, *BDC* morgue.

131. *"respectable but rather dreary":* Waugh, *A Little Learning,* 164–65.

131. *Nancy, Lady Astor: NYT,* July 10, 1929; Gerald Brown diary, courtesy of Gerald Brown.

132. *"A large number of Rhodes Scholars":* Lord Elton, ed., *The First Fifty Years of the Rhodes Trust and the Rhodes Scholarships,* 150.

132. *"drastic change":* Kaiser, 72.

133. *"rented the top part":* Wright, 91.

134. *"firestorm":* Michael Beschloss, *Kennedy and Roosevelt,* 178 (cited below as "Beschloss").

134. *"it has long been":* Ibid.

134. *"while it seemed to be unpopular":* James McGregor Burns, *John Kennedy,* 37.

134. *"Foolishly, he had":* Kaiser, 64.

135. *"gone to an eastern college":* Lawrence Leamer, *The Kennedy Women,* 261.

135. *"most exciting debutante":* Angela Lambert, *1939: The Last Season of Peace,* 133 (cited below as "Lambert").

135. *"to withold recognition":* Times (London), Mar. 13, 1939.

136. *"What do you expect":* For another account of the incident, see Bakal, 21.

136. *"He had one of the most":* Taplin interview.

137. *"baseball more than I did any other sport":* Wright, 90.

137. "Felix, qui potuit": *American Oxonian* (1939), 276. Compare Virgil, *Georgics* 2.490.

137. *"I borrowed":* Wright, 91.

138. *"the south Germans":* Ibid.

138. *"the sun setting":* Taplin interview.

138. *"You had the feeling":* Leo Damore, *The Cape Cod Years of John Fitzgerald Kennedy,* 50.

138. *"We got along":* Quoted in Hamilton, 269–70. See also Macdonald Oral History, JFKL.

140. *"It's the end":* Beschloss, 190.

140. *"Everything that I have believed":* Ibid.

142. *"Joe Kennedy":* Harold L. Ickes diary, Mar. 22, 1939, Reel 3, Box 04, Harold L. Ickes Papers.

143. *"It was hell":* Lambert, 136.

143. *"their studies":* Sept. 19, 1939.

CHAPTER 7. YALE AND DETROIT

146. *"the war situation":* Dean's Report 1939–40, Yale Law School, 3.

147. *"Equipment for competitive sports":* Yale Law School Catalog 1939–40, 39.

148. *"My football playing days":* Oct. 4, 1939.

148. *"made a very favorable impression":* New Haven Journal-Courier, Oct. 24, 1939.

150. *"switch in time":* Corwin to Homer S. Cummings, May 19, 1937, Corwin Papers (Princeton), quoted in William E. Leuchtenburg, "Comment: FDR's Court-Packing Plan: A Second Life, a Second Death," *Duke Law Journal* (1985): 673 n. 2. See also Michael Ariens, "A Thrice-Told Tale: Or Felix the Cat," *HLR* 107 (1994): 620, 623 n. 11, examining other claims to authorship of the phrase.

151. *a footnote:* 304 U.S. at 152–53 n. 4.

153. *"1. Substantive due process":* "Remarks at the 25th Anniversary of Byron White's Appointment to the Supreme Court, Apr. 25, 1987," courtesy of Judge Louis F. Oberdorfer (cited below as "Oberdorfer 'Remarks'").

153. *"the deflation of the due process clause"*: "The Supreme Court and Private Rights," *YLJ* 47: 1938: 1051, 1077.

154. *Their exchanges:* Oberdorfer "Remarks."

154. *"a healthy skepticism"*: Nicholas deB. Katzenbach, "Byron White's Appointment to the Supreme Court," *UCOLR* 58 (1987): 429.

154. *"His classes were intense"*: Byron R. White, "Mr. Justice White Recalls: To Students, the Deftness of a Master Surgeon," *Miami Law Review* 18 (1963): 1, 2.

155. *"What did Wesley teach"*: Grant Gilmore, "For Wesley Sturges: On the Teaching and Study of Law," *YLJ* 72 (1963): 646, 654.

155. *"think things, not words"*: Oliver Wendell Holmes, Jr., "Law in Science and Science in Law," in *Collected Legal Papers,* 238.

155. *"the 'rules' and doctrines"*: Arthur L. Corbin, "Sixty-Eight Years at Law," *Yale Law Report* 11 (1965):20, quoted in William L. Twining, *Karl Llewellyn and the Realist Movement,* 31–32. See especially Corbin, *Cases on the Law of Contracts,* 3d ed. (1947), Preface, vii; Corbin, "The Law and the Judges," *Yale Review* 3 (Jan. 1914): 234–50.

156. *"securing certain generally accepted social ends"*: Myres S. McDougal, "Fuller v. the American Legal Realists: An Intervention," *YLJ* 50 (1941):827, 836.

156. *"the judicial institution"*: Ibid., 837.

156. *"Yale Law School was"*: Wright, 92.

157. *"as a serious-minded"*: Potter Stewart to John Marshall Harlan, Apr. 14, 1970, Box 609, JMHP (background memoir for 1970 Yale Law School Association Citation of Merit, presented by Justice Harlan).

157. *"established in 1923"*: *Yale Law School Bulletin* (1940–41): 31, 52 (now awarded for the best paper written by a first-year student).

157. *"I waited table"*: *FC,* July 24, 1940.

158. *Mandel offered $7,500:* McDougal interview.

159. *"How come Whizzer White / apparently"*: Aug. 18, 1940.

159. *"about the only break"*: Aug. 20, 1940.

159. *"The reason"*: *PP,* Aug. 18, 1940.

160. *"I was chosen"*: Wright, 92.

162. *"hero on offense"*: Oct. 20, 1940.

162. *"courageous football"*: Oct. 20, 1940.

163. *"conscription is here to stay"*: Nov. 28, 1940.

165. *"There was the Whizzer"*: Aug. 28, 1941.

165. *"Although Whizzer White"*: Sept. 15, 1941.

166. *"Whizzer White Again Holds"*: *Detroit Sunday Times,* Sept. 21, 1941.

166. *"Although he could speak"*: Sept. 22, 1941.

166. *"Whizzer White—the one-man"*: Sept. 29, 1941.

166. *"He made brilliant"*: Oct. 13, 1941.

167. *"reached the end"*: *DFP,* Oct. 29, 1941.

167. we shouldn't be losing: Radovich interview.

167. *"the most satisfying"*: Nov. 17, 1941.

168. *"a perfect specimen"*: *DN,* Nov. 18, 1941.

170. *Like Ted Williams:* The classic account of Williams's memorable final game is by John Updike, published contemporaneously in the *New Yorker,* reprinted in Updike, *Assorted Prose,* and in Lawrence Baldassaro, *The Ted Williams Reader.*

CHAPTER 8. THE NAVY

172. *"I was driving":* Wright, 92.

173. *As the photographs:* See, for example, David Levy's photos in Robert J. Donovan, *PT 109* (cited below as "Donovan"), and Bill Barrett's "scrapbook picture" in Chandler Whipple, *Lt. John F. Kennedy—Expendable!* (cited below as "Whipple").

173. *"The whole base":* Joan and Clay Blair, Jr., *The Search for J. F. K.,* 177 (cited below as "Blairs").

174. *"weird and treacherous":* Tameichi Hara with Fred Saito and Roger Pineau, *Japanese Destroyer Captain,* 181–82 (cited below as "Hara").

175. *"Jack, how":* Blairs, 240.

175. *"Sinking of PT 109":* Hara, 305–8, reprints the report, which is filed archivally at the Naval Historical Center as Action Report, Serial 006(64341), dated Jan. 13, 1944.

175. *several minor points:* See Blairs, 217, 223.

175. *"PT-109 was the* only": Michael T. Isenberg, *Shield of the Republic,* 751 (cited below as "Isenberg").

176. *was lying down on deck:* Hamilton, 577.

176. *"the reason he was unable":* Blairs, 240.

177. *Squad Nine policy:* Ibid.

177. *it is not clear:* Compare Blairs, 237.

178. *MacArthur later denied:* Whipple, 121.

179. *"Part of the young JFK":* Isenberg, 750.

179. *tastes that White relished:* The camaraderie is recalled in Paul B. Fay, Jr., *The Pleasure of His Company,* especially 141.

179. *gash in his palm:* Donovan, 202.

179. *"I remember riding":* Wright, 92.

179. *"hopped a PT boast":* Harry interview.

179. *"Detach from MTB":* White, Byron R., Personnel Record, Naval Historical Center.

180. *"pictured Burke as a hotshot":* E. B. Potter, *Admiral Arleigh Burke,* 103 (cited below as "Potter").

180. the press never worries: Rothgerber interview.

180. *established a distinguished record:* Potter, 108–9.

181. *"large and rather bare":* Lee Fleming Reese, ed., *Men of the Blue Ghost,* 218.

182. *" 'Whizzer' White Rated":* June 8, 1944.

183. *"Whatever Whizzer White":* Reprinted in Daley, *The Daley Years,* 20–23.

183. *"goddamn lie":* Oberdorfer interview and correspondence.

183. *"I just got in":* FC, June 16, 1944.

185. "Two young intelligence officers": C. Vann Woodward, *The Battle for Leyte Gulf,* 138–39.

186. *"an American Hotspur and a Japanese Hamlet":* Woodward, *Thinking Back: The Perils of Writing History,* 47.

186. *"Carrier searches":* CTG 38.3 Action Report, Dec. 2, 1944, Naval Historical Center, copy courtesy of Carl Solberg.

187. *"I thought":* Bakal, 104. Burke was developing his own suspicions. See Thomas J. Cutler, *The Battle of Leyte Gulf,* 212 (cited below as "Cutler").

187. Mitscher listened: Harry interview. See the account in Cutler, 212–13.

187. *"immediately":* Clark G. Reynolds, *The Fast Carriers,* 278.

187. *reads like a brief:* The document is set out in full in Hanson W. Baldwin, *Battles Lost and Won,* 488. Halsey's prickly defensiveness is illustrated by the correspondence con-

tained in Box 35, Halsey Papers. He was especially incensed at Samuel Eliot Morison's account in the official history published in 1958: "I want to fight Morison on every point." Halsey to R. B. Carney, Nov. 10, 1958.

189. The guy lived: Petry interview.

190. I was below: Petry interview.

190. *"There were some fine stories":* James Kelley, *Admiral Arleigh (31-Knot) Burke,* 144. Harrowing photographs of the ship's devastation and of the rescue work, including pictures of fire fighting belowdecks, are contained in Keith Wheeler, *The Road to Tokyo,* 166–75.

190. *"White and two other officers":* June 29, 1945.

190. *"I remember one time": Pueblo Chieftain,* Mar. 29, 1962.

192. He's head-on: Cheston interview.

192. *"Hit the deck":* Potter, 257.

192. *"They held a formation":* Theodore Taylor, *The Magnificent Mitscher,* 299–300.

193. The First Line: *Silver & Gold,* Oct. 5, 1945.

193. *"He told his parents":* Associated Press, Dec. 18, 1945.

CHAPTER 9. SUPREME COURT: OCTOBER TERM 1946

194. *"Before the war":* Wright, 95.

195. *"most impressed":* Rodell to William O. Douglas, Mar. 19, 1946, Box 366, WODLC.

195. *"'Whizzer' White":* Burton diary, Mar. 18, 1946, reel 2, Burton Papers (microfilm).

195. *"Thanks a lot":* Box 366, WODLC.

196. *unprecedented breach:* See Dennis J. Hutchinson, "The Black-Jackson Feud," *SCR* (1986): 203.

197. *"White, who comes":* Douglas to Vinson, June 7, 1946, Box 254, WODLC, reprinted in Melvin I. Urowsky, ed., *The Douglas Letters,* 48.

197. *The size of the estate:* Probate File No. 3175 (Estate of Chas. S. White, Decd.), Audubon, Iowa, District Court.

197. *"Byron (Whizzer) White": BDC,* June 15, 1946. The *RMN* headline a day later read: "Whizzer White Weds Miss Marion Stearns."

199. Information Please: See generally Thomas A. DeLong, *Quiz Craze,* ch. 4.

200. *Kentucky Derby:* See Burton diary, May 3, 1947, reel 3, Burton Papers (microfilm).

200. *Sam Rayburn's campaign:* See C. Dwight Porough, *Mr. Sam,* 254–55.

201. *"You can't run the world":* Transcript of Recorded Interview with Howard J. Trienens and Newton N. Minow (Feb. 27, 1975), 29, Fred M. Vinson Oral History Project, University of Kentucky.

201. *He voted to grant:* Calculated by the author from Jan Palmer, *The Vinson Court Era: The Supreme Court's Conference Votes.*

203. *"seemed to think" / Reed scribbled:* Case 465, Box 30, SFRUK.

204. *Their convictions were affirmed: Trudell v. State,* 28 So. 2d 124 (1946); *Lewis v. State,* ibid. at 122 (1946).

204. *"cert should be denied":* Cases 1104, 1105, Box 32, SFRUK.

204. *Neither petitioner had raised:* 28 So. 2d at 122ff.

205. *"Court was reluctant":* Case 1356, Box 32, SFRUK.

205. *two members of the California Supreme Court: People v. Dorman and Smith,* 172 P. 2d 686, 692 (1946).

206. *"Petitioner relies":* Case 1356, Box 32, SFRUK.

207. *Frankfurter was impatient:* See Joseph Lash, *From the Diaries of Felix Frankfurter,* 274 (Oct. 19, 1946) (cited below as "Frankfurter 'Diaries'").

208. *Memorandum for the Conference:* Box 236, FMVUK.

208. *"Amen!":* Ibid.

209. *"thing which causes injury":* 154 F. 2d 703, 704 (1946), quoting *San Juan Light Co. v. Requena,* 224 U.S. 89, 98, 99 (1911).

209. *"not only incomplete":* Box 234, FMVUK.

210. *Harold Burton noted:* Burton diary, Oct. 10, 1946, reel 2, Burton Papers (microfilm).

210. *"stiff":* Frankfurter "Diaries," 304 (Nov. 23, 1946) (*U.S. v. Alcea Band of Tillamooks,* 329 U.S. 40 [1946]). Vinson's extreme sensitivity to criticism is a chronic theme in the diaries during this period.

211. *"generous":* John P. Frank, "Fred Vinson and the Chief Justiceship," *UCHILR* 21 (1954): 212; see also 241–43.

212. *"extremely interested":* Transcript of Recorded Interview with Karl R. Price (1975), 20, Fred M. Vinson Oral History Project, University of Kentucky Library.

212. *"The chips are down":* S. Sidney Fine, *Frank Murphy: The Washington Years,* 531 (cited below as "Fine").

212. *"is one of those block-buster":* Frank, "Fred Vinson," p. 217.

213. *"it broke a strike":* John P. Frank, "The United States Supreme Court: 1946–47," *UCHILR* 15 (1947): 1, 6.

213. *sellouts to political expediency:* Fred Rodell to William O. Douglas, n.d., Box 366, WODLC ("your position in this case [rates] as your biggest mistake since you've been on the Court").

213. *"The Chief Justice, of course":* Transcript in Box 228, FMVUK.

214. *"soldiering":* Burton diary, June 23, 1946, reel 3, Burton Papers (microfilm).

215. *"with too much vehemence and intensity":* Frankfurter to Conference, Apr. 25, 1947, Box 283, HLBLC, and other archives.

215. *"more readily justified":* Fine, 493.

215. *"The difficulty":* 331 U.S. at 197.

215. *"The dangers":* Ibid. at 155.

218. *"make the states topsy-turvy":* Roger K. Newman, *Hugo Black,* 355 n.

218. *"the striking aspect":* Frank, "United States Supreme Court," 24.

219. *"Certainly not":* *NYT,* June 30, 1972.

219. *"I should like":* White to Vinson, Mar. 5, 1958, Box 216, FMVUK.

219. *"You waited so long":* Vinson to White, May 17, 1948, Box 216, FMVUK.

220. *"a tangle on the squash courts":* White to Minow, May 10, 1951, Box 219, FMVUK.

220. *"pretty adept":* John Thompson to Vinson, Jan. 4, 1950, Box 216, FMVUK.

220. *he shut off Yale:* Vinson to Thompson, Jan. 6, 1950, Box 216, FMVUK.

220. *Sturges tried:* Vinson to Sturges, Jan. 6, 1950; Sturges to Vinson, Jan. 9, 1950; Box 216, FMVUK.

CHAPTER 10. DENVER: LAW AND LOCAL POLITICS

223. *"I think one":* Wright, 96.

224. *The region "jumped":* "The Mountain States, Cool to Boom in Energy Resources," *Business Week,* Jan. 27, 1975.

224. *"scenery, beet sugar":* John Gunther, *Inside U. S. A.,* 223–24.

224. *"Today Denver":* Perkin, in Ray B. West, Jr., ed., *Rocky Mountain Cities,* 281.

226. *"physically attacked a library":* Donald W. Hoagland, "Byron White As a Practicing Lawyer in Colorado," *UCOLR* 58: 365, 366.

226. *"Illegible notes":* Ibid., 365.

227. *cult stock:* Peter Fullam, "Locally Controlled Stock Has 'Cult' Following Here," *Indianapolis Business Journal,* May 12, 1986.

228. *required headlines: RMN,* Aug. 19, 1947.

228. *"outstanding young men":* FC, Dec. 28, 1947.

228. *new headline:* Mar. 21, 1948.

228. *bogus check:* AP, Mar. 19, 1948.

228. *"greatest native":* BDC, Aug. 25, 1953.

229. *neither replied:* Dinner Correspondence, Boxes 6–8, Grantland Rice Papers, Vanderbilt University. See generally Charles Fountain, *Sportswriter,* 275–77.

229. *"deeply touched":* Ibid., 277.

229. *"most influential man": RMN,* Feb. 8, 1994; see also *DP,* Jan. 30, 1994.

229. *"wolves":* New Haven Journal-Courier, Oct. 24, 1939.

230. *Every summer:* Wright, 96.

230. *"I had":* Ibid.

231. *"written several letters": RMN,* Oct. 28, 1945.

232. *"White was being groomed": Cervi's Rocky Mountain Journal,* June 19, 1952.

232. *"Every year after":* Wright, 96.

233. *"I didn't feel":* Ibid.

234. *"was an unqualified":* Dolan to Sorensen, May 22, 1957, Box 928, JFK Pre-Presidential Papers.

234. *"inner circle":* Sorensen to Dolan, Oct. 1, 1957, ibid.

234. *"damns with faint praise":* Dolan to Sorensen, Oct. 8, 1957, ibid.

235. *"A year ago": DP,* Feb. 25, 1958.

236. *"last step": RMN,* Feb. 25, 1958.

236. *"Whizzer White looks":* Dolan to Sorensen, Feb. 27, 1958, Box 928, JFK Pre-Presidential Papers.

236. *On April 22:* Dolan to Sorensen, April 22, 1959, ibid.

237. *"I had":* Dolan to Sorensen, April 28, 1959, ibid.

237. *"Larry [Henry] and I":* Dolan to Sorensen, April 30, 1959, ibid.

238. *Charles Byron:* Charles Byron (Barney) White was born July 22, 1953, in Denver. Nancy Pitkin White was born March 7, 1958, in Denver; "Pitkin" was the name of her maternal grandmother, daughter of Frederick W. Pitkin, the second governor of the state of Colorado (1879–83), a Republican.

239. *"who was sitting":* C-SPAN, Nov. 18, 1994.

239. *"Nixon won":* Christopher Mathews, *Kennedy and Nixon,* 74.

239. *"great American":* Ibid., 75.

240. *a comfortable elite:* The videotape of White's remarks to the U.S. attorneys' reunion is striking for the contemptuous way White pronounces the word "professors."

"Remarks, Reunion of U.S. Attorneys in the Kennedy Administration," C-SPAN, Nov. 18, 1994.

240. *"We are not as strong":* Sorensen and Wallace to JFK, June 24 (revised July 14), 1959, Box 928, JFK Pre-Presidential Papers.

240. *By the time Kennedy:* See Sorensen to Dolan, July 1, 1959, ibid.

CHAPTER 11. THE KENNEDY CAMPAIGN

241. *"political powers":* Sorensen and Wallace to JFK, June 24 (revised July 14), 1959, Box 928, JFK Pre-Presidential Papers.

242. *"Byron White and I":* Dolan to Sorensen, July 2, 1959, ibid.

242. *White was eager:* Sorensen to Dolan, July 1, 1959, ibid.

242. *Dolan wanted:* Dolan to Sorensen, June 24, 1959, ibid.

243. *"when we will kick off":* Dolan to Steve Smith, Aug. 20, 1959, ibid.

243. *"Whizzer Carries the Ball":* RMN, Nov. 22, 1959.

244. *"U.S. Lost":* DP, Nov. 29, 1959.

245. *"with the force":* RMN, Jan. 3, 1960.

245. *White issued:* RMN, Feb. 14, 1960.

246. *"That was a very":* White to RFK, Jan. 1, 1960, Box 31, RFK Pre-Administration Political Files.

246. *"We made":* "Remarks, Reunion of U.S. Attorneys in the Kennedy Administration," C-SPAN, Nov. 18, 1994.

247. *"from union officials":* RMN, Feb. 14, 1960.

247. *"I'd rather":* White to RFK, April 12, 1960, Box 31, RFK Pre-Administration Political Files.

247. *"we will be lucky":* Smith to RFK, May 23, 1960, Box 39, RFK Pre-Administration Political Files.

248. *"He took me":* Stewart Udall Oral History, 23.

248. *Ciancio brothers:* RMN, Jan. 8, 10, 1960.

249. *"What am I good for?":* Joe Dolan Oral History, 39–40.

249. *"But you":* T. H. White, *The Making of the President, 1960,* 143.

249. *"That is one reason":* DP, June 19, 1960.

249. *White denied / "Comer in Colorado Politics":* DP, June 29, 1960.

250. *"Every time [White]":* Joe Dolan Oral History, 45.

250. *"outstanding scholars":* Ibid., 48.

251. *"Ex–Grid Star":* DP, July 11, 1960.

251. *"We don't ask":* AP, July 20, 1960.

251. *White's first major task:* NYT, July 28, 29, Aug. 2 (photograph), 1960.

252. *"The Kennedys were ferocious":* See also Schlesinger, 211.

252. *Kaiser suggested:* Kaiser Oral History, 8; Kaiser, *Journeying Far and Wide,* 183–84; Sorensen, *Kennedy,* 188–89.

252. *"We went":* Orrick Oral History, 7.

253. *"to establish":* WP, July 27, 1960.

255. *"I want to re-emphasize":* Moyers to Salinger, Aug. 19, 1960, Box 34, RFK Pre-Administration Political Files.

256. *"As you know":* Box 34, ibid.

256. *"scorched":* Strobers, 36.

256. *"bomb-throwers":* Schlesinger, 217; Harris Wofford, *Of Kennedys and Kings,* 19 (attributed to John Seigenthaler).

257. *In fact, Mitchell:* Jack Bass, *Taming the Storm,* 169–71, is the most complete and accurate account. See also Bass, *Atlanta Journal and Constitution,* May 23, 1994; *Unlikely Heroes,* 162–63.

257. *"celebrated incidents":* Schlesinger, 214.

257. *"improper":* Nation, Nov. 19, 1960.

258. *"The encounter":* Wofford, *Of Kennedys and Kings,* 93–94; see also Wofford Oral History, 124.

259. *"Correction Please":* Box 34, RFK Pre-Administration Political Files.

CHAPTER 12. KENNEDY JUSTICE

260. *"a Jew":* Guthman & Shulman, 74.

260. *"on the record":* Schlesinger, 231.

261. *one of McNamara's conditions:* Paul B. (Red) Fay, a South Sea comrade of the president and active California campaigner, soon became an exception when he was named undersecretary of the navy.

261. *"I have nothing"* / *"in some defense capacity":* DP, Dec. 8, 1960.

262. Washington Post *guessed:* Dec. 15, 1960.

262. *"'I talked to the President'":* Seigenthaler Oral History, 331–33; for a somewhat different account, see Ronald Goldfarb, *Perfect Villains, Imperfect Heroes,* 24.

263. *"The appointment spoils":* WP, Dec. 17, 1960.

263. *ill-fated Ohio campaign:* Nixon carried Ohio and won its 25 electoral votes by almost 6 percentage points. Robert Kennedy expected his brother to win almost until the last few days of the campaign and asked Geoghegan more than once, *What happened? What happened?*

264. *consent decree:* See generally *English v. Cunningham,* 269 F. 2d 517 (CADC 1959).

264. *"I wish you'd come":* Orrick Oral History, 10.

264. *"Bob was looking":* Ibid., 10–11.

265. *"prepare formal":* Dick Maguire to Kenneth O'Donnell, Dec. 1, 1960, Box 66, AG's General Correspondence.

265. *Katzenbach came highly:* John Douglas to RFK, Jan. 16, 1961, Katzenbach Papers. The Katzenbach Papers do not carry box numbers.

265. *"politics figured":* Edwin O. Guthman, *We Band of Brothers,* 94 (cited below as "Guthman").

266. *Humphrey went to great length:* John Seigenthaler Oral History, 334.

266. *"would be at the center":* Guthman, 95; see also Kenneth O'Reilly, *"Racial Matters,"* 65, and Navasky, 52.

267. *never had until Kennedy:* Navasky, 40–41.

268. *"Byron's work":* Box 8, Robert L. Stearns Papers.

268. *"Bill":* Jan. 19, 1961, Box 16, RFK General Correspondence.

268. *"promoting Byron White":* Douglas to RFK, Dec. 21, 1960, Box 347, WODLC. See also Frank to Douglas, Dec. 19, 1960, ibid. Douglas was stretching the facts. White's name was mentioned during the course of the tangled debates over Sturges's successor, but he apparently was not a serious candidate. Frank now does not recall "promoting" White. Frank letter to author.

268. *"Please tell Bobbie"*: N.d., Box 16, RFK General Correspondence.

268. *Kennedy was more concerned:* Dolan interview.

268. judges were appointed: Joe Dolan, Duquesne Conference, April 12, 1996.

269. *The* New York Times Magazine: Robert Manning, "Someone the President Can Talk To," May 28, 1961, 22, 26, 28–29.

269. *"It was the most"*: Quoted in Schlesinger, 238–39.

269. *"contradictory career"*: *WES,* Jan. 15, 1961.

269. *"into the intercom"*: *WP,* Apr. 21, 1961.

270. *"Attorney General Finds"*: *NYT,* Mar. 3, 1961.

271. *"stamp his Administration"*: Robert Massie, "Many Rhodes to Washington," Apr. 16, 1961. A photo of White riding a bicycle in cap and gown at Oxford (see above, Chapter 6) appears on p. 56.

271. *"most of the hostesses"*: Apr. 7, 1961, Box 8, Robert L. Stearns Papers.

271. *"major"*: Guthman & Shulman, 422.

271. told many times: Taylor Branch, *Parting the Waters* (the riders); Guthman and Guthman & Shulman (the Department of Justice); Jack Bass, *Taming the Storm* (federal judge Frank M. Johnson).

273. *"the time is not right"*: May 10, 1961, Martin to Sorensen, Box 66, AG's General Correspondence.

274. *Robert Kennedy later admitted:* Guthman & Shulman, 82–83.

274. *"Well, we will probably / Where are you"*: Oberdorfer Oral History, 27.

275. *"As you know"*: Burke Marshall Oral History, 5.

275. *"All hell brok[e] loose"*: Quoted in Oberdorfer Oral History, 28.

276. *"take those marshals" / "We'll both go"*: Ibid.

276. *"other such means"*: The president's power was limited by the statute to situations where the "domestic violence" in a state "so hinders the execution of the laws of that State, and of the United States within the State," as to deprive any "class of its people a right, privilege, immunity, or protection named in the Constitution and secured by law, and the constituted authorities of the State are unable, fail, or refuse to protect that right, privilege, or immunity, or to give that protection; or opposes or obstructs the execution of the laws of the United States or impedes the course of justice under those laws." The questions were whether the riders had a protected federal right under the terms of the statute, and if so, whether obstruction of that right fell within the scope of the statute, and whether White's ad hoc federal force was authorized by the statute. During the Little Rock crisis, President Eisenhower relied on Section 334, which authorized the use of the "armed forces" when the president considered "it necessary . . . under this chapter."

276. attacked the books: For a glamorized account, see John P. Frank, *The Warren Court,* 149–50.

276. *"Byron, if this thing"*: Oberdorfer Oral History, 29.

277. *"White hedged"*: *MA,* May 21, 1961.

277. *"there were strong words"*: Bakal, 21.

277. *"In return, White was firm"*: More than a decade after the fact, Patterson declared in an interview with Howell Raines that he had so shaken White with his arguments that White immediately called the president directly, bypassing the attorney general, and urged that the marshals be withdrawn. Howell Raines, *My Soul Is Rested,* p. 310. (Civilian telephone operators at Maxwell Air Force Base eavesdropped on outgoing calls and passed on information to Patterson's aides, which White knew.) White telephoned the White House to report on his meeting but did not speak with the president. Telephone Memos, Box 5,

Record Group 87, Misc. Presidential Files, JFKL. Patterson also claimed that White told the president that "there was no reason to have federal forces here," which as a legal or tactical assessment is overwhelmingly against the weight of the evidence regardless of the auditor. Nothing in White's behavior, before or after the interview in the Capitol, is consistent with Patterson's tale, which sounds more wishful than plausible—an exercise in belated braggadocio. Nonetheless, others have accepted Patterson's account at face value. See Taylor Branch, *Parting the Waters*, at 454; James W. Hilty, *Robert Kennedy*, at 324.

278. *"I want you fellows"*: Oberdorfer Oral History, 31.

278. *"My God"*: Ibid., 31.

278. *"I wonder"*: Strobers, 298; Dolan interview. Compare Guthman & Shulman, 95.

279. *"We have committed"*: Dolan interview.

279. *Behind the scenes:* See Schlesinger, 299; Guthman & Shulman, 97.

279. *"Freedom Riders": MA,* May 23, 1961.

280. *"There have been no": Jackson Clarion-Ledger,* May 23, 1961.

280. *"White is about": Alabama Journal,* May 23, 1961.

280. *"Police, Klan, Mixers"*: June 3, 1961.

281. *"the worst examples": NYHT,* May 23, 1961.

281. *J. Skelly Wright's school desegregation decree:* See generally Liva Baker, *The Second Battle of New Orleans.*

281. *well-publicized strategy meeting: NYT,* Feb. 14, 1961.

282. *"the FBI was worthless"*: See also Navasky, 112. The FBI never reported the widespread rumors of the Klan's plan to attack the riders in Montgomery. See Hollinger F. Barnard, ed., *Outside the Magic Circle: The Autobiography of Virginia Foster Durr,* 298–99.

282. *memorandum to Burke Marshall:* Burke, TMLC. See correspondence from June 26 to Aug., 14, 1961.

282. *"situations where"*: See responses from Marshall to White, June 30 (Atlanta, Memphis, Dallas), Aug. 14 (Atlanta, Dallas, New Orleans), Burke Marshall Papers.

282. *SNCC:* Marshall to White, July 14, 1961, ibid.

282. *federal lawsuit:* See *NYT,* Dec. 12, 1982; *Bergman v. U.S.,* 565 Fed Supp 1353 (W. D. Mich., S.D., 1983).

282. *the most Marshall:* Marshall, Deposition, p. 69, in *Bergman v. U.S.,* ibid., courtesy of William H. Goodman.

283. *the resulting organization:* Navasky, 22 n.

284. *"a Negro can achieve"*: May 26, 1961, coverage in numerous newspapers.

284. *the whole affair:* See *MA,* May 30, 1961; *Atlanta Journal,* June 1, 1961.

285. *"Apart from the commission / endorsement of the legislation": NYT,* June 17, 1961.

285. *Robert Kennedy appeared:* AP, June 19, 20, 1961.

286. *"What RFK's ICC": Birmingham News,* May 30, 1961.

CHAPTER 13. KENNEDY JUDGES

288. *"ideal" / "inherent evil of communism": NYT,* Feb. 21, 1961.

289. *suicide of a Chicago man: Chicago Sun-Times,* Feb. 21, 1961.

289. *Kenny O'Donnell:* See Kenneth P. O'Donnell and David F. Powers, *"Johnny, We Hardly Knew Ye,"* 280.

289. *He appointed:* The issue of party affiliation in Kennedy's judicial appointments is detailed in Harold W. Chase, *Federal Judges: The Appointing Process,* 71–78 (cited below as "Chase").

289. *"I want for our courts"*: NYT, May 20, 1961, quoted in Chase, 51.

289. *"no aspect"*: Navasky, 244.

289. *"more than offset"*: Alexander M. Bickel, *Politics and the Warren Court,* 67 (cited below as "Bickel").

289. *"mechanism"*: Mary Hannah Curzan, "A Case Study in the Selection of Federal Judges, the Fifth Circuit, 1953–1963."

290. *"sacrificed its control"*: Ibid., 7–8.

290. *points that:* See Navasky, 255–56, 269–70. Others were less harsh in their assessments of the administration's performance. See Carl M. Brauer, *John F. Kennedy and the Second Reconstruction,* 123, 340. Arthur M. Scheslinger Jr. and others later pointed out that "the somewhat rigid Curzan criteria had the curious result of classifying Judge Frank Johnson as a segregationist." Scheslinger, 955 n. 125.

290. *"It was such"*: Bickel, 68.

290. *A Congress that could consider:* The classic study is Walter Murphy, *Congress and the Court.*

291. *"thought Cox would make"*: Oberdorfer to White, Aug. 16, 1961, Box 11, Oberdorfer Papers, Judge Book.

291. *"in the background"*: Ibid. On the Citizens' Council generally, see Neil R. McMillen, *The Citizens' Council.*

291. *Robert Kennedy personally:* Dolan interview; compare Schlesinger, 308; Guthman & Shulman, 109.

291. *Kennedy directed White:* Jack Bass, *Unlikely Heroes,* 165 (cited below as "Bass").

291. *Georgia and Alabama:* White to O'Donnell, Apr. 24, 1961, Presidential Office Files, Department of Justice File.

292. *"a bunch of chimpanzees"*: See Frank T. Read and Lucy McGough, *Let Them Be Judged,* 299.

292. *"out of Kafka"*: Bickel, 74. On Cox, see "Judge William Harold Cox and the Right to Vote in Clarke County, Mississippi," in Leon Friedman, ed., *Southern Justice.*

292. *Even Eastland:* Bass, 166–67.

292. *stalled for more than two years:* Ibid., 220–22.

292. *"one of the truly"*: *Davis v. East Baton Rouge Parish Board,* 214 F. Supp. 624. See also Bickel, 71–73.

292. *"didn't have"*: Guthman & Shulman, 114.

292. *Louis Oberdorfer later:* Oberdorfer Oral History, 23.

293. *nomination paved the way:* Navasky, 268.

293. *"Hill was adamant"*: Oberdorfer Oral History, 20.

293. *"a more extensive"*: Oberdorfer to White, Aug. 16, 1961, Judge Book.

293. *"inconceivable"*: Oberdorfer to White, Aug. 16, 25, 1961, ibid.

293. *"ABA people / "Advise and Consent"*: Oberdorfer to White, Aug. 22, 1961, ibid. The reference is to Allen Drury's novel of Washington confirmation politics, which won the Pulitzer Prize for fiction in 1960.

294. *"People began / Allgood became the judge"*: Oberdorfer Oral History, 20.

294. *"Senatorial pressure"*: Bickel, 71.

295. *Allgood served:* NYT, Dec. 2, 1991.

295. *but he yielded to Robert Kennedy:* Strobers, 196, quoting John Seigenthaler.

296. *Emanuel Celler:* One priority, Celler claimed, was the appointment of more women to the federal judiciary. Celler to Lawrence O'Brien, Sept. 12, 1961, Box 270, Celler Papers.

296. *test case of its judgment:* William Geoghegan Oral History, 31.

296. *backed him up:* See Chase, 16.

297. *"We could":* Geoghegan Oral History, 32.

297. *FBI could not verify:* Dolan interview.

297. *lost his temper:* Navasky, 363.

297. *final compromise:* Dolan interview.

297. *"a tremendous amount":* John Seigenthaler Oral History, 29.

298. *"Young men":* Geoghegan Oral History, 29. Schlesinger, p. 374.

298. *"Tell [the president]":* Schlesinger, 374.

298. *"I said":* Seigenthaler Oral History, 352–53.

298. *"frankly didn't confirm":* Geoghegan Oral History, 29.

298. *Kerr, who announced:* Jace Weaver, *Then to the Rock Let Me Fly,* 61.

299. *"Except on the theory":* Oberdorfer to White, Aug. 10, 1961, Judge Book.

300. *"The President of the United States":* Guthman & Shulman, 110.

300. *"aggressive, hard-headed":* Ramsey Clark Oral History.

301. *"impossible for anyone":* Santa Fe New Mexican, Nov. 22, 1996.

301. *"I guess":* Geoghegan interview.

301. *"Tell your brother":* Schlesinger, 308, quoting Robert Sherrill, *Gothic Politics in the Deep South,* 212.

303. *constantly peppering:* Among others suggested were Luther Youngdahl (Douglas to RFK, Nov. 28, 1961) and Hubert Will (July 24, 1961); Box 16, General Correspondence, RFK Personal Papers.

303. *which White received:* William Orrick to White, June 7, 1961, Box 5, William H. Orrick Papers.

303. *submission to the department:* Clair Engle to White (bcc: Orrick), ibid.

303. *Stanley A. Weigel:* Weigel had earlier asked Chief Justice Earl Warren to support his ambition for a federal judgeship. Weigel to Warren, Feb. 13, 1961; Warren to Weigel, Feb. 20, 1961; Box 662, EWLC.

303. *"the next Italian judge":* Alfonso J. Zirpoli, *Faith in Justice: Alfonso J. Zirpoli and the United States District Court for the Northern District of California* (interviews with Sarah L. Sharp), 116.

303. *used recess appointments:* See Chase, 86–88.

305. *"I have another":* James F. Schneider, "In Memoriam: Harrison L. Winter," *Maryland Law Review* 50: 1.

305. *"all business":* Ramsey Clark Oral History.

305. *for formal or informal rating:* Hearings before the Committee on the Judiciary, U. S. Senate, Apr. 11, 1962: Nomination of Byron R. White, 87th Cong., 2d Sess., 16.

305. *granting an interview: NYT,* Feb. 3, 1962.

306. *"odious": NYT,* Feb. 20, 1962; Chase, 28.

306. *He fretted:* Bernard Segal to White, June 17, 1961, Presidential Office Files, Department of Justice File.

306. *"in the integrity":* Bass, 168.

308. *"Fairly competent":* Judge Book.

308. *"liaison":* Dick Maguire to Kenneth O'Donnell, Dec. 1, 1960, Box 66, AG's General Correspondence.

308. *testimony and formal opinion letters:* See, for example, *U.S. v. Brecht,* 540 F. 2d 45 (CA2, 1976); *People v. USDA,* 427 F. 2d 561, 565 b. (CADC, 1970) (mandamus power, referring to SRept. No. 1992, 87th Cong., 2d Sess. [Jurisdiction and Venue of the U.S. District Courts in Actions against Government Officials], 5–7); *U. S. v. Merrigan,* 389 F. 2d 21, 21 n. 4 (CA 3, 1968) (government recovery and subrogation); H. Rept. No. 1086,

87th Cong., 1st Sess. (Amending the Immigration and Nationality Act) (judicial review of deportation orders), 24–25.

308. *wiretaps in criminal investigations: NYT,* July 5, 1961. White was a "hawk" on wiretapping (favoring use by state and federal criminal investigators as well as by national security agents), according to Joe Dolan, a self-professed "dove," who thought wiretaps appropriate only in national security cases. See generally Navasky, 74–76 (1961 legislation), 94–95, 448–49 (FBI authority for electronic surveillance).

308. *encouraging Archibald Cox:* Navasky, 297–322, esp. 301–2.

308. *cautioning the president:* Schlesinger, 381. President Kennedy invoked executive privilege only once in his administration. White's memorandum, as acting attorney general in Feb. 1962, argued that the executive's "managerial responsibility" needed to be "weigh[ed]" against "the needs of Congress for the information withheld. . . . The Executive branch has some tendency to hide its errors and many Congressional investigations have disclosed errors which would not otherwise have come to the attention of an agency head."

308. *than by memorandum:* For an example of the informal decision-making structure (and lack of archival records), see Theodore P. Kovaleff, "The Two Sides of the Kennedy Antitrust Policy," *Antitrust Bulletin* 7 (1992): 5.

308. *prodding Robert Kennedy:* For accounts of White's insistence to Robert Kennedy—despite a hostile reception—that the brother of an important Brooklyn congressman be prosecuted for obstruction of justice, see Navasky, 368–69, and Guthman, 146–47.

309. *knowing where:* White was remembered by colleagues in the department, as one later said without intended irony, for "keeping his eye on the ball." "It's nothing to come to an important job in government and be smart," White has been quoted as saying of his tenure in the Department of Justice. "The key is what you spend your time on." Navasky, 439.

309. *mixture of idealism:* After a year in office, White asked Edwin Guthman what he viewed as the attorney general's most important accomplishment, and then answered his own question: "This place has always been run like a big law office. For the first time, he's given it the sense of the public man." Guthman, 107.

CHAPTER 14. "THE IDEAL NEW FRONTIER JUDGE"

310. *told many times:* The principal accounts are James E. Clayton, *The Making of Justice,* 50–52 (cited below as "Clayton"); Schlesinger, 377–78; Nicholas Katzenbach Oral History, 56–71; Nicholas deB. Katzenbach, "Byron White's Appointment to the Supreme Court," *UCOLR* 58 (1987): 429, 430 (cited below as "Katzenbach"); Randy Lee Sowell, *Judicial Vigor: The Warren Court and the Kennedy Administration,* ch. 3.

310. *influencing the outcome:* Katzenbach (Katzenbach Oral History, 70–71; Katzenbach, 430); William O. Douglas (*The Court Years,* 122–27; compare William O. Douglas Oral History, interview by Walter F. Murphy, cassette 7b, transcript p. 152, cited below as "Princeton Interview"); Joe Dolan (interview with author; Duquesne Conference, cited below as "Duquesne"); Clark Clifford (*Counsel to the President,* 374–75, cited below as "Clifford").

310. *final nominee:* Katzenbach (Katzenbach Oral History, 62); Dolan (Duquesne); Bernard Segal (Navasky, 265).

310. *different accounts:* Compare Clayton, 50–52, and *NYT,* Apr. 1, 1962, with Gutman & Shulman, 115–18.

311. *since February 1:* Warren to Conference (except Frankfurter), Apr. 25, 1962, Box 124, TCCUT.

312. *called on Whittaker:* Warren Schedule, Box 32, EWLC.

312. *§372(a):* Section 372(a) of Title 28, United States Code (1958), provided:

> Any justice or judge of the United States appointed to hold office during good behavior who becomes permanently disabled from performing his duties may retire from regular active service, and the President shall, by and with the advice and consent of the Senate, appoint a successor.
>
> Any justice or judge of the United States desiring to retire under this section shall certify to the President his disability in writing.
>
> Whenever an associate justice of the Supreme Court desires to retire under this section, he shall furnish to the President a certificate of disability signed by the Chief Justice of the United States.

At age sixty-one, with eight years of active service as a federal judge, Whittaker was not eligible to retire at full pay on the basis of age and service under §371 (age seventy and ten years' service, or age sixty-five and fifteen years' service). Under another provision of §372, Whittaker was entitled to retire on disability at "one-half the salary of the office during the remainder of his lifetime." He did so for three years until he was retained by General Motors Corporation as a legal consultant; he then resigned his judicial office and forfeited his half pension. He later became an outspoken critic of the Court and of civil disobedience. See Charles E. Whittaker and William Sloane Coffin Jr., *Law, Order and Civil Disobedience.*

312. *"Having become":* Draft statement, "Dictated March 16, 1962, not used," Box 358, EWLC.

312. *refocused his ambitions:* Douglas, Princeton Interview, 155.

313. *on March 18:* Log of closed Presidential Office Files, Departments and Agencies, Justice, JFK Library.

313. *"A Negro should":* Box 52, RFK Pre-Administration Political Files.

314. *"most of the work":* Katzenbach Oral History, 57, 59–60.

314. *of suspect loyalty:* See generally John W. Poulos, "The Judicial Philosophy of Roger Traynor," *Hastings Law Journal* 46 (1995): 643.

314. *endorsing them:* Katzenbach Oral History, 61.

314. *"violently opposed":* Guthman & Shulman, 115.

314. *"just one more vote for Frankfurter":* Schlesinger, 377. Douglas provided three different accounts of his role in the Whittaker vacancy. In 1962, he told Walter Murphy that "Bobby Kennedy, an old, old friend of mine, came to see me about the vacancy" and suggested Hastie, who Douglas said was "pedestrian" (Princeton Interview, 155). In 1967, he told an interviewer for the Kennedy Library that he had not been contacted by the attorney general (Douglas Oral History, 25–26). In vol. 2 of his memoirs (1980), he claimed that the president asked his advice on the vacancy and that he recommended J. Skelly Wright, a "district judge . . . in Louisiana," but that Kennedy concluded he could "never get Wright by" Senator Eastland's Judiciary Committee (*The Court Years,* 122, 127). Douglas was incapacitated at the time he finished his memoirs and may have forgotten that Wright had already "gotten by" Eastland on Feb. 28, 1962, for a seat on the Court of Appeals for the District of Columbia, a position he had enjoyed under a recess appointment since Dec. 15, 1961—news conveyed to Douglas by the deputy attorney general, Byron White. Liva Baker, *The Second Battle of New Orleans,* 464.

314. *"Members of the Administration"*: Sorensen to JFK, Mar. 21, 1962, Box 88A, Presidential Office Files ("Supreme Court").

315. *"too obvious"*: Schlesinger, 377.

315. *"I thought"*: Ibid. Clifford later wrote in his memoirs that he thought Hastie's opinions were "shaky" and that "it would demean both the Court and the civil rights movement if he made an appointment which appeared to be based solely on the grounds of race." Clifford, 374.

315. *Leon Jaworski:* Jaworski told Joe Dolan that he *did not want to leave Texas* and did not wish to be considered for the appointment.

316. *"Associate of Hoodlums"*: Federal Bureau of Investigation Memo, Mar. 20, 1962, J. Edgar Hoover Official and Confidential File 96 (John F. Kennedy), quoted in Richard Reeves, *President Kennedy,* 289.

316. *"I said we had a lot"*: Katzenbach Oral History, 63.

317. *"to find out whether"*: Guthman & Shulman, 116.

317. *"the right of citizens"*: *DP,* March 29, 1962.

317. *"has advised us"*: *LAT,* Mar. 30, 1962.

317. *"Washington, D.C. is not America"*: *Pueblo Chieftain,* Mar. 30, 1962.

318. *"About all I can say"*: *DP,* Mar. 30, 1962.

318. *"a distinguished"*: *NYT,* Mar. 30, 1962.

318. *Sen. Richard B. Russell:* Schlesinger, 377; Schlesinger letter to the author.

319. *"I really think"*: Katzenbach Oral History, 71. See also Navasky, 255; Katzenbach, 430.

319. *"The ages of the eight"*: Sorensen, Memorandum for the President, Mar. 29, 1962, Box 88A, Presidential Office Files ("Supreme Court").

320. *"The best and most confidential"*: Bundy, Memorandum for the President, Mar. 30, 1962, ibid.

320. *another contemporary memo:* Bundy to the President, July 26, 1962, Box 88A, President's Office Files ("Supreme Court"), JFKL.

320. *the developing consensus:* The only holdout in the president's inner circle was Kenny O'Donnell, the appointments secretary, whose objections were more "sarcastic" than substantive. See Kenneth P. O'Donnell and David F. Powers, *"Johnny, We Hardly Knew Ye,"* 280:

> I had no objections to White's nomination, but I reminded the President that he had been getting a hard time from Bobby and his friends in the Justice Department whenever we tried to reward a nice young man, who had helped us politically, with an appointment to a federal judgeship. The Justice people always complained that our nominee was either too young, too inexperienced, had not served as a judge, or had not attended Harvard Law School. "And now Bobby wants to put Whizzer White on the Supreme Court," I said to the President. "I'm sure Whizzer will be fine on the Court, but it seems to me he doesn't have any of that Oliver Wendell Holmes background that the Justice Department is always demanding when we try to give somebody a judge's job."

321. *"a strong candidate"*: See also Navasky, 264–65.

321. *the rating they wanted:* Joel Grossman, *Lawyers and Judges,* 134–35; Navasky, 264–65.

321. *"Ordinarily our committee"*: AP, Mar. 31, 1962; Statement of Bernard G. Segal, Chairman, Standing Committee on the Federal Judiciary of the American Bar Association, Archives of the ABA, courtesy of Irene Emsellem, Governmental Affairs Office, ABA.

322. *"peeked around a door"*: AP, Mar. 30, 1962.

322. *" 'Well, Byron' "*: Schlesinger, 378.

322. *"wasn't very enthusiastic"*: Benjamin C. Bradlee, *Conversations with Kennedy,* 67.

322. *"White was no mere professor"*: Schlesinger, 378.

322. *"excelled"*: AP and numerous newspapers, Mar. 31, 1962.

322. *conferred by telephone:* Taylor Branch, *Parting the Waters,* 583–84.

322. *"Kennedy's Choice"*: WP, Mar. 31, 1962.

322. *"an able Supreme Court justice"*: UPI, Mar. 30, 1962.

323. *"one of those solid people"*: NYHT, Mar. 31, 1962.

323. *"splendid"*: AP, Mar. 31, 1962.

323. *dashing pictures:* The most comprehensive gallery was the *Sunday DP* Pictorial page, Apr. 1, 1962.

323. *cartoonists:* For example, *LAT,* Apr. 3, 1962; *WES,* Apr. 1, 1962.

323. *"truly first-rate choice"*: NYHT, Apr. 1, 1962.

323. *"excellent"*: WES, Apr. 1, 1962.

323. *"political henchman"*: WES, Apr. 2, 1962.

323. *"cautious and plodding"*: WES, Apr. 2, 1962.

323. *"liberal"* / *"the ideal justice"*: NYT, Apr. 1, 1962.

324. *"the appointment"*: TNR, Apr. 9, 1962, p. 7.

324. *"It's the logical outcome"*: DP, Mar. 31, 1962.

324. *"You shouldn't have to ask"*: RMN, Mar. 31, 1962.

324. *"industriousness"*: RMN, Apr. 1, 1962.

324. *Roscoe Fleming:* DP, Apr. 5, 1962.

324. *"most of Colorado"*: *Cervi's Rocky Mountain Journal,* Apr. 4, 1962.

325. *"vindictive"*: Bakal, 99.

326. *"The proof"*: WES, Mar. 31, 1962.

326. *"I guess we'll just have"*: FC, Apr. 1, 1962.

326. *"he will be"*: DP, Apr. 1, 1962.

327. *"ought to be somebody"*: Katzenbach Oral History, 64.

327. *"In picking"*: NYT, Apr. 2, 1962.

327. *"the Supreme Court"*: Katzenbach Oral History, 78.

327. *government financial aid:* Within a month of the inauguration, presidential aides sought advice from the Department of Justice on the feasibility of providing federal funds to students attending parochial schools, an initiative prompted by "Cuban refugee children in Miami" and plans by Gov. Nelson A. Rockefeller of New York to provide similar state aid there. Frederick G. Dutton to Archibald Cox, Feb. 23, 1961, Box 66, AG's General Correspondence. Even before Cox could respond, Theodore C. Sorensen, special counsel to the president, detailed the legal and political arguments against a federal program and closed with his "personal conviction that the first Catholic President, under fire from the Catholic Hierarchy, cannot now reverse his vote on the Morse Amendment in 1960 when he was a candidate to support the first aid-to-parochial schools Bill." Sorensen Memorandum ("In answer to questions"), March, 7, 1961, Box 66, ibid. Morse proposed an amendment to Kennedy's 1959 federal aid to education bill that would have allowed funds for nonpublic schools, but Kennedy called Morse's proposal "unconstitutional." Sorensen, *Kennedy,* 111.

328. *"He said"*: Katzenbach Oral History, 77.

328. *"I think John Kennedy's"*: Wofford Oral History, 16.

328. Now why: Dolan interview.

328. I guess they want: See also Jim Mann, *LAT,* Aug. 7, 1978.

328. *he paid a call:* Calendar of the Chief Justice, Box 32, EWLC.

329. *"Mrs. 'Whizzer' "*: WP, Mar. 31, 1962.

329. *"President Kennedy couldn't have":* Pittsburgh Post-Gazette, Mar. 31, 1962.

329. *"Over here in the all brawn":* Baltimore American, Apr. 22, 1962.

329. *"For every professional football":* WP, Apr. 17, 1962.

330. *"painfully modest":* NYT, May 1, 1962.

330. *journalist David Brinkley:* David Brinkley, *David Brinkley: A Memoir,* 152; see also William F. Buckley (column), *Houston Chronicle,* Oct. 19, 1991.

330. *"Frankly":* Hearings before the Committee on the Judiciary, U. S. Senate, April 11, 1962: Nomination of Byron R. White, 87th Cong., 2d Sess., 15 (cited below as "Hearings").

330. *"White, a reticent man":* WP, Apr. 12, 1962.

330. *"the first appointment" / "well-qualified":* Hearings, 20.

331. *"legislate[s]" / "I think":* Ibid., 23.

331. *executive session:* WES, Apr. 12, 1962.

331. *"genuine conservative constitutionalist":* NYT, Apr. 12, 1962.

CHAPTER 15. THE WARREN COURT: WHITE, J., DISSENTING

336. *"Justice White's New Home":* DP, Oct. 14, 1962.

336. *purchase price:* Fairfax County Tax Records, ID No. FX21-2-5-4A.

336. *controlling public appearances:* Early in his first full term, White turned down an invitation to deliver the prestigious James Madison Lecture at New York University. When a faculty member solicited Justice Brennan to encourage White to accept, Brennan declined and speculated that White's "reticence about accepting" was "because of some uncertainty that he is sufficiently seasoned to undertake the assignment. I've observed something of this modesty in him in our relationship." Brennan to Edmond Cahn, Jan. 29, 1963, Brennan Personal Correspondence (uncataloged), courtesy of Stephen J. Wermeil. White's modesty extended to ceremonial academic honors: after accepting an honorary doctorate from the University of Colorado in 1963, White adopted Justice Brandeis's practice and declined further honorary degrees. See Barrett McGurn, *America's Court,* 107.

337. *only sustained newspaper interview:* NYHT, Apr. 4, 1962.

338. *"Finally, I deem":* 370 U.S. at 689.

340. Every time someone: See, for example, the 1996 *RMN* interview, Appendix C.

340. *"High Court Bans":* WES, June 25, 1962.

340. *"Most Significant" / "put his weight":* NYT, July 2, 1962.

340. *"the real Warren Court":* Currie, 415.

341. *As the term wore on:* See, for example, *Yellin v. U.S.,* 374 U.S. 109, 123 (1963) (dissenting); *Gibson v. Florida Legislative Investigation Committee,* 372 U.S. 539, 583 (1963) (dissenting); *NAACP v. Button,* 371 U.S. 415, 447 (1963) (concurring in part and dissenting in part).

341. *He also wrote: Florida Lime & Avocado Growers v. Paul,* 373 U.S. 132, 159 (1963) (dissenting).

341. *"dogs":* Bernard Schwartz, *Super Chief,* 461 (cited below as "Schwartz"). Richard Posner, reviewing the uneven record of Justice Holmes's judicial work, observes—with firsthand knowledge—that "much of any judge's work, even that of a justice of the Supreme Court, is ephemeral—indeed, when viewed from the distance of a half century or a century, a bore." Posner, ed., *The Essential Holmes,* Introduction, xxii.

341. *"I wasn't exactly":* Schwartz, 430.

341. *"fair":* Ibid., 460–61.

342. *"During the winter":* James E. Clayton, *The Making of Justice,* 159 (cited below as "Clayton").

342. *Silver Anniversary: Sports Illustrated,* Dec. 10, 1962.

342. *Gold Medal: NYT,* Dec. 5, 1962.

342. *"M" Club:* Clayton, 159–160.

343. *might be impossible:* Judge Jerome Frank, recalling Mark Twain, likened the task to telling a jury to "stand in the corner and not think of a white elephant." *U.S. v. Antonelli Fireworks,* 155 F. 2d 631, 656 (CA2 1946).

343. *"'Fairness' used in [this]":* Black to White, Feb. 21, 1964, Box 379, HLBLC.

343. *"A state criminal procedure":* "The Supreme Court, 1963 Term," *HLR* 78 (1964): 143, 212.

343. *"plague[d]":* Kurland, "Enter the Burger Court: The Constitutional Business of the Supreme Court, O. T. 1969," *SCR* (1970): 1, 29.

344. *"overrated":* Kurland, *Politics, the Constitution, and the Warren Court,* 80–81.

344. *"In some unknown number":* 384 U.S. at 542–43.

344. *"soften the impact":* Schwartz, 594.

345. *"Neither the language / which must be decided": DP,* Aug. 18, 1966.

345. *"for such secondary purposes":* Fred Graham, *The Self-Inflicted Wound,* 312 (cited below as "Graham"); see also *NYT,* Aug. 4, 1967.

346. *"realized that the aging":* Graham, 312.

346. *"One of the current notions":* Harlan, "Thoughts at a Dedication: Keeping the Judicial Function in Balance," *ABA Journal* 49 (1963): 943, reprinted in David L. Shapiro, ed., *The Evolution of a Judicial Philosophy,* 289.

347. *by inappropriate means:* By sending an emissary from the Department of Justice to meet with a member of the Court ex parte to advocate rehearing. Schwartz, 750–51.

347. *aboveboard:* P. L. 91-452, 84 Stat. 935 (1970).

347. Camara *and* See: *Camara v. Municipal Court,* 387 U.S. 523 (1967); *See v. Seattle,* 387 U.S. 541 (1967). See Wayne LaFave, "Administrative Searches and the Fourth Amendment: The Camara and See Cases," *SCR* (1967): 1.

347. *"about my Dad":* White to Harlan, undated, Box 609, JMHP.

348. *enduring importance: United Mine Workers v. Pennington,* 381 U.S. 657 (1965) (intersection of antitrust and labor laws).

348. *handful of major: Avery v. Midland County,* 390 U.S. 474 (1968) (reapportionment and the equal protection clause); *Swain v. Alabama,* 380 U.S. 202 (1965) (racial discrimination in jury selection); *McLaughlin v. Florida,* 379 U.S. 184 (1964) (anti-interracial-cohabitation statute violates equal protection clause).

348. *"truly superb":* Box 183, WJBLC. Even Hugo Black, the self-styled absolutist protecting freedom of speech, was "happy to agree to your comprehensive discussion of vital and important issues involved in this case."

348. *"most distressing":* Currie, 420.

348. *"during the later":* Ibid., 419.

349. *"Though the opinion":* Ibid., 420.

349. *antibusing referenda: Washington v. Seattle School District No. 1,* 458 U.S. 457 (1982).

349. *trial court injunction: Coalition for Economic Equity v. Wilson,* 946 F. Supp. 1480 (N. D. Cal. 1996), vacated and remanded, 110 F. 3d 1431 (1997).

349. *"after stewing around":* White to Clark, Mar. 19, 1964, Box 154, Clark Papers. The case was *Mechling Barge v. U.S.,* 376 U.S. 375 (1964). For another example, see *U.S. v. Adams,* Draft of Feb. 11, 1966, Box 187, TCCUT, and compare 383 U.S. 39, 52 (1966), where White ultimately dissented without opinion.

350. *"I am still stewing":* White to Warren, May 7, 1963, Box 604, EWLC.

350. Bell v. Maryland: See Philip B. Kurland, *Politics, the Constitution, and the Warren Court*, 131ff.

350. *wound up in dissent:* See Roger Newman, *Hugo Black*, 544–48.

350. *but withdrew it:* White to Conference, June 20, 1964, Box A151, TCCUT.

350. *"nub of my reasons":* Draft opinion, June 17, 1964, ibid.

352. *That string would not be broken:* See Dennis J. Hutchinson, "Unanimity and Desegregation: Decision-Making in the Supreme Court, 1948–1958," *Georgetown Law Journal* 68: 1.

352. *White joined:* Schwartz, 534; see generally 533–40. The full account is Anthony Lewis, *Make No Law: The Sullivan Case and the First Amendment*.

352. *In subsequent terms: Rosenbloom v. Metromedia*, 403 U.S. 29, 59 (1971) (concurring); *Gertz v. Robert Welch*, 418 U.S. 323, 369 (1974) (dissenting); *Time v. Firestone*, 424 U.S. 448, 481 (1976) (dissenting); *Dun & Bradstreet v. Greenmoss Builders*, 472 U.S. 749, 765 (1985) (concurring); *Masson v. New Yorker Magazine*, 501 U.S. 496, 525 (1991) (concurring in part and dissenting in part). His most pointed statement after *Gertz* was *Greenmoss*. See also Bernard Schwartz, *The Unpublished Opinions of the Warren Court*, 288–97, reproducing White's unpublished opinion in *Time v. Hill*, 385 U.S. 374 (1967), on the intersection of privacy and the freedom of the press, and including the telling remark that "one who publishes the news and facts behind it has a constitutional right to do so, even if those he writes about would rather he had not written at all" (295).

353. *"John has devoted":* John V. ("Johnny Blood") McNally File, Library, National Football League Hall of Fame.

353. *annual private trek:* Ed Cray, *Chief Justice*, 298. See generally "Army-Navy football game" File, Box 657, EWLC.

354. *"Farewell":* White to Warren, June 29, 1969, Box 358, EWLC.

354. *Lance Liebman suggested:* Liebman, "A Tribute to Justice Byron R. White," *HLR* 107: 13, 15 n. 3.

CHAPTER 16. OCTOBER TERM 1971

355. *Three terms provide:* For a topical analysis of White's judicial career, there are two sustained studies by former clerks turned law professor: Kate Stith, "Byron White: Last of the New Deal Liberals," and Allan Ides, "The Jurisprudence of Justice Byron White," both in *YLR* 103. The *UCOLR* devoted an issue in volume 58 honoring White's twenty-fifth year on the Court, and it contains useful studies of his work to that point. The *BYULR* devoted an entire issue in 1994 to White and his judicial career a year after his retirement. The most perceptive snapshot of White during his active service on the Court remains Lance Liebman's study in the *New York Times Magazine*, Oct. 8, 1972.

356. *"A rough measure":* Lewin, "White's Flight: The Burger Court's Right-Hand Man: Justice Byron R. White," *TNR*, Aug. 27, 1984.

356. *White participated:* See Robert E. Riggs, "When Every Vote Counts: 5-4 Decisions in the United States Supreme Court, 1900–1990," *Hofstra Law Review* 21 (1993): 667, for preliminary figures.

356. *resignation in disgrace:* See Laura Kalman, *Abe Fortas*, ch. 15; John P. MacKenzie, *The Appearance of Justice*. See generally Robert Shogan, *A Question of Judgment*.

356. *shamelessly focused:* The search was a "clear-cut case of presidential contempt, utter contempt, for the Court" as well as for the Senate, whom Nixon was trying to "teach" a lesson for defeating his nominations of Judges Clement F. Haynsworth, Jr., and G. Harold

Carswell a year before. Henry J. Abraham, *Justices and Presidents,* 310. See the summary of the 1971 search, 20–23.

357. *"Minnesota Twins":* Kurland, "The 1971 Term: The Year of the Stewart-White Court," *SCR* (1972): 181, 185 (cited below as "Kurland").

357. *"lean years ahead": NYT,* Dec. 19, 1971.

357. *White also wrote:* Kurland, 183.

357. *cases of both:* On *U.S. District Court,* see Box 1553, WODLC, for Conference Notes and correspondence documenting the misassignment, and Phillip J. Cooper, *Battles on the Bench* (cited below as "Cooper"), 37; on *Loper v. Beto,* see Box 249, WJBLC; for Douglas's correspondence with Burger over *Roe v. Wade,* see Box 78, TMLC. See also Bob Woodward and Scot Armstrong, *The Brethren,* 170–72, 179–81, 187–89, 223.

358. *patent case: Deepsouth Packing v. Laitrim Corp.,* 406 U.S. 518 (1972).

358. *Federal Trade Commission case: FTC v. Sperry & Hutchinson,* 405 U.S. 508 (1972).

358. *Federal Power Commission: FPC v. Florida Power & Light,* 404 U.S. 453 (1972).

358. *admiralty case: Victory Carriers v. Law,* 404 U.S. 202 (1971).

358. Burns Int'l Security: See "The Supreme Court, 1971 Term," *HLR* 86 (1972): 1, 247–59. The other case was *NLRB v. Plasterers' Union Local No. 79,* 404 U.S. 453 (1972).

358. *present the Court's budget:* House Subcommittee on State, Justice, Commerce and Judiciary of the Committee on Appropriations, Hearings, Feb. 7, 1972, 92d Cong., 2d Sess.

358. *"physical changes":* Chief Justice to White, Thurgood Marshall, Harry Blackmun, Feb. 23, 1971, Box 78, TMLC.

358. *to search:* Chief Justice to Conference, Apr. 7, 1972, Box 1523, WODLC.

358. *to interview:* Chief Justice to Conference, Aug.. 1, 1972, Box 78, TMLC.

358. *to investigate:* Memo to Chief Justice, July 12, 1972, Box 78, TMLC. White and the three other justices appointed to the committee delegated the task to a clerk in each of their chambers. Eventually the Court decided to adopt a pool: each application would be the subject of a brief memorandum summarizing the issues and arguments, which would be distributed to all chambers in the pool. Thus, pool chambers would be freed from producing analytical memoranda for each application. When the process was adopted, all but three members of the Court (Brennan, Stewart, and Marshall) participated. The pool is discussed in H. W. Perry, *Deciding to Decide.*

359. *Justice Powell would often do:* See Paul W. Kahn, "The Court, the Community and the Judicial Balance: The Jurisprudence of Justice Powell," *YLJ* 97 (1987): 1.

360. *"We do not denigrate":* 405 U.S. at 74.

361. *"the essential difficulty":* Kurland, 284.

361. *"Neither are we now":* 408 U.S. at 697.

361. *thoughtful criticism:* For example, see Kurland, 241–46; Allan Ides, "The Jurisprudence of Justice Byron White," *YLJ* 103: 435–39.

362. *"The opinion of the Court":* 381 U.S. at 616.

362. *"counter-revolution":* Vincent Blasi, *The Burger Court: The Counter-Revolution That Wasn't.*

363. *"on perfection from police":* Kate Stith, "Byron R. White, Last of the New Deal Liberals," *YLJ* 103: 19, 29.

363. *widely admired by his colleagues:* William H. Rehnquist, "A Tribute to Justice Byron R. White," *YLJ* 103: 1; John Paul Stevens, "Justice Byron White," *BYULR* (1994): 209, 217.

365. *"inductive reasoner": WP,* March 20, 1993.

365. *"What about whatever clause"*: Lee Epstein and Joseph F. Kobylka, *The Supreme Court and Legal Change,* 180.

366. *only unequivocal vote:* David J. Garrow, *Liberty and Sexuality,* 528–32.

366. *provoked Douglas:* Ibid., 533–34.

366. Washington Post: July 4, 1972. See also Bernard Schwartz, *The Unpublished Opinions of the Burger Court,* ch. 4 (cited below as "Schwartz, 'Burger'"); Cooper, 45–46; Box 1588, WODLC; Box 78, TMLC.

366. *three-page dissent:* Schwartz, "Burger," 141; Box 281, WJBLC.

366. *"If a standard which refers"*: Schwartz, "Burger," 142.

367. *"for allowing the consensus"*: June 8, 1972, Box 1588, WODLC.

367. *"weighing one life"*: Stephanie Guitton and Peter Irons, ed., *May It Please the Court: Arguments on Abortion,* 31. The Guitton-Irons transcripts must be used with caution. On the page cited, Harry Blackmun is misidentified as White ("Well, do I get") and Potter Stewart is misidentified as White ("If it were") Stewart is also misidentified as White on the following page ("You certainly would").

367. *"choos[ing] to kill the innocent one"*: Ibid., 33.

368. *"The common claim"*: 410 U.S. at 221.

368. *"With all due respect"*: Ibid. at 221–22.

370. *"The integrity of the family unit"*: 405 U.S. at 651.

370. *circulated within the Court:* Schwartz, "Burger," 95–99 (Douglas on *Doe*), 126–27 (Blackmun on *Doe*).

371. *"[There is] little talk"*: Douglas Conference notes, Box 1552, WODLC.

372. *"Presented, thus"*: White to Conference, Feb. 24, 1972, Box 77, TMLC.

373. *"transparently erroneous"*: White to Conference, Mar. 3, 1972, Box 281, WJBLC; Box 1588, WODLC.

373. *Blackmun soon expressed:* Blackmun to White, Mar. 13, 1972, Box 1588, WODLC.

373. *"with the suggestion, however"*: White to Chief Justice, June 14, 1972, Box 1565, WODLC.

373. *The passage was dropped:* Compare 408 U.S. at 489 n. 16.

374. *even a friendly critic:* Anthony Amsterdam, "The Void-for-Vagueness Doctrine in the Supreme Court," *University of Pennsylvania Law Review* 109: 67, 75–85, 98–115.

374. *"vague-for-voidness cases"*: Kurland, *Politics, the Constitution, and the Warren Court,* 166; see the cases at 148–49 n. 152.

374. *when he disagreed:* See, for example, *NAACP v. Button,* 371 U.S. 415, 447 (1963) (White, J., concurring and dissenting); see also *Cameron v. Johnson,* 381 U.S. 741, 753 (1965) (White, J., dissenting); *Brown v. Louisiana,* 383 U.S. 131, 150 (1966) (White, J., dissenting).

375. *"root of the vagueness"*: 407 U.S. at 110.

375. *"where conduct and not merely speech"*: 413 U.S. at 615–16.

376. *reflecting views:* Box 1562, WODLC. White was one of the votes to grant certiorari.

376. *"A number of years ago"*: John Jenkins, "A Candid Talk with Justice Blackmun," *NYT Magazine,* Feb. 20, 1983, 6.

377. *"committee to draft"*: *NYT,* May 10, 1972.

377. *"I have several"*: *RMN,* May 9, 1972.

378. *chief justice had postponed:* Memorandum, Box 78, TMLC.

378. *habitually bore witness: NYT,* Jan. 9, 1975. White routinely attended observances marking the deaths of John and Robert Kennedy. He also attended the funerals of Walter

Lippman, W. Averell Harriman, Adm. Arleigh M. Burke, and many others, as well as that of J. Edgar Hoover. He swore in former clerks who became judges or sub–cabinet officers and even presided over the swearing-in of a former student campaign worker as a federal appellate judge (Carlos Lucero, head of Adams State College Students for Kennedy in 1960, became a member of the Tenth Circuit Court of Appeals on Aug. 21, 1995.). Friends also recall his unexpected attendance at employee award luncheons (such as Andrew Mair, Department of Agriculture) and swearing-ins. "I knew him slightly at Oxford," recalled B. Lane Timmons, "but he showed up when I was sworn in as an ambassador and I was both flattered and surprised. He is one of the most loyal men I have ever known; a most unusual friendship."

378. *"with our usual product":* Chief Justice to Conference, June 6, 1972, Box 1523, WODLC.

378. *penetrating portrait:* Gerald Holland, "Is That You Up There, Johnny Blood?," *Sports Illustrated,* Sept. 2, 1963, reprinted in Jack Newcombe, ed., *The Fireside Book of Football,* 140–46.

379. *"Look at Byron": PP,* May 21, 1972.

379. *"The dark horse is White!": Chicago Tribune,* May 25, 1972.

379. *Arthur Daley: NYT,* June 8, 1972.

379. *"The subject":* June 15, 1972.

379. *Bob Collins: RMN,* July 6, 1972.

379. *San Francisco:* July 3, 1972.

379. *Jim Murray:* July 11, 1972.

379. *"White for":* July 11, 1972.

379. *"A man of":* July 11, 1972.

380. *"Sometimes Justice White":* B. Drummond Ayres, June 30, 1972.

380. *"Is he on":* Lance Liebman, "Swing Man on the Supreme Court," *NYT Magazine,* Oct. 8, 1972.

380. *"White Acts": BDC,* Aug. 8, 1972.

CHAPTER 17. OCTOBER TERM 1981

382. *"One day": NYT,* June 2, 1978. More intemperately, the Northern California journalistic magazine *Feedback* presented White with its annual "Golden Zenger Award" (a golden typewriter with an axe buried in the keys) as the "person who did the most to discredit the First Amendment" for his opinion in *Zurcher.* UPI, Nov. 6, 1978.

383. *"'Properly applied'": NYT,* June 8, 1978.

383. *"naive refusal": Newsweek,* June 12, 1978.

383. *"controversy boiled": Newsweek.* Apr. 30, 1979.

383. *"sporting, if chilly":* O'Brien interview. On the leak, see *NYT,* Apr. 17, 1979.

383. *"jock": San Francisco Chronicle,* May 23, 1979.

383. *"better as running backs":* "Your Law-Baseball Quiz," *NYT,* Apr. 5, 1979, reprinted in *Yale Law Report,* fall 1986; Martha Minow, Michael Ryan, and Austin Sarat, eds., *Narrative, Violence, and the Law: The Essays of Robert Cover,* 249–52.

383. *"White: A Justice": National Law Journal,* Feb. 18, 1980.

384. *"in the end":* On the day between oral argument and the Court's conference to decide *Bakke,* White hand-delivered a three-page, single-spaced Memorandum for the Conference that largely focused on the statutory aspects of the case but also contained the quoted remark. White to Conference, Oct. 13, 1978, Box 204, TMLC. See also Mark Tushnet, "The Supreme Court and Race Discrimination, 1967–1991: The View from the Marshall Papers," *William & Mary Law Review* 36: 473, 518–19; Bernard Schwartz, *Behind Bakke,* 59.

384. *fully documented:* See Bernard Schwartz, *The Unpublished Opinions of the Burger Court; Behind Bakke: Affirmative Action and the Supreme Court; The Road to Swann: The School Busing Case and the Supreme Court; The Unpublished Opinions of the Warren Court.*

384. *"The Supreme Court term":* NYT, July 12, 1980.

385. *"the first of his colleagues":* National Law Journal, July 14, 1980.

385. *authors claimed:* WP, Dec. 9, 1979.

386. *Woodward claimed:* J. Anthony Lukas, "Interview: Bob Woodward," *Playboy,* Feb. 1989. See also Adrian Havill, *Deep Truth,* 128–35 (cited below as "Havill").

386. *Powell, who admitted:* John C. Jeffries, Jr., *Justice Lewis F. Powell, Jr.,* 390.

386. *Cooke, was canceled:* Havill, 136–50.

386. *Anthony Lewis even argued:* NYT, Apr. 19, 1981.

386. *Burger had discussed:* See WP, Dec. 12, 1981; compare John Erlichman, *Witness to Power,* 133.

386. *Frankfurter's indiscretions:* Philip Elman interviewed by Norman Silber, "The Solicitor General's Office, Justice Frankfurter, and Civil Rights Litigation, 1946–1960: An Oral History," *HLR* 100 (1987): 817.

386. *Fortas's revelations:* See Alexander Charns, *Cloak and Gavel: FBI Wiretaps, Bugs, Informers, and the Supreme Court,* ch. 4, 6–7; Athan Theoharis, ed., *From the Secret Files of J. Edgar Hoover,* 268–75.

386. *less than a decade old:* When Thurgood Marshall's papers were opened at his death, in 1993, less than two years after his retirement, even defenders of the new access were hard pressed to support disclosure of information that cast light—even for a short period of time—on pending issues if not pending cases. Nonetheless, no justice who had deposited working papers in archives withdrew them; the compromise was to restrict or prevent access for a period of ten years after the donor's death or retirement, and Justice White and Sandra Day O'Connor both did. See generally Dennis J. Hutchinson, "The Papers of Thurgood Marshall," *Appellate Law Review* 6 (1994).

387. *"so Delphic":* NYT, Aug. 10, 1981.

387. *"maybe":* WP, Dec. 5, 1982.

387. *"several of us":* WP, Aug. 10, 1981.

387. *"in the very near future":* William H., Rehnquist, *The Supreme Court: How It Was, How It Is,* 301.

389. *sovereign immunity: Florida Department of State v. Treasure Salvors,* 458 U.S. 670, 703 n. (1982) (concurring and dissenting).

389. *federal criminal law: Williams v. U.S.,* 458 U.S. 279, 291 (1982) (dissenting).

389. *retroactivity: U.S. v. Johnson,* 457 U.S. 537, 564 (1982) (dissenting).

389. *labor union: United Steelworkers of America v. Sadlowksi,* 457 U.S. 102, 121 (1982) (dissent).

389. *"excellent and persuasive":* Brennan to White, May 25, 1982, Box 597, WJBLC.

389. *regulation of charitable: Larson v. Valente,* 456 U.S. 228, 258 (1982) (dissenting).

389. *use, or misuse: Florida Department of State v. Treasure Salvors; U.S. v. Johnson; United Steelworkers of America v. Sadlowksi; Tibbs v. Florida.*

389. *factual predicate: Larson v. Valente,* 456 U.S. at 260.

389. *for the second time: U.S. v. Nixon,* 418 U.S. 683 (1974). The opinion was issued under the name of the chief justice but was a committee product; White wrote the section that treated the standard under Rule 17(c) of the Federal Rules of Criminal Procedure for securing a court order (subpoena duces tecum) to obtain evidence before trial. See 418 U.S. at 697–702; Woodward and Armstrong, 314ff.

389. *"I would not overrule":* 456 U.S. at 826–27.

390. *abrupt dissenting statement:* He would repeat the terse performance a few years later in the second of the "victim impact statement" cases, *South Carolina v. Gathers,* 490 U.S. 805, 812 (1989) (concurring), in which he refused to cast the deciding vote to overrule *Booth v. Maryland,* 482 U.S. 496, 515 (1987) (dissenting), which was only two years old at the time. *Booth* held in 1987 that testimony from surviving relatives of victims of capital crimes could not constitutionally be used in evidence when a jury was deciding between death and lesser sentences; White dissented. In *Gathers* in 1989, four members of the Court refused to apply *Booth* in similar but not identical circumstances. White refused to be the fifth vote to uphold the death sentence: he wrote that unless the four were willing to overrule *Booth* outright, he would not join in what he apparently viewed as a rear-guard attack on the precedent. In 1991, a majority of the Court—White included—was finally willing to take the step. *Payne v. Tennessee,* 501 U.S. 808.

391. *"right to read":* WP, March 3, 1982.

391. *"dangerous case":* Conference Notes, Box 574, WJBLC.

392. *"As your draft":* White to Brennan, May 10, 1982, ibid.

393. *"really that far":* Brennan to White, May 19, 1982, ibid.

393. *final two paragraphs:* See 457 U.S. at 870–72.

393. *"We should":* Compare 457 U.S. at 884.

393. *The* Wall Street Journal: Sept. 13, 1982.

394. *"11 years":* Powell to Brennan, June 22, 1982, Box 594, WJBLC.

394. *"wholly ignored":* Conference Notes, Box 574, WJBLC.

394. *"deterring National Geographic"* Undated note, Box 574, WJBLC.

394. *"stronger and more":* Stevens to White, June 4, 1982, Box 597, WJBLC.

394. *"right both on":* Brennan to Marshall, Blackmun, Stevens, June 4, 1982, ibid.

394. *"since 1919":* Frederick Schauer, "Codifying the First Amendment: New York v. Ferber," SCR (1982): 285.

395. *"relatively little practical":* NYT, July 9, 1982.

396. *"gutted":* Dan Fischel, "From MITE to CTS: State Anti-Takeover Statutes, the Williams Act, the Commerce Clause, and Insider Trading," SCR (1987): 47, 92.

396. *"advent and triumph":* Bowsher v. Synar, 478 U.S. 714, 761 (1986) (dissenting).

396. *"this worrisome case":* Powell to Chief Justice, Feb. 25, 1982, Mar. 9, 1982, Box 604, WJBLC.

396. *the vote in March:* Box 571, WJBLC.

396. *letter to Burger:* Blackmun to Chief Justice, June 25, 1982, Box 283, TMLC.

397. *"rare moments":* NYT, June 24, 1983.

398. *"vigilant oversight":* NYT, June 30, 1983 (op-ed).

398. *"remitted":* Choper, *Judicial Review and the National Political Process,* 263.

398. *"formalistic":* Donald Elliott, "INS v. Chadha: The Administrative Constitution, the Constitution, and the Legislative Veto," SCR (1983): 125, 135–36, 176.

398. *"Byron has":* Chief Justice to Brennan, Marshall, Blackmun, Powell, Stevens, O'Connor, May 27, 1983, Box 611, WJBLC.

398. *"There was a more":* Currie, 592–93.

398. *"how the underlying":* Allan Ides, "The Jurisprudence of Justice Byron White," YLJ 103: 425.

398. *"intellectual appeal":* Ibid., 426.

398. "White's appraisal": Ibid.; see Burger, 462 U.S. at 923–28.

398. *Congress produced:* Louis Fisher, "One Year after *INS v. Chadha:* Congressional and Judicial Developments" (Congressional Research Service, Government Division, June 23, 1984).

399. *"inconsequential":* Jessica Korn, *The Power of Separation,* 13.

400. *"Perhaps, as I have said":* 454 U.S. at 311.

400. *again and again:* See, for example, *First National Bank v. Bellotti,* 435 U.S. 765, 802 (1978) (dissenting); *Federal Election Commission v. National Conservative Political Action Committee,* 470 U.S. 480, 507 (1985) (dissenting).

400. *"persuaded":* O'Connor to White, Mar. 1, 1982, Box 283, TMLC. See also John Paul Stevens, "Justice Byron White," *BYULR* (1994): 209, 217.

400. *routine basis:* The first dissent from denial was in *Coates v. SEC,* 394 U.S. 976 (1969).

400. *Michael J. Broyde:* "The Inter Circuit Tribunal and Perceived Conflicts: An Analysis of Justice White's Dissents from Denial of Certiorari During the 1985 Term," *New York University Law Review* 62 (1987): 610.

400. *Arthur Hellman:* "By Precedent Unbound: The Nature and Extent of Unresolved Intercircuit Conflicts," *University of Pittsburgh Law Review* 56 (1995): 693.

401. *strong views:* See *NYT,* Sept. 14, 1982; *Criminal Justice Newsletter,* Sept. 27, 1982.

401. *David M. O'Brien:* "incredibly shrinking" plenary docket: "The Rehnquist Court's shrinking plenary docket," *Judicature* 81: 58 (1997).

401. *good faith exception:* White's dissent in *Stone v. Powell,* 428 U.S. 465, 538 (1976), was the first opinion to advocate "good faith" exception to the rule requiring unlawfully seized evidence from being admitted in criminal trials, although Justices Powell and Rehnquist had privately floated the idea in other conference deliberations during the same term. The lengthy trail from the 1976 cases to *Leon* and *Massachusetts v. Sheppard,* 461 U.S. 981 (1984), is traced carefully by Ross E. Davies, "*Mapp* and Good Faith" (seminar paper, University of Chicago Law School, 1997). On the doctrine, see Albert W. Alschuler, " 'Close Enough for Government Work': The Exclusionary Rule After Leon," (1984): *SCR* 309.

402. *one-sentence rumor: U.S. News & World Report,* Apr. 19, 1982.

402. *The press noted: NYT,* Mar. 22, 1982.

402. *"Fresh disclosures": U.S. News & World Report,* May 28, 1979.

403. *"government bonds":* Ibid.

403. *"most vivid example":* Fred Graham, *Happy Talk!,* 112 (cited below as "Graham").

403. *"Filth! Pornography!"* Ibid., 113.

403. *"liberate": Salt Lake City Tribune,* July 16, 1982 (photo, B11).

403. *Estes was actually subdued:* UPI, Sept. 14, 1982.

404. *"hit harder":* Graham, 114. The allusion was to the 1937 Colorado-Utah football game. See Chapter 3 above and Robert Leede Davis, "And He Can Take a Hit Too: Justice White's Utah Connection," (1994): *BYULR* 363.

404. *"droned through":* Graham, 114.

404. *"fullest extent": NYT,* Aug. 8, 1982.

404. *"extremely rude":* UPI, Sept. 14, 1982.

404. *"filth": Salt Lake City Tribune,* July 16, 1982.

404. *"ridiculous":* AP, Dec. 11, 1982.

404. *"direct action"* / Capricorn I: *Salt Lake City Tribune,* July 16, 1982.

404. *stray bullet struck:* Graham, 116–17.

404. *requested chauffeured automobiles:* UPI, Mar. 13, 1985.

405. *he pleaded:* UPI, Aug. 15, 1988.

405. *unsuccessful lawsuits: Estes v. Namba,* 74 F. 3d 1249 (CA 10, 1996); *Estes v. Warden,* 13 F. 3d 405 (1993); *Estes v. Warden,* 955 F. 2d 49 (1992). In all three cases, the district

court denied relief and the court of appeals affirmed without oral argument under Rule 34(a), Federal Rules of Appellate Procedure and 10th Circuit Rule 34.1.9.

405. *"Even in his feuds"*: McCloskey, in Leon Friedman and Jerold Israel, eds., *The Justices of the United States Supreme Court*, vol. 2, 2d ed., 545.

405. *series of denied certiorari petitions: Estes v. Namba,* 116 S. Ct. 1438 (1996); *Estes v. Van Der Veur,* 511 U.S. 1021 (1994); *Estes v. McCotter,* 506 U.S. 1063 (1993); *In Re Newton C. Estes,* 506 U.S. 812 (1992) (habeas corpus); *In Re Newton C. Estes,* 502 U.S. 1003 (1991); *Estes v. U.S.,* 471 U.S. 1044 (1985). The cases were so transparently frivolous that White recused himself only in the 1985 petition.

405. *ran stories:* Mar. 5, 1995.

406. *"John, old friend"*: Nov. 24, 1985, Library, National Football Hall of Fame.

CHAPTER 18. OCTOBER TERM 1991

407. *"the big news"*: Federal News Service, July 18, 1991 (cited below as "FNS-1991").

408. *his old high school: Wellington News,* Aug. 19, 1984, courtesy of Andrew Mair.

408. *"robust and still playing": LTW,* Apr. 20, 1987.

408. *"was reported"*: UPI, July 24, 1987.

408. *"leave the high court": NLJ,* July 4, 1988.

409. *only eleven justices:* By the time White retired in 1993, he was number ten on the list. Those serving longer were Douglas, Stephen J. Field, John Marshall, Hugo Black, John Marshall Harlan I, Joseph Story, William J. Brennan, James M. Wayne, and John McLean. McLean served a year longer than White, Douglas five years and five months longer.

409. *he kept for himself:* See Assignment Sheets, Box 513, TMLC.

409. *"The issue / anything new"*: FNS-1991.

411. *"he had said more": LTW,* Apr. 8, 1991.

411. *last paragraph of Part II:* See 499 U.S. at 287–88.

411. *Scalia's price:* Scalia to White, Jan. 17, 1991, Box 528, TMLC.

411. *"As I indicated"*: O'Connor to White, Nov. 29, 1990, Box 528, TMLC.

411. *joined that portion:* Scalia to Chief Justice, Jan. 7, 1991, Box 528, TMLC.

411. *"like Nino"*: O'Connor to Chief Justice, Jan. 9, 1991, Box 528, TMLC.

411. *"preferred to vote quickly"*: Jeffrey Rosen, "The Next Justice: How Not to Replace Byron White," *TNR,* Apr. 12, 1993.

412. *"bitterest legacy": NYT,* June 7, 1988.

413. *"Is it possible": DP,* May 18, 1988.

413. *"He scowls": LTW,* July 3, 1989.

413. *in 1988: L.A. Daily Journal,* July 5, 1988.

413. *end of the 1990 term:* Ibid., Sept. 24, 1991.

414. 40 Patriots: *Washington Times,* Nov. 13, 1991.

414. *"Metaphor is my business": WP,* Oct. 19, 1992.

414. *"it wouldn't be strange"*: FNS-1991.

415. *"This is Your Life"*: William F. Buckley, syndicated column, Nov. 19, 1991.

415. *"He's up against": WP,* Sept. 16, 1987.

415. *"What would you think": WP,* Sept. 23, 1987.

415. *"informal": Chicago Tribune,* Sept. 23, 1987.

415. *"unusual step": Congressional Record* 133: S14006 (Sept. 25, 1987, remarks of Senator McClure).

415. *"endorsement": Congressional Record* 133: S14169 (Oct. 13, 1987, remarks of Senator Armstrong).

416. *"majority":* Chief Justice to T. B. Dyk, Sept. 26, 1991, Box 525, TMLC.

416. *"I refused":* Blackmun to Chief Justice, Sept. 19, 1991, Box 525, TMLC.

416. *"one of the most"* / *"The Swearing-in":* UPI, Oct. 18, 1991.

416. *White announced: LTW,* Aug. 29, 1994.

417. *without even notifying: LTW,* Oct. 28, 1991.

417. *"with unseemly haste": Ibid.*

417. *"great repose": Ibid.*

417. *"The case has drawn": WP,* Dec. 12, 1991.

418. *ancien régime: Franklin,* 503 U.S. at 60.

419. *Report Card:* See, for example, Memorandum of the Chief Justice, June 19, 1991, Box 525, TMLC.

419. *"impatient, almost scolding": NYT,* Feb. 27, 1992.

420. *"nonpublic forum" analysis:* White's opinion for the Court in *Perry* created, over four dissents, a substantial qualification on the pre–World War II doctrine that "public places" (streets, sidewalks, parks, and so on) were largely immune from state regulation of the content of speech. White concluded that a school board could grant a recognized union access to the school district's internal mail system while excluding a contending union. He relied on prior case law that set different standards for regulating speech at nontraditional sites for debate, such as mailboxes or military bases. The case was an important doctrinal step and could have served as the basis in *Burson v. Freeman* for upholding regulations at polling places, which have not traditionally been sites of public debates. Justice Blackmun ignored the reasoning of *Perry,* although he cited the decision in the course of a rambling opinion that featured a largely irrelevant history of the Australian ballot.

421. *"differentiated between": Atlanta Journal & Constitution,* Nov. 7, 1991.

421. *"I've always said":* Aug. 5, 1993, Colorado Springs, Colo., broadcast on C-SPAN.

421. *"You may hold": LTW,* Aug. 29, 1994.

422. *"I remain convinced":* 472 U.S. at 767.

422. *Sofaer's handling:* See *Sharon v. Time, Inc.,* 599 F. Supp. 538 (1984).

423. *"My understanding":* 480 U.S. at 657.

423. *anxieties he had when* Bakke *arose:* White to Conference, Oct. 13, 1978, Box 204, TMLC. See Chapter 17.

424. *"strongly suggest[ed]": LTW,* March 22, 1993.

425. *but the case was settled:* The case was *NOPSI v. Council of the City of New Orleans,* cert. dismissed under Rule 46, 502 U.S. 954 (1991).

425. *worst Sartorial Strategy: LTW,* Dec. 28, 1992. White is wearing the same tie in the photos accompanying "Perspectives on White: A Roundtable," *ABA Journal,* Oct. 1993: 68, 70, 72, 73.

425. *"The fact is that the Court functions":* Jackson, *The Supreme Court in the American System of Government,* 16.

426. *White's assets: Chicago Daily Law Bulletin,* May 18, 1992.

427. *her mother's estate:* UPI, May 15, 1986.

427. "A great day" / "A positive": *Jet,* July 13, 1992.

428. *He asked only two questions:* Leon Friedman, ed., *The Supreme Court Confronts Abortion,* 336.

429. *"The distance between":* 505 U.S. at 943.

430. *"sharply worded separate opinion":* Akhil Amar, "The Case of the Missing Amendments: *R.A.V. v. City of St. Paul,"* HLR 106 (1992): 124, 129.

430. *"untried"*: Ibid., 129 n. 37.

430. *"the White Four"*: Ibid., 147–48, quoting White at 505 U.S. at 402.

431. *majority in eight:* Not five as the annual *Harvard Law Review* chart declares, *HLR* 106 (1992): 380.

431. *"Of great concern"*: *Washington Times,* June 30, 1992.

CHAPTER 19. "THE END OF THE RIDE"

433. *governor boasts:* States News Service, June 3, 1996.

433. *"Now I am too old"*: Norman Maclean, *A River Runs Through It and Other Stories,* 104.

433. *"haunted by waters"*: Ibid.

434. *"I haven't had"*: *NYT,* Mar. 22, 1982.

434. *"reached an extraordinary"*: John C. Jeffries Jr., *Justice Lewis F. Powell, Jr.,* 417 (cited below as "Jeffries"). Compare Bob Woodward and Scot Armstrong, *The Brethren,* 435.

435. *"decision to cut Douglas"*: Woodward and Armstrong, 445.

435. *William J. Brennan Papers:* According to Stephen J. Wermeil, Justice Brennan's authorized biographer, the memo from White is contained in Brennan's Personal Correspondence, which is not yet housed in the Library of Congress and which will be closed for twenty years even after it has been received and processed by the Library. Wermeil interview.

435. *"Powell followed the lead"*: Jeffries, 417.

437. *picked up a letter: LTW,* Apr. 12, 1993.

437. *White had contacted Klain: NYT,* Mar. 20, 1993.

437. *"that he intends"*: *Public Papers of the President, Weekly Compilation of Presidential Documents,* March 19, 1993, 454.

437. *"He has had"*: UPI, March 19, 1993.

437. *"Byron White, a year ago"*: Cable News Network (CNN) Text Transcript 662-2, Apr. 6, 1994.

438. *: "I have today"*: Reuter Transcript Report, March 19, 1993. White was the first justice ever to relinquish office space in the Supreme Court building simultaneously with taking retirement. At the time he retired, three former members of the Court retained chambers in the building—Chief Justice Warren E. Burger, William J. Brennan, and Lewis F. Powell, Jr.

438. *"many of the statements"* / *"feeling of personal loss"*: UPI, Mar. 19, 1993.

438. *Family photographs:* Pamela A. Stewart, ed., *The Whites: Soldiers to Statesmen,* 51.

439. *"You'll understand"*: *USA Today,* Apr. 27, 1993.

439. *"Since I remain"*: 114 S. Ct. CXIV (1993).

439. *"Minutes later"*: *LTW,* July 5, 1993.

440. *"The public ought"*: Aug. 5, 1993, Colorado Springs, Colo., broadcast on C-SPAN. White expressed similar views in 1986 to Phillip Cooper and Howard Ball of the University of Vermont. Multiple opinions with no majority, as in *Regents of the University of California v. Bakke,* 438 U.S. 265 (1978), leave "it up to the lawyers to interpret the opinions. I always thought that wasn't a bad way to do things. So I've never been upset by plurality opinions." And legal changes from a "fragmented Court" come "in small increments rather than in big steps." Cooper and Ball, *The United States Supreme Court,* 225.

440. *"old-fashioned liberal"*: Mar. 22, 1993.

440. *"was one of the more remarkable"*: Mar. 20, 1993. The tendentious coverage of White's career and retirement was criticized by Terry Eastland, "Presswatch: In Contempt," *American Spectator,* June 1993.

441. *leading authority: Antitrust: Broadcast Music v. Columbia Broadcasting,* 441 U.S. 1 (1979), is a sophisticated analysis of markets and price controls, rated by most experts as one of the most important antitrust decisions in a generation. *Albrecht v. The Herald Co.,* 390 U.S. 145 (1968), is such an analytically wooden treatment of resale price maintenance that antitrust scholars wonder even more at the later achievement of *Broadcast Music.* White also wrote important opinions for the Court defining the scope of relief available in private antitrust suits, both with respect to damages available (*Hanover Shoe v. United Shoe Machinery,* 392 U.S. 481 [1968]) and parties who could successfully sue (*Illinois Brick v. Illinois,* 431 U.S. 720 [1977]). See generally James T. Malysiak, "Justice White on Antitrust: Protecting Freedom to Compete," *UCOLR* 58 (1987): 497.

Labor: Vaca v. Sipes, 386 U.S. 171 (1967), is fundamental to defining a union's responsibilities in the bargaining process. *United Mine Workers v. Pennington,* 381 U.S. 657 (1965), forms half of the Noerr-Pennington doctrine. See Dan Fischel, "Antitrust Liability for Attempts to Influence Government Action: The Basis and Limits of the Noerr-Pennington Doctrine," *UCHILR* 45 (1977): 80. White also wrote major opinions in almost every area of labor law.

441. *modified by Congress:* Attorneys Fees Civil Rights Act of 1976 (P. L. 94-559, 90 Stat. 2641 [1976]), P. L. 96-440 (94 Stat. 1879 [1980]), Civil Rights Restoration Act of 1987 (P. L. 100-259, 102 Stat. 28 [1987]), Civil Rights Act of 1991 (P. L. 102-166, 105 Stat. 1071).

441. *"unleashed a string"*: Jeffrey Rosen, "The Next Justice: How Not to Replace Byron White," *TNR,* Apr. 12, 1993.

441. *"I agree with the conclusion"*: Quoting *Pennsylvania v. Union Gas,* 491 U.S. 26, 45 (White, J., concurring in the judgment in part and dissenting in part). White's statement in *Union Gas* was later called the "most unsettling phenomenon" in the 1988 term. John M. Rogers, "'I Vote This Way Because I'm Wrong': The Supreme Court Justice As Epimenides," *Kentucky Law Journal* 79 (1990–91): 439.

442. *"topsy-turvy world"*: Glendon, "Partial Justice: Jurisprudence on the Supreme Court," *Commentary,* Aug. 1994; see also Glendon, *A Nation Under Lawyers,* 170–73.

442. *"mainstream media"*: Casey, "Pope John XXIII Lecture (Sept. 30, 1994)," *Catholic University Law Review* 44 (1995): 821, 832.

443. *"We'll bid adieu": Nation,* Apr. 12, 1993.

CHAPTER 20. SERVICE AS LEGACY

444. *"conservative"*: ABC Transcript 3056, Mar. 19, 1993.

444. *"perfect cipher"*: Jeffrey Rosen, "The Next Justice: How Not to Replace Byron White," *TNR,* Apr. 12, 1993 (cited below as "Rosen").

444. *"nominated Byron White": Christian Science Monitor,* Oct. 29, 1996; compare Charles Roos, *RMN,* Mar. 31, 1996.

445. *"conservative drift"*: John C. Jeffries, Jr., *Justice Lewis F. Powell, Jr.,* 541.

445. *"The thumbnail sketch": LTW,* Mar. 22, 1993.

445. *William Nelson:* See "Byron White: A Liberal of 1960," in Mark Tushnet, ed., *The Warren Court in Historical and Political Perspective;* "Justice Byron R. White: A Modern Federalist and a New Deal Liberal," *BYULR* (1994): 313.

445. *Kate Stith:* "Byron White, Last of the New Deal Liberals," *YLJ* 103: 19, adapted from Leonard W. Levy, ed., *Encyclopedia of the American Constitution* (Supp. I 1992).

445. *"Civil rights":* *NYT,* Mar. 20, 1993. Similarly, Scot Armstrong stated: "More than any other justice we looked at [he and Bob Woodward, for *The Brethren*], his positions and values changed the least from the time he came to the time he left." Gannett News Service, Mar. 19, 1993.

445. *law journals probed:* See, for example, the essays of Judge Oberdorfer, Kenneth Starr, and Kate Stith in *YLJ* 103, no. 1 (1993).

446. *"interstitial":* "I recognize without hesitation that judges do and must legislate, but they can do so only interstitially; they are confined from molar to molecular motions." *Southern Pacific v. Jensen,* 244 U.S. 205, 221 (1921) (Holmes, J., dissenting).

446. *"fact-intensive":* Ides, "Realism, Rationality and Justice Byron White: Three Easy Cases," *BYULR* (1994): 283, 285, 289, discussing *San Antonio Independent School District v. Rodriguez,* 411 U.S. 1, 63 (1973) (dissenting); *New York Transit Authority v. Beezer,* 440 U.S. 568, 597 (1979) (dissenting); *Cleburne v. Cleburne Living Center,* 473 U.S. 432 (1985).

446. *"rule skepticism":* Jerome Frank, *Law and the Modern Mind* and *Courts on Trial.* See also Karl Llewellyn, "Some Realism About Realism—Responding to Dean Pound," *HLR* 44 (1931): 1222, 1239; but see Twining, *Karl Llewellyn and the Realist Movement,* 32, 408 nn. 19–22. For a sustained study of American legal realism that clarifies the lack of unity in the "movement," see Neil Duxbury, *Patterns of American Jurisprudence,* ch. 2.

446. *"I think the most":* *Newsday,* Mar. 20, 1993.

446. *New Deal:* See generally Alan Brinkley, *The End of Reform;* William E. Leuchtenburg, *In the Shadow of FDR* and *The Supreme Court Reborn.*

447. *"This is a very small":* 114 S. Ct. CXIV (1993).

447. *Harry Blackmun:* Correspondence Respecting the Retirement of Harry Blackmun, 114 S. Ct. 746, 747 (June 22, 1994).

447. *"Justice White does* not*":* Teri Grove to June Clark, Aug. 26, 1987, University of Colorado Foundation, Inc., University of Colorado Public Relations Files.

447. *"call him Whizzer":* *NYT,* July 25, 1988 (Eighth Circuit conference, St. Louis, Mo.).

447. *"we should discontinue":* *RMN,* May 27, 1961.

447. *"perhaps because":* Lee, "On Greatness and Constitutional Vision: Justice Byron R. White," *BYULR* (1994): 291, 296 n. 24.

448. *"Geez, don't call me that":* That is not to say that White did not enjoy hosting old teammates in Washington. Ned Mathews, another teammate with the Lions, found White unexpectedly generous when he telephoned the justice's chambers early one morning on a day when the Court was sitting: "He told us to come right over and he gave us a complete tour—in his robe—before Court started." Art Rooney told a similar story: "The first time we visited Washington after White's appointment to the Supreme Court I was a little hesitant about telephoning because it's a big job and I knew he was busy. But I went ahead and called and he was delighted and spent the entire day with us. I'll tell you another thing. After two minutes he was talking the old lingo like the rest of us." *Baltimore Sun,* June 26, 1971.

448. *at least until he retired:* He never attended the annual National Football League Players Association banquet, at which the Whizzer White Humanitarian Award is presented, even when his former next-door neighbor in suburban Virginia, Nick Lowery—the all-time NFL field-goal-kicking champion—won, in 1993. Apparently White was concerned that the banquet, which raised money for the Better Boys Foundation (now the Better Families Foundation) could be construed as unethical fund-raising. The banquet was

also held in late June, at the end of term, the worst time of the year for White to be absent from Washington, for both substantive and public relations reasons.

448. *"You have 60 seconds"*: *DP,* Aug. 1, 1995.

448. *"I would have chosen"*: Bob Curran, *Pro Football's Rag Days,* 183; *Pittsburgh Post-Gazette,* Feb. 3, 1969; see also Wright, 90.

449. *"few persons"*: *DP,* June 27, 1967.

449. *priced at up to $150:* Catalog, Larry Fritsch Cards, Inc. (Stevens Point, Wis.), Christmas 1997, 58.

449. *"He was anathema"*: *Boston Globe,* Mar. 20, 1993.

449. *"There appears"*: Kempton, "Thoughts Astray: Code Duello," *National Review,* June 8, 1979, 754 (cited below as "Kempton"); Kempton repeated the thought, more briefly, in *Newsday,* Nov. 21, 1991.

449. *"welcomed"*: Kempton, 756.

450. *inconvenient case:* The Court extended *Cox v. Cohn* to protect publication of a rape victim's name obtained by a reporter who was properly in a police station but who recorded and printed the name in violation of posted police regulations and state law in *Florida Star v. B. J. F.,* 491 U.S. 524 (1989). White dissented, ibid. at 542, and discussed his views on privacy in some detail, ibid. at 550f. He recorded his regret for the Court descent from *Time v. Hill,* 385 U.S. 374, 383-84 n. 7 (1967), through *Cox v. Cohn* to *Florida Star*—"the bottom of the slippery slope" (491 U.S. at 553). "I would find a place to draw the line higher on the hillside: a spot high enough to protect [the victim's] desire for privacy and peace-of-mind in the wake of a horrible personal tragedy."

450. *"selfish[ly]"*: Panel Discussion, Eighth Circuit judicial conference, Aug. 5, 1993, Colorado Springs, Colo., broadcast on C-SPAN, quoted by Tony Mauro, *LTW,* Sept. 6, 1993: "I am very pleased to walk around and very seldom am I recognized. It's very selfish, I know."

450. *"There are still things"*: *DP,* July 31, 1979.

451. *"professors"*: See Chapter 10. Kennedy Administration U.S. Attorneys Reunion, Nov. 18, 1994.

451. *"To the distress"*: *YLJ* 103: 19 n. 1, citing *Pennsylvania v. Union Gas,* 491 U.S. 1, 45 (1989) (concurring in part and dissenting in part); *South Carolina v. Gathers,* 490 U.S. 805, 812 (1989) (concurring); *Teague v. Lane,* 489 U.S. 288, 316 (1989) (concurring in part and dissenting in part); *U.S. v. Paradise,* 480 U.S. 149, 196 (1987) (dissenting).

451. *flooded the law reviews:* See Earl M. Maltz, "The Prospects for a Revival of Conservative Activism in Constitutional Jurisprudence," *Georgia Law Review* 24 (1995): 629, 645 n. 95, and works cited there, but as Judge Posner notes, almost all confine themselves to legal-doctrinal analysis. Posner, *Sex and Reason,* 347 n. 55. Michael Hardwick's first-person story of his case is in Peter Irons, *The Courage of Their Convictions,* 392–403.

451. *"vituperatively homophobic"*: David Garrow, *Nation* (book review), Feb. 27, 1995.

452. *sent a memo:* Brennan to Conference, Oct. 23, 1985, Box 714, WJBLC.

452. *November 4, 1985:* Certiorari granted, 474 U.S. 943.

452. *switched his vote:* Powell to Conference, Apr. 8, 1986, Box 714, WJBLC.

453. *next day, April 21:* White to Conference, Apr. 21, 1986, ibid.

453. *"Nor are we inclined"*: 478 U.S. at 194.

454. *famous for their reading lists:* Sheldon M. Novick, *Honorable Justice: The Life of Oliver Wendell Holmes;* Liva Baker, *The Justice from Beacon Hill: The Life and Times of Oliver Wendell Holmes;* but see Richard A. Posner, ed., *The Essential Holmes,* Introduction; Daniel J. Meador, *Mr. Justice Black and His Books.*

454. *"I get rather satiated"*: *RMN,* May 5, 1968. Years later, he would also claim, unconvincingly, "I never read stories about the Supreme Court. Why inflict more pain on myself than I already have?" *LTW,* June 29, 1987. He nonetheless was willing to pay for his own subscriptions to the *American Lawyer,* the *National Law Journal,* and the *Legal Times of Washington* when Chief Justice Burger raised the question of canceling personal subscriptions to the journals for each member of the Court. White to Roger Jacobs, Librarian (Copies to the Conference), June 30, 1980, Box 242, TMLC.

454. *only recorded fan letter: Boston Globe,* Sept. 26, 1991.

454. *Tulagi:* Fahey described traversing the Slot, in which White and John F. Kennedy both saw action, as "like going up an alley at night in tough sections of any big city. You have to be on your guard at all times." *Pacific War Diary,* 37. Fahey, whose book sold 120,000 copies in hardback and 200,000 softbound copies, donated all of his royalties to a missionary priest so that a Roman Catholic church could be built in a south India village.

455. *"Byron White: not a household name":* Mar. 28, 1993.

455. *"banalization of Holmes":* Rosen.

455. *Byron R. White Courthouse:* Some of the proceedings at the dedication, on Aug. 10, 1994, are published in *UCOLR* 66 (1995): 2, 5 (remarks of Justice Ruth Bader Ginsburg, David M. Ebel). White's modesty extended to ceremonial acedemic honors: after accepting an honorary doctorate from the University of Colorado in 1963, White adopted Justice Brandeis's practice and declined further honorary degrees. See Barrett McGurn, *America's Court,* 107.

455. *flattering portrait:* The artist was Frank Tauriello. Other formal portraits of White are exhibited in the Yale Law School Library, the Byron Rogers Federal Building in Denver, and the Supreme Court of the United States. The portrait at Yale was painted in 1969 by Gardner Cox and presented the following year "by Justice White's Law School Classmates and Department of Justice Colleagues." Box 11, Oberdorfer Papers. A black-and-white rendition appears in Bernice Loss, *Lawyers Painted by Gardner Cox,* 41. A 1964 portrait of Justice Potter Stewart, White's contemporary at Yale Law School, also hangs there (Loss, 37). The official portrait for the collection of the Supreme Court, subscribed by White's former law clerks, was painted by Chris Owen and presented to the Court in Nov. 1995. A black-and-white photograph of the portrait appears in *Yale Law Report,* Spring 1996, 33. Ms. Owen also painted the portrait in the Rogers Building, which was subscribed by the American, Colorado, and Denver Bar Associations, and presented in conjunction with the annual midwinter meetings of the ABA in Denver on Feb. 5, 1989.

455. *"Retired Justice Byron White":* WP, Jan. 23, 1997.

456. *"questions about legal matters":* RMN, Feb. 8, 1994.

457. *oil painting.* The painting, which is signed *S. Huertas,* can be seen in the photograph of White on page 72 of October 1993 issue of the *American Bar Association Journal.* White also owns a painting of a snowy mountain peak signed by the same artist. When asked from which gallery he obtained the works, he told more than one visitor, *Oh, just at a Starving Artists sale in San Francisco.*

SOURCES

Interviews and Correspondence

T *denotes telephone interview;* L *denotes letter;* TL *denotes both.*

Frank Altmar *T,* Gene Amole *L,* James A. Anderson III *L,* Richard Barkley, Paul Barrett *L,* Samuel A. Baugh *T,* John V. Bernard, Boris Bitker *T,* Dr. Wallace S. Brooke *L,* Judge Gerald Brown, Matthew J. Bruccoli *L,* Hugh A. Burns, Lloyd R. Cardwell *T,* E. Calvert Cheston, J. Hector Currie Jr. *L,* Richard W. Cutler *L,* Horace Davenport *L,* Ray Didinger *T,* John Doar, Joe Dolan, Evelyn Schmidt Ely, Myer Feldman, Larry Flanders, Fred Folsom, John P. Frank *L,* Anthony Furst *T,* William A. Geoghegan, Fred Gehrke *T,* Linda Greenhouse *L,* Erwin Griswold *L,* Chuck B. Hanneman *T,* Robert Harry, Frank Harraway, Chauncey Harris, Louis J. Hector *L,* Charles Jelinek, Philip M. Kaiser, John L. Kane, Tom Killefer *T,* Penn T. Kimball *T,* Robert T. Kingsley *L,* Rex Lee, Lou Liley, Andy Mair, Burke Marshall, Ned Mathews *T,* Wesley McCune, William S. McEwan *T,* Judge Robert H. McWilliams, Herbert J. Miller, Diane Montgomery, John Morton *T,* Ray Moses, R. M. Muir *L,* James K. Nance, John L. Noppenberg, O. T. Nuttall, Tim O'Brien *T,* Judge Louis Oberdorfer, Ed Pelz *TL,* Nicholas R. Petry, Shirley Povich *TL,* Mrs. Margaret Pryce, Edward Pringle *T,* Bill Radovich *T,* Patty Nash Ris, Ira Rothgerber, Jack D. Samuels *T,* Richard Schmidt, Arthur M. Schlesinger Jr. *TL,* Gerald Scofield *T,* Howard K. Smith *L,* Carl Solberg *L,* Theodore C. Sorensen, Carl Stern *L,* Luther Stringham *TL,* Leonard vB. Sutton *T,* Frank Taplin, Clarence L. Thompson *T,* Donald Thurman, B. Lane Timmons *T,* Nina Tottenberg *T,* John Tripson *T,* Alan Tu *T,* Robert F. Tyler *L,* Art Unger, Stephen J. Wermiel *T,* Dr. Clayton S. White, Wayne E. and Bernice White, Marshall Wolfe, Roger Wollenberg, Kenneth York.

All interviews were conducted between May 30, 1993, and August 31, 1997. In addition to the persons listed, others were interviewed but preferred not to be identified. More than fifty former clerks of Justice White were interviewed, including at least two clerks from each of the three focal terms discussed in Part IV; approximately a dozen former clerks of others justices were also interviewed.

Oral Histories

Bancroft Library, University of California, Berkeley. Alfonso J. Zirpoli (1982–83), published as *Faith in Justice: Alfonso J. Zirpoli and the United States District Court for the Northern District of California* (Berkeley: University of California, 1984).

John F. Kennedy Library, Boston. Major Sources: Ramsey Clark (1970), Joseph F. Dolan (1964), William O. Douglas (1969), William A. Geoghegan (1966), Burke Marshall (1964), Philip M. Kaiser (1966), Nicholas deB. Katzenbach (1964, 1969), "Kennedy's Call to King (1988)," Torbert H. McDonald (1965), Louis F. Oberdorfer (1964, 1970), Lawrence F. O'Brien (1985, 1987), Andrew F. Oehman (1970), William H. Orrick (1970), John H. Patterson (1967), John L. Seigenthaler (1964, 1966), John H. Sharon (1969), Theodore C. Sorensen (1964), Stewart L. Udall (1970), Robert A. Wallace (1968), Harris L. Wofford (1965, 1968). *Minor Sources:* Anthony B. Akers, James V. Bennett, Arleigh Burke, Arthur A. Chapin, Richardson Dilworth, Robert B. Docking, Frederick G. Dutton, Myer Feldman, Felix Frankfurter, William S. Gaud, Roswell L. Gilpatric, Camille F. Gravel, Kay Halle, John Harlee, E. William Henry, John Jay Hooker, Jr., John E. Horne, Ralph Horton, Rafer L. Johnson, John H. Kelso, Caroll Kilpatrick, Philip M. Klutznick, Anthony Lewis, Lee Loevinger, James H. Meredith, Frank B. Morrison, Joseph L. Rauh, Norbert A. Schlei, Charles Spalding, Walter Spolar, Frank Thompson, James W. Wine. (All minor-source interviews were conducted before 1971, except Bennett, who was interviewed in 1974.)

Margaret I. King Library, University of Kentucky (Special Collections). Howard Trienens and Newton Minow (1975), Karl R. Price (1975) (Frederick M. Vinson Oral History Project).

Wellington Public Library, Wellington, Colorado. Francis and Sylvia Bee (1978), Eldon Edwards (1989), Fred Hankins (1975), Grant Hubert Jones (n.d.), Mary Delle Kafka (1989), Barbara Leeper (1989), Andrew Mair (1989), Jack Mair (1989), Doyle Russell (1989), Jeannette Thimmig (1989), Mary Francis Wagers (1989), Eugene Wich (1989).

Manuscripts

Teller Ammons Papers, Colorado Historical Society
Aspen Institute Papers, Colorado Historical Society
Hugo L. Black Papers, Library of Congress
Charles Boettcher Papers, Colorado Historical Society
Claude Boettcher Papers, Colorado Historical Society
Harold H. Burton Papers, Library of Congress
William J. Brennan Papers, Library of Congress
John A. Carroll Papers, Auraria Library, Metropolitan State College, Denver
Emanuel Cellar Papers, Library of Congress
Tom C. Clark Papers, Tarlton Law Library, University of Texas at Austin
Edward S. Corwin Papers, Seeley G. Mudd Library, Princeton University
Congress on Racial Equality Papers (CORE), Library of Congress
William O. Douglas Papers, Library of Congress
Myer Feldman Papers, John F. Kennedy Library, Boston
F. Scott Fitzgerald Collection, University of Tulsa
William F. Halsey Papers, Library of Congress
John M. Harlan Papers, Seeley G. Mudd Manuscript Library, Princeton University
Stephen H. Hart Collection, Colorado Historical Society

Roy W. Howard Papers, Library of Congress
Harold L. Ickes Papers, Library of Congress
Nicholas deB. Katzenbach Papers, John F. Kennedy Library
John F. Kennedy Papers, John F. Kennedy Library
Robert F. Kennedy Papers, John F. Kennedy Library
Burke Marshall Papers, John F. Kennedy Library
Thurgood Marshall Papers, Library of Congress
Frank Murphy Papers, University of Michigan
Louis F. Oberdorfer Papers, John F. Kennedy Library
William H. Orrick Papers, John F. Kennedy Library
Lewis F. Powell Papers, Washington & Lee University
President's Office Papers, Western Collections and Archives, Norlin Library, University
    of Colorado at Boulder
Grantland Rice Papers, Vanderbilt University
Wiley B. Rutledge Papers, Library of Congress
Theodore C. Sorensen Papers, John F. Kennedy Library
Social Science Foundation Papers, Special Collections, Penrose Library, University of
    Denver
Robert Stearns Papers, Western Collections and Archives, Norlin Library, University of
    Colorado at Boulder
Earl Warren Papers, Library of Congress

Select Books

Abbott, Carl, Stephen J. Leonard, and David McComb. *Colorado: A History of the Centennial State.* Boulder: University Press of Colorado, 1982, 1994.

Abraham, Henry J. *Justice and Presidents: A Political History of Appointments to the Supreme Court.* 3d ed. New York: Oxford University Press, 1992.

Allen, Frederick S., and others. *The University of Colorado, 1876–1976.* New York: Harcourt, Brace, Jovanovich, 1976.

Anderson, Dave, and others. *The Heisman: Sixty Years of Tradition and Excellence.* Bronxville N.Y.: Adventure Quest, 1995.

Baker, Liva. *The Justice from Beacon Hill: The Life and Times of Oliver Wendell Holmes.* New York: HarperCollins, 1991.

———. *The Second Battle of New Orleans: The Hundred-Year Struggle to Integrate the Schools.* New York: HarperCollins, 1996.

Baldassaro, Lawrence, ed. *The Ted Williams Reader.* New York: Simon & Schuster/A Fireside Book, 1991.

Baldwin, Hanson W. *Battles Lost and Won: Great Campaigns of World War II.* New York: Smithmark Publishers, 1966, 1994.

Ball, Howard, and Phillip J. Cooper. *Of Power and Right: Hugo Black, William O. Douglas, and America's Constitutional Revolution.* New York: Oxford University Press, 1992.

Barker, Bill, and Jackie Lewin. *Denver! An Insider's Look at the High, Wide and Handsome City.* Garden City, N.Y.: Doubleday, 1972.

Barnard, Hollinger F., ed. *Outside the Magic Circle: The Autobiography of Virginia Durr.* University, Ala.: University of Alabama Press, 1985.

Barnes, Catherine A. *Journey from Jim Crow: The Desegregation of Southern Transit.* New [York: Colu]mbia University Press, 1983.

Bass, Jack. *Taming the Storm: The Life and Times of Judge Frank M. Johnson, Jr., and the South's Fight Over Civil Rights.* New York: Doubleday, 1993.

———. *Unlikely Heroes.* New York: Simon & Schuster, 1981.

Belknap, Michal R. *Federal Law and Southern Order: Racial Violence and Constitutional Conflict in the Post-Brown South.* Athens: University of Georgia Press, 1987.

Bernstein, Irving. *Promises Kept: John F. Kennedy's New Frontier.* New York: Oxford University Press, 1991.

Beschloss, Michael R. *Kennedy and Roosevelt: The Uneasy Alliance.* New York: Norton, 1980.

Bickel, Alexander M. *The Least Dangerous Branch: The Supreme Court at the Bar of Politics.* Indianapolis: Bobbs-Merrill, 1962.

———. *Politics and the Warren Court.* New York: Harper & Row, 1965.

———. *The Supreme Court and the Idea of Progress.* New York: Harper & Row, 1970.

———. *The Unpublished Opinions of Justice Brandeis.* Cambridge: Belknap, 1957.

Black, Elizabeth. *Mr. Justice and Mrs. Black: The Memoirs of Hugo L. Black and Elizabeth Black.* New York: Random House, 1986.

Black, Hugo, Jr. *My Father.* New York: Random House, 1975.

Blair, Joan, and Clay Blair, Jr. *The Search for J.F.K.* New York: Berkley, 1976.

Blasi, Vincent, ed. *The Burger Court: The Counter-Revolution That Wasn't.* New Haven: Yale University Press, 1983.

Borchard, Edwin M. *Convicting the Innocent: Errors in Criminal Justice.* New Haven: Yale University Press, 1932.

Boyne, Walter J. *Clash of Titans: World War II at Sea.* New York: Simon & Schuster/A Touchstone Book, 1995.

———. *Clash of Wings: World War II in the Air.* New York: Simon & Schuster/A Touchstone Book, 1994.

Bradlee, Benjamin C. *Conversations with Kennedy.* New York: Norton, 1975.

Branch, Taylor. *Parting the Waters: America in the King Years, 1954–63.* New York: Simon & Schuster, 1988.

Brauer, Carl M. *John F. Kennedy and the Second Reconstruction.* New York: Columbia University Press, 1977.

Breuer, William. *Devil Boats: The PT War Against Japan.* Novato, Calif.: Presidio, 1987.

Brinkley, Alan. *The End of Reform: New Deal Liberalism in Recession and War.* New York: Knopf, 1995.

Brinkley, David. *David Brinkley: A Memoir.* New York: Knopf, 1995.

Bronner, Ethan. *Battle for Justice: How the Bork Nomination Shook America.* New York: Norton, 1989.

Bulkley, Robert J., Jr. *At Close Quarters: A History of Motor Torpedo Boats in the United States Navy.* Washington, D.C.: U.S. Government Printing Office, 1962.

Burnham, David. *Above the Law: Secret Deals, Political Fixes, and Other Misadventures of the U.S. Department of Justice.* New York: Scribner, 1996.

Burns, James MacGregor. *John Kennedy: A Political Profile.* New York: Harcourt, Brace & World, 1961.

Camerer, Dave, ed. *The Best of Grantland Rice.* New York: Franklin Watts, 1963.

Caplan, Lincoln. *The Tenth Justice: The Solicitor General and the Rule of Law.* New York: Random House, 1987.

Carson, Clayborne. *In Struggle: SNCC and the Black Awakening of the 1960s.* Cambridge: Harvard University Press, 1981, 1995.

Casotti, Fred. *The Golden Buffaloes: Colorado Football.* Huntsville, Ala.: Strode Publishers, 1980.

Chappell, David L. *Inside Agitators: White Southerners in the Civil Rights Movement.* Baltimore: Johns Hopkins University Press, 1994.

Charns, Alexander. *Cloak and Gavel: FBI Wiretaps, Bugs, Informers, and the Supreme Court.* Urbana: University of Illinois Press, 1992.

Chase, Harold W. *Federal Judges: The Appointing Process.* Minneapolis: University of Minnesota Press, 1972.

Choper, Jesse. *Judicial Review and the National Political Process: A Functional Reconsideration of the Role of the Supreme Court.* Chicago: University of Chicago Press, 1980.

Christianson, Gale E. *Edwin Hubble: Mariner of the Nebulae.* New York: Farrar, Straus and Giroux, 1995.

Claassen Harold (Spike). *The History of Professional Football: Its Great Teams, Games, Players and Coaches.* Englewood Cliffs, N.J.: Prentice Hall, 1963.

Clark, Hunter. *Justice Brennan: The Great Conciliator.* New York: Carroll Publishing/A Birch Lane Press Book, 1995.

Clayton, James E. *The Making of Justice: The Supreme Court in Action.* New York: Dutton, 1964.

Clifford, Clark, with Richard Holbrooke. *Counsel to the President: A Memoir.* New York: Anchor, 1991, 1992.

Cohane, Tim. *The Yale Football Story.* New York: Putnam, 1951.

Colorado Agricultural Statistics, 1935. Denver: Colorado Cooperative Livestock Reporting Service, 1935.

Colorado: The Superstar State (Members of the Colorado Sports Hall of Fame). Baton Rouge, La.: Moran Publishing Corp., 1979.

Cooper, Phillip J. *Battles on the Bench: Conflict Inside the Supreme Court.* Lawrence: University Press of Kansas, 1995.

Cooper, Phillip [J.], and Howard Ball. *The United States Supreme Court: From the Inside Out.* Upper Saddle River, N.J.: Prentice Hall, 1996.

Cope, Myron. *The Game That Was: The Early Days of Pro Football.* New York: World, 1970.

Corbin, Arthur L. *Cases on the Law of Contracts.* St. Paul: West. 1st ed., 1921; 2d ed., 1937; 3d ed., 1947.

Craig, Barbara Harrison. *Chadha: The Story of an Epic Constitutional Struggle.* Berkeley: University of California Press, 1988.

Cray, Ed. *Chief Justice: A Biography of Earl Warren.* New York: Simon & Schuster, 1997.

Cruttwell, C. R. M. F. *A History of the Great War.* 2d ed. Chicago: Academy Chicago Publishers, 1991.

Curran, Bob. *Pro Football's Rag Days.* Englewood Cliffs, N.J.: Prentice Hall, 1969.

Current, Richard Nelson. *Phi Beta Kappa in American Life: The First Two Hundred Years.* New York: Oxford University Press, 1990.

Currie, David P. *The Constitution in the Supreme Court: The Second Century, 1888–1986.* Chicago: University of Chicago Press, 1990.

Cutler, Thomas J. *The Battle of Leyte Gulf: 23–26 October 1944.* New York: HarperCollins, 1994.

Daley, Arthur. *The Arthur Daley Years.* Edited by James Tuite. New York: Quadrangle Books, 1975.

———. *Pro Football's Hall of Fame.* New York: Grosset and Dunlap, 1963.

Dallek, Robert. *Franklin D. Roosevelt and American Foreign Policy, 1932–1945.* New York: Oxford University Press, 1995.

Daly, Dan, and Bob O'Donnell. *The Pro Football Chronicle.* New York: MacMillan/Collier Books, 1990.

Damore, Leo. *The Cape Cod Years of John Fitzgerald Kennedy.* New York: Four Walls Eight Windows, 1967, 1993.

Davis, John H. *The Kennedys: Dynasty and Disaster, 1848–1984.* New York: McGraw-Hill, 1984.

Davis, Richard. *Decisions and Images: The Supreme Court and the Press.* Englewood Cliffs: Prentice Hall, 1994.

Davis, William E. (Bud). *Glory Colorado! A History of the University of Colorado, 1858–1963.* Boulder: Pruett Press, 1965.

DeLoach, Cartha D. "Deke." *Hoover's FBI: The Inside Story by Hoover's Trusted Lieutenant.* Washington, D.C.: Regnery, 1995.

DeLong, Thomas A. *Quiz Craze: America's Infatuation with Game Shows.* New York: Praeger, 1992.

Didinger, Ray. *The Pittsburgh Steelers.* New York: Macmillan, 1974.

Dodd, Walter F. *Cases and Other Authorities on Constitutional Law.* St. Paul: West, 1937. Cumulative Supplement, 1940.

Donovan, Hedley. *Right Places, Right Times: Forty Years in Journalism Not Counting My Paper Route.* New York: Henry Holt, 1989.

Donovan, Robert J. *PT 109: John F. Kennedy in World War II.* New York: McGraw-Hill, 1961.

Dorough, C. Dwight. *Mr. Sam.* New York: Random House, 1962.

Douglas, William O. *The Court Years: The Autobiography of William O. Douglas.* New York: Random House, 1980.

Drury, Allen. *Advise and Consent.* New York: Doubleday, 1959.

Dunne, Gerald T. *Hugo Black and the Judicial Revolution.* New York: Simon & Schuster, 1977.

Dunnigan, James F., and Albert A. Nofi. *Victory at Sea: World War II in the Pacific.* New York: Morrow, 1995.

Duxbury, Neil. *Patterns of American Jurisprudence.* Corr. ed. Oxford: Clarendon Press, 1997.

Ehrlichman, John. *Witness to Power: The Nixon Years.* New York: Simon & Schuster, 1982.

Eisler, Kim Isaac. *A Justice for All: William J. Brennan, Jr., and the Decisions That Transformed America.* New York: Simon & Schuster, 1993.

Elliff, John T. *The United States Department of Justice and Individual Rights, 1937–1962.* New York: Garland, 1987.

Ellsworth, Ralph E. ed. *A Voice from Colorado's Past for the Present: Selected Writings of George Norlin.* Boulder: Colorado Associated University Press, 1985.

Elton, Lord, ed. *The First Fifty Years of the Rhodes Trust and the Rhodes Scholarships.* Oxford: Basil Blackwell, 1956.

Epstein, Lee, and Joseph F. Kobylka. *The Supreme Court and Legal Change: Abortion and the Death Penalty.* Chapel Hill: University of North Carolina, 1992.

Epstein, Lee, Jeffrey A. Segal, Harold J. Spaeth, and Thomas G. Walker. *The Supreme Court Compendium: Data, Decisions, and Developments.* 2d ed. Washington, D.C.: Congressional Quarterly, 1996.

Evans, Howard Ensign, and Mary Alice Evans. *Cache La Poudre: The Natural History of a Rocky Mountain River.* Niwot: University Press of Colorado, 1991.

Fahey, James J. *Pacific War Diary, 1942–1945: The Secret Diary of an American Sailor.* Boston: Houghton-Mifflin, 1963, 1991.

Farley, Edward J. *PT Patrol: Wartime Adventures in the Pacific and the Story of PT's in World War II.* New York: Exposition Press, 1958.

Farmer, James. *Lay Bare the Heart: An Autobiography of the Civil Rights Movement.* New York: Arbor House, 1985.

Fassett John D. *New Deal Justice: The Life of Stanley Reed of Kentucky.* New York: Vantage, 1994.

Faux, Marian. *Roe v. Wade: The Untold Story of the Landmark Supreme Court Decision That Made Abortion Legal* New York: Macmillan, 1988.

Fay, Paul B., Jr. *The Pleasure of His Company.* New York: Harper & Row, 1966.

Fine, Sidney. *Frank Murphy: The Washington Years.* Ann Arbor: University of Michigan Press, 1984.

Foster, Simon. *Okinawa 1945: The Final Assault on the Empire.* London: Arms and Armour Press, 1994.

Fountain, Charles. *Sportswriter: The Life and Times of Grantland Rice.* New York: Oxford University Press, 1993.

Fradkin, Philip L. *A River No More: The Colorado River and the West.* Expanded and updated ed. Berkeley: University of California Press, 1996.

Frank, Jerome. *Courts on Trial: Myth and Reality in American Justice.* Princeton: Princeton University Press, 1949.

———. *Law and the Modern Mind.* Garden City, NY: Anchor Books/Doubleday, 1930, 1949.

Frank, John P. *The Warren Court.* New York: Macmillan, 1964.

Fried, Charles. *Order and Law: Arguing the Reagan Revolution—A Firsthand Account.* New York: Simon & Schuster, 1991.

Friedelbaum, Stanley H. *The Rehnquist Court: In Pursuit of Judicial Conservatism.* Westport: Greenwood Press, 1994.

Friedman, Leon, ed. *Southern Justice.* New York: Pantheon, 1965.

———, ed. *The Supreme Court Confronts Abortion: The Briefs, Argument, and Decision in Planned Parenthood v. Casey.* New York: Farrar, Straus and Giroux, 1993.

Friedman, Leon, and Jerold Israel. *The Justices of the United States Supreme Court: Their Lives and Major Opinions.* New York: Chelsea House, 2d ed. 1997.

Fuller, Helen. *Year of Trial: Kennedy's Crucial Decisions.* New York: Harcourt, Brace and World, 1962.

Gailey, Harry A. *The War in the Pacific: From Pearl Harbor to Tokyo Bay.* Novato, Calif.: Presidio Press, 1995.

Garrow, David J. *Bearing the Cross: Martin Luther King., Jr., and the Southern Christian Leadership Conference.* New York: Morrow, 1986.

———. *The FBI and Martin Luther King, Jr.: From "Solo" to Memphis.* New York: Norton, 1981.

———. *Liberty and Sexuality: The Right to Privacy and the Making of* Roe v. Wade. New York: Macmillan, 1994.

Gelfand, David. *8 Men and a Lady: Profiles of the Justices of the Supreme Court.* Bethesda, Md.: National Press, 1990.

Gentry, Curt. *J. Edgar Hoover: The Man and the Secrets.* New York: Norton, 1991.

Gibson, Barbara, and Ted Schwarz. *Rose Kennedy and Her Family: The Best and Worst of Their Lives and Times.* New York: Carroll Publishing/A Birch Lane Press Book, 1995.

Glendon, Mary Ann. *A Nation Under Lawyers: How the Crisis in the Legal Profession Is Transforming American Society.* New York: Farrar, Straus and Giroux, 1994.

Golden, Harry. *Mr. Kennedy and the Negroes.* Cleveland: World, 1964.

Goldfarb, Ronald. *Perfect Villains, Imperfect Heroes: Robert F. Kennedy's War Against Organized Crime.* New York: Random House, 1995.

Gorman, Joseph Bruce. *Kefauver: A Political Biography.* New York: Oxford University Press, 1971.

Graham, Fred [P.]. *Happy Talk: Confessions of a TV Newsman.* New York: Norton, 1990.
———. *The Self-Inflicted Wound.* New York: Macmillan, 1970.

Graham, Hugh Davis. *The Civil Rights Era: Origins and Development of National Policy.* New York: Oxford University Press, 1990.

Grange, Harold (Red), as told to Ira Morton. *The Red Grange Story: An Autobiography.* Urbana: University of Illinois Press, 1953, 1981, 1993.

Gray, Kenneth E. *A Report on Politics in Denver, Colorado.* Cambridge: Joint Center for Urban Studies of MIT and Harvard, 1959.

Green, Jerry. *Detroit Lions.* New York: Macmillan, 1973.

Greenberg, Jack. *Crusaders in Court: How a Dedicated Band of Lawyers Fought for the Civil Rights Revolution.* New York: Basic Books, 1994.

Grossman, Joel B. *Lawyers and Judges: The ABA and the Politics of Judicial Selection.* New York: John Wiley and Sons, 1965.

Gugin, Linda C., and James E. St. Clair. *Sherman Minton: Cold War Justice.* Indianapolis: Indiana Historical Society, 1997.

Gunther, John. *Inside U.S.A.* New York: Harper Brothers, 1947.

Guthman, Edwin. *We Band of Brothers: A Memoir of Robert F. Kennedy.* New York: Harper and Row, 1971.

Guthman, Edwin O., and Jeffrey Shulman, eds. *Robert F. Kennedy in His Own Words: The Unpublished Recollections of the Kennedy Years.* New York: Bantam, 1988.

Hamilton, Nigel. *JFK: Reckless Youth.* New York: Random House, 1992.

Hara, Tameichi, with Fred Saito and Roger Pineau. *Japanese Destroyer Captain.* New York: Ballantine Books, 1961.

Harper, Fowler V. *Justice Rutledge and the Bright Constellation.* Indianapolis: Bobbs-Merrill, 1965.

Harrington, Denis J. *The Pro Football Hall of Fame: Players, Coaches, Team Owners and League Officials, 1963–1991.* Jefferson, N.C.: McFarland and Co., 1991.

Harrison, Brian, ed. *The History of the University of Oxford.* Vol. 8, *The Twentieth Century.* Oxford: Clarendon Press, 1994.

Havill, Adrian. *Deep Truth: The Lives of Bob Woodward and Carl Bernstein.* New York: Birch Lane, 1993.

Healey, Denis. *The Time of My Life.* New York: Norton, 1989, 1990.

Hendel, John. *Kansas Jayhawks: History-Making Basketball.* Lenexa, Kans.: Quality Sports Publications, 1991.

Henderson, Deirdre, ed. *Prelude to Leadership: The European Diary of John F. Kennedy: Summer 1945.* Washington, D.C.: Regnery, 1995.

Hendrie, Laura. *Stygo.* New York: Scribner Paperback, 1995.

Hersh, Burton. *The Education of Edward Kennedy: A Family Biography.* New York: William Morrow, 1972.

Higham, Charles. *Rose: The Life and Times of Rose Fitzgerald Kennedy.* New York: Simon & Schuster/Pocket Books, 1995.

Hilty, James W. *Robert Kennedy: Brother Protector.* Philadelphia: Temple, 1997.

Hirsch, H. N. *The Enigma of Felix Frankfurter.* New York: Basic Books, 1981.

History of Audubon, Iowa, 1878–1978. Audubon, Iowa.: Centennial History Book Committee, 1978.

Hoffman, Joyce. *Theodore H. White and Journalism As Illusion.* Columbia: University of Missouri Press, 1995.

Hogrogian, John. *All-Pros: The First 40 Years.* North Huntingdon, Pa.: Professional Football Researchers Association, 1995.

Holmes, Oliver Wendell, Jr. *Collected Legal Papers.* Selected by Harold Laski. New York: Harcourt, Brace, 1920.

Hosokawa, Bill. *Thunder in the Rockies: The Incredible Denver Post.* New York: Morrow, 1976.

Howard, J. Woodford. *Mr. Justice Murphy: A Political Biography.* Princeton: Princeton University Press, 1968.

Howarth, Stephen. *August 39: The Last Four Weeks of Peace.* San Francisco: Mercury House, 1989.

Hoyt, Edwin P. *The Battle for Leyte Gulf.* New York: Jove, 1972, 1983.

Hutchinson, Earl Ofari. *Betrayed: A History of Presidential Failure to Protect Black Lives.* Boulder: Westview Press, 1996.

Ickes, Harold L. *The Secret Diary of Harold L. Ickes.* Vol. 2, *The Inside Struggle, 1936–1939.* New York: Simon & Schuster, 1954.

Irons, Peter. *The Courage of Their Convictions: Sixteen Americans Who Fought Their Way to the Supreme Court.* New York: Free Press, 1988.

Irons, Peter, and Stephanie Guitton, eds. *May It Please the Court: Arguments on Abortion.* New York: New Press, 1995.

————, eds. *May It Please the Court: The Most Significant Oral Arguments Made Before the Supreme Court Since 1955.* New York: New Press, 1993.

Isenberg, Michael T. *Shield of the Republic: The United States Navy in the Era of Cold War and Violent Peace, 1945–1962.* New York: St. Martin's, 1993.

Jackson, Kenneth T. *The Ku Klux Klan in the City, 1915–1930.* Chicago: Elephant Paperbacks/Ivan R. Dee, 1967, 1992.

Jackson, Robert H. *The Supreme Court in the American System of Government.* Cambridge: Harvard University Press, 1955.

Jeffries, John C., Jr. *Justice Lewis F. Powell, Jr.: A Biography.* New York: Scribner, 1994.

Jenkins, Roy. *A Life at the Center: Memoirs of a Radical Reformer.* New York: Random House, 1991.

Kaiser, Philip M. *Journeying Far and Wide: A Political and Diplomatic Memoir.* New York: Scribner, 1992.

Kalman, Laura. *Abe Fortas: A Biography.* New Haven: Yale University Press, 1990.

————. *Legal Realism at Yale, 1927–1960.* Chapel Hill: University of North Carolina Press, 1986.

Keating, Bern. *The Mosquito Fleet.* New York: Scholastic Book Services, 1963.

Kelley, George V. *The Old Gray Mayors of Denver.* Boulder: Pruett Press, 1974.

Kelley, James. *Admiral Arleigh (31-Knot) Burke.* Radnor, Pa.: Chilton Books, 1962.

Keresey, Dick. *PT 105.* Annapolis: Naval Institute Press, 1996.

Korn, Jessica. *The Power of Separation: American Constitutionalism and the Myth of the Legislative Veto.* Princeton: Princeton University Press, 1996.

Krock, Arthur. *Memoirs: Sixty Years on the Firing Line*. New York: Funk and Wagnalls, 1968.

Kunstler, William M. *Deep in My Heart*. New York: William Morrow, 1966.

Kurland, Philip B. *Politics, the Constitution, and the Warren Court*. Chicago: University of Chicago Press, 1970.

———. *Watergate and the Constitution*. Chicago: University of Chicago Press, 1978.

Laing, Margaret. *The Next Kennedy*. New York: Coward-McCann, 1968.

Lamb, Charles M., and Stephen C. Halpern, eds. *The Burger Court: Political and Judicial Profiles*. Urbana: University of Illinois Press, 1991.

Lambert, Angela. *1939: The Last Season of Peace*. New York: Weidenfield and Nicholson, 1989.

Langhorne, Elizabeth. *Nancy Astor and Her Friends*. New York: Praeger, 1974.

Larkin, Philip. *Jill*. Woodstock, N.Y.: Overlook Press, 1976, 1984.

Lash, Joseph P., ed. *From the Diaries of Felix Frankfurter*. New York: Norton, 1975.

Lawson, F. H. *The Oxford Law School, 1850–1965*. Oxford: Clarendon Press, 1968.

Leamer, Laurence. *The Kennedy Women: The Saga of an American Family*. New York: Villard Books, 1994.

Leckie, Robert. *Okinawa: The Last Battle of World War II*. New York: Viking, 1995.

Leonard, Stephen J., and Thomas J. Noel. *Denver: Mining Camp to Metropolis*. Niwot, Colo.: University Press of Colorado, 1990.

Lerner, Max. *Nine Scorpions in a Bottle: Great Judges and Cases of the Supreme Court*. Edited by Richard Cummings. New York: Arcade, 1994.

Leuchtenburg, William E. *In the Shadow of FDR: From Harry Truman to Bill Clinton*. Ithaca: Cornell University Press, 1983.

———. *The Supreme Court Reborn: The Constitutional Revolution in the Age of Roosevelt*. New York: Oxford University Press, 1995.

Levy, Leonard W. *Against the Law: The Nixon Court and Criminal Justice*. New York: Harper and Row, 1974.

———. ed. *Encyclopedia of the American Constitution*, Supp. I. New York: Macmillan, 1992.

———. ed. *The Supreme Court Under Earl Warren*. New York: Quadrangle Books, 1972.

Lewis, Anthony. *Gideon's Trumpet*. New York: Random House, 1964.

———. *Make No Law: The Sullivan Case and the First Amendment*. New York: Random House, 1991.

———. *Portrait of a Decade: The Second American Revolution*. New York: Random House, 1964.

Lieberson, Goddard, and Joan Meyers, eds. *John Fitzgerald Kennedy As We Remember Him*. London: J. M. Dent, 1965.

Loss, Bernice. *Lawyers Painted by Gardner Cox*. Cambridge: Harvard Law School, 1984.

Lowitt, Richard. *The New Deal and the West*. Norman: University of Oklahoma Press, 1984, 1993.

Lowitt, Richard, and Maurine Beasley, eds. *One Third of a Nation: Lorena Hickok Reports on the Great Depression*. Urbana: Illinois, 1981.

McCarty, Bernie. *All-America: The Complete Roster of Football's Heroes*. Vol. 1, *1889–1945*. University Park, Ill.: Bernie McCarty, 1991.

McCloskey, Robert G. *The American Supreme Court*. Revised by Sanford Levinson. Chicago: University of Chicago Press, 1994.

McCune, Wesley. *The Nine Young Men*. New York: Harper Brothers, 1947.

McFeeley, Neil D. *Appointment of Judges: The Johnson Presidency.* Austin: University of Texas, 1987.

McGurn, Barrett. *America's Court: The Supreme Court and the People.* Golden, Colo.: Ful.rum, 1997.

MacKenzie, John P. *The Appearance of Justice.* New York: Charles Scribner's Sons, 1974.

Maclean, Norman. *A River Runs Through It and Other Stories.* Chicago: University of Chicago Press, 1976.

McMillen, Neil R. *The Citizens' Council: Organized Resistance to the Second Reconstruction, 1954–1964.* Urbana: University of Illinois Press, 1971.

Manchester, William. *American Caesar: Douglas MacArthur, 1880–1964.* Boston: Little, Brown, 1978.

————. *The Death of a President: November, 1963.* New York: Harper and Row, 1967.

————. *Portrait of a President: John F. Kennedy in Profile.* Boston: Little, Brown, 1962.

Mann, Robert. *The Walls of Jericho: Lyndon Johnson, Hubert Humphrey, Richard Russell, and the Struggle for Civil Rights.* New York: Harcourt, Brace, 1996.

Martin, Ralph G. *A Hero for Our Time: An Intimate Story of the Kennedy Years.* New York: Macmillan, 1983.

————. *Seeds of Destruction: Joe Kennedy and His Sons.* New York: Putnam, 1995.

Mathews, Christopher. *Kennedy and Nixon: The Rivalry That Shaped Postwar America.* New York: Simon & Schuster, 1996.

Meador, Daniel J. *Mr. Justice Black and His Books.* Charlottesville: University Press of Virginia, 1974.

Miller, Nathan. *War at Sea: A Naval History of World War II.* New York: Scribner/A Lisa Drew Book, 1995.

Milner, Clyde A. ed. *A New Significance: Re-envisioning the History of the American West.* New York: Oxford University Press, 1996.

Minow, Martha, Michael Ryan, and Austin Sarat, eds. *Narrative, Violence, and the Law: The Essays of Robert Cover.* Ann Arbor: University of Michigan Press, 1993.

Morgan, Anne Hodges. *Robert S. Kerr: The Senate Years.* Norman: University of Oklahoma Press, 1977.

Morison, Samuel Eliot. *History of the United States Naval Operations in World War II.* Vol. VII, *Aleutians, Gilberts and Marshalls, June 1942–April 1944.* Vol. VIII, *New Guinea and the Marianas, March 1944–August 1944.* Vol. XII, *Leyte, June 1944–January 1945.* Vol. XIV, *Victory in the Pacific, 1945.* Boston: Little, Brown, 1958.

————. *The Two-Ocean War: A Short History of the United States Navy in the Second World War.* Boston: Little, Brown, 1963.

Murphy, Bruce Allen. *Fortas: The Rise and Ruin of a Supreme Court Justice.* New York: Morrow, 1988.

Murphy, Walter F. *Congress and the Court.* Chicago: University of Chicago Press, 1962.

Murray, Mike, ed. *Lions Pride: 50 Years of Detroit Lions Football.* Dallas: Taylor Publishing, 1993.

Nash, Gerald D. *The American West Transformed: The Impact of the Second World War.* Lincoln: University of Nebraska Press/A Bison Book, 1985.

Navasky, Victor S. *Kennedy Justice.* New York: Atheneum, 1971.

Neft, David S., and Richard M. Cohen. *The Football Encyclopedia: The Complete History of Professional NFL Football from 1892 to the Present.* New York: St. Martin's, 1991.

Nelson, David M. *Anatomy of a Game: Football, the Rules, and the Men Who Made the Game.* Newark, Del.: University Press of Delaware, 1994.

Newcombe, Jack, ed. *The Fireside Book of Football.* New York: Simon and Schuster, 1964.

Newfield, Jack. *Robert Kennedy: A Memoir.* New York: Plume, 1988.

Newman, Roger K. *Hugo Black: A Biography.* New York: Pantheon, 1994.

Norlin, George. *Things in the Saddle: Selected Essays and Addresses.* Cambridge: Harvard University Press, 1940.

Novick, Sheldon. *Honorable Justice: The Life of Oliver Wendell Holmes.* Boston: Little, Brown, 1989.

Oakes, Bernard F. *Football Line Play—Revised.* 2nd ed. New York: A. S. Barnes, 1948.

O'Donnell, Kenneth P., and David F. Powers, with Joe McCarthy. *"Johnny, We Hardly Knew Ye."* New York: Pocket Books, 1972.

Opie, John. *The Law of the Land: Two Hundred Years of American Farmland Policy.* Lincoln: University of Nebraska Press, 1987, 1994.

O'Reilly, Kenneth. *Black Americans: The FBI Files.* Edited by David Gallen. New York: Carroll and Graf, 1994.

———. *"Racial Matters": The FBI's Secret File on Black America, 1960–1972.* New York: Free Press, 1989.

Packer, Billy, and Roland Lazenby. *The Golden Game.* Dallas: Taylor Publishing for Jefferson Street Press, 1991.

Palmer, Jan. *The Vinson Court Era: The Supreme Court's Conference Votes.* New York: AMS, 1990.

Perrin, Tom. *Football: A College History.* Jefferson, N.C.: McFarland and Co., 1987.

Perry, H. W., Jr. *Deciding to Decide: Agenda Setting in the United States Supreme Court.* Cambridge: Harvard University Press, 1991.

Peterson, Robert W. *Pigskin: The Early Years of Pro Football.* New York: Oxford University Press, 1997.

Plimpton, George, ed. *American Journey: The Times of Robert Kennedy.* Interviews by Jean Stein. New York: Harcourt, Brace, Jovanovich, 1970.

Posner, Richard A. *The Essential Holmes: Selections from the Letters, Speeches, Judicial Opinions, and Other Writings of Oliver Wendell Holmes, Jr.* Chicago: University of Chicago Press, 1992.

———. *Sex and Reason.* Cambridge: Harvard University Press, 1992.

Potter, E. B. *Admiral Arleigh Burke: A Biography.* New York: Random House, 1990.

———. *Bull Halsey.* Annapolis: Naval Institute Press, 1985.

———. *Nimitz.* Annapolis: Naval Institute Press, 1976.

Povich, Shirley. *All These Mornings.* Englewood Cliffs, N.J.: Prentice Hall, 1969.

Powers, Richard Gid. *Secrecy and Power: The Life of J. Edgar Hoover.* New York: Free Press, 1987.

Powledge, Fred. *Free at Last? The Civil Rights Movement and the People Who Made It.* Boston: Little, Brown, 1991.

Prados, John. *Combined Fleet Decoded: The Secret History of American Intelligence and the Japanese Navy in World War II.* New York: Random House, 1995.

Pritchett, C. Herman. *Civil Liberties and the Vinson Court.* Chicago: University of Chicago Press, 1954.

Propst, Nell Brown. *Uncommon Men and the Colorado Prairie.* Caldwell, Idaho: Caxton Printers, 1992.

Raines, Howell. *My Soul Is Rested: Movement Days in the Deep South Remembered.* New York: Putnam, 1977.

Read, Frank T., and Lucy S. McGough. *Let Them Be Judged: The Judicial Integration of the Deep South.* Scarecrow Press: Metuchen, N.J., 1978.

Reese, Lee Fleiming, ed. *Men of the Blue Ghost: USS Lexington CV-16.* San Diego: Lexington Book Co., 1980.

Reeves, Richard. *President Kennedy: Profile of Power.* New York: Simon & Schuster, 1993.

Reeves, Thomas C. *A Question of Character: A Life of John F. Kennedy.* New York: Free Press, 1991.

Register: Department of Justice and the Courts of the United States. 46th ed. Washington, D.C.: U.S. Department of Justice, 1962.

Register of Rhodes Scholars, 1903–1945. London: Oxford University Press, 1950.

Rehnquist, William H. *The Supreme Court: How It Was, How It Is.* New York: Morrow, 1987.

Reisner, Marc. *Cadillac Desert: The American West and Its Disappearing Water.* Rev. and updated ed. New York: Penguin, 1993.

Reynolds, Clark G. *The Fast Carriers: The Forging of an Air Navy.* Annapolis: Naval Institute Press, 1968, 1992.

Rice, Grantland. *The Tumult and the Shouting: "My Life in Sport."* New York: A. S. Barnes and Co., 1954.

Rogers, Warren. *When I Think of Bobby: A Personal Memoir of the Kennedy Years.* New York: Harper Collins, 1993.

Rosenberg, Morton M. *Iowa on the Eve of the Civil War: A Decade of Frontier Politics.* Norman: University of Oklahoma Press, 1972.

Rotberg, Robert I., with the collaboration of Miles F. Shore. *The Founder: Cecil Rhodes and the Pursuit of Power.* New York: Oxford University Press, 1988.

Rowan, Carl T. *Dream Makers, Dream Breakers: The World of Justice Thurgood Marshall.* Boston: Little, Brown, 1993.

Rudko, Frances Howell. *Truman's Court: A Study in Judicial Restraint.* New York: Greenwood, 1988.

Russell, Fred. *"I'll Go Quietly."* Nashville: McQuiddy Press, 1944.

Salinger, Pierre. *With Kennedy.* New York: Doubleday, 1966.

Savage, David G. *Turning Right: The Making of the Rehnquist Supreme Court.* New York: John Wiley, 1992.

Sayler, Richard H., Barry B. Boyer, and Robert E. Gooding, Jr., eds. *The Warren Court: A Critical Analysis.* New York: Chelsea House, 1969.

Schlegel, John Henry. *American Legal Realism and Empirical Social Science.* Chapel Hill: University of North Carolina Press, 1995.

Schlesinger, Arthur M., Jr. *Robert Kennedy and His Times.* Boston: Houghton Mifflin, 1978.

———. *A Thousand Days: John F. Kennedy in the White House.* Boston: Houghton Mifflin, 1965.

Schwartz, Bernard. *The Ascent of Pragmatism: The Burger Court in Action.* Reading, Mass.: Addison-Wesley, 1990.

———. *Behind Bakke: Affirmative Action and the Supreme Court.* New York: New York University Press, 1988.

———. *Swann's Way: The School Busing Case and the Supreme Court.* New York: Oxford University Press, 1986.

———. *Super Chief: Earl Warren and His Supreme Court—A Judicial Biography.* New York: New York University Press, 1983.

————. *The Unpublished Opinions of the Burger Court.* New York: Oxford University Press, 1988.

————. *The Unpublished Opinions of the Rehnquist Court.* New York: Oxford University Press, 1996.

————. *The Unpublished Opinions of the Warren Court.* New York: Oxford University Press, 1985.

————, ed. *The Warren Court: A Retrospective.* New York: Oxford University Press, 1996.

Schwartz, Herman, ed. *The Burger Years: Rights and Wrongs in the Supreme Court, 1969–1986.* New York: Viking, 1987.

Shapiro, David L., ed. *The Evolution of a Judicial Philosophy: Selected Opinions and Papers of Justice John M. Harlan.* Cambridge: Harvard University Press, 1969.

Shogan, Robert. *A Question of Judgment: The Fortas Case and the Struggle for the Supreme Court.* Indianapolis: Bobbs-Merrill, 1972.

Sidey, Hugh. *John F. Kennedy, President.* New York: Atheneum, 1964.

Simon, James F. *The Antagonists: Hugo Black, Felix Frankfurter and Civil Liberties in Modern America.* New York: Simon & Schuster, 1989.

————. *The Center Holds: The Power Struggle Inside the Rehnquist Court.* New York: Simon & Schuster, 1995.

————. *Independent Journey: The Life of William O. Douglas.* New York: Harper & Row, 1980.

Smith, Howard K. *Events Leading Up to My Death: The Life of a Twentieth-Century Reporter.* New York: St. Martin's, 1996.

Smith, Robert. *Pro Football: The History of the Game and the Great Players.* New York: Doubleday, 1963.

Smolla, Rodney A., ed. *A Year in the Life of the Supreme Court.* Durham: Duke University Press, 1995.

Solberg, Carl. *Decision and Dissent: With Halsey at Leyte Gulf.* Annapolis: Naval Institute Press, 1995.

Sorensen, Theodore C. *Kennedy.* New York: Harper and Row, 1965.

————. *The Kennedy Legacy.* New York: Macmillan, 1969.

————, ed. *"Let the Word Go Forth": The Speeches, Statements, and Writings of John F. Kennedy, 1947 to 1963.* New York: Dell, 1988.

Stadtman, Verne A. *The University of California, 1868–1968.* New York: McGraw-Hill, 1970.

Stampp, Kenneth. *America in 1857: A Nation on the Brink.* New York: Oxford University Press, 1990.

Stannard, Martin. *Evelyn Waugh: The Early Years, 1903–1939.* New York: Norton, 1986.

Staudohar, Paul D. and James A. Mangan. *The Business of Professional Sports.* Urbana: University of Illinois Press, 1991.

Stebenne, David L. *Arthur J. Goldberg: New Deal Liberal.* New York: Oxford University Press, 1996.

Steinel, Alvin T., with D. W. Working. *History of Agriculture in Colorado, 1858 to 1926.* Fort Collins: State Agricultural College, 1926.

Steward, Roger. *Cyclone Memories: 100 Years of Iowa State Football.* Webster City, Iowa: S&RS Publishers, 1991.

Stowers, Carlton. *Cotton Bowl Classic: The First Fifty Years.* Dallas: Taylor Publishing, 1986.

Strickler, George, ed. *1941 Official National Football League Roster and Record Manual.* Chicago: NFL, 1941.

———, ed. *1942 Official National Football League Record and Roster Manual.* Chicago: NFᵀ, 1942.

Strober, Gerald S. and Deborah H. *"Let Us Begin Anew": An Oral History of the Kennedy Presidency.* New York: HarperCollins, 1993.

Sykes, Christopher. *Nancy: The Life of Lady Astor.* New York: Harper and Row, 1972.

Sykes, Hope Williams. *Second Hoeing.* Lincoln: University of Nebraska Press/A Bison Book, 1982.

Taylor, Theodore. *The Magnificent Mitscher.* Annapolis: Naval Institute Press, 1954, 1991.

Theoharis, Athan, ed. *From the Secret Files of J. Edgar Hoover.* Chicago: Ivan R. Dee, 1991.

Thomas, Evan. *The Man to See: Edward Bennett Williams: Ultimate Insider; Legendary Trial Lawyer.* New York: Simon & Schuster, 1991.

Tuite, James, ed. *Sports of the Times: The Arthur Daley Years.* New York: Quadrangle Books, 1975.

Tushnet, Mark. *Making Constitutional Law: Thurgood Marshall and the Supreme Court, 1961–1991.* New York: Oxford University Press, 1997.

———, ed. *The Warren Court in Historical and Political Perspective.* Charlottesville: University Press of Virginia, 1993.

Twining, William. *Karl Llewellyn and the Realist Movement.* Norman: University of Oklahoma Press, 1973, 1985.

Tyler, Daniel. *The Last Water Hole in the West: The Colorado–Big Thompson and the Northern Colorado Water Conservancy District.* Boulder: University Press of Colorado, 1992.

Updike, John. *Assorted Prose.* New York: Knopf, 1965.

Urofsky, Melvin I., ed. *The Douglas Letters.* Bethesda: Adler and Adler, 1987.

van der Vat, Dan. *The Pacific Campaign: The U.S.-Japanese Naval War, 1941–1945.* New York: Simon & Schuster/A Touchstone Book, 1991.

Walsh, Christy, ed. *College Football and All America Review.* Culver City, Calif.: Murray and Gee, 1949.

Ware, Gilbert. *William Hastie: Grace Under Pressure.* New York: Oxford University Press, 1984.

Wasby, Stephen L., ed. *"He Shall Not Pass This Way Again": The Legacy of Justice William O. Douglas.* Pittsburgh: University of Pittsburgh Press, 1990.

Watkins, T. H. *Righteous Pilgrim: The Life and Times of Harold L. Ickes, 1874–1952.* New York: Henry Holt, 1990.

Waugh, Evelyn. *Decline and Fall, An Illustrated Novellette.* Rev'd uniform ed. London: Chapman and Hall, 1962.

———. *A Little Learning: The First Volume of an Autobiography.* London: Chapman and Hall, 1964.

Weaver, Jace. *Then to the Rock Let Me Fly: Luther Bohanon and Judicial Activism.* Norman: University of Oklahoma Press, 1993.

Wechsler, Herbert. *The Nationalization of Civil Liberties.* Austin: University of Texas at Austin, 1968.

Weddington, Sarah. *A Question of Choice.* New York: Putnam, 1992.

West, Ray B., Jr. *Rocky Mountain Cities.* New York: Norton, 1949.

Westin, Alan F., and Barry Mahoney. *The Trial of Martin Luther King.* New York: Thomas Y. Crowell, 1974.

Whalen, Richard J. *The Founding Father: The Story of Joseph P. Kennedy.* Washington, D.C.: Regnery Gateway, 1964, 1993.

Wheeler, Keith. *The Road to Tokyo.* Vol. 19 of *World War II.* Alexandria, Va.: Time-Life Books, 1979.

Whipple, Chandler. *Lt. John F. Kennedy—Expendable!* New York: Nova Books, 1964.

White, Theodore H. *The Making of the President, 1960: A Narrative History of American Politics in Action.* New York: Atheneum, 1961.

———. *The Making of the President, 1972: A Narrative History of American Politics in Action.* New York: Atheneum, 1973.

White, William L. *They Were Expendable.* New York: Harcourt, 1943.

Whittaker, Charles E., and William Sloane Coffin Jr. *Law, Order and Civil Disobedience.* Washington, D.C.: American Enterprise Institute, 1967.

Whittingham, Richard. *What a Game They Played.* New York: Harper and Row, 1984.

Wickens, James F. *Colorado in the Great Depression.* New York: Garland, 1979.

Wilkinson, Charles F. *Crossing the Next Meridian: Land, Water, and the Future of the West.* Washington, D.C.: Island, 1992.

Wilson, Derek. *The Astors: 1763–1992.* New York: St. Martin's 1993.

Wofford, Harris. *Of Kennedys and Kings: Making Sense of the Sixties.* New York: Farrar, Straus and Giroux, 1980.

Wolfe, Jane. *The Murchisons: The Rise and Fall of a Texas Dynasty.* New York: St. Martin's, 1989.

Woodward, Bob, and Scot Armstrong. *The Brethren.* Simon & Schuster, 1979.

Woodward, C. Vann. *The Battle for Leyte Gulf.* New York: Macmillan, 1947.

———. *Thinking Back: The Perils of Writing History.* Baton Rouge: Louisiana State University Press, 1986.

Wooldridge, E. T. *Carrier Warfare in the Pacific: An Oral History Collection.* Washington, D.C.: Smithsonian Institution, 1993.

Worster, Donald. *Rivers of Empire: Water, Aridity, and the Growth of the American West.* New York: Oxford University Press, 1985.

The WPA Guide to 1930s Colorado. Introduction by Thomas J. Noel. Lawrence: University Press of Kansas, 1987.

Yarbrough, Tinsley. *John Marshall Harlan: Great Dissenter of the Warren Court.* New York: Oxford University Press, 1992.

Y'Blood, William T. *The Little Giants: U.S. Escort Carriers Against Japan.* Annapolis: Naval Institute Press, 1987.

Young, Andrew. *An Easy Burden: The Civil Rights Movement and the Transformation of America.* New York: HarperCollins, 1996.

Select Periodical Articles

Allen, Francis, "Chief Justice Vinson and the Theory of Constitutional Government: A Tentative Appraisal," *Northwestern Law Review* 49 (1954): 3.

Alschuler, Albert W. "'Close Enough for Government Work': The Exclusionary Rule After Leon." *Supreme Court Review* (1984): 309.

Amar, Akhil. "The Case of the Missing Amendments: *R.A.V. v. City of St. Paul.*" *Harvard Law Review* 106 (1992): 124.

Amsterdam, Anthony. "The Void-for-Vagueness Doctrine in the Supreme Court." *University of Pennsylvania Law Review* 109: 67.

Ariens, Michael. "A Thrice-Told Tale: Or Felix the Cat." Harvard Law Review 107 (1994): 620.

Armstrong, Michael J. "A Barometer of Freedom of the Press: The Opinions of Mr. Justice White." *Pepperdine Law Review* 8 (1980): 157.

Bakal, Carl. "New Man on the Big Bench." *True,* July 1962.

Bernard, John V. "Our Best High Schools: Science in the Small School—Green River, Wyoming." *Atlantic,* Apr. 1965.

Borchard, Edwin. "The Supreme Court and Private Rights." *Yale Law Journal* 47 (1938): 1051.

Broyde, Michael J. "The Inter Circuit Tribunal and Perceived Conflicts: An Analysis of Justice White's Dissents from Denial of Certiorari During the 1985 Term." *New York University Law Review* 62 (1987): 610.

Casey, Lee. "When the Klan Controlled Colorado." *Rocky Mountain News,* June 17, 18, 19, 1946.

Casey, Robert P. "Pope John XXIII Lecture (Sept. 30, 1994)." *Catholic University Law Review* 44 (1995): 821.

Corbin, Arthur L. "Sixty-Eight Years at Law." *Yale Law Report* 11 (1965): 20.

Coughlin, John J. "Common Sense in Formation for the Common Good—Justice White's Dissents in the Parochial School Aid Cases: Patron of Lost Causes or Precursor of Good News." *St. John's Law Review* 66 (1992): 261.

Davis, Robert Leede. "And He Can Take a Hit Too: Justice White's Utah Connection." *Brigham Young University Law Review* (1994): 363.

Daye, Charles E. "Justice Byron R. White." *North Carolina Central Law Journal* 12 (1981): 260.

Eastland, Terry. "Presswatch: In Contempt." *American Spectator,* June 1993.

Ebel, David M. "Justice White: A Brief Sketch." *Washburn Law Journal* 33 (1993): 1.

Elliott, Donald. "INS v. Chadha: The Administrative Constitution, the Constitution, and the Legislative Veto." *Supreme Court Review* (1983): 125.

Elman, Philip (interviewed by Norman Silber). "The Solicitor General's Office, Justice Frankfurter, and Civil Rights Litigation, 1946–1960: An Oral History." Harvard Law Review 100 (1987): 817.

Fischel, Dan. "Antitrust Liability for Attempts to Influence Government Action: The Basis and Limits of the Noerr-Pennington Doctrine." *University of Chicago Law Review* 45 (1977): 80.

———. "From MITE to CTS: State Anti-Takeover Statutes, the Williams Act, the Commerce Clause, and Insider Trading." *Supreme Court Review* (1987): 47.

Frank, John P. "Fred Vinson and the Chief Justiceship." *University of Chicago Law Review* 21 (1954): 212.

———. "The United States Supreme Court: 1946–47." *University of Chicago Law Review* 15 (1947): 1.

Gilmore, Grant. "For Wesley Sturges: On the Teaching and Study of Law." *Yale Law Journal* 72 (1963): 646.

Glendon, Mary Ann. "Partial Justice: Jurisprudence on the Supreme Court." *Commentary,* Aug. 1994.

Hellman, Arthur. "By Precedent Unbound: The Nature and Extent of Unresolved Intercircuit Conflicts." *University of Pittsburgh Law Review* 56 (1995): 693.

Herz, Michael. "Justice Byron White and the Argument that the Greater Includes the Lesser." *Brigham Young University Law Review* (1994): 227.

Hoagland, Donald W. "Byron White As a Practicing Lawyer in Colorado." *University of Colorado Law Review* 58: 365.

Holland, Gerald. "Is That You Up There, Johnny Blood?" *Sports Illustrated,* Sept. 2, 1963.

Horan, Dennis J., Clarke D. Forsythe, and Edward R. Grant. "Two Ships Passing in the Night: An Interpretavist Review of the White-Stevens Colloquy on Roe v. Wade." *Saint Louis University Public Law Review* 6 (1987): 229.

Hutchinson, Dennis J. "The Black-Jackson Feud." *Supreme Court Review* (1986): 203.

———. "The Papers of Thurgood Marshall." *Appellate Law Review* 6 (1994): 72.

———. "Unanimity and Desegregation: Decision-Making in the Supreme Court, 1948–1958." *Georgetown Law Journal* 68: 1.

Hutton, Mary Christine. "The Unique Perspective of Justice White: Separation of Powers, Standing and Section 1983 Cases." *Administrative Law Review* 40 (1988): 377.

Ides, Allan. "The Jurisprudence of Justice Byron White." *Yale Law Journal* 103 (1993): 419.

———. "Realism, Rationality and Justice Byron White: Three Easy Cases." *Brigham Young University Law Review* (1994): 283.

Jenkins, John. "A Candid Talk with Justice Blackmun." *New York Times Magazine,* Feb. 20, 1983, 6.

Kahn, Paul W. "The Court, the Community and the Judicial Balance: The Jurisprudence of Justice Powell." *Yale Law Journal* 97 (1987): 1.

Katzenbach, Nicholas deB. "Byron White's Appointment to the Supreme Court." *University of Colorado Law Review* 58 (1987): 429.

Kempton, Murray. "Thoughts Astray: Code Duello." *National Review,* June 8, 1979, 754

Kovaleff, Theodore P. "The Two Sides of the Kennedy Antitrust Policy." *Antitrust Bulletin* 7 (1992): 5.

Kurland, Philip B. "The 1971 Term: The Year of the Stewart-White Court." *Supreme Court Review* (1972): 181.

Lee, Rex, and Richard G. Wilkins. "On Greatness and Constitutional Vision: Justice Byron R. White." Brigham Young University Law Review (1994): 291.

Leuchtenburg, William E. "Comment: FDR's Court-Packing Plan: A Second Life, a Second Death." *Duke Law Journal* (1985): 673.

Lewin, Nathan. "White's Flight: The Burger Court's Right-Hand Man: Justice Byron R. White." *New Republic,* Aug. 27, 1984.

Liebman, Lance. "Swing Man on the Supreme Court." *New York Times Magazine,* Oct. 8, 1972.

Llewellyn, Karl. "Some Realism About Realism—Responding to Dean Pound." *Harvard Law Review* 44 (1931): 1222.

Lukas, J. Anthony. "Interview: Bob Woodward." *Playboy,* Feb. 1989.

McDougal, Myres S. "Fuller v. the American Legal Realists: An Intervention." *Yale Law Journal* 50: 827.

Maltz, Earl M. "The Prospects for a Revival of Conservative Activism in Constitutional Jurisprudence." *Georgia Law Review* 24 (1995): 629.

Malysiak, James T. "Justice White on Antitrust: Protecting Freedom to Compete." *University of Colorado Law Review* 58 (1987): 497.

Massie, Robert. "Many Rhodes to Washington." *New York Times,* Apr. 16, 1961.

May, Clifford. "Interview: Byron R. White." *Rocky Mountain News,* June 30, 1996.

Moore, Ralph. "Remembering Whizzer White." *Denver Post,* Apr. 4, 1962.

Moss, Irv. "The Duke of Wellington." *Denver Post,* Jan. 30, 1994.

Nelson, William E. "Justice Byron R. White: A Modern Federalist and a New Deal Liberal." *Brigham Young University Law Review* (1994): 313.

Newcombe, Jack. "Whizzer White." *Sport,* Dec. 1962, 76.

Nichol, Gene R., Ruth Bader Ginsburg, and David M. Ebel. "Dedication of the Byron White United States Courthouse." *University of Colorado Law Review* 66 (1995): 1.

Oberdorfer, Louis F. "Justice White and the Yale Legal Realists." *Yale Law Journal* 103 (1993): 5.

O'Brien, David M. "The Rehnquist Court's Shrinking Plenary Docket." *Judicature* 81 (1997): 58.

O'Donnell, Pierce. "The Hands of Justice: A Law Clerk Fondly Remembers Byron R. White." *Washburn Law Journal* 33 (1993): 12.

"Perspectives on White: A Roundtable." *ABA Journal,* Oct. 1993, 68.

Peth, Gus. "White, Mair Visit Old School." *Wellington News,* Aug. 9, 1984.

Poulos, John W. "The Judicial Philosophy of Roger Traynor." *Hastings Law Journal* 46 (1995): 643.

Powell, Lewis F., Jr., Rhesa H. Barksdale, David M. Ebel, Lance Liebman, and Charles Fried. "A Tribute to Justice Byron R. White." *Harvard Law Review* 107 (1993): 1.

Price, Monroe. "A Justice of Studied Unpredictability." *National Law Journal,* Feb. 18, 1980.

Rehnquist, William H. "A Tribute to Justice Byron R. White." *Yale Law Journal* 103 (1993): 1.

Rehnquist, William H., Harry A. Blackmun, David H. Souter, George Bush, and Gerald Ford. "Tributes." *Washburn Law Journal* 33 (1993): 5.

Riggs, Robert E. "When Every Vote Counts: 5-4 Decisions in the United States Supreme Court, 1900–1990." *Hofstra Law Review* 21 (1993): 667.

Rosen, Jeffrey. "The Next Justice: How Not to Replace Byron White." *New Republic,* Apr. 12, 1993.

Ritter, Robert. "Court Split on Marshall Papers." *Quill,* Oct. 1993.

Rogers, John M. "'I Vote This Way Because I'm Wrong': The Supreme Court Justice as Epimenides." *Kentucky Law Journal* 79 (1990–91): 439.

Ruebner, Ralph. "Police Interrogation: The Privilege Against Self-Incrimination, the Right to Counsel, and the Incomplete Metamorphosis of Justice White." *Miami Law Review* 48 (1994): 511.

Schauer, Frederick. "Codifying the First Amendment: New York v. Ferber." *Supreme Court Review* (1982): 285.

Schneider, James F. "In Memoriam: Harrison L. Winter." *Maryland Law Review* 50: 1.

Seymour, Whitney North. "Mr. Justice White." *ABA Journal* 48 (May 1962): 450.

Smith, Thomas G. "Civil Rights on the Gridiron: The Kennedy Administration and the Desegregation of the Washington Redskins." *Journal of Sports History* 14 (1987): 189.

Starr, Kenneth W. "Byron R. White: The Last New Dealer." *Yale Law Journal* 103 (1993): 37.

Stevens, John Paul, Warren E. Burger, William J. Brennan Jr., and Harry A. Blackmun, "'Cheers' A Tribute to Justice Byron R. White." *Brigham Young University Law Review* (1994): 209.

Stier, Serena. "Privileging Empiricism in Legal Dialogue: Death and Dangerousness." *U. C. Davis Law Review* 21 (1988): 271.

Stith, Kate. "Byron White: Last of The New Deal Liberals." *Yale Law Journal* 103 (1993): 19.

"The Supreme Court, 1971 Term." *Harvard Law Review* 86 (1972): 1.

Trillin, Calvin. "Adieu, Whizzer." *Nation,* Apr. 12, 1993.

Tushnet, Mark. "The Supreme Court and Race Discrimination, 1967–1991: The View from the Marshall Papers." *William & Mary Law Review* 36: 473.

Wallace, Francis. "Pigskin Preview." *Saturday Evening Post,* Sept. 25, 1937, 65.

White, Byron R. "Mr. Justice White Recalls: To Students, the Deftness of a Master Surgeon." *Miami Law Review* 18 (1963): 1.

Worthen, Kevin J. "Shirt-Tales: Clerking for Byron White." *Brigham Young University Law Review* (1994): 349.

Wright, Alfred. "A Modest All-American Who Sits on the Highest Bench." *Sports Illustrated,* Dec. 10, 1962.

Zylstra, Don. "When the Ku Klux Klan Ran Denver." *Sunday Denver Post,* Jan. 5, 1958, Roundup section.

Newspapers

Alabama Journal, Atlanta Journal, Audubon (Iowa) Advocate-Republican, Birmingham News, Boston Globe, Boston Herald, Boston Transcript, Boston Traveler, Boulder Daily Camera, Brooklyn Eagle, Buffalo Evening News, Cervi's Rocky Mountain Journal, Chicago Tribune, Chicago Daily News, Christian Science Monitor, Cincinnati Enquirer, Cleveland Plain Dealer, Cleveland Press, Colorado Springs Gazette & Gazette-Telegraph, Daily Express (London), *Daily Herald* (London), *Daily Mail* (London), *Daily Telegraph* (London), *Daily Worker* (New York), *Dallas Morning News, Dallas Times-Herald, Denver Post, Deseret News, Detroit Free Press, Detroit News, Detroit Times, Evening Star* (Washington, D.C.), *Fort Collins Coloradoan, Fort Collins Leader, Fort Collins News-Leader, Grand Junction Sentinel, Larimer County Sun* (Wellington, Colo.), *Laramie (Wyoming) Daily Boomerang and Daily Bulletin, Long View* (Fort Collins), *Los Angeles Times, Montgomery Advertiser, New Haven Journal-Courier, New Orleans States-Item, New Orleans Times-Picayune, News-Chronicle* (London), *New York Daily News, New York Daily Mirror, New York Herald-Tribune, New York Journal-American, New York Morning Telegraph, New York Post, New York Sun, New York Times, New York World-Telegram, New York World-Telegram & Sun, Philadelphia Evening Bulletin, Philadelphia Inquirer, Philadelphia Record, Pittsburgh Post-Gazette, Pittsburgh Press, Pittsburgh Sun-Telegraph, Pueblo Chieftain, Rocky Mountain News, Salt Lake City Tribune, San Francisco Chronicle, Silver & Gold* (University of Colorado), *Sunday Times* (London), *Times* (London), *Triangle Review* (Wellington), *Tulsa World, Washington Post, Wellington Hi-Lites, Wellington Sun, Wyoming State Tribune* (Cheyenne).

Magazines

American Mercury, American Oxonian, American Scholar, Atlantic, Collier's, Liberty, Library of Congress Bulletin, Life, Nation, National Review, New Yorker, New Republic, Saturday Evening Post, School and Society, Sport, Sports Illustrated, Time, True, U.S. News & World Report.

Unpublished Materials

Dissertations. Mary Hannah Curzan, "A Case Study in the Selection of Federal Judges, the Fifth Circuit, 1953–1963" (Yale, 1968); Paul Governali, "The Professional Football Player: His Vocational Status" (Columbia Teachers College, 1951); Randy Lee Sowell, "Judicial Vigor: The Warren Court and the Kennedy Administration" (Kansas, 1992).

Seminar Papers (University of Chicago Law School). John Cashman, "Byron White and Antitrust" (1994); Ross E. Davies, "*Mapp* and Good Faith" (1997); Joan Radovich, "From *New York Times* to *Dun & Bradstreet:* A Study in Activism and Restraint" (1997).

Court Records. Probate File No. 3175 (Estate of Chas. S. White, Decd.), Audubon (Iowa) District Court; Deposition of Burke Marshall, United States District Court (S.D.N.Y.), Peck v. United States, No. 76 Civ. 983(CES).

Privately Printed Works

Genealogies. Charles Sumner White, *Ephriam Godfrey White and His Descendants* (1946); Pamela A. Stewart, ed., *The Whites: Soldiers to Statesmen* (Family History and Genealogical Research Center, Brigham Young University, for the Tenth Circuit Judicial Conference, 1982).

Yearbooks. The Coloradoan (University of Colorado, 1934, 1936, 1937, 1938); *The Kynewisbok* (Denver University 1937, 1938).

Newspaper Morgues

Boulder Daily Camera; Fort Collins Coloradoan.

Public Relations Offices

University of Colorado (Office of Public Relations, Office of Sports Information); Detroit Lions Football Club; Pittsburgh Steelers Football Club; Public Information Office, Supreme Court of the United States.

Libraries

Public. Audubon, Iowa, Public Library (Iowa Room); Boulder Public Library (Carnegie Branch for Local History); Denver Public Library (Western History Collection); Fort Collins Public Library (Local History Department); Wellington Public Library (Oral History Collection).

University. Western Collections and Archives, Norlin Library (University of Colorado); Penrose Library, Archives and Special Collections (University of Denver); Watson Library (University of Kansas); Margaret I. King Library Special Collections (University of Kentucky); Hatcher Graduate Research Library (University of Michigan); Seeley G. Mudd Library (Princeton University); Tarlton Library, Jamail Research Center (University of Texas School of Law).

Other. Archives II (National Archives and Records Service [NARS], Textual Services, College Park, Md.); John F. Kennedy Library (NARS) (Boston); Hart Library, Colorado Historical Society (Denver); Edward J. and Gena G. Hickox Library, Basketball Hall of Fame (Springfield, Mass.); Library of Congress, Manuscript Division (Washington, D.C.); Library, Professional Football Hall of Fame (Canton, Ohio); Naval Historical Center (Washington, D.C.).

Privately Held Papers

Correspondence. Gerald Brown, Joe Dolan.
Scrapbooks and Miscellaneous Clippings. John V. Bernard, James K. Nance, O. T. Nuttall, Wayne E. White.

Television Broadcasts

Stephenson Lecture, University of Kansas (Lawrence, Kans., Apr. 1, 1996*); *This Honorable Court,* Program Two: "Inside the Supreme Court" (WETA, 1988); Portrait Presentation, Midwinter Meetings, American Bar Association, Feb. 5, 1989 (privately produced; courtesy Clerk's Office, U.S. District Court for the District of Colorado); Kennedy Administration U.S. Attorneys Reunion (Nov. 18, 1994*); Judicial Conference for the Eighth Circuit, Colorado Springs, Colo. (August 5, 1993*); Speech, Dedication of John Giffen Weinmann Law School Building, Tulane University (New Orleans, La., Nov. 16, 1995*); Symposium, "Kennedy Justice," Duquesne University, Apr. 12, 1996 (Pittsburgh, Pa.).

---

* Broadcast by C-SPAN and transcribed by Mrs. Delores Jackson, New Collegiate Division, University of Chicago.

ACKNOWLEDGMENTS

My principal debts are to B. J. Schwartz for his research assistance and to David Currie, Katy Hutchinson, and David Roe for their generous editorial advice. The University of Chicago provided research support, thanks to Dean John Boyer of The College, and Dean (now Provost) Geoffrey R. Stone and Dean Douglas G. Baird of The Law School. Others also provided assistance, which I gratefully acknowledge:

Librarians and Archivists: Fred Casotti (former director of Sports Information, University of Colorado), Marty Covey and David Hay (Western History and Archives, Norlin Library, University of Colorado), Stephen P. Ehrlich (chief deputy clerk, United States District Court for the District of Colorado), Connie Fleischer (D'Angelo Law Library, University of Chicago), William H. Goodman (attorney at law, Detroit, Michigan), John N. Jacob (archivist, Washington & Lee University School of Law), Rhaeva Massey (Local History Department, Fort Collins Public Library), Diane Montgomery (Wellington Public Library), June Payne and Maura Porter (John F. Kennedy Library), Dave Plati (director of Sports Information, University of Colorado), Mike Walker (Naval Historical Center), Mike Widener (Archives and Special Collections, Tarlton Law Library, University of Texas at Austin School of Law), David Wigdor (assistant chief, Manuscript Division, Library of Congress), and Evelyn Wiges (clerk of the District Court, Audubon, Iowa).

Permissions to Examine Papers: Nicholas deB. Katzenbach (John F. Kennedy Library) and Louis F. Oberdorfer (John F. Kennedy Library).

Permissions to Quote from Papers: In addition to Katzenbach and Oberdorfer, Sir Anthony Kenny, Warden of Rhodes House (Rhodes House Files of

Deceased Rhodes Scholars); Seeley G. Mudd Library, Princeton University (John Marshall Harlan Papers); and Tarlton Law Library, University of Texas at Austin (Tom C. Clark Papers).

Research Assistants and Other Colleagues: Student research assistants: Matthew Buttrick, Nicole M. McGinnis, Heidi L. Rummel, and Wendy Saltzman. *Other colleagues who provided editorial advice or other assistance:* William A. Fletcher, Ken Gormley, Barney P. Hutchinson, Allan Ides, Delores Jackson, Emily E. Kadens, Gregory A. Mark, Steven McAllister, Abner J. Mikva, Richard A. Posner, David M. Quammen, Lorrie Ragland, and Diane P. Wood.

CASE INDEX

Cases in text are italicized; cases in notes are in roman.

Adamson v. California, 332 U.S. 46 (1947), 216–218, 339

Adarand Contractors v. Pena, 515 U.S. 200 (1995), 424

Aguilar v. Texas, 378 U.S. 108 (1964), 401–402

Albrecht v. The Herald Co., 390 U.S. 145 (1968), 513n

Alderman v. U.S., 394 U.S. 154 (1969), 347

Alyeska Pipeline Service Co. v. Wilderness Society, 421 U.S. 240 (1975), 441

Apodaca v. Oregon, 406 U.S. 404 (1972), 360–362

Arizona v. Fulminante, 499 U.S. 279 (1991), 409–412

Avery v. Alabama, 308 U.S. 444 (1940), 206

Avery v. Midland County, 390 U.S. 474 (1968), 502n

Baggett v. Bullitt, 377 U.S. 360 (1964), 374–375

Baker v. Carr, 369 U.S. 186 (1962), 308, 340

Banco National de Cuba v. Sabbatino, 376 U.S. 398 (1964), 410

Bell v. Burson, 402 U.S. 535 (1971), 370

Bell v. Hood, 327 U.S. 678 (1946), 418

Bell v. Maryland, 378 U.S. 226 (1964), 350

Bergman v. U.S., 565 F. Supp. 1353 (W.D. Mich., S.D., 1983), 494

Betts v. Brady, 316 U.S. 455 (1942), 206, 339

Board of Education v. Allen, 392 U.S. 236 (1968), 348

Board of Education, Island Trees v. Pico, 457 U.S. 853 (1982), 390–393, 440

Booth v. Maryland, 482 U.S. 496, 515 (1987) (dissenting), 508n

Bowers v. Hardwick, 478 U.S. 186 (1986), 437, 446, 451–454

Bowsher v. Synar, 478 U.S. 714 (1986), 397, 508n

Boynton v. Virginia, 364 U.S. 454 (1960), 283–284

Branzburg v. Hayes, 408 U.S. 665 (1972), 361, 382–383, 441, 450

M/S Bremen v. Zapata Off-Shore Company, 407 U.S. 1 (1972), 376

Broadcast Music v. Columbia Broadcasting, 441 U.S. 1 (1979), 513n

Broadrick v. Oklahoma, 413 U.S. 601 (1973), 375–376, 441

Brown v. Board of Education, 347 U.S. 483 (1954), 283, 292, 307–308, 340, 351–352

Brown v. Board of Education [II], 349 U.S. 294 (1955), 283, 351

Brown v. Louisiana, 383 U.S. 131 (1966), 505n

Buckley v. Valeo, 424 U.S. 1 (1976), 8, 399–400, 409, 447

Burson v. Freeman, 504 U.S. 191 (1992), 420, 511n

California v. Greenwood, 486 U.S. 535 (1988), 412–413, 450

California v. Krivda, 409 U.S. 33 (1972), 204

Camara v. Municipal Court, 387 U.S. 523 (1967), 347, 502n

Cameron v. Johnson, 381 U.S. 741 (1965), 505n

Cannon v. University of Chicago, 441 U.S. 677 (1979), 418

Carey v. Population Services International, 431 U.S. 678 (1977), 452–453

Carter v. Carter Coal Co., 298 U.S. 238 (1936), 200

Chambers v. Maroney, 399 U.S. 42 (1970), 389

Chapman v. California, 386 U.S. 18 (1967), 410–411

Citizens Against Rent Control v. City of Berkeley, 454 U.S. 290 (1981), 400

Cleburne v. Cleburne Living Center, 473 U.S. 432 (1985), 514n

Coalition for Economic Equity v. Wilson, 946 F. Supp. 1480 (N. D. Cal. 1996), vacated and remanded, 110 F. 3d 1431 (1997), 502n

Coates v. City of Cincinnati, 402 U.S. 611 (1971), 375

Coates v. SEC, 394 U.S. 976 (1969), 509n

Cohen v. Cowles Media, 501 U.S. 663 (1991), 412

Coker v. Georgia, 433 U.S. 584 (1977), 395

Colten v. Kentucky, 407 U.S. 104 (1972), 374–375

Connick v. Myers, 461 U.S. 138 (1983), 400

Cooper v. Aaron, 358 U.S. 1 (1958), 290

Cox Broadcasting Corp. v. Cohn, 420 U.S. 469 (1975), 450, 515n

Craig v. Harney, 331 U.S. 367 (1947), 213

CTS Corp. v. Dynamic Corp. of America, 481 U.S. 69 (1987), 396

Davis v. East Baton Rouge Parish Board, 214 F. 2d 624 (E. D. La. 1963), 495n

Davis v. Smith, 329 U.S. 789, cert. denied., 203

Davis v. U.S., 328 U.S. 582 (1946), 214

DeBartolo Corp. v. Florida Gulf Coast Building Council, 485 U.S. 568 (1988), 413

In Re Debs, 158 U.S. 564 (1895), 276

Deepsouth Packing v. Laitrim Corp., 406 U.S. 518 (1972), 504n

Doe v. Bolton, 410 U.S. 179 (1973), 366

Dombrowski v. Eastland, 387 U.S. 82 (1967), 391

Dombrowski v. Pfister, 380 U.S. 479 (1965), 372

Duncan v. Louisiana, 391 U.S. 145 (1968), 347, 360, 362

Dun & Bradstreet v. Greenmoss Builders, 472 U.S. 749 (1985), 421–422, 503n

Edgar v. MITE Corp., 457 U.S. 624 (1982), 395–396, 401

Edwards v. Arizona, 451 U.S. 477 (1981), 390

Eisenstadt v. Baird, 405 U.S. 438 (1972), 362–363, 452

Engel v. Vitale, 370 U.S. 421 (1962), 340

English v. Cunningham, 269 F. 2d 517 (CADC 1959), 492n

Enmund v. Florida, 458 U.S. 782 (1982), 395

Erie Railroad v. Tompkins, 304 U.S. 64 (1938), 150, 151, 156

Escobedo v. Illinois, 378 U.S. 478 (1964), 342, 345, 348

Estes v. McCotter, 506 U.S. 1063 (1993), 510n

Estes v. Namba, 74 F. 3d1249 (CA 10, 1996), 509n

Estes v. Namba, 116 S. Ct. 1438 (1996), 510n

In Re Newton C. Estes, 502 U.S. 1003 (1991), 510n

In Re Newton C. Estes, 506 U.S. 812
(1992) (habeas corpus), 510n
Estes v. Texas, 381 U.S. 532 (1965),
361–362
Estes v. U.S., 471 U.S. 1044 (1985), 510n
Estes v. Van Der Veur, 511 U.S. 1021
(1994), 510n
Estes v. Warden, 955 F. 2d 49 (1992),
509n
Estes v. Warden, 13 F. 3d 405 (1993),
509n
Everson v. Board of Education, 330 U.S. 1
(1947), 211, 216, 348

Federal Communications Commission v.
Midwest Video, 440 U.S. 689
(1979), 383
Federal Election Commission v. Democratic
Senatorial Campaign Committee,
454 U.S. 27 (1981), 399–400
Federal Election Commission v. National
Conservative Political Action Com-
mittee, 470 U.S. 480 (1985), 509n
Federal Power Commission v. Florida
Power & Light, 404 U.S. 453
(1972), 504n
Federal Trade Commission v. Sperry &
Hutchinson, 405 U.S. 508 (1972),
504n
Ferber v. New York, 458 U.S. 747 (1982),
394–395, 403
First National Bank v. Bellotti, 435 U.S.
765 (1978), 509n
Florida Department of State v. Treasure
Salvors, 458 U.S. 670 (1982), 507n
Florida Lime & Avocado Growers v. Paul,
373 U.S. 132 (1963), 501n
Florida Star v. B. J. F., 491 U.S. 524
(1989), 515n
Foucha v. Louisiana, 112 S. Ct. 1780
(1992), 417
Frank v. Mangum, 237 U.S. 309 (1915),
206
Franklin v. Gwinnett County Public School,
112 S. Ct. 1028 (1992), 417–419
Freeman v. Pitts, 503 U.S. 467 (1992),
424–425
Fullilove v. Klutznick, 448 U.S. 448
(1980), 424

Furman v. Georgia, 408 U.S. 238 (1972),
362–363

Gastellum-Quinones v. Kennedy, Attorney-
General, 374 U.S. 469 (1963), 341
Gertz v. Robert Welch, Inc., 418 U.S. 323
(1974), 422n, 503n
Gibson v. Berryhill, 411 U.S. 564 (1973),
372–373
Gibson v. Florida Legislative Investigation
Committee, 372 U.S. 539 (1963),
329, 501n
Green v. New Kent County Board of Educa-
tion, 391 U.S. 430 (1968),
351–352, 424–425
Griswold v. Connecticut, 381 U.S. 479
(1965), 370–372, 452
Grove City v. Bell, 465 U.S. 555 (1984),
441

Hanover Shoe v. United Shoe Machinery,
392 U.S. 481 (1968), 513n
Harris v. U.S., 331 U.S. 145 (1947),
214–215
Hazelwood School District v. Kuhlmeir, 484
U.S. 260 (1988), 413
Herbert v. Lando, 441 U.S. 153 (1979),
382–383, 441, 450
Hickman v. Taylor, 329 U.S. 495 (1947),
211
Hicks v. Miranda, 422 U.S. 332 (1975), 372
Hunter v. Erickson, 393 U.S. 385 (1969),
349, 351

Illinois v. Gates, 462 U.S. 213 (1983), 401
Illinois Brick v. Illinois, 431 U.S. 720
(1977), 513n
Immigration and Naturalization Service v.
Chadha, 462 U.S. 919 (1983), 388,
396–399, 401, 411, 446–447

Jackson v. Denno, 378 U.S. 368 (1964),
342–343, 347
Jacobson v. U.S., 503 U.S. 540 (1992),
420–421
Jesionowski v. Boston & Maine R. R., 329
U.S. 452 (1947), 209–210
Johnson v. Louisiana, 406 U.S. 356 (1972),
360–361

Johnson v. Transportation Agency, Sanata CLara Co., 480 U.S. 616 (1987), 423–424

Katz v. U.S., 389 U.S. 347 (1967), 390
Kennedy v. Mendoza-Martinez, 372 U.S. 144 (1963), 329
Kennedy v. Silas Mason, 334 U.S. 249 (1948), 391

Larson v. Valente, 456 U.S. 228 (1982), 507n
Lee v. Wiseman, 505 U.S. 577 (1992), 429
Lewis v. State, 28 So. 2d 122 (Miss. 1946), 488n
Lindsey v. Normet, 405 U.S. 56 (1972), 360
Loew's v. Cinema Amusements, 210 F. 2d 86 (CA10 1954), 226
Lochner v. New York, 198 U.S. 45 (1905), 152, 153, 339
Lombard v. Louisiana, 373 U.S. 267 (1963), 351
Loper v. Beto, 405 U.S. 473 (1972), 504n
Louisiana ex rel. Francis v. Resweber, 329 U.S. 459 (1947), 211, 216–217, 339
Lucas v. South Carolina Coastal Council, 505 U.S. 1003 (1992), 428

McCollum v. Board of Education, 333 U.S. 203 (1948), 216
McGautha v. California, 402 U.S. 183 (1971), 363
McLaughlin v. Florida, 379 U.S. 184 (1964), 502n
Malloy v. Hogan, 378 U.S. 1 (1964), 342, 345–346
Mapp v. Ohio, 367 U.S. 642 (1961), 344–345
Massachusetts v. Sheppard, 461 U.S. 981 (1984), 509n
Massiah v. United States, 377 U.S. 201 (1964), 342, 345
Masson v. New Yorker Magazine, 501 U.S. 546 (1991), 412, 503n
Mechling Barge v. U.S., 376 U.S. 375 (1964), 502n
Metro Broadcasting v. FCC, 497 U.S. 547 (1990), 424

Meyer v. Nebraska, 262 U.S. 390 (1923), 370
Michigan v. Long, 463 U.S. 1032 (1983), 204n
Minnick v. Mississippi, 498 U.S. 146 (1990), 390
Miranda v. Arizona, 384 U.S. 436 (1966), 3, 8, 344–346, 348, 390, 446
Mistretta v. United States, 488 U.S. 361 (1989), 397
Mitchum v. Foster, 407 U.S. 225 (1972), 372
City of Mobile v. Bolden, 446 U.S. 55 (1980), 395
Moore v. City of East Cleveland, 431 U.S. 494 (1977), 452–453
Morrissey v. Brewer, 408 U.S. 471 (1972), 362, 373
Morrison v. Olson, 487 U.S. 654 (1988), 397
Murphy v. Waterfront Commission, 378 U.S. 52 (1964), 342, 347

NAACP v. Button, 371 U.S. 415 (1963), 501n, 505n
Neagle, In Re, 135 U.S. 1 (1890), 405
New York Times v. Sullivan, 376 U.S. 254 (1964), 352, 421
New York Transit Authority v. Beezer, 440 U.S. 568, 597 (1979) (dissenting), 514n
Nixon v. Fitzgerald, 457 U.S. 731 (1982), 389
NLRB v. Burns Int'l Security Services, 406 U.S. 272 (1972), 358, 370
NLRB v. Jones & Laughlin, 301 U.S. 1 (1937), 149, 152
NLRB v. Plasters' Union Local No. 79, 404 U.S. 453 (1972), 504n
NOPSI v. Council of the City of New Orleans, cert. dismissed under Rule 46, 502 U.S. 954 (1991), 511n
Northern Pipeline Construction Company v. Marathon Pipe Line Company, 458 U.S. 50 (1982), 396–397, 399

Palko v. Connecticut, 302 U.S. 319 (1937), 153, 217–218
Palmer v. Thompson, 403 U.S. 217 (1971), 430
Papachristou v. City of Jacksonville, 405 U.S. 156 (1972), 375

Parker v. Fleming, 329 U.S. 565 (1947), 207–210

Payne v. Tennessee, 501 U.S. 808 (1991), 508n

Pennsylvania v. Union Gas, 491 U.S. 1 (1989), 513n, 515n

People v. Dorman and Smith, 172 P. 2d 686, 692 (1946), 489n

People v. USDA, 427 F. 2d 561 (CADC, 1970), 496n

Perry Education Association v. Perry Local Educators' Association, 460 U.S. 37 (1983), 420, 441, 511n

Peters v. Kiff, 407 U.S. 493 (1972), 359

Peterson v. City of Greenville, 373 U.S. 244 (1963), 350–351

Pierce v. Society of Sisters, 268 U.S. 510 (1925), 370

Planned Parenthood of Southeastern Pennsylvania v. Casey, 505 U.S. 833 (1992), 428–429, 431, 434

Plyler v. Doe, 457 U.S. 202 (1982), 388

Powell v. Alabama, 287 U.S. 45 (1932), 203, 205

Quill Corp. v. North Dakota, 504 U.S. 298 (1992), 425

Radovich v. National Football League, 352 U.S. 445 (1957), 251

R.A.V. v. City of St. Paul, 505 U.S. 377 (1992), 429–430

Red Lion Broadcasting v. FCC, 395 U.S. 367 (1969), 348, 383

Regents of the University of California v. Bakke, 438 U.S. 265 (1978), 384, 423, 512n

Reitman v. Mulkey, 387 U.S. 369 (1968), 348–349, 351

Robbins v. California, 453 U.S. 420 (1981), 389–390

Robinson v. California, 370 U.S. 660 (1962), 338–339, 367–368

Robinson v. Florida, 378 U.S. 153 (1964), 350

Rodgers v. Lodge, 458 U.S. 613 (1982), 395

Roe v. Wade, 410 U.S. 113 (1973), 8, 365–371, 384, 399, 407, 429, 437, 440, 446, 452, 504n

Romer v. Evans, 116 S. Ct. 1620 (1996), 349

Rosenbloom v. Metromedia, 403 U.S. 29 (1971), 503n

San Antonio Independent School District v. Rodriquez, 411 U.S. 1, 63 (1973) (dissenting), 514n

San Juan Light Co. v. Requena, 224 U.S. 89 (1911), 489n

Schmerber v. California, 384 U.S. 757 (1966), 344

(Dred) Scott v. Sandford, 19 Howard 393 (1857),

Securities and Exchange Commission v. Chenery, 332 U.S. 194 (1947), 218

See v. Seattle, 387 U.S. 541 (1967), 347, 502n

Sharon v. Time, Inc., 599 F. Supp. 538 (1984), 422–423, 511n

Sierra Club v. Morton, 405 U.S. 727 (1972), 357

Skinner v. Oklahoma, 316 U.S. 535 (1942), 370

Smith v. California, 331 U.S. 852 (1947), cert. denied, 205

Smith v. Goguen, 415 U.S. 566 (1974), 451

Smith v. O'Grady, 312 U.S. 329 (1941), 206

South Carolina v. Gathers, 490 U.S. 805 (1989), 508n, 515n

Southern Pacific v. Jensen, 244 U.S. 205, 221 (1921) (Holmes, J., dissenting), 446

Spinelli v. U.S., 393 U.S. 419 (1969), 401–402

Stanley v. Illinois, 405 U.S. 645 (1972), 369–372

Stone v. Powell, 428 U.S. 465 (1976), 402, 509n

Swain v. Alabama, 380 U.S. 202 (1965), 502n

Swift v. Tyson, 16 Peters 1 (1842), 151

Teague v. Lane, 489 U.S. 288 (1989), 515n

Thornburgh v. American College of Obstetricians and Gynecologists, 476 U.S. 747 (1986), 452–453

Tibbs v. Florida, 457 U.S. 31 (1982), 389, 507n

Time, Inc. v. Firestone, 424 U.S. 448 (1976), 503n

Time, Inc. v. Hill, 385 U.S. 374 (1967), 503n, 515n

Townsend v. Sain, 372 U.S. 293 (1963), 329

Trudell v. Mississippi, 331 U.S. 785 (1947), cert. denied, 204

Trudell v. State, 28 So. 2d 124 (Miss. 1946), 488n

Trupiano v. U.S., 334 U.S. 699 (1948), 215

Twining v. New Jersey, 211 U.S. 78 (1908), 218

United Mine Workers v. Pennington, 381 U.S. 657 (1965), 502n, 513n

United Public Workers v. Mitchell, 330 U.S. 75 (1947), 211

U.S. v. 12 200-Feet Reels of Super 8mm Film, 373

U.S. v. Adams, 383 U.S. 39, 52 (1966), 502n

U.S. v. Alcea Band of Tillamooks, 329 U.S. 40 (1946), 489n

U.S. v. Antonelli Fireworks, 155 F. 2d 631 (CA2 1946), 502n

U.S. v. Ballard, 329 U.S. 187 (1946), 211

U.S. v. Biswell, 406 U.S. 311 (1972), 370

U.S. v. Brecht, 540 F. 2d 45 (CA2, 1976), 496n

U.S. v. Brewster, 408 U.S. 501 (1972), 364

U.S. v. Carolene Products, 304 U.S. 144 (1938), 151

U.S. v. Dixon, 509 U.S. 688 (1993), 439–440

U.S. v. Fordice, 505 U.S. 717 (1992), 425–429

U.S. v. Gravel, 408 U.S. 606 (1972), 364

U.S. v. Johnson, 457 U.S. 537 (1982), 507n

U.S. v. Leon, 468 U.S. 897 (1984), 402, 509n

U.S. v. Merrigan, 389 F. 2d 21 (CA 3, 1968), 496n

U.S. v. Nixon, 418 U.S. 683 (1974), 507n

U.S. v. Paradise, 480 U.S. 149 (1987), 515n

U.S. v. Ross, 456 U.S. 798 (1982), 389

U.S. v. United Mine Workers, 330 U.S. 258 (1947), 211–213

U.S. v. U.S. District Court, 407 U.S. 297 (1972), 357, 357n, 359, 504n

U.S. v. Vuitch, 402 U.S. 62 (1971), 365–369

United Steelworkers of America v. Sadlowski, 457 U.S. 102 (1982), 507n

United Steelworkers v. Weber, 443 U.S. 193 (1979), 423

Vaca v. Sipes, 386 U.S. 171 (1967), 513n

Victory Carriers v. Law, 404 U.S. 202 (1971), 504n

Wards Cove Packing Co. v. Atonio, 490 U.S. 642 (1989), 441

Washington v. Davis, 426 U.S. 229 (1976), 384

Washington v. Seattle School District No. 1, 458 U.S. 457 (1982), 502n

Weeks v. U.S., 232 U.S. 383 (1914), 345

West Coast Hotel v. Parrish, 300 U.S. 379 (1937), 149, 152

West Virginia Board of Education v. Barnette, 319 U.S. 624 (1943), 393

White v. Ragen, 324 U.S. 760 (1945), 203

Williams v. Florida, 399 U.S. 78 (1970), 360

Williams v. Kaiser, 323 U.S. 471 (1945), 203, 204

Williams v. U.S., 458 U.S. 279 (1982), 507n

Wisconsin v. Yoder, 406 U.S. 205 (1972), 371–372

Woods v. Nierstheimer, 328 U.S. 211 (1946), 202

Wygant v. Jackson Board of Education, 476 U.S. 267 (1986), 423–424

Yellin v. U.S., 374 U.S. 109 (1963), 501n

Younger v. Harris, 401 U.S. 37 (1971), 372

Zurcher v. Stanford Daily, 436 U.S. 547 (1978), 382–383, 441, 450

GENERAL INDEX

ABC News, 383, 444
Abernathy, Rev. Ralph David, 276, 277
Ackerman, Bruce, 455
Adams, Alva B., 81
Adams, Franklin P., 199
Adams, John N., 225
Adams, No. 18 (dry fly), 432
Adams County, 248
Advise and Consent (Drury), 294
affirmative action, 423. *See also* Constitution, Fourteenth Amendment
Afghanistan, 450
AFL-CIO, 236
Agency, Iowa, 12, 13
Agricultural Adjustment Administration, 146
Agricultural College (Colorado). *See* Colorado A & M
Agriculture, U. S. Department of, 17
Ainsworth, Robert A., 293
Air Force Academy, United States, 244
Air Force One, 295
Airborne Warning and Control System (AWACS) aircraft, 388
Alabama, 263, 271–277, 281, 283–284, 291–292, 302, 304, 351
Alabama Journal, 280
Alabama National Guard, 279
Alabama State Board of Optometry
Alaska, 292
Albany Hotel, 237

Albert, Lee, 374
Albuquerque, 247, 324, 410
Alger, Horatio, 53, 324
All-American Board of Football, 58
all-American football teams, 32 (1928), 36 (1935), 56, 57, 58 (1937); *see also* Rice, Grantland
Allen, C(arleton). K., 91, 93, 127–128, 132, 140
Allen, Francis A. (Frank), 170, 199–200, 202, 212, 215, 219, 454
Allen, F. Aley, 195
Allen, Dr. Forrest C. (Phog), 73, 74
Allgood, Clarence, 292–295
Allott, Gordon, 233, 240
All-Stars, College (1938), 101, 102
Alpha Chi Omega sorority, 88
Altmar, Frank, 114
Amagiri, 174, 175, 176
Amar, Akhil, 430
Amateur Athletic Union (AAU), 230, 239, 240
American Bar Association (ABA), 287–295, 516n; American Bar Center, 346; Canons of Professional Ethics, 258; Convention, 387; House of Delegates, 287, 288, 305; Standing Committee on the Federal Judiciary, 288, 295–297, 301–302, 305–306, 313, 318, 321, 323, 330, 357

547

American College of Trial Lawyers, 306
American Family Association, 414
American Lawyer, 413, 516n
American Municipal Association, 243
American Political Science Association, 153
American University, 252
Amery, L.S., 126
Ames, Iowa, 22
Amherst College, 313
Ammons, Governor Teller (Colorado), 56
Anderson, Clinton, 301
Anderson, James A., 479n
Andretta, Salvatore A. (Sal), 267, 303
Andrews Air Force Base, 437
Ann Arbor, Michigan, 168
Anniston, Alabama, 274
Anonymous, 391
Anschluss, 82–83
anti-Fascism, 132
Antoine's, 118
Antonio, Joe, 49, 68
Arcaro, Eddie, 120
Arizona, 248, 293
Arizona Supreme Court, 411
Arkansas, 264, 281, 285, 403
Arkansas River, 230
Armstrong, Ike, 50
Armstrong, Neil, 432
Armstrong, Scott, 2, 384, 514n
Armstrong, William, 511n
Army-Navy game, 353
Arnold, Thurman, 146–147, 226
Aspen Institute for Humanistic Studies, 228, 309
Aspinall, Wayne, 241
Associated Press (AP), 32, 50, 52, 54, 59–60, 64–66, 69, 79, 80–81, 92, 99, 101, 111, 118–119, 123–125, 144, 157, 170, 178, 193, 270–271, 318, 323, 380
Associated Students of the University of Colorado (ASUC), 28, 41, 45, 48, 82, 86
Association of American Universities, 25
Astor, Nancy, Lady, 131, 132
Athenia, 141–142
Athens, Georgia, 304
Atlanta, 256, 307

Attorneys Fees Civil Rights Act of 1976, 441
Auden, W. H., 136
Audubon, Iowa, 14, 100, 118, 197
Audubon County, Iowa, 13, 14, 22
USS Charles S. Ausburne, 179
Australia, 173
Austria, 82, 88
AVON, 386
Aydelotte, Frank, 140

Babcock, Robert S., 137
Bachelor of Civil Law (B.C.L.), 138
Bachrach, Fabian, 219
Badger (American destroyer), 142
Bailyn, Bernard, 364
Baker, Bobby, 298
Baker, Terry, 37
Baker & Botts, 376
Baldwin, Stanley, 93
Balliol College, 129
Baltimore American, 329
Baltimore Orioles, 427, 429
Bank of Denver, 242
Bankruptcy Code, 295
Barbarossa, Operation, 164
"Barbs." *See* University of Colorado, social life
Barnard, Robert C., 138
Barnett, Ross, 279
Barkley, Richard, 479n
Basrak, Mike, 113, 116, 122
Bass, Jack, 206, 479n
Batchelor, E. A., 60
Battisti, Frank J., 300–301
Battles, Cliff, 100
Bauer, Gary, 431
Baugh, Sammy, 53, 60, 61, 75, 80, 98–99, 101, 111, 117, 163, 171
Bay of Pigs, 271, 273, 284
Bazelon, David, 315
Beasley, 136
Beaverbrook, Lord (Max Aitkin), 142
Beet Holiday. *See* sugar beets
Belgium, 88
Bell, Bert, 86
Bell, Griffin B., 257, 304
Beresford, Howard (Ham), 34
Berkeley, 400

Berlin, 27, 84, 139
Berlin, University of, 27
Bernard, John V., 18–23
Berwanger, Jay, 59
Best Short Stories by Negro Writers, 391
Better Boys Foundation (Better Families Foundation), 514n
Bible, Dana X., 33
Bickel, Alexander M., 260, 269, 289–290, 292–294, 447
Bierman, Bernie, 229
Big Blackfoot River, 433
Big Six Conference, 36, 44, 73
Big Ten, 32, 98, 102
Big Thompson River, 15
Bilboism, 446
Bill of Rights. *See* Constitution
Bingham, Joseph W., 152
"Bird Island,"177
Birmingham, 137, 264, 271, 274–275, 277, 282, 292–294
Birmingham Board of Education, 294
Birmingham News, 286
Biskupic, Joan, 436
Bismarck Islands, 180
Black, Charles, 349
Black, Hugo, L., 195, 196, 200, 201, 206–210, 212–213, 216–218, 220, 263, 268, 293, 294, 314, 319, 323, 325, 328–329, 338–343, 348–351, 356, 358, 454, 502n, 510n
Black, Hugo L., Jr., 195
Black Boy, 391
"black vote," 255, 272
Blackett Strait, 174
Blackmun, Harry A., 356, 366, 367, 370, 371, 373, 376, 387, 390–391, 394, 396, 401, 404, 414, 416, 418–421, 426, 428–429, 431, 434, 435, 436, 437, 447, 452, 505n
Blanc, Ronald, 337
Blasi, Vincent, 446
"Blood, Johnny." *See* McNally, John Victor
"Blood and Sand," 80
Bloomfield Hills, Michigan, 158
Boalt Hall. *See* California, University of, at Berkeley
Boettcher family, 223, 227; Boettcher Foundation, 224; Boettcher Scholars, 337

Bohanon, Luther L., 297–300
Boorstin, Daniel, 454
Borah, William E., 17
Borchard, Edwin, 153, 164
Bordeaux, 141
Border Patrol. *See* Justice, U. S. Department of, Bureaus (Immigration and Naturalization)
Bork, Robert H., 409, 415
Boston, 297, 305
Boston Globe, 379
Boston Post, 58
Boston Shamrocks, 111
Boston Transcript, 111
Bougainville, 180
Boulder, Colorado, 4, 25, 27, 34–35, 48, 54, 61, 71–72, 74, 82, 86–87, 92, 157–158, 164, 179, 197, 230, 239, 244
Boulder Canyon, 89
Boulder Daily Camera, 34–35, 52, 71, 86, 92–93, 102, 125, 130, 197, 337, 380
Bountiful, Utah, 403
Bowles, Chester, 255
Boxelder Creek, 15
Boxelder Valley, 16
Boy Scouts of America, 227, 228
Boyle, Havey, 108, 159
Braden, Tom, 252
Bradlee, Ben, 322, 328
Bradley University, 74
Brady, Dave, 269–270, 335
Brandeis, Louis D., 2, 151, 320
Brannan, Charles, 242
Bregman, Bo, 100
Bremen, The (M/S), 376
Brennan, William J., 8, 323, 325, 338, 340, 344, 348, 350–352, 356, 358–359, 367, 370–371, 382, 386, 389–394, 396, 401, 403, 407, 412, 423, 434, 438, 441, 451, 452, 454, 501n, 504n, 510n, 512n
Brennan, William J., Papers, 435
Brethren, The, 2, 6, 384–386, 435
Brideshead Revisited, 132
Briggs Stadium, 164, 169–170
Brigham Young University (BYU), 30, 45,
Brill, Marty, 69

Brinkley, David, 330–331, 415
Britt, Maurice (Footsy), 182
Broadmoor Hotel, 234
Broeg, Bob, 379
Brogan, Denis, 135
Bronze Star, 29
Brooklyn College, 54
Brooklyn Dodgers (football team), 60,
        108, 111–112, 114–116, 122, 166,
        171
Brooklyn Eagle, 74–75 , 109, 113
Brown, Dyke (Franklin M.), 141
Brown, Edmund G. (Pat), 234, 252, 302,
        303
Brown, Gerald, 94, 129, 132, 140–141,
        145–148, 153, 156, 483n, 485n
Brown, Harold, 303
Brown, John R., 307
Brown Palace Hotel, 86
Browning, James R., 295–296
Browning, Robert (poet), 21
Broyde, Michael J., 400
Brozgold, Lee, 414
Buckley, William F., 415
Budge, Don, 112
Buffalo, New York, 101, 107–108, 227
Buffalo Evening News, 107
Bunche, Ralph, 318
Bundy, McGeorge, 315, 319, 320
USS Bunker Hill, 188–192
Bureau of Alcohol, Tobacco and Firearms
        (ATF), Treasury department, 275,
        277
Bureau of Prisons. *See* Justice, U. S. De-
        partment of
Bureau of Reclamation, 17
Burger, Maude. *See* White, Maude Burger
Burger, Warren E., 353, 356, 358, 366,
        367, 373, 378, 386–387, 389–391,
        393, 396–398, 403, 407–408, 434,
        435, 438, 451, 512n, 516n
Burke, Arleigh, 179, 180–182, 184,
        187–191, 193, 271, 454, 506n
Burke, Roberta G. (Bobbie), 190
Burnette, Tom, 116
Burns, Hugh, 229, 330–331
Burton, Harold H., 195–196, 200, 208,
        210, 212, 214, 216–217, 265, 335
Bush, Barbara, 414

Bush, George, 377
Bush administration, 418
Byrd, Harry Flood ("Bird Machine"), 254,
        298
Byron, George Gordon, Lord, 216
        ("Julia")

Cache La Poudre River, 15, 230
Caffrey, Andrew J., 289
Cahn, Edmond, 501n
Cahn, Leonard, 31
Calhoun, John C., 281
California, 239, 251–253, 293, 302, 338,
        348, 400
California Supreme Court, 205, 313,
California, University of, at Berkeley, 63,
        449; School of Law (Boalt Hall),
        195, 413
California, University of, at Davis, Medical
        School, 384
Cambridge, England, 137
Cambridge, Massachusetts, 320
Cambridge University, 29, 132
Camden Yards, 427, 429
Camp, Walter (all-America football team),
        44
Camp Chief Ouray for Children, 227
Campbell, Judith, 316
Canadians in England, 137
Cannes, 139
Cannon, George, 448
Canton, Ohio, 121, 352
Cape Cod, 236
Cape Engaño, battle of, 186
Cape St. George, battle of, 180
Capitol Hill, 253, 263
Capitol Theater, 76
Capricorn I, 404
Cardozo, Benjamin N., 153, 217, 318,
        320
Cardwell, Lloyd, 160, 162, 164, 166
Carlson, Eddie, 432
Carlson, George A., 28, 93, 128
Carlson, Harry, 84, 229
Carnegie Tech, 108, 112, 117
Carroll, John, 232–236, 240, 242, 245,
        250, 263, 301, 330–331
Carswell, G. Harold, 503–504n
Carter, James M., 303

Carter, Jimmy, 199, 380–381, 387, 450
Carter administration, 388
Casey, Robert P., 442, 455
Castro, Fidel, 271
Catholic Church, 301
Catholicism, as political issue, 233–235, 241, 253, 297, 500n
Cavender, George, 238, 238n
CBS News, 403
Cedar Creek, battle of, 13
Celler, Emanuel, 273, 296, 311, 312, 495n
Central Intelligence Agency (CIA), 336
Centre College, 200
Cervi, Eugene, 231–232, 324, 325
Cervi's Rocky Mountain Journal, 232, 324
Chamberlain, Neville, 129, 134–135, 140, 142
Chapman, Ben, 58
Charge of the Light Brigade, 187
Charleston, West Virginia, 117
Chattanooga, Tennessee, 116, 310
Chavez, Dennis, 301
Cheek, James, 427
Chenowith, J. Edgar, 335
Chesterfield cigarettes, 120
Cheston, E. Calvert, 181, 185–187, 189–191, 193, 271
Cheyenne, Wyoming, 14, 15, 119, 244
Chez François, 378
Chicago, University of, 25, 62, 140, 449; Law School, 149, 265, 302, 315, 413, 471
Chicago, 60, 74, 81, 93, 99, 101, 103, 134, 148, 158, 172, 224, 251–252, 268, 287, 289, 302, 305, 316, 379, 449
Chicago and Northwestern Railway, 13
Chicago Bears, 103, 116, 162–163, 166–168, 171–172
Chicago Cardinals, 60, 162–163, 166, 168–171, 227, 449
Chicago Cubs, 115
Chicago Daily News, 65, 182, 188, 236
Chicago Tribune, 51, 68, 81, 87, 93, 99–101, 103, 379
Chicago Tribune All-Star (football) game, 87, 93, 99–103
Chief of Naval Operations, 193, 231

child pornography. *See* Constitution, First Amendment
Child Protection Act of 1984, 420
Childress, Alice, 391
Choper, Jesse, 398, 413
Church, Frank, 247
Ciancio, Don, 248
Ciancio, Frank, 248
Cincinnati, 116, 251, 253–254, 263
Cincinnati Bengals, 264
Circus Saints and Sinners Dinner, 120
Citizens Caucus, 23
Citizens for Kennedy-Johnson (and other Committees), 251–254, 256, 258
City College of New York, 72
Civic Auditorium (Denver), 235
Civil Rights Act of 1957, 285
Civil Rights Act of 1964, 350; Title VII, 423
Civil Rights Act of 1991, 441
Civil Rights Commission, U. S., 284
Civil Rights Division. *See* Justice, U. S., Department of
Civil Rights Restoration Act of 1987, 441
Civil War, 12, 22
Clark, Charles, 146–147, 150, 152
Clark, Earl Harry (Dutch), 32–33, 36, 40, 44, 47, 51–52, 58–60, 74, 76, 84, 104, 110, 158, 160–162, 353
Clark, George (Potsy), 158, 160–164
Clark, Joe, 235, 252, 273
Clark, Ramsey, 266, 268, 293, 300, 305
Clark, Tom C., 266, 343, 348, 350, 358
Clark Fork River, 230
Clayton, James E., 262, 263, 318, 342
Cleaver, Eldridge, 391
Clements, R. Canon (Sam), 90
Cleveland, 99, 101, 214, 225
Cleveland Plain Dealer, 116
Cleveland Rams, 60, 116–118, 162, 166–167, 171
Clifford, Clark M., 261, 315, 320, 435, 499n
Clinton, Bill, 2, 199, 436, 437, 455
Cliveden, 132
"Cliveden set," 132
Cohn family, 450
Coleman, James Plemon (J. P.), 279, 291
Collier's, 44, 58–59, 229

Collins, Bob, 379
Collins, Bud, 379
Collins, Harold, 241
Colorado, 14, 15, 25, 28, 31, 48, 67, 69,
    80, 113, 119, 168, 172, 224, 227,
    231–234, 236–240, 241–243, 245,
    247, 249, 254, 293, 300–301, 309,
    316–317, 322, 324, 328, 330–331,
    335–336, 403, 408, 413, 415, 433,
    471–472
Colorado, chief justice of, 61
Colorado, University of (CU), 4, 24,
    28–30, 33, 36, 40, 43–45, 48–55,
    58, 61, 63–64, 68–70, 72–75,
    77–78, 80, 84, 88, 93, 112, 125,
    128, 157, 161, 193, 195, 198,
    224–225, 228–229, 244, 259, 324,
    330, 337, 408, 432, 438, 442, 449;
    history, 25–28; athletic mascot
    ("Buffalo"), 30; Board of Regents,
    87; College of Arts & Sciences, 26,
    37, 43, 86; *Law Review,* 3; Depart-
    ment of Psychology, 24; Executive
    Council, 41, 73; School of Law, 48,
    140, 148, 157, 159 (summer
    school), 193; social life ("Greeks"
    and "Barbs"), 28, 41–42
Colorado A & M ("Aggies"), 18, 26, 30,
    39, 42, 45
Colorado and Southern Railroad (C&S),
    14, 18
Colorado Bar Association (CBA), 219,
    227, 228, 330, 516n
Colorado–Big Thompson Project, 16
Colorado College, 30, 32, 39, 51–55, 61
Colorado Daily, 337
Colorado General Assembly, 236
Colorado Jaycees, 228
Colorado National Guard, 231
Colorado School of Mines, 26, 30, 33, 39,
    45, 61
Colorado Sports Hall of Fame, 353, 456
Colorado Springs, 117, 234, 240, 245,
    247, 439
Colorado Springs Evening Telegraph, 113
Colorado State College (Greeley), 20, 30,
    84
"Colorado [architectural] Style," 26
Columbia, Missouri, 73

Columbia Broadcasting System (CBS),
    193, 199
Columbia Law School, 149, 446
Communist Party, 129
Condon, Dave, 379
Conference of Chief Justices, 345
Congress, U. S., 83, 200, 216, 237, 239,
    258, 272, 285, 290, 303, 323, 331,
    347, 359, 373, 388, 395–399, 418,
    424, 440–441, 455
Congressional Medal of Honor, 182, 188
Connecticut, 147, 260
Connecticut Sportswriters' Alliance, 148
Connor, Eugene (Bull), 274
Conservative Club, 130
Considine, Bob, 65
Constitution, U. S., 215, 217, 268, 289,
    303, 313, 325, 331, 351, 359–360,
    365–366, 388, 397–398, 435, 452,
    453, 454; commerce clause, 425;
    dormant commerce clause, 395;
    separation of powers, 388, 396,
    399; speech and debate clause, 364
Bill of Rights, 361
First Amendment, 348, 400, 412,
    420, 422, 440, 447, 450; alternate
    to *New York Times* rule, 422; and
    broadcasting, 383; campaign fi-
    nancing, 399; child pornography,
    394; defamation, 352, 382, 421,
    441, 449; "fighting words," 430;
    privacy, 450, 515n; public forum
    doctrine, 511n; religion clauses,
    216–217 (school prayer, 340; invo-
    cations, benedictions, 429;
    parochial schools, government aid
    to, 327, 500n; "released time,"
    216); journalistic privilege, 361,
    382, 440; and police searches of
    newsrooms, 382, 441; school li-
    braries, 391–393
Fourth Amendment, 202, 214, 345,
    347; administrative searches, 347;
    automobile searches, 389–390,
    441; exclusionary rule, 401–402,
    441, 509n
Fifth Amendment, 217, 344; double
    jeopardy, 217; self-incrimination,
    217, 342, 344, 346–347, 390

Sixth Amendment, 344; right to counsel, 339, 342; trial by jury, 347, 360; nonunanimous jury verdicts, 360–361

Eighth Amendment, 338, 395; cruel and unusual punishment, 338–339

Ninth Amendment, 365

Eleventh Amendment, 389

Thirteenth Amendment, 430

Fourteenth Amendment, 202, 217, 339, 345, 350–351, 359, 395; equal protection clause, 348, 371, 430; due process clause, 338, 453; affirmative action programs, 384; criminal due process, 217, 338–339; substantive due process, 339, 343; intent requirement, 384

Cook, Walter Wheeler, 152

Cooke, Alistair, 123

Cooke, Janet, 386

Coolidge, Calvin, administration, 290

Cooper, Irving Ben, 296

Coors, 223

Corbett, Mack, 50

Corbin, Arthur Linton, 148–149, 155–156, 445–446

CORE (Congress of Racial Equality), 273, 274

Corpus Christi Call-Times, 213

Corum, Bill, 67, 109

Corwin, Edward S., 150

Cosmopolitan Hotel, 243

Cotton Bowl, 4, 52, 54, 56–57, 63, 65, 69, 71, 73–74, 89, 377, 408, 449

Counter, Jim (Duke), 39

courts of appeals, federal, 438–439; 147, 301, 304, 311 (second); 301, 313 (third); 291, 292, 304, 425–426 (fifth); 302 (seventh); 311, 420 (eighth); 196, 293, 295–296, 302, 388 (ninth); 61, 226, 293, 301, 403, 472, 506n (tenth); 304, 315 (District of Columbia)

Cover, Robert, 383

Covington & Burling, 266

Cox, Archibald, 263, 266, 308, 315–316, 335, 500n

Cox, Forrest (Frosty), 73–75, 78

Cox, Gardner, 516n

Cox, William Harold, 291–292, 301–302

Cox Broadcasting Corporation, 450

Craig, Colorado, 471

Cranbrook School, 158

Crimean War, 12

Cripple Creek, Colorado, 149

Cross, Harry, 51

cruel and unusual punishment. *See* Constitution, Eighth Amendment

Cruttwell, C. M. R. F., 90–91

Cuba, 271, 273, 278, 284, 500n (refugees)

Cullen, Edgar M., Prize, 157

Curran, Bob, 104

Currie, David P., 340, 348–349, 398

Currie, J. H., 141

Curzan, Mary M., 289, 495n

Customs Service, U. S., 420

Cutler, Lloyd, 198

Czechoslovakia, 82, 88, 129, 139, 142

Daily Express (London), 125, 127

Daily Herald (London), 125–126

Daily Oklahoman, 298

Daily Worker, 75–76, 239

Daley, Arthur J., 78, 182–183, 330, 379

Daley, Richard J., Daley machine, 254, 302

Dallas, Texas, 61, 64, 69, 71, 74, 295

Dallas Morning News, 57

Dallas Times-Herald, 66

Dapper Dan Dinner (Pittsburgh), 121, 353

Dartmouth College, 172

Davenport, William B., 157

Davies, Ronald N., 290

Davis, Richard M., 225

Davis, Willie, 203

Dawson, Congressman William, 256

Decatur, Illinois, 254, 302

Decline and Fall (Waugh), 91

defamation. *See* Constitution, First Amendment

Defense, U. S. Department of, 261; Secretary of Defense, 261; Secretary of the Air Force, 261; Secretary of the Army, 261, 264

Democratic Club Monday Forum (Denver), 243

Democratic National Committee (DNC), 253, 256, 273

Democratic National Convention, 250
(Los Angeles, 1960), 377 (Miami
Beach, 1972)
Democratic Party of Colorado, 231, 233,
236
Democratic Party (Denver), 232–233
Dempsey, Jack, 353
Denmark, 88
Denver, 1, 3, 4, 22, 27, 34, 46, 61, 165,
178, 189, 190, 219, 223–226, 230,
232, 234, 236, 238, 240, 243–245,
248, 254, 259, 263, 276, 317–318,
328, 330, 335, 345, 349, 379, 399,
409, 421, 424, 448, 455, 456, 479n
Denver Bar Association, 227, 516n
Denver Broncos, 448
Denver Chamber of Commerce, 227
Denver Elks Lodge, 72
Denver Kiwanis Club, 94
Denver National Bank, 225, 226
Denver Post, 4, 30, 31, 35, 50–51, 80, 83,
87, 94, 102, 112, 119–121, 125,
228, 242, 244, 249–251, 317–318,
324, 326, 336, 345, 448
Denver University (DU), 30, 33–34,
39–40, 42, 51, 54–56, 61, 66, 69,
225, 227, 235, 321; Board of
Trustees, 225; Graduate School of
International Studies, 228; Social
Science Foundation, 227, 235, 309,
317, 321
Denver Welfare Council, 227
DePaul University, 198
Depression, 18, 26, 28
Dershowitz, Alan M., 357, 383
Des Moines College of Law, 22
desegregation, 307
Deseret News, 48, 50
Destroyer Squadron 23, 179, 181
Detroit, 224, 282
Detroit, University of, Stadium, 105, 161,
164
Detroit Free Press, 161, 170
Detroit Lions, 32–33, 51, 60, 76, 101,
104–105, 115–116, 158–159,
161–162, 164–172, 182, 194, 251,
330, 335, 448–449, 514n
Detroit News, 60, 162–163, 169
Detroit Times, 161, 162, 165–168, 170

Deutschland uber Alles, 139
Devitt, Edward J., 405
Dewey, Thomas E., 188
Dickinson, Angie, 254
Didinger, Ray, 113
DiMaggio, Joe, 75
Dingfelder, Frank, 191
Dirksen, Everett M., 322
DiSalle, Michael, 234, 251, 300
DiSapio, Carmine, 251
Disney, Walt, 77
Distilled Spirits Institute, 146
District of Columbia Court of Appeals,
200
District of Columbia Touchdown Club,
342
Doar, John, 270, 275, 276, 278, 281, 283,
377
Dobbs, James K., Sr., 432
Dodd, Walter, 154
Dolan, Beverly, 432
Dolan, Joe, 234–238, 240–247, 249–250,
252–254, 259, 263, 265, 267–268,
276, 278–279, 289, 291, 295–296,
298–302, 304–305, 313, 318,
320–321, 325, 330, 335, 479n,
494n, 496n, 497n, 499n, 500n
Dominions Fellowship Trust, 132
Donovan, Robert J., 337
Douglas, Helen Gahagan, 239
Douglas, John W., 265
Douglas, Paul H., 235, 265, 288, 289, 302
Douglas, William O., 146–147, 152–153,
156, 195–197, 200, 208–209,
212–213, 215, 219–220, 224,
261–262, 268, 302, 311, 314, 323,
325, 328–329, 338–340, 349, 353,
358, 366–367, 375–376, 389,
407–409, 434, 435, 436, 447, 472,
498n, 510n
Douglas Fairbanks Award, 67
Down These Mean Streets (Thomas), 391
Downtown Athletic Club of New York
City, 37, 60
Doyle, Ted, 116, 270
Doyle, William E., 301
Drake, John, 162
Drake University, 22
Drury, Allen, 495n

Dubofsky, Jean, 387
Duke University, 54
Duniway, Ben. C., 303
Duquesne University School of Law, 80
Durango, 245, 248–251, 259, 324
Durex condom factory (Birmingham),
    baseball team, 137
Dutton, Frederick G., 252, 254
Dyde, Dr. Walters Farrell, 45–47
Dyer, Braven, 36
Dyer, David, 302

Eagle Forum, 414
Early, General Jubal, 13
East China Sea, 188
Eastland, James O., 267, 277, 279,
    284–285, 289, 291–292, 296,
    301–302, 311–312, 314, 322, 330,
    499n
East-West Shrine Game, 36
Ebbets Field, 111, 166
Ebel, David, 516n
Eckersall, Walter (all-American football
    player, University of Chicago,
    1904–1906), 85
Economic Stabilization, Office of, 200
Edmondson, J. Howard, 298
Edwards, Bill, 164–165, 167
Edwards, Ralph, 228–229
Eisenhower, Arthur, 311
Eisenhower, Dwight D., 274, 284,
    288–290, 305, 307, 310, 444, 493n
Elks Club, 20
Ellender, Allen J., 285
Elliott, E. Donald, 398
Elman, Phil, 268, 386
Emergency Court of Appeals, 207
Emergency Price Control Act of 1942, 207
Empire State Building, 78
employment discrimination, 421
Empress Augusta Bay, battle of, 180
Emsellem, Irene, 499n
Encaenia, 137
Encampment River, 433
England, 46, 135
Engle, Clair, 302–303
USS English, 191
English Law and Its Background (Fifoot),
    127

USS Enterprise, 173, 191, 192
entrapment, 420
Equal Employment Opportunity Com-
    mission (EEOC), 414
Erickson, Leif, 178
Erlichman, John, 386
Ervin, Sam J., 330
Esso Building, 253, 261
Estes, Newton C., 403–405
Ethics in Government Act of 1978, 402,
    426
Eton College, playing field of, 235
SS Europa, 124
Evanston, Illinois, 172

Fadiman, Clifton, 199
Fahey, James J., 454
Fairman, Charles, 218
"fairness doctrine," 348
Family Research Council, 431
Farrar, Harry, 482n
Farrell, (Edward Francis, Jr.) Scrapper, 116
Faubus, Orville, 281
Fay, Paul B. (Red), 303, 492n
Federal Aviation Administration (FAA),
    276
Federal Bureau of Investigation (FBI), 267,
    272, 275, 277, 282, 297, 301, 316,
    322, 359, 378, 386, 408; White ru-
    mored as director, 358–359, 378,
    402, 408
Federal Center (Denver), 224
Federal Communications Commission
    (FCC), 266, 348, 383, 424
Federal Election Campaign Act, 399, 400,
    409
Federal Employers Liability Act (FELA),
    209–210, 341
Federal Home Loan administrator, 200
Federal Power Commission (FPC), 358
Federal Rules of Civil Procedure, 151, 211
Federal Trade Commission (FTC), 295,
    358
Feikens, John, 289, 304
Feldman, Myer (Mike), 311, 312, 327
Field, Stephen J., 405, 434, 510n
field hockey, American Olympic team, 450
Fifoot, C. H. S., 28, 127–129, 138, 229
Fiji, 173

Filchock, Frankie, 98, 107, 116, 122
Finance Committee, U. S. Senate,
    297–298
Finland, 164
First Baptist Church (Montgomery), 276
"First Line, The," 193
Fisher's Hill, battle of, 13
Fisk, Bill, 169
Fixer, The, 391
Flatley, James, 187, 192
Fleeson, Doris, 323, 325
Fleet Street, 5
Fleming, Ian, 454
Fleming, Roscoe, 324
Florida, 11, 121, 239, 291, 302
"Flyte, Sebastian," 132–133
Folsom, Fred, 32, 33
Folsom Field, 239
Football Line Play (Oakes), 33
Football Writers Association of America,
    109, 353
Forbes Field, 85, 98, 104, 115–118
Fordham University, 54
Fordice, Kirk, 425
Foreign Assistance Act of 1961, 299
Forest Lumber Company, 14
"formalism," 156
Formosa, 183, 184, 189
Fort Benning, Georgia, 278
Fort Collins (Colorado), 2, 14–15, 17–19,
    23–24, 230, 309
Fort Collins Coloradoan, 182, 188, 326
Fort Morgan (Colorado), 14
Fort Collins Public Library, 479n
Fort Collins Public Library Oral History
    Program, 2
Fort Collins Rotary Club, 84
Fort Sumter (South Carolina), 12
Fort Worth, 63–64, 66–67
Fortas, Abe, 146, 153, 344, 356, 386, 402,
    414, 435
Fortune, 211
40 Patriots/Countless Americans, 414
Foster, Jack, 447
"Four Horsemen" (Notre Dame football),
    44, 229, 449
Fowler, H. H., 315
Fox-Movietone newsreel, 53
France, 88, 137–138, 237

Franco, Francisco, 134–135
Frank, Clint, 57–60, 67, 147–148, 229,
    329
Frank, Jerome, 446 ("rule skepticism"),
    502n
Frank, John P., 212, 213, 218, 220, 268,
    492n
Frankfurter, Felix, 137, 149, 153, 195,
    196, 200, 207, 210, 212, 213–216,
    220, 260, 268, 310–311, 314, 320,
    324, 328, 335, 340, 386
Franklin, Walter B. (Walt), 80, 83
Frederick, David, 457
freedom of contract. See Constitution,
    Fourteenth Amendment, substan-
    tive due process
Freedom Rides, Riders, 6, 271–272,
    274–275, 279, 280–285, 291,
    307–308, 494n
French Riviera, 133
Freund, Paul A., 261, 314–315, 318–320,
    327, 387, 453
Frick, Ford, 378
Friendly, Henry J., 315, 318
"Frothy Facts." See Tom Meany
Fryingpan-Arkansas Project, 16, 318
Ft. Knox, 317
Fulbright Scholarships, 471
Fuld, Stanley, 315
Fulminante, Oreste, 411
Furman, Jack, 196

Gaius (Institutes), 128
Galbraith, John Kenneth, 250
Gallico, Paul, 100
"Galloping Ghost." See Harold (Red)
    Grange
Garden City Hotel, 112
Garfield Street, Wellington, Colorado, 458
Gartner, Murray, 195
Gates Rubber, 223
Gavin, Tom, 245, 247, 326, 412–413
Gehrig, Lou, 75
Gehrke, Fred, 481n, 484n
General Services Administration (GSA),
    278
Gentry, Byron, 119
Geoghegan, William, 263, 268, 293,
    296–298, 328, 479n, 492n

Georgetown, 261
Georgetown University Hospital, 269, 271
Georgia, University of, 273
Georgia, 256, 272–273, 291, 304, 318, 366, 450
Germany, 14, 88, 134, 137–140, 164
Gewin, Walter P., 304
Giancana, Sam, 316
Gibson, S. Elizabeth, 471
Gilmore, Grant, 155
Ginsburg, Ruth Bader, 516n
Gizo Island, 174
Gleason, Bill, 449
Glendon, Mary Ann, 442
Glenwood Springs, Colorado, 18
Go Ask Alice, 391
Go East, Young Man, 219
Goebbels, Dr. Josef, 138–139
Golay, John, 63
Goldberg, Arthur L., 311, 314–316, 318–319, 335, 336, 340, 341, 344, 402
Goldberg, Marshall (Biggie), 57, 227, 229
Golenpaul, Ann, 199
Gonzaga, 108
Good Housekeeping, 46
Goodman, Louis M., 303
Goodman, William H., 494n
Goodwin, Richard, 281
Gore, Albert, 436
Gould, Alan, 32, 52, 59
Gould Lumber Company, 14
Grady, J. Harold
Graham, Donald S., 225
Graham, Fred, 346, 403–404
Graham, Henry V., 279–281
Grand Army of the Republic, 13, 22
Grand Canyon, 62, 109
Grand Junction, Colorado, 28, 89, 244–245
Grange, Harold (Red), 33, 36–37, 57, 101, 103–104, 133
Grant, James B., 225
Grant, Gen. U. S., 13, 276
Grayson, Bobby, 36
Great Britain, 139, 142, 164
Great Marianas Turkey Shoot, 184
Great Western Sugar Refining Company, 14, 17, 224

Greeley, Colorado, 20, 245, 448
Green Bay Packers, 60, 98, 101, 117, 129, 165, 167
Green, Billy, 252
Greenberg, Hank, 112
Greenhouse, Linda, 384, 397, 479n
Greenwich Steps, 193
Gressman, Eugene, 195, 206, 219
Gridiron Club, 313
Grier, Robert C., 434
Griffith Stadium, 193
Grinnell College, 69
Griswold, Erwin N., 7, 318
Grooms, Harlan H., 294
Guadalcanal, 173
Guam, 183, 192
Guffey Coal Act, 200
Guinan, Texas, 109
Gulf of Mexico, 376
Gulliver, Ashbel, 147
Gunnels, Larry, 337
Gunnison, 232
Gunther, John, 224
Guthman, Edwin O., 264–266, 275, 449, 497n

habeas corpus, 339
Haight, Walter, 81
Halaby, Najeeb, 276
Halas, George, 120
Hall, David, 337
Halsey, William F. (Bull), 174, 179–181, 184–187, 189, 192, 487n–488n
Hamilton, Nigel, 479n
Hamilton, Walton Hale, 154, 195
Hamilton County, Ohio, 251
Hammel's (Washington, D.C., restaurant), 1
Hanneman, Chuck, 160–167
Harding, Warren G., administration, 290
Harlan, John Marshall, 343–345, 347–348, 350, 356, 358, 384
Harlan, John Marshall, I, 510n
Harlow, Dick, 57
harmless error rule, 410, 411
Harper, Fowler V., 220
Harriman, W. Averill, 251–252, 506n
Harris, George, 214
Harry, Robert H., 147, 155, 225–226, 246, 487n

Hart, Phillip, 330
Harvard University, 57, 148, 150; Harvard
    College, 133–134; *Harvard Law
    Review,* 313, 343, 349; Harvard
    Law School, 63, 137, 140, 149,
    152, 195–196, 225, 260, 263, 300,
    314, 318–319, 383, 442, 499n
Harvey, Jack, 79
Haskell, Floyd, 406
Hastie, William H., 301, 313–315,
    318–319, 321–322, 499n
Hatch Act of 1938, 211
Hawaii, 289, 293, 335
Hawaiian Room (Roosevelt Hotel), 118
Hawks, Rex, 299
Haynsworth, Clement, 403, 503n
Healey, Denis, 129–130
Health, Education and Welfare (HEW),
    U. S. Department of, 312, 319
Hearst News, 118
Hector, Louis, 141, 293
Hegel, G. W. F., 419
Heisman Trophy, 37, 56–57, 59–60,
    147
Hellman, Arthur, 400–401
Helms Foundation, 228
Henderson, Greg, 438
Hendricks, Don, 77–78
Hendrie, Laura, 480n
Henkin, Louis, 195
Henry, Lawrence (Larry), 233, 236–237,
    241, 244–245, 247
Henry, S. Arthur, 225
Hentoff, Nat, 412
Hero Ain't Nothing But a Sandwich, A, 391
Herring, Donald G., 482n
Hersey, John, 198
Hertford College (Oxford), 29, 90–93,
    125–128, 229, 342
Heslet, Valetta Evalyn, 193
Hewitt, Bill, 103
Hickory Hill, 246, 262, 336, 354
Higginbotham, A. Leon, 295
Hill, Anita, 414, 416
Hill, Lister, 292, 293, 294
Hillerman, Tony, 454
Hinckley, John, 403
Hinkle, Clark, 67

Hitler, Adolph, 27, 82–83, 129–130, 134,
    139–140, 143, 164
Hoagland, Donald W., 225, 233, 329, 335
Hoak, James K., Sr., 432
Hoffa, James R., 287
Hogan, Gorman, 53, 61–62, 87
Hogg, Quentin, 129
"Hold That Co-ed," 84
Holland, 88
Hollings, Ernest F. (Fritz), 255
Holme, Peter H., 61
Holmes, Hamilton, 273
Holmes, Oliver Wendell, Jr., 7, 27, 31,
    155, 198, 326, 408, 434, 446, 454,
    455, 499n, 501n
Honolulu, 345–346
Hoover, Herbert, 212n, 290
Hoover, J. Edgar, 267, 282–283, 315,
    (funeral) 378
Hopkinson, Charles, 27
Horne, John, 254
Hotel Fort Pitt, 105
Houghton, Charlie, 133
Houghton Mifflin, 454
House, Toni, 415
House of Commons, 131, 140
House of Representatives, U. S., 82, 200,
    231, 266, 358, 388; Judiciary Com-
    mittee, 311; Rules Committee, 318;
    Select Committee Investigating
    Lobbying and Campaign Finance,
    263
Houston, 307, 315, 376
Houston Chronicle, 67
Houston Post, 69
Hovde, F. L. (Ted), 483n
Howard, A. E. Dick, 417
Howard University, 427
Hoyt, E. Palmer (Ep), 242
Hubble, Edwin, 62
Huertas, S., 516n
Hughes, Charles Evans, 149, 196, 318,
    349, 377, 434
Hughes, Hubbard & Reed, 226
Hughes, Langston, 391
Hughes, Sarah Tilghman, 295
Humphrey, Hubert H., 234, 242, 247,
    249, 266

Hundley, William G., 287
Hungary, 88, 244
Hunter, Charlayne, 273
Hutchins, Robert Maynard, 140, 146
Hutson, Don, 167

Iba, Henry, 73
Ickes, Harold, 142, 214
Idaho, 17, 293
Ideal Cement Company, 223, 225
Ideological Origins of the American Revolution, 364
Ides, Allan, 398, 446, 503n
Illinois, 254, 259, 288, 301, 322, 369
Illinois, University of, 33, 36
Illinois Supreme Court, 313
Illustrated Football Annual, 44
Immigration and Naturalization Service
    (INS). *See* Justice, U. S. Department of
immunity from prosecution, 346–347
incorporation doctrine, 217–218, 339,
    347, 359, 360
Indiana University, 98, 116
USS Independence, 185
Indianola, Texas, 13
Indochina, 244
"Information, Please!" 168, 199
Interior, U. S. Department of, 146, 335
Internal Revenue Service (IRS), 299
Internal Security Act of 1950, 267
International Business Machines (IBM),
    226
International News Service (INS), 58,
    118–119
Interstate Commerce Commission (ICC),
    284–286, 341
"In the Wake of the News," 379
Iowa, 12, 13, 69
Iowa, University of, 37, 70, 150
Iowa State College, 22
Iowa Territory, 11
Ireland, 11, 143
Irish, Ned, 113
Iron Curtain, 244
Isbell, Cecil, 102
Isocrates, 25, 269
Italy, 139, 182

Ivy League, 32, 147
Iwo Jima, 188, 189

Jackson, Mississippi, 279, 291, 292
Jackson, Robert H., 195, 196, 200,
    209–210, 213–216, 218, 363, 385,
    393, 425
Jacob Jones (American destroyer), 142
Jacobs, Eli, 427
Jacobson, Keith, 420
Jaffe, Harry, 100
Jaworski, Leon, 291, 315, 499n
"Jeeves," 137
Jefferson, Billy, 165
Jefferson, Thomas, 216, 364
Jefferson-Jackson Day, 242
Jelinek, Charles, 133, 136, 484n
Jensen, Jackie, 383
Jersey City, New Jersey, 117
Jesionowski, Stanley, 209
Jews, German oppression of, 134
Jill (Larkin), 132
"Jim Crow," 205, 286, 307, 352
Johnson, Edwin Carl (Big Ed), 81,
    231–233, 241, 249–250
Johnson, Frank M., 276, 278, 279, 280,
    307, 494n
Johnson, Lyndon B., 241, 247–249, 250n,
    255, 266, 293, 295, 297, 444
Johnson, William, 408
Joint Chiefs of Staff, 181
Jones-Costigan Act of 1934, 17
Journal of the Supreme Court, 216
Judges Act of 1925, 358
judicial code, 312
judicial conferences, Eighth Circuit,
    421, 439; Tenth Circuit, 354,
    407–410, 414, 479n
Judiciary Committee, U. S. Senate, 150,
    164, 267, 311, 330
Justice, U. S. Department of, 5, 261, 263,
    269–271, 274, 279, 281–283,
    288–289, 295–296, 299–300, 305,
    308–309, 311–313, 315, 319–320,
    322–323, 327–328, 335, 337, 347,
    350, 388, 389, 448–449, 499n
    attorney general, 261, 262, 297, 388
    deputy attorney general, 102, 260,

Justice, U. S. Department of (*continued*)
    261, 262, 270, 297, 299, 311, 325,
    336, 447
  solicitor general, 261, 263, 268, 335, 428
  assistant attorneys general (AAG), 102,
    308; Administrative AAG, 267;
    Antitrust Division, 146, 264, 265,
    266, 268, 296, 438; Civil Division,
    264, 265, 280, 296; Civil Rights
    Division, 257, 264–266, 270, 281,
    283; Criminal Division, 264; Inter-
    nal Security, 267; Lands Division,
    264, 265, 266; Office of Legal
    Counsel (OLC), 264, 265, 311,
    313, 314; Tax Division, 264, 275
  Bureaus, Prisons, 275; Immigration
    and Naturalization, 388 (Border Pa-
    trol, 278)
  Executive Office for United States At-
    torneys, 268
  Organized Crime Task Force, 287
Justinian (Institutes), 128
Jutland, battle of, 184

Kaese, Harold, 111
Kai, Lt. Tomai, 192
Kaiser, Philip, 129, 130, 132, 134, 137,
    252, 254, 259, 266
Kakasic, George (Bunko), 116
kamikaze, 188, 189, 190, 191, 192
Kamisar, Yale, 412
Kane, John L., 248, 259
Kansas, 293
Kansas, University of, 36, 73, 424, 481n
Kansas City, Missouri, 311
Karcis, Bill, 108–109, 112, 115
Karpowich, Ed (*aka* Ed Karp), 113, 116
Katzenbach, Nicholas deB., 154, 265,
    313–316, 318–321, 326–327
Kaufman, Irving R., 304
KDKA Radio (Pittsburgh), 99
Keating, Kenneth, 285
Keck, Harry, 107–108
Kefauver, Estes, 234–235, 248, 261, 310,
    318
Kelley, Paul, 210
Kemp, Naomi, 11
Kempton, Murray, 449–450
Kendall, David E., 365

Kennedy, Anthony M., 390, 407, 412,
    418, 425–429, 439, 472
Kennedy, Edward M. (Teddy), 142,
    246–248
Kennedy, Ethel, 330, 336, 342
Kennedy, Eunice, 135, 142–143
Kennedy, Jean (Smith), 142, 263
Kennedy, John F. (JFK), 1, 2, 133,
    134–135, 138–140, 142, 173–179,
    198, 230, 234–245, 247–256,
    258–259, 260–263, 272, 274–275,
    287, 289, 290, 297, 299–301, 308,
    310–311, 313, 315–318, 320–329,
    354, 399, 412, 442, 444, 445, 448,
    451, 497n, 500n, 505n, 516n
Kennedy, John F. (Library), 2
Kennedy, Joseph P., 126, 133–135,
    140–143, 198, 252, 261, 268, 296;
    anti-Semitism, 143, 252
Kennedy, Joseph P., Jr., 63, 135, 140, 142
Kennedy, Kathleen (Kick), 133, 135, 140,
    142
Kennedy, Patricia, 142
Kennedy, Robert F. (RFK), 6, 246–247,
    250–258, 260–281, 284–285, 287,
    289–293, 295, 297–299, 301,
    303–305, 308–317, 319–320,
    327–328, 336, 342, 354, 492n,
    497n–498n, 505n
"Kennedy hounds," 479n
Kennedy Justice (Navasky), 290, 364
Kenny, Sir Anthony, 483n, 484n
Kentucky, University of (Library), 202
Kentucky Derby, 200
Kerr, Aubrey, 297
Kerr, Robert S., 297–299
Khrushchev, Nikita S., 273, 281
Kieran, John, 77, 199
Kiesling, Walt, 353
kikusui, 189
Kiley, Roger J., 302
Killefer, Tom, 63, 432
Killefer, Wade (Red), 63
Kimball, Penn, 137
Kinard, (Bruiser), 166
King, Rev. Martin Luther, Jr., 255–258,
    272, 276–279, 322
King, Mrs. Martin Luther (Coretta),
    256–257, 304

Kinkaid, Rear Adm. Thomas C., 185
Kirksey, Andrew, 177
Klain, Ron, 437
Klauder, Charles, 26
Klauder and Day, 26
Kolombangara, 173–175, 178, 180
Koonce, Harold, 31
Korn, Jessica, 398
Kourlis, Rebecca Love, 471
Kristallnacht, 134
Ku Klux Klan, 27, 233, 271–272, 276,
        278, 282–283, 291, 494n
Kurita, Admiral Takeo, 184–186
Kurland, Philip B., 343–344, 357, 358, 361
Kyushu, 191

Labor, U. S. Department of, 335, 340, 378
Labor Management Relations Act, 337
Labour Club, 130
Labour Party, 129
Lain, Ernie, 57, 68–69
Lam, William C. (Kayo), 35–36
Lambert, William, 264
Lambu Lambu Cove, 178
Landis, James M., 195
Landrum-Griffin Act, 263
Lane, French, 51
Larimer County Collection, Fort Collins
        Public Library, 479n
Larimer County (Colorado) Hospital, 14
Larkin, Philip, 132
Larson, Lloyd, 329
Latin, 88, 89, 128, 138
Latin America, 244
Law of Property Act 1925, 128
Lawrence, David (columnist), 284, 323
Lawrence, David (Pa. Gov.), 234
Lawrence, William H., 260
Lawson, Marjorie, 256
Leadville Corporation, 227
Least Dangerous Branch, The, 447
Lee, Rex, 340, 349, 352, 374–375, 406,
        424, 447, 454, 471
Lee, Vice-Adm. Willis A. (Chink), 185
Leemans, Alphonse (Tuffy), 103, 118
legal realism, 7, 146, 149, 152, 154,
        445–446
Legal Times of Washington, 408, 410–411,
        425, 439, 445, 516n

legislative vetoes, 388, 397–399
Lehman, Herbert H., 251
Leigh, Vivien, 76, 123
Levant, Oscar, 199, 256
Levi, Edward H., 315, 318
Lewin, Nathan, 356
Lewis, Anthony, 297, 318, 340, 383, 386
Lewis, Grant & Davis, 225
Lewis, Grant, Newton, Davis & Henry,
        225
Lewis, John L., 211–213
Lewis & Grant, 225
USS Lexington, 181, 182
Leyte (island), 184–185
Leyte Gulf, battle of, 184, 188
Liberal Club, 130
Liberal Party, 129
Liberty Magazine, 67, 111
Library of Congress (Manuscript Divi-
        sion), 2, 435, 512n
Liebenow, William F., 175, 177
Liebman, Lance, 354, 380, 503n
Life, 53, 198
Lileks, James, 455
Liley, Lou, 56, 67, 69, 482n
Lincoln, Abraham, 22, 30
Lincoln Hotel, 75–76
Lincoln Memorial, 354
Lindsay, A. D. (Sandy), 129
Lindsay, Vachel, 375
Lion's Club (Boulder), 71
Lippman, Walter, 378, 505n–506n
"Little Beavers." *See* Destroyer Squadron
        23
Little Rock, Arkansas, 274–275, 281, 283,
        290, 493n
Liuzzo, Mrs. Viola, 282
Llewellyn, Karl N., 152
Lodge, Henry Cabot, 257
Lodge, Herman, 395
Loeb Classical Library, 25
Loevinger, Lee, 265, 266
Loftus, Charles, 55, 66
Logan, John (Slim), 133
Lombardi, Vince, 120
London, 140, 142, 376
Long, Edward V., 331
Long, Russell, 292, 304
Long Island, 257

Long Island University (LIU), 72, 74
Look, 198, 220
Loretto, Pensylvania, 101, 270
Los Angeles, 36, 54, 65, 117, 240, 248, 250
Los Angeles Bulldogs, 117
Los Angeles Times, 36, 64, 93, 379
Lothian, Lord (Philip H. Kerr, 11th Marquess), 135
Louisa, Kentucky, 200
Louisiana, 13, 130, 285, 291–293, 302
Love, John A., 471
Lovelace Medical Foundation, 3, 324
Lowery, Nick, 514n
Lubyanka, 449
Lucero, Carlos, 506n
Luisetti, Hank, 32, 72–73
Lumberi, 174
Luzon (Philippine Islands), 183, 184
Lynch, Thomas, 252
Lynne, Seybourn H., 294
Lyons, Leonard, 210–211

MacArthur, Douglas, 177–178, 180, 183–185
Macdonald, Torbert (Torby), 133, 138–139, 148
McAfee, George (One-Play), 171
McAllister, Thomas F., 208
McBride, Thomas J., 303
McCabe, Charles, 383
McCain, Vice-Admiral John S., 186
McCarthy, Joseph, 235, 239, 267; Permanent Subcommittee on Investigations of the Senate Government Operations Committee, 267
McClellan, John, 264, 284–285, 295
McCloskey, Robert G., 405
McClure, J.C., 175
McConnell, Michael W., 413
McCree, Wade H., 301–302
McCune, Wes, 197
McDonald, Miss, of Sleat, 132–133
McDonald, Russell, 63, 128, 133
McDonough, Paul, 49, 116, 120
McDougal, Myres S., 153–154, 156, 446, 486n
McEwan, William, 63, 484n
McGrory, Mary, 455

McKay, Monroe, 403
McKaye, Milton, 85
McKenna, Joseph, 434
McLaughlin, John, 415
McLean, John, 510n
McLean, Virginia, 246, 336
M'Lemore, Henry, 47–48, 50–52, 65, 110–111
McMillen, Thomas R., 302
McMillin, Bo, 101–102
McNally, John Victor (Johnny Blood), 79–80, 83, 86–87, 93, 97–98, 100–101, 104, 108–109, 111, 113–114, 117, 119–122, 133, 163, 269–270, 335, 352, 353, 358, 378, 379, 405, 406; characteristics, 98, 121; White for President, 358, 378–379
McNamara, Patrick V., 289
McNamara, Robert, 261
McNichols, Stephen L. R., 233, 236, 241, 245, 247, 249
McRae, William A., 302
McWilliams, Robert H., 61, 472
Mabus, Ray, 425
Maclean, Norman, 433
Madrid, 135
Magruder, Calvert, 208
Mahoning County Common Pleas Court, 300
Maidenhead, 132
Mair, Andrew, 31, 480n, 506n, 510n
Madison, James, Lecture (New York University), 501n
Madison Square Garden, 72–73, 77–79, 84, 113
Malamud, Bernard, 391
Manchester, 137
Manchester, William, 479n
Mandel, Freddie, 158–159, 163, 165, 167, 169, 172, 335
Manders, Clarence (Pug), 171
SS Manhattan, 141–143
Manhattan College, 109
Mann, Floyd, 278, 279
Mansfield, Mike, 296, 322
Manske, Ed (Eggs), 116
Mantz, Clark, 100
Manufacturers Association of Colorado, 317

Mara, Tim, 144, 148, 157–158
Marcantonio, Vito, 239
Mariana Islands, 183
Marine Corps, 164
Maris, Albert, 208
Maritime Commission, United States, 143
Mark VIII torpedoes, 177
Marshall, Burke, 266, 267, 274–275, 279, 281–285, 292–293, 308, 327, 433
Marshall, George C., 27
Marshall, George Preston, 98, 100, 101
Marshall, John, 31, 510n
Marshall, Thurgood, 4, 204–205, 301, 304, 311, 318, 358–359, 390–391, 393–394, 401, 403, 407, 414, 434, 436, 438, 452, 454, 479n, 504n
Marshall, Thurgood, federal judiciary building, 4, 438
Marshall, Thurgood, Papers, 435, 479n, 507n
Marshall Scholarships, 471
Martin, Louis, 273
Martindale-Hubbell *Law Directory*, 297
Maryland "M" Club, 342
Mason-Dixon Line, 255
Massachusetts, 263, 289, 296
Mathews, Ned, 514n
Matisi, Tony, 116
Maupin, Armistead, 193
Mauro, Tony, 408, 425, 439
Maxwell, Robert W. (Tiny) Memorial Football Club, 57, 329
Maxwell Air Force Base, 276–280, 493n
Mayhew, (Hayden L.) Lindy, 116
Meany, George, 319
Meany, Tom ("Frothy Facts"), 73
Medicare Bill (1962), 316
Medicine Bow Mountains, 15 (Colorado), 433 (Wyoming)
Meehan, Chick, 109
Memphis, 403
Merriwell, Frank, 53
Metcalf, Lee, 295–296
Metro-Goldwyn-Mayer (MGM) studios, 123; newsreel, 53
Metropolitan Basketball Writers' Association of New York, 72–73, 77
Metropolitan Denver Democratic Dinner, 243

Miami, 379, 500n
Miami, University of, Law School, 154
Michigan, 289, 301
Michigan, University of, 37, 140, 159, 168, 195, 412
Middle East, 235, 244
Midway, battle of, 173
Miller, Herbert J. (Jack), 264, 287, 308, 389
Milliken, Colorado, 28
Milwaukee Sentinel, 329
Minneapolis, 335
Minneapolis Star-Tribune, 405
Minnesota, supreme court of, 266
Minnesota, University of, 37, 229
Minnesota Twins, 357
Minow, Newton, 220
Mississippi, 13, 273, 279, 280, 282, 284, 291, 302, 425, 427
Mississippi, University of, 166
Mississippi River, 12, 36, 57
Mississippi State University, 165
Missouri, 12–13, 331
Missouri, University of, 35–36, 44–45
Missouri River, 36
Missouri Valley Conference, 73
Mitchell, Oscar, 457
Mitscher, Marc A. (Pete), 181, 183–192
Mollenhoff, Clark, 264
Montana, 126, 230, 293, 295, 302, 322, 403, 433
Montana, University of, 33
Montana State College, 30
"Monte," 34
Montgomery, Alabama, 271, 275–277, 280, 282, 307, 494n
Montgomery Advertiser, 277, 280
USS Montpelier, 454
Moore, Gene, 47
Moore, James William, 148–149, 152, 157
Moore, Underhill, 148–149, 152–153, 156, 446
Morison, Samuel Eliot, 454, 488n
Morley, Clarence, 27
Morris, Desmond, 391
Morris, Everett, 78–79
Morris, Glen, 84
Morrissey, Francis X., 296–297, 305

Morse [Wayne] Amendment, 500n
Morton, Robert, 31, 41
Moscow, 139
Moscow Radio, 281
Mottley, Charles C., 377
Moyers, Bill, 255
Muir, R. M., 72
Mullin, Willard, 75
Munich, Germany, 137–140
Munich Agreement, 129, 132, 134, 137, 142–143
Murphy, Bob, 168
Murphy, Frank, 195, 201, 205–206, 208–209, 212, 214–216, 218
Murphy, Walter, 498n
Murrah, Alfred P., 297, 298
Murray, Jim, 379
Mutual Broadcasting Network, 199

Naked Ape, The, 391
Nance, James K., 67, 69, 376–377
Nash, Patty (Ris), 86
Nashville, 274
Nation, The, 257, 443
National Association for the Advancement of Colored People (NAACP), 291
National Association for the Advancement of Colored People (NAACP) Legal Defense and Education Fund, Inc., 204, 307
National Broadcasting Company (NBC), 78
National Collegiate Athletic Association (NCAA), 55, 72, 353; Theodore Roosevelt Award, 353
National Conference of Citizens for Religious Freedom, 252
National District Attorneys Association Foundation, 345
National Education Association, 240
National Endowment for the Arts (NEA), 414
National Farmers Union (NFU), 234–236, 241
National Football Foundation, 342, 352
National Football Hall of Fame, 228
National Football League (NFL), 1, 4, 32–33, 59–61, 71, 80–81, 83, 85, 99, 104–105, 110, 119, 123,
144–145, 148, 158, 161–162, 165, 167, 171, 181, 183, 227, 329, 353, 378; 1937 draft, 59–60; brutal play, 99–100, 102, 115, 166
National Football League Hall of Fame, 121, 166, 352, 353
National Football League Players Association, 353, 514n; Byron "Whizzer" White Humanitarian Award, 353, 514n
National Geographic, 394
National Invitational (basketball) Tournament (NIT), 72, 74, 80, 82, 84, 157, 449
National Labor Relations Board (NLRB), 358
National Law Journal, The, 383, 408, 516n
National Press Club, 377
National Presbyterian Church, 378
National Professional Football Writers Association (NPFWA), 109
National Review, 449
National Road, 11
National socialism, 139
Naval Academy, U. S., 61
Naval Intelligence, 168–169, 172, 182, 185
Navasky, Victor S., 289, 290, 364
Navy Cross, 180, 182
Navy League, 134
Neagle, David, 405
Nebraska, University of, 160, 270
Nelson, Chester (Red), 48, 52, 55, 62, 84–85
Nelson, William, 445
Neuborne, Burt, 413
Nevada, 126, 128, 293
Nevada, University of, 63
New Deal, 7, 17, 146, 150–151, 156, 164, 231, 348, 445–446, 449, 453
New England College of Law, 437
New Frontier, 444. See also White, Byron: Image
New Georgia, 173, 174, 178
New Georgia Sound. See Slot, the
New Guinea, 173, 174, 180
New Haven, Connecticut, 141, 143–144, 148, 156, 226
New Haven Journal-Courier, 148

New Jersey, 147, 252

New Mexico, 293

New Orleans, 116–118, 273, 280–281, 292, 304, 307, 387, 402

New Republic, The, 260, 323, 356, 441, 444

New York (state), 147, 254, 285, 315

New York City, 73, 75, 84, 105, 112, 122, 142–143, 156–157, 172, 194, 224, 226, 251–252, 257, 303, 305, 313

New York Court of Appeals, 157

New York Daily Mirror, 75, 82

New York Daily News, 58, 77, 80, 112, 115, 125

New York Giants, 51, 60, 103–105, 107, 109, 112–115, 117–119, 124, 144, 148, 157, 159, 167, 172, 193

New York Herald-Tribune, 51, 75–77, 142, 323, 337

New York Journal-American, 67, 75, 79, 109

New York Post, 74

New York Pro Football Writers Dinner, 353

New York Sun, 75–76, 125

New York Sunday News, 162

New York Times, 17, 46, 50, 64, 75, 77, 115, 126, 143, 182, 260, 270, 297, 305, 318, 323, 327, 330, 337, 340, 346, 379, 382, 384, 386, 395, 397, 405, 412, 419, 440, 445, 454; Man in the News, 379–380

New York Times Magazine, 269, 271, 380

New York University (NYU), 72, 74, 77, 337, 400, 413, 445

New York World-Telegram, 57–59, 64, 67, 73, 75, 77, 79, 109, 110–111, 113–114, 125

New York Yankees, 98, 427

New Yorker, 198

Newhouse News Service, 455

News-Chronicle (London), 125

Newsday, 449

Newspaper Enterprise Association (NEA), 54–55, 58

Newsweek, 3, 322

Newton, Davis & Henry, 219, 224

Newton, Quigg, 224, 225, 228, 232, 233, 236

Neyland, (Major) Bob, 33

Niccolai, Armand, 113, 119

SS Niew Amsterdam, 88

Nikkel, Harold, 30–31

Nimitz, Admiral Chester, 185, 186, 187

Nine Young Men (McCune), 197

Nishimura, Vice-Admiral Shoji, 185

Nixon, Richard M., 239–240, 251, 255, 257, 258, 259, 289, 347, 356, 357, 380, 382, 386, 389, 503n

Nolan, Betty, 125

Noppenberg, John, 165

Norlin, George, 25–28, 47–48, 51–52, 56, 64, 73, 82, 193, 269

Norman, Oklahoma, 35

Norris-LaGuardia Act, 212, 213

North American Newspaper Alliance (NANA), 58

North Carolina, 273

North Dakota, 290, 425

North Platte River, 433

Northwestern University, 167, 220

Norway, 88

Notre Dame University, football team, 23, 44, 229; law school, 257, 258

Noumea, New Caledonia, 173

Novak, Robert, 260

Nuremberg (trials), 195, 196, 200, 216

Nuttall, O. T., 49, 66, 69, 481n, 482n

Oakes, Bernard F. (Bunny), 33–36, 47–48, 52–53, 55–57, 64, 66–69, 74, 111, 121, 229

Oberdorfer, Louis F., 2, 3, 7, 153, 155, 183, 195, 218–219, 263–264, 274–276, 291–294, 299, 302, 307, 377, 397, 485n, 487n; Judge Book, 302

O'Brien, Davey, 57–58

O'Brien, David M., 401

O'Brien, Lawrence (Larry), 252, 268

O'Brien, Tim, 479n

O'Connor, Sandra Day, 387, 389–391, 393–394, 396, 400, 403, 407, 411, 416, 418–419, 421, 426–429, 431, 507n

Odd Fellows (Wellington), 23

O'Donnell, Kenneth P. (Kenny), 289, 499n

Oerter, Al, 240
Ohio, 214, 234, 254, 263, 293, 300
Okinawa, 184, 189, 191–192
Oklahoma, 255, 293, 296, 297, 299
Oklahoma City, Oklahoma, 297, 298
Oklahoma State University, 56, 73–74, 78
Oklahoma University, 35–36, 39
Oliphant, Herman, 152
Olympics, Berlin (1936), 84; Moscow
    (1980), 450
Omnibus Judgeship Bill of 1961, 272,
    289, 291, 295–296, 299–301,
    304–305
"One Minute to Play," 133
One on One, 415
Oral History Program (John F. Kennedy
    Library), 2, 310
Orange Bowl, 52–53
Oregon, University of, 228
Oregon Forcible Entry and Wrongful De-
    tainer Statute, 360
Oregon State University, 37
Orrick, William, 102, 252–253, 264–265,
    280, 293, 302–303
Ottenberg, Miriam, 269, 325
Owen, Chris, 516n
Oxford City, 130
Oxford Mail, 125
Oxford University, 5, 28, 45–46, 60–62,
    65, 71–72, 75, 80–82, 85–92, 105,
    109, 119, 121, 123–132, 134–138,
    140–141, 143, 145, 147, 159, 195,
    197, 243, 252, 265, 323, 342, 448,
    506n; antiprofessionalism, 126;
    curricula: 128 (law curriculum),
    129 (Politics, Philosophy, and
    Economics [PPE]); rugby, 72,
    124–125; "scouts," 130, 136; terms
    (Michaelmas, Hilary, Trinity) and
    vacations ("vacs"), 128
Ozawa, Admiral Jizaburo, 184, 185, 186

Pacific War Diary 1942–1945, 454
Paepcke, Walter, 228
Palace Hotel (San Francisco), 63
Palau Islands, 183
Palm Beach, Florida, 134, 260, 262
Palm Springs, California, 316, 405
Pan-American Games, 239

Panic of 1857, 12
Paramount Motion Pictures (Pittsburgh), 93
Paris, France, 134, 139
parochial schools, government aid to. *See*
    First Amendment
Parsons, C. L. (Poss), 35, 52, 53, 70, 94,
    483n
Parsons, James B., 301, 302
Pathé newsreel, 53
Patterson, Edwin W., 152
Patterson, John, 272, 275, 277, 279, 281,
    284, 493n
Peace Convocation, 82
Peace Corps, 281
Peale, Norman Vincent, 252
Pearl Harbor, 172–173, 185, 188,
    192–193, 483n
Pearson, Drew, 211, 213–214
Peckham, Rufus, 152
Peipul, Milt, 165–166
Peltason, Jack, 307
Pelz, Edward, 61, 63
Pennsylvania, 11, 254, 295
Pennsylvania, University of, Law School,
    220
Pennsylvania Abortion Control Act, 428
Pennsylvania Hotel, 109
Pennsylvania Human Relations Commis-
    sion, 295
Pepper, Claude, 239
Perkin, Robert L. (Bob), 224, 228, 243
Petersburg, Pennsylvania, 11
Petry, Nicholas R., 432, 433, 488n
Phi Beta Kappa honorary fraternity, 1, 48,
    50, 54, 60–61, 67, 69, 83, 91, 313
Phi Delta Phi gold medal (chemistry), 37
Phi Gamma Delta fraternity, 29, 158, 259
Philadelphia, 104, 252, 288, 295, 329,
    353, 397
Philadelphia Eagles, 60, 86, 101, 103, 107,
    110, 116–117, 162, 167–168
Philadelphia Inquirer, 80
Philippine Islands, 173, 178, 180–181,
    183–184, 187
Philippine Sea, battle of, 183, 187
Philippine Sea, second battle of, 202
Phoenix, 235, 268
Piranian, George, 127, 136, 484n
Pitkin, Frederick W., 490n

Pitt, William (the Younger), 85
Pittsburgh, University of (Pitt), 52, 54,
      56–57, 80, 97, 108, 111–112, 117,
      227; School of Law, 400
Pittsburgh (baseball) Pirates, 104, 115, 159
Pittsburgh Pirates (Steelers as of 1940), 4,
      60, 76, 79, 81–82, 85, 89, 92–93,
      97–98, 100–101, 103–119, 122,
      124, 129, 159, 161, 165, 168, 264,
      269–270, 329, 353, 449; rumors of
      jealousy over White's salary, 104,
      108–109, 111, 122; White rejects
      rumors, 110, 113; New York writer
      accuses players, who reply,
      112–113; John Doar's views, 270
Pittsburgh Post-Gazette, 100, 102, 104,
      108, 114, 159, 353
Pittsburgh Press, 85, 104, 108, 116, 120,
      159
Pittsburgh Sun-Telegraph, 107, 120
Poe, Luke Harvey, 254
Poland, 139–140, 143
Politics, Philosophy, and Economics (PPE).
      See Oxford University, curricula
Polo Grounds, 112, 114–115, 193, 483n
Pomponio, Mike, 241
Pond, Raymond (Ducky), 147
Pony Express. See Union Pacific
Poole, Cecil, 303
Pope, Walter L., 295, 302
Pope John XXIII Lecture, Catholic Uni-
      versity, 442
Port Gibson, battle of, 12
Portland, Oregon, 264
Portsmouth Spartans, 32, 158
Posner, Richard A., 401, 501n
Postal Service, U. S., 420
Potts, Frank, 39
Pound, Roscoe, 152
Povich, Shirley, 58, 60, 99–101, 111,
      329–330, 335, 483n; questions
      motives for choice of White as all-
      American, 58–59; reports dissen-
      sion over White's salary, 100;
      ghostwriter for Sammy Baugh, 111
Powell, Lewis F., Jr., 4, 356–357, 359, 386,
      387, 390–391, 393–396, 403, 407,
      408, 409, 434, 445, 452, 457,
      509n, 512n

Powers, Jimmy, 115
PPE. See Oxford University, curricula
Prague, 139
Prendergast, Michael H., 251
Press Radio Bureau, 78
Price, Cotton, 162, 165, 166
Price, Karl R., 141, 145–146, 197, 199,
      202, 212
Price, Monroe E., 383
Price Administration, Office of, 207
Princeton University, 150, 229, 265
Pro Football Chronicle, 122
Prohibition, 214
Propaganda Ministry (Nazi), 138
Providence, Rhode Island, 103
PT 59, 178
PT 109, 173–179, 198, 337
Public Law 96–440, 441
Public Works and Appropriations Com-
      mittee, U. S. Senate, 298
Pueblo American Legion, 82
Pueblo, Colorado, 14, 32, 244, 245
Pueblo Sertoma Club, 317
Puerto Rico, 343
Pulitzer Prize, 269, 386
Purple Heart, 29

SS Queen Mary, 135
Quinn, Mary Ellen, 198

Rabaul, 174, 180, 181
Rabbit Ears Range (Colorado), 15
Rabun, Hank, 52–53, 99, 111
racial discrimination, 348–352
Radin, Max, 195–196
Radovich, Bill, 160–161, 167, 169, 251,
      486n
Raines, Howell, 493n
USS Randolph, 192
Raton, New Mexico, 15
Rayburn, Sam, 200, 266
Rea, Howard, 225
Read, William A. (Gus), 191
Reader's Digest, 198
Reagan, Ronald, 388, 397, 415, 416, 441,
      452; and Nancy Reagan, 414
Reagan administration, 388
Rebekah Lodge (Wellington), 23
Reconstruction, 276, 307, 359, 430

Reed, Stanley F., 195, 202–203, 208, 210, 311, 335
Reed, Walter, Army Hospital, 311, 312, 329
Rehnquist, Natalie Cornell (Nan), 416
Rehnquist, William H., 356, 357, 390–391, 393, 396, 407, 409–411, 416–417, 419, 426–429, 431, 441, 445, 451, 452, 479n, 509n
Rehnquist Court, 413
Reidsville state prison, 258
Reilly, John R., 268, 287, 307, 479n
Rendova Island, 174, 178
Republican Party, 377
res ipsa loquitur, 209, 226
Reston, James, 318, 323, 325, 382, 383
Reynolds, Clark G., 187
Rheinbayern, 14
Rhodes, Cecil, 46, 85, 126, 271
Rhodes scholar, Rhodes Scholarships, 1, 4, 28, 31, 44–47, 53, 60–61, 64–65, 71–72, 75–79, 83, 85, 87–88, 91, 93, 105, 111, 119, 126–133, 135–136, 138, 140–141, 143, 145–146, 168, 197, 229, 254, 265, 271, 302, 413, 442, 448, 471, 472; selection criteria, 46, 62, 271
Rhodes Trust and Trustees, 46, 90, 92–93, 125–126, 135, 140, 227, 229; Rhodes House, 124, 127, 132, 135, 140–141 (Warden of, 91, 93, 127–128, 132, 140)
Rhône-Alpes, 133
Ribicoff, Abraham, 260, 312, 317, 318
Rice, Grantland, 44, 68, 110–111, 229; Collier's all-American team, 36, 44, 58, 229 (reunion)
Rice Institute, 56–58, 67–69
Richards, George A. (Dick), 101, 158, 160
Richmond School Board, 394
Rio Grande River, 230
River Runs Through It, A, 433
Rives, Richard T., 307
Roanoke, Virginia, 116
Robinson, Nancy Jane, 13
Rock, George, 242, 245
Rockefeller, Nelson A., 500n
Rockefeller Center, 78
Rockne, Knute, 23, 449

Rocky Mountain Conference, 30, 45, 48, 50, 55–56
Rocky Mountain News, 4, 31, 34–35, 39, 46, 48, 50, 52–54, 61–63, 83–85, 87, 93, 99, 111, 113, 224, 231, 243, 245, 247, 324, 379, 447, 454, 456, 457
Rocky Mountains, 15–16, 84, 456, 458
Rodell, Fred, 195, 196, 220
Rogers, Byron G., 335
Rogers, Byron, Federal Building (Denver), 516n
Rogers, James Grafton, 148
Rogers, Will, 86
Roman law, 89, 128, 138–139, 145
Romer, Roy, 471
Rooney, Arthur J. (Art), 60–61, 69, 75, 79, 80, 83–87, 93, 97–101, 104–110, 113–122, 127, 144, 158–159, 163, 329, 353, 514n; reasons for drafting White, 60–61; financial resources, 97, 115–117; reactions to rumors about players not blocking for White, 108; exploitation of White, 120; sells White to Detroit Lions, 159
Roosevelt, Eleanor, 17
Roosevelt, Franklin D., 47, 134, 135, 137, 139–143, 146, 150, 164, 187–188, 196, 200, 231, 297, 453; Court-packing plan, 150, 453; "Four Freedoms," 164; lend lease, 164
Roosevelt, Theodore, Professor of American History and Institutions (Berlin), 27
Roosevelt Hotel (New Orleans), 118
Rose Bowl, 47, 52, 65
Rose Memorial Hospital, 227
Rosen, Jeffrey, 441–442, 444
Rosslyn, Virginia, 404
Rostow, Eugene V., 318
Rothgerber, Ira C., Jr., 2–3, 5–6, 226, 233, 248, 301, 346, 351, 354, 368, 385, 399, 430, 437, 445, 447, 479n, 487n
Routt, Joseph, 59
Rowe, Gary Thomas, 282
Russell, Richard B., 256, 318, 330
Russell, Robert, 256

Russell Islands, 173
Russia, 17
Rutledge, Wiley B., 150, 195, 196, 201,
    205, 208–209, 212, 214, 216, 218
"Ryder, Charles," 133
Ryder, Lady Frances, 132

Sabo, John, 170
Sacramento, 303
Sailors, Kenny, 32
Saipan, 183, 184
Saliman's Grill, 259
Salinger, Pierre, 251, 255, 264
Salsinger, H. G., 169
Salt Lake City, 45, 47–48, 50, 403
Salt Lake City Tribune, 48–49
Samar Island, 185
Samoa, 173
Samsonite. *See* Schwayder Brothers, 223
San Bernardino Strait, 185, 187
San Francisco, 31, 36, 46, 61, 64, 193,
    252–253, 264, 303, 379
San Francisco Chronicle, 64, 383
Sanders, Barry, 56
Sanford, J. Curtis, 52–54, 56
Santa Barbara, 264
Santa Clara, University of, 54
Santa Fe, N. M., 301
Saratoga, Wyoming, 433
Saturday Evening Post, 44
Saudi Arabia, 388
Saunders, (Navy) Bill, 33
Savannah, 305
Savarine Hotel, 172
Scalia, Antonin (Nino), 397, 407, 411,
    417–420, 423, 426–430, 439
Schaefer, Walter V., 314, 315, 318
Schauer, Frederick, 394
Schlafly, Phyllis, 414
Schlesinger, Arthur M., Jr., 211, 250, 254,
    315, 322, 495n
Schmidt, Evelyn (Ely), 18, 20–22
Schmidt, Richard, 240
school desegregation, 351–352
school prayer. *See* Constitution, First
    Amendment
Schorr, Daniel, 387
Schreiber, Mark, 36, 44, 47

Schultz, Andy, 406, 410
Schwartz, Bernard, 384, 386, 398
Schwartz, Jim (Swisher), 74, 78–79
Schwayder Brothers, 223
Scofield, Gerald R. (Jerry), 29
"Scone College," 91
Scotland, 142
Scott, General Winfield, 11
Scottsboro Boys, 203
Scribner's Magazine, 85, 91
Scripps-Howard Newspapers, 85
Seattle, Washington, 264, 432
Second Hoeing (Williams), 17
Securities and Exchange Commission
    (SEC), 143, 146, 224–225
Segal, Bernard G., 288, 291, 294, 295,
    305, 306, 313, 321, 330
Seigenthaler, John, 262, 264, 274–275,
    282, 297–298, 319
Selective Service, 214
Sell, Jack, 114
Seminole War (Second), 11
Senate, U. S., 82, 164, 231, 236, 261, 272,
    277, 285, 289, 291, 297–299, 301,
    303, 304, 314, 325, 330–331, 356,
    364, 388, 414, 415
Sesape, 173
Seth, Oliver, 301
Seymour, Whitney North, 315
Shakespeare, 98
Shaner's, 228
Sharon, Ariel, 422–423
Sharp, Tom, 259
Shaw, George Bernard, 132
Shea, Francis M. (Frank), 327
Shearer, Norma, 107
Shearer, Shorty, 19
Sheer, Harry, 182–183
Shenandoah Valley, Virginia, 13
Sheridan, General Philip, 13
"Sheridan, Lee," 126
Sherman Act, 226
Shields, Don, 79
Shigure, 175
Shorey, Paul, 25
Shreveport, 305
Shriver, R. Sargent, 255–256, 261,
    264–265, 289, 313

Shulman, Harry, 148–149, 153

Silver & Gold, 30–31, 35–37, 39, 41, 43–45, 47, 50, 54, 58, 72, 82, 84, 88, 94; all-American campaign, 36–37; criticizes White's ASUC presidency, 45; various nicknames for White, 39

Silver Glade Room (Cosmopolitan Hotel), 243

Silver Star, 29, 191

Sinatra, Frank, 414

sit-in cases, 350

Slaughterhouse-Five, 391

Slot, the, 173, 174, 178, 180, 516n

Small Business Administration, 424

Smathers, George, 239

Smith, Gov. Al, 78

Smith, Ben, 133

Smith, Chester L., 85

Smith, Howard K., 130

Smith, Stephen (Steve), 242, 247

Smith, Stu, 122

Smith Act of 1940, 267

Smithsonian, 385

"Sniggs," 91

Snow, Paul, 49

Snow White, 77

Snowmass, Colorado, 479n

Social Science Foundation. *See* Denver University

Sofaer, Abraham, 422

Soldier Field, 93, 102

Solomon Islands, 173, 178–180, 182–183, 237–238

Sommerset County, Pennsylvania, 11

Sorensen, Theodore C. (Ted), 234–240, 241–243, 249, 252, 273, 312, 314, 319–320, 322, 327, 500n

Soul on Ice, 391

Souter, David H., 407, 415–416, 418, 421, 426–429, 437

South Carolina, 255, 273

South High School (Denver), 229

South Platte River, 15

South Platte River Valley, 17

Southampton, 124, 141

Southern California, University of (USC), 63, 119, 141

Southern California Rugby Football Union, 71

Southern California Striders, 240

Southern Methodist University (SMU), 56–58

Southwest Conference (SWC), 54, 57–58

Soviet Union. *See* U.S.S.R.

Spaeth, Nicholas J., 425

Spain, 134–135

Spanish Civil War, 27, 82

Sparkman, John, 254

Special Senate Committee Investigating Lobbying and Campaign Finance, 263

Speech and Debate Clause. *See* Constitution

Sport, 337

Sporting News, 75

Sports Illustrated, 2–3, 24, 46, 113, 230, 337, 342, 377–378; Silver Anniversary All-America team, 342, 377

"Sports of the Times," 77

Sprague, Rear Admiral Clifton, 185

Sproul, Robert G., 63

Spruance, Admiral Raymond, 187, 191

St. John's Episcopal Church, 197

St. Louis, 319, 379

St. Louis (baseball) Cardinals, 75

St. Louis Post-Dispatch, 379

St. Regis Paper, 432

St. Rosalia Prep School, 103

Stahr, Elvis, 137, 264

standing, 347n

Stagg, Amos Alonzo, 229

Stanford Law Review, 218

Stanford University, 32, 36, 63, 72, 73, 471

Stapleton, Benjamin F., 225

stare decisis, 389–390

Starr, Kenneth, 428

"Starving Artists," 516n

State, U. S. Department of, 102, 141, 239

state action, 350

State Fair Park Stadium, 53

Statler Hilton Hotel, 313

Steadman, John, 329

Stearns, Marion Lloyd. *See* Marion White

Stearns, Robert L., 48, 82, 193, 225, 228, 267–268, 324, 335; and Stearns, Amy Pitkin, 228, 335

Sterling Advocate, 88

Stern, Richard H. (Dick), 337, 339
Stevens, John Paul, 387, 389–391, 393–394, 401, 407, 418, 421, 426, 428, 438
Stevenson, Adlai, 234, 236, 241, 242, 249–250, 250n, 252, 261, 314, 325, 344
Stewart, Potter, 157, 311, 324, 341, 343, 344, 348, 357, 358, 367, 371, 380, 385, 386, 387, 389, 390, 402, 407, 434, 504n, 505n, 516n
"Stewart-White Court," 358
Stibes Tavern, 89
Stith, Kate, 363, 445, 451, 503n
Stone, Harlan Fiske, 196, 201
Stone, William M. (Iowa Governor), 12
Stortet, Wilbur, 118
Story, Joseph, 151, 510n
Stowaway restaurant, 141
Strangers' Gallery (House of Commons), 140
Stringham, Luther, 42
Stubbs, Donald S., 225
Student Nonviolent Coordinating Committee (SNCC), 282
Students for Kennedy (Colorado), 248
Sturges, Wesley A., 146, 152, 154–155, 219–220, 268, 446, 492n
substantive due process. See Constitution, Fourteenth Amendment
Subyuan Sea, 184
Sudetenland, 82, 129
Sugar Act of 1937, 17
Sugar Bowl, 53
sugar beets, 14, 15; Beet Holiday, 15; characteristics of the industry, 16–17
Suits, Frederick, 94
summit conference, U.S.-U.S.S.R., 274, 275
Sun Bowl, 54
Sunday Chronicle (London), 124
Superior Court of Cook County, 302
Supreme Court of Colorado, 226, 387, 471
Supreme Court of Mississippi, 204
Supreme Court of the United States, 1, 3–4, 6–7, 31, 82, 120, 137, 146, 149, 151, 156, 170, 179, 194–197, 199–207, 210–218, 248, 260–261, 263, 266, 268, 283, 289, 291, 296,

298, 307, 309–315, 321–331, 335–336, 338–344, 348–352, 354–378, 380, 382–391, 393–397, 400–405, 407–431, 432, 434–442, 445, 446, 447, 449, 450, 451, 452, 453, 454, 455, 457, 499n, 512n, 516n; certiorari, 217, 358 (cert pool), 387, 400 (White's dissents from denial, 400–401, 431, 451, 452); content of docket, 339–340, 358; Chief Justice's Report Card, 419, 426; in forma pauperis docket, 201–203, 204, 206; police force, 414, 427; Public Information Office, 415, 438; Rule of Four, 393
Supreme Court of the United States (Office of the Curator), 6
Supreme Court Review, 349, 357
Surigao Strait, 185
Sutton, Leonard vB., 61
Swarthmore College, 26, 140
Sweden, 88
Switzerland, 265
Swygert, Luther M., 302
Sykes, Hope Williams, 17
Symington, Stuart, 234, 236, 241–242, 247–249, 250n

Taft-Hartley Act of 1947, 213, 216, 244
Tales of the City, 193
Tammany Hall, 251
Tännhauser, 139
Taplin, Frank, 141, 153, 157, 485n
Tarzan's Revenge, 84
Task Force (TF) 34, 184–186
Task Force (TF) 38, 184–186, 192
Task Force (TF) 58, 181, 188, 191–192
TASS, 164
Tauriello, Frank, 516n
Tavares, C. Nils, 289
Taylor, Robert, 76, 123–124
Taylor, Stuart, 413, 424, 431, 445
Taylor, General Zachary, 11
Teamsters Union, 264, 287
Telegraph Hill, 193
Temple University, 74, 78–79
Tennessee, 145, 310
Tennessee, University of, 33
Tennyson, Alfred Lord, 77

Terry, David, 405

Texas, 13, 17, 67, 232, 255, 259, 291, 295, 366, 388

Texas, University of, School of Law, 377

Texas A & M University, 59, 162

Texas Christian University (TCU), 37, 53, 57, 64, 66

Textron, 432

This is Your Life! 228

Thom, Lennie, 176

Thomas, Clarence, 407, 414–418, 421, 426–428, 437, 472

Thomas, Helen, 416

Thomas, Piri, 391

Thompson, Clarence (Tuffy), 98, 103, 107, 114, 118, 122, 484n

Thompson, Frank (Topper), 252, 254

Thoreau, Henry David, 375

Thornton, Colorado, 248

Thornton, Dan, 232–233

Thorpe, Jim, 229, 449

Thurman, Don, 157, 481n, 483n

Tibet, 244

Tigar, Michael E., 439

Time, 197, 198, 422–423

Timmons, B. Lane, 506n

Timnath, Colorado, 15

Tinian Island, 183

Title IX of Education Amendments of 1972, 417

"Tokyo Express," 174, 180

Tolstoy, 20

Topeka [Kansas] Daily Capital, 88

Topping, Dan, 114–115

Topps Company, 449

Toscanini, Arturo, 142

Totenberg, Nina, 395

Tracy, Spencer, 107

Trafalgar Day, 134, 142

Transportation, U. S. Department of, 424

Traynor, Roger, 314, 315, 318

Treasury, secretary of, 196, 200

Treasury, U. S. Department of the, 197

Tresner, Charlene, 479n

Triangle Review (Wellington-Fort Collins), 337

Trillin, Calvin, 443

Trinidad, Colorado, 89, 335

Tripson, John R., 182, 448

True, 337

Truman, Harry, 196, 200, 213, 288, 294, 295, 301, 307, 313, 315

Tu, Alan, 479n

Tucson, Arizona, 66

Tulagi Island, 173, 174, 178, 454

"Tulagi Tech," 244

Tulsa, Oklahoma, 29

Turl, 125

Turner, Bulldog, 158

Turner, Wallace, 264

Tuttle, Elbert P., 307

Twain, Mark, 502n

22d Regiment of Iowa Volunteers, 12–13

Tydings, Joseph D., 305

Tyler, Harold (Ace), 283

Tyler, Robert F., 48

UCLA School of Law, 383

Udall, Stewart, 248, 249, 335, 471

Unger, Art, 32, 38–40, 42, 74, 448

Union Pacific, 50; Pony Express, 61–62

Union Station (Washington, D.C.), 80

United Fund, 227

United Mine Workers, 211, 213

United Nations, 281, 318, 344

United Press (UP), 44, 47, 57–58, 75–76, 84, 86, 110, 119, 162, 196

United Press International (UPI), 318, 408, 416, 437–438

United States Reports, 211–212, 401

United States Society, 134

Unity (Bible magazine), 324

Universal Service Syndicate, 65

University Club (Denver), 27, 61

Updike, John, 486

Urban League (Denver), 227

USA Today, 415

U.S. News & World Report, 402

U.S.S.R., 164, 235, 272–273

Utah, 126, 293, 403–404

Utah, University of, 30, 33–34, 39–40, 45–52, 65–66, 69, 74, 110, 116

Utah Agricultural College (Utah State), 30, 40, 45, 52, 63

Utah Bar Association, 403, 404

"vagueness," "overbreadth" doctrines, 374–376

Val D'Isère, 133
Valentine, Alan C., 482n
Valentino, Rudolph, 80
"Valley City" (Fort Collins, Colorado), 17
Vanderbilt University, 67
Vandiver, Ernest, 256, 257, 272
Vanzo, Fred, 167
Vassar College, 193
Vella Lavella, 173, 178–179, 182
Le Verdon, 141
Vermont, 137
Vicksburg, Mississippi, 12–13
Vienna, 139, 275
Vila, 174
Villanova University, 54
Vinson, Frederick M., 5, 170, 196–202,
        206–216, 218, 219–220, 266, 328,
        339, 359, 385, 489n
Vinson, Fred M. Oral History Project, 2,
        212–220
Virgil, 137
Virgin Islands, U.S., 313
Virginia, 13, 254, 273, 298, 302
Virginia, University of, 401, 417
Virginia Board of Education, 394
Virginia Supreme Court of Appeals, 203
Voice of America, 284
Volga German immigrants, 17
Vonnegut, Kurt, 391
Voting Rights Act of 1965, 395

Wagner, Martin, 482n
Waldorf-Astoria Hotel, 352
"Walker, Mrs.," 145
Walker, Wyatt Tee, 322
Wall Street Journal, 260, 337, 393, 440
Wallace, Francis, 44
Wallace, Henry, 446
Wallace, Robert A. (Bob), 238–242, 249,
        265
Walsh, Christy, 58
Walter, Lewis H., 170
Waltham, Massachusetts, 454
Wapello County, Iowa, 12, 13
War and Peace (Tolstoy), 20
War Mobilization and Reconversion, Of-
        fice of, 200
Ward, Arch, 68
Ward, Charles, 161

Ward, Dallas, 229
Ward, Gene, 112–114, 120, 122
Warren, Chief Justice Earl, 8, 217, 312,
        314, 317, 319, 323, 325, 329, 335,
        338, 340–342, 344, 349, 352–354,
        356, 357, 360, 380
Warren Court, 318, 340, 344, 346,
        348–349, 352–353, 356, 357, 360,
        380, 390, 401, 444
Washington (state), 293
Washington, D.C., 5, 13, 80–81, 83–84,
        111, 193, 194, 225, 231, 238, 253,
        258, 261–266, 270, 273–274, 278,
        280, 284, 317, 321–323, 328, 330,
        336, 343, 365, 381, 382, 389, 438,
        448
Washington, George T., 315
Washington, University of, 34
Washington Evening Star, 83, 269, 323,
        340
Washington Post, 5, 58, 60, 64, 81, 99,
        111, 253, 262, 269, 318, 322,
        329–330, 335, 337, 342, 367, 384,
        386, 387, 412, 417, 436, 437, 455
Washington Redskins, 53, 60, 93, 98–102,
        116–118, 129, 162, 193
Washington State University, 34
Washington Touchdown Club Hall of
        Fame, 376
Watergate, 399
Waterloo, Battle of, 14, 235
Waugh, Evelyn, 91, 131, 132
Waverly, Colorado, 14
WAVES, 193
Wayne, James M., 510n
Weaver, Robert C., 311, 319
Webb & Knapp, 124
Webster, Bethuel M., 315
Wechsler, Herbert, 315
Weddington, Sarah, 365–367
Weigel, Stanley A., 303, 496n
Weinstock, Izzy, 108, 112
Weld County, 245
Wellington, Duke of (Arthur Wellesley,
        nee Wesley, 1st Duke), 6
Wellington (Colorado), 14–18, 20–24, 28,
        30–31, 34, 64, 87, 92–93,
        118–119, 140, 147, 178, 188, 193,
        197, 458

Wellington Chamber of Commerce, 23
Wellington Federated Church, 23
Wellington High School, 24
Wellington High School Alumni Association, 4, 408
Wellington Public Library Oral History Collection, 2, 15
Wellington Sun, 31
Welsh Union, 126
Wermeil, Stephen J., 479n, 501n, 512n
Wessel, Horst, 139
West, E. Gordon, 292–295
West Publishing Company, 405
West Virginia American Legion convention, 228
West Virginia Democratic Primary (1960), 245–247
Western Athletic Conference, 353
Western Reserve University, 164
Western Reserve University Law School, 225
Western State (Colorado) College, 30
Western States Democratic Conference, 247
Westin Hotels, 432
Weston, Harris K., 195
White, Alpha Albert, 14–15, 20, 22–23, 64, 94, 197, 324, 347
White, Byron Brown, 12
White, Byron R., Courthouse, 455
White, Byron Raymond, 7, 11, 15–22, 24, 29–30, 33–69, 71–94, 97–194, 196–212, 215, 218–220, 223–233, 235–240, 242–272, 274–306, 308–309, 311, 313–331, 335–354, 355, 357–385, 387–431, 432, 433, 434, 435, 436, 437, 438, 439, 440, 441, 442, 443, 444, 445, 446, 447, 448, 449, 450, 451, 452, 453, 454, 455, 456, 457, 472, 479n, 493n–494n, 497n, 504n, 505n, 506n, 507n, 508n, 509n, 512n, 516n
    appearance: description, 101, 125, 136, 157, 178, 197, 280, 455; general physique, 136 (hands, 109–110, 229, 280); oil portraits, 376, 455, 516n
    character and characteristics: antipathy to academics, 451; biography and autobiography, 5, 19 (self-effacing recollections, 46, 105, 110, 118, 230, 450); charitable work, 227; compassion and tenderness, 395, 406, 433; competitiveness, 39, 79, 89, 108, 121, 147–148, 230, 239, 325, 365; curt manner, 21, 42, 76, 99; discomfort with, and antipathy to, press, 2, 4–5, 40–41, 74, 76–77, 80–82, 99, 127, 133, 269, 336, 337, 383, 448, 450; discomfort with being used in advertisements, 120 (clothing, cigarettes); disposition, public, 413; frustration with public relations duties, 110; generosity and selflessness, 118, 191; hostility to nickname "Whizzer," 1, 35, 237, 447–448 (mistaken as "Buzzer," 44, 61, 291, 296); idealized view of politics, 239; impatience, 42, 230, 233, 305, 347, 421, 453, 455; incrementalism, 7, 359, 375–376, 419–420, 440, 512n; lack of judicial ambition, 322, 328–329, 456; loyalty, 120–121, 229; modesty, 2, 7, 64, 82, 330, 409, 421, 427, 450, 455 (as to athletic career, 3, 81–82, 109–110, 181, 227, 237, 269, 447; as to intellectualism, 92; as to war record, 183, 187, 188; as to legal career, 305; emphasizes "ordinariness," 455; "judicial modesty," 454–455); noncommittal tendency, 82, 89, 93, 269, 433; passion for privacy (especially family), 3, 7, 227, 228, 336, 448, 450; passion for football, 92, 121, 168–169, 193; physical courage, 166, 190–191; pragmatism, 258; public service, esteems, 456; as public speaker, 233; oral histories, resistance to, 2; religious affiliations, 23, 251, 324 (parents); reserve and reticence, 326, 330; self-criticism, 421; stubbornness, 411–412; sense of humor, 246, 421, 439; sentiment, 406, 408; shyness, 2, 42; smoking habit, 18, 42, 280, 330, 381; unpretentiousness, 168

family: 197, 228, 238, 243, 438–439.
    See also White, Alpha Albert;
    White, Maude Burger; White, (Dr.)
    Clayton Samuel; White, Marion
    Lloyd Stearns; White, Charles
    Byron; White, Nancy Pitkin
finances: 29–30, 61, 75, 80, 157–159,
    336, 403, 426–427
health and injuries: 35, 45, 104, 115,
    157, 162, 166, 179, 269, 271,
    274–275, 288, 409
image: as New Frontier symbol, 46,
    270–271, 322; semiheroic figure,
    355; "storybook figure," 442; role
    model, 448; personal hero,
    448–449; local hero, 455
judicial philosophy: resists using Consti-
    tution to set social policy, 338; nar-
    row view of issues, 341; importance
    of unbiased decision-maker,
    342–343; view of Court's role, 355;
    incrementalism, self-effacing opin-
    ions, 359; strategy toward incorpo-
    ration doctrine, 360; prefers
    concrete facts to hypothetical risks,
    215, 361–362, 450; trusts good
    faith of public officials, 215, 363;
    meticulous attention to questions of
    jurisdiction, 372–373; growing
    concern for stare decisis, 389; aver-
    sion to precipitous decisions on
    constitutional issues, 391–393,
    440; deference to Congress, 397;
    INS v. Chada as epitome of philoso-
    phy, 397; anxieties over legitimacy,
    434–446, 452; philosophy summa-
    rized (Mary Ann Glendon), 442.
    See also opinion practices and tac-
    tics, above; Constitution
personal relationships: with John F.
    Kennedy, 133; shared affinities,
    133, 142; PT-109, 174–178; rea-
    sons for Supreme Court nomina-
    tion, 327–328; anguish over
    assassination, 354; with Robert F.
    Kennedy, 246 (common style); ad-
    vice on Martin Luther King,
    257–258; 246, 270, 342 (annual
    skiing trips); alter ego at Depart-

ment of Justice, 271; point man for
    Freedom Rides, 272–281; impact
    on departmental operations,
    308–309; effect of assassination,
    354; with Earl Warren, 341–342,
    349, 353–354; with William O.
    Douglas, 218–219, 268, 340,
    434–436; with John Marshall Har-
    lan, 346–347; others, 98, 121,
    269–270, 352–353, 358, 378–379,
    405–406 ("Johnny Blood"), 60–61,
    117, 120–121 (Art Rooney),
    431–432 (annual fishing party)
recreation: 20, 35, 38, 42, 84, 87, 89,
    127, 131, 133, 136–137, 147–148,
    230, 246, 270, 316, 342, 403,
    432–433
views
    pre-judicial: 31–32, 81–82, 130, 136,
        233, 258; political party affiliation,
        243; "liberals," 233, 259, 269,
        325–326, 346, 444
    as judge: model, 326; sparse pre-judi-
        cial record, 330; role of Supreme
        Court, 331, 351; wiretapping, 347,
        359, 497n; death penalty, 363; role
        of history, 364; abortion, 365–369;
        constitutional protection for chil-
        dren and family, 370–372; "vague-
        ness/overbreadth," 374–376;
        confidentiality within Court,
        384–385; child pornography,
        394–395; separation of powers,
        397–399; elections and First
        Amendment, 399–400; retirement,
        408–409; coerced confessions,
        409–411; entrapment, 420–421;
        defamation, 422–423; affirmative
        action, 423–424; nonmajority deci-
        sions, 439–440; sports as personal
        challenge, 448; substantive due
        process, 452–454; legacy, 455–456;
        "pivotal" justices, blocs, 457;
        antitrust, 513n; labor, 513n
    work habits: pre-judicial: 19–20,
        29–30, 31, 38, 129, 133, 156–157,
        159–160, 165, 226, 308–309, 358;
        as a judge: assigning opinions, 409,
        417–418; announcing opinions in

White, Byron Raymond (*continued*)
court, 397, 410–411; with law
clerks, 3, 5–6, 363–364, 418–419,
439, 452–453; opinions: writing
practices and tactics, 338, 346–348,
350–351, 356, 359, 363–365,
372–374, 380, 384, 389, 397,
411–412, 418–419, 441, 451, 454,
479n, 513n, 515n; 12 day/12 page
deadline, 419, 452; oral argument,
365–367, 380; reading tastes, 364,
454, 516n
White, Charles Byron (Barney), 4, 238,
432
White, Charles Sumner, 13, 22, 118, 197
White, (Dr.) Clayton Samuel, 3, 7, 14,
18–24, 26, 28–31, 45–46, 62, 80,
85, 87, 89–94, 119, 124, 128, 165,
197, 324, 335; and Mrs. Margaret
Reeve White, 335
White, Ephraim Godfrey, 11–12, 22
White, James Getty, 13
White, Marion (Lloyd Stearns), 2, 193,
194, 197, 271, 322, 329, 335, 336,
342, 427, 438
White, Maude Burger, 14, 20, 23, 64, 193,
197, 354
White, Milton Cramer, 12
White, Nancy Pitkin, 238, 450
White, Samuel Kirkwood, 13
White, Sid, 54
White Citizens' Council, 291
"White Court," 419
"White for President." *See* McNally, John
Victor ("Johnny Blood")
White House, 275, 316, 320, 322, 416,
437, 438
White House Correspondents' Dinner,
337
White House Initiative on Historical Black
Colleges and Universities, 427
Whittaker, Charles E., 309–313, 316–319,
322–323, 329, 335, 337, 498n
Who's Who, 85
Wicker, Tom, 412
Wiethe, John, 160–162, 167, 251
Wildmon, Rev. Donald, 414
Will, George F., 383
Will, Hubert L., 302, 496n

Williams Act, 395
Williams, Joe, 59, 67
Williams, Ted, 170
Williamsburg, Virginia, 321
Wilson, Billy, 108
Wilson, Woodrow, 398
Winchester, battle of, 13
Winter, Harrison, 304
wiretapping, 347, 359, 497n
Wisconsin, 254, 267, 270, 283
Wisconsin Democratic Primary (1960),
245–247
Wisdom, John Minor, 307, 376
Witty, Irwin, 77
Wofford, Harris, 255–258, 266–267, 281,
313, 328
Wolfson, Richard F., 195
Wollenberg, Roger, 195
Wood, Jimmy, 109
Woodcock, Leonard, 319
Woodhouse, P. G., 137
Woodward, Bob, 2, 384, 385, 386
Woodward, C. Vann, 185, 186
"Wooster, Bertie," 137
Works Progress Administration (WPA),
27, 136
World Series, 98, 104, 200
World War I, 16, 62, 91, 132, 177
World War II, 19, 29, 132, 149, 156, 194,
223, 232–233, 237, 270, 274, 300,
339, 377, 438
Wright, Gordon, 228
Wright, J. Skelly, 281, 304, 498n
Wright, Richard, 391
Wright, Richard W. (Dick), 88, 89
Wyoming, 243, 247, 293
Wyoming, University of, 30, 32, 35, 72

Xavier University, 160

Yale, Elihu, 198
Yale Bowl, 47
Yale Corporation, 150
Yale Daily News, 150
Yale Law School, 1, 4–5, 140–141,
143–147, 149–150, 152–153,
156–157, 159–160, 163, 168, 170,
172, 193–199, 202, 219–220,
224–225, 260, 263, 265–266, 268,

276, 295, 301, 398, 430, 434, 445, 446, 447, 455, 516n; curriculum, 153 (1939–1940), 163 (1940–1941); *Yale Law Journal,* 156, 160, 163, 183, 196, 265; World War II impact on enrollment, 146

Yale University, 57, 141, 147–148, 150, 156, 198, 224, 236

Yank at Oxford, A, 76, 123–125, 127

Yarmolinsky, Adam, 219, 266

Yeagley, J. Walter, 267

Yeats, William Butler, 136

YMCA (Denver), 227

YMCA (San Francisco), 63

York, Kenneth C., 41

Youngdahl, Luther, 496n

Youngstown, Ohio, 300

Zeckendorf, William, 124

Zeno the Stoic, 348

Zirpoli, Alfonso J., 303

Zubrow, Ruben, 224

Zuckerman, Sollie (Sir), 90

Zuikaku, 186

Zuppke, Robert C. (Bob), 36, 37